KARL MARX
FREDERICK ENGELS
COLLECTED WORKS
VOLUME
23

KARL MARX
FREDERICK ENGELS

COLLECTED
WORKS

INTERNATIONAL PUBLISHERS

NEW YORK

KARL MARX
FREDERICK ENGELS

Volume
23

MARX AND ENGELS: 1871-74

INTERNATIONAL PUBLISHERS

NEW YORK

This volume has been prepared jointly by Lawrence & Wishart Ltd., London, International Publishers Co. Inc., New York, and Progress Publishers, Moscow, in collaboration with the Institute of Marxism-Leninism, Moscow.

Editorial commissions:
GREAT BRITAIN: Eric Hobsbawm, John Hoffman, Nicholas Jacobs, Monty Johnstone, Martin Milligan, Jeff Skelley, Ernst Wangermann.
USA: Louis Diskin, Philip S. Foner, James E. Jackson, Leonard B. Levenson, Victor Perlo, Betty Smith, Dirk J. Struik.
USSR: for Progress Publishers—A. K. Avelichev, N. P. Karmanova, V. N. Sedikh, M. K. Shcheglova; for the Institute of Marxism-Leninism— P. N. Fedoseyev, L. I. Golman, A. I. Malysh, M. P. Mchedlov, V. N. Pospelova, G. L. Smirnov.

Library of Congress Cataloging in Publication Data

Marx, Karl, 1818-1883.

Karl Marx, Frederick Engels: collected works.

1. Socialism—Collected works. 2. Economics— Collected works. I. Engels, Friedrich, 1820-1895. Works. English. 1975. II Title
HX 39.5 A 16 1975 335.4 73-84671
ISBN 0-7178-0523-9 (v. 23)

Printed in the Union of Soviet Socialist Republics

Contents

Preface XV

KARL MARX AND FREDERICK ENGELS
WORKS
October 1871-July 1874

1871

1. *K. Marx.* General Rules and Administrative Regulations of the International Working Men's Association 3

2. *F. Engels.* Resolution of the General Council Expelling Gustave Durand from the International Working Men's Association 21

3. *F. Engels.* To Enrico Bignami, Editor of *La Plebe* ....: 22

4. *K. Marx.* Declaration of the General Council on Nechayev's Misuse of the Name of the International Working Men's Association 23

5. *K. Marx.* Resolution of the General Council on the Rules of the French Section of 1871 24

6. *F. Engels.* On the Progress of the International Working Men's Association in Italy and Spain. Engels' Record of His Report at the General Council Meeting of October 17, 1871 28

7. *F. Engels.* To the Editors of the *Gazzettino Rosa.* Covering Letter to the "Declaration of the General Council on Nechayev's Misuse of the Name of the International Working Men's Association" ....: 30

8. *F. Engels.* Statement by the General Council Concerning Alexander Baillie Cochrane's Letter 31

9. *F. Engels.* On the Company Swindle in England 34

10. *K. Marx.* Resolution of the General Council on the French Section of 1871 37

11. *F. Engels.* Giuseppe Garibaldi's Statement and Its Effects on the Working Classes in Italy. Engels' Record of His Report at the General Council Meeting of November 7, 1871 43

12. *F. Engels.* Working Men's Congress at Rome.—Bebel's Speeches in the Reichstag. Engels' Record of His Report at the General Council Meeting of November 14, 1871 46

13. *K. Marx.* Declaration 50

14. *K. Marx.* Statement Sent by the General Council to the Editors of the *Frankfurter Zeitung und Handelsblatt* 52

15. *F. Engels.* To the Federal Council of the Spanish Region in Madrid 53

16. *F. Engels.* To the Editors of *Il Proletario Italiano* 54

17. *F. Engels.* Credentials for Giuseppe Boriani 56

18. *F. Engels.* The Position of the Danish Members of the International on the Agrarian Question. Engels' Record of His Report at the General Council Meeting of December 5, 1871 57

19. *F. Engels.* On the Position of the International's Sections in European Countries 59

20. *F. Engels.* Declaration Sent by the General Council to the Editors of Italian Newspapers Concerning Mazzini's Articles about the International 60

21. *K. Marx.* To the Editor of *The Eastern Post* 62

1872

22. *F. Engels.* The Congress of Sonvillier and the International 64

23. *K. Marx.* To the Editor of *The Eastern Post* 71

24. *K. Marx.* To the Editor of *The Eastern Post* 72

25. *F. Engels.* Letter to the Editors of the *Gazzettino Rosa* 74

26. *F. Engels.* To the Section of Commercial Employees in Barcelona 76

27. *K. Marx and F. Engels.* Declaration of the General Council of the International Working Men's Association 77

28. *K. Marx and F. Engels.* Fictitious Splits in the International. Private Circular from the General Council of the International Working Men's Association 79

    I 79
    II 84
    III 94
    IV 102

V 114

VI 116

VII 119

29. *K. Marx.* Resolutions on the Split in the United States' Federation Passed by the General Council of the I.W.A. in Its Sittings of 5th and 12th March, 1872 124

30. *K. Marx.* To the Editor of *La Liberté* 127

31. *K. Marx.* Resolutions of the Meeting Held to Celebrate the Anniversary of the Paris Commune 128

32. *F. Engels.* To the Spanish Federal Council 129

33. *K. Marx.* The Nationalisation of the Land 131

34. *F. Engels.* To Citizen Delegates of the Regional Spanish Congress Assembled at Saragossa 137

35. *F. Engels.* To the Saragossa Congress 139

36. *K. Marx.* Declaration of the General Council of the International Working Men's Association Concerning Cochrane's Speech in the House of Commons 140

37. *F. Engels.* To the Society of Ferrarese Workers 146

38. *F. Engels.* Letters from London.—I. The English Agricultural Labourers' Strike 148

39. *F. Engels.* On the Police Persecution of the Member of the International Theodore Cuno 151

40. *F. Engels.* To the Society of Ferrarese Workers 153

41. *F. Engels.* Relations Between the Irish Sections and the British Federal Council. Engels' Record of His Report at the General Council Meeting of May 14, 1872 154

42. *K. Marx.* Declaration of the General Council Concerning the Universal Federalist Council 157

43. *K. Marx.* Stefanoni and the International Again 160

44. *K. Marx.* Reply to Brentano's Article 164

45. *F. Engels.* To the *Emancipation of the Proletarian* Society in Turin 168

46. *F. Engels.* Announcement of the General Council on the Convocation and the Agenda of the Congress at The Hague 170

47. *K. Marx and F. Engels.* Preface to the 1872 German Edition of the *Manifesto of the Communist Party* 174

48. *F. Engels.* Resolutions of the Sub-Committee on Mikhail Bakunin and the Alliance 176

49. *F. Engels.* The International in America 177

50. *F. Engels.* To Citizen Vincenzo Spotti, Secretary of the Committee for the Emancipation of the Working Classes in Parma 184

51. *K. Marx.* To the Striking Miners of the Ruhr Valley 185

52. *K. Marx.* The General Council's Reply to the Protest of the Jura Federation Against the Convening of a Congress at The Hague 188

53. *K. Marx.* Reply to Brentano's Second Article 190

54. *K. Marx.* Amendments to the General Rules and Administrative Regulations of the International Working Men's Association Adopted by the General Council in the Summer of 1872 198

55. *F. Engels.* The General Council to All the Members of the International Working Men's Association 205

56. *K. Marx and F. Engels.* To the Spanish Sections of the International Working Men's Association 211

57. *K. Marx.* To the Editor of *The Times* 214

58. *F. Engels.* The General Council to the New Madrid Federation 215

59. *F. Engels.* On the Rimini Conference 216

60. *F. Engels.* Address of the General Council to the Italian Sections of the International Working Men's Association Concerning the Rimini Conference 217

61. *K. Marx.* Resolution on the Behaviour of Members of the General Council at the Congress 218

62. *K. Marx.* Report of the General Council to the Fifth Annual Congress of the International Working Men's Association Held at The Hague, from the 2nd to the 7th September 1872 219

63. *F. Engels.* Report on the Alliance of Socialist Democracy Presented in the Name of the General Council to the Congress at The Hague 228

64. *F. Engels.* Motion for the Procedure of Debate on the General Rules and Administrative Regulations 239

65. *K. Marx and F. Engels.* Proposal on the Transfer of the Seat and on the Composition of the General Council for 1872-1873 240

66. *K. Marx and F. Engels.* Resolutions of the General Congress Held at The Hague from the 2nd to the 7th September, 1872 243

    I. Resolution Relative to the General Rules 243

    II. Resolutions Relating to the Administrative Regulations 244

    III. Resolutions Relating to the Internationalisation of Trades' Societies 245

    IV. Resolutions Relating to the Admission of Sections 246

    V. Audit of the Accounts of the General Council 248

1873

85. *K. Marx.* Political Indifferentism 392

86. *K. Marx.* To the Editor of *The Times* 398

87. *F. Engels.* The "Crisis" in Prussia 400

88. *K. Marx.* Reply to the Second Circular of the Self-styled Majority of the British Federal Council 406

39. *F. Engels.* News on the Activities of the International on the Continent 409

    I 409

    II 411

    III 411

    IV 412

0. *F. Engels.* Notes for the General Council 414

1. *F. Engels.* The Republic in Spain 417

2. *F. Engels.* On Authority 422

3. *F. Engels.* News on the International Labour Movement 426

    I 426

    II 427

    III 429

    IV 431

    V 433

    VI 434

F. Engels. To the General Council of the International Working Men's Association 437

F. Engels. On the Articles in the *Neuer Social-Demokrat.* (From a Letter to A. Hepner) 439

F. Engels. The International and the *Neuer* 442

F. Engels. Communication from the Continent 446

F. Engels. To the General Council of the International Working Men's Association 447

F. Engels. From the International 448

F. Engels. Note on a Review of E. Renan's *L'Antéchrist* 452

F. Engels. Comment upon Giuseppe Garibaldi's Letter to Prospero Crescio 453

K. Marx and F. Engels. The Alliance of Socialist Democracy and the International Working Men's Association. Report and Documents Published by Decision of the Hague Congress of the International 454

    I. Introduction 454

    II. The Secret Alliance 459

    III. The Alliance in Switzerland 470

Contents

    VI. Powers Issued by the General Council, and by Fede: Councils ....

    VII. Resolutions Relating to the Alliance ....

  VIII. Residence and Composition of the Next General Cc cil ....

    IX. Place of Meeting of Next Congress ....

    X. Committee to Draw up the Minutes ....

67. *K. Marx.* On the Hague Congress. A Correspondent's R: of a Speech Made at a Meeting in Amsterdam on tember 8, 1872 ....

68. *K. Marx.* To the Editor of *Le Corsaire* ....

69. *K. Marx.* To the Editor of *The Daily News* ....

70. *F. Engels.* On the Hague Congress of the International ..

71. *F. Engels.* The Congress at The Hague (Letter to Bignami) ....

72. *F. Engels.* Imperative Mandates at the Hague Congress

73. *F. Engels.* Letters from London.—II. More about the Congress ....

74. *F. Engels.* To the British Federal Council, Inte: Working Men's Association Concerning Portuguese Stri

75. *K. Marx.* To the Editors of *Der Volksstaat* ....

76. *F. Engels.* Report to the General Council of the upon the Situation in Spain, Portugal and Italy ....

77. *F. Engels.* To the Workers' and Peasants' Association Lombardy (Section of the International) in Lodi ....

78. *F. Engels.* Letters from London.—III. Meeting Park ....

79. *F. Engels.* Mandate to E. Larroque ....

80. *F. Engels.* Letters from London.—IV. Meeting Park.—Situation in Spain ....

81. *K. Marx and F. Engels.* To the Editor of *The Herald* ....

82. *F. Engels.* The Manchester Foreign Section to All Members of the British Federation ....

83. *K. Marx.* Address of the British Federal Cc Sections, Branches, Affiliated Societies and Me International Working Men's Association ....

84. *F. Engels.* The Housing Question ....

    Part   I. How Proudhon Solves the Housing Qu

    Part II. How the Bourgeoisie Solves the Housi

    Part III. Supplement on Proudhon and the tion ....

94

95

96
97
98.

99.
100.
101.

102.

IV. The Alliance in Spain 486
V. The Alliance in Italy 497
VI. The Alliance in France 504
VII. The Alliance After the Hague Congress 508
VIII. The Alliance in Russia 515
    1. The Nechayev Trial 515
    2. *The Revolutionary Catechism* 544
    3. Bakunin's Appeal to the Officers of the Russian
       Army 549
IX. Conclusion 554
X. Appendix 556
    1. Bakunin's Hegira 556
    2. Bakunin's Pan-Slav Manifesto 558
    3. Bakunin and the Tsar 561
XI. Documents 567
103. *F. Engels.* The Bakuninists at Work. An Account of the
Spanish Revolt in the Summer of 1873 581
    I 581
    II 584
    III 590
    IV 595
104. *F. Engels.* Varia on Germany 599
    I. Introduction 1500-1789 599
       1789-1815 603
    Varia on Germany 1789-1873 604

1874

105. *F. Engels.* The English Elections 611
106. *F. Engels.* The Imperial Military Law 617
    I 617
    II 619
107. *F. Engels.* Supplement to the Preface of 1870 for *The Peasant
War in Germany* 626

FROM THE PREPARATORY MATERIALS

108. *K. Marx.* Notes on the Condition of the Refugees from the
Commune 635
109. *K. Marx.* American Split 636
110. *K. Marx.* Extracts from the Minutes of the General Council
for June 1870-April 1872 644

NOTES AND INDEXES

Notes.. 655
Name Index.. 726
Index of Quoted and Mentioned Literature..................................... 761
Index of Periodicals... 787
Subject Index... 796

ILLUSTRATIONS

Title page of the English edition of the General Rules and Administrative Regulations of the International Working Men's Association 5

Title page of Marx's and Engels' pamphlet *Fictitious Splits in the International*.. 81

Page of Marx's manuscript *The Nationalisation of the Land*................ 133

Page of Engels' manuscript with the announcement of the General Council on the convocation of the I.W.M.A.'s Congress at The Hague 171

Pages of the French edition of the General Rules and Administrative Regulations of the First International with corrections by Marx 199

Facsimile of Marx's manuscript with a proposal to transfer the seat of the General Council to New York 241

Page of the manuscript of the Hague Congress' resolutions............... 251

Title page of the separate reprint of Engels' *The Housing Question*, Part I, with the author's dedication to Laura Lafargue................. 315

Title page of Marx and Engels' pamphlet *The Alliance of Socialist Democracy and the International Working Men's Association* 455

Page of the manuscript *Varia on Germany*....................................... 605

Mandate issued to Marx by New York Section No. 1 for him to take part in the Hague Congress 647-48

Mandate issued to Engels by the Breslau Section for him to take part in the Hague Congress 649-50

Mandate issued to Engels by New York Section No. 6 for him to take part in the Hague Congress 651-52

TRANSLATORS:

DAVID FORGACS: Works 3, 7, 19, 25, 37, 38, 43, 50, 60,
    77, 80
GEOFFREY NOWELL-SMITH: Works 85
JOHN PEET: Works 44, 53
BARRIE SELMAN: Works 30, 59, 87, 90, 91, 95, 96, 100,
    104, 106; From the Preparatory Materials 108
SERGEI SYROVATKIN: Works 40, 99; From the Pre-
    paratory Materials 109
VERONICA THOMSON: Works 15, 26, 32
JOAN and TREVOR WALMSLEY: Works 9, 49, 51

Preface

Volume 23 of the *Collected Works* of Karl Marx and Frederick Engels contains pamphlets, articles, documents of the International Working Men's Association (the First International) and other items written between October 1871 and July 1874.

These years mark an important stage in the development of the international working-class movement. After the Paris Commune of 1871 the general socio-political situation, and the shifts that had occurred in the movement itself, intensified the need for independent proletarian parties capable of leading the workers' class struggle in the specific conditions of their own countries. The activities of the First International helped to prepare the ideological and organisational ground for the formation of such parties. And it was to this historic task that Marx and Engels devoted their efforts.

The materials in this volume show the all-round development and promulgation in these years of the basic principles of the scientific proletarian worldview, the struggle waged by Marx and Engels against trends hostile to the proletariat.

Their main thrust is towards the theoretical generalisation of the historical experience of the Paris Commune, a task Marx had begun in his *The Civil War in France* (see present edition, Vol. 22). Basing themselves on the experience of the Commune, Marx and Engels develop and enrich their theory of the state, the position and role of the working class in bourgeois society, the conditions required for its winning of political power, and the functions of the proletarian state. Inseparably linked with these

problems are those relating to the character and tasks of the
proletarian parties. And it is precisely these problems that provide
the battleground for the fight against the non-proletarian socialist
trends—Proudhonism, Lassalleanism, Bakuninism, and others.

The volume begins with the new edition of the "General Rules
and Administrative Regulations of the International Working
Men's Association", drawn up by Marx and Engels soon after the
London Conference of 1871 and issued by the General Council in
three languages. This document played a crucial role in
spreading the ideological and organisational principles of the
International in the period following the Paris Commune. In the
light of its lessons the programmatic proposition contained in the
Rules on the role of political struggle in the emancipation of
the working class, which had more than once been distorted in
Proudhonist publications, was of especial importance.

Marx's desire to deepen the programme of the International,
and to perfect its organisational structure in the spirit of
democratic centralism, is expressed in the "Amendments to the
General Rules and Administrative Regulations of the International
Working Men's Association". These Amendments, made in
preparation for the Hague Congress, reproduced in substance the
resolution passed by the London Conference of the International on
political action by the working class. As a result, for the first time ever,
a fundamental conclusion arrived at earlier by Marxist thought and
confirmed by the analysis of the Paris events of 1871 was
incorporated into a programmatic document of the International
Working Men's Association—the conclusion that to ensure the
victory of the proletarian revolution the working class had to have its
own political party.

Marx and Engels never tired of explaining to the working class
the world historic significance of the Paris Commune. For
example, in the resolutions written in March 1872 for the mass
meeting of members of the International and the Commune
refugees in London, Marx pointed out that the proletariat would
regard the Commune "as the dawn of the great social revolution
which will for ever free the human race from class rule" (see this
volume, p. 128).

In contrast to the reformists, who tried to gloss over the
revolutionary essence of the Commune, and to the anarchists, who
interpreted it as an example of the destruction of the state as such,
Marxism saw it as the first attempt by the working class not only to
break the bourgeois state machine, but to replace it by

a state of a new, proletarian type—an instrument for the socialist transformation of society. Attaching exceptional importance to this historical lesson, Marx and Engels in 1872 found it necessary to make a special addition to the *Manifesto of the Communist Party*. In the preface to the new German edition they noted that the Commune had proved that "the working class cannot simply lay hold of the ready-made State machinery", and that to achieve its aims it would therefore have to set up a truly democratic state system of an entirely different class nature (p. 175).

In his article "Political Indifferentism" Marx exposed the theoretical bankruptcy and political harmfulness of the Proudhonist doctrine preached by the Bakuninists that the working class should renounce political struggle, and of the anarchist idea of the immediate "abolition of the State". He showed that in practice these ideas disarm the workers and condemn them to the status of obedient servants of the bourgeoisie. Criticising these anarchist views, Marx demonstrates the historical need to replace the dictatorship of the bourgeoisie by the revolutionary dictatorship of the working class.

The Marxist propositions on the attitude of the proletarian revolution to the state are also substantiated in the essay "On Authority" by Engels. The essay shows that the anarchists' repudiation of authority, of any kind of guiding or organising principle, is in deep contradiction to real life, to the actual conditions of material production. Organisation of modern industry, transport and agriculture, Engels observes, is impossible without authority. There is also an obvious necessity for authority in the future socialist society, which must be based on highly developed, scientifically organised production requiring strict regulation and control.

Engels demonstrated the anti-scientific and anti-revolutionary essence of the anarchist idea that political authority should be abolished as the first act of the social revolution, that the political state should be "abolished at one stroke", even before the destruction of all the social relations that engendered it. "A revolution is certainly the most authoritarian thing there is; it is the act whereby one part of the population imposes its will upon the other part by means of rifles, bayonets and cannon—authoritarian means, if such there be at all... Would the Paris Commune have lasted a single day if it had not made use of this authority of the armed people against the bourgeois? Should we not, on the contrary, reproach it for not having used it freely enough?" (p. 425).

One of the sources that enriched revolutionary theory was the experience of the bourgeois revolution in Spain, 1868-74, especially the culminating stage of its development. During this stage the republican system was established at the beginning of 1873 and cantonal revolts were instigated in the summer of that year by the extremist group of the left-wing bourgeois republicans, the "Intransigents", and their Bakuninist allies. The article by Engels "The Republic in Spain" and his series of articles *The Bakuninists at Work* analyse these events. Both works are a contribution to Marxist theory on working-class tactics in the bourgeois-democratic revolution.

In the first of these works, while opposing idealisation of the bourgeois republic, Engels nevertheless argues that this type of republic is in a certain sense more advantageous to the proletariat than to the bourgeoisie because it is "the type of state that frees the class struggle from its last fetters" (p. 419). An indispensable condition for successful opposition to the rule of the bourgeoisie, he notes, is the ideological maturity of the working-class movement, a maturity which the Spanish workers had not at that time achieved. Warning against precipitate action, Engels insistently advises the workers to use the republican system to consolidate and organise their ranks. If they did so, the bourgeois republic would have prepared "the ground in Spain for a proletarian revolution" (p. 420).

In his series of articles *The Bakuninists at Work* Engels notes that one of the most pernicious aspects of Bakuninist tactics was that they ignored the bourgeois-democratic tasks of the revolution. The Bakuninists, who at that time had the support of a considerable section of the Spanish proletariat, were incapable of evolving a correct political orientation and in practice were inevitably destined to fall in with the extremist wing of the bourgeois republicans. It was their fault that the Spanish workers, who represented a real force, capable of influencing the course of events in a democratic spirit, were drawn into the adventuristic actions of the instigators of local revolts. The result was a grievous defeat. "The Bakuninists in Spain," Engels stressed, "have given us an unparalleled example of how a revolution should *not* be made" (p. 598).

To the Bakuninist position Engels contrasts the tactical line that should have been adopted by the advanced workers in a country where the conditions for the transference of power to the working class had not yet matured. He believed that energetic participation in the democratic revolution and intense political activity by the proletarian masses could accelerate the maturing process, that representatives of the working class should enter the revolutionary government in order to coordinate popular action from below with the actions of the revolutionary organs of power from above. Since matters had got to the point of armed struggle, Engels noted, the struggle should have been waged according to the rules of military art, without which no armed uprising could succeed. Above all, it was essential to prevent the insurgent forces from splitting up and getting out of touch, to establish centralised leadership and, by means of offensive action, to prevent the concentration of government troops and spread the uprising across the whole country.

Some essential aspects of the theory of socialist revolution were highlighted in the speech made by Marx in Amsterdam on September 8, 1872, at the meeting of members of the International that followed the Hague Congress. When choosing the tactical means and forms of struggle for establishing working-class power and building a socialist society, Marx said, one had to take into consideration the specific historical conditions proceeding from general revolutionary principles—"the institutions, customs and traditions in the different countries must be taken into account" (p. 255). Developing the thesis he had proposed in the 1850s, on the possibility of different roads—non-peaceful and peaceful—for the advance of the proletarian revolution, Marx admitted that in some countries where at that time there was no powerful military-bureaucratic state apparatus, specifically, in Britain and the USA, the proletariat could achieve its class aims by peaceful means. On the other hand, taking into account the situation obtaining in the majority of European countries at that time, Marx emphasised, "it is force which must be the lever of our revolution" (ibid.). He also envisaged the possibility of a situation in which the peaceful course of a revolution in Britain or other similarly placed countries might be interrupted by the resistance of the exploiting classes with the result that the working class would have to wage an armed struggle with its enemies.

Engels' *The Housing Question,* one of the most important works of scientific socialism, substantiates and defends a number of fundamental propositions of Marxist theory. Written in polemical form, this work is aimed both against the petty-bourgeois ideologists who saw the housing shortage as the basic evil of the whole capitalist system, and against the bourgeois social reformists who thought they could save and perpetuate the existing system of exploitation by relieving the workers of the worst consequences of capitalist development, specifically by improving their living conditions. Engels scathingly criticised the views of the German Proudhonist Mülberger, who had advanced the utopian idea of turning every worker into the owner of his dwelling as a means of solving the social problem in the spirit of the Proudhonist ideal of "eternal justice". Revealing the flaws in this remedy, Engels shows the petty-bourgeois nature and anti-scientific nature of the views held by Proudhon and his followers. In this work Engels thus continued the criticism of Proudhonism, which Marx had begun in his *The Poverty of Philosophy*, characterising Proudhonism as one of the most typical expressions of petty-bourgeois socialism; Engels also struck a blow at its other varieties. He considered the tendency to camouflage defence of the capitalist system with apparent concern for the good of the working people as a characteristic feature of many bourgeois studies of the housing question, and regarded their authors as representatives of bourgeois socialism. Like the petty-bourgeois ideologists, he wrote, the bourgeois socialists are deeply hostile to the revolutionary working-class movement, sidetrack the workers away from the class struggle, and preach the false idea of the harmony of class interests. "Bourgeois socialism extends its hand to the petty-bourgeois variety" (p. 340).

The housing shortage, Engels tells us, is a logical consequence of the capitalist system. It does not become any less acute with the development of capitalism. However, while affecting the vital interests of the workers and also many categories of the middle strata, the housing question is not the main and decisive social problem. The crucial contradictions of capitalism are to be sought not in the sphere of the relations between the tenant and the house-owner. They are rooted in the sphere of production, in the conditions of the exploitation of labour power by the capitalists. To prove these truths Engels expounds in simple terms the main propositions of *Capital*. As in a number of his other works, he writes as an indefatigable propagandist of Marx's economic theory. He stresses that to do away with the housing shortage, solve the housing question and other social questions generated by the capitalist system, the capitalist mode of production must be abolished and the conditions for the exploitation of wage labour removed. This means that the working class has to win political power, and that the political and economic domination of the bourgeoisie must be eliminated. To achieve these aims the proletariat needs an independent political party armed with the theory of scientific socialism and pursuing a consistent class policy (see p. 372).

Dealing with the question of the possible roads towards the socialist transformation of society, Engels put forward the fruitful idea that these roads would depend on the specific historical conditions of the given country. These conditions would, in particular, determine how and in what form the socialisation of the instruments and means of production owned by the capitalists would be effected by the victorious proletariat (see pp. 385-87).

Engels linked the socialist transformation of society with the problem of eliminating the antithesis between town and country. Arguing against Mülberger's proposition that this antithesis is "natural", and that the desire to get rid of it "utopian", Engels shows that the abolition of the exploiting classes as a result of the socialist revolution will clear the road towards the complete solution of this problem. In socialist society the close intrinsic connection between industrial and agricultural production will lift the rural population out of its millennia of isolation and backwardness.

In "The Nationalisation of the Land", one of Marxism's programmatic documents on the agrarian question, Marx showed that the economic development, growth and concentration of the population would by natural necessity demand the use of collective labour in agriculture. A stable expansion of agricultural production could be attained only on the basis of broad application of the achievements of science and technology. "...The scientific knowledge we possess," Marx stressed, "and the technical means of agriculture we command, such as machinery, etc., can never be successfully applied but by cultivating the land on a large scale" (p. 132).

In defining the socio-economic significance of the nationalisation of the land, Marx proceeded from analysis of the peculiarities of the agrarian systems in various countries. For Britain, where the land was not owned by peasants but concentrated in large estates, land nationalisation had become, in Marx's view, "a social necessity". At the same time, Marx exposed the reformist notions that the agrarian question could be completely solved within the framework of capitalist society by means of land nationalisation. Only in a state where the working class held power, he emphasised, would "agriculture, mining, manufacture, in one word, all branches of production ... gradually be organised in the most adequate manner. *National centralisation of the means of production* will become the national basis of a society composed of associations of free and equal producers, carrying on the social business on a common and rational plan" (p. 136).

Many of the works and documents included in this volume expose the sectarian activity of the Bakuninists, who had become particularly active at that time. Expressing the moods of the petty bourgeoisie who were going bankrupt and thrown into the ranks of the proletariat, especially in such economically backward countries as Italy and Spain, and peddling the "leftist" phrases that went down well in such circles, the Bakuninists made a fresh bid to impose their dogmas on the working-class movement and take over its leadership. Their activities created a serious threat to the unity and solidarity of the International and could have weakened its resistance to the all-round offensive launched by the forces of reaction. The danger became particularly acute when the Bakuninist attacks on the leadership of the International and its line were backed by other sectarian and reformist trends—the Belgian Proudhonists, the bourgeois and petty-bourgeois reformists in the USA, the British reformists, and the German followers of Lassalle.

The struggle between the Marxist trend in the International and anarchism flared up after the London Conference (1871), whose resolution on the need for the working class to win political power and set up independent working-class parties had been furiously opposed by Bakunin's followers. In November 1871, the Bakuninist congress in Sonvillier countered this resolution with the doctrine that the workers should abstain from political activity, and put forward the principle of complete autonomy and repudiation of discipline. As Engels noted in his article "The Congress of Sonvillier and the International", the Bakuninist dogmas tended to deprive the proletariat of any organisation of its own. The incompatibility of Bakunin's ideas with the aims of the International, with the task of creating independent political parties of the proletariat, made the ideological defeat of anarchism in the working-class movement a matter of great urgency.

The General Council's private circular, *Fictitious Splits in the International,* which was written by Marx and Engels, struck a blow at Bakuninism. This work was designed to uphold proletarian party principles in contrast to anarchist sectarianism. The actions of the Bakuninist Alliance of Socialist Democracy, states the circular, are imbued with the spirit of bellicose sectarianism and aimed at undermining the International—the true militant organisation of the proletarians of all countries, "united in their common struggle against the capitalists and the landowners" (p. 107). Marx and Engels showed that sectarianism was a characteristic feature of the early, immature stage of the working-class movement, and regarded the Bakuninists' attempt to revive it as thoroughly retrograde.

Exposing the anarchists' pseudo-revolutionary phraseology, Marx and Engels show that their programme "is nothing but a heap of pompously worded ideas long since dead" (ibid.). All the basic tasks of the working-class struggle for emancipation—the winning of state power and using it to build a classless society with the further prospect of the withering away of the state—were ignored by the anarchists, who proposed beginning the revolution by destroying all state apparatus. Most damaging of all for the working-class movement was the attempt to sow anarchy in the ranks of the movement itself, a tactic which amounted to disarming the proletariat in their struggle with the exploiters, who had at their disposal all the power of the state apparatus. The Bakuninist attacks on the principles of democratic centralism and party discipline, their demand that the functions of the General Council be reduced to the role of a mere correspondence and statistical bureau, which amounted to robbing the International of centralised leadership, were fraught with disorganisation. The campaign that Marx and Engels waged against the anarchists on the question of the functions and powers of the General Council was, in essence, a campaign for the organisational principles of the proletarian party.

After *Fictitious Splits in the International* had been published, the campaign against the Bakuninists entered a new phase. Marx and Engels began receiving information to the effect that the Alliance of Socialist Democracy which the Bakuninists claimed to have disbanded had in fact been kept going as a strictly conspiratorial society. The very people who accused the General Council of "authoritativeness", Engels observed, "in practice, constitute themselves as a secret society with a hierarchical organisation, and under a, not merely authoritative, but absolutely dictatorial leadership" (p. 206).

The existence within the International Working Men's Association of a secret international organisation of Bakuninists with its own rules and programme meant that Bakunin and his supporters were in practice splitting the Association. "For the first time in the history of the working-class struggles," Engels wrote, "we stumble over a secret conspiracy plotted in the midst of that class, and intended to undermine, not the existing capitalist *régime,* but the very Association in which that *régime* finds its most energetic opponent" (p. 209). The task of the leaders of the International now was not only to bring about the ideological defeat of the Bakuninist Alliance but also

to substantiate and carry out organisational measures to rid the
Association's ranks of this alien body.

As can be seen from a number of documents published in this
volume, specifically, the appeal "The General Council to All the
Members of the International Working Men's Association" and the
"Report on the Alliance of Socialist Democracy Presented in
the Name of the General Council to the Congress at The Hague",
Marx and Engels acted promptly to expose the true face of the
secret Bakuninist Alliance before all members of the International,
to show the harm that was being done to the working-class organisation by the illegal existence within its ranks of this secret
society. They both attached especial importance to unmasking the
Bakuninists in the eyes of the workers of Spain and Italy. In their
appeal "To the Spanish Sections of the International Working Men's
Association" they explained that the aims and character of the
Alliance, its activities, were in glaring contradiction to the spirit
and letter of the Rules of the International. The attempt by anarchistic groups in Italy to usurp the name of the International was
rebuffed in the address written by Engels to the Italian sections
concerning the Rimini Conference (see p. 217), and other documents.

While exposing the anti-proletarian activity of the Bakuninists,
Marx and Engels and their supporters also had to wage a
campaign to root out other elements alien to the revolutionary
working-class movement who were trying to use the International
Working Men's Association for their own purposes. When such an
attempt was made by the bourgeois and petty-bourgeois reformists
in the USA, for example, Marx and Engels resolutely opposed these
forays against the proletarian character of the International. Their
position on this question was reflected in the "Resolutions on the
Split in the United States' Federation Passed by the General Council
of the I.W.A. in Its Sittings of 5th and 12th March, 1872", written by
Marx, in his manuscript "American Split", and in Engels' article
"The International in America" (see pp. 124-26, 636-43 and
177-83).

Marx and Engels also had to beat off the attacks by bourgeois
politicians and journalists who were trying to distort the aims and
purposes of the International Working Men's Association and to
discredit its leaders. In the statements with which the General
Council reacted to the speeches of the British M.P., Alexander
Cochrane, in letters to *The Eastern Post* of December 20, 1871, *Le
Corsaire* of September 12, 1872, and in the article "Stefanoni and
the International Again" and other documents, they exposed the

dishonest slanders of the working-class movement put about in bourgeois circles.

The documents and articles connected with the Congress of the International at The Hague (September 2-7, 1872) form one of the most important group of items in the volume.

The Hague (fifth) Congress of the I.W.M.A. was a crucial landmark in the long struggle waged by Marx and Engels and advanced workers in various countries to establish the foundations of the revolutionary proletarian worldview in the international working-class movement. Through 1872 Marx and Engels did an enormous amount of work in preparation for the Congress, and the agenda and dates of the Congress were those that they proposed.

The Congress assembled more than a year after the fall of the Paris Commune, when international reaction was on the rampage. The Congress proceedings enjoyed the direct guidance of Marx and Engels and their most active participation. An acute ideological conflict developed between the advocates of the revolutionary proletarian line, grouped round Marx and Engels, and the anarchist delegates, who were supported by the British reformists. The discussion centred on two inseparably connected issues: open recognition, as a programmatic proposition of the International, of the idea that the proletariat should win state power, and proclamation as a guiding principle of the international working-class movement that political mass parties of the proletariat should be set up independently of the bourgeois parties. The solution of these problems in the spirit of the proposals made by Marx and Engels and their comrades meant that the key ideas of Marxism were embodied in the I.W.M.A. programme and marked the victory of Marxist theory over anarchist and reformist ideology.

The report that Marx presented to the Congress on behalf of the General Council gave a profound analysis of the situation facing the International after the Commune, and the qualitative changes that had taken place in the working-class movement as a result of I.W.M.A. activities (see pp. 219-27).

Most of the resolutions of the Hague Congress were written by Marx and Engels; the rest were based on proposals they made at the General Council meetings during preparations for the Congress. By decision of the Congress the basic content of the above-mentioned resolution of the London Conference on working-class political action was incorporated in the General Rules of the International, and the articles specifying and expanding the powers of the General Council were included in the Administrative Regulations. The resolution on the Bakuninist Alliance of Socialist Democracy in fact declared this organisation incompatible with the International and expelled the Alliance leaders—Bakunin and Guillaume—from the International Working Men's Association.

At the proposal of Marx and Engels, who based themselves on the actual historical situation that had taken shape in the Europe of the early 1870s, a resolution was passed transferring the seat of the General Council to New York (see p. 240). This step was also prompted by the danger that if it remained in London, the Council might be saddled with a majority of British reformists, or émigré Blanquists bent on adopting adventuristic conspiratorial tactics.

Taken together, the Congress decisions defined the tasks and prospects of the working-class movement in the new historical conditions. They laid the theoretical foundation for the formation in the immediate future of mass proletarian parties within the framework of the national states.

Directly related to the documents of the Hague Congress is the group of articles written by Marx and Engels in order to publicise the key decisions of the Congress. They include the above-mentioned speech by Marx at the meeting of International members in Amsterdam, the articles by Engels "On the Hague Congress of the International", "The Congress at The Hague (Letter to Enrico Bignami)", "Letters from London.—II. More about the Hague Congress", and "Imperative Mandates at the Hague Congress".

In their published writings on the Hague Congress, Marx and Engels showed its historical significance and revealed the essence of the struggle that had taken place there between the revolutionary-proletarian trend and the anarchist-reformist bloc.

They summed up the results of the battle against the Bakuninists in the pamphlet *The Alliance of Socialist Democracy and the International Working Men's Association*, written at the request of the Hague Congress. On the basis of numerous documents this pamphlet presented an exhaustive picture of the Bakuninist Alliance's disorganising activities within the International and exposed the intrigues and subterfuges to which the leaders of the Alliance had resorted in order to assert their dominance in the I.W.M.A.

After making a critical analysis of the programmatic documents of the Alliance and what its leaders were publishing in the press, the authors of the pamphlet revealed the futility of the Bakuninists' ideological arsenal, their petty-bourgeois levelling notions of the future society in the spirit of "barrack communism", their calls for rebellion and general destruction, and their orientation on the déclassé sections of society as allegedly the most revolutionary force. Marx and Engels regarded as totally unworthy of revolutionaries the contempt which the Alliance leaders showed for the ethical standards accepted in the working-class movement, their indiscriminate choice of methods of struggle, their use of mystification and deceit, and their actions based on the principle of "the end justifies the means".

The chapter "The Alliance in Russia" demonstrated the harm that Bakunin's and Nechayev's adventuristic activities had done to the Russian revolutionary movement. Marx and Engels contrasted to the Bakuninists' line the Russian revolutionary trend that was taking shape under the influence of Nikolai Chernyshevsky, of whom they wrote with great respect. As we see from his correspondence, it was at this time that Marx had the idea of writing a biography of that Russian revolutionary democrat and socialist.

The pamphlet noted that after the Hague Congress the anarchistic sectarians had launched a hostile campaign aimed at discrediting its decisions and openly refused to submit to them at their separate congresses and local rallies. Their example was followed by the British reformists. The answer to these splitting actions came with the resolutions passed on January 26 and May 30, 1873, by the New York General Council, which signalled the final organisational disassociation from the anarchists. According to these resolutions, all federations, sections and individuals who refused to recognise the decisions of the Hague Congress were declared to have placed themselves outside the ranks of the International Working Men's Association.

A substantial body of materials included in the volume reflect the systematic support that the founders of Marxism gave to the activities of the International's national organisations. Before the Hague Congress they had performed this work mainly as corresponding secretaries of the General Council for several countries—Marx for Germany and Russia, Engels for Italy, Spain, and Portugal. In this capacity they wrote numerous documents and appeals addressed to the sections of the International and individual members, explaining the various tasks that faced the international proletarian organisation and publicising its decisions (see pp. 54-56, 60-61, 74-76, 137-38, 153, 168-69, 184, 211-13, 217, 288-93). At meetings of the General Council Marx and Engels reported regularly on the state of the working-class movement in various countries. After the Congress in The Hague and the General Council's move to New York these activities did not cease, although they assumed a different character. Marx and Engels constantly helped the Council as its representatives in Europe and supplied it with important information (see, for example, the "Notes for the General Council" compiled by Engels, pp. 414-16).

Because of the great moral authority they enjoyed, they exerted a direct influence on the working-class movement in various countries. They strengthened their connections with the leaders of national contingents of the working class, and their correspondence with them became even more intensive.

The contribution of the founders of Marxism to the working-class press of various countries, their journalistic writings continued to play an important part in rallying and providing revolutionary training for those who participated in the proletariat's struggle. Articles and despatches from Marx and Engels were published in the German newspaper *Der Volksstaat*, and in the *Arbeiter Zeitung*, which came out in German in the USA, in the British papers *The Eastern Post* and *The International Herald*, in the Spanish *La Emancipacion*, the Portuguese *O Pensamento Social*, the Italian *La Plebe*, *Gazzettino Rosa*, and others.

The contributions that Engels made to the Italian paper *La Plebe*, for example, were of great importance in establishing the Italian working-class movement. His articles about English agricultural labourers' strike, the Hague Congress, the actions of the Irish members of the International in defence of arrested Fenians, and the situation in Spain (see pp. 148-50, 283-84, 294-96, 298-300), published under the general title of "Letters from London", kept Italian workers informed about the proletarian movement in other countries and helped Italy's working class to strengthen its international ties and overcome anarchist influence.

Some of the documents published in this volume are connected with the part Marx and Engels continued to play in those years in the British working-class movement. The position of the International, which openly declared its solidarity with the Paris Commune, brought about the final break between the General Council and a number of trade union leaders who had taken part in the founding and activities of the International Working Men's Association but were negative in their attitude to the Commune. The British Federal Council, set up in October 1871 by decision of

the London Conference of the International, gave Marx and
Engels a stronghold in the struggle for the broad masses of the
British working class from 1871 to 1873. Making every effort to
boost the revolutionary trend in the British working-class movement, they helped the British Federal Council to consolidate its
ties with the workers, popularised the ideas of scientific socialism
through its members, and guided the struggle against the
reformist elements that had infiltrated the Council.

Marx and Engels did all they could to draw the participants in
the Irish working-class movement into the International. They
supported the idea of creating an independent Irish organisation
of the International, regarding it as the basis for the future
formation of an Irish working-class party independent of the
bourgeois nationalists. Marx and Engels fought hard to overcome
the hostility between English and Irish workers that was being
artificially inflamed by the English bourgeoisie, and to dispel the
chauvinistic prejudices spread by the English reformist leaders. "If
members of a conquering nation called upon the nation they had
conquered and continued to hold down to forget their specific
nationality and position, to 'sink national differences' and so forth,
that was not Internationalism, it was nothing else but preaching to
them submission to the yoke, and attempting to justify and to
perpetuate the dominion of the conqueror under the cloak of
Internationalism," Engels said at the meeting of the General
Council on May 14, 1872 (p. 155).

For Marx and Engels, one of the crucial means of influencing
the British workers in the struggle against reformist ideology was
their contributing to the newspaper *The International Herald*, which
was in practice the organ of the British Federal Council. In an
effort to use this paper to broaden the outlook of British
working-class readers and awaken their interest in the emancipation struggle of their class brothers in other countries, Engels
published in several of its issues in 1873 the "Communication from
the Continent" and "News on the International Labour Movement".

Actions by the reformist elements against the decisions of the
Hague Congress brought the internal conflict in the British
Federation to a higher pitch, and in December 1872 this led to a
split in the British Federal Council. A number of documents
reflect the efforts of Marx and Engels to rally the revolutionary
forces in the British organisations of the International. The "Address of the British Federal Council to the Sections, Branches, Affiliated Societies and Members of the International Working Men's

Association", and the "Reply to the Second Circular of the Self-styled Majority of the British Federal Council", both of which were written by Marx, and the appeal composed by Engels and entitled "The Manchester Foreign Section to All Sections and Members of the British Federation" showed up the splitting activities of the reformists who had been expelled from the International. Marx and Engels helped to consolidate the victory over the reformists at the Manchester Congress of the British Sections, held in June 1873. The decisions of this congress—recognition of the need to set up a working-class party, and to nationalise all the means of production, recognition of the workers' right to offer armed resistance to the exploiters, proclamation of the red banner, the banner of the British organisations in the International, etc.—testified to the acceptance of Marxist ideas by the vanguard of Britain's working class. Engels pointed out that "no English workers' congress has ever advanced such far-reaching demands" (p. 449). The activities of the British Federation of the International, guided by Marx and Engels, kept alive the revolutionary tendency in the British working-class movement, despite the temporary dominance of reformism in the movement.

Marx and Engels saw the causes of the increasing influence of reformist ideology on union-organised British workers in the peculiar development of British capitalism, in the economic situation in Britain at that time. In his article "The English Elections", written in February 1874, Engels noted that "no separate political working-class party has existed in England since the downfall of the Chartist Party in the fifties. This is understandable in a country in which the working class has shared more than anywhere else in the advantages of the immense expansion of its large-scale industry. Nor could it have been otherwise in an England that ruled the world market..." (p. 613). Emphasising that, in the mass, the English workers participated in political struggle "almost exclusively as the extreme left wing of the 'great Liberal Party'", Engels pointed out that the English proletariat was confronted with the task of organising a strong independent working-class party.

Marx and Engels attached exceptional importance to developing the German proletariat's emancipation struggle. The course of events after the Franco-Prussian war and the Paris Commune increasingly confirmed Marx's and Engels' conclusion that the centre of the European working-class movement was shifting from France to Germany, where the first ever national working-class party to accept the revolutionary principles of the International had been operating since 1869. They saw the German Social-Democratic Workers' Party as a bastion for rallying the forces of the international working class, as its vanguard contingent. In current conditions it was a task of utmost urgency to get German Social-Democracy on to a sounder theoretical basis, to inoculate it against petty-bourgeois tendencies, and strengthen its ties with the masses. Marx and Engels maintained permanent contact with Bebel, Liebknecht and other party leaders, and helped them to work out a tactical platform and to overcome individual mistakes; they became regular contributors to the party's central organ—*Der Volksstaat*. Engels was a particularly frequent contributor. He explained to the German workers the situation in the international working-class movement and exposed the Lassalleans' slanderous attempts to misrepresent the campaign waged by the revolutionary proletarians against the Bakuninists at the Hague Congress and after it (see "From the International", "On the Articles in the *Neuer Social-Demokrat*", "The International and the *Neuer*", etc.).

Engels used the opportunities afforded by the Social-Democratic press as a means of training the German working class and its party to be irreconcilable towards the reactionary internal system and the aggressive foreign policy of the ruling classes, towards militarism and chauvinism. In his articles "The 'Crisis' in Prussia" and "The Imperial Military Law" he showed that the German Empire, created in 1871 under the aegis of the Prussia of the Junkers, was a military police state, a forcing ground for the arms race and preparations for new wars of aggression. Engels noted the hostility towards the masses, especially the proletariat, of the policy pursued by Bismarck's government, its desire to provide maximum protection for the interests of the most reactionary class—the Junkers, who were clinging to their feudal privileges. Engels poured scorn on the liberal bourgeoisie and its crawling subservience to Bismarck. "The Prussian bourgeoisie," he wrote, "does not *want* political dominance; rotten without having reached maturity, ... it has already arrived, without ever having ruled, at the same stage of degeneration that the French bourgeoisie has attained after eighty years of struggles and a long period of dominance" (p. 405).

In his works of those years Engels laid bare the Bonapartist nature of the state system of the German Empire and the policies of its upper crust. He noted that the form of state that had developed in Prussia, and in Germany's imperial structure which was built according to the same pattern, "is pseudo-constitutionalism, a form which is at once both the present-day form of the dissolution of the old absolute monarchy and the form of existence of the Bonapartist monarchy" (p. 363). Taking as an example the Prussian-Bismarckian version of the Bonapartist state, Engels singled out the essential features of Bonapartism: ma-noeuvring between the main contesting classes of bourgeois society, concentration of power in the hands of the military-bureaucratic caste, apparent independence of the state apparatus, decay and corruption of the ruling clique, etc.

A profound analysis of the socio-political situation that had arisen in the Germany of the early 1870s is to be found in the supplement Engels wrote in 1874 to the Preface of 1870 for *The Peasant War in Germany.* Proceeding from this analysis, Engels formulated the tasks confronting the advanced German workers. Lenin described the thoughts he expressed in this connection as "recommendations to the German working-class movement, which had become strong, practically and politically" (V. I. Lenin, *Collected Works,* Vol. 5, Progress Publishers, Moscow, 1977, p. 370). Engels showed the immense importance of revolutionary theory for the socialist working-class movement. He pointed out that the proletarian party could fulfil its historic mission only if it were armed with the theory of scientific socialism and had learned to dovetail this theory with the practice of revolutionary struggle. "...Socialism," Engels wrote, "since it has become a science, demands that it be pursued as a science, that is, that it be studied. The task will be to spread with increased zeal among the masses of workers the ever more lucid understanding thus acquired and to knit together ever more strongly the organisation both of the party and of the trade unions" (p. 631). Defining the three inseparably linked directions in which the working-class struggle should be pursued—theoretical, political and economico-practical—Engels stressed that the warrant of success lay in the unity of these three forms of class struggle.

Engels put a high priority on implanting the ideas of proletarian internationalism among the German workers. He indicated that German Social-Democracy, as the most highly organised contingent of the international working-class movement, bore a special responsibility. He urged it "to safeguard the true international spirit, which allows no patriotic chauvinism to arise and which readily welcomes every new advance of the proletarian movement, no matter from which nation it comes" (ibid.).

Linked with the published works of Engels are his manuscript

"Varia on Germany", which emerged from an unaccomplished plan to write a detailed historical study that would help the German workers to draw correct lessons from their country's past. In these "Varia" the Marxist conception of German history from the late Middle Ages is expounded in compact form. Engels reveals the causes of Germany's fragmentation, its political and economic backwardness, and the historical roots of reaction. The adventuristic, anti-popular policy of the ruling classes of the German states, particularly Junker Prussia, the inability of the German burghers and their heirs, the bourgeoisie, to find a revolutionary solution in the struggle with feudalism had resulted in Germany's being unable right up to the middle of the 19th century to complete the process of bourgeois reforms. Engels compared Germany's historical development with that of several other European countries and offered profound thoughts on the process of the formation of nations and national states, and also on German culture, literature and philosophy.

Looking into the future, Engels predicted the collapse of the Prussian-German militarist state.

By the autumn of 1873, during preparations for the Congress of the International in Geneva, Marx and Engels came to the conclusion that the International Working Men's Association, as an organisation for uniting the militant forces of the proletariat, no longer measured up to the new historical conditions. They were both as free of dogmatism over matters concerning the organisation of the proletarian struggle as they were in other matters. They believed that the very process of its development generated the need to change its organisational forms. This development virtually brought the activities of the International Working Men's Association to an end in late 1873, although it was not officially disbanded until 1876. "The First International had played its historical part, and now made way for a period of a far greater development of the labour movement in all countries in the world, a period in which the movement grew in *scope,* and *mass* socialist working-class parties in individual national states were formed" (V. I. Lenin, *Collected Works,* Vol. 21, 1977, p. 49).

The First International, guided by Marx and Engels, performed its historical tasks. It gave an enormous impulse to the development of the working-class struggle for emancipation and rallied tens of thousands of proletarians in Europe and America round the banner of proletarian internationalism. For the first time, the working-class movement emerged on the international scene as a powerful factor of social progress, as a standard-bearer in the struggle for peace, democracy and socialism. Thanks to the efforts of Marx and Engels and their comrades, an important step was taken towards imbuing the broad masses with the ideas of scientific socialism. During the years of the International the ideological arsenal of revolutionary theory was itself notably enriched with new conclusions and generalisations. Various kinds of pre-Marxist petty-bourgeois socialism were defeated and loosing their influence. A revolutionary proletarian party was founded in Germany and the ground was prepared for the setting up of similar parties in other countries. A whole galaxy of proletarian revolutionaries—organisers, journalists, propagandists—was formed in the ranks of the International Working Men's Association under the guidance of Marx and Engels. The International performed a great service in evolving the tactics of proletarian organisations, in establishing trade unions, and in developing the working-class press. Its revolutionary traditions of solidarity action by the workers of different countries in defence of the economic and political interests of the working people, of opposing aggressive wars and supporting national-liberation movements have been of enduring value to subsequent generations of proletarian fighters. "It is unforgettable, it will remain for ever in the history of the workers' struggle for their emancipation" (V. I. Lenin, *Collected Works*, Vol. 29, 1977, p. 240).

* * *

The volume contains 110 works by Marx and Engels. Of these, 40 were written in English, 25 in German, 16 in French, 20 in Italian, and 8 in Spanish; one work was written in the mixture of English, French and German. Twenty-eight works are published in English for the first time.

Any misprints or slips of the pen have been corrected in the text with explanations in footnotes where necessary.

Foreign words and expressions in the text of the original have been preserved in the form in which they were used by the authors, and are given in italics, with the translation usually supplied in a footnote. The English words and expressions used by Marx and Engels in texts written in German, French and other languages, are given in small caps; large passages written in English are marked with initial and closing asterisks.

The volume was compiled, the text prepared and the preface and notes were written, the index of quoted and mentioned

literature, and the subject index were prepared by Tatyana
Vasilyeva. The name index and the index of periodicals were
prepared by Yelizaveta Ovsyannikova. The volume was edited by
Lev Golman (Institute of Marxism-Leninism of the CC CPSU).

The translations were made by David Forgacs, John Peet,
Barrie Selman, Veronica Thomson, Joan and Trevor Walmsley
(Lawrence & Wishart); Geoffrey Nowell-Smith; Sergei Syrovatkin
(Progress Publishers), and edited by Nicholas Jacobs (Lawrence &
Wishart), Yelena Kalinina, Mzia Pitskhelauri, Jane Sayer, Victor
Schnittke, Andrei Skvarsky, Anna Vladimirova, Yelena Vorotnikova
(Progress Publishers) and scientific editor Vladimir Mosolov
(Institute of Marxism-Leninism of the CC CPSU).

The volume was prepared for the press by Margarita
Lopukhina, Lyudmila Mikhailova, Alla Varavitskaya and Yelena
Vorotnikova (Progress Publishers).

KARL MARX
and
FREDERICK ENGELS

WORKS

October 1871-July 1874

Karl Marx

[GENERAL RULES AND ADMINISTRATIVE REGULATIONS OF THE INTERNATIONAL WORKING MEN'S ASSOCIATION][1]

GENERAL RULES
OF THE INTERNATIONAL WORKING MEN'S ASSOCIATION

Considering,

That the emancipation of the working classes must be conquered by the working classes themselves; that the struggle for the emancipation of the working classes means not a struggle for class privileges and monopolies, but for equal rights and duties, and the abolition of all class-rule;

That the economical subjection of the man of labour to the monopolizer of the means of labour, that is the sources of life, lies at the bottom of servitude in all its forms, of all social misery, mental degradation, and political dependence;

That the economical emancipation of the working classes is therefore the great end to which every political movement ought to be subordinate as a means;

That all efforts aiming at that great end have hitherto failed from the want of solidarity between the manifold divisions of labour in each country, and from the absence of a fraternal bond of union between the working classes of different countries;

That the emancipation of labour[a] is neither a local nor a national, but a social problem, embracing all countries in which modern society exists, and depending for its solution on the concurrence, practical and theoretical, of the most advanced countries;

That the present revival of the working classes in the most industrious countries of Europe, while it raises a new hope, gives solemn warning against a relapse into the old errors, and calls for

---

[a] The German edition has "the emancipation of the working class".— *Ed.*

the immediate combination of the still disconnected movements;

For these Reasons—

The International Working Men's Association has been founded.

It declares:

That all societies and individuals adhering to it will acknowledge truth, justice, and morality, as the basis of their conduct towards each other and towards all men, without regard to colour, creed, or nationality;

That it acknowledges *no rights without duties, no duties without rights;*

And in this spirit the following rules have been drawn up.

1. This Association is established to afford a central medium of communication and co-operation[a] between Working Men's Societies existing in different countries and aiming at the same end; viz., the protection, advancement, and complete emancipation of the working classes.

2. The name of the Society shall be "The International Working Men's Association".

3. There shall annually meet a General Working Men's Congress, consisting of delegates of the branches of the Association. The Congress will have to proclaim the common aspirations of the working class, take the measures required for the successful working of the International Association, and appoint the General Council of the Society.

4. Each Congress appoints the time and place of meeting for the next Congress. The delegates assemble at the appointed time and place without any special invitation. The General Council may, in case of need, change the place, but has no power to postpone the time of meeting. The Congress appoints the seat and elects the members of the General Council annually. The General Council thus elected shall have power to add to the number of its members.

On its annual meetings, the General Congress shall receive a public account of the annual transactions of the General Council. The latter may, in cases of emergency, convoke the General Congress before the regular yearly term.

5. The General Council shall consist of working men from the different countries represented in the International Association. It shall from its own members elect the officers necessary for the

---

[a] The German edition has "systematic co-operation".— *Ed.*

GENERAL RULES

AND

ADMINISTRATIVE REGULATIONS

OF THE

INTERNATIONAL WORKING-MEN'S ASSOCIATION.

OFFICIAL EDITION, REVISED BY THE GENERAL COUNCIL.

LONDON:

Printed for the General Council by

EDWARD TRUELOVE, 256, HIGH HOLBORN.

1871.

Title page of the English edition of the General Rules and Administrative Regulations of the International Working Men's Association

transaction of business, such as a treasurer, a general secretary, corresponding secretaries for the different countries, etc.

6. The General Council shall form an international agency between the different national and local groups of the Association, so that the working men in one country be constantly informed of the movements of their class in every other country: that an inquiry into the social state of the different countries of Europe be made simultaneously, and under a common direction[a]; that the questions of general interest mooted in one society be ventilated by all; and that when immediate practical steps should be needed—as, for instance, in case of international quarrels—the action of the associated societies be simultaneous and uniform. Whenever it seems opportune, the General Council shall take the initiative of proposals to be laid before the different national or local societies. To facilitate the communications, the General Council shall publish periodical reports.

7. Since the success of the working men's movement in each country cannot be secured but by the power of union and combination, while, on the other hand, the usefulness of the International General Council must greatly depend on the circumstance whether it has to deal with a few national centres of working men's associations, or with a great number of small and disconnected local societies; the members of the International Association shall use their utmost efforts to combine the disconnected working men's societies of their respective countries into national bodies, represented by central national organs. It is self-understood, however, that the appliance of this rule will depend upon the peculiar laws of each country, and that, apart from legal obstacles, no independent local society shall be precluded from directly corresponding with the General Council.

8. Every section has the right to appoint its own secretary corresponding with the General Council.

9. Everybody who acknowledges and defends the principles of the International Working Men's Association is eligible to become a member. Every branch is responsible for the integrity of the members it admits.

10. Each member of the International Association, on removing his domicile from one country to another, will receive the fraternal support of the Associated Working Men.

11. While united in a perpetual bond of fraternal co-operation,

---

[a] The French edition has "in a common spirit".— Ed.

the working men's societies joining the International Association will preserve their existent organizations intact.

12. The present rules may be revised by each Congress, provided that two-thirds of the delegates present are in favour of such revision.

13. Everything not provided for in the present rules will be supplied by special regulations, subject to the revision of every Congress.

ADMINISTRATIVE REGULATIONS,
REVISED IN ACCORDANCE
WITH THE RESOLUTIONS PASSED
BY THE CONGRESSES (1866 TO 1869),
AND BY THE LONDON CONFERENCE (1871)

I

The General Congress

1. Every member of the International Working Men's Association has the right to vote at elections for, and is eligible as, a delegate to the General Congress.

2. Every branch, whatever the number of its members, may send a delegate to the Congress.

3. Each delegate has but one vote in the Congress.

4. The expenses of the delegates are to be defrayed by the branches and groups which appoint them.

5. If a branch be unable to send a delegate, it may unite with other neighbouring branches for the appointment of one.

6. Every branch or group consisting of more than 500 members may send an additional delegate for every additional 500 members.

7. Only the delegates of such societies, sections, or groups as form parts of the International, and shall have paid their contributions to the General Council, will in future be allowed to take their seats and to vote at Congresses. Nevertheless, for such countries where the regular establishment of the International may have been prevented by law, delegates of trades' unions and working men's co-operative societies will be allowed to participate in Congress debates on questions of principle, but not to discuss, or to vote on, administrative matters.

8. The sittings of the Congress will be twofold—administrative sittings, which will be private, and public sittings, reserved for the

discussion of, and the vote upon, the general questions of the Congress programme.

9. The Congress programme, consisting of questions placed on the order of the day by the preceding Congress, questions added by the General Council, and questions submitted to the acceptance of that Council by the different sections, groups, or their committees, shall be drawn up by the General Council.

Every section, group, or committee which intends to propose, for the discussion of the impending Congress, a question not proposed by the previous Congress, shall give notice thereof to the General Council before the 31st of March.

10. The General Council is charged with the organization of each Congress, and shall, in due time, through the medium of the Federal Councils or Committees, bring the Congress programme to the cognizance of the branches.

11. The Congress will appoint as many committees as there shall be questions submitted to it. Each delegate shall designate the committee upon which he may prefer to sit. Each Committee shall read the memorials presented by the different sections and groups on the special question referred to it. It shall elaborate them into one single report, which alone is to be read at the public sittings. It shall moreover decide which of the above memorials shall be annexed to the official report of the Congress transactions.

12. In its public sittings, the Congress will, in the first instance, occupy itself with the questions placed on the order of the day by the General Council, the remaining questions to be discussed afterwards.

13. All resolutions on questions of principle shall be voted upon by division (*appel nominal*).

14. Two months[a] at latest before the meeting of the annual Congress, every branch or federation of branches shall transmit to the General Council a detailed report of its proceedings and development during the current year. The General Council shall elaborate these elements into one single report, which alone is to be read before Congress.

II

The General Council

1. The designation of General Council is reserved for the Central Council of the International Working Men's Association.

---

[a] The French edition has "one month".— *Ed.*

The Central Councils of the various countries, where the International is regularly organized, shall designate themselves as Federal Councils, or Federal Committees, with the names of the respective countries attached.

2. The General Council is bound to execute the Congress Resolutions.

3. As often as its means may permit, the General Council shall publish a *bulletin* or report embracing everything which may be of interest to the International Working Men's Association.

For this purpose it shall collect all the documents to be transmitted by the Federal Councils or Committees of the different countries and such others as it may be able to procure by other means.

The *bulletin*, drawn up in several languages, shall be sent gratuitously to the Federal Councils or Committees, which are to forward one copy to each of their branches.

In case the General Council should be unable to publish such *bulletins*, it shall every three months send a written communication to the different Federal Councils or Committees, to be published in the newspapers of their respective countries, and especially in the International organs.

4. Every new branch or society intending to join the International, is bound immediately to announce its adhesion to the General Council.

5. The General Council has the right to admit or to refuse the affiliation of any new branch or group, subject to appeal to the next Congress.

Nevertheless, wherever there exist Federal Councils or Committees, the General Council is bound to consult them before admitting or rejecting the affiliation of a new branch or society within their jurisdiction; without prejudice, however, to its right of provisional decision.

6. The General Council has also the right of suspending, till the meeting of next Congress, any branch of the International.

7. In case of differences arising between societies or branches of the same national group, or between groups of different nationalities, the General Council shall have the right of deciding such differences, subject to appeal to the next Congress, whose decision shall be final.

8. All delegates appointed by the General Council to distinct missions shall have the right to attend, and be heard at, all meetings of Federal Councils or Committees, district and local

Committees, and local branches, without, however, being entitled to vote thereat.

9. English, French, and German editions of the General Rules and Regulations are to be reprinted from the official texts published by the General Council.

All versions of the General Rules and Regulations in other languages shall, before publication, be submitted to the General Council for approval.

III

Contributions to Be Paid to the General Council

1. An annual contribution of One Penny[a] per member shall be levied from all branches and affiliated societies for the use of the General Council. This contribution is intended to defray the expenses of the General Council, such as the remuneration of its General Secretary, costs of correspondence, publications, preparatory work for Congresses, etc. etc.

2. The General Council shall cause to be printed uniform adhesive stamps representing the value of one penny each, to be annually supplied, in the numbers wanted, to the Federal Councils or Committees.

3. These stamps are to be affixed to a special sheet of the *livret* or to a copy of the Rules which every member of the Association is held to possess.[b]

4. On the 1st of March of each year, the Federal Councils or Committees of the different countries[c] shall forward to the General Council the amounts of the stamps disposed of, and return the unsold stamps remaining on hand.

5. These stamps, representing the value of the individual contributions, shall bear the date of the current year.

---

[a] The French and German editions have "10 centimes" and "one groschen" respectively.— *Ed.*

[b] In the German and French editions Article 3 reads as follows: "The Federal Councils or Committees shall provide the local Committees, or, in their absence, their respective branches, with the number of stamps corresponding to the number of their members." Then follow articles 4, 5 and 6 which correspond to articles 3, 4 and 5 in the English edition.— *Ed.*

[c] The French edition has "of the different countries or localities".— *Ed.*

IV

Federal Councils or Committees

1. The expenses of the Federal Councils or Committees shall be defrayed by their respective branches.

2. The Federal Councils or Committees shall send one report at least every month to the General Council.

3. The Federal Councils or Committees shall transmit to the General Council every three months a report on the administration and financial state of their respective branches.

4. Any Federation may refuse to admit or may exclude from its midst societies or branches. It is, however, not empowered to deprive them of their International character, but it may propose their suspension to the General Council.

V

Local Societies, Branches, and Groups

1. Every branch is at liberty to make rules and bye-laws for its local administration, adapted to local circumstances and the laws of its country. But these rules and bye-laws must not contain anything contrary to the General Rules and Regulations.

2. All local branches, groups, and their committees are henceforth to designate and constitute themselves simply and exclusively as branches, groups, and committees of the International Working Men's Association, with the names of their respective localities attached.

3. Consequently, no branches or groups will henceforth be allowed to designate themselves by sectarian names,— such as Positivists, Mutualists, Collectivists, Communists, etc., or to form separatist bodies, under the name of *sections of propaganda,* etc., pretending to accomplish special missions distinct from the common purposes of the Association.

4. Art. 2 of this division does not apply to affiliated Trades' Unions.

5. All sections, branches, and working men's societies affiliated to the International are invited to abolish the office of President of their respective branch or society.

6. The formation of female branches amongst the working class is recommended. It is, however, understood that this resolution

does not at all intend to interfere with the existence, or formation of branches composed of both sexes.

7. Wherever attacks against the International are published, the nearest branch or committee is held to send at once a copy of such publication to the General Council.

8. The addresses of the offices of all International Committees and of the General Council are to be published every three months in all the organs of the Association.

VI

General Statistics of Labour

1. The General Council is to enforce Article 6 of the Rules[a] relating to general statistics of the working class, and the Resolutions of the Geneva Congress, 1866, on the same subject.

2. Every local branch is bound to appoint a special Committee of Statistics, so as to be always ready, within the limits of its means, to answer any question which may be put to it by the Federal Council or Committee of its country or by the General Council.

It is recommended to all branches to remunerate the secretaries of the Committees of Statistics, considering the general benefit the working class will derive from their labour.

3. On the 1st of August of each year the Federal Councils or Committees will transmit the materials collected in their respective countries to the General Council, which, in its turn, is to elaborate them into a general report, to be laid before the Congresses or Conferences annually held in the month of September.[b]

4. Trades' Unions and International branches refusing to give the information required, shall be reported to the General Council, which will take action thereupon.

5. The Resolutions of the Geneva Congress, 1866, alluded to in Article 1 of this division are the following.[2]

One great International combination of efforts will be a statistical inquiry into the situation of the working classes of all civilized countries[c] to be instituted by the working classes

---

[a] The reference is to Article 6 of the "Provisional Rules of the Association" (present edition, Vol. 20, pp. 15-16). The French edition refers to Article 5 of the *Statuts et Règlements*, London, 1866, p. 5 (cf. *Rules of the International Working Men's Association*, London [1867], p. 5. See present edition, Vol. 20, p. 443).— *Ed.*

[b] The words "annually held in the month of September" are omitted in the French edition.— *Ed.*

[c] The French edition has "of different countries".— *Ed.*

themselves. To act with any success, the materials to be acted upon must be known. By initiating so great a work, the working men will prove their ability to take their own fate into their own hands.

The Congress therefore proposes that in each locality where branches of our Association exist, the work be immediately commenced, and evidence collected on the different points specified in the subjoined scheme of inquiry; the Congress invites the working men of Europe and the United States of America to co-operate in gathering the elements of the statistics of the working class; reports and evidence to be forwarded to the General Council. The General Council shall elaborate them into a report, adding the evidence as an appendix. This report, together with its appendix, shall be laid before the next annual Congress, and after having received its sanction, be printed at the expense of the Association.

General scheme of inquiry, which may of course be modified by each locality. 1. Industry, name of. 2. Age and sex of the employed. 3. Number of the employed. 4. Salaries and wages; (a) apprentices; (b) wages by the day or piece work; scale paid by middle men. Weekly, yearly average. 5. (a) Hours of work in factories. (b) The hours of work with small employers and in home work,[a] if the business be carried on in those different modes. (c) Nightwork and daywork. 6. Meal-times and treatment. 7. Sort of workshop and work; overcrowding, defective ventilation, want of sunlight, use of gaslight, cleanliness, etc. 8. Effect of employment upon the physical condition. 9. Moral condition. Education. 10. State of trade: whether season trade, or more or less uniformly distributed over the year, whether greatly fluctuating, whether exposed to foreign competition—whether destined principally for home or foreign consumption, &c.[b]

APPENDIX

The Conference held at London from 17th to 23rd September, 1871, has charged the General Council to issue a new, authentic and revised edition, in English, French, and German, of the "General Rules and Regulations of the International Working Men's Association"; for the following reasons:—

---

[a] The rest of the sentence is omitted in the French edition.— Ed.

[b] The French and German editions add Point 11: "Particular laws on the relations between the worker and the employer". The German edition has Point 12: "The dietary and housing conditions of the workers".— Ed.

I. General Rules

The Geneva Congress (1866) adopted, with a few additions, the Provisional Rules of the Association, published at London in November, 1864. It also decided (see "Congrès ouvrier de l'Association Internationale des Travailleurs, tenu à Genève du 3 au 8 Septbre., 1866", Genève, 1866, p. 27, note), that the General Council should publish the official and obligatory text of the Rules as well as of the Regulations voted by the Congress.[a] The General Council was prevented from executing this order by the seizure, on the part of the Bonapartist Government, of the minutes of the Geneva Congress on their transit through France.[3] When at last, through the intercession of Lord Stanley, then British Foreign Secretary, the minutes were recovered, a French edition had already been issued at Geneva, and the text of the Rules and Regulations contained in it was at once reproduced in all French-speaking countries. This text was faulty in many respects.

1. The Paris edition of the London Provisional Rules had been accepted as a true translation; but the Paris Committee to which this translation is due, had not only introduced most important alterations[4] in the preamble of the Rules which, on the interpellation of the General Council, were represented as changes unavoidable under the existing political state of France. From an insufficient acquaintance with the English language, it had also misinterpreted some of the articles of the Rules.

2. The Geneva Congress having to give a final character to the Provisional Rules, the Committee appointed for this purpose simply struck out all passages in which anything of a provisional nature was alluded to, without noticing that several of these passages contained most important matter of no provisional character whatever. In the English edition published after the Lausanne Congress (1867) the same omissions are repeated.

II. Administrative Regulations

The Administrative Regulations hitherto published conjointly with the Rules, are but those voted by the Geneva Congress (1866). It thus became necessary to codify the further regulations voted by subsequent Congresses and by the late London Conference.

---

[a] The French edition adds here: "in its report on the Congress".— Ed.

3*

The following publications have been made use of for the present revised edition:—

"Address and Provisional Rules of the International Working Men's Association", &c. London. 1864.

"Rules of the International Working Men's Association". London. 1867.

"Congrès ouvrier de l'Association Internationale des Travailleurs, tenu à Genève du 3 au 8 Septbre., 1866". Genève, 1866.[a]

"Procès-verbaux du Congrès de l'Association Internationale des Travailleurs, réuni à Lausanne, du 2 au 8 Septbre., 1867". Chaux-de-Fonds. 1867.

"Troisième Congrès de l'Association Internationale des Travailleurs (Brussels Congress)—Compte-rendu officiel". Bruxelles. 1868.

"The International Working Men's Association. Resolutions of the Congress of Geneva, 1866, and the Congress of Brussels, 1868". London. 1869.

"Compte-rendu du 4me Congrès International, tenu à Bâle en Septbre., 1869". Bruxelles. 1869.

"Report of the Fourth Annual Congress of the International Working Men's Association, held at Basel, 1869". Published by the General Council. London. 1869.

"Quatrième Congrès de l'Association Internationale des Travailleurs, tenu à Bâle, 1869. Rapport du délégué des Sections de la Fabrique à Genève". Genève. 1869.

"Resolutions of the Conference of Delegates of the International Working Men's Association, assembled at London, 1871". London. 1871.

For the Basel Congress, the German report of the Congress proceedings, published in fly-sheets at Basel, and the notes taken during the Congress by the General Secretary,[b] have also been consulted.

How these various sources have been made use of for the purposes of the present revised edition will appear from the following statement.[c]

---

[a] The French edition has an additional source: "Compte-rendu du Congrès de Genève" (publié d'après les procès-verbaux par le Conseil général dans le *Courrier international*, Londres, mars et avril 1867).— *Ed.*

[b] J. G. Eccarius.— *Ed.*

[c] In the French edition this paragraph reads as follows: "In the following report, next to the articles of the present Rules and Regulations, the corresponding articles of previous editions are indicated, as well as information relating to administrative resolutions, compiled here for the first time. The changes in the French text, made by the decision of the Conference, to bring it into accord with the English one, have not been indicated."— *Ed.*

GENERAL RULES

Preamble.—After the words, "*For these reasons*", there have been restored the words, "the International Working Men's Association has been founded". See Provisional Rules, p. 13.[a]

The passage, "They hold it the duty of a man", &c., has been omitted, because there exist two equally authentic versions of it, irreconcilable with each other. The true meaning of it is, besides, already contained in the passage immediately preceding, and in that immediately following: "No rights without duties", &c.[5]

Art. 3 is restored from Art. 3 of Provisional Rules.

Art. 4.—Part of Art. 3 and the whole of Art. 4 of Rules, London, 1867.

Art. 5.—Introductory part of Art. 3, Rules, 1867. The words "a president" have been omitted, in agreement with Administrative Resolution I. of Basel Congress.[6]

Art. 6.—Art. 5, Rules, 1867. The words "Co-operating Associations" have been changed into "national and local groups of the Association", because the expression, in some translations, has been misinterpreted as meaning co-operative societies.[b]

Art. 7.—Art. 6, Rules, 1867.

Art. 8.—Art. 10, Rules, 1867.

Art. 10.—Art. 8, Rules, 1867.

Art. 12 forms Art. 13 of the Administrative Regulations in "Rules, 1867".[c]

Art. 13.—Art. 12, Rules, 1867.

Art. 7, Rules, 1867, has been omitted, because its insertion was contrary to a resolution of the Lausanne Congress. See "Procès-verbaux du Congrès de Lausanne", p. 36.[d]

ADMINISTRATIVE REGULATIONS

I. The General Congress

Art. 1.—Art. 11 of Regulations voted by Geneva Congress ("Congrès de Genève", Genève, 1866, p. 26, [27] &c); Art. 10, Rules, &c, 1867, which is incomplete.

---

[a] See present edition, Vol. 20, pp. 14-15. The reference to the "Provisional Rules" is omitted in the German edition.— *Ed.*

[b] The sentence is omitted in the French edition.— *Ed.*

[c] The French edition refers to another source: "Règlement administratif. Art. 15, Congrès ouvrier de Genève".— *Ed.*

[d] This point is omitted in the French edition.— *Ed.*

Art. 2.—Art. 9, Congrès de Genève; Art. 6, Rules, &c, 1867.

Art. 3.—Art. 13, Congrès de Genève; Art. 11, Rules, &c, 1867.

Art. 4.—Art. 10, Congrès de Genève; Art. 9, Rules, &c, 1867.

Art. 5.—Art. 9, Congrès de Genève; Art. 7, Rules, &c, 1867.

Art. 6.—Art. 12, Congrès de Genève; Art. 8, Rules, &c, 1867.

Art. 7.—Basel Administrative Regulations, VIII.

Art. 8.—For this article the Guide pratique pour le Congrès de l'Internationale (Compte-rendu du Congrès de Bâle, Bruxelles, 1869) has been completed by the other materials on the Basel Congress, quoted above.

Art. 9.—First part as for Art. 8. Second part, Resolution of Lausanne Congress (Procès-verbaux, p. 74, 1).

Art. 10.—Art. 1b, Congrès de Genève; Art. 1b, Rules, &c, 1867.

Art. 11.—Guide Pratique, Basel Congress, Art. 3 and 11.

Art. 12.—Guide Pratique, &c, Art. 10.

Art. 13.—Guide Pratique, &c, Art. 7.

Art. 14.—Guide Pratique, &c, Art. 4.

II. The General Council

Art. 1.—London Conference, 1871, II. 1.

Art. 2.—Congrès de Genève, Art. 1; Rules, &c, 1867, Art. 1.

Art. 3.—The two first Alineas, Art. 2 and Art. 1a; Congrès de Genève, and Rules, &c, 1867. Third Alinea, Art. 3, Congrès de Genève. Last Alinea, Lausanne Congress, Procès-verbaux, p. 37, Art. 2.

Arts. 4 to 7.—Basel Administrative Resolutions, IV. to VII.

Art. 8.—London Conference, III.

Art. 9.—Resolution of London Conference, sittings of 18th and 22nd September.

III. Contributions to Be Paid to the General Council

Art. 1.—First Alinea, Lausanne Congress, Procès-verbaux, p. 37, 3; and Art. IX., Basel Administrative Resolutions. Second Alinea, Art. 4, Congrès de Genève, and Rules, 1867.

Arts. 2 to 6.—London Conference, IV., 1 to 5.

IV. Federal Councils or Committees

Art. 1.—Art. 6, Congrès de Genève, and Rules, 1867.

Art. 2.—Art. 5, ditto.

Art. 3.—Brussels Congress, "Compte-rendu Officiel", p. 50, Appendice, Séances Administratives, Resolution № 3.
Art. 4.—Art. VI., Basel Administrative Resolutions.

V. Local Societies, Branches, and Groups

Art. 1.—Art. 14, Congrès de Genève; Art. 12, Rules, &c, 1867.
Arts. 2 to 4.—London Conference, II., 2 to 4.
Art. 5.—Art. I., Basel Administrative Resolutions.
Art. 6.—London Conference, V.
Art. 7.—Art. II., Basel Administrative Resolutions.
Art. 8.—Art. III., ditto.

VI. General Statistics of Labour

Arts. 1 to 4.—London Conference, VI., 1 to 4.
Art. 5.—Resolution of Geneva Congress (London edition of Geneva and Brussels Congress Resolutions, p. 4).

By order, and in the name of the London Conference, 1871,

The General Council

R. Applegarth, M. J. Boon, Fred. Bradnick, G. H. Buttery, V. Delahaye, Eugène Dupont (on mission), *Wm. Hales, G. Harris, Hurliman, Jules Johannard, Harriet Law, Fred. Lessner, Lochner, Ch. Longuet, C. Martin, Zévy Maurice, Henry Mayo, George Milner, Ch. Murray, Pfänder, John Roach, Rühl, Sadler, Cowell Stepney, Alfred Taylor, W. Townshend, E. Vaillant, John Weston.*[a]

Corresponding Secretaries

Leó Frankel, for Austria and Hungary; *A. Herman,* Belgium; *T. Mottershead,* Denmark; *A. Serraillier,* France; *Karl Marx,* Germany and Russia; *Charles Rochat,* Holland; *J. P. McDonnell,* Ireland; *Fred. Engels,* Italy and Spain; *Walery Wróblewski,* Poland;

------

[a] Both the French and German editions have the names of Ant. Arnaud, F. Cournet and G. Ranvier among the General Council members, and the German edition, Vitale Regis as well; besides that the words "(on mission)" after the name of Eugène Dupont are omitted in the German edition.— *Ed.*

Hermann Jung, Switzerland; *J. G. Eccarius,* United States; *Le Moussu,* for French Branches of United States.

Charles Longuet, Chairman
Hermann Jung, Treasurer
John Hales, General Secretary

256, High Holborn, W.C., London,
24th October, 1871

Drawn up in October 1871

First published as pamphlets in English and French in November-December 1871, and in German in February 1872

Reproduced from the English pamphlet checked with the French and German editions

Frederick Engels

[RESOLUTION OF THE GENERAL COUNCIL EXPELLING GUSTAVE DURAND FROM THE INTERNATIONAL WORKING MEN'S ASSOCIATION][7]

The General Council having received full evidence that Gustave Durand, working jeweller of Paris, ex-delegate of the jewellers to the Federal Chamber of Paris Working Men,[8] ex-chief of Battalion of the National Guards, ex-chief cashier at the Delegation of Finance under the Commune, passing as a refugee in London, has served, and is now serving, as a spy for the French police upon the Communal refugees and especially upon the General Council of the International Working Men's Association, and has already received 725 francs for his services.

The said Gustave Durand is therefore branded as infamous[a] and expelled from the International Association.

This resolution to be published in all the organs of the International.

Adopted by the General Council on October 7, 1871

First published in *The Eastern Post*, No. 159 and *Der Volksstaat*, No. 83, on October 14, 1871

Reproduced from the Minute Book of the General Council checked with the newspapers

---

[a] *Der Volksstaat* has "a traitor" instead of "infamous".— *Ed.*

28 VENDEMMIALE 80 — LODI — 19 OTTOBRE 1871

LA PLEBE

GIORNALE REPUBBLICANO

I coal deMi Grandi aan poso tali os nop parshò nei
siamo in ginocchioi leviaghooi.   Lamdalaf.

Frederick Engels

[TO ENRICO BIGNAMI, EDITOR OF *LA PLEBE*] [9]

London, October 13 [1871]

Citizen Editor of *La Plebe*,

The General Council has entrusted me with sending you the enclosed resolution[a] and requesting that you publish it in the columns of your esteemed newspaper.

I remain yours sincerely,

Frederick Engels,
Secretary for Italy

First published in *La Plebe*, No. 122, October 19, 1871

Printed according to the newspaper

Translated from the Italian

---

[a] F. Engels, "Resolution of the General Council Expelling Gustave Durand from the International Working Men's Association" (see this volume, p. 21).— *Ed.*

Karl Marx

[DECLARATION OF THE GENERAL COUNCIL ON NECHAYEV'S MISUSE OF THE NAME OF THE INTERNATIONAL WORKING MEN'S ASSOCIATION][10]

International Workingmen's Association

The Conference of the Delegates of the International Workingmen's Association, assembled at London from the 17th to the 23d September 1871, has charged the General Council to declare publicly:

that *Netschajeff* has never been a member or an agent of the International Workingmen's Association;

that his assertions[a] to have founded a branch at Brussels and to have been sent by a Brussels branch on a mission to Geneva, are false;

that the above said Netschajeff has fraudulently used the name of the International Workingmen's Association in order to make dupes and victims in Russia.

By order of the General Council, etc.

14 October 1871

Adopted by the General Council on October 16, 1871

First published in *Qui vive!*, No. 14, October 18, 1871 and in *Der Volksstaat*, No. 88, November 1, 1871

Reproduced from the manuscript checked with the text in *Der Volksstaat*

---

[a] *Der Volksstaat* has the following words inserted here: "(made known through the political process in St. Petersburg)".— *Ed.*

Karl Marx

[RESOLUTION OF THE GENERAL COUNCIL ON THE RULES OF THE FRENCH SECTION OF 1871][11]

INTERNATIONAL WORKING MEN'S ASSOCIATION
256, High Holborn, London.—W.C.

RESOLUTION OF THE GENERAL COUNCIL ADOPTED AT THE MEETING OF OCTOBER 17, 1871

TO CITIZEN MEMBERS OF THE FRENCH SECTION OF 1871

Citizens,

Considering the following articles of the administrative resolutions voted on by the Basle Congress: Article 4. "Every new section or society which comes into existence and wishes to join the International must immediately notify the General Council of its adherence."

Article 5. "The General Council is entitled to accept or to refuse the affiliation of every new society or group, etc."[a]

The General Council confirms the Rules of the French Section of 1871 with the following modifications:

I. That in Article 2 the words "*justify his means of existence*" be erased and that it should simply be said: in order to be admitted as member of the section a person must present guarantees of morality, etc.

Article 9 of the General Rules states:

"Everybody who acknowledges and defends the principles of the International Working Men's Association is eligible to become a member. Every branch is responsible for the integrity of the members it admits."[b]

---

[a] *Compte-rendu du IVe Congrès international, tenu à Bâle en septembre 1869*, Brussels, 1869, p. 172.— *Ed.*

[b] Here and further on Marx quotes the 1867 English edition of the General Rules and Regulations, published in accordance with the Geneva Congress decisions— *Rules of International Working Men's Association*, London [1867] (see present edition, Vol. 20, p. 444). In the manuscript the last sentence in this paragraph is repeated in English in brackets.— *Ed.*

In dubious cases a section may well take information about means of existence as "guarantee of morality", while in other cases, like those of the refugees, workers on strike, etc., absence of means of existence may well be a guarantee of morality. But to ask candidates to justify their means of existence as a general condition to be admitted to the International, would be a bourgeois innovation contrary to the spirit and letter of the General Rules.

II. (1) Considering that Article 4 of the General Rules states: "The Congress elects the members of the General Council with power to add to their numbers"[a]; that consequently the General Rules only recognise two ways of election for General Council members: either their election by the Congress, or their co-option by the General Council; that the following passage of Article 11 of the Rules of the French Section of 1871: "One or several delegates shall be sent to the General Council" is therefore contrary to the General Rules which give no branch, section, group or federation the *right* to send delegates to the General Council.

That Article 12 of the Regulations prescribes: "Every section is at liberty to make Rules and Bye-Laws for its local administration, suitable to the peculiar circumstances and laws of the different countries. *But these Bye-Laws must not contain anything contrary to the General Rules.*"[b]

For these reasons:

The General Council cannot admit the above-mentioned paragraph of the Rules of the "French Section of 1871".

(2) It is quite true that the different sections existing in London had been invited to send delegates to the General Council which, so as not to violate the General Rules, has always proceeded in the following manner:

It has first determined the number of delegates to be sent to the General Council by each section, reserving itself the right to accept or refuse them depending on whether it considered them able to fulfil the general functions it has to perform. These delegates became members of the General Council not by virtue of the fact that they were delegated by their sections but by virtue of the right of co-opting new members accorded to the Council by the General Rules.

Having acted up to the decision taken by the last Conference

---

[a] Cf. this volume, p. 4 and present edition, Vol. 20, p. 442. In the manuscript this sentence is in English; it is repeated in French in brackets.— *Ed.*

[b] Cf. present edition, Vol. 20, p. 446.— *Ed.*

both as the General Council of the International Working Men's Association and as the Central Council for England,[12] the Council in London thought it useful to admit, besides the members that it co-opted directly, members originally delegated by their respective sections.

It would have been a big mistake to identify the electoral procedure of the General Council of the International Working Men's Association with that of the Paris Federal Council which was not even a national Council nominated by a national Congress like, for example, the Brussels Federal Council or that of Madrid.

The Paris Federal Council being only a delegation of the Paris sections, the delegates of these sections could well be invested with an imperative mandate on a council where they had to defend the interests of their section. The General Council's electoral procedure is, on the contrary, defined by the General Rules and its members would not accept any other imperative mandate than that of the General Rules and Regulations.

(3) The General Council is ready to admit two delegates from the "French Section of 1871" on the terms prescribed by the General Rules and never contested by the other sections existing in London.

III. In Article 11 of the Rules of the "French Section of 1871", this paragraph appears:

"Each member of the section should not accept any delegation to the General Council other than that of his section."

Interpreted literally, this paragraph could be accepted since it says only that a member of the "French Section of 1871" should not present himself to the General Council as delegate from another section.

But if we take into consideration the paragraph that precedes it, Article 11 means nothing else but completely changing the General Council's composition and making out of it, contrary to Article 3 of the General Rules, a delegation of London sections where the influence of local groups would be substituted for that of the whole *International Working Men's Association.*

The meaning of the paragraph in Article 11 from the Rules of the "French Section of 1871" is clearly confirmed by the obligation which it imposes for opting between the title of member of the Section and the function of member of the General Council.

For these reasons the General Council cannot admit the above-mentioned paragraph since it is contrary to the General

Rules and deprives it of its right to recruit forces everywhere in the general interest of the International Working Men's Association.

IV. The General Council is sure that the "French Section of 1871" will understand the necessity for the proposed modifications and will not hesitate to bring its Rules into conformity with the letter and spirit of the General Rules and Regulations and that it will thereby forestall any discord which, in the present circumstances, could only hinder the progress of the International Working Men's Association.

Greetings and equality.

In the name and by order of the General Council

Auguste Serraillier,
Corresponding Secretary for France

Adopted by the General Council on October 17, 1871

Printed according to A. Serraillier's manuscript

First published in: Marx and Engels, *Works,* Second Russian Edition, Vol. 17, Moscow, 1960

Translated from the French

The Eastern Post.

No 160.   LONDON, SATURDAY, OCTOBER 21, 1871   ONE PENNY.

Frederick Engels

[ON THE PROGRESS OF THE INTERNATIONAL WORKING MEN'S ASSOCIATION IN ITALY AND SPAIN

ENGELS' RECORD OF HIS REPORT
AT THE GENERAL COUNCIL MEETING OF OCTOBER 17, 1871][13]

The news from Italy was of a most cheering character, the spread of the Association being really wonderful in that country. Three months ago Mazzini stated that there was only one town in Italy, where the International counted numerous adherents.[a] Now, from one end of the country to the other, it is fully established. It is represented in the press by one, if not two, daily papers in Rome; a daily paper in Milan; a semi-weekly one in Turin; weekly papers in Ravenna, Lodi, Pavia, Girgenti, and Catania, besides a number of other papers published in smaller localities. These papers are subject to incessant Government prosecutions; one of them the *Proletario Italiano* of Turin had six consecutive numbers seized by the Police, and one or more actions at law brought against it for each number seized; nevertheless, these papers continue undaunted in their crusade against the Priests, the capitalists, and Mazzini, who has been attacking the International because it was not religious.[b] The Government has dissolved two International sections in Florence and Naples, but the result has only been the immediate formation of new sections all over the country. In Girgenti, the new section has just published its rules,[c] preceded by the translation of the Statutes, published by the General Council,[d] in Ravenna six Republican and Working Men's Societies, have organised themselves into sections of the International, with a common Council.

---

[a] G. Mazzini, "Agli operai italiani", *La Roma del Popolo*, No. 20, July 13, 1871.— *Ed.*

[b] Ibid.— *Ed.*

[c] *Statuto e Regolamento della Società Internazionale degli Operai seguiti dal Regolamento interno della Sezione Girgentina*, Girgenti, 1871.— *Ed.*

[d] *Statuts et règlements. 1866*, London [1866].— *Ed.*

Garibaldi's letters, in which he gives his adhesion to the Association, are everywhere reprinted and commented on, and have evidently helped a great many waverers to make up their minds in favour of the International.[a] The power of Mazzini over the workmen of Italy is thoroughly broken.

In Spain the progress of the Association has been as rapid as in Italy. The Spanish trades' unions, having been created almost exclusively by the International, form an essential part of its organisation. The trades' unions of each locality have a local trades' council, corresponding directly with the Spanish Federal Council at Madrid, on general matters relating to the International; while each trade all over the country again is under the direction of a Central Board, corresponding with the Spanish Federal Council on all matters relating to its trade.

This organisation, as finally settled by the Conference of Valencia, held from the 10th to the 18th of September, 1871, is now being carried out all over Spain.[14] There is scarcely a single large town in Spain without its local "Trades' Council", and a great many small towns are organized upon the same principle. New sections are forming everywhere, and individual adhesions are coming in by hundreds. The Republican party, which only a short time ago attacked the International as a party of "Jesuits", has been made to feel its power acutely. The rising of the Commune in Paris had already split the Republican party in two camps. The middle class section took the side of Versailles, while the younger elements and the Republican working men, supported the Commune. This latter section has been drawn, naturally, nearer and nearer to the International, and will soon enter its ranks, thus strengthening it by the adhesion of numerous and valuable new elements. The Republican papers belonging to this section begin to advocate the nationalization of the land, and other socialistic tenets; to these belong La Asociacion, of Leon; El Comunero, of Madrid; La Justicia, of Malaga; El Trabajo, of Ferrol, and others. At a great Republican meeting, held in Madrid October 15th, the proposal for joint action with the International was cheered enthusiastically.

First published in The Eastern Post,   Reproduced from the newspaper
No. 160, October 21, 1871

---

[a] The reference is to G. Garibaldi's letters of August 20, 1871 to the editorial boards of Il Romagnolo and Il Proletario Italiano, and to his letter of September 20, 1871 to The Echo in London, which were reprinted by other newspapers.— Ed.

GAZZETTINO ROSA

MONITOR QUOTIDIANO

Abbonamento per un Anno, Milano L. 12
Idem   id.   Provincia ▪ 20
Semestre e trimestre in proporzione.
Inviare vaglia postale all'Ufficio del Giornale.

Bisordica in terza pagina Cent. 70 per linea
Idem   in quarta Id.   ▪   30   ▪
Inserzioni vaglia postale all'Ufficio del Agenzia
Giornalisti Londra &c. via Pietro Torri, L.

CENTESIMI **5** MILANO E PROVINCIA ✦ L'Ufficio e in Milano, via S. Pietro all'Orto. 23 ✦ UN NUMERO ARRETRATO CENT. **10**

Frederick Engels

[TO THE EDITORS OF THE *GAZZETTINO ROSA*

COVERING LETTER TO THE "DECLARATION OF THE GENERAL COUNCIL ON NECHAYEV'S MISUSE OF THE NAME OF THE INTERNATIONAL WORKING MEN'S ASSOCIATION"]

In the trial, known by the name of Nechayev, conducted several months ago before the Court of Assizes of St. Petersburg, a number of assertions relating to the International Working Men's Association were made, assertions which naturally attracted the attention of the Conference of Delegates of this Association in session in London.

The Conference consequently took the following decision, ordering it to be published in the organs of the International.[a]

London, October 20, 1871

Certified copy
Frederick Engels,
Secretary for Italy

First published in *Gazzettino Rosa,* No. 306, November 3, 1871 and in *L'Eguaglianza,* No. 18, November 12, 1871

Printed according to *Gazzettino Rosa*

Translated from the Italian

Published in English for the first time

---

[a] This is followed by the text of the "Declaration of the General Council on Nechayev's Misuse of the Name of the International Working Men's Association" in Engels' translation (see p. 23 of this volume).— *Ed.*

Frederick Engels

[STATEMENT BY THE GENERAL COUNCIL CONCERNING ALEXANDER BAILLIE COCHRANE'S LETTER] [15]

TO THE EDITOR OF *THE EASTERN POST*

Sir,—A letter appeared in *The Times* on October 31st on the International, signed Alexander Baillie Cochrane, which I ask space to reply to in your columns. In the first instant, Mr. A. B. C. is

"ignorant whether Mr. Odger is still president of the English branch of this society".

Ever since September, 1867, the office of president of the General Council of the International, which Mr. A. B. C. calls the English branch of this society, has been abolished.[16] It is well-known that after the publication of our manifesto on the civil war in France[a] (in June last) Mr. Odger withdrew from the General Council.

Having read some continental gossip about the composition of our conference of delegates, held in London last September, Mr. A. B. C. applies this information to the public meeting held in St. Martin's Hall, on the 28th September, 1864. At that meeting, as the writer in *The Times* of October 27th correctly stated,[b] the provisional council of the International Working Men's Association was elected, but not "Mr. Odger elected president, Mr. Cremer and Mr. Wheeler, Secretary" as Mr. A. B. C. says.

---

[a] K. Marx, *The Civil War in France.*—*Ed.*

[b] [J. G. Eccarius,] "The International Working Men's Association", *The Times*, No. 27205, October 27, 1871.—*Ed.*

Mr. A. B. C. then proceeds to prove the trustworthiness of his information by the following "authentic document"—
Firstly—

"The red flag is the symbol of universal love."

This authentic document is nothing but the preamble of one of the innumerable forgeries, lately published, in the name of the International by the Paris police, and disowned at the time by the General Council.
Secondly—

"The programme of Geneva, under the presidency" (it is rather hard to make out how a programme can be under a presidency) "of the Russian Michael Bakounine was accepted by the General Council of London, July 1869."

This programme of Geneva is nothing else but the statutes of the "Alliance de la Démocratie Socialiste", of Geneva, already quoted in Jules Favre's circular on the International. Now, in reply to that circular I stated, (see *The Times*, of June 13th) the General Council never issued such a document.[a] On the contrary, it issued a document which quashed the original statutes of the Alliance.[b]
I may now add that the conference, lately held at London, has finally disposed of the Alliance, founded by Michael Bakounine,[c] and that the *Journal de Genève*, this worthy representative of the party tenets of Mr. A. B. C., has taken up the defence of the Alliance against the International.[d]
Thirdly—Mr. A. B. C. pulls out of his bundle of "authentic documents" some garbled extract from private letters written by our friend Eugène Dupont, long since published by the Bonapartist ex-procureur Oscar Testut.[17] Before Mr. A. B. C. set out for the Continent in search of this "trustworthy information", it had already gone the round of the English Press.

---

[a] K. Marx and F. Engels, "Statement by the General Council on Jules Favre's Circular" (published in *The Times* under the signature of John Hales).— *Ed.*
[b] K. Marx, "The International Working Men's Association and the International Alliance of Socialist Democracy".— *Ed.*
[c] See present edition, Vol. 22, pp. 429-30.— *Ed.*
[d] "La Liberté dans l'Association Internationale des Travailleurs. Confédération Suisse. Genève, le 27 octobre 1871", *Journal de Genève*, No. 254, October 27, 1871.— *Ed.*

Mr. Alexander Baillie Cochrane calls our society "infamous". How am I to call a society which instructs the business of law-making to that same Alexander Baillie Cochrane?

I am, Sir,
Yours obediently,

John Hales,
General Secretary

International Working Men's Association
256, High Holborn

Written on October 31, 1871

Adopted by the General Council on
October 31, 1871

First published in *The Eastern Post,*
No. 163, November 11, 1871

Reproduced from the newspaper

№ 91.   Sonnabend, den 11. November.   1871.

Der Volksstaat

Organ der sozial-demokratischen Arbeiterpartei und der Internationalen Gewerksgenossenschaften.

Frederick Engels

[ON THE COMPANY SWINDLE IN ENGLAND]

London, November 4.—We here are now in the full swing of prosperity and thriving business—*we,* i.e., official England, the big capitalists. There is a surplus of capital on the market and it is looking everywhere for a profitable home; bogus companies, set up for the happiness of mankind and the enrichment of the entrepreneurs, are shooting up out of the ground like mushrooms. Mines, asphalt quarries, horse-drawn tramways for big cities, and iron works seem to be the most favoured at the moment. Mines are being offered for sale on the Volga and in New Mexico; people are buying asphalt quarries in Savoy, the Jura and Hanover; Lisbon and Buenos Aires are to have horse-drawn tramways, and so on. The sole aim of all these joint-stock companies is, of course, briefly to raise the value of the stock so the entrepreneurs can rid themselves of their share at a profit; what then becomes of the stockholders does not bother them: "After us the deluge!"[a] In three or four years, five-sixths of these companies will have gone the way of all flesh and, with them, the money of the ensnared stockholders. As always, it will be mainly small people who put their savings into these "most reliable and profitable" enterprises and always, when the swindle has forced the stock up to its peak on the market—and it serves them right. The stock exchange swindle is one of the most effective ways of transferring the ostensibly, and in part probably genuinely, self-earned assets of the small people into the pockets of the big capitalists, so even the most stupid can see that, in the social order of today, there can be no such thing as capital "earned by one's

---

a These words are attributed to Louis XV and Mme. de Pompadour.—*Ed.*

own labour"; that all existing capital is nothing other than the fruit of other people's work taken without payment. And if the practice of swindling people out of their money by setting up bogus companies has, of late, got really into its stride in Germany and Austria, if princes and Jews, imperial chancellors and petty clerics are in joint pursuit of the savings of the small people, we can only welcome this.

This deluge of capital on the money market reflects, however, only the way big industry is blossoming. In almost all branches of production work is going ahead at a brisker pace than it has for many a year. This is the picture in England's two main industries, where iron and cotton are the raw materials.

At last, the Lancashire spinners again have enough cotton to be able to extend their mills on a massive scale; and they will not let the opportunity slip. In the small town of Oldham alone there are fifteen new mills under construction, with an average of fifty thousand spindles each—a total of 750,000 spindles, almost as many as there are (excluding Alsace) in the whole of the Customs Union [18]! A corresponding number of weaving-looms is being provided, and the picture is the same in the other Lancashire towns. The machine factories have work for months ahead, in some cases a year, and can demand any price, if only they can deliver. In short, things again look as they did in 1844, after the Chinese market was opened up,[19] when the manufacturers' only fear was that they might not be able to satisfy the huge demand. As they said at the time, they had to make clothes for 300 million people! Then came the reverses of 1845 and 1847, when it suddenly turned out that the 300 million Chinese had, so far, been making their own clothing, thank you very much, and huge surpluses of English-made goods accumulated on all markets, with no one to buy them, while the manufacturers and speculators went bankrupt in their hundreds. That is what will happen again this time; these people never learn anything, and even if they do, they are forced by the intrinsic law of capitalist production constantly to repeat the old, familiar cycle of boom, overproduction and crisis, and to repeat it on an ever-increasing scale until, finally, the proletariat rises and liberates society from enduring this absurd cycle.

In the *Volksstaat,* one Herr *Schwitzguébel* demands,[a] on behalf of some federal committee in Romance Switzerland of which I have

---

[a] A. Schwitzguébel, "An die Redaktion des *Volksstaat* in Leipzig", *Der Volksstaat,* No. 81, October 7, 1871.— *Ed.*

no knowledge, that I explain what I published in the *Volksstaat* concerning Herr *Elpidin*.[a] I have had no dealings whatsoever with Herr Schwitzguébel and cannot be answerable in this matter to just any third party who chooses to take issue with me. If, however, Herr Elpidin himself should contact the editor's office on this matter, I shall place myself at his disposal and, in that event, shall ask the editor of the *Volksstaat* to inform Herr Elpidin of my address, so he may contact me directly.

Written on November 4, 1871

First published in *Der Volksstaat*, No. 91, November 11, 1871

Printed according to the newspaper

Published in English for the first time

---

[a] F. Engels, "The Address *The Civil War in France* and the English Press", *Der Volksstaat*, No. 54, July 5, 1871 (Elpidin was accused of espionage in the last paragraph of the article).— *Ed.*

Karl Marx

[RESOLUTION OF THE GENERAL COUNCIL ON THE FRENCH SECTION OF 1871][20]

International Working Men's Association

RESOLUTIONS OF THE GENERAL COUNCIL ADOPTED AT ITS MEETING OF NOVEMBER 7, 1871

I. *Preliminary remarks*

The General Council considers that the ideas expressed by the "French Section of 1871" about a radical change to be made in the articles of the General Rules concerning the constitution of the General Council have no bearing on the question which it ought to discuss.

With regard to the insulting references to the General Council made by that section, these will be judged for what they are worth by the councils and federal committees of the various countries.

The Council merely wishes to note:

That *three years* have not yet elapsed since the Basle Congress (which met on September 6-11, *1869*), as the above-mentioned section deliberately asserts;

That in 1870, on the eve of the Franco-Prussian war, the Council addressed a general circular to all the federations, including the Paris Federal Council, proposing that the seat of the General Council be transferred from London[a];

That the replies received were unanimously in favour of retaining the present seat of the Council and of prolonging its term of office;

That in 1871, as soon as the situation permitted, the General Council summoned a Conference of Delegates, this being the only action possible in the given circumstances;

That at this Conference delegates from the Continent gave voice[b] to the misgivings in their respective countries that the

---

[a] See K. Marx, *Confidential Communication to All Sections.—Ed.*

[b] In the second manuscript this sentence begins as follows: "That at this Conference, held in London on September 17-23, 1871, delegates from the Continent, as members of the French section are fully aware, gave voice...".— *Ed.*

co-option of too large a number of French refugees would destroy
the international character of the General Council;

That the Conference (see its "Resolutions, etc." XV[a]) "leaves it
to the discretion of the General Council to fix, according to events,
the day and place of meeting of the next Congress or Conference
which might replace it".

With regard to the said section's claim to exclusive representation of "the French revolutionary element", because its members
include ex-presidents of Paris workers' societies, the Council
remarks:

The fact that this or that person has in the past been president
of a workers' society may well be taken into account by the
General Council, but does not in itself constitute the "right" to a
seat on the Council or to represent the "revolutionary element"
on that body. If this were so, the Council would be obliged to
grant membership to M. Gustave Durand, former President of the
Paris Jewellers' Society and secretary of the French section in
London. Moreover, members of the General Council are bound to
represent the principles of the International Working Men's
Association, rather than the opinions and interests of this or that
corporation.

II. Objections presented by the "French Section of 1871" at the General Council meeting of October 31 to the resolutions of October 17

1) With respect to the following passage from Article 2 of the
section's Rules:

"In order to be admitted as member of the section, a person must justify his
means of existence, present guarantees of morality, etc."

the section remarks:

"The General Rules make the sections responsible for the morality of their
members and, as a consequence, recognise the right of sections to demand the
guarantees *they think necessary.*"

On this argument, a section of the International founded by
TEETOTALLERS could include in its own rules this type of article: "To be
admitted as member of the section, a person must swear to abstain
from all alcoholic drinks." In short, it would be always possible for
individual sections to impose in their local rules the most absurd

---

[a] Cf. present edition, Vol. 22, p. 429.— *Ed.*

and incongruous conditions of admittance into the International, under the pretext that they "think it necessary in this way" to discharge their responsibility for the integrity of their members.

In its Resolution I of October 17, the General Council stated that there may be "cases in which the absence of means of existence may well be a guarantee of morality". It is of the opinion that the section repeated this point unnecessarily when it said that "refugees" are "above suspicion by virtue of the eloquent proof of their poverty".

As to the phrase that strikers' "means of existence" consist of "the strike fund" this might be answered by saying, first, that this "fund" is often fictitious.[a]

Moreover, official English inquiries have shown that the majority of English workers who, generally speaking, enjoy better conditions than their brothers on the Continent, are forced as a result of strikes and unemployment, or because of insufficient wages or terms of payment and many other causes, to resort incessantly to pawnshops or to *borrowing*, that is, to "means of existence" about which one cannot demand information without interfering in an unqualified manner in a person's private life.

There are two alternatives.

Either the section sees "means of existence" purely as "guarantees of morality",[b] in which case the General Council's proposal that "to be admitted as member of the section a person must present guarantees of morality" serves the purpose since it assumes (see Resolution I of October 17) that "in dubious cases a section may well take information about means of existence *as guarantee of morality*".

Or in Article 2 of its Rules the section deliberately refers to the furnishing of information about "means of existence" as a condition for admission, over and above the "guarantees of morality" which it is empowered to require, in which case the General Council affirms that "it is a bourgeois innovation contrary to the letter and spirit of the General Rules".

2) With respect to the General Council's rejection of the following clause of Article 11 of the section's Rules:

"One or several delegates shall be sent to the General Council"

---

[a] The second manuscript continues as follows: "and is it not the case that strikes invariably result in deprivation and suffering for the strikers, which fact appears to have been ignored by the 1871 Section."— *Ed.*

[b] The second manuscript continues as follows: "in order to avoid its responsibility".— *Ed.*

the section states:

"We are not unaware ... that the literal sense of the General Rules confers on it" (the General Council) "the right to accept or reject delegates."

This is a patent demonstration of the fact that[a] the section is not familiar with the literal sense of the General Rules.

In actual fact, the General Rules, which recognise only *two* ways of election to the General Council, namely, election by the Congress or co-option by the Council itself, *nowhere* state that the Council has the right to accept or reject delegates from the sections or groups.

The admission of delegates initially proposed by the London sections has always been a purely *administrative measure* on the part of the General Council, which in this case only made use of its power of co-option (see Resolution II, 2, of the General Council of October 17). The exceptional circumstances which led the General Council to have recourse to co-option of this kind were explained at sufficient length in its resolutions of October 17.

In the same resolution (II, 3) the Council declared that it would admit delegates from the "French Section of 1871" *on the same conditions* as those from the London sections. It cannot, however, be expected to give serious consideration to a demand that would grant this section a privileged position contrary to the General Rules.

By the inclusion of the following paragraph in Article 11 of its Rules:

"One or several delegates *shall be sent* to the General Council",

the "French Section of 1871" is claiming the right to send delegates to the General Council allegedly basing itself on the General Rules. It acted as though fully convinced that it possessed this imaginary right, and even before the section had been recognised by the General Council (see Article VI of the Administrative Resolutions of the Basle Congress[b]), it did not hesitate to send "by right" to the General Council meeting of October 17 two delegates,[c] armed with "imperative mandates" in the name of the 20 full members of the section. Finally, in its latest communication it again insists on "the duty and right to send delegates to the General Council".

---

[a] The second manuscript continues as follows: "on this point as on many others".— *Ed.*

[b] *Compte-rendu du IVe Congrès international, tenu à Bâle, en septembre 1869,* Brussels, 1869, p. 172.— *Ed.*

[c] Chautard and Camélinat.— *Ed.*

The section attempts to justify its claims by seeking a precedent in the position of Citizen Herman on the General Council. It pretends to be unaware of the fact that Citizen Herman was co-opted into the General Council at the recommendation of the *Belgian Congress,*[21] and in no way represents a Liège section.[a]

3) With respect to the General Council's refusal to recognise the following passage in the section's Rules:

"Each member of the section should not accept any delegation to the General Council other than that of his section",

the section states:

"In response to this, we shall limit ourselves to the observation that our Rules pertain to our section alone; our agreements are of no concern or relevance to anyone but ourselves, and this claim in no way contradicts the General Rules which include no provision on this subject."

It is difficult to comprehend how the Rules which include no provision on the right of delegation to the General Council, should suddenly specify the conditions of this delegation. On the other hand, it is not so difficult to see that the section's own Rules do not apply outside its field of competence. Nevertheless, it cannot be admitted that the specific rules of any section "are of no concern or relevance to anyone but that section alone".[b] For were the General Council to approve Article 11 of the Rules of the "French Section of 1871", for example, it would be obliged to insert it into the rules of all the other sections, and this article, once it began to apply generally, would completely nullify the right of co-option conferred on the Council by the General Rules.[c]

For these reasons:

I) The General Council reaffirms in their entirety its resolutions of October 17, 1871[d];

---

[a] The second manuscript continues as follows: "although he is in fact a member of it".— *Ed.*

[b] The second manuscript continues as follows: "This kind of argument would mean, firstly, the negation of the homogeneity and of the principle of solidarity uniting the groups and committees of the International and, secondly, it would fetter the Federal Councils as well as the General Council."— *Ed.*

[c] The second manuscript continues as follows: "Finally, if this article were adopted, the Federal Councils and even the national Congresses would be restricted to the utmost in their activity owing to its delegates being faced with the alternative of remaining members of their section or of the delegation. This would be the case with the Belgian national Congress and the Liège section, to which Citizen Herman belongs, if this article were included in its Regulations, as the French Section of 1871 seems to demand." — *Ed.*

[d] In the second manuscript the next paragraph II is crossed out, and in paragraph I "reaffirms and declares final" is substituted for "reaffirms in their entirety".— *Ed.*

II) In the event of these resolutions not being accepted by the section before the Council's meeting on November 21, the corresponding secretaries should bring the following documents to the notice of the Federal Councils or Committees of the various countries or, where these do not exist, to the notice of the local groups: the Rules of the "French Section of 1871", the mandate of that section's delegates presented to the General Council at its meeting on October 17, the General Council's resolutions of October 17, the reply of the "French Section of 1871" presented to the General Council at its meeting on October 31, and the Council's final resolutions of November 7.

London, November 7, 1871

In the name and by order
of the General Council[a]

First published in: Marx and Engels, *Works*, Second Russian Edition, Vol. 17, Moscow, 1960

Printed according to Marx's manuscript checked with Delahaye's manuscript (second manuscript)

Translated from the French

---

[a] In the second manuscript there follow the signature and the addressee: "Corresponding Secretary for France *Auguste Serraillier*. To Citizen Members of the French Section of 1871."—Ed.

Frederick Engels

[GIUSEPPE GARIBALDI'S STATEMENT
AND ITS EFFECTS
ON THE WORKING CLASSES IN ITALY

ENGELS' RECORD OF HIS REPORT
AT THE GENERAL COUNCIL
MEETING OF NOVEMBER 7, 1871][22]

The news from Italy was of a peculiar interest, letters were received from a number of Italian cities, amongst whom were Turin, Milan, Ravenna, and Girgenti. These confirmed in every respect the immense strides with which the Association was advancing in Italy. The working-classes, in the towns at least, were rapidly abandoning Mazzini, whose denunciations of the International had no effect whatever upon the masses.[a] But Mazzini's denunciations had produced one good effect; they had caused Garibaldi, not only to pronounce himself entirely in favour of our Association, but also, on this very question, to come to an open rupture with Mazzini. In a long letter addressed to M. Petroni,[b] a Sardinian lawyer, who has been since elected president of the Italian Working Men's Congress,[23] now sitting at Rome, Garibaldi expresses his indignation that the Mazzinians should venture to speak of him as of an old fool, who always had done what ever the men surrounding him, his satellites and flatterers, had persuaded him to do. Who were these satellites, he asks? Were they the men of his staff that came with him from South America in 1848, those he found at Rome in '49, or those of his staff of '59 and '60, or those who fought with him recently against the Prussians?[24] If so, he maintains they were men whose names will for ever live in the memory of grateful Italy. But let them re-enter these satellites and flatterers.

---

[a] See G. Mazzini, "Il moto delle classi artigiane e il congresso", "L'Internazionale Svizzera", and "L'Internazionale. Cenno storico", *La Roma del Popolo*, Nos. 28-31, September 7, 14, 21 and 28, 1871.—*Ed.*

[b] G. Garibaldi's letter was published in *La Favilla*, No. 255, October 31, 1871, and other newspapers.—*Ed.*

"I repeat it, you have not even the merit of originality, when you dig up again my satellites and flatterers have always led that grey-headed baby from Nice by the nose. And while you, Petroni, were suffering for eighteen years in the prisons of the Inquisition, the people of your sect (the Mazzinians) were the very men accused by the Royalists, of being my satellites and followers. Read all the dynastic trash published especially since 1860, and there you will find Garibaldi might be good for something if he had not the misfortune of being led by Mazzini, and to be surrounded by the Mazzinians. This is all false, and you may ask those that have known me more closely and more intimately, whether they ever found a man more obstinate than myself when I had made up my mind to do something which I had recognised to be right. Ask Mazzini himself, whether he has found me to be easily persuaded whenever he attempted to draw me over to some of his impracticable realities. Ask Mazzini whether the origin of our disagreement is not this, that, in 1848, I told him he was doing wrong in holding back in the city, under one pretext or another, the youth of Milan, while our army was fighting the enemy on the Mincio. And Mazzini is a man who never forgives if any one touches his infallibility."

Garibaldi then states that Mazzini, in 1860, did everything in his power to frustrate and to render abortive the general's expedition to Sicily, which ended in the unification of Italy; that when Mazzini heard of Garibaldi's success, he insisted upon the latter proclaiming the Republic in Italy, a thing absurd and utterly foolish under the circumstances, and he[a] finally reproaches "the great exile, whom everybody knew to be in Italy", with his meanness in bespattering the fallen of Paris,[b] the only men who in this time of tyranny, of lies, of cowardice and degradation have waved high, even while dying, the sacred banner of rights and justice. He continues,

"You cry anathema upon Paris, because Paris destroyed the Vendôme Column and the house of Thiers. Have you ever seen a whole village destroyed by the flames for having given shelter to a volunteer, or a franc-tireur? And that not only in France, the same in Lombardy, in Venetia. As to the palaces set fire to in Paris by petroleum, let them ask the priests who, from their intimate acquaintance with the hell-fire about which they preach, ought to be good judges, what difference there is between petroleum fire and those fires which the Austrians lit in order to burn down the villages in Lombardy and Venetia, when those countries were still under the yoke of the men who shot Ugo Bassi, Ciceruacchio and his two sons, and thousands of Italians who committed the sacrilege of demanding a free Rome and a free Italy.

"When the light of day shall once have dispersed the darkness which covers Paris, I hope that you, my friend, will be more indulgent for the acts caused by the desperate situation of a people which, certainly, was badly led, as it generally happens to nations, who allow themselves to be allured by the phraseology of the *doctrinaires*, but who, in substance, fought heroically for their rights. The detractors

---

[a] G. Garibaldi.— *Ed.*

[b] G. Mazzini, "Il Comune di Francia", *La Roma del Popolo*, No. 9, April 26, 1871.— *Ed.*

of Paris may say what they like, they will never succeed in proving that a few miscreants and foreigners—as they said of us in Rome in 1849—have resisted for three months against a grand army, backed as it was by the most potent armies of Prussia.

"And the International? What need is there to attack an Association almost without knowing it? Is that Association not an emanation of the abnormal state of society all over the world? A society where the many have to slave for bare subsistence, and where the few, by lies and by force, appropriate the greater portion of the produce of the many, without having earned it by the sweat of their brow, must not such a society excite the discontent, and the vengeance of the suffering masses.

"I wish that the International should not fare as did the people of Paris—that is to allow itself to be circumvented by the concoctors of doctrines which would drive it to exaggerations, and finally to ridicule; but that it should well study, before trusting them, the character of the men who are to lead it on the path of moral and material improvement."

He returns for a moment to Mazzini,

"Mazzini and I, we are both old; but no one speaks of reconciliation between him and me. Infallible people die, but they do not bend. Reconciliation with Mazzini? there is only one possible way for it—to obey him; and of that I do not feel myself capable."

And finally the old soldier proves by referring to his past, that he has always been a true International, that he has fought for liberty everywhere and anywhere, first in South America, then offering his services to the Pope[a] (aye, even to the Pope, when he played the liberal), then under Victor Emmanuel, lastly in France, under Trochu and Jules Favre—and he concludes,

"I and the youth of Italy are ready to serve Italy, also side by side with you, the Mazzinians, if it should be necessary."

This crowning letter of Garibaldi's, coming as it does after a number of others, in which he has plainly expressed his sympathies for the International, but abstained from speaking plainly as to Mazzini, has had an immense effect in Italy, and will induce many recruits to rally round our banner.

It was also announced that a full report of the working men's Congress at Rome would be laid before the next meeting of the Council.[b]

First published in *The Eastern Post*,
No. 163, November 11, 1871

Reproduced from the newspaper

---

[a] Pius IX.—*Ed.*
[b] On November 14, 1871.—*Ed.*

4—1006

Frederick Engels

[WORKING MEN'S CONGRESS AT ROME.— BEBEL'S SPEECHES IN THE REICHSTAG

ENGELS' RECORD OF HIS REPORT AT THE GENERAL COUNCIL MEETING OF NOVEMBER 14, 1871][25]

From Italy numerous communications had again come to hand. From them it appeared that the so-called Working Men's Congress at Rome was but a dodge of Mazzini's, intended to deceive the public as to the giant strides with which the International is advancing in Italy. In the course of last summer the local leaders of the well-organised Mazzinian party in many large Italian towns, for the first time, and quite unexpectedly, became aware of the fact that they were losing the absolute hold they had hitherto possessed over the working-classes. The sound instinct of the Italian working men had enabled them to see that the working men of Paris, under the Commune, execrated as they were by the common voice of the ruling classes of Europe, had been in reality but the champions of the cause of the whole proletariat; and when Mazzini gave the word to his followers to join in the general middle-class outcry against the people of Paris,[a] he himself destroyed the foundation of his hitherto almost undisputed sway over the Italian workmen. The working people of the Italian towns then began to see that they had class interests reaching beyond Mazzini's republic; that these interests were the same for all workmen all over the civilised world; and that there was a vast society in existence for the upholding of these common interests— the International. Moreover, they had been tired, for some time, of Mazzini's religious preachings, quite out of place as they were in the most priest-ridden country in Europe, and of his everlastingly reminding them that the grand object of their lives was the

---

[a] G. Mazzini, "Il Comune di Francia", *La Roma del Popolo*, No. 9, April 26, 1871.— *Ed.*

performance of duties, while he never spoke of their rights. Mazzini thought it best to nip this counter-movement in the bud. He had, for the last twenty years, virtually directed the mutual benefit societies of working-men, the Oddfellows, Foresters, and Druids of Italy, societies in which politics were officially forbidden, and where even the commonest objects of an ordinary trades' union were rigorously excluded. The presidents, secretaries, and boards of these societies were generally Mazzinian, and with their help some demonstration in favour of decrying Mazzinianism might be got up. Now, up to 1864 these societies had held annual Congresses; the last was held in Naples in the above year, when an act of fraternization was agreed to, embodying a kind of constitution, with a central committee for common affairs, &c. But since then no Congress had been called. By the assistance of the societies in Liguria, Mazzini now had a new Congress called, which met at Rome, on the 1st of November. How this Congress was composed is best shown by what happened in the Roman Working Men's Society. There the board happened to be anti-Mazzinian, and, because the invitation of the Ligurians had called upon the Congress to discuss political questions, this board refused to send delegates because the discussion of politics was against the general rules. In fact, wherever the boards of the workmen's societies were not composed of Mazzinians, no delegates were sent, as the Mazzinian papers themselves aver; from which it is pretty clear that the delegates sent were elected, not by the members, but by the boards of the various societies. Under these circumstances the mass of the Italian Internationals protested against this Congress if it should pretend to represent the mass of the Italian working men. A few only assisted at its meetings, in order to be able to watch the proceedings.

The Congress opened its sittings on the 1st November. Mazzini and Garibaldi were elected honorary presidents, and that a week after Garibaldi's letter to Petroni appeared, in which he had finally broken with Mazzini![a] Then the act of fraternisation of the Naples Congress was re-discussed. On this occasion a delegate proposed that it should be amended by adding a declaration that the Congress adhered expressly to the principles of Giuseppe Mazzini. The debate was long, but the old Mazzinian organisation at last prevailed. Thirty-four voted yes, nineteen no, six abstained, ten were absent. By a majority of fifteen upon the number of votes given, but by a minority of one upon the total number of

---

[a] See this volume, pp. 43-45.—Ed.

delegates sent to the Congress, the Italian Oddfellows and Druids have bound themselves, for the space of one year, to whatever Mazzini may say or do. Needless to say that the three representatives of International sections retired under protest immediately.[a] We may add that already in the first preliminary meeting of Congress it had been privately settled that neither the question of the International nor any religious question should be discussed. The standing orders were to be suspended in favour of Mazzini only!

The other votes of the Congress were of interest to the Mazzinians alone. They represent attempts to galvanise back into life the dying influence of Mazzini, attempts utterly fruitless in presence of the immense International movement now pervading the Italian working class. The Radical Italian press in Rome, especially *La Capitale* and *Il Tribuno*,[b] severely blame the Congress for its implicit note of confidence in Mazzini. The latter paper says:

"This vote was a verdict upon the plot between Mazzini and Garibaldi; between the theological notions of the high priest, and the downright affirmations of the working man's rights." It was intended to say to Garibaldi:—"You are wrong in denying the principles of Mazzini, which are those of the Italian working class; it was intended to say to the vanquished of the Commune that the Royalist squires of Versailles were right in shooting them down; it was intended to say to the International that the various Governments did right in trying to kill it, and that Italy would oppose a dam to the torrents coming down upon privilege and monopoly. It would have been well if the Italian workmen, in Congress united, had thoroughly discussed, and well examined every proposition, but instead of this the exceptions taken even before the questions themselves arose, the Ait Philosophus,[c] the word of the master accepted as a gospel, constitutes acts damaging no one but that party which was compelled to recur to similar means in order to get rid of a propaganda it could not otherwise vanquish."

The same paper has a remarkable article on the Agricultural labours or small peasants in Italy, which demanded that all the immense estates now uncultivated or left in the state of bogs, should be declared the property of the labouring class, unless reclaimed and cultivated by their owners within a limited time.

In the German Parliament, our friend Bebel has spoken twice.[d] In the first speech, he attacked the increasing military expenditure.

---

[a] C. Cafiero, G. Montel and A. Tucci.—*Ed.*
[b] *Ciceruacchio. Il Tribuno.*—*Ed.*
[c] Said the philosopher.—*Ed.*
[d] A. Bebel's speeches at the Reichstag sittings of October 30 and November 8, 1871, *Der Volksstaat*, Nos. 91 and 92, November 11 and 15, 1871.—*Ed.*

All this vast army, he said, is needed principally against the working people at home. But you, gentlemen of the middle class, with the rapid increase of your factories and workshops, you yourselves created such a rapid increase of the numbers of the working-class that you will never be able to increase your army at the same rate.

In the second speech, upon the Liberal motion that all German States should be bound to have representative institutions, Bebel said that all constitutions of the German States, great and small, were not worth the paper upon which they were written; the Prussian Executive Covernment were supreme and did what they liked all over Germany, and he wished that all the small states, falsely supposed to be the last refuges of liberty, were swallowed up by Prussia, so as to place the people for once face to face with their true enemy, the Prussian Government. Upon his declaring that he did not except the constitutions of the German Empire from this sweeping condemnation, the House, upon the motion of the speaker,[a] stopped him in the midst of his speech.

This is liberty of discussion, as understood by the aristocrats, bureaucrats, capitalists, and lawyers of the German Parliament. The one working-man amongst them is so much a match for the whole of the rest that they have to put him down by main force.

First published in *The Eastern Post,* No. 164, November 18, 1871; reprinted in the second issue, November 19, 1871

Reproduced from the newspaper

---

[a] Dr. Simpson.— *Ed.*

Karl Marx

DECLARATION [26]

I Karl Marx of 1 Maitland park Road Haverstock Hill in the County of Middlesex, Secretary for Germany of the General Council of the International Working Men's Association, do solemnly and sincerely declare as follows

1) That the German Social Democratic Working Men's Party whose Committee in the beginning of September One thousand eight hundred and seventy was still seated at Brunswick [27] has never demanded to be enrolled as part and parcel or as a Section of the International Working Men's Association.

2) That for this reason such an enrolment has never taken place.

3) That many members of the aforesaid German Social Democratic Working Men's Party have on their demand been individually admitted as Members of the International Working Men's Association.

4) That this Declaration is made at the request of Wilhelm Bracke a Merchant at Brunswick and himself a Member of the International Working Men's Association.

And I make this solemn Declaration conscientiously believing the same to be true and by virtue of the provisions of an Act made and passed in the Session of Parliament of the fifth and sixth years of the reign of His late Majesty King William the Fourth, intituled "An Act to Repeal an Act of the present Session of Parliament intituled An Act for the more effectuell abolition of Oaths and Affirmations taken and made in various departments of the State, and to substitute Declarations in lieu thereof, and for the more entire suppression of voluntary and extra judicial Oaths and Affidavits and to make other provisions for the abolition of unnecessary Oaths."

Subscribed and Declared at the Mansions House in the City of London this seventeenth day of November 1871.

Karl Marx

Before me Sills John Gibbons, Lord Mayor

First published, in English, in *Der Proceß gegen den Ausschuß der Socialdemokratischen Arbeiterpartei*, Brunswick, 1871, p. 151

Reproduced from the book

Karl Marx

[STATEMENT SENT BY THE GENERAL COUNCIL TO THE EDITORS OF THE *FRANKFURTER ZEITUNG UND HANDELSBLATT*][28]

On page 2 of the *Frankfurter Zeitung,* No. 326, is a report, dated *London,* November 18, which runs as follows:

"At its last meeting the London section of the *International* passed the following resolution: 'The outstanding services of Sir Charles Dilke to the people's cause give him the right to recognition by the people; therefore he is invited to accept the title of honorary member of the international working men's union.' At an earlier meeting Kossuth was elected member."

The *International* does not recognise any honorary membership. In all probability the above-mentioned decision relates to a small London society, which first called itself "The International Democratic Association" and later changed its name to the "Universal Republican League".[29] It has no connection whatsoever with the *International.*

In the name of the General Council of the International Working Men's Association
                    Corresponding Secretary for Germany,
                                                            Karl Marx

Written on November 24, 1871

First published in *Frankfurter Zeitung und Handelsblatt,* No. 333, November 28, 1871

Printed according to the newspaper checked with the manuscript

Frederick Engels

TO THE FEDERAL COUNCIL OF THE SPANISH REGION IN MADRID

London, November 25, 1871

Since the return of Citizen Lorenzo from the last conference[a] we have not had any news from you. I have written two letters to you; the last one, dated the eighth of this November, which was registered, asked you to write to us immediately to explain this long silence. We have not yet received any answer but we have heard that a small minority of members of the International, seeking to sow divisions in the ranks of the association, is conspiring against the resolutions of the Conference and the General Council, spreading calumnies of all sorts.[30] We have no doubt that your mysterious silence is caused by your having received letters of this type. If this is the case, we want you to inform us of the accusations and insinuations expressed against us, as is your duty, so that we can refute them.

In any case, you cannot prolong this silence which is contrary to our General Rules which instruct you to send us regular reports. We ask for an immediate reply to this letter; if you do not reply to it, we shall have to conclude that your silence is deliberate and that you believe the calumnies which we have mentioned, without having the courage to inform us of them. And we shall have to proceed in that case in the manner which the interest of the International will dictate.

First published in: Marx and Engels, *Works*, First Russian Edition, Vol. XXVI, Moscow, 1935

Printed according to the rough manuscript

Translated from the Spanish

Published in English for the first time

---

[a] London Conference.— *Ed.*

Frederick Engels

TO THE EDITORS
OF *IL PROLETARIO ITALIANO*[31]

Citizens,

In your issue No. 39 you publish an announcement by Turin workers which contains the following:

"We hereby publicly announce that the decision of the Grand Council in London to subordinate socialism to politics was communicated to us by the editors of the *Proletario* immediately after it was made and that the decision was not of an official nature since it was withdrawn by the Grand Council in view of the fact that many European associations would have rejected it outright, as would we."

This assertion obliges the General Council to declare:

1) that it never took any decision to subordinate socialism to politics,

2) that it therefore could not have withdrawn such a decision,

3) that no European or American association could reject such a decision, or has indeed rejected any other decision of the General Council.

The position of the General Council as regards the political action of the proletariat is sufficiently well defined.

It is defined:

1) By the General Rules, in which the fourth paragraph of the *preamble* runs: "That the economical emancipation of the working classes is the great end *to which every political movement ought to be subordinate as a means.*" [a]

2) By the text of the Inaugural Address of the Association (1864), this official and essential commentary on the Rules, which says:

---

a See this volume, p. 3.— *Ed.*

"The lords of land and the lords of capital will always use their political privileges for the defence and perpetuation of their economical monopolies. So far from promoting, they will continue to lay every possible impediment in the way of the emancipation of labour... To conquer political power has therefore become the great duty of the working classes." [a]

3) By the resolution of the Congress of Lausanne (1867) to the effect that: "The social emancipation of the workmen is inseparable from their political emancipation." [b]

4) By Resolution IX of the London Conference (September 1871) which, in agreement with the above, reminds the members of the International that in the struggle of the working classes their economical movement and their political action are indissolubly united. [c]

The Council has always followed the line of conduct thus prescribed and will do so in future. It therefore declares the above communication made by persons unknown to the editors of the *Proletario* to be false and slanderous.

By order and in the name of the General Council

Secretary for Italy,

F. E.

P. S. I have just received *La Révolution Sociale* from Geneva which says that a small group in the Jura has rejected the decisions of the London Conference.[32] The General Council has received no official communication as yet. As soon as it does, it will take the necessary measures.

November 29, 1871

First published in: Marx and Engels, *Works,* First Russian Edition, Vol. XXVI, Moscow, 1935

Printed according to the rough manuscript

Translated from the Italian

---

[a] See present edition, Vol. 20, p. 12.— *Ed.*

[b] *Procès-verbaux du Congrès de l'Association Internationale des Travailleurs réuni à Lausanne du 2 au 8 septembre 1867,* La Chaux-de-Fonds, 1867, p. 19.— *Ed.*

[c] See present edition, Vol. 22, pp. 426-27.— *Ed.*

Frederick Engels

[CREDENTIALS FOR GIUSEPPE BORIANI] [33]

November 30, 1871

Citizen Giuseppe Boriani is accepted member of the International Working Men's Association and is authorised to admit new members and form new sections, on condition that he, and the members and sections newly admitted, recognise as obligatory the official documents of the Association, namely:

The General Rules and Administrative Regulations,
The Inaugural Address,
Resolutions of the Congresses,
The resolutions of the London Conference of September 1871.

By order and in the name of the General Council
Secretary for Italy,
Frederick Engels[a]

First published in: Max Nettlau, *Bakunin e l'Internazionale in Italia dal 1864 al 1872*, Geneva, 1928

Printed according to the manuscript

Translated from the Italian

---

[a] The document bears the stamp "International Working Men's Association, 256, High Holborn, London.— W. C." and the oval seal "International Working Men's Association. General Council. London".— *Ed.*

Frederick Engels

[THE POSITION OF THE DANISH MEMBERS OF THE INTERNATIONAL ON THE AGRARIAN QUESTION

ENGELS' RECORD OF HIS REPORT AT THE GENERAL COUNCIL MEETING OF DECEMBER 5, 1871][34]

A report was received from Denmark referring chiefly to the condition of the agricultural labourers, and the agitation taking place amongst them. In Denmark there are but two official political parties—the *"Doctrinaires"* who represent the capitalist class, and the *"Peasants Friends"*, as they call themselves, who represent the landed proprietors including the landed nobility, and the large peasant owner. They also pretend to represent the agricultural labourers, but as a matter of course nothing was ever done for them. The nobility are comparatively powerless in Denmark, so the large peasant holders form the bulk of the *"Peasants Friends"* party. The small farmers and labourers have hitherto been led by them, for though a few representatives of the latter class had been elected to Parliament, they acted under the influence of the large peasant holders, and were used as mere instruments by them.

The International aims at freeing the small peasants and agricultural labourers from this submission to the men who grow rich out of their labour, and is endeavouring to form them into an independent party—distinct from the so-called *"Peasants Friends"*, but in intimate union with the working men of the towns. This new labourer's party starts with the basis laid down by the Congress of Basle, *the Nationalisation of the Land.*[35]

"It is a truth more and more acknowledged," says *Socialisten*, our Copenhagen organ, "that the land is the common property of the people, that the people ought to cultivate it in common, enjoy its common produce, and hand over its excess (rent) to the state for common purposes."[a]

---

[a] L. Pio, "Om vore Landboforhold", *Socialisten*, No. 17, November 4, 1871.— *Ed.*

But as the land in Denmark is principally the property of a numerous class of Peasant Proprietors, each holding from 50 to 100 acres of good soil, the immediate expropriation of such a considerable body would be impossible. A plan has therefore been proposed, which offers many advantages to the holder as well as to the labourers, that is, to establish Agricultural Co-operative Societies consisting of peasant holders and labourers, for the common cultivation of the land, now cultivated by them individually. The small and medium farms would thus be replaced by farms of 500 acres and upwards, and would allow of the introduction of agricultural implements, steam culture, and other modern improvements, which cannot be taken advantage of, when agriculture is conducted on a small scale. The necessary capital is to be advanced by the state on the security of the land belonging to each association; these propositions are necessarily of a very elementary character, but they appear to be well adapted to the intellect and capacity of the agricultural population, whilst the constant reference to the *Nationalisation of the land as the ultimate end of the movement,* will powerfully assist in breaking up that political subserviency in which the large landowners, with the help of the parson, the village schoolmaster, and the government official, have hitherto held the agricultural labourers.

First published in *The Eastern Post,*   Reproduced from the newspaper
No. 167, December 9, 1871

Frederick Engels

[ON THE POSITION OF THE INTERNATIONAL'S SECTIONS IN EUROPEAN COUNTRIES] [36]

With regard to the Conference's resolution on politics,[a] I am pleased to announce that the Spanish federation has fully accepted it, as can be seen from the latest issues of the *Emancipacion* of Madrid and the *Federacion* of Barcelona (December 3).[b] The transformation of the *International* in Spain into a distinct and independent political party is now secure. We are doing wonderfully in Spain: from 19 to 20,000 new members in under three months! In Denmark the *International* has only been in existence for three months and it has 2,000 members in the capital alone, a smaller city than Milan. The peasants are joining in large numbers too, and a big campaign is being prepared for the forthcoming elections, which promise to give us a strong and respectable representation in the Danish Parliament.

We are doing well in Germany and Holland. In France we have 26 newspapers and the sections are re-forming behind M. Thiers' back.

Written between December 5 and 10, 1871

First published in *La Plebe*, No. 144, December 12, 1871

Printed according to the newspaper

Translated from the Italian

Published in English for the first time

---

[a] The reference is to Resolution IX ("Political Action of the Working Class") of the London Conference of the International (see present edition, Vol. 22, pp. 426-27).— *Ed.*

[b] "La politica de la Internacional", *La Emancipacion*, No. 24, November 27, 1871; reprinted in *La Federacion*, No. 120, December 3, 1871.— *Ed.*

Frederick Engels

[DECLARATION SENT BY THE GENERAL COUNCIL TO THE EDITORS OF ITALIAN NEWSPAPERS CONCERNING MAZZINI'S ARTICLES ABOUT THE INTERNATIONAL][37]

INTERNATIONAL WORKING MEN'S ASSOCIATION,
256, High Holborn, London.— W.C.
December 6, 1871

TO THE EDITOR OF *LA ROMA DEL POPOLO*

Dear Sir,

I count on you having the honesty to publish the enclosed declaration. If we are going to fight, let's fight honestly.

Yours most respectfully,
F. Engels,
General Council Secretary for Italy

INTERNATIONAL WORKING MEN'S ASSOCIATION

TO THE EDITORS OF *LA ROMA DEL POPOLO*

In number 38 of *La Roma del Popolo* Citizen Giuseppe Mazzini publishes the first of a series of articles entitled "Documents about the International".[a] Mazzini notifies the public:

"I ... have gathered from all the sources I was able to refer to all its resolutions, all the spoken and written declarations of its influential members."

And these are the documents he intends publishing. He begins by giving two samples.

I. "The abstention" (from political action) "went so far that some of the French founders [of the International] promised Louis Napoleon that they would renounce all political action provided he grant the workers I don't know what sum of material aid."

---

[a] Published on November 16, 1871; the next two articles of the series appeared in *La Roma del Popolo*, Nos. 39 and 41, November 23 and December 7, 1871.— *Ed.*

We defy Citizen Mazzini to prove this assertion which we regard as calumnious.

II. "In a speech at the Berne Congress of the League of Peace and Freedom in 1868, Bakunin said: 'I want the equalisation of individuals and classes: without this an idea of justice is impossible and peace will not be established. The worker must no longer be deceived with lengthy speeches. *He must be told what he o u g h t to want, if he doesn't know himself.* I'm a collectivist, not a communist, and if I demand the abolition of inheritance rights, I do so to arrive at social equality more quickly'."

Whether Citizen Bakunin pronounced these words or not is quite immaterial for us. What is important for the General Council of the International Working Men's Association to establish is:

1) that these words, as Mazzini himself asserts, were spoken at a congress not of the International but of the bourgeois League of Peace and Freedom;

2) that the International congress, which met at Brussels in September 1868, disavowed this same congress of the *League of Peace and Freedom* by a special vote[38];

3) that when Citizen Bakunin pronounced these words, he was not even a member of the International;

4) that the General Council has always opposed the repeated attempts to substitute for the broad programme of the International Working Men's Association (which has made membership open to Bakunin's followers) Bakunin's narrow and sectarian programme, the adoption of which would automatically entail the exclusion of the vast majority of members of the International;

5) that the International can therefore in no way accept responsibility for the acts and declarations of Citizen Bakunin.

As for the other documents about the International, which Citizen Mazzini intends to publish shortly, the General Council hereby declares that it is only responsible for its official documents.

By order and in the name of the General Council of the International Working Men's Association,

Secretary for Italy,

Frederick Engels

First published in *La Plebe*, No. 144, December 12, 1871; *Gazzettino Rosa*, No. 345, December 12, 1871; *La Roma del Popolo*, No. 43, December 21, 1871

Printed according to *La Roma del Popolo* checked with Engels' rough manuscript

Translated from the Italian

Karl Marx

TO THE EDITOR OF *THE EASTERN POST*[39]

Sir,—In his last epistle to you, Mr. Charles Bradlaugh makes the report of the sitting of the General Council of December 12th,[a]—a sitting from which I was absent in consequence of illness—the pretext for discharging upon me his ruffianism. He says,

"I feel indebted to Karl Marx for his enmity."[b]

My enmity to Mr. Charles Bradlaugh! Ever since the publication of the "Address on the Civil War in France", Mr. Bradlaugh's voice has chimed in with the world-wide chorus of slander against the "International" and myself. I treated him, like the other revilers, with contemptuous silence. This was more than the grotesque vanity of that huge self-idolater could stand. I "calumniated" him because I took no notice of his calumnies. My silence drove him mad; in a public meeting he denounced me as *a Bonapartist* because, in the "Address on the Civil War", I had, forsooth, laid bare the historic circumstances that gave birth to the Second Empire. He now goes a step further and transforms me into a *police agent of Bismarck.* Poor man! He must needs show that the lessons he has recently received at Paris from the infamous Emile de Girardin and his *clique* are not lost upon him. For the present, I shall "betray him" to the German public by giving the greatest possible circulation to his epistle. If he be kind enough to

---

[a] J. Hales, "International Working Men's Association", *The Eastern Post*, No. 168, December 16, 1871.—*Ed.*

[b] C. Bradlaugh, "To the Editor of *The Eastern Post*", *The Eastern Post*, No. 168 (second edition), December 17, 1871.—*Ed.*

clothe his libels in a more tangible shape, I shall "betray him" to an English law-court.

I am, Sir,

Yours obediently,

Karl Marx

London, December 20th

First published in *The Eastern Post*, No. 169, December 23, 1871

Frederick Engels

THE CONGRESS OF SONVILLIER
AND THE INTERNATIONAL[40]

It is hardly necessary to enlarge upon the present position of the International Working Men's Association. On the one hand, owing to the tremendous events in Paris,[a] it has become stronger and more widespread than ever before; on the other we find almost all the European governments united against it—Thiers and Gorchakov, Bismarck and Beust, Victor Emmanuel and the Pope,[b] Spain and Belgium. A general drive against the International has been launched, all the powers of the old world, the courts-martial and civil courts, the police and the press, squires from the backwoods and bourgeois, vie with each other in persecuting it, and there is hardly a spot on the entire continent where every means is not used to outlaw this fear-inspiring great brotherhood of workers.

At this very moment of general and inevitable disorganisation caused by the forces of the old society, when unity and solidarity are more indispensable than ever, at this very moment a small number of the Internationals—whose number by their own admission is steadily diminishing—in some corner of Switzerland has chosen to throw an apple of discord in the shape of a public circular among the members of the International. These people—they call themselves the *Federation of the Jura*—are essentially the same who under the leadership of Bakunin have continuously undermined the unity in the French-speaking part of Switzerland for more than two years and who through their assiduous private correspondence with kindred notabilities in various countries have

---

[a] The proletarian revolution of March 18, 1871 and the Paris Commune.— *Ed.*
[b] Pius IX.— *Ed.*

obstructed concerted action in the International. So long as these intrigues were confined to Switzerland or done on the quiet we did not want to give them wide publicity, but this circular compels us to speak.

Because this year the General Council has not convened a Congress but a Conference,[a] a circular to all sections of the International has been adopted by the Federation of the Jura at its Congress at Sonvillier on November 12. Large numbers of the circular were printed and mailed in all directions requesting all sections to press for the immediate convocation of a Congress. Why a Conference *had* to take the place of a Congress is perfectly clear, at least to us in Germany and Austria. If we had been represented at a Congress our delegates on their return would have been immediately apprehended and placed into safe custody, and the delegates from Spain, Italy and France would have been in the same position. But a Conference which held no public debates but only committee meetings could very well take place, for the names of the delegates would not be published. It had the disadvantage that it could not decide fundamental issues or make any changes in the General Rules, that it had no legislative power at all and could pass merely administrative decisions designed to facilitate the putting into practice of the organisational measures laid down by the General Rules and Congress resolutions. But nothing more was required under the circumstances, it was merely a question of adopting measures to deal with the present emergency, and a Conference was sufficient for the purpose.

The attacks on the Conference and its decisions, however, were merely a pretext. In fact, the present circular only makes passing mention of them. It considers, on the contrary, that the evil is far more deep-rooted. It asserts that according to the General Rules and the original Congress resolutions the International is nothing but "a free federation of autonomous" (independent) "sections", whose aim is the emancipation of the workers by the workers themselves

"without any directing authority, even if set up by voluntary agreement".

The General Council therefore was nothing but "a simple statistical and correspondence bureau". But this original basis was very soon distorted, first by conferring on the General Council the right to co-opt new members, and even more by the resolutions of

---

[a] The London Conference of the International held on September 17-23, 1871.— *Ed.*

the Basle Congress, which gave the General Council the right to
suspend individual sections till the next Congress and to decide
controversies provisionally until the Congress adopted a relevant
resolution.[a] This placed dangerous powers in the hands of the
General Council and turned the free association of independent
sections into a hierarchical and authoritarian organisation of
"disciplined sections", so that

"the sections are entirely under the control of the General Council, which can
arbitrarily either refuse to admit them or suspend their work".

To our German readers, who know only too well the value of an
organisation that is able to defend itself, all this will seem very
strange. And this is quite natural, for Mr. Bakunin's theories,
which appear here in their full splendour, have not yet penetrated
into Germany. A workers' association which has inscribed upon its
banner the motto of struggle for the emancipation of the working
class is to be headed, not by an executive committee, but merely by
a statistical and correspondence bureau! For Bakunin and his
companions, however, the struggle for the emancipation of the
working class is a mere pretext; their real aim is quite different.

"The future society should be nothing but a universalisation of the organisation
which the International will establish for itself. We must therefore try to bring this
organisation as close as possible to our ideal... The International, embryo of the
future human society, must henceforth be the faithful image of our principles of
liberty and federation, and must reject any principle leading to authoritarianism, to
dictatorship."

We Germans have earned a bad name for our mysticism, but we
have never gone the length of such mysticism. The International is
to be the prototype of a future society in which there will be no
executions à la Versailles, no courts-martial, no standing armies,
no inspection of private correspondence, and no Brunswick
criminal court [41]! Just now, when we have to defend ourselves with
all the means at our disposal, the proletariat is told to organise not
in accordance with requirements of the struggle it is daily and
hourly compelled to wage, but according to the vague notions of a
future society entertained by some dreamers. Let us try to imagine
what our own German organisation would look like according to
this pattern. Instead of fighting the government and the
bourgeoisie, it would meditate on whether each paragraph of our
General Rules and each resolution passed by the Congress

---

[a] *Report of the Fourth Annual Congress of the International Working Men's
Association, Held at Basle, in Switzerland. From the 6th to the 11th September 1869,*
London [1869], p. 21.— Ed.

presented a true image of the future society. In place of our
executive committee there would be a simple statistical and
correspondence bureau; it would have to deal as best it knew with
the independent sections, which are so independent that they can
accept no steering authority, be it even one set up by their own
free decision; for they would thus violate their primary duty—that
of being a true model of the future society. Co-ordination of
forces and joint action are no longer mentioned. If in each
individual section the minority submits to the decision of the
majority, it commits a crime against the principles of freedom and
accepts a principle which leads to authority and dictatorship! If
Stieber and all his associates, if the entire black cabinet,[42] if all
Prussian officers were ordered to join the Social-Democratic
organisation in order to wreck it, the committee, or rather the
statistical and correspondence bureau, must by no means keep
them out, for this would amount to establishing a hierarchical
and authoritarian organisation! And above all, there should be
no disciplined sections! Indeed, no party discipline, no centralisation
of forces at a particular point, no weapons of struggle! But what,
then, would happen to the model of the future society? In short,
where would this new organisation get us? To the cowardly, servile
organisation of the early Christians, those slaves, who gratefully
accepted every kick and whose grovelling did indeed after 300
years win them the victory of their religion—a method of
revolution which the proletariat will surely not imitate! Like the
early Christians, who took heaven as they imagined it as the model
for their organisation, so we are to take Mr. Bakunin's heaven of
the future society as a model, and are to pray and hope instead of
fighting. And the people who preach this nonsense pretend to be
the only true revolutionaries!

As far as the International is concerned, all this is still a long
way off. Until the Congress passes new decisions it is the duty of
the General Council to carry out the Basle resolutions and it will
do its duty. Just as it did not hesitate to expel the Tolains and
Durands, so it will see to it that admission to the International will
remain barred for the Stiebers & Co., even if Mr. Bakunin should
consider this dictatorial.

But how did these reprehensible Basle resolutions come into
being? Very simply. The Belgian delegates proposed them, and *no
one supported them more ardently than Bakunin and his friends,*
especially Schwitzguébel and Guillaume, who signed the circular in
question! But then matters were of course quite different. These
gentlemen then hoped to secure a majority and that the General

Council would be dominated by them. At that time they wanted to make the General Council as strong as possible. And now—now it is quite a different matter. Now the grapes are sour, and the Council is to be reduced to a simple statistical and correspondence bureau, so that Bakunin's chaste future society should not have to blush.

These people, professional sectarians, who, with all their mystical early-Christian doctrines, form an insignificant minority in the International, have the effrontery to reproach the General Council and its members with wanting

"to make their particular programme, their personal tenets the predominant ones in the International; they regard their private ideas as the official theory which alone should be entitled to full recognition in the Association".

This is indeed bold language. Anyone who has been able to follow the internal history of the International knows that for nearly three years now these people have been mainly occupied in trying to force their sectarian doctrine on the Association as its general programme, and having failed in this they underhandedly seek to pass off Bakunin's phrases as the general programme of the International. Nevertheless, the General Council protested only against this insinuation but has so far never challenged their right to belong to the International or freely to propagate their sectarian humbug as such. How the General Council will look upon their latest circular is yet to be seen.

These people have themselves brilliantly demonstrated what they have achieved by their new organisation. Wherever the International did not encounter the violent resistance of reactionary governments, it has made enormous advances since the Paris Commune. What do we see, on the other hand, in the Swiss Jura, where these gentlemen were free to run things their own way during the last eighteen months? Their own report to the Sonvillier Congress (printed in the Geneva journal *La Révolution Sociale* of November 23) says:

"These terrible events could not but exert a *partly demoralising* and partly beneficial influence on our sections... Then the gigantic struggle which the proletariat has to wage against the bourgeoisie will begin, and that makes people think ... some withdraw (*s'en vont*) and hide their cowardice, others rally closer than ever in support of the regenerating principle of the International.—This is at present the dominant fact of the internal history of the International in general and of our Federation in particular." [a]

a "Rapport du Comité fédéral romand. Siégeant à St.-Imier-Sonvillier, présenté au Congrès régional de la fédération romande de l'Internationale, tenu à Sonvillier, le 12 novembre 1871". [Signed:] Adhémar Schwitzguébel, *La Révolution Sociale*, No. 5, November 23, 1871.— *Ed.*

What is new here is the statement that this happened in the International in general, where just the opposite took place. It is true that this happened in the Jura Federation. According to these gentlemen themselves, the Moutier section has suffered least of all, but has achieved nothing:

> "Though no new sections were set up, it is to be hoped that, etc." ... and this section was after all "in a particularly favourable position because of the excellent temper of the population" ... "the Grange section has been reduced to a small nucleus of workers".

Two sections in Biel never answered the letters of the Committee, and the same applies to the sections in Neuchâtel and one in Locle; the third section in Biel

> "is for the time being dead" ... although "there is still some hope of the International in Biel reviving".

The Saint-Blaise section is dead; that of Val de Ruz has vanished, no one knows how; after a prolonged agony the central section at Locle was dissolved, but has managed to reconstitute itself, evidently for the purpose of the Congress elections; that of La Chaux-de-Fonds is in a critical position; the watch-makers' section in Courtelary is now transforming itself into a trades association and adopting the rules of the association of Swiss watch-makers; it thus adopts the rules of an organisation which is not part of the International; the central section at the same district has suspended its activities because its members have formed separate sections at Saint-Imier and Sonvillier (which has not prevented this central section from sending two delegates to the Congress, in addition to the delegates from Saint-Imier and Sonvillier); after an outstanding career the Catébat section had to dissolve itself as a result of intrigues by the local bourgeois, and the same happened to the Corgémont section; finally in Geneva one section is still in existence.

That is what in eighteen months the representatives of a free federation of independent sections headed by a statistical and correspondence bureau have done to a flourishing, though not widespread or numerous, Federation. And that in a country where they had complete freedom of action and at a time when everywhere else the International had made gigantic advances. And at the very moment when they themselves exhibit this picture of their miserable failure, when they utter this cry of helplessness and dissolution, they demand that we should divert the International from the course it has hitherto followed, a course which has made it what it is now, and lead it along the path which brought the Jura Federation from a comparatively flourishing state to complete dissolution.

Written not later than January 3, 1872

First published in *Der Volksstaat*, No. 3, January 10, 1872

Printed according to the newspaper

Karl Marx

TO THE EDITOR OF *THE EASTERN POST*

Sir,— In *The National Reformer* of January 7th, Mr. Charles Bradlaugh says:

"We only meant to allege that Dr. Marx had, in former times, given information to his own Government." [a]

I simply declare that this is a calumny, as ridiculous as it is infamous. I call upon Mr. Bradlaugh to publish any fact that could afford him even the slightest pretext for his statement. For his personal tranquility I add that he shall not be "challenged".

I am, Sir, yours obediently,

Karl Marx

January 16th

First published in *The Eastern Post*, No. 173, January 20, 1872   Reproduced from the newspaper

---

[a] C. Bradlaugh, "Rough Notes and Readings", *The National Reformer*, No. 1, January 7, 1872.— *Ed.*

Karl Marx

TO THE EDITOR OF *THE EASTERN POST*[a]

Sir,— In his immortal poem, Dante says that one of the most cruel tortures of an exile is the necessity of having to rub elbows with all sorts of people.[b] I have deeply felt the truth of his complaint when being forced to enter for a moment into a public controversy with men like Messrs. Charles Bradlaugh and Co. I shall, however, no longer allow him to turn the quarrel he has fastened upon me into the cheap and convenient means of advertising himself abroad.

He published against me an accusation which, if published in Germany, would have made him the laughing-stock of all parties.[c] I thereupon challenged him to publish such facts as might have lent him the slightest pretext for a calumny as ridiculous as it is infamous. I did so in order, not to justify myself, but to expose him. With the low cunning of a solicitor's clerk he tries to escape this liability by inviting me to a "Court of Honour".

Does he really fancy that a Bradlaugh, or the editors of the Paris *demi-monde* Press, or those of the Bismarckian papers at Berlin, or the *Tages-Presse* at Vienna, or the *Criminal-Zeitung* at New York, or the *Moscow Gazette*,[d] have only to slander me, in order to make me amenable to clear my public character, and even to do so before a "Council of Honour", of which the friends of those "honourable" gentlemen must form part?

---

[a] The letter is provided with the editor's headline: "Dr. Karl Marx and Mr. Bradlaugh".— *Ed.*

[b] Dante, *The Divine Comedy*, Paradise, Canto XVII.— *Ed.*

[c] See this volume, p. 71.— *Ed.*

[d] *Московскія вѣдомости.—Ed.*

I have done with Mr. Charles Bradlaugh, and leave him to all the comforts he may derive from the quiet contemplation of his own self.

I am, Sir,
Yours obediently,
Karl Marx

Written before January 28, 1872

First published in *The Eastern Post*, No. 174, January 28 (second edition), 1872

Reproduced from the newspaper

Frederick Engels

[LETTER TO THE EDITORS OF THE *GAZZETTINO ROSA*][43]

INTERNATIONAL WORKING MEN'S ASSOCIATION
256, High Holborn, London.— W. C.
London, February 7

TO THE CITIZEN EDITOR OF THE *GAZZETTINO ROSA*

Citizen,

For several months now, the *Libero Pensiero* of Florence has not ceased to attack the International, as if the great workers' association could get jealous of the society of rationalist prebendaries promoted by this newspaper. Up till now it seemed superfluous for me to reply to these attacks, but when the aforementioned publication sinks to the level of spreading rumours of a Bismarckian sort in Italy against the International and its General Council, it is time to protest. I have therefore sent the following letter to the *Libero Pensiero*, and I should like you to publish it in the *Gazzettino Rosa* as well.

Fraternal greetings,

F. Engels,

General Council Secretary for Italy

TO MR. LUIGI STEFANONI, EDITOR OF *IL LIBERO PENSIERO*

Dear Sir,

Issue number 1 of the *Libero Pensiero*, January 4, 1872, contains an article, "L'Internazionale ed il Consiglio supremo di Londra", to which I must submit a brief reply.

It says in the article:

"We should like to ask what mandate Mr. Engels has to represent Italy."

I do not claim and have never claimed to represent Italy. I have the honour of being, in the General Council, the secretary with special responsibility for corresponding with Italy, a capacity in which it is my duty to represent the Council, not Italy.

The article then gives translations of several items of correspondence from London taken from the *Neuer Social-Demokrat* of Berlin, items which are full of the most infamous slanders against the General Council and the whole International. To these I shall not reply. One does not engage in dispute with that newspaper. It is well known throughout Germany what the *Neuer Social-Demokrat* is: a newspaper funded by Bismarck, the organ of Prussian governmental socialism. If you require more detailed information about this paper, write to your correspondent Liebknecht in Leipzig and you will get all you want. Allow me merely to add that if you are keen to have such slanders against the International you will find them in abundance in the *Figaro, Gaulois, Petit-Journal* and the other newspapers of the Parisian *demi-monde*, in the London *Standard*, the *Journal de Genève*, the Vienna *Tages-Presse* and the *Moscow Gazette*,[a] authorities which will relieve you of having to quote this poor devil Schneider.

In an editorial note it says:

"Perhaps this alludes to the communist secret society set up by Karl Marx in Cologne in 1850; when it was uncovered, as usual, many poor devils fell into the clutches of the Prussian police, while the principal organisers fled in safety to London."

Whoever told you this was lying. I was a member of this society.[44] It was founded neither by Marx, nor in 1850, nor in Cologne. It was already in existence at least ten years previously. Marx and I had already been in England for a year, exiles driven out by the Prussian government, when the Cologne section, through its own imprudence, fell into police hands. If you want further information you can ask Mr. Becker, mayor of Dortmund and member of the Prussian and German parliaments; Klein, doctor and municipal councillor in Cologne; Bürgers, editor of the *Wiesbadener Zeitung*; Lessner, tailor and member of the General Council of the International in London. All of these were sentenced in this trial against the communists.[45]

I beg you to publish this correction in your next issue.

Yours sincerely,

Frederick Engels

First published in *Gazzettino Rosa*, No. 50, February 20, 1872 and in *Il Libero Pensiero*, February 22, 1872

Printed according to the *Gazzettino Rosa*

Translated from the Italian

---

[a] *Московскія вѣдомости.—Ed.*

Frederick Engels

TO THE SECTION OF COMMERCIAL EMPLOYEES IN BARCELONA [46]

Citizens,[a]

In reply to your letter of January 23, I regret that I cannot give you the addresses of the sections of your occupation because no such sections are known to us. What you say, relating to your country, about commercial employees being very opposed to proletarian progress also applies to other countries: this class generally consists of lackeys of the bourgeoisie who expect sooner or later to become bourgeois themselves. There are many honourable exceptions; but I believe that you are the first to succeed in forming a section of your profession.

If you also want to send me about twenty copies of your circular, I will disseminate them in the big commercial cities of Europe and America and it will serve well for propaganda.

Greetings and Social Revolution.

Written on February 16, 1872

First published in: Marx and Engels, *Works*, Second Russian Edition, Vol. 33, Moscow, 1964

Printed according to the rough manuscript

Translated from the Spanish

Published in English for the first time

---

[a] In the rough manuscript there is a note in Engels' hand: "Barcelona 23 January 72. Section of commercial employees. Answered. 16 February. The reply enclosed."— *Ed.*

Karl Marx and Frederick Engels

DECLARATION OF THE GENERAL COUNCIL OF THE INTERNATIONAL WORKING MEN'S ASSOCIATION [47]

The Swiss authorities have thought proper, upon a simple reclamation of the Russian Foreign Office, sent in violation of the Federal Constitution direct to a magistrate at Iverdun, to search the house of Citizen Outine at Geneva, under the infamous pretext that he might be implicated in the forgery of Russian paper money — a scandalous affair, in which, wonderful to say, the Russian State Councillor, Kamensky, charged to prosecute the forgers, figures at the same time as their ringleader. They seized the papers of Outine, and exposed all his Russian, German, and English correspondence to the scrutiny of a Russian translator, whose very name they refused to give. Citizen Outine, up to December 1871, was editor of the International organ, *L'Égalité*, and consequently his correspondence was for the greater part that of the International, and provided with the stamps of its different committees. Had it not been for the interference of his legal adviser, Citizen Amberny, to whom the Council tenders its best thanks, Outine's papers and himself would have been handed over to the Russian Government, with which Switzerland has not even a treaty of extradition.

The Russian Government, met at home by a daily growing opposition, has taken advantage of the sham conspiracies of men like Netchayeff, who did not belong to the International, to prosecute opponents at home under the pretext of being Internationals. Now it takes another step in advance. Supported by its faithful vassal, Prussia, it commences an intervention in the internal concerns of Western nations by calling upon their magistrates to hunt down in its service the International. It opens its campaign in a Republic, and the Republican authorities hastened to make themselves the humble servants of Russia. The General Council considers it sufficient to denounce the designs of the Russian Cabinet, and the subserving of its Western helpmates, to the workmen of all nations.

Written on February 20, 1872

First published in *The Eastern Post*, No. 178, February 24, 1872 (second edition) and in *The International Herald*, No. 1, March 2, 1872

Reproduced from *The Eastern Post*

Karl Marx and Frederick Engels

FICTITIOUS SPLITS IN THE INTERNATIONAL

PRIVATE CIRCULAR FROM THE GENERAL COUNCIL OF THE INTERNATIONAL WORKING MEN'S ASSOCIATION [48]

Until now the General Council has completely refrained from any interference in the International's internal conflicts and has never replied publicly to the overt attacks launched against it during more than two years by some members of the Association.

But if the persistent efforts of certain meddlers to deliberately maintain confusion between the International and a society[a] which has been hostile to it since its origin allowed the General Council to maintain this reserve, the support which European reaction finds in the scandals provoked by that society at a time when the International is undergoing the most serious crisis since its foundation obliges it to present a historical review of all these intrigues.

I

After the fall of the Paris Commune, the General Council's first act was to publish its Address on *The Civil War in France*[b] in which it came out in support of all the Commune's acts which, at the moment, served the bourgeoisie, the press and the governments of Europe as an excuse to heap the most vile slander on the vanquished Parisians. A part of the working class still failed to realise that their cause was lost. The Council came to understand

---

[a] International Alliance of Socialist Democracy.— *Ed.*
[b] K. Marx, *The Civil War in France.— Ed.*

the fact, among other things, by the resignation of two of its members, Citizens Odger and Lucraft, who repudiated all support of the Address. It may be said that the unity of views among the working class regarding the Paris events dates from the publication of the Address in all the civilised countries.

On the other hand, the International found a very powerful means of propaganda in the bourgeois press and particularly in the leading English newspapers, which the Address forced to engage in the polemic kept going by the General Council's replies.[49]

The arrival in London of numerous refugees from the Commune made it necessary for the General Council to constitute itself as a Relief Committee and for more than eight months perform this function, which lay quite outside its regular duties.[50] It goes without saying that the vanquished and exiles from the Commune had hothing to hope for from the bourgeoisie. As for the working class, the appeals for aid came at a difficult moment. Switzerland and Belgium had already received their contingent of refugees whom they had either to support or send on to London. The funds collected in Germany, Austria and Spain were sent to Switzerland. In England, the big fight for the nine-hour working day, the decisive battle of which was fought at Newcastle,[51] had exhausted both the workers' individual contributions and the funds set up by the Trades Unions, which could be used, incidentally, according to the rules, only for labour conflicts. Meanwhile, by tireless work and active correspondence, the Council succeeded in raising, bit by bit, a certain amount of money, which it distributed weekly. The American workers responded more generously to its appeal. It is unfortunate that the Council could not avail itself of the millions which the terrified bourgeoisie believed the International to have amassed in its safes!

After May 1871, some of the Commune's refugees were asked to join the Council,[52] in which, as a result of the war, the French side was no longer represented. Among the new members were some old Internationals and a minority composed of men known for their revolutionary energy whose election was an act of homage to the Paris Commune.

Along with all these preoccupations, the Council had to prepare for the Conference of Delegates that it had just called.[53]

The violent measures taken by the Bonapartist government against the International had prevented the holding of the Congress at Paris, which had been provided for by a resolution of

LES

PRÉTENDUES SCISSIONS

DANS

L'INTERNATIONALE

CIRCULAIRE PRIVÉE

DU

CONSEIL GÉNÉRAL

DE

L'ASSOCIATION INTERNATIONALE DES TRAVAILLEURS

GENÈVE

IMPRIMERIE COOPÉRATIVE, RUE DU CONSEIL-GÉNÉRAL, 8

—

1872

Title page of Marx's and Engels' pamphlet *Fictitious Splits in the International*

the Basle Congress. Using the right conferred upon it by Article 4 of the Rules,[a] the General Council, in its circular of July 12, 1870, convened the Congress at Mainz.[54] In letters addressed at the same time to the various federations, it proposed that the General Council should transfer its seat from England to another country and asked that the delegates be provided with imperative mandates to that effect. The federations unanimously insisted that it should remain in London.[55] The Franco-Prussian war, which broke out a few days later, made holding of any congress impossible. It was then that the federations which we consulted authorised us to fix the date of the next Congress depending on the course of events.

As soon as the political situation permitted, the General Council called a private Conference, acting on the precedents of the 1865 Conference[56] and the private administrative meetings of each Congress. A public Congress was impossible and could only have resulted in the continental delegates being denounced at a moment when European reaction was celebrating its orgies; when Jules Favre was demanding from all governments, even the British, the extradition of refugees as common criminals; when Dufaure was proposing to the Rural Assembly a law banning the International,[57] a hypocritical counterfeit of which was later presented by Malou to the Belgians; when, in Switzerland, a Commune refugee[b] was put under preventative arrest while awaiting the federal government's decision on the extradition order; when hunting down members of the International was the ostensible basis for an alliance between Beust and Bismarck, whose anti-International clause Victor Emmanuel was quick to adopt; when the Spanish Government, putting itself entirely at the disposal of the butchers of Versailles, was forcing the Madrid Federal Council to seek refuge in Portugal[58]; at a time, lastly, when the International's prime duty was to strengthen its organisation and to accept the gauntlet thrown down by the governments.

All sections in regular contact with the General Council were invited in good time to the Conference, which, even though it was not to be a public meeting, nevertheless faced serious difficulties. In view of the internal situation France was, of course, unable to elect any delegates. In Italy, the only organised section at the time

---

[a] *Rules of the International Working Men's Association. Founded September 28th, 1864*, London [1867].— *Ed.*

[b] A. E. Razoua.— *Ed.*

was that of Naples; but just as it was about to nominate a delegate it was broken up by armed force. In Austria and Hungary, the most active members were imprisoned. In Germany, some of the more well-known members were persecuted for the crime of high treason, others landed in gaol, and the party's funds were spent on aid to their families.[59] The Americans, though they sent the Conference a detailed Memorandum on the situation of the International there, employed the delegation's money for maintaining the refugees.[60] All federations, in fact, recognised the necessity of substituting the private Conference for a public Congress.

After meeting in London from September 17 to 23, 1871, the Conference authorised the General Council to publish its resolutions; to codify the Administrative Regulations and publish them with the General Rules, as reviewed and corrected, in three languages; to carry out the resolution to replace membership cards with stamps; to reorganise the International in England[61]; and, lastly, to provide the necessary money for these various purposes.

Following the publication of the Conference proceedings, the reactionary press of Paris and Moscow, of London and New York, denounced the resolution on working-class policy[62] as containing such dangerous designs—*The Times* accused it of "a cold and calculating judgment[a]—that it was necessary to outlaw the International with all possible speed. On the other hand, the resolution that dealt a blow at the fraudulent sectarian sections[63] gave the international police a long-awaited excuse to start a noisy campaign ostensibly for the unrestricted autonomy of the workers whom it professed to protect against the despicable despotism of the General Council and the Conference. The working class felt itself so "heavily oppressed", indeed, that the General Council received from Europe, America, Australia and even the East Indies, reports regarding the admission of new members and the formation of new sections.

II

The denunciations in the bourgeois press, like the lamentations of the international police, found a sympathetic echo even in our Association. Some intrigues, directed ostensibly against the Gener-

---

[a] *The Times*, No. 27200, October 21, 1871, p. 7.—*Ed.*

al Council but in reality against the Association, were hatched in its midst. At the bottom of these intrigues was the inevitable *International Alliance of Socialist Democracy*, fathered by the Russian Mikhail Bakunin. On his return from Siberia, the latter began to write in Herzen's *Kolokol* preaching the ideas of Pan-Slavism and racial war,[a] conceived out of his long experience. Later, during his stay in Switzerland, he was nominated to the steering Committee of the League of Peace and Freedom founded in opposition to the International. When this bourgeois society's affairs went from bad to worse, its president, Mr. G. Vogt, acting on Bakunin's advice, proposed to the International's Congress which met at Brussels in September 1868 to conclude an alliance with the League. The Congress unanimously proposed two alternatives: either the League should follow the same goal as the International, in which case it would have no reason for existing; or else its goal should be different, in which case an alliance would be impossible. At the League's Congress held in Berne a few days after, Bakunin made an about-face. He proposed a makeshift programme whose scientific value may be judged by this single phrase: *"economic and social equalisation of classes"*.[64] Backed by an insignificant minority, he broke with the League in order to join the International, determined to replace the International's General Rules by his makeshift programme, which had been rejected by the League, and to replace the General Council by his personal dictatorship. To this end, he created a special instrument, the *International Alliance of Socialist Democracy*, intended to become an International within the International.

Bakunin found the necessary elements for the formation of this society in the relationships he had formed during his stay in Italy, and in a small group of Russian emigrants, serving him as emissaries and recruiting officers among members of the International in Switzerland, France and Spain. Yet it was only after repeated refusals of the Belgian and Paris Federal Councils to recognise the *Alliance* that he decided to submit for the General Council's approval his new society's rules, which were nothing but a faithful reproduction of the "misunderstood" Berne programme. The Council replied by the following circular dated December 22, 1868[65]:

---

[a] М. А. Бакунинъ, «Русскимъ, польскимъ и всѣмъ славянскимъ друзьямъ», *Колоколъ*, No. 122/123, February 15, 1862, supplement.— *Ed.*

The General Council
to the International Alliance of Socialist Democracy

Just about a month ago a certain number of citizens formed in Geneva the *Central Initiative Committee* of a new international society named *The International Alliance of Socialist Democracy*, stating it was their *"special mission* to study political and philosophical questions on the basis of the grand principle of *equality,* etc.".

The programme and rules published by this Initiative Committee were communicated to the General Council of the International Working Men's Association only on December 15, 1868. According to these documents, the said Alliance is "absorbed entirely in the International", at the same time as it is established entirely outside the Association. Besides the General Council of the *International,* elected successively at the Geneva, Lausanne and Brussels congresses, there is to be, in line with the rules drawn up by the Initiative Committee, another General Council in Geneva, which is self-appointed. Besides the local groups of the *International,* there are to be local groups of the *Alliance,* which through their national bureaus, operating independently of the national bureaus of the *International, "will ask the Central Bureau of the Alliance to admit them into the International"*; the *Alliance* Central Committee thereby takes upon itself the right of admittance to the *International.* Lastly, the *General Congress of the International Working Men's Association* will have its counterpart in the *General Congress of the Alliance,* for, as the rules of the Initiative Committee state, at the annual working men's congress the delegation of the International Alliance of Socialist Democracy, as a branch of the International Working Men's Association, *"will hold its meetings in a separate building".*

Considering,

that the existence of a second international body operating within and outside the International Working Men's Association would be the surest means of its disorganisation;

that every other group of individuals, anywhere, would have the right to imitate the Geneva initiative group, and, under more or less plausible excuses, to bring into the International Working Men's Association other international associations with other special missions;

that the International Working Men's Association would thereby soon become a plaything of any meddlers of whatever nationality or party;

that the Rules of the International Working Men's Association furthermore admit only local and national branches into its membership (see Article I and Article VI of the Rules)[a];

that sections of the International Working Men's Association are forbidden to adopt rules or administrative regulations contrary to the General Rules and Administrative Regulations of the International Working Men's Association (see Article XII of the Administrative Regulations);

that the Rules and Administrative Regulations of the International Working Men's Association can be revised by the General Congress only, provided two-thirds of the delegates present vote in favour of such a revision (see Article XIII of the Administrative Regulations);

that a decision on this question is already contained in the resolutions against the *League of Peace*, unanimously passed at the General Congress in Brussels;

that in these resolutions the Congress declared that there was no justification for the existence of the *League of Peace* since, according to its recent declarations, its aim and principles were identical with those of the International Working Men's Association;

that a number of members of the initiative group of the Alliance, as delegates to the Brussels Congress, had voted for these resolutions;

The General Council of the International Working Men's Association unanimously resolved at its meeting of December 22, 1868, that:

1) All articles of the rules of the International Alliance of Socialist Democracy, defining its relations with the International Working Men's Association, are declared null and void;

2) The International Alliance of Socialist Democracy may not be admitted as a branch of the International Working Men's Association.

G. Odger, Chairman of the meeting
R. Shaw, General Secretary

London, December 22, 1868

A few months later, the Alliance again appealed to the General Council and asked whether, *yes or no*, it accepted its *principles*. If yes, the Alliance was ready to dissolve itself into the International's sections. It received a reply in the following circular of March 9, 1869[66]:

---

[a] *Rules of the International Working Men's Association. Founded September 28th, 1864*, London [1867].— Ed.

The General Council to the Central Committee
of the International Alliance
of Socialist Democracy

According to Article I of our Rules, the Association admits all working men's societies aiming at the same end, viz., *the mutual protection, progress and complete emancipation of the working class.*

The sections of the working class in the various countries finding themselves in different conditions of development, it follows necessarily that their theoretical opinions, which reflect the real movement, should also differ.

The community of action, however, established by the International Working Men's Association, the exchange of ideas facilitated by the public organs of the different national sections, and, lastly, the direct debates at the General Congresses, are sure gradually to engender a common theoretical programme.

Consequently, it is not the function of the General Council to subject *the programme of the Alliance to a critical examination.* We have not to inquire whether, *yes or no*, it is an adequate expression of the proletarian movement. All we have to establish is whether it may contain anything contrary to the *general tendency* of our Association, that is, *the complete emancipation of the working class.* There is one sentence in your programme which fails in this respect. Article 2 reads:

"It" (Alliance) "seeks, above all, the *political, economic, and social equalisation of classes.*"

The *equalisation of classes*, literally interpreted, means *harmony between Capital and Labour* so persistently preached by the bourgeois socialists. It is not the logically impossible *equalisation of classes*, but on the contrary the *abolition of classes*, this true secret of the proletarian movement, which forms the great aim of the *International Working Men's Association.*

Considering, however, the context, in which the phrase *equalisation of classes* occurs, it seems to be a mere slip of the pen. The General Council feels confident that you will be anxious to remove from your programme a phrase which may give rise to such dangerous misunderstandings.[a] The principles of our Association

---

[a] In accordance with the General Council's demand Article 2 of the programme of the Alliance was amended as follows: "It aims above all at the complete and final abolition of classes and the political, economic and social equalisation of men and women."— *Ed.*

permit every section freely to shape its own theoretical programme, except in cases when the general policy of our Association is contradicted.

There exists, therefore, no obstacle to the *transformation* of the sections of the Alliance into sections of the International Working Men's Association.

The dissolution of the Alliance, and the entrance of its sections into the International once settled, it would, according to our Regulations, become necessary *to inform the Council of the seat and the numerical strength of each new section.*

Meeting of the General Council
of March 9, 1869

Having accepted these conditions, the Alliance was admitted to the International by the General Council, misled by certain signatures affixed to Bakunin's programme and supposing the Alliance was recognised by the Romance Federal Committee in Geneva which, on the contrary, had always refused to have any dealings with it. Thus, it had achieved its immediate goal: to be represented at the Basle Congress. Despite the dishonest means employed by his supporters, means used on this and solely on this occasion, in an International Congress, Bakunin was deceived in his expectation of seeing the Congress transfer the seat of the General Council to Geneva and give an official sanction to the old Saint-Simonian rubbish, to the immediate abolition of hereditary rights which he had made the practical point of departure of socialism. This was the signal for the open and incessant war which the Alliance waged not only against the General Council but also against all International sections which refused to adopt this sectarian clique's programme and particularly the doctrine of total abstention from politics.

Even before the Basle Congress, when Nechayev came to Geneva, Bakunin got together with him and founded, in Russia, a secret society among students. Always hiding his true identity under the name of various "revolutionary committees", he sought autocratic powers based on all the tricks and mystifications of the time of Cagliostro. The main means of propaganda used by this society consisted in compromising innocent people in the eyes of the Russian police by sending them communications from Geneva in yellow envelopes stamped in Russian on the outside "Secret Revolutionary Committee". The published accounts of the Nechayev trial[67] bear witness to the infamous abuse of the

International's name.*

The Alliance commenced at this time a public polemic directed against the General Council, first in the Locle *Progrès*, then in the Geneva *Égalité*, the official newspaper of the Romance Federation, onto which several members of the Alliance had wiggled their way following Bakunin. The General Council, which had scorned the attacks published in the *Progrès*, Bakunin's personal organ, could not ignore those from the *Égalité*, which it was bound to believe were approved by the Romance Federal Committee. It therefore published the circular of January 1, 1870 [a] which said:

"We read in the *Égalité* of December 11, 1869:

     " 'It is *certain* that the General Council is neglecting extremely important matters. We remind it of its obligations under Article 1 of the Regulations: The General Council is *commissioned* to carry the resolutions of the Congress into effect, etc. We could put enough questions to the General Council for its replies to make up quite a long report. They will come later... Meanwhile, etc. ...'

"The General Council does not know of any article, either in the Rules, or the Regulations, which would oblige it to enter into correspondence or into polemic with the *Égalité* or to provide 'replies to questions' from newspapers. The Federal Committee of Geneva alone represents the branches of Romance Switzerland vis-à-vis the General Council. When the Romance Federal Committee addresses requests or reprimands to us through the only legitimate channel, that is to say through its secretary, the General Council will always be ready to reply. But the Romance Federal Committee has no right either to abdicate its functions in favour of the *Égalité* and *Progrès*, or to let these newspapers usurp its functions. Generally speaking, the General Council's administrative correspondence with national and local committees cannot be published without greatly prejudicing the Association's general interests. Consequently, if the other organs of the International were to follow the example of the *Progrès* and the *Égalité*, the General Council would be faced with the alternative of either discrediting itself publicly by its silence or violating its obligations by replying publicly. The *Égalité* joins the *Progrès* in *inviting* the *Travail* (Paris paper) to denounce, on its part, the General Council. That is almost a League of Public Welfare.[68]"

     * An extract from the Nechayev trial will be published shortly. The reader will find there a sample of the maxims, both stupid and infamous, which Bakunin's friends have laid at the door of the *International*.

---

     [a] See K. Marx, *The General Council to the Federal Council of Romance Switzerland* (present edition, Vol. 21, pp. 84-85).— *Ed.*

Meanwhile, before having read this circular, the Romance Federal Committee had already expelled supporters of the Alliance from the editorial board of the *Égalité.*

The January 1, 1870 circular, like those of December 22, 1868 and March 9, 1869, was approved by all International sections.

It goes without saying that none of the conditions accepted by the Alliance have ever been fulfilled. Its sham sections have remained a mystery to the General Council. Bakunin sought to retain under his personal direction the few groups scattered in Spain and Italy and the Naples section which he had detached from the International. In the other Italian towns he corresponded with small cliques composed not of workers but of lawyers, journalists and other bourgeois doctrinaires. At Barcelona some of his friends maintained his influence. In some towns in the South of France the Alliance made an effort to found separatist sections under the direction of Albert Richard and Gaspard Blanc, of Lyons, about whom we shall have more to say later. In a word, the international society within the International continued to operate.

The big blow—the attempt to take over the leadership of Romance Switzerland—was to have been executed by the Alliance at the Chaux-de-Fonds Congress, opened on April 4, 1870.

The battle began over the right to admit the Alliance delegates, which was contested by the delegates of the Geneva Federation and the Chaux-de-Fonds sections.

Although, on their own calculation, the Alliance supporters represented no more than a fifth of the Federation members, they succeeded, thanks to repetition of the Basle manoeuvres, to procure a fictitious majority of one or two votes, a majority which, in the words of their own organ (see the *Solidarité* of May 7, 1870),[a] represented no more than *fifteen* sections, while in Geneva alone there were thirty! On this vote, the Romance Congress split into two groups which continued their meetings independently. The Alliance supporters, considering themselves the legal representatives of the whole of the Federation, transferred the Romance Federal Committee's seat to La Chaux-de-Fonds and founded at Neuchâtel their official organ, the *Solidarité,* edited by Citizen Guillaume. This young writer had the special job of decrying the Geneva "factory workers",[69] those odious "bourgeois", of waging war on the *Égalité,* the Romance Federation newspaper, and of preaching total abstention from politics. The authors of the most

---

[a] "Deux organes socialistes...", *La Solidarité,* No. 5, May 7, 1870.— *Ed.*

important articles on this theme were Bastelica in Marseilles, and Albert Richard and Gaspard Blanc in Lyons, the two big pillars of the Alliance.

On their return, the Geneva delegates convened their sections in a general assembly which, despite opposition from Bakunin and his friends, approved their actions at the Chaux-de-Fonds Congress. A little later, Bakunin and the more active of his accomplices were expelled from the old Romance Federation.

Hardly had the Romance Congress closed when the new Chaux-de-Fonds Committee called for the intervention of the General Council in a letter signed by F. Robert, secretary, and by Henri Chevalley, president, who was denounced two months later as a *thief* by the Committee's organ the *Solidarité* of July 9.[a] After having examined the case of both sides, the General Council decided on June 28, 1870 to keep the Geneva Federal Committee in its old functions and invite the new Chaux-de-Fonds Federal Committee to take a local name.[b] In the face of this decision which foiled its plans, the Chaux-de-Fonds Committee denounced the General Council's *authoritarianism*, forgetting that it had been the first to ask for its intervention. The trouble that the persistent attempts of the Chaux-de-Fonds Committee to usurp the name of the Romance Federal Committee caused the Swiss Federation obliged the General Council to suspend all official relations with the former.

Louis Bonaparte had just surrendered his army at Sedan. From all sides arose protests from International members against the war's continuation. In its address of September 9, the General Council, denouncing Prussia's plans of conquest, indicated the danger of her triumph for the proletarian cause and warned the German workers that they would themselves be the first victims.[c] In England, the General Council organised MEETINGS which condemned the pro-Prussian tendencies of the court. In Germany, the International workers organised demonstrations demanding recognition of the Republic and "an honourable peace for France"....

Meanwhile, his bellicose nature gave the hot-headed Guillaume (of Neuchâtel) the brilliant idea of publishing an *anonymous*

---

[a] "Communications du Comité fédéral romand", *La Solidarité*, No. 14, July 9, 1870.— *Ed.*

[b] K. Marx, *General Council Resolution on the Federal Committee of Romance Switzerland.—Ed.*

[c] K. Marx, *Second Address of the General Council of the International Working Men's Association on the Franco-Prussian War.—Ed.*

manifesto as a supplement and under cover of the official newspaper *Solidarité*, calling for the formation of a Swiss volunteer corps to fight the Prussians, something which he had always been prevented from doing doubtlessly by his abstentionist convictions.[70]

Then came the Lyons uprising.[71] Bakunin rushed there and, supported by Albert Richard, Gaspard Blanc and Bastelica, installed himself on September 28 in the Town Hall, where he *refrained* from posting a guard, however, lest it would be viewed as a political act. He was driven out in shame by several National Guards at the moment when, after a difficult accouchement, his decree on the *abolition of the State* had just seen the light of day.

In October 1870, the General Council, in the absence of its French members, co-opted Citizen Paul Robin, a refugee from Brest, one of the best-known supporters of the Alliance, and, what is more, the instigator of several attacks in the *Égalité* against the General Council where, since that moment, he acted constantly as official correspondent of the Chaux-de-Fonds Committee. On March 14, 1871, he suggested the calling of a private Conference of the International to sift out the Swiss trouble. Foreseeing that important events were in the making in Paris, the Council flatly refused. Robin returned to the question on several occasions and even suggested that the Council take a definite decision on the conflict. On July 25, the General Council decided that this affair would be one of the questions for the Conference due to be convened in September 1871.

On August 10, the Alliance, hardly eager to see its activities looked into by a Conference, declared itself dissolved as from the 6th of August.[72] But on September 15, it reappeared and requested admission to the Council under the name of the *Atheist Socialist Section*, According to Administrative Resolution No. V of the Basle Congress,[a] the Council could not admit it without consulting the Geneva Federal Committee, which was exhausted after its two years of struggle against the sectarian sections. Moreover, the Council had already told the English Christian workers' societies (YOUNG MEN'S CHRISTIAN ASSOCIATION) that the International did not recognise theological sections.

On August 6, the date of the dissolution of the Alliance, the Chaux-de-Fonds Federal Committee renewed its request to enter into official relations with the Council and said that it would continue to ignore the June 28 resolution and to regard itself, in

---

[a] See *Compte-rendu du IVe Congrès international, tenu à Bâle, en septembre 1869*, Brussels, 1869, p. 172.— *Ed.*

relation to Geneva, as the Romance Federal Committee, and "that
it was up to the General Congress to judge this affair". On
September 4, the same Committee challenged the Conference's
competence, even though it had been the first to call for its
convocation. The Conference could have replied by questioning
the competence of the Paris Federal Committee which the
Chaux-de-Fonds Committee had requested before the siege of
Paris to deliberate on the Swiss conflict.[73] But it confined itself to
the General Council decision of June 28, 1870 (see the motives
expounded in the *Égalité* of Geneva, October 21, 1871[74]).

III

The presence in Switzerland of some of the outlawed French
who had found refuge there put some life back into the Alliance.
The Geneva members of the International did all they could for
the emigrants. They came to their aid right from the beginning,
initiated a wide campaign and prevented the Swiss authorities
from serving an extradition order on the refugees as demanded
by the Versailles government. Several risked the grave danger by
going to France to help the refugees to gain the frontier. Imagine
the surprise of the Geneva workers when they saw several of the
ringleaders such as B. Malon* immediately come to an understanding with the Alliance people and with the help of
N. Zhukovsky, ex-Secretary of the Alliance, try to found at
Geneva, outside of the Romance Federation, the new "Section of
Propaganda and Revolutionary Socialist Action".[75] In the first article
of its rules it

---

* Do the friends of B. Malon, who have been advertising him in a stereotyped
way for the last three months as *the founder of the International*, who have called his
book [*La troisième défaite du prolétariat français*] the *only independent work on the
Commune*, know the attitude taken by this assistant of the Mayor of Batignolles on
the eve of the February elections? At that time, B. Malon, who did not yet foresee
the Commune and saw nothing more than the success of his election to the
Assembly, plotted to get himself put on the list of the four committees as a member
of the International. To these ends he insolently denied the existence of the Paris
Federal Council and submitted to the committees the list of a section founded by
himself at Batignolles as coming from the entire Association.—Later, on March 19,
he insulted in a public document the leaders of the great Revolution accomplished
on the eve.—Today, this anarchist from top to toe prints or has printed what he
was saying a year ago to the four committees: I am the International! B. Malon has
hit on a way of parodying Louis XIV and Perron the chocolate manufacturer at
one and the same time. It was Perron who declared that his chocolate was the *only*
... edible chocolate!

"pledges allegiance to the General Rules of the International Working Men's Association, *while reserving for itself the complete freedom of action* and initiative to which it is entitled as a logical consequence of the principle of autonomy and federation recognised by the Rules and *Congresses* of the Association".

In other words, it reserves for itself full freedom to continue the work of the Alliance.

In a letter from Malon, of October 20, 1871, this new section for the third time asked the General Council for admission into the International. Conforming to Resolution V of the Basle Congress, the Council consulted the Geneva Federal Committee which vigorously protested against the Council recognising this new "seedbed of intrigues and dissentions". The Council acted, in fact, in a rather "authoritarian" manner so as not to bind the whole Federation to the will of B. Malon and N. Zhukovsky, the Alliance's ex-Secretary.

The *Solidarité* having gone out of business, the new Alliance supporters founded the *Révolution Sociale* under the supreme management of Madame André Léo who had just said at the Lausanne Peace Congress that

"Raoul Rigault and Ferré were the two sinister figures of the Commune who, up till then" (up till the execution of the hostages), "had not stopped calling for bloody measures, albeit always in vain".[a]

From its very first issue, the newspaper hastened to put itself on the same level as the *Figaro, Gaulois, Paris-Journal* and other disreputable sheets, reproducing the mud they were throwing at the General Council. It thought the moment opportune to fan the flames of national hatred, even within the International. It called the General Council a German committee led by a Bismarckian brain.[*]

After having definitely established that certain General Council members could not boast of being *"Gauls first and foremost"* the *Révolution Sociale* could find nothing better than to take up the second slogan put in circulation by the European police and to denounce the Council's *authoritarianism.*

What, then, were the facts on which this childish rubbish rested? The General Council had let the Alliance die a natural death and,

---

[*] Here is the national composition of the Council: 20 Englishmen, 15 French, 7 Germans (of whom five are foundation members of the International), 2 Swiss, 2 Hungarians, 1 Pole, 1 Belgian, 1 Irishman, 1 Dane and 1 Italian.

---

[a] A. Léo, *La guerre sociale. Discours prononcé au Congrès de la Paix à Lausanne (1871)*, Neuchâtel, 1871, p. 7.— *Ed.*

in accord with the Geneva Federal Committee, had prevented it from being resurrected. Moreover, it had suggested to the Chaux-de-Fonds Committee to take a name which would permit it to live in peace with the great majority of International members in Romance Switzerland.[76]

Apart from these "authoritarian" acts, what use did the General Council make, between October 1869 and October 1871, of the fairly extensive powers that the Basle Congress had conferred upon it?

1) On February 8, 1870, the Paris "Society of Positivist Proletarians" applied to the General Council for admission. The Council replied that the principles of the positivists, the part of the society's special rules concerning capital, were in flagrant contradiction with the preamble of the General Rules; that the society had therefore to drop them and join the International not as "positivists" but as "proletarians", while remaining free to reconcile their theoretical ideas with the Association's general principles. Realising the justness of this decision, the section joined the International.

2) At Lyons, there was a split between the 1865 section and a recently-formed section in which, amidst honest workers, the Alliance was represented by Albert Richard and Gaspard Blanc. As had been done in similar cases, the judgment of a court of arbitration, formed in Switzerland, was turned down. On February 15, 1870, the recently-formed section, besides requesting the General Council to resolve the conflict by virtue of Resolution VII of the Basle Congress, sent it a ready-made resolution excluding and branding the members of the 1865 section, which was to be signed and sent back by *return mail*. The Council condemned this unprecedented procedure and demanded that the evidence be produced. In reply to the same request, the 1865 section said that the accusatory documents against Albert Richard, which had been submitted to the court of arbitration, had been seized by Bakunin, who refused to give them up. Consequently, it could not completely satisfy the desires of the General Council. The Council's decision on the affair, dated March 8, met with no objection from either side.[77]

3) The French branch in London, which had admitted people of a more than dubious character, had been gradually transformed into a sleeping partners concern run by Mr. Félix Pyat. He used it to organise damaging demonstrations calling for the assassination of Louis Bonaparte, etc., and to spread his absurd manifestos in France under cover of the International. The

General Council confined itself to declaring in the Association's organs that Mr. Pyat was not a member of the International and it could not be responsible for his actions.[a] The French branch then declared that it no longer recognised either the General Council or the Congresses; it plastered the walls of London with bills proclaiming that with the exception of itself the International was an anti-revolutionary society. The arrest of French members of the International on the eve of the plebiscite, on the pretext of a conspiracy, plotted in reality by the police and to which Pyat's manifestos gave an air of credibility, forced the General Council to publish in the *Marseillaise* and *Réveil* its resolution of May 10, 1870,[b] declaring that the so-called French branch had not belonged to the International for over two years, and that its agitation was the work of police agents.[78] The need for this *démarche* was proved by the declaration of the Paris Federal Committee, published in the same newspapers, and by that of the Paris members of the International during their trial, both declarations referring to the Council's resolution. The French branch disappeared at the outbreak of the war, but like the Alliance in Switzerland, it was to reappear in London with new allies and under other names.

During the last days of the Conference, a "French Section of 1871", about 35 members strong, was formed in London among the Commune refugees. The first "authoritarian" act of the General Council was to publicly denounce the secretary of this section, Gustave Durand, as a French police spy.[c] The documents in our possession prove the intention of the police to assist Durand, firstly, to attend the Conference and then to secure for him membership in the General Council. Since the rules of the new section directed its members not to "accept any delegation to the General Council other than that of their section", Citizens Theisz and Bastelica withdrew from the Council.

On October 17, the section delegated to the Council two of its members, holding imperative mandates; one was none other than Mr. Chautard, ex-member of the artillery committee. The Council refused to admit them prior to an examination of the rules of the

---

[a] K. Marx, *Resolution of the General Council on Félix Pyat's Provocative Behaviour.—Ed.*

[b] K. Marx, *Draft Resolution of the General Council on the "French Federal Section in London".—Ed.*

[c] See this volume, p. 21.— *Ed.*

"1871 section".* Suffice it to recall here the principal points of the debate to which these rules gave rise. Article 2 states:

"In order to be admitted as member of the section, a person must justify his means of existence, present guarantees of morality, etc."

In its resolution of October 17, 1871,[a] the Council proposed deleting the words *"justify his means of existence"*.

"In dubious cases," said the Council, "a section may well take information about means of existence as 'guarantee of morality', while in other cases, like those of the refugees, workers on strike, etc., absence of means of existence may well be a guarantee of morality. But to ask candidates to justify their means of existence as a general condition to be admitted to the International, would be a bourgeois innovation contrary to the spirit and letter of the General Rules." The section replied:

"The General Rules make the sections responsible for the morality of their members and, as a consequence, recognise the right of sections to demand the guarantees *they think necessary.*"

To this the General Council replied, November 7[b]:

"On this argument, a section of the International founded by TEETOTALLERS (*société de tempérance*) could include in its own rules this type of article: To be admitted as member of the section, a person must swear to abstain from all alcoholic drinks. In a word, the most absurd and most incongruous conditions of admittance into the International could be imposed by sections' rules, always on the pretext that they intend, in this way, to be assured of the morality of their members... 'The means of existence of strikers,' adds the French Section of 1871, 'consist of the strike fund.' This might be answered by saying, first, that this fund is often fictitious... Moreover, official English questionnaires have proved that the majority of English workers ... is forced—by strikes or unemployment, by insufficient wages or terms of payment, as well as many other causes—to resort incessantly to pawnshops or to *borrowing*. These are means of existence about which one cannot demand information without interfering in an unqualified manner in a

---

* A little later, this Chautard whom they had wanted to put on the General Council was expelled from his section as an agent of Thiers' police. He was accused by the same people who had judged him worthy among all others of representing them on the General Council.

---

a See this volume, pp. 24-27.— *Ed.*
b Cf. ibid., pp. 37-42.— *Ed.*

person's private life. There are thus two alternatives: either the section is only to seek guarantees of morality through means of existence, in which case the General Council's proposal serves the purpose... Or the section, in Article 2 of its rules, intentionally says that the members have to provide information as to their means of existence as a condition of admission, *over and above* the guarantees of morality, in which case the Council affirms that it is a bourgeois innovation, contrary to the letter and spirit of the General Rules."

Article 11 of their rules states:

"One or several delegates shall be sent to the General Council."

The Council asked for this article to be deleted "because the International's General Rules do not recognise any right of the sections to send delegates to the General Council". "The General Rules," it added, "recognise only two ways of election for General Council members: either their election by the Congress, or their co-option by the General Council..."

It is quite true that the different sections existing in London had been invited to send delegates to the General Council which, so as not to violate the General Rules, has always proceeded in the following manner: it has first determined the number of delegates to be sent by each section, reserving itself the right to accept or refuse them depending on whether it considered them able to fulfil the general functions assigned to them. These delegates became members of the General Council not by virtue of their nomination by their sections, but by virtue of the right that the Rules accord the Council to co-opt new members. Having operated up to the decision taken by the last Conference both as the International Association's General Council and as the Central Council for England, the London Council thought it expedient to admit, besides the members that it co-opted directly, also members nominated initially by their respective sections. It would be a serious mistake to identify the General Council's electoral procedure with that of the Paris Federal Council which was not even a national Council nominated by a national Congress like, for example, the Brussels Federal Council or that of Madrid. The Paris Federal Council was only a delegation of the Paris sections... The General Council's electoral procedure is defined in the General Rules ... and its members would not accept any other imperative mandate than that of the Rules and General Regulations... If we take into consideration the article that precedes it, Article 11 means nothing else but a complete change of the

General Council's composition, turning it, contrary to Article 3 of the General Rules, into a delegation of the London sections, in which the influence of local groups would be substituted for that of the whole International Working Men's Association. Lastly, the General Council, whose first duty is to carry out the Congress resolutions (see Article 1 of the Geneva Congress's Administrative Regulations), said that it "considers that the ideas expressed by the 'French Section of 1871' about a radical change to be made in the articles of the General Rules concerning the constitution of the General Council have no bearing on the question..."

Moreover, the Council declared that it would admit two delegates from the section on the same conditions as those of the other London sections.

The "1871 section", far from being satisfied with this reply, published on December 14 a "declaration"[a] signed by all its members, including the new secretary who was shortly expelled as a scoundrel from the refugee society. According to this declaration, the General Council, by refusing to usurp the legislative functions, was accused of "a gross distortion of the social idea".

Here are some samples of the good faith displayed in the drawing up of this document.

The London Conference approved the conduct of the German workers during the war.[79] It was apparent that this resolution, proposed by a Swiss delegate,[b] seconded by a Belgian delegate[c] and approved unanimously, only referred to the German members of the International who paid and are still paying for their anti-chauvinist behaviour during the war by imprisonment. Furthermore, in order to avoid any possible misinterpretation, the Secretary of the General Council for France had just explained the true sense of the resolution in a letter published by the journals *Qui Vive!*,[d] *Constitution, Radical, Émancipation, Europe*,[e] etc. Nonetheless, eight days later, on November 20, 1871, fifteen members of the French Section of 1871 inserted in *Qui Vive!* a "protest" full of abuse against the German workers and denounc-

---

[a] *Déclaration de la Section française fédéraliste de 1871, siégeant à Londres*, London, 1871. Although it was refused admission by the General Council the section put the words "International Working Men's Association" before the title of the pamphlet. E. Navarre signed the declaration as the section's secretary.— *Ed.*

[b] Nikolai Utin.— *Ed.*

[c] Alfred Herman.— *Ed.*

[d] A. Serraillier, "Au citoyen Vermersch, rédacteur du *Qui Vive!*", *Qui Vive!*, No. 39, November 16, 1871.— *Ed.*

[e] Presumably *Courrier de l'Europe.—Ed.*

ing the Conference resolution as irrefutable proof of the General Council's "pan-Germanic idea". On the other hand, the entire feudal, liberal and police press of Germany seized avidly upon this incident to demonstrate to the German workers how their international dreams had come to naught. In the end the November 20 protest was endorsed by the entire 1871 section in its December 14 declaration.

To show "the dangerous slope of authoritarianism down which the General Council was slipping" the declaration cited "the publication by the very same *General Council* of an *official* edition of the General Rules as *revised by it*".

One glance at the new edition of the Rules is enough to see that each new article has, in the appendix, reference to the original sources establishing its authenticity[a]! As for the words "*official* edition", the first Congress of the International decided that "the *official and obligatory* text of the Rules and Regulations would be published by the General Council" (see *Congrès ouvrier de l'Association Internationale des Travailleurs, tenu à Genève du 3 au 8 septembre 1866*, page 27, note).

Naturally enough, the 1871 section was in continuous contact with the dissidents of Geneva and Neuchâtel. One Chalain, a member who had shown more energy in attacking the General Council than he had ever shown in defending the Commune, was unexpectedly rehabilitated by B. Malon, who quite recently levelled very grave charges against him in a letter to a Council member. The French Section of 1871, however, had scarcely launched its declaration when civil war exploded in its ranks. First Theisz, Avrial and Camélinat withdrew. Thereafter the section broke up into several small groups, one of which was led by Mr. Pierre Vésinier, expelled from the General Council for his slander against Varlin and others, and then cast out of the International by the Belgian Commission appointed by the Brussels Congress of 1868. Another of these groups was founded by B. Landeck who had been relieved by the sudden flight of police prefect Piétri, on September 4, of his obligation,

"scrupulously fulfilled, not to engage any more in *political affairs*, nor in the International in France!" (see *Troisième procès de l'Association Internationale des Travailleurs de Paris*, 1870, p. 4).

On the other hand, the mass of French refugees in London have formed a section which is in complete harmony with the General Council.

---

[a] See this volume, pp. 3-20.— *Ed.*

IV

The men of the Alliance, hidden behind the Neuchâtel Federal Committee and determined to make another effort on a vaster scale to disorganise the International, convened a Congress of their sections at Sonvillier on November 12, 1871.— Back in July two letters from *maître* Guillaume to his friend Robin had threatened the General Council with the same kind of campaign if it did not agree to recognise them to be in the right "*vis-à-vis* the Geneva bandits".

The Sonvillier Congress was composed of sixteen delegates claiming to represent nine sections in all, including the new "Section of Propaganda and Revolutionary Socialist Action" of Geneva.

The Sixteen made their début by publishing the anarchist decree declaring the Romance Federation dissolved, and the latter hastened to restore to the Alliance members their "autonomy" by driving them out of all sections. However, the Council has to recognise that a stroke of good sense brought them to accept the name of the Jura Federation that the London Conference had given them.

The Congress of Sixteen then proceeded to "reorganise the International" by attacking the Conference and the General Council in a circular to all federations of the International Working Men's Association.

The authors of the circular accuse the General Council first of all of having called in 1871 a Conference instead of a Congress. The preceding explanations show that these attacks were made directly against the International as a whole, which had unanimously agreed to convene a Conference at which, incidentally, the Alliance was properly represented by Citizens Robin and Bastelica.

The General Council has had its delegates at every Congress; at the Basle Congress, for example, it had six. The Sixteen claim that

"the majority of the Conference was fraudulently assured in advance by the admission of six General Council delegates with deciding vote".

In actual fact, among the General Council delegates at the Conference, the French refugees were none other than the representatives of the Paris Commune, while its English and Swiss members could only take part in the sessions on rare occasions, as is attested to by the Minutes which will be submitted before the next Congress. One Council delegate had a mandate from a national federation.[a] According to a letter addressed to the Conference, the mandate of another was withheld because of the news of his death in the papers.[b] That left one delegate. Thus, the Belgians alone outnumbered the Council by 6 to 1.

The international police, who in the person of Gustave Durand were kept out, complained bitterly about the violation of the General Rules by the convening of a "secret" conference. They were not conversant enough with our General Regulations to know that the administrative sittings of the Congresses *have to be in private.*

Their complaints, nonetheless, found a sympathetic echo with the Sonvillier Sixteen who cried out:

"And on top of it all, a decision of this Conference declares that the General Council will itself fix the time and place of the next Congress or of the *Conference to replace it*; thus, we are threatened with the suppression of the General Congresses, these great public sessions of the International."

The Sixteen refused to see that this decision had no other purpose but to show to the various governments that, despite all the repressive measures, the International was firmly resolved to hold its general meetings one way or another.

At the general assembly of the Geneva sections, held on December 2, 1871, which gave a bad reception to Citizens Malon and Lefrançais, the latter put forward a proposal confirming the decrees passed by the Sonvillier Sixteen and censuring the General Council, as well as disavowing the Conference.[80]—The Conference had resolved that "the Conference resolutions not intended for publicity *will be* communicated to the *Federal Councils of the various countries by* the corresponding secretaries of the *General Council"*. This resolution, which was in complete conformity with the General Rules and Regulations, was fraudulently revised by B. Malon and his friends to read as follows:

"*Some* Conference resolutions *shall* be communicated *only* to the Federal Councils *and* to the corresponding secretaries."

They further accused the General Council of having "violated *the principle of sincerity*" in refusing to hand over to the police, by means of "*publicity*", the resolutions which were aimed exclusively at reorganising the International in the countries where it is proscribed.

Citizens Malon and Lefrançais complain further that

---

[a] A. Herman held a mandate of the Liège sections (Belgium).— *Ed.*
[b] This refers to Marx.— *Ed.*

"the Conference had aimed a blow at freedom of thought and its expression ... in conferring upon the General Council the right to denounce and disavow any publicity organ of the sections and federations that discussed either the principles on which the Association rests, or the respective interests of the sections and federations, or finally the general interests of the Association as a whole (see the *Égalité* of October 21)".

What, then, had the *Égalité* of October 21 published? It had published a resolution in which the Conference "gives warning that henceforth the General Council will be bound to publicly denounce and disavow all newspapers calling themselves organs of the International which, following the example of the *Progrès* and the *Solidarité*, should discuss in their columns, before the middle-class public, questions exclusively reserved for the local or Federal Committees and the General Council, or for the private and administrative sittings of the Federal or General Congresses".[a]

To appreciate properly the sour-sweet lamentation of B. Malon we must bear in mind that this resolution puts an end once and for all to the attempts of some journalists who wished to substitute themselves for the responsible committees of the International and to play therein the role that the journalists' Bohemia is playing in the bourgeois world. As a result of one such attempt the Geneva Federal Committee had seen some members of the *Alliance* edit the *Égalité*, the official organ of the Romance Federation, in a manner completely hostile to the latter.

Incidentally, the General Council had no need of the London Conference to "publicly denounce and disavow" the improper use of the press, for the Basle Congress had decided (Resolution II) that:

"All newspapers containing attacks on the Association must be immediately sent by the sections to the General Council."[b]

"It is evident," says the Romance Federal Committee in its December 20, 1871 declaration (*Égalité*, December 24) "that this article was adopted not in order that the General Council might keep in its files newspapers which attack the Association, but to enable it to reply, and to nullify in case of need, the pernicious effect of slander and malevolent denigrations. It is also evident that this article refers in general to all newspapers, and that if we do not want to leave the attacks of the bourgeois papers without retaliation, it is all the more necessary to disavow, through our main representative body, i.e., the General Council, those newspapers whose attacks against us are made under cover of the name of our Association."

Let us note, in passing, that *The Times*, that Leviathan of the capitalist press, the *Progrès* (of Lyons), a publication of the liberal

---

[a] K. Marx, *Resolution of the London Conference relating to the Split in Romance Switzerland* (cf. present edition, Vol. 22, pp. 421-22).

[b] *Compte-rendu du IVᵉ Congrès international, tenu à Bâle, en septembre 1869*, Brussels, 1869, p. 172.— *Ed.*

bourgeoisie, and the *Journal de Genève,* an ultra-reactionary paper, have brought the same charges against the Conference and used virtually the same terms as Citizens Malon and Lefrançais.

After having challenged the convocation of the Conference and, later, its composition and its allegedly secret character, the Sixteen's circular challenged even the Conference resolutions.

Stating first that the Basle Congress had surrendered its rights

"having authorised the General Council to grant or refuse admission to, or to suspend, the sections of the International",

it accuses the Conference, farther on, of the following sin:

"This Conference has ... taken resolutions ... which tend to turn the International, which is a free federation of autonomous sections, into a hierarchical and authoritarian organisation of disciplined sections placed entirely under the control of a General Council which may, at will, refuse their admission or suspend their activity!!"

Still farther on, the circular once more takes up the question of the Basle Congress which had allegedly "distorted the nature of the General Council's functions".

The contradictions contained in the circular of the Sixteen may be summed up as follows: the 1871 Conference is responsible for the resolutions of the 1869 Basle Congress, and the General Council is guilty of having observed the Rules which require it to carry out Congress resolutions.

Actually, however, the real reason for all these attacks against the Conference is of a more profound nature. In the first place, it thwarted, by its resolutions, the intrigues of the *Alliance* men in Switzerland. In the second place, the promoters of the Alliance had, in Italy, Spain and part of Switzerland and Belgium, created and upheld with amazing persistence a calculated confusion between *Bakunin's makeshift programme and the programme of the International Working Men's Association.*

The Conference drew attention to this deliberate misunderstanding in its two resolutions on proletarian policy and sectarian sections. The motivation of the first resolution, which makes short work of the political abstention preached by Bakunin's programme, is given fully in its recitals, which are based on the General Rules, the Lausanne Congress resolution and other precedents.*

---

* The Conference resolution on the *political action of the working class* reads as follows:

"Considering the following passage of the original Rules: 'The economical emancipation of the workmen is the great end to which every political movement ought to be subordinate *as a means*';

We now pass on to the sectarian sections:

The first phase of the proletariat's struggle against the bourgeoisie is marked by a sectarian movement. That is logical at a time when the proletariat has not yet developed sufficiently to act as a class. Certain thinkers criticise social antagonisms and suggest fantastic solutions thereof, which the mass of workers is left to accept, preach and put into practice. The sects formed by these initiators are abstentionist by their very nature, i.e., alien to all real action, politics, strikes, coalitions, or, in a word, to any united movement. The mass of the proletariat always remains indifferent or even hostile to their propaganda. The Paris and Lyons workers did not want the Saint-Simonians, the Fourierists, the Icarians,[81] any more than the Chartists and the English trades unionists

"That the Inaugural Address of the International Working Men's Association (1864) states: 'The lords of land and the lords of capital will always use their political privileges for the defence and perpetuation of their economical monopolies. So far from promoting, they will continue to lay every possible impediment in the way of the emancipation of labour... To conquer political power has therefore become the great duty of the working classes';

"That the Congress of Lausanne (1867) has passed this resolution: 'The social emancipation of the workmen is inseparable from their political emancipation';

"That the declaration of the General Council relative to the pretended plot of the French Internationals on the eve of the plebiscite (1870) says: 'Certainly by the tenor of our Rules, all our branches in England, on the Continent, and in America have the special mission not only to serve as centres for the militant organisation of the working class, but also to support, in their respective countries, every political movement tending towards the accomplishment of our ultimate end—the economical emancipation of the working class';

"That inaccurate translations of the original Rules have given rise to false interpretations which have been harmful to the development and action of the International Working Men's Association;

"In presence of an unbridled reaction which violently crushes every effort at emancipation on the part of the working men, and pretends to maintain by brute force the distinction of classes and the political domination of the propertied classes resulting from it;

"Considering, besides,

"That against this collective power of the propertied classes the working class cannot act, as a class, except by *constituting itself into a political party, distinct from, and opposed to, all old parties formed by the propertied classes*;

"That this constitution of the working class into a political party is indispensable in order to ensure the triumph of the Social Revolution and its ultimate end—the abolition of classes;

"That the combination of forces which the working class has already effected by its economical struggles ought at the same time to serve as a lever for its struggles against the political power of its exploiters.

"The Conference recalls to the members of the *International*:

"That in the militant state of the working class, its economical movement and its political action are indissolubly united."

wanted the Owenists. These sects act as levers of the movement in the beginning, but become an obstruction as soon as the movement outgrows them; after which they become reactionary. Witness the sects in France and England, and lately the Lassalleans in Germany who, after having hindered the proletariat's organisation for several years, ended by becoming simple instruments of the police. To sum up, we have here the infancy of the proletarian movement, just as astrology and alchemy are the infancy of science. If the International were to be founded it was necessary that the proletariat would go through this phase.

Contrary to the sectarian organisations with their vagaries and rivalries, the International is a genuine and militant organisation of the proletarian class of all countries united in their common struggle against the capitalists and the landowners, against their class power organised in the state. The International's Rules, therefore, speak of only simple "working men's societies", all following the same goal and accepting the same programme, which presents a general outline of the proletarian movement, while leaving its theoretical elaboration to be guided by the needs of the practical struggle and the exchange of ideas in the sections, unrestrictedly admitting all shades of socialist convictions in their organs and Congresses.

Just as in every new historical phase old mistakes reappear momentarily only to disappear forthwith, so within the International there followed a resurrection of sectarian sections, though in a less obvious form.

The Alliance, while considering the resurrection of the sects a great step forward, is in itself conclusive proof that their time is over: for, if initially they contained elements of progress, the programme of the Alliance, in tow of a "Mohammed without the Koran", is nothing but a heap of pompously worded ideas long since dead and capable only of frightening bourgeois idiots or serving as evidence to be used by the Bonapartist or other prosecutors against members of the International.*

The Conference, at which all shades of socialism were represented, unanimously acclaimed the resolution against sectarian sections, fully convinced that this resolution, bringing the Interna-

---

* Recent police publications on the *International*, including the Jules Favre circular to foreign powers and the report of Sacase, a deputy in the Rural Assembly, on the Dufaure project, are full of quotations from the Alliance's pompous manifestos.[82] The phraseology of these sectarians, whose radicalism is wholly restricted to verbiage, is extremely useful for promoting the aims of the reactionaries.

tional back to its true ground, would mark a new stage of its development. The Alliance supporters, whom this resolution dealt a fatal blow, construed it only as the General Council's victory over the International, through which, as their circular pointed out, the General Council assured "the domination of the special programme" of some of its members, "their personal doctrine", "the orthodox doctrine", "the official theory, and the sole permissible within the Association". Incidentally, this was not the fault of those few members, but the necessary consequence, "the corrupting effect", of the fact that they were members of the General Council, for

"it is absolutely impossible for a person who has power" (!) "over his fellows to remain a moral person. The General Council is becoming a hotbed of intrigue".

According to the opinion of the Sixteen, the General Rules of the International should be censured for the grave mistake of authorising the General Council to co-opt new members. Thus authorised, they claim,

"the Council could, whenever it saw fit, co-opt a group numerous enough to completely change the nature of its majority and its tendencies".

They seem to think that the mere fact of belonging to the General Council is sufficient to destroy not only a person's *morality*, but also his common sense. How else can we suppose that a majority will transform itself into a minority by voluntary co-options?

At any rate, the Sixteen themselves do not appear to be very sure of all this, for they complain further on that the General Council has been

"composed for five years running of *the same persons, continually re-elected*",

and immediately afterwards they repeat:

"*most of them* are not regular mandatories, *not having been elected by a Congress*".

The fact is that the body of the General Council is constantly changing, though some of the founding members remain, as in the Belgian, Romance, etc., Federal Councils.

The General Council must fulfil three essential conditions, if it is to carry out its mandate. In the first place, it must have a numerically adequate membership to carry on its diverse functions; secondly, a membership of "working men belonging to the different nations represented in the International Association"; and, lastly, workers must be the predominant element therein. Since the exigencies of the worker's job incessantly cause changes in the membership of the General Council, how can it fulfil all these indispensable conditions without the right of co-option? The Council nonetheless considers a more precise definition of this right necessary, as it indicated at the recent Conference.

The re-election of the General Council's original membership, at successive Congresses, at which England was definitely under-represented, would seem to prove that it has done its duty within the limits of the means at its disposal. The Sixteen, on the contrary, view this only as a proof of the "blind confidence of the Congresses" carried at Basle to the point of

"a sort of voluntary abdication in favour of the General Council".

In their opinion, the Council's "normal role" should be "that of a simple correspondence and statistical bureau". They justify this definition by adducing several articles extracted from an incorrect translation of the Rules.

Contrary to the rules of all bourgeois societies, the International's General Rules touch only lightly on its administrative organisation. They leave its development to practice, and its regularisation to future Congresses. Nevertheless, inasmuch as only the unity and joint action of the sections of the various countries could give them a genuinely international character, the Rules pay more attention to the General Council than to the other bodies of the organisation.

Article 5 of the original Rules[a] states:

"The General Council shall form an *international agency* between the different" national and local groups,

and proceeds to give some examples of the manner in which it is to function. Among these examples is a request to the Council to see that

"when immediate practical steps should be needed, as, for instance, in case of international quarrels, the action of the associated societies be simultaneous and uniform".

The article continues:

"Whenever it seems opportune, the General Council shall take the initiative of proposals to be laid before the different national or local societies."

In addition, the Rules define the Council's role in convening and arranging Congresses, and charge it with the preparation of certain reports to be submitted thereto. In the original Rules so little distinction is made between the spontaneous action of various

---

[a] Here and further on the authors quote from the *Rules of the International Working Men's Association* (present edition, Vol. 20, p. 443).— *Ed.*

groups and unity of action of the Association as a whole, that Article 6 states:

"Since the success of the working men's movement in each country cannot be secured but by the power of union and combination, while, on the other hand, the activity of the General Council will be more effective ... the members of the International Association shall use their utmost efforts to combine the disconnected working men's societies of their respective countries into national bodies, represented by central organs."

The first administrative resolution of the Geneva Congress (Article I) says:

"The General Council is commissioned *to carry* the resolutions of the Congress *into effect*." [a]

This resolution legalised the position that the General Council has held ever since its origin: that of the Association's *executive delegation*. It would be difficult to carry out orders without enjoying moral "authority" in the absence of any other "freely recognised authority". The Geneva Congress at the same time charged the General Council with publishing "the official and obligatory text of the Rules".

The same Congress resolved (Administrative Resolution of Geneva, Article 14):

"Every section has the right to draw up its own rules and regulations adapted to local conditions and to the laws of its own country, but they must not contain anything contrary to the General Rules and Regulations" [p. 27].

Let us note, first of all, that there is not the least allusion either to any special declarations of principles, or to any special tasks which this or that section should set itself apart from the common goal pursued by all the groups of the International. The issue simply concerns the right of sections to adapt the General Rules and Regulations "to local conditions and to the laws of their country".

In the second place, who is to establish whether or not the local rules conform to the General Rules? Evidently, if there would be no "authority" charged with this function, the resolution would be null and void. Not only could police or hostile sections be formed, but also the intrusion of declassed sectarians and bourgeois philanthropists into the Association could warp its character and, by force of numbers at Congresses, crush the workers.

---

[a] *Congrès ouvrier de l'Association Internationale des Travailleurs, tenu à Genève du 3 au 8 septembre 1866*, Geneva, 1866, p. 26.— *Ed.*

Since their origin, the national and local federations have exercised in their respective countries the right to admit or reject new sections, according to whether or not their rules conformed to the General Rules. The exercise of the same function by the General Council is provided for in Article 6 of the General Rules, which allows *local independent societies*, i.e., societies formed outside the federal body in the country concerned, the right to establish direct contacts with the General Council. The *Alliance* did not hesitate to exercise this right in order to fulfil the conditions set for the admission of delegates to the Basle Congress.

Article 6 of the Rules deals further with legal obstacles to the formation of national federations in certain countries where, consequently, the General Council is asked to function as a Federal Council (see *Procès-verbaux du Congrès, etc., de Lausanne, 1867*, p. 13 [a]).

Since the fall of the Commune, these legal obstacles have been multiplying in the various countries, making action by the General Council therein, designed to keep doubtful elements out of the Association, more necessary than ever. Thus, for instance, the French committees recently demanded the General Council's intervention to rid themselves of informers, and why, in another great country,[b] members of the International requested it not to recognise any section which has not been formed by its direct mandatary or by themselves. Their request was motivated by the necessity of ridding themselves of *agents-provocateurs*, whose burning zeal manifested itself in the rapid formation of sections of unparalleled radicalism. On the other hand, the so-called anti-authoritarian sections do not hesitate to appeal to the Council the moment a conflict arises in the midst, nor even to ask it to deal severely with their adversaries, as in the case of the Lyons conflict. More recently, since the Conference, the Turin Working Men's Federation decided to declare itself a section of the International. As the result of the split that followed, the minority formed a society called "Emancipation of the Proletarian".[83] It joined the International and began by passing a resolution in favour of the Jura people. Its newspaper, *Il Proletario*, is filled with outbursts against all authoritarianism. When sending in the society's subscriptions,

---

[a] A slip of the pen. Article 6 of the General Rules was adopted at the 1866 Geneva Congress of the International. See *Congrès ouvrier de l'Association Internationale des Travailleurs, tenu à Genève du 3 au 8 septembre 1866*, Geneva, 1866, pp. 13-14.— *Ed.*

[b] Austria.— *Ed.*

the secretary[a] warned the General Council that the old federation would probably also send its subscriptions. Then he continues:

"As you will have read in the *Proletario*, the *Emancipation of the Proletarian* society ... has declared ... its rejection of all solidarity with the bourgeoisie, who, under the mask of workers, are organising the *Working Men's Federation*",

and begs the Council to

"communicate this resolution to all sections and to refuse the 10 centimes in subscriptions in the event of their being sent".*

Like all the International's groups, the General Council is required to carry on propaganda. This it has accomplished through its manifestos and its agents, who laid the basis for the first organisations of the International in North America, in Germany and in many French towns.

Another function of the General Council is to aid strikers and organise their support by the entire International (see General Council reports to the various Congresses). The following fact, *inter alia*, indicates the importance of its intervention in the strike movement. The Resistance Society of the English Foundrymen is in itself an international Trades Union with branches in other countries, notably in the United States. Nonetheless, during a strike of American foundrymen, the latter found it necessary to invoke the intercession of the General Council to prevent English foundrymen being brought into America.[84]

The growth of the International obliged the General Council and all Federal Councils to assume the role of arbiter.

The Brussels Congress resolved that:

"The Federal Councils shall transmit to the General Council every three months a report on the *administration* and *financial state* of their respective branches" (Administrative Resolution No. 3[b]).

Lastly, the Basle Congress, which provokes the bilious wrath of the Sixteen, occupied itself solely with regulating the administra-

---

* At this time these were the *apparent* ideas of the Emancipation of the Proletarian society, represented by its corresponding secretary, a friend of Bakunin. Actually, however, this section's tendencies were quite different. After expelling this double-dealing traitor for embezzlement and for his friendly relations with the Turin police chief, the society set forth its explanations, which cleared up all misunderstanding between it and the General Council.

---

[a] Carlo Terzaghi.— *Ed.*

[b] *Troisième Congrès de l'Association Internationale des Travailleurs. Compte-rendu officiel*, Brussels, September 1868. Supplement to the journal *Le Peuple Belge*, p. 50.— *Ed.*

tive relations engendered by the Association's continuing development. If it extended unduly the limits of the General Council's
powers, whose fault was it if not that of Bakunin, Schwitzguébel,
F. Robert, Guillaume and other delegates of the Alliance, who
were so anxious to achieve just that? Or will they accuse
themselves of "blind confidence" in the London General Council?
Here are two resolutions of the Basle Congress:

"No. IV. Each new section or society which is formed and wishes to be part of
the International, must immediately announce its adhesion to the General
Council",
and "No. V. The General Council has the right to admit or reject the affiliation
of any new society or group, subject to appeal at the next Congress."

As for local independent societies formed outside the federal
body, these articles only confirm the practice observed since the
International's origin, the maintaining of which is a matter of life
or death for the Association. But extending this practice and
applying it indiscriminately to every section or society in the
process of formation is going too far. These articles do authorise
the General Council to intervene in the internal affairs of the
federations; but they have never been applied in this sense by the
General Council. It defies the Sixteen to cite a single case where it
has intervened in the affairs of new sections desirous of affiliating
themselves with existing groups or federations.

The resolutions cited above refer to sections in the process of
formation, while the resolutions given below refer to sections
already recognised:

"VI. The General Council has equally the right to suspend until the next
Congress any section of the International."
"VII. When conflicts arise between the societies or branches of a national
group, or between groups of different nationalities, the General Council shall have
the right to decide the conflict, subject to appeal at the next Congress which will
decide definitely." [a]

These two articles are necessary for extreme cases, although up
to the present the General Council has never had recourse to
them. The review presented above shows that the Council has
never suspended any section and, in cases of conflict, has only
acted as arbiter at the request of the two parties.

We arrive, at last, at a function imposed on the General Council
by the needs of the struggle. However shocking this may be for
supporters of the Alliance, it is the very persistence of the attacks

---

[a] *Compte-rendu du IVe Congrès international, tenu à Bâle, en septembre 1869,* Brussels,
1869, p. 172.— *Ed.*

to which the General Council is subjected by all the enemies of the proletarian movement that has placed it in the vanguard of the defenders of the International Working Men's Association.

V

Having dealt with the International such as it is, the Sixteen proceed to tell us what it should be.

Firstly, the General Council should be nominally a simple correspondence and statistical bureau. Once it has been relieved of its administrative functions, its correspondence would be concerned only with reproducing the information already published in the Association's newspapers. The correspondence bureau would thus become needless. As for statistics, that function is possible only if a strong organisation, and especially, as the original Rules expressly say, a common direction are provided. Since all that smacks very much of "authoritarianism", however, there might perhaps be a bureau, but certainly no statistics. In a word, the General Council would disappear. The Federal Councils, the local committees and other "authoritarian" centres would go by the same token. Only the autonomous sections would remain.

What, one may ask, will be the purpose of these "autonomous sections", freely federated and happily rid of all superior bodies, "even of the superior body elected and constituted by the workers"?

Here it becomes necessary to supplement the circular by the report of the Jura Federal Committee submitted to the Congress of the Sixteen.

"In order to make the working class the real representative of humanity's new interests", its organisation must be "guided by the idea that will triumph. *To evolve* this idea from the needs of our epoch, from mankind's vital aspirations, by a consistent study of the phenomena of social life, *to then carry* this idea to our workers' organisations,—such should be our aim, etc." Lastly, there must be created "amidst our working population a real revolutionary socialist *school*".

Thus, the autonomous workers' sections are in a trice converted into *schools*, of which these gentlemen of the Alliance will be the masters. They *evolve the idea* by "consistent studies" which leave no trace behind. They then "*carry* this idea to our workers' organisations". To them, the working class is so much raw material, a chaos into which they must breathe their Holy Spirit before it acquires a shape.

All of which is but a paraphrase of the old Alliance program-me [85] beginning with these words:

"The socialist minority of the League of Peace and Freedom, having broken away from this League", proposes to found "a new Alliance of Socialist Democracy ... adopting as its *special mission* the study of political and philosophical questions..."

This is the *idea* that is being "*evolved*" therefrom!

"Such an enterprise ... would provide sincere socialist democrats of Europe and America with the *means* of being understood and of affirming *their ideas*." *

That is how, on its own admission, the minority of a bourgeois society slipped into the International shortly before the Basle Congress with the exclusive aim of utilising it *as a means* for posing before the working masses as a hierarchy of a secret science that may be expounded in four phrases and whose culminating point is "the economic and social equality of the classes".

Apart from this "theoretical mission", the new organisation proposed for the International also has its practical aspect.

"The future society," says the circular of the Sixteen, "should be nothing but a universalisation of the organisation which the International will establish for itself. We must therefore try to bring this organisation as close as possible to our ideal."

"How could one expect an egalitarian and free society to grow out of an authoritarian organisation? That is impossible. The International, embryo of the future human society, must henceforth be the faithful image of our principles of liberty and federation."

In other words, just as the medieval convents presented an image of celestial life, so the International must be the image of the New Jerusalem, whose "embryo" the Alliance bears in its womb. The Paris Communards would not have failed if they had understood that the Commune was "the embryo of the future human society" and had cast away all discipline and all arms, that is, the things which must disappear when there are no more wars!

Bakunin, however, the better to establish that despite their "consistent studies" the Sixteen did not hatch this pretty project of

---

* The gentlemen of the Alliance, who continue to reproach the General Council for calling a private Conference at a time when the convocation of an open Congress would be the height of treachery or folly, these absolute proponents of clamour and publicity organised within the International, in contempt of our Rules, a real secret society directed against the International itself with the aim of bringing its sections, unbeknown to them, under the sacerdotal direction of Bakunin.

The General Council intends to demand at the next Congress an investigation of this secret organisation and its promoters in certain countries, such as Spain, for example.

disorganisation and disarmament in the International when it was fighting for its existence, has just published the original text of that project in his report on the International's organisation (see *Almanach du Peuple pour 1872*, Geneva).[a]

VI

Now turn to the report presented by the Jura Committee at the Congress of the Sixteen.

"A perusal of the report," says their official organ, *Révolution Sociale* (November 16), "will give the *exact measure* of the devotion and practical intelligence that we can expect from the Jura Federation members."[b]

It begins by attributing to "these terrible events"—the Franco-Prussian war and the Civil War in France—a "somewhat *demoralising*" influence ... "on the situation within the International's sections".

If, in fact, the Franco-Prussian war could not but lead to the *disorganisation* of the sections because it drew great numbers of workers into the two armies, it is no less true that the fall of the empire and Bismarck's open proclamation of a war of conquest provoked in Germany and England a violent struggle between the bourgeoisie, which sided with the Prussians, and the proletariat, which more than ever demonstrated its international sentiments. This alone should have been sufficient for the International to have gained ground in both countries. In America, the same fact produced a split in the vast German proletarian émigré group; the internationalist party definitely dissociating itself from the chauvinist party.

On the other hand, the advent of the Paris Commune gave an unprecedented boost to the expansion of the International and to a vigorous support of its principles by sections of all nationalities, except the Jura sections, whose report continues thus: "The beginning of the gigantic struggle ... has caused people to think... Some go away to hide their weakness... For many this situation" (within their ranks) "is a sign of decrepitude", but "on the contrary ... this *situation is capable of transforming the International completely*" according to their own pattern. This modest wish will be

---

a M. Bakounine, "L'Organisation de l'Internationale", *Almanach du Peuple*, 1872.— *Ed.*

b "Le Congrès de Sonvillier", *La Révolution Sociale*, No. 4, November 16, 1871.— *Ed.*

understood after a deeper examination of so propitious a situation.

Leaving aside the dissolved Alliance, replaced since by the Malon section, the Committee had to report on the situation in twenty sections. Among them, seven simply turned their backs on the Alliance; this is what the report has to say about it:

"The section of *box-makers* and that of *engravers and guillocheurs of Bienne* have never replied to *any* of the communications that we sent them.

"The sections of *Neuchâtel* craftsmen, i.e., *joiners, box-makers, engravers and guillocheurs,* have made *no* reply to letters from the Federal Committee.

"We have not been able to obtain *any* news of the *Val-de-Ruz* section.

"*The section of engravers and guillocheurs of Locle* has given *no* reply to letters from the Federal Committee."

That is what is described as *free* intercourse between the autonomous sections and their Federal Committee.

Another section, that

"of *engravers and guillocheurs* of the *Courtelary* district after three years of stubborn perseverance ... at the present time ... is forming a resistance society"

independent of the International, which does not in the least deter them from sending two delegates to the Congress of the Sixteen.

Next come four completely defunct sections:

"The *central section of Bienne* has currently been *dissolved*; one of its devoted members wrote to us recently, however, saying that *all hope* of seeing the rebirth of the International at Bienne *is not lost.*

"The *Saint-Blaise* section has been *dissolved.*

"The Catébat section, after a brilliant existence, *has had to yield* to the intrigues woven by the masters" (!) "of this district in order to dissolve this *valiant*" (!) "section.

"Lastly, the Corgémont section also has *fallen victim* of intrigues on the part of the employers."

The *central section of Courtelary district* follows, which

"took the wise step of *suspending* its activity",

which did not deter it from sending two delegates to the Congress of the Sixteen.

Now we come to four sections whose existence is more than problematical.

"The *Grange* section has been reduced to a *small nucleus* of socialist workers... Their local action is paralysed by their numerically modest membership.

"The *central section of Neuchâtel has suffered considerably* from the events, and *would have inevitably disbanded* if it were not for the dedication and activity of some of its members.

"*The central section of Locle, hovering between life and death* for some months, ended up by *being dissolved.* It has been reconstituted quite recently, however", evidently for the sole purpose of sending two delegates to the Congress of the Sixteen.

"The *Chaux-de-Fonds section of socialist propaganda* is in a *critical situation...* Its position, far from getting better, *tends rather to deteriorate.*"

Next come two sections, the *study-circles of Saint-Imier* and of *Sonvillier,* which are only mentioned in passing, without so much as a word about their circumstances.

There remains the model section, which, to judge by its name of *central* section, is nothing but the residue of other defunct sections.

"The central section of *Moutier* is certainly the one that has suffered least... Its Committee has been in constant contact with the Federal Committee... *No sections have yet been founded...*"

That is easily explained:

"The activity of the Moutier section was especially *facilitated* by the *excellent attitude* of a working population ... with a traditional life style; we would like to see the working class of this district make itself still more independent of political elements."

One can see, in fact, that this report

"gives the *exact measure* of the devotion and *practical intelligence* that we can expect from the Jura Federation members".

They might have rounded it off by adding that the workers of La Chaux-de-Fonds, the original seat of their committee, have always refused to have anything to do with them. Just recently, at the general assembly of January 18, 1872, they replied to the circular of the Sixteen by a unanimous vote confirming the London Conference resolutions, as also the Romance Congress resolution of May 1871:

"To exclude forever from the International Bakunin, Guillaume and their supporters."

Is it necessary to say anything more about the gallantry of this sham Sonvillier Congress which, in its own words, "caused war, open war within the International"?

Certainly these men, who make more noise than their stature warrants, have had an incontestable success. The whole of the liberal and police press has openly taken their side; they have been backed in their personal slander of the General Council and the insipid attacks aimed against the International by ostensible reformers in many lands:—by the bourgeois republicans in England, whose intrigues were exposed by the General Council; by the dogmatic free-thinkers in Italy, who, under the banner of Stefanoni, have just formed a "Universal Society of Rationalists", with obligatory seat [headquarters] in Rome, an "authoritarian" and "hierarchical" organisation, monasteries for atheist monks and nuns, whose rules provide for a marble bust in the Congress hall for every bourgeois who donates ten thousand francs[86]; and, lastly, by the Bismarck socialists in Germany, who, apart from their police mouthpiece, the *Neuer Social-Demokrat*, played the role of "white shirts"[87] for the Prusso-German empire.

The Sonvillier conclave requests all sections of the International, in a pathetic appeal, to insist on the urgency of an immediate Congress "to curb the consistent encroachments of the London Council", according to Citizens Malon and Lefrançais, but actually to replace the International with the Alliance. This appeal received such an encouraging response that they immediately set about falsifying a resolution voted at the last Belgian Congress. Their official organ (*Révolution Sociale*, January 4, 1872) writes as follows:

"Lastly, which is even more important, the Belgian sections met at the Congress of Brussels on December 24 and 25 and voted unanimously for a resolution identical with that of the Sonvillier Congress, on the urgency of convening a General Congress."

It is important to note that the Belgian Congress voted the very opposite. It charged the Belgian Congress, which was not due to meet until the following June, to draft new General Rules for submission to the *next Congress* of the International.[88]

In accordance with the will of the vast majority of members of the International, the General Council is to convene the annual Congress only in September 1872.

VII

Some weeks after the Conference, Messrs. Albert Richard and Gaspard Blanc, the most influential and most ardent members of the *Alliance*, arrived in London. They came to recruit, among the French refugees, aides willing to work for the restoration of the Empire, which, according to them, was the only way to rid themselves of Thiers and to avoid being left destitute. The General Council warned all concerned, including the Brussels Federal Council, of their Bonapartist plots.

In January 1872, they dropped their mask by publishing a pamphlet entitled *L'Empire et la France nouvelle. Appel du peuple et de la jeunesse à la conscience française,* by Albert Richard and Gaspard Blanc. Brussels, 1872.

With the modesty characteristic of the charlatans of the Alliance, they declaim the following humbug:

"We who have built up the great army of the French proletariat ... we, the most influential leaders of the International in France,* ... happily, we have not been shot, and we are here to flaunt in their face (to wit: *ambitious parliamentarians, smug republicans, sham democrats of all sorts*) the banner under which we are fighting, and despite the slander, threats, and all manner of attacks that await us, to hurl at an amazed Europe the cry that comes from the very heart of our conscience and that will soon resound in the hearts of all Frenchmen: *'Long live the Emperor!'*

"Napoleon III, disgraced and scorned, must be splendidly reinstated";

and Messrs. Albert Richard and Gaspard Blanc, paid out of the secret funds of Invasion III, are specially charged with this restoration.

Incidentally, they confess:

"It is the normal evolution of our ideas that has made us imperialists."

Here is a confession that should give pleasure to their co-religionists of the *Alliance.* As in the heyday of the *Solidarité,* A. Richard and G. Blanc mouth again the old clichés regarding "abstention from politics" which, on the principle of their "normal evolution", can become a reality only under the most absolute despotism, with the workers abstaining from any meddling in politics, much like the prisoner abstaining from a walk in the sun.

---

* Under the heading "Au Pilori!", *L'Égalité* (of Geneva), February 15, 1872, had this to say:

"The day has not yet come to describe the story of the defeat of the movement for the Commune in the South of France; but what we can announce today, we, most of whom witnessed the deplorable defeat of the Lyons insurrection on April 30,[89] is that one of the reasons for the insurrection's failure was the cowardice, the treachery and the thievery of G. Blanc, who intruded everywhere carrying out the orders of A. Richard, who kept in the shade.

"By their carefully prepared manoeuvres these rascals intentionally compromised many of those who took part in the preparatory work of the insurrectionary Committees.

"Further, these traitors managed to discredit the International at Lyons to such an extent that by the time of the Paris Revolution the International was regarded by the Lyons workers with the greatest distrust. Hence the total absence of organisation, hence the failure of the insurrection, a failure which was bound to result in the fall of the Commune which was left to rely on its own isolated forces! It is only since this bloody lesson that our propaganda has been able to rally the Lyons workers around the flag of the International.

"Albert Richard was the pet and prophet of Bakunin and company."

"The time of the revolutionaries," they say, "is over ... communism is restricted to Germany and England, especially Germany. That, moreover, is where it had been developed in earnest for a long time, to be subsequently spread throughout the International, and this disturbing expansion of *German influence* in the Association has in no small degree contributed to retarding its development, or rather, to giving it a new course in the sections of central and southern France, whom no German has ever supplied with a slogan."

Perhaps this is the voice of the great hierophant,[a] who has taken upon himself, ever since the Alliance's foundation, in his capacity as a Russian, the special task of representing the *Latin races?* Or do we have here the "true missionaries" of the *Révolution Sociale* (November 2, 1871) denouncing

"the backward march which the German and Bismarckian minds endeavour to foist upon the International"?

Fortunately, however, the true tradition has survived, and Messrs. Albert Richard and Gaspard Blanc have not been shot! Thus, their own "contribution" consists in "setting a new course" for the International in central and southern France to follow, by an effort to found Bonapartist sections, *ipso facto* basically "autonomous".

As for the constitution of the proletariat as a political party, as recommended by the London Conference,

"*after the restoration of the Empire, we*"—Richard and Blanc—"shall quickly deal not only with the socialist theories but also with any attempts to implement them through revolutionary organisation of the masses".

Briefly, exploiting the great "autonomy principle of the sections" which "constitutes the real strength of the International ... especially in the *Latin* countries (*Révolution Sociale,* January 4)",

these gentlemen base their hopes on anarchy within the International.

Anarchy, then, is the great war-horse of their master Bakunin, who has taken nothing from the socialist systems except a set of labels. All socialists see anarchy as the following programme: once the aim of the proletarian movement, i.e., abolition of classes, is attained, the power of the State, which serves to keep the great majority of producers in bondage to a very small exploiter minority, disappears, and the functions of government become simple administrative functions. The Alliance reverses the whole process. It proclaims anarchy in proletarian ranks as the most infallible means of breaking the powerful concentration of social

---

[a] Mikhail Bakunin.— *Ed.*

and political forces in the hands of the exploiters. Under this pretext, it asks the International, at a time when the old world is seeking a way of crushing it, to replace its organisation with anarchy. The international police want nothing better for perpetuating the Thiers republic, while cloaking it in a royal mantle.*

General Council:

R. Applegarth, Antoine Arnaud, M. J. Boon, F. Bradnick, G. H. Buttery, F. Cournet, Delahaye, Eugène Dupont, W. Hales, Hurliman, Jules Johannard, Harriet Law, F. Lessner, Lochner, Marguerittes, Constant Martin, Zévy Maurice, Henry Mayo, George Milner, Charles Murray, Pfänder, Vitale Regis, J. Rozwadowski, John Roach, Rühl, G. Ranvier, Sadler, Cowell Stepney, Alf. Taylor, W. Townshend, Ed. Vaillant, John Weston, F. J. Yarrow.

Corresponding Secretaries:

Karl Marx, Germany and Russia; *Leó Frankel*, Austria and Hungary; *A. Herman*, Belgium; *Th. Mottershead*, Denmark; *J. G. Eccarius*, United States; *Le Moussu*, French sections in the United States; *Aug. Serraillier*, France; *Charles Rochat*, Holland; *J. P. MacDonnell*, Ireland; *Fred. Engels*, Italy and Spain; *Walery Wróblewski*, Poland; *H. Jung*, Switzerland.

* In the report on the Dufaure law, Sacase, the Rural Assembly deputy, attacks above all the International's "organisation". He positively hates that organisation. After having verified "the mounting popularity of this formidable Association", he goes on to say: "This Association rejects ... the shady practices of the sects that preceded it. Its organisation was created and modified quite openly. Because of the power of this organisation ... it has steadily extended its sphere of activity and influence. It is expanding throughout the world." Then he gives a "short description of the organisation" and concludes: "Such is, in its wise unity ... the plan of this vast organisation. Its strength lies in its very conception. It also rests in its numerous adherents, who are linked by their common activities, and, lastly, in the invincible impulse which drives them to action."

Charles Longuet, **Chairman of the meeting**
Hermann Jung, **Treasurer**
John Hales, **General Secretary**

33, Rathbone Place, W.
London, March 5, 1872

Written between mid-January and March 5, 1872

First published as a pamphlet in Geneva in 1872

Printed according to the pamphlet

Translated from the French

Karl Marx

RESOLUTIONS ON THE SPLIT
IN THE UNITED STATES' FEDERATION
PASSED BY THE GENERAL COUNCIL OF THE I.W.A.
IN ITS SITTINGS OF 5TH AND 12TH MARCH, 1872 [90]

I. THE TWO FEDERAL COUNCILS

Art. 1. Considering, that Central Councils are but instituted in order to secure, in every country, to "the Working Men's movement the power of union and combination" (Art. 7 of the General Rules)[a]; that, consequently, the existence of two rival Central Councils for the same federation is an open infraction of the General Rules;

The General Council calls upon the two provisional Federal Councils at New York to re-unite and to act as one and the same provisional Federal Council for the United States until the meeting of an American General Congress.

Art. 2. Considering, that the efficiency of the Provisional Federal Council would be impaired if it contained too many members who have only quite recently joined the International Working Men's Association;

The General Council recommends that such new-formed sections as are numerically weak, should combine amongst each other for the appointment of a few common delegates.

II. GENERAL CONGRESS
OF THE UNITED STATES' FEDERATION

Art. 1. The General Council recommends the convocation, for the 1st of July 1872, of a General Congress of the delegates of sections and affiliated societies of the United States.

Art. 2. To this Congress will belong the appointment of the

---

[a] See this volume, p. 7.— *Ed.*

members of the Federal Council for the United States. It may, if convenient, empower the Federal Council thus appointed to add to itself a certain limited number of members.

Art. 3. This Congress will have the sole power of determining the bye-laws and regulations for the organisation of the I.W.A. in the United States, "but such bye-laws and regulations must not contain anything contrary to the General Rules and Regulations of the Association" (Adm. Reg., V. Art. 1).[a]

III. SECTIONS[b]

Art. 1. Considering, that Section No. 12 at New York has not only passed a formal resolution by virtue of which "each section" possesses "the independent right" to construe, according to its fancy, "the proceedings of the several congresses" and the "General Rules and Regulations",[c] but moreover has fully acted up to this doctrine which, if generally adopted, would leave nothing of the I.W.A. but its name;

that the same section has never ceased to make the I.W.A. the vehicle of issues some of which are foreign to, while others are directly opposed to, the aims and purposes of the I.W.A.;

For these reasons the General Council considers it its duty to put in force Administrative Resolution VI of the Bâle Congress[d] and to declare Section No. 12 *suspended* till the meeting of the next General Congress of the I.W.A. which is to take place in September 1872.

Art. 2. Considering, that the I.W.A., according to the General Rules, is to consist exclusively of "working men's societies" (see Art. 1, Art. 7 and Art. 11 of the General Rules);

that, consequently, Art. 9 of the General Rules to this effect: "Everybody who acknowledges and defends the principles of the I.W.A. is eligible to become a member", although it confers upon the active adherents of the *International*, who are no working men,[e] the right either of individual membership or of admission to working men's sections, does in no way legitimate the foundation

---

[a] Cf. ibid., p. 12.— *Ed.*

[b] In the *Woodhull & Claflin's Weekly* this part is headed "Section XII".— *Ed.*

[c] "Appeal of Section No. 12", *Woodhull & Claflin's Weekly*, No. 19 (71), September 23, 1871.— *Ed.*

[d] *Compte-rendu du IVe Congrès international, tenu à Bâle, en septembre 1869,* Brussels, 1869, p. 172.— *Ed.*

[e] The words "who are no working men" are omitted in the *Woodhull & Claflin's Weekly.*— *Ed.*

of sections, exclusively or principally composed of members not belonging to the working class;

that for this very reason the General Council was some months ago precluded from recognising a Slavonian section, exclusively composed of students[91];

that, according to the General Regulations V, 1, the General Rules and Regulations are to be adapted "to local circumstances of each country";

that the social conditions of the United States, though in many other respects most favourable to the success of the working-class movement, peculiarly facilitate the intrusion into the *International* of bogus reformers, middle-class quacks and trading politicians;

For these reasons the General Council recommends that in future there be admitted no new[a] American section of which two-thirds at least do not consist of wage-labourers.

Art. 3. The General Council calls the attention of the American Federation to Resolution II, 3, of the London Conference relating to "sectarian[b] sections" or "separatist bodies pretending to accomplish special missions" distinct from the common aim of the Association,[c] viz., to emancipate the man of labour from his "economical subjection to the monopoliser of the means of labour", which "lies at the bottom of servitude in all its forms, of all social misery, mental degradation, and political dependence" (see Preamble of the General Rules).[d]

Written on about March 5, 1872

First published in *La Emancipacion*, No. 43, April 6, 1872; *Woodhull & Claflin's Weekly*, No. 103, May 4, 1872; *Der Volksstaat*, No. 37, May 8, 1872

Reproduced from the manuscript checked with the *Woodhull & Claflin's Weekly*

---

[a] The word "new" is omitted in the *Woodhull & Claflin's Weekly.—Ed.*

[b] The word "sectarian" is omitted in the *Woodhull & Claflin's Weekly.—Ed.*

[c] K. Marx and F. Engels, *Resolutions of the Conference of Delegates of the International Working Men's Association Assembled at London from 17th to 23rd September 1871* (present edition, Vol. 22, pp. 423-24).—*Ed.*

[d] See this volume, p. 3.—*Ed.*

Karl Marx

TO THE EDITOR OF *LA LIBERTÉ*

London, March 12, 1872

Dear Sir,

In the book by Citizen *G. Lefrançais, Sur le mouvement communaliste*, which only came to my attention a few days ago, I find on page 92 the following passage:

"The letter subsequently written to Citizen Serraillier by Karl Marx, the principal inspirer of the German section of the International, on the subject of the elections of February 8, in which he criticises with some bitterness the intervention of the French section in these elections, is sufficient evidence that rightly or wrongly the International was then reluctant to become involved in active politics."

Immediately after the publication of my alleged letter to Serraillier I declared in *The Times*, the *Courrier de l'Europe*, the *Zukunft* of Berlin, etc., that this letter was a fabrication of the *Paris-Journal*.[92] From his part, Serraillier publicly denounced the police journalist who was the true author of this letter. Since almost all the organs of the International and even some Parisian newspapers have taken note of our statements, I am really astonished to see Citizen Lefrançais publicly endorse the falsehood circulated by Henri de Pène.

Yours faithfully,

Karl Marx

First published in *La Liberté*, No. 11, March 17, 1872

Printed according to the newspaper

Translated from the French

Published in English for the first time

Karl Marx

RESOLUTIONS OF THE MEETING
HELD TO CELEBRATE THE ANNIVERSARY
OF THE PARIS COMMUNE[93]

[I]

"That this meeting assembled to celebrate the anniversary of the 18th March last, declares, that it looks upon the glorious movement inaugurated upon the 18th March, 1871, as the dawn of the great social revolution which will for ever free the human race from class rule."

[II]

"That the incapacity and the crimes of the middle classes, extended all over Europe by their hatred against the working classes, have doomed old society no matter under what form of government—Monarchical or Republican."

[III]

"That the crusade of all governments against the International, and the terror of the murderers of Versailles as well as of their Prussian conquerors, attest the hollowness of their successes, and the presence of the threatening army of the proletariat of the whole world gathering in the rear of its heroic vanguard crushed by the combined forces of Thiers and William of Prussia."

Written between March 13 and 18, 1872

First published in *La Liberté*, No. 12, March 24, 1872 and in *The International Herald*, No. 3, March 30, 1872

Reproduced from *The International Herald*

Frederick Engels

TO THE SPANISH FEDERAL COUNCIL

We have received your letter of March 15, and we thank you for the detailed report about the present state of our Association in Spain, a very satisfying state in the circumstances at the moment.[94] We will publish the most important elements of this report, we will send you a letter for the Saragossa Congress, and we will send you a telegram[a] later. The telegram will be in the name of the General and British Federal Councils. As for France, with the Dufaure law[95] against the International, there is no way to maintain a Federal Council, but we will write to Paris so that the "Ferré Section"[96] sends you a letter for the Congress—there will be no signatures but you will receive it signed "Ferré Section", which will be in order. In Germany the recent trials have disorganised the Association for the moment, and as you will know Liebknecht and Bebel have been condemned to two years in prison, mainly because of involvement with the International[97]; sending a telegram from there would be impracticable at the moment; however we have sent your letter to Germany.

There is no problem about stamps. Ask for as many stamps as you think you will need, and send us the quotas or parts of the quotas *received* before the 1st July; then two or three weeks before the General Congress you can send us the rest with the stamps which you have not used. We have a large quantity and it will not matter if your delegates at the Congress return us a thousand or two.

Yesterday afternoon Jung the treasurer did not come to the Council. I have sent him the receipt to sign and when I have it

---

[a] See this volume, pp. 137-39.— *Ed.*

back from him I shall send it with the letter for the Saragossa Congress.

We hope that you will submit the resolutions of the London Conference to the Regional Congress for their approval. These resolutions have so far been recognised by the German, Romance, German-Swiss (Zurich), English, Dutch and American federations and by the French and Irish sections.

Written on March 27, 1872

First published in: Marx and Engels, *Works*, First Russian Edition, Vol. XXVI, Moscow, 1935

Printed according to the rough manuscript

Translated from the Spanish

Published in English for the first time

Karl Marx

THE NATIONALISATION OF THE LAND[98]

The property in the soil is the original source of all wealth, and has become the great problem upon the solution of which depends the future of the working class.[a]

I do not intend discussing here all the arguments put forward by the advocates of private property in land, by jurists, philosophers and political economists, but shall confine myself firstly to state that they have tried hard to disguise the primitive fact of conquest under the cloak of *"Natural Right"*. If conquest constituted a natural right on the part of the few, the many have only to gather sufficient strength in order to acquire the natural right of reconquering what has been taken from them.

In the progress of history the conquerors found it convenient to give to their original titles, derived from brute force, a sort of social standing[b] through the instrumentality of laws imposed by themselves.

At last comes the philosopher and demonstrates that those laws imply and express the universal consent of mankind.[c] If private property in land be indeed founded upon such an universal consent, it will evidently become extinct from the moment the majority of a society dissent from warranting it.

However, leaving aside the so-called "rights" of property, I assert that the economical development of society, the increase and concentration of people, the very circumstances that compel the capitalist farmer to apply to agriculture collective and organised

---

[a] In the rough manuscript the sentence is preceded by the note "Ad p. 1".— *Ed.*

[b] The rough manuscript has "sanction" instead of "standing".— *Ed.*

[c] The rough manuscript has "society" instead of "mankind".— *Ed.*

labour, and to have recourse to machinery and similar contrivances, will more and more render the nationalisation of land a "*Social Necessity*", against which no amount of talk about the rights of property can be of any avail. The imperative wants of society will and must be satisfied, changes dictated by social necessity will work their own way, and sooner or later adapt legislation to their interests.

What we require is a daily increasing production and its exigencies cannot be met by allowing a few individuals to regulate it according to their whims and private interests, or to ignorantly exhaust the powers of the soil. All modern methods, such as irrigation, drainage, steam ploughing, chemical treatment and so forth, ought to be applied to agriculture at large. But the scientific knowledge we possess, and the technical means of agriculture we command, such as machinery, etc., can never be successfully applied but by cultivating the land on a large scale.

If cultivation on a large scale proves (even under its present capitalist form, that degrades the cultivator himself to a mere beast of burden) so superior, from an economical point of view,[a] to small and piecemeal husbandry, would it not give an increased impulse to production if applied on national dimensions?

The ever-growing wants of the people on the one side, the ever-increasing price of agricultural produce on the other, afford the irrefutable evidence that the nationalisation of land has become a social necessity.

Such a diminution of agricultural produce as springs from individual abuse, will, of course, become impossible whenever cultivation is carried on under the control[b] and for the benefit of the nation.

All the citizens I have heard here today during the progress of the debate, on this question, defended the nationalisation of land, but they took very different views of it.[c]

France was frequently alluded to, but with its *peasant proprietorship* it is farther off the nationalisation of land than England with its landlordism.[d] In France, it is true, the soil is accessible to all who can buy it, but this very facility has brought about a division

---

[a] The words "from an economical point of view" are not to be found in the rough manuscript.— *Ed.*

[b] In the rough manuscript the end of the sentence reads: "at the cost and for the benefit of the nation".— *Ed.*

[c] The phrase, presumably, belongs to Dupont since it is absent in the rough manuscript.— *Ed.*

[d] In the rough manuscript the sentence is preceded by the note "+p. 5".— *Ed.*

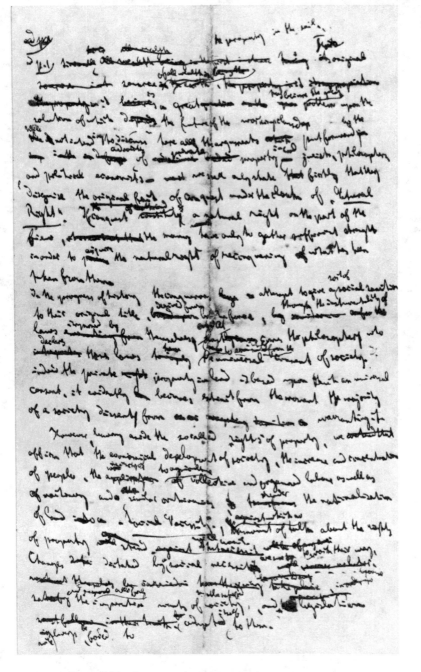

Page of Marx's manuscript *The Nationalisation of the Land*

into small plots cultivated by men with small means and mainly relying upon the land by exertions of themselves and their families. This form of landed property and the piecemeal cultivation it necessitates, while excluding all appliances of modern agricultural improvements, converts the tiller himself into the most decided enemy to social progress and, above all, the nationalisation of land. Enchained to the soil upon which he has to spend all his vital energies in order to get a relatively small return, having to give away the greater part of his produce to the state, in the form of taxes, to the law tribe in the form of judiciary costs, and to the usurer in the form of interest, utterly ignorant of the social movements outside his petty field of employment; still he clings with fanatic fondness to his bit of land and his merely nominal proprietorship in the same. In this way the French peasant has been thrown into a most fatal antagonism to the industrial working class.

Peasant proprietorship being then the greatest obstacle to the nationalisation of land, France, in its present state, is certainly not the place where we must look to for a solution of this great problem.

To nationalise the land, in order to let it out in small plots to individuals or working men's societies, would, under a middle-class government, only engender a reckless competition among themselves and thus result in a progressive increase of "*Rent*" which, in its turn, would afford new facilities to the appropriators of feeding upon the producers.

At the International Congress of Brussels, in 1868, one of our friends said:

> "Small private property in land is doomed by the verdict of science, large land property by that of justice. There remains then but one alternative. The soil must become the property of rural associations or the property of the whole nation. The future will decide that question." [a]

I say on the contrary [b]; the social movement will lead to this decision that the land can but be owned by the nation itself. To give up the soil to the hands of associated rural labourers, would be to surrender society to one exclusive class of producers.

The nationalisation of land will work a complete change in the

---

[a] Marx quotes César De Paepe's report on land property at the meeting of the Brussels Congress of the International Working Men's Association on September 11, 1868 (see *Troisième Congrès de l'Association Internationale des Travailleurs. Compte-rendu officiel*, Brussels, 1868, p. 35 et seq.).— *Ed.*

[b] In the rough manuscript the end of the sentence reads: "the future will decide that the land cannot be owned but nationally".— *Ed.*

relations between labour and capital, and finally, do away with the capitalist form of production, whether industrial or rural. Then class distinctions and privileges will disappear together with the economical basis[a] upon which they rest. To live on other people's labour will become a thing of the past. There will be no longer any government or state power, distinct from society itself! Agriculture, mining, manufacture, in one word, all branches of production, will gradually be organised in the most adequate manner. *National centralisation of the means of production* will become the national[b] basis of a society composed of associations of free and equal producers, carrying on the social business on a common and rational plan. Such is the humanitarian[c] goal to which the great economic movement of the 19th century is tending.

Written in March-April 1872

First published in *The International Herald*, No. 11, June 15, 1872

Reproduced from the newspaper checked with the rough manuscript

---

[a] In the rough manuscript the end of the sentence reads: "from which they originate and society will be transformed into an association of free producers".— *Ed.*

[b] The rough manuscript has "natural" instead of "national".— *Ed.*

[c] This word is crossed out in the rough manuscript.— *Ed.*

NO MAS DEBERES SIN DERECHOS: NO MAS DERECHOS SOIN EBERES.

LA EMANCIPACION.

PERIODICO SOCIALISTA.

SE PUBLICA TODOS LOS SABADOS.

| Año II. | Precio de suscricion: 4 rs. trimestre. Administracion: San Pedro, 16, 3.° | Madrid 13 de abril de 1872. | Para suscriciones dirigirse á la librería de San Martin, Puerta del Sol. | Num. 44. |

Frederick Engels

TO CITIZEN DELEGATES
OF THE REGIONAL SPANISH CONGRESS
ASSEMBLED AT SARAGOSSA [99]

London, April 3, 1872

Citizens,

The General Council of the International Working Men's Association has asked me to congratulate you on its behalf on the occasion of the second congress of the Spanish sections. You are indeed to be congratulated for the results you have obtained in so short a time. The International, founded in Spain less than three years ago, now covers the whole country with its sections and federations, is established in all the towns and is penetrating into the countryside. Thanks to your efforts, and also to the senseless and ridiculous persecution by successive governments of your country, it has been possible to obtain these fine results and make the International a real force in Spain. We ought not to forget, at the same time, that these results are also due to the special constitution of our Association which leaves every national or local federation complete freedom of action, granting the central organs only such powers as are absolutely essential to enable them to safeguard the unity of the programme and common interests, and to prevent the Association from becoming a plaything of bourgeois intrigues and police machinations.[a]

You have probably still to come in for further persecutions. Remember then that there are other countries, like France, Germany, and Austria and Hungary, where the members of the

---

[a] The rough copy of the letter continues: "No bourgeois association would ever be able to subsist in such conditions; the merit of the modern proletariat is that it organised for the common struggle an association embracing all civilised countries and yet in no way restricting the autonomy of each federation." — Ed.

International suffer even harsher government repression and yet
do not bow their heads, knowing, as you know, that persecution is
the best means of propaganda for our Association, and that there
is no force in the world strong enough to suppress the
ever-growing revolutionary movement of the modern proletariat.
In order to destroy the International it would be necessary to
destroy the soil of which it is the natural product: modern society
itself.

    Greetings and fraternity,
    On behalf of the General Council
                   Secretary for Spain,
                                 Frederick Engels

First published in *La Emancipacion*,
No. 44, April 13, 1872 and in other
newspapers of the International

Printed according to the newspaper checked with the rough
copy of the letter in French

Translated from the Spanish

Frederick Engels

[TO THE SARAGOSSA CONGRESS] [100]

London, April 6 [1872]

The General Council and the British Federal Council greet the Congress of Saragossa. Long live the emancipation of the proletariat!

Engels

First published in *La Emancipacion*, No. 44, April 13, 1872

Printed according to the newspaper

Translated from the Spanish

Karl Marx

[DECLARATION OF THE GENERAL COUNCIL OF THE INTERNATIONAL WORKING MEN'S ASSOCIATION CONCERNING COCHRANE'S SPEECH IN THE HOUSE OF COMMONS][101]

The performances of the Versailles Rural Assembly, and of the Spanish Cortes, with intent to extinguish the International, very properly aroused a noble spirit of emulation in the breasts of the representatives of the Upper Ten Thousand in the British House of Commons. Accordingly, on the 12th April, 1872, Mr. B. Cochrane, one of the most representative men, as far as Upper Class intellect is concerned, called the attention of the House to the sayings and doings of that formidable society. Being a man not much given to reading, he had qualified himself for his task by a journey of inspection to a few of the Continental headquarters of the International, undertaken last autumn, and had, on his return, hastened to secure, by a letter to *The Times*, a kind of provisional protection for his right of priority to this subject.[a] His speech in Parliament betrays, what in any other man would be considered a wilful and premeditated ignorance of what he is talking about. With one exception the many official publications of the International are unknown to him; in their stead, he quotes a jumble of passages from petty publications by private individuals in Switzerland, for which the International, as a body, is as much responsible as the British Cabinet is for the speech of Mr. Cochrane. According to that speech,

"the great majority of those who joined the society in England, and their number was 180,000, was totally ignorant of the principles it was intended to carry out, which were carefully concealed from them while they were giving their subscriptions".[b]

---

[a] A. B. Cochrane, "To the Editor of *The Times*", *The Times*, No. 27208, October 31, 1871, p. 6.— *Ed.*

[b] Here and below Cochrane's speech in the House of Commons on April 12, 1872 is cited from *The Times*, No. 27350, April 13, 1872.— *Ed.*

Now, the principles intended to be carried out by the International, are laid down in the preamble to the General Rules, and Mr. Cochrane is in happy ignorance of the fact that no one can enter the Association without giving his express adhesion to them. Again,

> "the society, as originally constituted, was founded upon the principles of the Trades' Unions, and no political element was then introduced into it".

Not only does the preamble to the original General Rules contain a strong political element, but the political tendencies of the Association are very fully developed in the Inaugural Address, published in 1864, contemporaneously with these Rules.[102] Another wonderful discovery is this, that Bakounine was "charged" to reply, in the name of the International, to the attacks of Mazzini, which is simply an untruth. After giving a quotation from Bakounine's pamphlet,[a] he continues:

> "We might smile at such bombastic nonsense, but when these papers emanated from London" (from which they did *not* emanate) "was it surprising that Foreign Governments should take alarm?"

And is it surprising that Mr. Cochrane should become their spokesman in England? Another charge is that the International had just started "a newspaper" in London, which is another untruth. However, let Mr. Cochrane console himself, the International has plenty of organs of its own in Europe and America, and in almost all civilised languages.

But the gist of the whole speech is contained in the following:

> "He should be *able to show* that the Commune and the International Association were, in reality, one, and that the International Society located" (?) "in London, had given orders to the Commune to burn Paris, and to murder the Archbishop of that City."

And now for the proofs. Eugène Dupont, as chairman of the Brussels Congress of September, 1868, truly stated that the International aimed at a social revolution. And what is the secret link between this statement of Eugène Dupont in 1868 and the deeds of the Commune in 1871? That

> "only last week Eugène Dupont was arrested in Paris, to which he had gone secretly from this country. Now, this M. Eugène Dupont was a member of the Commune and also a member of the International Society".

---

[a] This refers to Bakunin's *Risposta d'un Internazionale a Giuseppe Mazzini*, published in Milan in 1871.— *Ed.*

Unfortunately for this very conclusive mode of reasoning, A. Dupont, the member of the Commune, who has been arrested in Paris, was not a member of the International, and E. Dupont, the member of the International, was not a member of the Commune. The second proof is:

"Bakounine said, at Geneva, July, 1869, when the Congress met under his presidency:—'The International proclaims itself Atheist'."

Now there never took place an International Congress at Geneva, in July, 1869; Bakounine never presided at any International Congress, and was never charged to make declarations in its name. Third proof:— The *Volksstimme*, the International organ at Vienna, wrote:

"For us the red flag is the symbol of universal love, let our enemies beware, lest they turn it into the symbol of universal terror."

The same paper, moreover, stated in so many words that the General Council in London was, in fact, the General Council of the International, that is to say, its central administrative delegation. Fourth proof:— In one of the French trials of the International, Tolain ridiculed the assertion of the public prosecutor, that

"it was sufficient for the president of the International" (who does not exist) "to raise his finger to command obedience over the whole surface of the globe".

The muddling brain of Mr. Cochrane turns Tolain's denial into a confirmation. Fifth proof:— The manifesto of the General Council on the Civil War in France,[a] from which Mr. Cochrane quotes the defence of the reprisals against the hostages, and of the use of fire, as measures of warfare, necessary under the circumstances. Now, as Mr. Cochrane approves of the massacres committed by the Versaillese, are we to infer that he had *ordered* them, although he is surely innocent of the murder of anything but game? Sixth proof:

"There was a meeting held between the leaders of the International and the Commune before the burning of Paris."

This is exactly as true as the report which a short time ago went the round of the Italian press to the effect that the General Council of the International had sent, on a tour of inspection to the Continent, its truly and well-beloved Alexander Baillie-Cochrane, who reported most satisfactorily on the flourishing state

---

[a] K. Marx, *The Civil War in France.—Ed.*

of the organisation, and stated that it counted seventeen millions of members. Final proof:

"In the decree of the Commune which commanded the destruction of the Column of the Place Vendôme, the approval of the International is signified."

Nothing of the kind is stated in that decree, although the Commune was, no doubt, fully aware that the whole International all over the world would applaud this resolution.

Such then is the, according to *The Times* newspaper, irrefutable evidence for Cochrane's statement that the Archbishop of Paris[a] was killed and Paris burnt by the direct order of the General Council of the International in London. Compare his incoherent rant to the report of M. Sacase, on the law against the International in Versailles,[103] and you will be able to realise the distance still existing between a French Rural and a British Dogberry.[b]

Of Mr. Cochrane's *fidus Achates*, Mr. Eastwick, we should say with Dante: "Look at him and pass on",[c] were it not for his absurd assertion that the International is responsible for the *Père Duchêne* of Vermersch, whom the learned Mr. Cochrane calls Vermuth.

If it is an unmixed pleasure to have an opponent like Mr. Cochrane, it is a grievous calamity to have to undergo the patronage, as far as it goes, of Mr. Fawcett. If he is bold enough to defend the International against forcible measures, which the British Government neither dare not care to take, he has at the same time that sense of duty and high moral courage which compel him to pass upon it his supreme professional condemnation. Unfortunately the pretended doctrines of the International which he attacks, are but concoctions of his own poor brain.

"The State," he says, "was to do this and that, and find money to carry out all their projects. The first article of the programme was that the State should buy up all the land, and all the instruments of production, and let them out at a fair and reasonable price to the people."[d]

As to the buying up of the land by the State under certain circumstances and the letting of it out to the people at a fair and reasonable price, let Mr. Fawcett settle that with his theoretical

---

[a] Georges Darboy.— *Ed.*

[b] Dogberry—a character in Shakespeare's comedy *Much Ado about Nothing*.— *Ed*.

[c] Dante, *The Divine Comedy*, Hell, Canto III.— *Ed.*

[d] Here and below Fawcett's speech in the House of Commons on April 12, 1872 is cited from *The Times*, No. 27350, April 13, 1872.— *Ed.*

teacher Mr. John Stuart Mill, and with his political Chief Mr. John Bright. The second article

"proposes that the State should regulate the hours of labour".

The historical learning of our Professor shines out brilliantly when he makes the International the author of the British Factory and Workshops' Acts, and his economical proficiency comes out to equal advantage in his appreciation of those acts. Third article—

"That the State should provide gratuitous education."

Such broad facts as the existence of gratuitous education in the United States and Switzerland, and their beneficial results, what are they compared to the gloomy vaticinations of Professor Fawcett? Fourth article—

"That the State should lend capital to co-operative societies."

There is here a slight mistake; Mr. Fawcett mixes up the demands put forth by Lassalle, who died before the foundation of the International, with the principles of the International. By the by, Lassalle invoked the precedent of the State loans, which, under the pretext of agricultural improvements, and by the instrumentality of Parliament, the British landed proprietors had so generously granted to themselves. Fifth article—

"as the coping-stone, it was proposed that the whole revenue of the country should be raised by a graduated tax upon property".

This is really too bad; to make the demands of Mr. Robert Gladstone and his Liverpool middle-class Financial Reformers the "coping-stone" of the International!

This great political economist, Mr. Fawcett, whose claim to scientific fame rests entirely upon a vulgarisation, for the use of schoolboys, of Mr. John Stuart Mill's compendium of political economy,[a] confesses that "the confident predictions" (for the free-traders) "of five and twenty years ago had been falsified by facts".

At the same time he is confident of his ability to allay the giant proletarian movement of our days by repeating over and over again, in a still more diluted form, the very same stale phrases by which those false predictions of twenty-five years ago were propped up. His sham defence of the International, which is, in reality, an humble apology for his former pretended sympathies with the working classes, will, it is to be hoped, open the eyes of

---

[a] J. St. Mill, *Principles of Political Economy with Some of Their Applications to Social Philosophy*, Vols. 1, 2, London, 1848.—*Ed.*

such English working men as are still taken in by the sentimentalism, under which Mr. Fawcett hitherto tried to hide his scientific nullity.

Now if Mr. B. Cochrane represents the political intellect, and Mr. Fawcett the economical science of the British House of Commons, how does this "pleasantest of all London Clubs" compare with the American House of Representatives, which, on the 13th December, 1871, passed an act for the establishment of a Labour Statistics Office,[104] and declared that this act was passed at the express desire of the International Working Men's Association, which the House recognised as one of the most important facts of the present age?

The General Council:

R. Applegarth, A. Arnaud, M. Barry, M. J. Boon, F. Bradnick, G. H. Buttery, F. Cournet, E. Delahaye, Eugène Dupont, W. Hales, Hurliman, Jules Johannard, C. Keen, Harriet Law, F. Lessner, Lochner, C. Longuet, Marguerittes, C. Martin, Zévy Maurice, H. Mayo, G. Milner, Ch. Murray, Pfänder, J. Rozwadowski, V. Regis, J. Roach, Rühl, G. Ranvier, Sadler, Cowell Stepney, A. Taylor, W. Townshend, E. Vaillant, J. Weston, De Wolfers, F. J. Yarrow

Corresponding Secretaries:

Leó Frankel, for Austria and Hungary; *A. Herman*, Belgium; *T. Mottershead*, Denmark; *A. Serraillier*, France; *Karl Marx*, Germany and Russia; *C. Rochat*, Holland; *J. P. McDonnell*, Ireland; *F. Engels*, Italy and Spain; *Walery Wróblewski*, Poland; *Hermann Jung*, Switzerland; *J. G. Eccarius*, United States; *Le Moussu*, for French Branches of United States; *J. Hales*, General Secretary

Written between April 13 and 16, 1872

First published as a leaflet on April 17, 1872, and later on in some organs of the International

Reproduced from the leaflet

Frederick Engels

TO THE SOCIETY OF FERRARESE WORKERS[105]

Citizens,

In reply to your kind letter of March 3 I thank you, on behalf of the General Council, for your adherence to the International Working Men's Association. I must at the same time inform you that before accepting it, the Council requires clarification of the significance of the reservation you make about your "autonomy".

When an association is formed, the first requirement is to draw up rules and administrative regulations such as you yourselves possess, and as the International possesses too. You are perhaps not familiar with the latter and I am therefore enclosing a copy in French. Kindly submit them to your society and, if you agree to abide by them, let me know. These General Rules and Administrative Regulations are the only laws which our association possesses and which could limit your autonomy. But as you yourselves must realise, there cannot be two sorts of section in the International, one which accepts the collective laws and one which rejects them.[a] I hope, though, that you will have no difficulty in agreeing to these laws, made by the workers of the whole of Europe after seven years of annual meetings and recognised by all.

Administrative Regulation V, Article 1, says that "every branch is at liberty to make rules and bye-laws for its local administration, adapted to local circumstances and the laws of its country".[b] But these rules and bye-laws must not contain anything contrary to the

---

[a] Further on it is crossed out in the rough copy: "preserving its autonomy".— *Ed.*

[b] See this volume, p. 12.— *Ed.*

General Rules and Regulations.[a] Administrative Regulation II, Article 5, which leaves to the General Council the responsibility for accepting or rejecting each new section, entrusts it with the task of checking whether the rules and regulations of these new sections are in accordance with this article. I should be grateful, therefore, if you would send the Council a copy of your rules so that this formality can be carried out.

Written on April 16, 1872

First published in: Marx and Engels, *Works*, First Russian Edition, Vol. XXVI, Moscow, 1935

Printed according to the rough copy of the letter

Translated from the Italian

Published in English for the first time

---

[a] Further on it is crossed out in the rough copy: "As Italy does not yet have a regular Federal Council, the General Council reserves the right to check the rules and bye-laws of the Italian sections." — *Ed.*

Frederick Engels

LETTERS FROM LONDON [106]

I

[THE ENGLISH AGRICULTURAL LABOURERS' STRIKE]

London, April 20, 1872

The labour movement in England has made enormous progress in the last few days. It has established itself—solidly—among the agricultural labourers. In Great Britain, as is well known, all the land belongs to an extremely small number of large landowners who receive, in the form of rent, annual incomes ranging from 100,000 lire in the case of the poorest to several million for the richest. The Marquis of Westminster enjoys an annual income of over 10 million lire.

The land is divided up into large lots, worked by a small number of agricultural labourers, with the aid of machines, on behalf of the tenant farmer. There are no small peasant proprietors. The number of agricultural workers, already small in proportion to the area of land they cultivate is decreasing every year as a result of the introduction of new machinery. Hence the English agricultural labourers—ignorant, slaves of the soil as were never seen before and at the same time victims of competition—form the lowest paid class of the population. On several occasions they have rebelled against their hard fate. In 1831, in the south of England, they burned the farmers' corn and hay ricks.[107] A few years ago they did the same thing in Yorkshire. From time to time there have been attempts at setting up resistance societies among them, but with no real results. The present movement, however, has in a few weeks assumed dimensions which guarantee it an enormous success. This movement began among the labourers of Warwickshire. They demanded a rise in their wages from 11 or 12 shillings (13 or 14 francs) a week to 16 shillings (19 francs). In order to obtain it they formed a resistance society and went on strike.[108] There was general horror among the landowners,

farmers and Tories of the county; the labourers, slaves in body
and mind, after over a thousand years were daring to rebel against
the authority of the masters! And they really did rebel. They
struck with such effect that in two or three weeks the rebellion
spread to all the labourers not just of Warwickshire but of the
eight neighbouring counties. The union of agricultural labourers
was for the frightened landlords and farmers what the *International* is for the reactionary governments of Europe: the scarecrow at
the mere mention of whose name they quake. And they mounted
an opposition, but in vain; the union, helped by the counsel and by
the experience of the resistance societies of the industrial workers,
grew and became more solid every day. It was supported,
moreover, by the public opinion of the bourgeoisie itself. The
bourgeoisie, despite its contract of political alliance with the
aristocracy, permanently wages a sort of little economic war with
it. Since at present it is enjoying a state of great industrial
prosperity in which it needs many workers, nearly all the
agricultural labourers on strike found themselves transported to
the towns, where they were employed and paid much better than
they could have been on the land. Hence the strike was completely
successful, with the landlords and farmers of all England
spontaneously raising labourers' wages by 25 and 30 per cent.
From this first great victory will date a new era in the intellectual
and social life of the rural proletariat, which has entered as a mass
into the movement of the urban proletarians against the tyranny
of capital.

Last week, the English Parliament discussed the *International*.
Mr. Cochrane, a rabid reactionary, accused the terrible workers'
association of having ordered the Paris Commune to murder the
archbishop[a] and set fire to the city! He then demanded repressive
measures against the General Council which is based, for the
moment, in London. Naturally the government replied that the
members of the International, like all the inhabitants of England,
are responsible before the law alone, and as they have not yet
broken it there was no reason to persecute them.[b] It is believed

---

[a] Georges Darboy.— *Ed.*

[b] This refers to the reply of Bruce, Home Secretary, at the sitting of the House of
Lords on April 12, 1872 in connection with A. B. Cochrane's speech against the
International Working Men's Association (*The Times*, No. 27350, April 13,
1872).— *Ed.*

that the General Council of the Association will be replying to Mr. Cochrane's falsehoods.[a]

Written on April 20, 1872

First published in *La Plebe*, No. 48, April 24, 1872

Signed: *F. E.*
"Our correspondence"

Printed according to the newspaper

Translated from the Italian

---

[a] See this volume, pp. 140-45.— *Ed.*

Frederick Engels

[ON THE POLICE PERSECUTION OF THE MEMBER OF THE INTERNATIONAL THEODORE CUNO] [109]

It has been known for some time that a conspiracy had been entered into by the Governments of Germany, Austria, and Italy, for the purpose of hunting down the Internationals. How this conspiracy works may be seen from the following facts:—A prominent member of the International at Milan, Citizen Theodore Cuno, a native of Prussia and an engineer, having lost his place in a large machine shop, was, on the 25th February, arrested, and all his papers, and all photographs in his possession (including that of his father, &c.) were seized. He was transported, in chains, to Verona, where he was kept in prison for nearly a month amongst thieves and murderers, and treated exactly as they were, while his papers were sent to Rome to be examined. On the 29th March, chained to a common criminal, he was transported to the frontier, and handed over to the Austrian authorities. Here, for the first time, he was allowed to learn the reason which had caused all this. What was his astonishment when he read that he had been arrested because

"he was in Milan idle, a vagabond, and without means of existence, and, moreover, a dangerous agent of the International Socialist party, and for all these reasons expelled from the kingdom of Italy"!

Now, so far from being idle, he was, on the 1st of March, to have entered upon a very lucrative place at Como as manager of a factory, and so far from being without means of existence, the Italian authorities on parting with him, had to hand him over 111 francs of his own money! The Austrians could not make out this contradiction, but, instead of letting him free gave him in charge of a policeman who had to see him, at Cuno's expense, to the

Bavarian frontier; and thus, Cuno had not only to pass another seven nights in prison, but to spend the greater part of his money too. At the Bavarian frontier, thanks, no doubt, to the want of proper instructions, as also to the homely stupidity of the Bavarian police, he obtained intelligence that a telegram was sent to his relatives and on receipt of a satisfactory reply, he was at last set at liberty. Thus, it appears, that the European police league against the International is a reality. Cuno could have been sent to the Swiss frontier, and there set at liberty; but instead, he must be handed over to the Austrians, and by them to the Bavarians, to be sent from prison to prison as a common criminal. There is the liberalism of "free" Constitutional monarchies.

Written on April 22-23, 1872   Reproduced from *The Eastern Post*

First published in *The Eastern Post*,
No. 187, April 27, 1872 and in *Gazzettino
Rosa*, No. 127, May 7, 1872

Frederick Engels

TO THE SOCIETY OF FERRARESE WORKERS[110]

[*Draft letter*]

[London,] May 10 [1872]

Confirmation given that the reservation concerning autonomy is sufficiently outlined in this letter. Promise to send all our publications.

Request for report on their strength, position, etc.

I inform that the General Council will soon devote itself to preparations for the Congress and that the Congress will take place in September.

First published in: Marx and Engels, *Works*, Second Russian Edition, Vol. 33, Moscow, 1964

Printed according to the original

Published in English for the first time

Frederick Engels

[RELATIONS BETWEEN THE IRISH SECTIONS AND THE BRITISH FEDERAL COUNCIL

ENGELS' RECORD OF HIS REPORT
AT THE GENERAL COUNCIL MEETING
OF MAY 14, 1872] [111]

Citizen Engels said the real purport of this motion was to bring the Irish sections under the jurisdiction of the British Federal Council, a thing to which the Irish sections would never consent, and which the Council had neither the right nor the power to impose upon them. According to the Rules and Regulations, this Council had no power to compel any section or branch to acknowledge the supremacy of any Federal Council whatsoever. It was certainly bound, before admitting or rejecting any new branch, within the jurisdiction of any Federal Council, to consult that Council. But he maintained that the Irish sections in England were no more under the jurisdiction of the British Federal Council than the French, German or Italian sections[a] in this country. The Irish formed, to all intents and purposes, a distinct nationality of their own, and the fact that they used the English language could not deprive them of the right, common to all, to have an independent national organisation within the International.

Citizen Hales had spoken of the relations between England and Ireland as if they were of the most idyllic nature, something like those between England and France at the time of the Crimean war, when the ruling classes of the two countries never tired of praising each other, and everything breathed the most complete harmony. But the case was quite different. There was the fact of seven centuries of English conquest and oppression of Ireland, and so long as that oppression existed, it was an insult to Irish working men to ask them to submit to a British Federal Council.

---

[a] The Minute Book of the General Council has: "French, German, Italian or Polish sections".— Ed.

The position of Ireland with regard to England was not that of an equal, it was that of Poland with regard to Russia. What would be said if this Council called upon Polish sections to acknowledge the supremacy of a Russian Federal Council in Petersburg, or upon Prussian Polish, North Schleswig, and Alsatian sections to submit to a Federal Council in Berlin? Yet what it was asked to do with regard to Irish sections was substantially the same thing. If members of a conquering nation called upon the nation they had conquered and continued to hold down to forget their specific nationality and position, to "sink national differences" and so forth, that was not Internationalism, it was nothing else but preaching to them submission to the yoke, and attempting to justify and to perpetuate the dominion of the conqueror under the cloak of Internationalism. It was sanctioning the belief, only too common among the English working men, that they were superior beings compared to the Irish, and as much an aristocracy as the mean Whites of the Slave States considered themselves to be with regard to the Negroes.

In a case like that of the Irish, true Internationalism must necessarily be based upon a distinctly national organisation; the Irish, as well as other oppressed nationalities, could enter the Association only as equals with the members of the conquering nation, and under protest against the conquest. The Irish sections, therefore, not only were justified, but even under the necessity to state in the preamble to their rules that their first and most pressing duty, as Irishmen, was to establish their own national independence. The antagonism between Irish and English working men in England had always been one of the most powerful means by which class rule was upheld in England. He recollected the time when he saw Feargus O'Connor and the English Chartists turned out of the Hall of Science in Manchester by the Irish.[112] Now, for the first time, there was a chance of making English and Irish working men act together in harmony for their common emancipation, a result attained by no previous movement in their country. And no sooner had this been effected, than they were called upon to dictate to the Irish, and to tell them they must not carry on the movement in their own way, but submit to be ruled by an English Council! Why, that was introducing into the International the subjugation of the Irish by the English.

If the promoters of this motion were so brimful of the truly International spirits, let them prove it by removing the seat of the British Federal Council to Dublin, and submit to a Council of Irishmen.

As to the pretended collisions between Irish and English branches, they had been provoked by attempts of members of the British Federal Council to meddle with the Irish sections, to get them to give up their specific national character and to come under the rule of the British Council.

Then the Irish sections in England could not be separated from the Irish sections in Ireland; it would not do to have some Irishmen dependent upon a London Federal Council and others upon a Dublin Federal Council. The Irish sections in England were our base of operations with regard to the Irish working men in Ireland; they were more advanced, being placed in more favourable circumstances, and the movement in Ireland could be propagated and organised only through their instrumentality. And were they to wilfully destroy their own base of operations and cut off the only means of which Ireland could be effectually won for the International? For it must not be forgotten that the Irish sections, and rightly so, would never consent to give up their distinct national organisation and submit to the British Council. The question, then, amounted to this: were they to leave the Irish alone, or were they to turn them out of the Association? If the motion was adopted by the Council, the Council would inform the Irish working men, in so many words, that, after the dominion of the English aristocracy over Ireland, after the dominion of the English middle class over Ireland, they must now look forth to the advent of the dominion of the English working class over Ireland.

Written on about May 14, 1872

First published in: Marx and Engels, *Works*, Second Russian Edition, Vol. 18, Moscow, 1961

Reproduced from the manuscript checked with the Minute Book of the General Council

Karl Marx

DECLARATION OF THE GENERAL COUNCIL CONCERNING THE UNIVERSAL FEDERALIST COUNCIL [113]

Some weeks ago a pamphlet was published under the title "Universal Federalist Council of the International Working Men's Association and of the Republican Socialist Societies adhering". This pamphlet pretends nothing less than to inaugurate a *coup d'état* within the International. It announces the formation of a second General Council, and it denounces both the organisation of the International, and the administration of its General Council. Now, who are the members of this new self-constituted Council, and the authors of these denunciations? Among the names affixed to the document we find, firstly, that of Citizen John Weston, a member of the General Council, and its former treasurer, who, in a letter to the Council, declares his name to have been made use of without his authority. Secondly, six delegates from the Universal Republican League,[114] a society entirely foreign to the International. Thirdly, two delegates from an "International Republican Federalist Section", which section is totally unknown to the International. Fourthly, two delegates from the Land and Labour League,[115] which society does not form any part of the International. Fifthly, two self-styled delegates of the German Arbeiter-Bildungs-Verein, but, in fact, delegates of a few Germans who were excluded from that society on account of their openly avowed hostility to the International.[116] Lastly, four delegates of two French societies counting together less than a score of members, and which the General Council had declined to admit as branches; amongst these we find M. Vésinier, excluded from the International by a committee appointed by the Brussels Congress in 1868,[117] and M. Landeck, whom the hasty flight of Louis

Bonaparte's prefect of police,[a] on the 4th of September, 1870, liberated from the engagement he had voluntarily taken towards that officer, and "scrupulously kept, not to occupy himself any more, in France, either with politics or with the International" (see the published report of the third trial of the International at Paris[b]) and who only lately was expelled from the Society of the Communard Refugees in London.

It must be evident, even to the signatories of this document, that a conclave of such entire strangers to the International has exactly as much right to meddle with its organisation and to constitute itself its General Council, as the General Council of the International has to interfere with the organisation, and to declare itself the Board of Directors of the Great Northern Railway.

No wonder that these men are utterly ignorant of the history and organisation of the International. How should they be expected to know that according to our rules the General Council has to render its accounts to the General Congresses, and not to them? or that, when in 1870 the breaking out of the war prevented the Congress meeting an unanimous vote of all federations empowered the General Council to continue in office until political circumstances should permit the convocation of a public Congress? As to the fund collected by the General Council in favour of the refugees, the sum total received has, from time to time, been acknowledged in the published reports of the Council meetings, and our treasurer, Citizen Jung, 4, Charles-street, Northampton-square, Clerkenwell, holds the receipts for every farthing expended, which receipts, as well as the accounts, can be inspected any day by any of the donors. Such an inspection will show not only that the Council has devoted a great portion of its time to this object, quite foreign to its regular functions, but also that itself, as a body, and its individual members, have contributed to the refugee fund within the limits of their means.

Since the growth and power of the International have become what they are, the only way in which rival and hostile societies can attempt to attack it with any chance of success is to usurp its name in order to undermine its strength. This has been so well understood by the whole press-gang of the Governments, and of the ruling classes, that the same papers, from police press to so-called democratic and republican, which carefully suppress

---

[a] J. M. Piétri.— Ed.

[b] Troisième procès de l'Association Internationale des Travailleurs à Paris, Paris, 1870, p. 4.— Ed.

every official declaration of the General Council, always hasten to keep all Europe well-informed of insignificant and ridiculous manifestations like that of this "Universal Federalist. Council".

The General Council:

R. Applegarth, A. Arnaud, M. Barry, M. J. Boon, F. Bradnick, G. H. Buttery, E. Delahaye, Eugène Dupont, J. G. Eccarius, W. Hales, Hurliman, Jules Johannard, C. Keen, Harriet Law, F. Lessner, Lochner, C. Longuet, Marguerittes, C. Martin, Zévy Maurice, H. Mayo, G. Milner, T. Mottershead, Pfänder, J. Rozwadowski, V. Regis, J. Roach, Rühl, G. Ranvier, Sadler, G. Sexton, Cowell Stepney, A. Taylor, W. Townshend, E. Vaillant, J. Weston, De Wolfers, F. J. Yarrow.

Corresponding Secretaries:

Leó Frankel, for Austria and Hungary; *A. Herman,* Belgium; *F. Cournet,* Denmark; *A. Serraillier,* France; *Karl Marx,* Germany and Russia; *C. Rochat,* Holland; *J. P. McDonnell,* Ireland; *F. Engels,* Italy and Spain; *Walery Wróblewski,* Poland; *Hermann Jung,* Switzerland; *Le Moussu,* for French Branches of United States.

C. Murray, Chairman,
H. Jung, Treasurer,
John Hales, Gen. Sec.

33, Rathbone-place, London, W.
May 20th, 1872

First published in *The Eastern Post,* No. 191, May 26, 1872 (second edition) and in other newspapers of the International

Reproduced from *The Eastern Post*

Karl Marx

STEFANONI AND THE INTERNATIONAL AGAIN
(LETTER TO THE EDITORS OF THE *GAZZETTINO ROSA*)[118]

London, May 23, 1872

Dear Editor,

In the *Libero Pensiero* of March 28, Mr. Stefanoni rightly foresaw that, despite his misfortune with Liebknecht,[119] I would continue to reply with silence to his incessant slanders. If I now break this silence, it is because Mr. Karl Vogt, a man whom I politically and morally assassinated in Germany with my book *Herr Vogt*, is revealed to be the inspiration behind the assertions of his coreligionist Stefanoni.

Mr. Stefanoni cites, taking it from Vogt's book[a] against me and the German communist party in general, the fairy story about my relations with the spy Cherval. Yet he takes care to suppress the letter from J. Ph. Becker of Geneva which exposes Vogt's crass inventions in the most humorous fashion (see *Herr Vogt*, p. 21).[b]

This slander and others of like nature, with which Vogt fills his smutty book, were reproduced a few days after it was published in the *National Zeitung* of Berlin. I immediately commenced legal proceedings for libel in London. In accordance with Prussian law, I had to go first through a preliminary procedure, in other words, obtain permission from the courts to prosecute the editor[c] of the *National Zeitung*. I therefore had to go up the entire ladder of the tribunals, from the investigating magistrate to the supreme court, with absolutely no result. In a word, they prohibited me from embarking on a trial that would have been so compromising for

---

[a] C. Vogt, *Mein Prozess gegen die Allgemeine Zeitung*, Geneva, December 1859.— *Ed.*

[b] See present edition, Vol. 17, pp. 60-64.— *Ed.*

[c] F. Zabel.— *Ed.*

Mr. Vogt (who in his *Politische Studien*[a] had precisely invited Prussia to take possession of the rest of Germany by force of arms), and also so compromising for a newspaper which did the government's work under the mask of a fictitious opposition, and which later revealed itself to be the most servile tool of Bismarck—a trial, finally, that would give full satisfaction to a man who was torn to shreds, on command from above, by the entire prostituted press of Germany.

All the episodes of my struggle with the Prussian tribunals, together with the documents I submitted to them in support of my case, are to be found printed in my book *Herr Vogt*, and must therefore be familiar to the worthy Mr. Stefanoni too.

Mr. Stefanoni also cites my *Revelations Concerning the Communist Trial in Cologne* (1853)[b] in order to prove what? That I had relations with the German communists. Of that I am proud.

Besides, the true purpose of that publication was to show that the Communist League was not a secret society according to the definition of the penal code, and that for this reason the Prussian government was forced to get the notorious Stieber and his go-betweens to fabricate a series of false documents attributed to me and the accused.[120] Today, in Germany, there is nobody, not even among the Bismarckians, who dares to deny this fact. That Mr. Stefanoni should make common cause not only with Vogt but also with Stieber is too rich, even for an *esprit fort* of Stefanoni's calibre.

In your newspaper of April 18, Mr. Stefanoni renews the attack. I had given abundant proof in my book that in 1859 Mr. Vogt sold himself to Bonaparte, taking up the role of his principal agent in Germany and Switzerland. Ten years later, the indiscretion of his friends Jules Favre and Co. merely served to verify the fact.[121]

It is utterly false that I, through some supposed Germanic interest, took up the defence of Austria against Mr. Vogt, the valiant champion of Italy. In the *Neue Rheinische Zeitung* in 1848-49 I backed the cause of Italy against the majority in the German parliament and press.[c] Later, in 1853 and at other times, I assumed in the *New-York Tribune* the defence of a man with

---

[a] A reference to C. Vogt's *Studien zur gegenwärtigen Lage Europas*, Geneva and Berne, 1859, pp. 152-53 et seq.— *Ed.*

[b] See present edition, Vol. 11, pp. 395-457.— *Ed.*

[c] Ibid., Vols. 7-9.— *Ed.*

whose principles I was in permanent opposition—Mazzini.[a] In a word, I always took the side of revolutionary Italy against Austria.

But the war of 1859 was a different matter altogether. I denounced it because it would prolong the Bonapartist empire for another decade, subject Germany to the regime of the Prussian horde and make Italy what it is today.[122] Mazzini, for once, was of my opinion (see *Pensiero e Azione* of 2 to 15 May 1859[b]). He, like me, was assailed at that time by the inevitable Mr. Vogt.

Although I was ready to denounce Mr. Vogt as a Bonapartist agent, I nevertheless had to deny the authorship of an anonymous circular launched against him by Mr. Karl Blind. Mr. Stefanoni quotes, following Vogt, the declarations which the latter obtained from the publisher[c] and printers with the aim of proving that Blind was not the author of the circular and that it had not been printed by the aforementioned publisher.

Yet if Mr. Stefanoni had read my book, as he claims, he would have found reproduced on pages 186-187[d] the *declarations made under oath to the English court* by the aforementioned printer and one of his colleagues,[e] asserting that it was precisely Karl Blind who was the author of the anonymous circular!

From Vogt, Mr. Stefanoni passes to Herzen. First of all he asserts that Herzen attended the foundation meeting of the International, and he gives the date of the Association's foundation as 1867. Everybody knows that the International was founded in September 1864 at a meeting in Longacre, at which Herzen was not present. The evangelist of rationalism, Mr. Stefanoni, handles details of time and place exactly like his predecessors in the New Testament eighteen centuries ago. Nearly ten years before the founding of the International I refused to speak on the same platform as Mr. Herzen, the Russian Panslavist, at a public demonstration.[f]

Herzen, in a posthumous book brought to light by his son,[g] a book brimming with lies about me,[123] does not dare to say that I

---

[a] This refers to Marx's correspondence published in the *New-York Daily Tribune* on December 12, 1853 and also to his article "Mazzini and Napoleon" (present edition, Vol. 12, pp. 511-12; Vol. 15, pp. 485-89).—*Ed.*

[b] G. Mazzini, "La Guerra", *Pensiero e Azione*, No. 17, May 12-16, 1859.—*Ed.*

[c] Fidelio Hollinger.—*Ed.*

[d] See present edition, Vol. 17, pp. 128-30.—*Ed.*

[e] Wiehe and Vögele.—*Ed.*

[f] See present edition, Vol. 39, pp. 522-25.—*Ed.*

[g] A. A. Herzen. A reference to *Сборникъ посмертныхъ статей Александра Ивановича Герцена*, Geneva, 1870.—*Ed.*

designated him as a *Russian spy*, as the veracious Mr. Stefanoni maintains. Besides, those who thirst for enlightenment about the esteem in which the amateur socialist Herzen is to be held have only to read Serno-Solovyovich's pamphlet *Our Internal Affairs*.[a]

I have the honour, Sir, of being your devoted

Karl Marx

Written on May 23, 1872

First published in *Gazzettino Rosa*, No. 148, May 28, 1872 and in *Il Libero Pensiero*, August 1, 1872

Printed according to the newspaper

Translated from the Italian

Published in English for the first time

---

[a] А. Серно-Соловьевичъ, «*Наши домашнія дѣла. Отвѣтъ* г. Герцену на статью „Порядокъ торжествуетъ"» (III. *Колоколъ*, No. 233), Vevey, 1867.— *Ed.*

Karl Marx

[REPLY TO BRENTANO'S ARTICLE][124]

TO THE EDITORS OF *DER VOLKSSTAAT*

A friend[a] has sent me, from Germany, *Concordia. Zeitschrift für die Arbeiterfrage*, No. 10, dated March 7, in which this "organ of the German Manufacturers' Association" publishes an editorial entitled *"How Karl Marx Quotes"*.

In the Inaugural Address of the International Working Men's Association I quote, amongst other material, a portion of Gladstone's budget speech of April 16, 1863, which is not contained in Hansard's semi-official report of parliamentary debates.[125] On this basis, with comfortable manufacturers' logic the *Concordia* concludes: "This sentence is nowhere to be found in Gladstone's speech", and jubilates in the fullness of its heart with this mocking sentence in manufacturers' German, printed in mocking bold face:

"Marx has added the sentence lyingly, both in form and in content."

It would, in fact, be extremely strange if the Inaugural Address, originally printed in English in London under Gladstone's very eyes, had placed in his mouth a sentence interpolated by me, a sentence that, for seven and a half years, circulated unchallenged in the London press, to be finally detected by the "learned men" of the German Manufacturers' Association in Berlin.

The sentence in question of the Inaugural Address reads as follows:

"THIS INTOXICATING AUGMENTATION OF WEALTH AND POWER IS ENTIRELY CONFINED TO CLASSES OF PROPERTY" (P. 6, INAUGURAL ADDRESS etc.).[b] (In the

---

[a] W. Liebknecht.— *Ed.*

[b] See present edition, Vol. 20, p. 7.— *Ed.*

German translation literally: *"Diese berauschende Vermehrung von Reichtum und Macht ist ganz und gar beschränkt auf Eigentumsklassen."*)

In an article in *The Fortnightly Review* (November 1870), which attracted great attention and was discussed by all the London press, Mr. Beesly, Professor of History at the university here, quoted as follows, p. 518:

"AN INTOXICATING AUGMENTATION OF WEALTH AND POWER, AS MR. GLADSTONE OBSERVED, ENTIRELY CONFINED TO CLASSES OF PROPERTY." (In the German translation: *"Eine berauschende Vermehrung von Reichtum und Macht, wie Herr Gladstone bemerkte, ganz und gar beschränkt auf Eigentumsklassen."*)[a]

Yet Professor Beesly's article appeared six years later than the Inaugural Address! Good! Let us now take a specialised publication, intended solely for the City and published not only *before* the appearance *of the Inaugural Address,* but even *before the International Working Men's Association was founded.* It is entitled: THE THEORY OF EXCHANGES. THE BANK CHARTER ACT OF 1844. London 1864, published by T. Cautley Newby, 30, Welbeck Street.[b] It examines Gladstone's budget speech at length and p. 134 gives the following quotation from this speech:

"THIS INTOXICATING AUGMENTATION OF WEALTH AND POWER IS ENTIRELY CONFINED TO CLASSES OF PROPERTY." (In the German translation: *"Diese berauschende Vermehrung von Reichtum und Macht ist ganz und gar beschränkt auf Eigentumsklassen"*),

that is, word for word, exactly what I quoted.

This proves irrefutably that the German Manufacturers' Association *"lied both in form and in content"* in decrying this "sentence" as a fabrication "by me"!

Incidentally: honest old *Concordia* printed in bold face another passage, in which Gladstone prattled about an elevation of the English working class, over the last 20 years, that was supposedly "extraordinary and unparalleled in all countries and in all periods". The bold-face type is supposed to indicate that I had suppressed this passage. On the contrary! In the Inaugural Address I emphasised most strongly the screaming contrast between this shameless phrase and the "APPALLING STATISTICS", as

---

[a] E. S. Beesly, "The International Working Men's Association", *The Fortnightly Review,* Vol. XLVII, November 1, 1870.— *Ed.*

[b] Its author is Henry Roy.— *Ed.*

Professor Beesly rightly calls them, contained in the official English reports on the same period.*

The author of the THEORY OF EXCHANGES quoted, like myself, not from Hansard, but from a London newspaper which, on April 17, published the April 16 budget speech. In my collectanea of cuttings for 1863, I have searched in vain for the relevant extract and thus, also, for the name of the newspaper that published it. This is, however, not important. Although the parliamentary reports of the London newspapers always differ from one another, I was certain that none of them could completely suppress such a striking quotation from Gladstone. So I consulted *The Times* of April 17, 1863—it was then, as now, Gladstone's organ—and there I found, on p. 7, column 5, in the report on the budget speech:

"THAT IS THE STATE OF THE CASE AS REGARDS THE WEALTH OF THIS COUNTRY. I MUST SAY FOR ONE, I SHOULD LOOK ALMOST WITH APPREHENSION AND WITH PAIN UPON THIS INTOXICATING AUGMENTATION OF WEALTH AND POWER, IF IT WERE MY BELIEF THAT IT WAS CONFINED TO CLASSES WHO ARE IN EASY CIRCUMSTANCES. THIS TAKES NO COGNIZANCE AT ALL OF THE CONDITION OF THE LABOURING POPULATION. THE AUGMENTATION I HAVE DESCRIBED, AND WHICH IS FOUNDED, I THINK, UPON ACCURATE RETURNS, IS AN AUGMENTATION ENTIRELY CONFINED TO CLASSES OF PROPERTY."

In the German translation: "So steht's mit *dem Reichtum dieses Landes.* Ich für meinen Teil würde beinahe mit Besorgnis und mit Pein auf *diese berauschende Vermehrung von Reichtum und Macht blicken,* wenn ich sie auf die *wohlhabenden Klassen* beschränkt glaubte.** Es ist hier gar keine Notiz genommen von der arbeitenden Bevölkerung. *Die Vermehrung, die ich beschrieben habe"* (which he now characterised as *"diese berauschende Vermehrung von Reichtum und Macht")* "*ist ganz und gar beschränkt auf Eigentumsklassen".*

So, on April 16, 1863, Mr. Gladstone declared *"both in form and in content"* in the House of Commons, as reported in his own organ, *The Times,* on April 17, 1863 that *"this intoxicating augmentation of wealth and power is entirely confined to the classes possessed of property",* and his apprehension gives him a sort of shiver, but only because of his scruples that this was confined to one part of this class, the part in really easy circumstances.

Italiam, Italiam![a] Finally we arrive at *Hansard.* In its edition, here botchily corrected, Mr. Gladstone was bright enough clumsily

---

* Other whimsical apologetics from the same speech are dealt with in my work *Capital* (P. 638, 639).[126]

** The words "EASY CLASSES", "CLASSES IN EASY CIRCUMSTANCES" were apparently first introduced BY *Wakefield* for the really rich portion of the propertied class [E. G. Wakefield, *England and America. A Comparison of the Social and Political State of Both Nations,* Vols. I-II, London, 1833].

---

[a] Virgil, *Aeneid,* III.— Ed.

to excise the passage that would be, after all, compromising on the lips of an English Chancellor of the Exchequer. This is, incidentally, traditional English parliamentary practice, and by no means the invention of little Lasker versus Bebel.[127] A careful comparison of Gladstone's speech itself, as it appeared in *The Times*, and its subsequent form, as distorted by the same Gladstone, would provide an amusing description of this unctuous, phrase-mongering, quibbling and strictly-religious bourgeois hero, who timidly displays his piousness and his liberal ATTITUDES OF MIND.

One of the most infuriating things in my work *Capital* consists in the masses of official proof describing how manufacturers work, something in which no scholar could previously find a thing wrong. In the form of a rumour this even reached the ears of the gentlemen of the German Manufacturers' Association, but they thought:

> "Was kein Verstand der Verständigen sieht,
> Das übet in Einfalt ein kindlich' Gemüt."[a]

No sooner said than done. They find a suspicious-looking quotation in the Inaugural Address and turn for information to a business friend in London, the first best Mundella, and he, being a manufacturer himself, rushes to despatch overseas, in black and white, the extract from Hansard's Parliamentary Debates. Now they have my fabrication secret. I manufacture not only the text, but the quotations too. Drunk with victory, they trumpet out to the world *"How Karl Marx Quotes!"* So my *wares* were discredited, once and for all, and, as is fitting for manufacturers, in the way of normal business, without the expense of learned men.

The irksome subsequent events will perhaps teach the Manufacturing Associates that, however well they may know how to fake goods, they are as well fitted to judge literary goods as a donkey is to play the lute.

Karl Marx

London, May 23, 1872

First published in *Der Volksstaat*, No. 44, June 1, 1872

Printed according to the newspaper

Published in English for the first time

---

[a] "What the knowledge of the knowing cannot find,
May be seen by an innocent childish mind."
Fr. Schiller, *Die Worte des Glaubens.*—*Ed.*

Frederick Engels

TO THE *EMANCIPATION OF THE PROLETARIAN* SOCIETY IN TURIN[128]

[*Outline of a letter*]

In Milan, Ferrara, Naples, everywhere there are friends of Bakunin. As for the *Fascio Operaio*[a] of Bologna, we have never had a word from it. The Jura party, abandoned everywhere, seems to want to make Italy its great fortress. This party has formed within the International a secret society[b] for the purpose of dominating it; we have in our possession proofs as regards Spain, it must be the same thing in Italy. These men, who always have on their lips the words autonomy and free federation, treat the workers like a flock of sheep which is good only for being directed by the heads of this secret society and used to attain ends unknown to the masses. You have had a good example of this in Terzaghi (investigations are being made concerning the handing over of the letter). The Jura Committee, having revolted against the whole organisation of the International, and knowing that it would have had great difficulty in justifying itself at the Congress in the coming September, is now searching everywhere for letters and mandates originating from the General Council in order to fabricate a false accusation against us. We fully agree to all our letters being read at the Congress but it does not suit us to learn that the same letters which we wrote to this or that section have been placed at the disposal of these gentlemen.[c][129]

Meanwhile we ask you to postpone any decision and then act as the interests of the International dictate to you; I hope that you

---

a Workers' Union.— *Ed.*

b This refers to the International Alliance of Socialist Democracy.— *Ed.*

c The record published in the Russian edition further has: "The circular [*Fictitious Splits in the International*] informs".— *Ed.*

will discover that it was not the General Council, but certainly these Jura men, acting exclusively in the interest of the ambition of Bakunin, the head of the secret society, who sowed the discord.

(Request an immediate reply concerning the letter.)

Written on June 14, 1872

First published in: Marx and Engels, *Works*, First Russian Edition, Vol. XXVI, Moscow, 1935

Printed according to *La Corrispondenza di Marx e Engels con italiani 1848-1895*, Milan, 1964, pp. 226-27

Translated from the Italian

The International HERALD.

Official Organ of the British Section of the International Working Men's Association.

No. 13   SATURDAY, JUNE 29, 1872.   One Penny.

Frederick Engels

[ANNOUNCEMENT OF THE GENERAL COUNCIL ON THE CONVOCATION AND THE AGENDA OF THE CONGRESS AT THE HAGUE][130]

1. Considering the resolution of the Basel Congress fixing the seat of the next Congress at Paris, also the resolution of the General Council dated July 12th, 1870, by which, it being then impossible to hold a Congress at Paris, and conformably with Art. 4 of the General Rules, the Congress was convoked to meet at Mayence.

Considering further that up to this day the government persecutions[a] directed against the International in France, as well as in Germany, render impossible the meeting of a Congress either in Paris or in Mayence.

Conformably with Art. 4 of the General Rules[b] which confers upon the General Council the rights of changing, in case of need, the place of meeting of the Congress, the General Council convokes the next Congress of the I.W.M.A. for Monday, September 2nd, at The Hague, Holland.

2. Considering that the questions contained in the programme of the Congress which was to be held at Mayence on the 5th September 1870[c] do not correspond with the present wants of the International, these wants having been profoundly affected by the great historic events which have taken place since then.

That numerous sections and federations belonging to various countries have proposed that the next Congress should occupy itself with the revision of the General Rules and Regulations.

---

[a] The manuscript has "prosecutions".— Ed.

[b] See this volume, p. 4.— Ed.

[c] Cf. K. Marx, "Programme for the Mainz Congress of the International".— Ed.

1872

Page of Engels' manuscript with the announcement of the General Council on the convocation of the I.W.M.A.'s Congress at The Hague

That the persecutions to which the International finds itself exposed at this moment in almost all European countries, impose upon it the duty of strengthening its organization:

The General Council, while reserving to itself the faculty of drawing up hereafter a more extensive programme, to be completed by the propositions of the sections and federations, places on the order of the day, as the most important questions to be discussed by the Congress of The Hague, the revision of the General Rules and Regulations.

Written between June 18 and 28, 1872

First published in *The International Herald*, No. 13, June 29, 1872

Reproduced from the newspaper checked with Engels' rough manuscript

Karl Marx and Frederick Engels

PREFACE TO THE 1872 GERMAN EDITION
OF THE *MANIFESTO*
OF THE COMMUNIST PARTY[131]

The Communist League,[132] an international association of workers, which could of course be only a secret one under the conditions obtaining at the time, commissioned the undersigned, at the Congress held in London in November 1847, to draw up for publication a detailed theoretical and practical programme of the Party. Such was the origin of the following *Manifesto*, the manuscript of which travelled to London, to be printed, a few weeks before the February Revolution.[a] First published in German, it has been republished in that language in at least twelve different editions in Germany, England and America.[133] It was published in English for the first time in 1850 in *The Red Republican*, London, translated by Miss Helen Macfarlane, and in 1871 in at least three different translations in America.[134] A French version first appeared in Paris shortly before the June insurrection of 1848[135] and recently in *Le Socialiste* of New York. A new translation is in the course of preparation. A Polish version appeared in London shortly after it was first published in German. A Russian translation was published in Geneva in the sixties. Into Danish, too, it was translated shortly after its first appearance.[136]

However much the state of things may have altered during the last twenty-five years, the general principles laid down in this *Manifesto* are, on the whole, as correct today as ever. Here and there some detail might be improved. The practical application of the principles will depend, as the *Manifesto* itself states, everywhere and at all times, on the obtaining historical conditions, and, for that reason, no special stress is laid on the revolutionary

---

[a] The 1848 revolution in France.— *Ed.*

measures proposed at the end of Section II. That passage would, in many respects, be very differently worded today. In view of the gigantic strides of Modern Industry in the last twenty-five years, and of the accompanying improved and extended party organisation of the working class, in view of the practical experience gained, first in the February Revolution, and then, still more, in the Paris Commune, where the proletariat for the first time held political power for two whole months, this programme has in some details become antiquated. One thing especially was proved by the Commune, *viz.*, that "the working class cannot simply lay hold of the ready-made State machinery, and wield it for its own purposes". (See *The Civil War in France. Address of the General Council of the International Working Men's Association,* German edition, p. 19, where this point is further developed.[a]) Further, it is self-evident that the criticism of socialist literature is deficient in relation to the present time, because it comes down only to 1847; also, that the remarks on the relation of the Communists to the various opposition parties (Section IV), although in principle still correct, yet in practice are antiquated, because the political situation has been entirely changed, and the progress of history has swept from off the earth the greater portion of the parties there enumerated.

But, then, the *Manifesto* has become an historical document which we have no longer any right to alter. A subsequent edition may perhaps appear with an introduction bridging the gap from 1847 to the present day; this reprint was too unexpected to leave us time for that.

Karl Marx
Frederick Engels

London, June 24, 1872

First published in *Das kommunistische Manifest. Neue Ausgabe mit einem Vorwort der Verfasser,* Leipzig, 1872

Printed according to the pamphlet

---

[a] See present edition, Vol. 22, p. 328.— *Ed.*

Frederick Engels

[RESOLUTIONS OF THE SUB-COMMITTEE ON MIKHAIL BAKUNIN AND THE ALLIANCE] [137]

1. That it would not reply to Bakunin's letter. [a] [138]

2. Citizen Engels was to write to Valencia, to the Federal Council, to ask it to account for its relations with the *Alliance*, since the Council had at least three of its members belonging to this society. [b]

3. The Sub-Committee was to request the General Council to propose the expulsion of Bakunin and the members of the Alliance at the next Congress.

Adopted at the sitting of the Sub-Committee on July 5, 1872

Printed according to the original

Translated from the French

First published, in Russian, in *Generalny Sovet Pervogo Internatsionala. 1871-1872*, Moscow, 1965

---

[a] M. Bakounine, "Aux compagnons rédacteurs du *Bulletin de la Fédération jurassienne*", *Bulletin de la Fédération jurassienne...*, No. 10-11, June 15, 1872.— *Ed.*

[b] See this volume, pp. 211-13.— *Ed.*

Frederick Engels

THE INTERNATIONAL IN AMERICA [139]

Our readers will already be aware from our American correspondence that a split has occurred amongst the members of the
International in the United States. What has happened in New
York in the last few months is, in fact, so unique in the history of
the International that it is worth presenting it in context. For that
purpose, we shall base what we have to say on an article from the
Emancipacion, published in Madrid (June 22),[a] and will supplement
it with the original documents at our disposal.

It is a well-established fact that, in Europe, the bourgeoisie and
the governments made the International into a fearful bogey that
has subsequently properly fulfilled its task and so alarmed all good
citizens that no one need fear that the International will ever be
diverted from its original aims by a mass influx of bourgeois
elements. Things take a different course in America. That which
sends European bourgeois and governments into convulsions
appears, by contrast, interesting there. A society that has grown up
on a purely bourgeois foundation, without a landowning nobility
or a monarchy, laughs at the childish mortal terror of the
European bourgeoisie which—even in France, intellectually at
least—has still not outgrown the scourge of the monarchy and the
nobility. The more fearful, therefore, the International appeared
in Europe and the more monstrously it was presented by the
correspondents of the American press—and no one is more adept
at painting a lurid picture than these gentlemen—the more

---

[a] [P. Lafargue,] "La burguesia y la Internacional en los Estados-Unidos", *La
Emancipacion*, No. 54, June 22, 1872.— *Ed.*

widespread the view became in America that the time was now right for making both financial and political capital out of it.

The extent to which American society is ahead of European is strikingly exemplified by the fact that it was two American *ladies* who first discovered this and attempted to set up a business on the basis of it. Whilst the men of the European bourgeoisie trembled in fear of the International, two female members of the American bourgeoisie, Mrs. Victoria Woodhull and her sister Miss Tenni Claflin (who publish *Woodhull & Claflin's Weekly*) conceived the plan of exploiting this society of horrors—and they almost got away with it.

Both these sisters, millionairesses, advocates of women's emancipation and especially "free love", resolutely joined the International. Section No. 9 was set up under the leadership of Miss Claflin, Section No. 12 under that of Mrs. Woodhull; new sections soon followed in the most diverse parts of America, all set up by adherents of the two sisters. According to the currently valid arrangements, every section had the right to send a delegate to the Central Committee, which met in New York. The consequence was that, very soon, this federal council, which had originally been made up of German, Irish and French workers, was swamped by a whole host of bourgeois American adventurers of all sorts and of both sexes. The workers were pushed into the background; victory for the two speculating sisters seemed assured. Then Section No. 12 took centre stage and explained to the founders of the American International what it was really all about.

On August 30, 1871, Section 12 issued its own manifesto over the signature of W. West, secretary. It reads:

"The object of the International is simply to emancipate the labourer, male and female, by the conquest of political power. It involves, first, the Political Equality and Social Freedom of men and women alike. *Political Equality* means the personal participation of each in the preparation, administration and execution of the laws by which all are governed. *Social Freedom* means absolute immunity from impertinent intrusion in all affairs of exclusively personal concernment, such as religious belief, the *sexual relation, habits of dress, etc.* The proposition involves, secondly, the establishment of an *Universal Government*" for the whole world. "Of course, the *abolition* of [...] even *differences of language* are embraced in the programme."[a]

So there might be no misunderstanding as to the aim involved, a form of organisation is called for, according to which

"if practicable, for the convenience of political action, there should be a section

---

[a] "Appeal of Section No. 12", *Woodhull & Claflin's Weekly*, No. 19 (71), September 23, 1871.— *Ed.*

formed in every ... election district. There must ... be instituted in every town a municipal Committee or Council, corresponding with the Common Councils; in every State a State Committee or Council, corresponding with the State legislature, and in the Nation a National Committee or Council, corresponding with the United States National Congress... The work of the International, includes nothing less than the institution, within existing forms, of another form of Government, which shall supersede them all."

It is not, then, for the overthrow, but for the exploitation of the principles of the existing state, that, according to this, the International has come into existence. Mr. West was, in fact, right in proclaiming (*Woodhull & Cl. Weekly*, March 2, 1872):

"The issue of the 'Appeal' of Section 12 was a *new departure* in the history of the International!"

In order to accomplish this "new departure" it was, above all, necessary to shake off the fetters of the previous General Rules and Congress decisions, the validity of which had remained uncontested. Accordingly, Section No. 12 proclaimed (*W. & C. Weekly*, October 21, 1871)

"the independent right of each section" freely to interpret the congress decisions and the Rules and Regulations of the General Council (it should read the General Rules and Administrative Regulations of the Association) "each section being alone responsible for its own action".[a]

The nonsense now went too far. Instead of sections of workers, sections consisting of all kinds of bourgeois swindlers, free-lovers, spirit-rappers, spirit-rapping shakers,[140] etc., were set up, and so Section No. 1, the first section of the International to be formed in America (Germans), finally issued an appeal in which, in contrast to this swindle, emphasis was laid on the essentially proletarian character of the Association. The American parent section, No. 12, replied immediately. In *W. & C. W.* of November 18, 1871, it declares, through its secretary West:

"The extension of equal citizenship to women, the world over, must *precede any general change in the* [...] *relations of capital and labour...* Section 12 would also remonstrate against the vain assumption, running all through the Protest" (of Section 1) "under review, that the International Working Men's Association is *an organisation of the working classes.*"

On November 25, there followed another protest from Section 12, which says:

"The statement" (contained in the General Rules) that the working classes can

---

[a] "The Internationals", *Woodhull & Claflin's Weekly*, No. 23 (75), October 21, 1871.— *Ed.*

only be emancipated by their own efforts, "cannot be denied, yet it is true so far as it describes the fact that *the working classes cannot be emancipated against their will.*" [a]

War finally broke out between the exploiters of the state, place-seekers, free-lovers, spirit-rappers and other bourgeois swindlers, on the one hand, and, on the other, the workers who, in their naïveté, actually imagined that the International Working Men's Association was an organisation not of the bourgeois, but of the working class in America too. The German Section No. 1 demanded that the Central Committee exclude Section 12 and the delegates of all sections that did not consist, at least two-thirds, of wage labourers. This demand caused a split in the Central Committee; some of the Germans and the Irish together with some Frenchmen supported Section 1, whilst the Americans, together with the majority of the French and two German (Schweitzer) sections formed a new central committee.

On December 4, the old committee (which we shall call No. I) issued a circular describing the circumstances as follows:

"In the Central Committee, which is supposed to be a defence against all reformist swindles, the majority finally consisted of reformists and benefactors of the nation who had already almost sunk into oblivion, and thus it came about that the people who preached the gospel of free love sat most fraternally beside those who want to bless the whole world with a common language; supporters of land co-operatives, spiritualists, atheists, and deists, each trying to ride his own particular hobby-horse. Particularly Section 12 (Woodhull)... The first step that has to be taken here, in order to advance the movement, is to organise and, at the same time, to stimulate the revolutionary element, which lies in the conflict of interests of worker and capitalist... The delegates of sections 1, 4, 5, 7, 8, 11, 16, 21, 23, 24, 25 and other sections, having seen that all efforts to direct this nonsense were in vain, therefore decided, after the old Central Committee had been indefinitely adjourned (December 3, 1871) to found a new one, *which consists of actual workers.*" [b]

In the meantime, central committee No. II (Woodhull) continued to meet and filled its places with a host of delegates from allegedly new sections that had been established mainly by virtue of the efforts of sections 9 and 12, but were, in the main, so weak that they scarcely had enough members to fill the barest minimum of officers' positions (secretary, treasurer, etc.).

Both committees appealed to the General Council in London. In the meantime, various sections (e.g., French No. 10 and all the Irish sections) withdrew from both committees pending the decision of the General Council.

---

a "Protest of Section 12", *Woodhull & Claflin's Weekly*, No. 2 (80), November 25, 1871.— *Ed.*

b *New-Yorker Demokrat*, December 9, 1871.— *Ed.*

On March 5 and 12, the General Council passed the resolutions that have already been published in the *Volksstaat* (No. 37).[a] They suspended Section 12, advised that both committees combine until an American Congress was held to decide the matter, and recommended for the future that all sections not consisting, at least two-thirds, of wage labourers should not be admitted. Although, for good reasons, these resolutions almost exclusively took the form of recommendations, they determined the future of the International in America. By supporting as they did committee No. I, they made it impossible for the bourgeois of committee No. II to continue exploiting the name of the International for their own particular purposes.

Since the beginning of the split and in direct contravention of Resolution No. 17 of the London Conference, which laid down that all internal affairs of the Association should be dealt with only within the sections and federations and not in public,[b] committee No. II had been inviting reporters from the New York press to all its proceedings, and had seen to it that the whole matter was discussed in the most disreputable bourgeois papers. The same thing happened at this point, when this committee set about the General Council, which it had imagined it had duped. The activities of committee No. II made it possible for the worst of the New York newspapers, such as the *Herald*, etc., to declare the whole thing a squabble between Germans and Frenchmen, between communism and socialism, etc., and the opponents of the workers in New York were jubilant at the alleged destruction of the International in America.

However, in all that, committee No. II was constantly at pains to inform the world that the International was not a workers' organisation, but a bourgeois one. As early as December 16, 1871, its organ *Woodhull & Claflin's Weekly* declared:

"Where *our* committee is concerned, there is no need to prove that two-thirds or any part of a section shall be *wages-slaves, as if it were a crime to be free*";

and on May 4, 1872, it declared again:

"In this decree of the General Council its authors presume to recommend that in future no American section be admitted, of which two-thirds at least are not *wages-slaves*. Must they be *politically slaves* also? As well one thing or the other. [...]

---

[a] See this volume, pp. 124-26.— *Ed.*

[b] Karl Marx and Frederick Engels, *Resolutions of the Conference of Delegates of the International Working Men's Association*, XVII. Split in the French-speaking Part of Switzerland (see present edition, Vol. 22, pp. 430-31).— *Ed.*

The intrusion of 'bogus reformers, benefactors of the nation, middle-class quacks and trading politicians' is mostly to be feared from that class of citizens who have nothing better to depend upon than the *proceeds of wages-slavery*."

This was committee No. II's last word on one count. Not only was it absurd to believe that the International Working Men's Association was an association of workers—in addition to that, it could only fulfil its purpose really properly if it excluded all workers and wages-slaves, or at least declared them suspect.

What, precisely, is the purpose of the International Working Men's Association (without working men) in America? This, too, is now explained to us. The elections for a new President of the United States were approaching.

On March 2, 1872, those two ladies' paper *W. & C. W.*, forever with us, carried an article entitled "The Coming Combination Convention" in which it may be read that:

"There is a proposition under consideration by the representatives of the various reformatory elements of the country looking to a grand consolidated convention to be held in this city in May... Indeed, if this convention acts wisely, who can say that the fragments of the defunct Democratic" (i.e., sympathetic towards slavery) "Party may not make themselves known and take part in it... Everybody of *Radicals* should be represented at it", etc.

Week after week the same paper carries appeals to all kinds of world reformers:

"Labour, Land, Peace and Temperance reformers, and Internationals and Women Suffragists, [...] as well as all others, who believe that the time has come" to carry out the principles of true morality and religion (sic!),[a]

signed first of all by Victoria Woodhull, then by Th. H. Banks, R. W. Hume, G. R. Allen, W. West, G. W. Maddox, T. Millot, in short by the main people of committee No. II. All these appeals expressly state that the delegate convention would nominate candidates for the presidency and vice-presidency of the United States.

On May 9, 10, and 11, at the Apollo Hall in New York, this monstrous delegate convention finally got underway. All the male and female cranks of America assembled there. Committee No. II was present in a body. It was decided that *Mrs. Victoria Woodhull* should be nominated *as candidate for the presidency of the United States*, and, in fact, in the *name of the International*!

The whole of America responded with resounding laughter. Of

---

[a] [Woodhull, V. C. et al.] "The Party of the People to Secure and Maintain Human Rights, to Be Inaugurated in the U.S, in May, 1872", *Woodhull & Claflin's Weekly*, Nos. 21-25 (99-103), April 6, 13, 20, 27 and May 4, 1872.—*Ed.*

course, those Americans who had a vested interest and were indulging in speculation, did not allow this to divert them. It was a different story with the Germans and Frenchmen who had allowed themselves to be talked into it. Section 2 (French) withdrew its delegate from committee No. II and declared its support for the resolutions of the General Council. Section 6 (German) likewise withdrew its delegate, Dr. Grosse, former private secretary to the Berliner Schweitzer, from committee No. II, and refused to have anything to do with committee No. II until it declared its support for the resolutions of the General Council. On May 20, a further eight sections—French and German—withdrew from committee No. II, which now represents only the well-known, ambiguous American elements, which, in fact, had belonged together even before they had joined the International—Madame Victoria Woodhull, together with assorted accomplices. They now declare that they intend to establish a separate, exclusively American International, which, of course, they are free to do.

In the meantime, in response to an inquiry from the German section in St. Louis and the French section in New Orleans, the General Council has declared that it only recognises committee No. I (now the provisional Federal Council of the United States).[141] Thus, Madame Victoria Woodhull's campaign to conquer the International has achieved its ultimate goal.

The *Emancipacion* adds:

"Having heard these facts, all impartial observers must wonder: when and how might this scandal have ended, if there had been no General Council with authority to uphold the basic principles of the International and to suspend sections and federations who sought to change the character of the Association for their own political or personal ends."

Written not later than July 9, 1872

First published in *Der Volksstaat*, No. 57, July 17, 1872

Printed according to the newspaper

Frederick Engels

TO CITIZEN VINCENZO SPOTTI, SECRETARY OF THE COMMITTEE FOR THE EMANCIPATION OF THE WORKING CLASSES IN PARMA [142]

INTERNATIONAL WORKING MEN'S ASSOCIATION
33, Rathbone Place, London

July 18, 1872

Dear Citizen,

From your kind letter dated June 7 (postmarked Parma, July 9 and delivered here on July 13), I conclude that your Society wishes to become affiliated to the great International Working Men's Association.

As your rules [a] do not contain anything contrary to the General Rules and Regulations of the Association, there is no obstacle to your affiliation. It will only be necessary for you to adhere to the General Rules and Regulations of the Association, of which I enclose a copy in French (there being no complete and authentic edition in Italian).

I should be grateful if you would discuss this proposal and let me know the outcome if affirmative so that I may complete the necessary formalities for your affiliation.

Fraternal greetings.

In the name of the General Council

Secretary for Italy,

Frederick Engels

Write to the address I sent you last time, i.e. that of my place, so that your letter reaches me sooner.

First published in: Marx and Engels, *Works*, First Russian Edition, Vol. XXVI, Moscow, 1935

Printed according to the manuscript checked with the text in *La corrispondenza de Marx e Engels...*

Translated from the Italian

Published in English for the first time

---

[a] *Comitato per l'Emancipazione delle Classi Lavoratrici. Statuto*, Parma [1872].— *Ed.*

Karl Marx

TO THE STRIKING MINERS
OF THE RUHR VALLEY [143]

The German capitalist press is calling on you to drop your demands for an eight-hour shift and a 25 per cent wage increase, and is saying that you should resume work so that German industry might avoid having to get its coal from England, thus letting German money go abroad instead of using it to pay for German labour.

This is the eternal miserable whine of the bourgeois, heard whenever the workers get up on their own feet and try to make any demands. In England, where they have been telling the same old story for forty years or so now, nobody takes any notice any more. In this particular instance, however, it is worth pointing out that the capitalist press is deliberately trying to mislead you, by telling you that all the mine-owners and manufacturers need to do is just to write to England to get all the coal they want.

In England, coal consumption has increased since 1869 at an unprecedented rate, owing to the general upturn that has occurred in English industry since then, to the increase in the number of factories, the enlarged consumption by the railways, the immense growth of marine steam-ship traffic—but mainly owing to the colossal extension of the iron industry, which, in the last three years, has far outstripped all previous periods of prosperity. *The Daily News*, a liberal capitalist paper (edition of July 15[a] of this year) has this to say on the subject:

"One of the principal reasons for the recent advance in the price of coal is undoubtedly the sudden and unexampled improvement in the iron trade. [...] The

---

[a] *Der Volksstaat* mistakenly has: "July 12". Further on Marx quotes from "The Position of the British Coal Trade", *The Daily News*, No. 8179, July 15, 1872.— *Ed.*

North of England raises about one-fourth of the total quantity of coal produced in Great Britain. A large portion of this" goes to "London and the South and East of England with fuel. It has also been extensively used for steam-ship purposes; but more recently the development of the iron trade in Cleveland" (quite close to the mines) "caused a sudden demand for coal for local purposes. The growth of a trade requiring now at the rate of, perhaps, not less than from *five to six millions of tons** of coal per annum, naturally gave a great stimulus to the coal trade [...]. In addition to this, however, we have to consider the rapid rise of the west-coast hematite iron district. The blast-furnaces in Cumberland and Lancashire derive their fuel almost exclusively from the Durham coal-field," and, according to moderate estimates, need "*one million and a half tons* of coal" annually [...]. "In the North of England alone the new blast-furnaces now in course of erection [...] would require [...] *three-quarters of a million tons* of coal per annum. Then there are new rolling mills and several blast-furnaces in the west-coast district. It is no matter of surprise, therefore, that the fuel question became a subject of vital importance in the whole North of England, and the natural result was that prices speedily went up. In South Staffordshire, Scotland, South Wales, Derbyshire, the West Riding, and other parts of the country, the same causes operated to bring about higher prices of fuel."

Under these circumstances, the English miners did the same as you: they demanded higher wages and shorter working hours. The English mine-owners, as always superior to their German competitors in insight and worldly wisdom, put up no serious resistance, but rather accepted all the demands. Hear what *The Daily News* says further on this point:

"Wages were advanced from time to time... The miners also went in for systematic shortening of [...] a day's work. Altogether it is asserted by practical men that the quantity of coal now raised is not more per man than about 60 per cent of what was produced when trade was dull and wages were [...] much lower than they are now. This difficulty might be met by the employment of more men, but the men are not to be had all at once. It is true they are being drafted in to some extent from the agricultural districts; but pitmen want a good deal of training, so that the amount of relief thus to be obtained will be comparatively small and slow in its operation. At this moment the men *have succeeded* in some parts of the country in getting a reduction of the hours of labour *to eight per day,* whilst *in all parts advances in wages are succeeding each other so rapidly* that there seems no alternative but higher selling prices."

Then there is another circumstance to be borne in mind. *Almost throughout England the topmost coal seams are exhausted* and the mines have to be sunk deeper and deeper. Hear, again, the article in *The Daily News*:

"the best portions of these valuable deposits" in South Staffordshire "have been worked out. In many parts of that once rich mineral tract, the mines are exhausted, and the pit mounds are fast being converted into arable and grazing land, though thousands of acres" (pit mounds) "yet remain an almost desolate

* The English ton is almost the exact equivalent of 2,000 *Zollpfunds* or 1,000 kilos.

waste. The resources of the district are not, however, yet used up. Mines are being sunk to greater depths round the confines of the coal field... But under existing circumstances, even with improved modern appliances for mining purposes, it is increasingly expensive to raise material, besides which it has now to be carried further before it reaches the iron manufacturer... What we have said about South Staffordshire applies also to many other parts of the country. The coal has now to be won from greater depths, and has to be conveyed longer distances to the works where it is principally consumed."

The consequence is that, as *The Daily News* points out, coal prices at the pit-head "have doubled", and that *there is now a real shortage of coal*, which is claiming the attention of the whole country. Another paper, the English capitalists' main economic journal *The Economist*, says in its July 13[a] edition:

"Since the beginning of the present year coal has been rising rapidly in price, till it is now between 60 and 100 per cent dearer than it was twelve months ago... Before a week or two is over, the whole rise may be a good deal more than 100 per cent, with little sign of any immediate check to the movement. Coal exports in June of this year were 1,108,000 tons, or 4 per cent more than in June last year, but its value was £758,000, or 53 per cent more. This year the value of the coal exports in June was on average 13s 9d" (or 4 thalers 17$1/2$ groschen) "per ton; last year it was 9s 4d" (or 3 thalers 3$1/2$ groschen).

The Spectator, a third capitalist paper (July 20), also reports that, in London, good house coal has increased in price from 23s, or 7 thalers 20 groschen, to 35s, or 11 thalers 20 groschen.

From these facts you can see what to make of the mine-owners' and manufacturers' threat to get their coal from England. **Mr. Alfred Krupp can issue as many ukases as he wishes; he will have to pay dearer for English coal than for Ruhr coal, and it is very questionable too whether he will get it at all.** In my capacity as Secretary for Germany of the General Council of the International Working Men's Association I considered it my duty to bring these facts to your notice.

Karl Marx

London, July 21, 1872[b]

First published in *Der Volksstaat*, No. 60, July 27, 1872

Printed according to the news-paper

Published in English for the first time

---

[a] *Der Volksstaat* mistakenly has: "July 20". What follows is Marx's summary of a passage from "The Great Rise in the Price of Coal", *The Economist*, No. 1507, July 13, 1872.— *Ed.*

[b] In *Der Volksstaat* mistakenly: "1871".— *Ed.*

Karl Marx

[THE GENERAL COUNCIL'S REPLY TO THE PROTEST OF THE JURA FEDERATION AGAINST THE CONVENING OF A CONGRESS AT THE HAGUE] [144]

GENERAL COUNCIL OF THE INTERNATIONAL
WORKING MEN'S ASSOCIATION

33, Rathbone Place,
Oxford Street, London

To Citizen Schwitzguébel, Corresponding Secretary
of the Jura Federal Committee

I have placed your letter of July 15 inst. before the General Council and it has instructed me to inform you that its decision to hold the next Congress at The Hague was reached after due consideration of all the arguments contained in your letter, and that this choice was dictated by the following considerations:

The Congress could not be held in Switzerland, since that is the place of origin and focal point of the disputes; the Congress is always influenced to some extent by the place in which it is held; in order to add more weight to its decisions and enhance the wisdoms of its debates, the local character must be avoided, for which it was necessary to choose a place remote from the main centre of disputes.

You can scarcely be ignorant of the fact that three of the last four Congresses were held in Switzerland,[a] and that at Basle the Belgian delegates were most insistent that the next Congress should be held either at Verviers or in Holland.

In spite of the relative freedom which she enjoys, Switzerland can hardly claim the right to monopolise Congresses.

---

[a] In Geneva (1866), Lausanne (1867) and Basle (1869).—*Ed.*

The Romance Federal Council has also expressed its dissatisfaction with the General Council's choice and does not approve it.

Greetings and equality,

H. Jung,
Corresponding Secretary for Switzerland

July 28, 1872

First published in *Bulletin de la Fédération jurassienne...*, No. 14, August 1, 1872

Printed according to the newspaper

Translated from the French

Karl Marx

[REPLY TO BRENTANO'S SECOND ARTICLE] [145]

TO THE EDITORS OF *DER VOLKSSTAAT*

In the *Concordia* of July 4, the German Manufacturers' Association attempted to prove to me that its "learned men" were as well fitted to judge literary goods as the Association was to fake commercial ones.

With reference to the passage from Gladstone's budget speech of April 16, 1863, as quoted in the Inaugural Address of the International, the manufacturers' organ (No. 10) stated:

"Marx has added the sentence lyingly, both in form and in content."

It thus declares that I fabricated the sentence in both form and content, with hair and bones. Even more: it knows exactly how I did so. The paper writes: "The fact that Gladstone mentioned this, etc., *was utilised by Marx in order to have Gladstone say*, etc." By quoting the sentence from a work published *before* the Inaugural Address, the THEORY OF EXCHANGES, I exposed the crude lie of the manufacturers' organ.[a] As the paper itself tells, it then ordered from London this work, which it did not know, and convinced itself of the facts of the matter. How could it lie itself out of the situation? See here:

"When we stated that Marx had lyingly added the sentence in question to Gladstone's speech, we did not claim, either in form or in content, *that he himself had also fabricated it.*"

Here we obviously have a case of equivocation peculiar to the mind of manufacturers. For example, when a manufacturing swindler, in agreement with business colleagues, sends out into the

---

a See this volume, pp. 164-67.— *Ed.*

world rolls of ribbon that contain, instead of the alleged three dozen ells only two dozen, then he has in fact *lyingly added* one dozen ells, precisely because he "*has not fabricated*" them. Why, moreover, should lyingly added sentences not behave just like lyingly added ells? "The understandings of the greater part of men," says Adam Smith, "are necessarily formed by their ordinary employments",[a] the understandings of the manufacturer included.

Through the *Volksstaat*, I extended the erudite materials of the manufacturers' organ, not only with the quotation from the THEORY OF EXCHANGES, but also with the pages from my work *Capital* concerning Gladstone's budget speeches. Now, from the material with which I provided it, the paper attempts to prove that I did not quote the disputed passage from a "London newspaper", but from the THEORY OF EXCHANGES. The chain of arguments is another sample of manufacturers' logic.

I told the manufacturers' sheet that the THEORY OF EXCHANGES quotes on page 134 exactly as I quoted, and it discovers—that I quoted exactly as the THEORY OF EXCHANGES quotes on page 134.

And further!

"And the glosses too, which Marx bases on the contradiction contained in this version, are already contained in that book."

This is simply a lie. On page 639 of *Capital*, I give my glosses to the words in Gladstone's speech:

"While the rich have been growing richer, the poor have been growing less poor. Whether the extremes of poverty are less, I do not presume to say."

My remark on this is: "How lame an anti-climax! If the working-class has remained 'poor', only 'less poor' in proportion as it produces for the wealthy class 'an intoxicating augmentation of wealth and power', then it has remained relatively just as poor. If the extremes of poverty have not lessened, they have increased, because the extremes of wealth have." [146] And these "glosses" are nowhere to be found in the THEORY OF EXCHANGES.

"And the glosses too ... are already contained in that book, *in particular also* the quotation from Molière given in Note 105 on p. 640 of *Capital*." [147]

So "in particular also" I quote Molière, and leave it up to the "learned men" of the *Concordia* to detect and communicate to the public the fact that the quotation comes from the THEORY OF

---

[a] A. Smith, *An Inquiry into the Nature and Causes of the Wealth of Nations*, Vol. 2, London, 1776, Book V, Ch. I, Art. 2, p. 366.— *Ed.*

EXCHANGES. In fact, however, I state expressly in Note 105, p. 640 of *Capital* that the author of the THEORY OF EXCHANGES "*characterises with the following quotation from Molière*" the "continual crying contradictions in Gladstone's Budget speeches".

Finally:

"...in the same way the statement of the LONDON ORPHAN ASYLUM about the rising prices of foodstuffs quoted by Marx appears on p. 135 of that book, though Marx bases his claim for its correctness not on that book, but on that book's sources (see *Capital*, p. 640, Note 104)".

The *Concordia* advisedly forgets to inform its readers that "that book" gives *no sources*. What was it trying to prove? That I took from that "book" a passage from Gladstone's speech without knowing its source. And how does the *Concordia* prove it? By the fact that I really did take a quotation from that book, and checked it with the original sources, independent of the book!

Referring to my quotation from Professor Beesly's article in *The Fortnightly Review* (November 1870), the *Concordia* remarks:

"This article by Professor Beesly deals, in fact, with the history of the International, and as the author himself informs every enquirer, was written on the basis of material provided him by *Marx* himself."

Professor Beesly states:

"To no one is the success of the association so much due as to Dr. Karl Marx, who, in his acquaintance with the history and statistics of the industrial movement in all parts of Europe, is, I should imagine, without a rival. I am LARGELY indebted to him for the information contained in this article."[a]

All the material with which I supplied Professor Beesly referred exclusively to the history of the International, and not a word concerned the Inaugural Address, which he had known since its publication. The context in which his above remark stood left so little doubt on this point that *The Saturday Review*, in a review of his article,[b] more than hinted that *he himself* was the author of the Inaugural Address.[*]

The *Concordia* asserts that Professor Beesly did not quote the passage in question from Gladstone's speech, but only stated "*that the Inaugural Address contained that quotation*". Let us look into this.

* Professor Beesly drew my attention, in writing, to this *quid pro quo.*

---

a E. S. Beesly, "The International Working Men's Association", *The Fortnightly Review*, Vol. XLVII, November 1, 1870, pp. 529-30.— *Ed.*

b "Mr. Beesly and the International Association", *The Saturday Review of Politics, Literature, Science, and Art*, No. 785, November 12, 1870, pp. 610-11.— *Ed.*

Professor Beesly states:

"The address [...] is probably the most striking and powerful statement of the workman's case as against the middle class that has ever been compressed into a dozen small pages. I wish I had space for copious extracts from it."

After mentioning the "frightful statistics of the Blue Books",[148] to which the Address refers, he goes on:

"From these appalling statistics the address passes on to the income-tax returns, from which it appeared that the taxable income of the country had increased in eight years twenty per cent, 'an intoxicating augmentation of wealth and power', *as Mr. Gladstone observed,* 'entirely confined to classes of property'."[a]

Professor Beesly sets the words: "*as Mr. Gladstone observed*" outside quotation marks, saying these words on his own behalf, and thus proves to the *Concordia* with the greatest clarity that he knows Gladstone's budget speech—solely from the quotation in the Inaugural Address! As the London business friend of the German Manufacturers' Association, he is the only man who knows Gladstone's budget speeches, just as he, and he alone, knows: "Persons with an income under 150 pounds sterling, in fact, pay no income tax in England." (See the *Concordia*, Nos. 10 and 27.) Yet English tax officials suffer from the *idée fixe* that this tax only stops at incomes *under* **100** pounds sterling.

Referring to the disputed passage in the Inaugural Address, the manufacturers' paper stated:

"*Yet this sentence is nowhere to be found in Gladstone's speech.*" I proved the contrary with a quotation from the *Times* report of April 17, 1863. I gave the quotation in the *Volksstaat* in both English and German, since a commentary was necessary on account of Gladstone's assertion that he would "look almost with apprehension and with pain upon *this intoxicating augmentation of wealth and power,* if it were my belief that it was confined to the CLASSES WHO ARE IN EASY CIRCUMSTANCES". Basing myself on Wakefield, I declared that the "CLASSES WHO ARE IN EASY CIRCUMSTANCES"—an expression for which there is no German equivalent—means the "really rich", "the really prosperous portion" of the propertied classes. Wakefield actually calls the real middle class "THE UNEASY CLASS", which is in German roughly "die ungemächliche Klasse".*

The manufacturers' worthy organ not only suppresses my

---

*"THE MIDDLE OR UNEASY CLASS" ("ENGLAND AND AMERICA", London, 1833, v. I, P. 185).

---

[a] E. S. Beesly, op. cit., p. 518; italics by Marx.— *Ed.*

exposition, it ends the passage I quoted with the words: "Marx quotes *The Times* to this point", thus leaving the reader to suppose that it had quoted from my translation; in fact, however, the paper, leaving my version aside, does not translate "CLASSES WHO ARE IN EASY CIRCUMSTANCES" as "wohlhabenden Klassen"[a] but as "Klassen, die sich in *angenehmen Verhältnissen befinden*".[b] The paper believes its readers capable of understanding that not all sections of the propertied class are "prosperous", though it will always be a "pleasant circumstance" for them to possess property. Even in the translation of my quotation, as given by the *Concordia*, however, Gladstone describes the progress of capitalist wealth as "*this intoxicating augmentation of wealth and power*", and remarks that here he has "*taken no cognizance at all* of the condition of the labouring population", closing with words to the effect that this "*augmentation is entirely confined to the classes possessed of property*". Once the "learned man" of the German Manufacturers' Association has, in the report of *The Times* of April 17, 1863, thus had Gladstone say "both in form and in content", the same as I had him say in the Inaugural Address, he strikes his swollen breast, brimming with conviction, and blusters:

> "*Yet despite this ... Marx has the impudence* to write in the *Volksstaat* of June 1: '*Both in form and in content* Mr. Gladstone declared on April 16, 1863 in the House of Commons, as reported in his own organ, *The Times*, on April 17, 1863 that '*this intoxicating augmentation of wealth and power is entirely confined to the classes possessed of property*'."

The "learned man" of the German Manufacturers' Association obviously knows exactly what to offer his readership!

In the *Volksstaat* of June 1, I remarked that the *Concordia* was trying to make its readers believe I had suppressed in the Inaugural Address Gladstone's phrases about the improvement in the condition of the British working class, though in fact the exact opposite was the case, and I stressed there with great emphasis the glaring contradiction between this declamation and the officially established facts. In its reply of July 4, the manufacturers' paper repeated the same manoeuvre. "Marx quotes *The Times* to this point," the paper says, "we quote further." In confrontation with the paper, I needed only to quote the disputed passage, but let us look for a moment at the "further".

After pouring forth his panegyric on the increase of capitalist wealth, Gladstone turns to the working class. He takes good care

---

[a] Prosperous classes.— *Ed.*

[b] Classes finding themselves in *pleasant circumstances.—Ed.*

not to say that it had shared in the "*intoxicating augmentation of wealth and power*". On the contrary, he goes on, according to *The Times*: "Now, *the augmentation of capital* is of indirect benefit to the labourer, etc." He *consoles* himself further on with the fact "that while the rich have been growing *richer* the poor have been growing *less poor*". Finally, he asserts that he and his enriched parliamentary friends "have the *happiness* to know" the opposite of what parliamentary enquiries and statistical data prove to be the fact, viz.,

"that the average condition of the British labourer has improved during the last 20 years in a degree which we know to be extraordinary, and which we may almost pronounce to be unparalleled in the history of any country and of any age".

Before Mr. Gladstone, all his predecessors "*had the happiness*" to supplement the picture of the augmentation of capitalist wealth in their budget speeches with self-satisfied phrases about the improvement in the condition of the working class. Yet he gives the lie to them all; for the millennium dates only from the passing of the Free Trade legislation. The correctness or incorrectness of Gladstone's reasons for consolation and congratulation is, however, a matter of indifference here. We are concerned solely with this: that, from his standpoint, the pretended "extraordinary" improvement in the condition of the working class in no way contradicts the "intoxicating augmentation of wealth and power that is entirely confined to the classes possessed of property". On the contrary. It is the orthodox doctrine of the mouthpieces of capital—Mr. Gladstone being one of the best paid—that the most infallible means for working men *to benefit themselves* is—*to enrich* their exploiters.

The shameless stupidity or stupid shamelessness of the manufacturers' organ culminates in its assurance: "The report in *The Times* just gives, formally more contracted, what the shorthand report by Hansard gives *verbatim*." * Now let us see both reports:

I	II
From Gladstone's speech of April 16, 1863, printed in "The Times" of April 17, 1863	*From Gladstone's speech of April 16, 1863, printed by Hansard, Vol. 170, parliamentary debates of March 27 to May 28, 1863*

---

* The manufacturers' paper appears actually to believe that the big London newspapers employ no shorthand writers for their parliamentary reports.

"That is the state of the case as regards the wealth of this country. I must say for one, I should look almost with apprehension and with pain upon *this intoxicating augmentation of wealth and power* if it were my belief that it was confined to the CLASSES WHO ARE IN EASY CIRCUMSTANCES. This takes no cognisance at all of the condition of the labouring population. *The augmentation I have described ... is an augmentation entirely confined to the classes possessed of property.*[a] Now the augmentation of capital is of indirect benefit to the labourer etc."

"Such [...] is the state of the case as regards the general progress of accumulation; but, for one, I must say that I should *look with some degree of pain,* and with much apprehension, upon *this extraordinary and* **almost** *intoxicating growth,* if it were my belief that it is confined to THE CLASS OF PERSONS WHO MAY BE DESCRIBED AS IN EASY CIRCUMSTANCES. The figures which I have quoted take little or no cognizance of the condition of those who do not pay income tax; or, in other words, sufficiently accurate for *general truth* (!), they do not take cognizance of the *property* (!) of the labouring population, *or* (!) of the increase of its *income.* Indirectly, indeed, the mere augmentation of capital is of the *utmost* advantage to the labouring class, etc."

I leave it to the reader himself to compare the stilted, involved, complicated CIRCUMLOCUTION OFFICE[b] style of the Hansard publication with the report in *The Times.*

Here it is enough to establish that the words of the *Times* report: " *This intoxicating augmentation of wealth and power ... the augmentation I have described ... is an augmentation entirely confined to the classes possessed of property*", are in part garbled by Hansard and in part completely suppressed. Their emphatic *"exact wording"* escaped no earwitness. For example:

"The Morning Star", April 17, 1863 (Gladstone's budget speech of April 16, 1863).

"I must say, for one, I should look with apprehension and with pain upon *this intoxicating augmentation of wealth and power,* if it were my belief that it was confined to the CLASSES WHO ARE IN EASY CIRCUMSTANCES. THIS GREAT INCREASE OF WEALTH takes no cognizance at all of the condition of the labouring population. THE AUGMENTATION IS AN AUGMENTATION ENTIRELY CONFINED TO THE CLASSES POSSESSED OF PROPERTY. BUT THAT AUGMENTATION must be of indirect benefit to the labouring population, etc."

"The Morning Advertiser", April 17, 1863 (Gladstone's budget speech of April 16, 1863).

"I must say, for one, I should look almost with apprehension and ALARM upon *this intoxicating augmentation of wealth and power,* if it were my belief that it was

---

a Marx's italics.— *Ed.*
b The name is taken from Ch. Dickens' *Little Dorrit.—Ed.*

confined to the CLASSES WHO ARE IN EASY CIRCUMSTANCES. *This great increase of wealth* takes no cognisance at all of the condition of the labouring population. THE AUGMENTATION STATED *is an augmentation entirely confined to the* CLASSES POSSESSED OF PROPERTY. THIS AUGMENTATION must be of indirect benefit to the labouring population, etc."

Thus, Gladstone subsequently filched away from the semi-official Hansard report of his speech the words that he had uttered in the House of Commons on April 16, 1863: "*This intoxicating augmentation of wealth and power ... is an augmentation entirely confined to the classes possessed of property.*" The *Concordia* did not, therefore, find this in the excerpt provided by their business friend in London, and trumpeted:

"Yet this sentence is nowhere to be found in Gladstone's speech. **Marx has added the sentence lyingly, both in form and in content.**"

It is no surprise that they now weepingly tell me that it is the critical "*custom*" to quote parliamentary speeches as officially falsified, and not as they were actually delivered. Such a "custom" in fact accords with the "general" Berlin "education", and the limited thinking of the German Manufacturers' Association, which is typical of Prussian subjects.[149] Lack of time forces me to end, once and for all, my pleasurable exchange of opinions with the Association, but as a farewell, another nut for its "learned men" to crack. In what article did a man—and what was his name—utter to an opponent of a rank at least equal with that of the *Concordia*, the weighty words: "*Asinus manebis in secula seculorum*" *?

Karl Marx

London, July 28, 1872

First published in *Der Volksstaat,* No. 63, August 7, 1872

Printed according to the newspaper

Published in English for the first time

* "Thou wilt remain an ass for evermore."

Karl Marx

[AMENDMENTS TO THE GENERAL RULES AND ADMINISTRATIVE REGULATIONS OF THE INTERNATIONAL WORKING MEN'S ASSOCIATION ADOPTED BY THE GENERAL COUNCIL IN THE SUMMER OF 1872][150]

GENERAL RULES OF THE INTERNATIONAL WORKING MEN'S ASSOCIATION

Art 1. This Association is *founded* to *organise common action by the workers* of different countries[151] aiming at the same end; viz., the protection, advancement, and complete emancipation of the working classes.

Art. 4. Each Congress appoints the time and place of meeting for the next Congress. The delegates assemble at the appointed time and place without any special invitation. The General Council may, in case of need, change the place *and the date of the Congress and, with the sanction of the majority of the federations, may replace it with a private Conference which shall have the same powers. However, the Congress or the Conference which may replace it must meet within three months after the date fixed by the previous Congress.*

The Congress appoints the seat and elects the members of the General Council annually, *three from each nationality. The Council thus elected has the power to replace members who have resigned or who are unable, for one reason or another, to carry out their duties, and to co-opt members when the Congress elects fewer members than stipulated by the Rules.*

On its annual meetings, the General Congress shall receive a public account of the annual transactions of the General Council. The latter may, in cases of emergency, convoke the General Congress before the regular yearly term.

Art. 7. Since the success of the working men's movement in each country cannot be secured but by the power of union and combination, while, on the other hand, the usefulness of the International General Council must greatly depend on the

Que tous les efforts tendant à ce but ont jusqu'ici échoué, faute de solidarité entre les travailleurs des différentes professions dans le même pays et d'une union fraternelle entre les classes ouvrières des divers pays ;

Que l'émancipation du travail, n'étant un problème ni local ni national, mais social, embrasse tous les pays dans lesquels existe la société moderne, et nécessite, pour sa solution, le concours théorique et pratique des pays les plus avancés ;

Que le mouvement qui vient de renaître parmi les ouvriers des pays les plus industrieux de l'Europe, tout en réveillant de nouvelles espérances, donne un solennel avertissement de ne pas retomber dans les vieilles erreurs et de combiner le plus tôt possible les efforts encore isolés ;

Pour ces raisons,

L'*Association Internationale des Travailleurs* a été fondée.

Elle déclare,

Que toutes les sociétés et individus y adhérant reconnaîtront comme base de leur conduite envers tous les hommes, sans distinction de couleur, de croyance et de nationalité, la *Vérité*, la *Justice* et la *Morale*.

Pas de devoirs sans droits, pas de droits sans devoirs.

C'est dans cet esprit que les statuts suivants ont été conçus :

Art. 1er. — L'Association est fondée pour créer un point central de communication et de coopération entre les sociétés ouvrières des différents pays aspirant au même but, savoir : le concours mutuel, le progrès et le complet affranchissement de la classe ouvrière.

Art. 2. — Le nom de cette association est : *Association Internationale des Travailleurs.*

Art. 6. — Tous les ans aura lieu un Congrès ouvrier général composé de délégués des branches de l'Association. Ce Congrès proclamera les aspirations communes de la classe ouvrière, prendra l'initiative des mesures nécessaires pour le succès de l'œuvre de l'Association Internationale, et en nommera le Conseil général.

Art. 7. — Chaque Congrès fixera la date et le siège de la réunion du Congrès suivant. Les délégués se réuniront de plein droit aux lieu et jour désignés, sans qu'une convocation spéciale soit nécessaire. En cas d'urgence, le Conseil général pourra changer le lieu du Congrès sans en remettre toutefois la date.

Tous les ans, le Congrès réuni indiquera le siège du Conseil général, en nommera les membres. Le Conseil général ainsi élu aura le droit de s'adjoindre de nouveaux membres.

À chaque Congrès annuel, le Conseil général fera un rapport public de ses travaux. Il pourra, au cas de besoin, convoquer le Congrès avant le terme fixé.

Art. 8. — Le Conseil général se composera de travailleurs appartenant aux différentes nations représentées dans l'Association Internationale. Il choisira dans son sein les membres du bureau nécessaires pour la gestion des affaires, tels que trésorier, secrétaire général, secrétaires particuliers pour les différents pays, etc.

Art. 9. — Le Conseil général fonctionnera comme agent international entre les différents groupes nationaux et locaux, de telle sorte que les ouvriers de chaque pays soient constamment au courant des mouvements de leur classe dans les autres pays ; qu'une enquête sur l'état social soit faite simultanément et dans un même esprit ; — que les questions d'intérêt général,

Pages of the French edition of the General Rules and Administrative Regulations of the First International with corrections by Marx

circumstance whether it has to deal with a few national centres of working men's associations, or with a great number of small and disconnected local societies; the members of the International Association shall use their utmost efforts to combine the disconnected working men's societies of their respective countries into national bodies, represented by central national organs *which, as far as possible, should be international in their composition.* It is self-understood, however, that the appliance of this rule will depend upon the peculiar laws of each country, and that, apart from legal obstacles, no independent local society shall be precluded from directly corresponding with the General Council.

Art. 8.[152] *In its struggle against the collective power of the propertied classes, the working class cannot act as a class except by constituting itself into a political party, distinct from, and opposed to, all old parties formed by the propertied classes.*

This constitution of the working class into a political party is indispensable in order to insure the triumph of the social revolution, and of its ultimate end, the abolition of classes.

The combination of forces which the working class has already effected by its economical struggles ought, at the same time, to serve as a lever for its struggles against the political power of its exploiters.

The lords of land and the lords of capital will always use their political privileges for the defence and perpetuation of their economical monopolies, and for the enslavement of labour. The conquest of political power has therefore become the great duty of the working class.

Art. 9. Everybody who acknowledges and defends the principles of the International Working Men's Association is eligible to become a member.

However, in order to guarantee the proletarian character of the Association, no less than two-thirds of the members of each branch must consist of wage-workers.[153]

Every branch is responsible for the integrity of the members it admits.

Art. 11. The working men's *resistance* societies joining the International Association *may* preserve their existent organisations intact.[154]

ADMINISTRATIVE REGULATIONS,
REVISED IN ACCORDANCE
WITH THE RESOLUTIONS PASSED
BY THE CONGRESSES (1866 TO 1869),
AND BY THE LONDON CONFERENCE (1871)

I

The General Congress

1. Every member *of a branch* of the International Working Men's Association has the right to vote at elections for the General Congress, and *every member of the Association* is eligible as a delegate.

2. *Every branch or group of branches consisting of not less than 50 members may send a delegate to the Congress.*

3.[a] *Every branch or group of branches numbering more than 50 members may send an additional delegate for every additional 10 members.*

7. The sittings of the Congress will be twofold—administrative sittings, which will be private, and public sittings, reserved for the discussion of, and the vote upon, the questions *of principle* of the Congress programme.

8. The Congress *official* programme, consisting of questions placed on the order of the day by the preceding Congress, questions added by the General Council, and questions submitted to the acceptance of that Council by the different sections, groups, or their committees, *and which it will accept*, shall be drawn up by the General Council.

Every section, group, or committee which intends to propose, for the discussion of the impending Congress, a question not proposed by the previous Congress, shall give notice thereof to the General Council before the 31st of March.

II

The General Council

2. The General Council is bound to execute the Congress resolutions *and to take care that in every country the basic principles of the International are strictly observed.*

---

[a] With the introduction of this new article the subsequent articles of this section have been renumbered.— *Ed.*

3. *The General Council shall publish a report of its proceedings every week.*

4. Every *group which is outside federal associations* intending to join the International is bound immediately to announce its adhesion to the General Council.

6.[155] The General Council has also the right to suspend *branches, sections, Federal Councils or committees, and federations of the International,* till the meeting of the next Congress.

Nevertheless, in the case of sections belonging to a federation, the General Council will exercise this right only after having consulted the respective Federal Council.

In the case of the dissolution of a Federal Council, the General Council shall, at the same time, call upon the sections of the respective Federation to elect a new Federal Council within 30 days at most.

In the case of the suspension of an entire federation, the General Council shall immediately inform thereof the whole of the federations. If the majority of them demand it, the General Council shall convoke an extraordinary conference, composed of one delegate for each nationality, which shall meet within one month and finally decide upon the question.

Nevertheless, it is well understood that the countries where the International is prohibited shall exercise the same rights as the regular federations.

8. All delegates appointed by the General Council to distinct missions shall have the right to attend, and be heard at, all *federal or local* meetings *of the organisations of the International,* without, however, being entitled to vote thereat.

V

Local Societies, Branches, and Groups

2. *Conformity of the local rules and regulations with the General Rules and Regulations shall be established by the Federal Councils and, for branches outside the federal associations, by the General Council.*[a]

9. The addresses of the *Federal Committees* and of the General Council are to be published every three months in all the organs of the Association.

---

[a] With the introduction of this new article the subsequent articles of this section have been renumbered.— *Ed.*

VI

General Statistics of Labour

General scheme of inquiry, which may of course be modified by each locality

1. Industry, *which?*
5. (a) Hours of work in factories. (b) The hours of work with small employers and in home work. (c) Nightwork and daywork. (d) *Hours of rest.*
6. *Regulations in workshops.*
12. *Habitation and nourishment.*

Drawn up in June-August 1872

First published, in Russian, in *Problemy mira i sotsializma*, No. 4, 1964

Reproduced from the 1871 English edition of the General Rules and Administrative Regulations. The amendments made in Marx's hand in the French copy of the Rules and Regulations are translated from the French

Frederick Engels

THE GENERAL COUNCIL TO ALL THE MEMBERS OF THE INTERNATIONAL WORKING MEN'S ASSOCIATION [156]

Citizens,

The General Council finds itself under the necessity of publicly denouncing to you the existence, within the International, of intrigues which, although in full work for several years past, have never been even suspected by the majority among you.

In our private circular dated 5th March 1872, on "the pretended divisions within the International",[a] we were compelled to call your attention to the manoeuvres of the so-called "Alliance of Socialist Democracy", manoeuvres aiming at the creation of discord in our ranks, and at the handing over, in an underhand manner, of the supreme direction of our Association to a small clique directed by Michael Bakounine.

The Alliance of Socialist Democracy, you will recollect, published, at its very origin, a set of rules which, if we had sanctioned them, would have given it a double existence, within and without the International at the same time. It would have had its own sections, federations and congresses at the side of the sections, federations and congresses of the International, and yet it pretended to take part in the latter. Its aim was to supersede our General Rules by the special programme of M. Bakounine and to force upon our Association his personal dictatorship.

The General Council, by its circular of the 22 December 1868, repelled these pretentions.[b] It admitted the Alliance of Socialist

---

[a] See this volume, pp. 79-123.— Ed.

[b] K. Marx, "The International Working Men's Association and the International Alliance of Socialist Democracy". Below, Engels sets forth the Council's second letter, also written by Marx, dated March 9, 1869, "The General Council of the International Working Men's Association to the Central Bureau of the Internation-

Democracy into the International on the express condition only, that it should cease to be an international body; that it should dissolve its organisation; that its sections should enter simply as local sections. These conditions were formally accepted by the Alliance. But of all its pretended sections, only the Central Section of Geneva entered into our Association. The others remained a mystery to the General Council, thus leaving it under the impression that they did not exist.

And now, three years later, we are put in possession of documents which prove irrefragably that this same Alliance of Socialist Democracy, in spite of its formal promise, has continued and does continue to exist as an international body within the International, and that in the shape of a secret society; that it is still directed by M. Bakounine; that its ends are still the same, and that all the attacks which for the last twelve months have been directed apparently against the London Conference and the General Council, but in reality against the whole of our organisation, have had their source in this Alliance. The same men who accuse the General Council of authoritativeness without ever having been able to specify one single authoritative act on its part, who talk at every opportunity of the autonomy of sections, of the free federation of groups; who charge the General Council with the intention of forcing upon the International its own official and orthodox doctrine and to transform our Association into a hierarchically constituted organisation—these very same men, in practice, constitute themselves as a secret society with a hierarchical organisation, and under a, not merely authoritative, but absolutely dictatorial leadership; they trample under their feet every vestige of autonomy of sections and federations; they aim at forcing upon the International, by means of this secret organisation, the personal and orthodox doctrine of M. Bakounine. While they demand that the International should be organised from below upwards, they themselves, as members of the Alliance, humbly submit to the word of command which is handed down to them from above.

Need we say that the very existence of such a secret society within the International is a flagrant breach of our General Rules? These Rules know only one kind of members of the International, with rights and duties equal for all; the Alliance separates them into two classes, the initiated and the profane, the latter destined

---

al Alliance of Socialist Democracy". Both documents are included into *Fictitious Splits in the International* (see this volume, pp. 86-87 and 88-89).—*Ed.*

.to be led by the first, by means of an organisation whose very existence is unknown to them. The International demands of its adherents to acknowledge Truth, Justice and Morality as the basis of their conduct; the Alliance imposes upon its adepts, as their first duty, mendacity, dissimulation and imposture, by ordering them to deceive the profane Internationals as to the existence of the secret organisation and to the motives and ends of their own words and actions. The programme of the International is laid down in our Rules and known to all; that of the Alliance has never been avowed and is unknown up to this day.

The nucleus of the Alliance is in the federation of the Jura. From it the watchword is issued which is taken up and repeated immediately by the other sections and by the newspapers belonging to the secret organisation. In Italy, a certain number of societies are controlled by it. These societies call themselves International sections, but have never either demanded their admission, or paid any contributions, or fulfilled any of the other conditions prescribed by our Regulations. In Belgium, the Alliance has a few influential agents. In the South of France, it has several correspondents, among them pluralists, who couple their functions of correspondents to the Alliance with the office of clerk to the inspector of police. But the country where the Alliance is organised most effectively, and where it has the most extended ramifications is Spain. Having managed to slip itself quietly and from the commencement into the ranks of the Spanish Internationals, it has managed to control, most of the time, the successive Federal Councils and Congresses. The most devoted Internationals in Spain were induced into the belief that this secret organisation existed everywhere within our Association and that it was almost a duty to belong to it. This delusion was destroyed by the London Conference where the Spanish delegate,[a] himself a member of the Alliance, could convince himself that the contrary was the fact, and by the lies and violent attacks which, immediately afterwards, Bakounine ordered his faithful flock to launch against the Conference and the General Council. After a prolonged struggle within the Alliance, those of its Spanish members who had more at heart the International than the Alliance, retired from the latter. Immediately they were assaulted by the most atrocious insults and calumnies on the part of those who remained faithful to the secret society. Twice they were expelled from the local federation of Madrid, in open violation of the existing regulations. When they

---

[a] Anselmo Lorenzo.— *Ed.*

proposed constituting themselves as the "New Federation of Madrid",[157] the Federal Council refused its authorisation and returned the contributions they had proffered. And here we must state that out of eight members of that Federal Council there are five (Vicente Rossell, Peregrin Montoro, Severino Albarracin, Francisco Tomás, and Franco Martinez) whom we know to be members of the Alliance; it is moreover likely that there are others besides these. Thus the sections and local federations of Spain, so proud of their autonomy, are led like a flock of sheep, without even suspecting it, by secret orders sent from Switzerland, which the Federal Council has to carry out without a murmur, under penalty of being outlawed by the Alliance.

The Spanish Federal Council, in order to ensure the election, as delegates for the Congress at The Hague, of members of the Alliance, has sent to the sections and local federations a private circular dated 7th July, in which it calls upon them for an extraordinary contribution with which to defray the expenses of the delegates, and moreover orders them, authoritatively, to vote for a certain number of delegates, to be elected by the whole of the Spanish Internationals; all voting papers to be sent to the Federal Council which would ascertain the result of the election.[a] In this manner, the success of the candidates of the Alliance was placed beyond all doubt. Moreover, the Federal Council announced that it will draw up instructions[b] by which the delegates elected shall be bound. As soon as we had cognisance of this plot to have the delegates of the Alliance sent to the Congress with the money of the International, and had received, besides, the proofs of the complicity of the Spanish Federal Council in the manoeuvres of the secret society, we have summoned it, on the 24th July:

1) To hand us in a list of all members of the Alliance in Spain, with the designation of such offices as they may hold in the International;

2) To institute an inquiry into the character and action of the Alliance in Spain, as well as into its organisation and its ramifications beyond the frontier;

3) To send us a copy of their private circular of July 7th[c];

---

[a] In the French manuscript the end of the sentence reads: "orders them, authoritatively, to elect these delegates by voting for a list for the whole of Spain, so that the Federal Council itself will be charged with polling the votes".— Ed.

[b] The French manuscript has "a mandate imperative for all" instead of "instructions".— Ed.

[c] Federación Regional Española. Circular reservada, Valencia, July 7, 1872.— Ed.

4) To explain to us how they reconciliated with their duties towards the International, the presence, in the Federal Council, of at least three notorious members of the Alliance;

5) To send a categorical reply by return.[a]

This reply could have been in our hands on the 1st August at latest. But only on the 5th August we received a letter dated Valencia, Aug. 1st (postmark illegible), in which a reply was deferred under the pretence that the members of the Council did not understand our letter which was written in French, and that time was required to translate it. That same Council, in its letter of June 15th, had requested us to send them our publications, etc., as much as possible in French, they (the members of the Council) being somewhat familiarised with that language! Thus the pretence is false; all that is wanted is to make us lose time while it is precious.

We are therefore under the necessity of denouncing to all the members of the Association, and above all to the Spanish Internationals, the Spanish Federal Council as *traitors towards the International Working Men's Association.* Instead of faithfully fulfilling the mandate entrusted to them by the Spanish Internationals, they have made themselves the organ of a society not only foreign, but hostile to the International. Instead of obeying the General Rules and Regulations, and the resolutions of the General and Spanish Congresses, they obey to secret orders emanating from M. Bakounine. The very existence of a Federal Council composed, in its majority, of members of a secret society foreign to the International, is a flagrant violation of our General Rules.

These are, Citizens, the facts which we have to lay before you before the elections for the Congress take place. For the first time in the history of the working-class struggles, we stumble over a secret conspiracy plotted in the midst of that class, and intended to undermine, not the existing capitalist[b] *régime*, but the very Association in which that *régime* finds its most energetic opponent. It is a conspiracy got up to hamper the proletarian movement. Thus, wherever we meet it, we find it preaching the emasculating doctrine of absolute abstention from political action; and while the plain profane Internationals are persecuted and imprisoned over nearly all Europe, the valiant members of the Alliance enjoy a quite exceptional immunity.

Citizens, it is for you to choose. What is at stake at this moment,

---

[a] See this volume, pp. 211-13.— *Ed.*

[b] The French manuscript has "exploiter".— *Ed.*

is neither the autonomy of sections, nor the free federation of groups, nor the organisation from below upwards, nor any other formula equally pretentious and sonorous; the question today is this: Do you want your central organs composed of men who recognise no other mandate but yours, or do you want them composed of men elected by surprise, and who accept your mandate with the resolution to lead you, like a flock of sheep, as they may be directed by secret instructions emanating from a mysterious personage in Switzerland?

To unveil the existence of this secret society of dupers, is to crush its power. The men of the Alliance themselves are not foolish enough to expect that the great mass of the Internationals would knowingly submit to an organisation like theirs, its existence once made known. Yet there is complete incompatibility between the dupers and those who are intended for the dupes, between the Alliance and the International.

Moreover, it is time once and for all to put a stop to those internal quarrels provoked every day afresh within our Association, by the presence of this parasite body. These quarrels only serve to squander forces which ought to be employed in fighting the present middle-class *régime*. The Alliance, in so far as it paralyses the action of the International against the enemies of the working class, serves admirably the middle class and the governments.

For these reasons, the General Council will call upon the Congress of The Hague to expel from the International all and every member of the Alliance and to give the Council such powers as shall enable it effectually to prevent the recurrence of similar conspiracies.[a]

Written on August 4-6, 1872

First published in: Marx and Engels, *Works*, First Russian Edition, Vol. XIII, Part II, Moscow, 1940

Reproduced from the English manuscript checked with the French manuscripts

---

[a] The French manuscript further has: "The General Council".— *Ed.*

Karl Marx and Frederick Engels

TO THE SPANISH SECTIONS OF THE INTERNATIONAL WORKING MEN'S ASSOCIATION [158]

London, August 8, 1872

In view of the intrigues launched against the *International Working Men's Association* by some members of the Alliance secret society, the Executive Committee of the General Council had, at its meeting of July 24, 1872, instructed Citizen F. Engels, Secretary for Spain, to write the Spanish Federal Council in Valencia the following letter:

TO THE SPANISH FEDERAL COUNCIL

Citizens,

We hold proof that within the International, and particularly in Spain, there exists a secret society called the *Alliance of Socialist Democracy*. This society, whose centre is in Switzerland, considers it its special mission to guide our great Association in keeping with its own particular tendencies and lead it towards goals unknown to the vast majority of International members. Moreover, we know from the Seville *Razon* that at least three members of your Council belong to the Alliance.

When this society was formed in 1868 as a public society, the General Council was obliged to refuse it admission to the International, so long as it preserved its international character, for it pretended to form a second international body functioning within and without the *International Working Men's Association*. The Alliance was admitted to the International only after promising to limit itself to being purely a local section in Geneva (see the private circular of the General Council on *Fictitious Splits etc.*, p. 7 onwards[a]).

---

[a] See this volume, pp. 86-87.—*Ed.*

If the organisation and character of this society were already contrary to the spirit and the letter of our Rules, when it was still public, its secret existence within the International, in spite of its promise, represents no less than treason against our Association. The International knows but one type of members, all with equal rights and duties; the Alliance divides them into two classes, the initiated and the uninitiated, the latter doomed to be led by the former by means of an organisation of whose very existence they are unaware. The International demands that its adherents should acknowledge Truth, Justice and Morality as the basis of their conduct; the Alliance obliges its supporters to hide from the uninitiated members of the International the existence of the secret organisation, the motives and the aim of their words and deeds. The General Council had already announced in its private circular that at the coming Congress it would demand an inquiry into this Alliance, which is a veritable conspiracy against the International. The General Council is also aware of the measures taken by the Spanish Federal Council on the insistence of the men of the Alliance in the interests of their society, and is determined to put an end to this underhand dealing. With this end in view, it requests from you for the report it will be presenting at the Hague Congress:

1) a list of all the members of the Alliance in Spain, with indication of the functions they fulfil in the International;

2) information about the nature and activities of the Alliance, and also about its organisation and ramifications outside Spain;

3) a copy of your private circular of July 7[a];

4) an explanation of how you reconcile your duties towards the International with the presence in your Council of at least three notorious members of the Alliance.

Unless it receives *a categoric and exhaustive answer by return*, the General Council will be obliged to denounce you publicly in Spain and abroad for having violated the spirit and the letter of the General Rules, and having betrayed the International in the interests of a secret society that is not only alien but hostile to it.

Greetings and fraternity.

On behalf of the General Council

Secretary for Spain,

Frederick Engels

33, Rathbone Place, W.

London, July 24, 1872

---

[a] *Federación Regional Española. Circular reservada,* Valencia, July 7, 1872.—*Ed.*

The Spanish Federal Council replied to the inquiries of the General Council in a letter dated "Valencia, August 1", and received in London on August 5. It ran as follows:

"Comrades, we have received your last letter, but as it is in French we are unable to acquaint ourselves with its contents since our usual translator is not in Valencia. We have asked another comrade to translate it as soon as possible so that we can answer it."

At its meeting of August 8, 1872, the Executive Committee of the General Council decided that pending the receipt of the requested information from the Spanish Federal Council, it was necessary to publish the above letter in order to move all the Spanish federations and sections to undertake their general inquiries into the existence, acts and aims of the Alliance secret society.

The Executive Committee
of the General Council:

Leó Frankel, Corresponding Secretary for	Austria and Hungary
J. P. McDonnell	Ireland
F. Engels	Spain and Italy
A. Serraillier	France
Le Moussu	America
Hermann Jung	Switzerland
Karl Marx	Germany and Russia

Chairman of the meeting

Walery Wróblewski, Secretary for Poland

Secretary of the meeting

F. Cournet, Secretary for Holland

Written on August 8, 1872

First published in *La Emancipacion*, No. 62, August 17, 1872

Printed according to the newspaper checked with the rough manuscript in French

Translated from the Spanish

Karl Marx

TO THE EDITOR OF *THE TIMES*[159]

Sir,—In your issue of to-day I find a paragraph headed "The International", containing, after "the Paris papers", a pretended circular of the "Grand Council" of that Association, and bearing my signature as "General Secretary".

I beg to state, in reply, that this document is from beginning to end a forgery. No such circular was ever issued by the General Council of the International Working Men's Association, nor could I have signed anything of the sort as General Secretary, inasmuch as I have never occupied that position.

I request you to publish the above in your next number, and remain, Sir, your obedient servant,

Karl Marx

[London] 1, Maitland-park-road, N. W., Aug. 15 [1872].

First published in *The Times*, No. 27457, August 16, 1872

Reproduced from the newspaper

Frederick Engels

THE GENERAL COUNCIL
TO THE NEW MADRID FEDERATION [160]

The Executive Committee, entrusted by the General Council with temporarily carrying out all the administrative business of the Association,

in view of the New Madrid Federation's letter of August 5, requesting its recognition by the General Council;

in view of the Spanish regional Federal Council's resolution of July 16, refusing to admit the said federation;

considering that, formally, it would be absurd to share in this matter the attitude of a regional Federal Council, the majority of which are members of a secret society hostile to the International, and which the General Council intends opposing at the Congress;

considering that, essentially, the founders of the New Madrid Federation are the very people who were the first in Spain to dare disassociate themselves from this secret society called the *Alliance of Socialist Democracy*, and disclose and thwart its schemes.

For these reasons,

the Executive Committee, on behalf of the General Council, has resolved to recognise the New Madrid Federation and enter into regular and direct relations with it.

London, August 15, 1872

In the name of the Executive Committee
Secretary for Spain,
Frederick Engels

First published in *La Emancipacion*, No. 63, August 24, 1872

Printed according to the newspaper

Translated from the Spanish

Frederick Engels

[ON THE RIMINI CONFERENCE]¹⁶¹

The *Bakuninists* have now finally placed themselves outside the International. A conference (ostensibly of the International, in reality of the Italian Bakuninists) has been held in *Rimini*. Of the 21 sections represented, only *one*, that from Naples, really belonged to the International. The other 20, in order not to endanger their "autonomy", had deliberately *neglected to take all the measures* on which the Administrative Regulations of the International make admission conditional; they had neither written to the General Council requesting admission, nor sent their subscriptions. And these 21 "International" sections decided unanimously in Rimini on August 6:

"The Conference solemnly declares to all workers of the world that the Italian Federation of the International Working Men's Association severs all solidarity with the General Council in London, proclaiming instead, all the louder, its economic solidarity with all workers, and urges all sections that do not share the authoritarian principles of the General Council *to send* their representatives on September 2, 1872 *not to The Hague, but to Neuchâtel in Switzerland* in order to open the general anti-authoritarian Congress there on the same day."

First published in *Der Volksstaat*, No. 68, August 24, 1872

Printed according to the newspaper

Published in English for the first time

Frederick Engels

[ADDRESS OF THE GENERAL COUNCIL TO THE ITALIAN SECTIONS OF THE INTERNATIONAL WORKING MEN'S ASSOCIATION CONCERNING THE RIMINI CONFERENCE][162]

33, Rathbone Place, London
August 23, 1872

We have received a resolution, dated Rimini, August 6, from the Conference of what claims to be the Italian Federation of the International Working Men's Association, breaking all solidarity with the General Council in London and calling *on its own authority* an anti-authoritarian Congress[a] in Neuchâtel, Switzerland, to which all sections of the same opinion are invited to send delegates, instead of to The Hague, where the regular Congress of the International is to be held.

It should be pointed out that of the 21 sections whose delegates have signed this resolution, there is *only one* (Naples) which belongs to the International. None of the other 20 sections has ever fulfilled any of the conditions prescribed by our General Rules and Regulations for the admission of new sections. An Italian federation of the Working Men's Association therefore does not exist. Those who want to found it, form their own international outside the great Working Men's Association.

It will be the task of the Hague Congress to deliberate on these usurpations.

In the name and by order of the General Council
Secretary for Italy,

Frederick Engels[b]

First published in part in *La Plebe*, No. 95, August 28, 1872 and in *Il Ladro*, September 3, 1872; and in full in *Il Popolino*, No. 20, September 29, 1872

Printed according to *Il Popolino* checked with the rough copy of the letter

Translated from the Italian

---

[a] The rough copy of the letter has "a so-called anti-authoritarian Congress".— *Ed.*

[b] In *Il Popolino* the letter begins with the address: "To the Turin Sections"; there is the postscript after the signature: "*N.B.* The letter containing the 25 lire was not received."— *Ed.*

Karl Marx

[RESOLUTION ON THE BEHAVIOUR OF MEMBERS OF THE GENERAL COUNCIL AT THE CONGRESS] [163]

No member of the General Council should have the right to accuse another before the International Working Men's Congress until discussion of the election of members of the General Council.

Adopted at the sitting of the Sub-Committee on August 28, 1872

First published, in Russian, in *Generalny Sovet Pervogo Internatsionala. 1871-1872*, Moscow, 1965

Printed according to the manuscript

Translated from the French

Karl Marx

REPORT OF THE GENERAL COUNCIL TO THE FIFTH ANNUAL CONGRESS OF THE INTERNATIONAL WORKING MEN'S ASSOCIATION, HELD AT THE HAGUE,

FROM THE 2nd TO THE 7th SEPTEMBER 1872 [164]

[*The International Herald*, No. 27, October 5, 1872]

Citizens,[a]—Since our last Congress at Basel, two great wars have changed the face of Europe: the Franco-German War and the Civil War in France. Both of these wars were preceded, accompanied, and followed by a third war—the war against the International Working Men's Association.

The Paris members[b] of the International had told the French people publicly and emphatically, that voting the plebiscite [165] was voting despotism at home and war abroad.[c] Under the pretext of having participated in a plot for the assassination of Louis Bonaparte, they were arrested on the eve of the plebiscite, the 23rd of April, 1870. Simultaneous arrests of Internationalists took place at Lyons, Rouen, Marseilles, Brest, and other towns. In its declaration of May 3rd, 1870, the General Council stated [d]:

"This last plot will worthily range with its two predecessors of grotesque memory. The noisy and violent measures against our French sections are exclusively intended to serve one single purpose—the manipulation of the plebiscite." [e]

---

[a] The leaflet and *Der Volksstaat* have "working men" instead of "citizens".—*Ed.*

[b] In *L'Internationale*, *La Liberté* and other newspapers this sentence begins as follows: "When the empire demanded that France should sanctify its existence with a new plebiscite, the Paris members..."—*Ed.*

[c] "Manifeste antiplébiscitaire des sections parisiennes fédérées de l'Internationale et de la chambre fédérale des sociétés ouvrières. A tous les travailleurs français" published in *La Marseillaise*, No. 125, April 24, 1870, and as a leaflet in Paris, 1870.—*Ed.*

[d] K. Marx, "Concerning the Persecution of the Members of the French Sections" (cf. present edition, Vol. 21, p. 128).—*Ed.*

[e] Here the leaflet and *Der Volksstaat* have: "We were right."—*Ed.*

In point of fact, after the downfall of the December empire its governmental successors published documentary evidence[a] to the effect that this last plot had been fabricated by the Bonapartist police itself, and that on the eve of the plebiscite, Ollivier, in a private circular, directly told his subordinates,

"The leaders of the International must be arrested or else the voting of the plebiscite could not be satisfactorily proceeded with."

The plebiscitary farce once over, the members of the Paris Federal Council were indeed condemned, on the 8th of July, by Louis Bonaparte's own judges, but for the simple crime of belonging to the International and not for any participation in the sham plot.[166] Thus the Bonapartist government considered it necessary to initiate the most ruinous war that was ever brought down upon France, by a preliminary campaign against the French sections of the International Working Men's Association. Let us not forget that the working class in France rose like one man to reject the plebiscite. Let us no more forget that

"the stock-exchanges, the cabinets, the ruling classes, and the press of Europe celebrated the plebiscite as a signal victory of the French emperor over the French working class."—(Address of General Council on the Franco-Prussian War, 23rd July, 1870.)

A few weeks after the plebiscite, when the imperialist press commenced to fan the warlike passions amongst the French people, the Paris Internationalists, nothing daunted by the government persecutions, issued their appeal of the 12th of July, "to the workmen of all nations", denounced the intended war as a "criminal absurdity", telling their "brothers of Germany", that

their "division would only result in the complete triumph of despotism on both sides of the Rhine", and declaring that "we, the members of the International Association, know of no frontiers."[b]

Their appeal met with an enthusiastic echo from Germany, so that the General Council was entitled to state,

"The very fact that while official France and Germany are rushing into a fratricidal feud, the workmen of France and Germany send each other messages of peace and good will—this great fact, unparalleled in the history of the past—opens the vista of a brighter future. It proves that in contrast to old society with

a *Papiers et correspondance de la Famille impériale*, Vol. 1, Paris, [1870-]1871, pp. 314-26.— *Ed.*

b "Aux travailleurs de toutes les nations", *Le Réveil*, No. 409, July 12, 1870.— *Ed.*

its economical miseries and its political delirium, a new society is springing up whose international rule will be *peace*, because its national ruler will be everywhere the same— *Labour*. The pioneer of that new society is the International Working Men's Association."—(Address of July 23rd, 1870.)

Up to the proclamation of the Republic, the members of the Paris Federal Council remained in prison, while the other members of the Association were daily denounced to the mob as traitors acting in the pay of Prussia.

With the capitulation of Sedan, when the second empire ended as it began, by a parody,[167] the Franco-German War entered upon its second phase. It became war against the French people. After her repeated solemn declarations to take up arms for the sole purpose of repelling foreign aggression, Prussia now dropped the mask and proclaimed a war of conquest. From that moment she found herself compelled not only to fight the Republic in France, but simultaneously the International in Germany. We can here but hint at a few incidents of that conflict.

[*The International Herald*, No. 28, October 12, 1872]

Immediately after the declaration of war, the greater part of the territory of the North German Confederation, Hanover, Oldenburg, Bremen, Hamburg, Brunswick, Schleswig-Holstein, Mecklenburg, Pomerania, and the province of Prussia, were placed in a state of siege, and handed over to the tender mercies of General Vogel von Falckenstein. This state of siege, proclaimed as a safeguard against the threatening foreign invasion, was at once turned into a state of war against the German Internationals.

The day after the proclamation of the Republic at Paris, the Brunswick Central Committee of the German Democratic Socialist Working Men's Party, which forms a section of the International within the limits imposed by the law of the country, issued a manifesto (5th September) calling upon the working class to oppose by all means in their power the dismemberment of France, to claim a peace honourable for that country, and to agitate for the recognition of the French Republic.[168] The manifesto denounced the proposed annexation of Alsace and Lorraine as a crime tending to transform all Germany into a Prussian barracks, and to establish war as a permanent European institution. On the 9th September, Vogel von Falckenstein had the members of the Brunswick Committee arrested, and marched off in chains, a distance of 600 miles, to Loetzen, a Prussian fortress, on the Russian frontier, where their ignominious treatment was to serve as a foil to the ostentatious feasting of the Imperial guest at Wilhelmshöhe.[169] As arrests, the hunting of workmen from one German state to another, suppression of proletarian papers, military brutality, and police-chicane in all forms, did not prevent the International vanguard of the German working class from acting up to the Brunswick manifesto, Vogel von Falckenstein, by an ukase of September 21st,[a] interdicted all meetings of the Democratic Socialist party. That interdict was cancelled by another ukase of October 5th, wherein he naively commands the police spies

"to denounce to him personally all individuals who, by public demonstrations, shall encourage France in her resistance against the conditions of peace imposed by Germany, so as to enable him to render such individuals innocuous during the continuance of the war".

Leaving the cares of the war abroad to Moltke, the King of Prussia contrived to give a new turn to the war at home. By his personal order of the 17th October, Vogel von Falckenstein was to lend his Loetzen captives to the Brunswick District Tribunal, the which, on its part, was either to find grounds for their legal durance, or else return them to the safe keeping of the dread general.

Vogel von Falckenstein's proceedings were, of course, imitated throughout Germany, while Bismarck, in a diplomatic circular, mocked Europe by standing forth as the indignant champion of the right of free utterance of opinion, free press, and free meetings, on the part of the peace party in France. At the very same time that he demanded a freely-elected National Assembly for France, in Germany he had Bebel and Liebknecht imprisoned for having, in opposition to him, represented the International in the German Parliament, and in order to get them out of the way during the impending general elections.[170]

His master, William the Conqueror,[b] supported him, by a decree from Versailles, prolonging the state of siege, that is to say, the suspension of all civil law, for the whole period of the elections. In fact, the King did not allow the state of siege to be raised in Germany until two months after the conclusion of peace with France.[171] The stubbornness with which he was insisting upon the state of war at home, and his repeated personal meddling with his own German captives, prove the awe in which he, amidst the din of victorious arms and the frantic cheers of the whole middle class,

---

[a] 1870.— *Ed.*
[b] William I.— *Ed.*

held the rising party of the proletariat. It was the involuntary homage paid by physical force to moral power.

If the war against the International had been localised, first in France, from the days of the plebiscite to the downfall of the Empire, then in Germany during the whole period of the resistance of the Republic against Prussia, it became general since the rise, and after the fall, of the Paris Commune.

On the 6th of June, 1871, Jules Favre issued his circular to the Foreign Powers demanding the extradition of the refugees[a] of the Commune as common criminals, and a general crusade against the International as the enemy of family, religion, order, and property, so adequately represented in his own person.[172] Austria and Hungary caught the cue at once. On the 13th June, a raid was made on the reputed leaders of the Pesth Working Men's Union, their papers were seized, their persons sequestered, and proceedings were instituted against them for high treason.[173] Several delegates of the Vienna International, happening to be on a visit to Pesth, were carried off to Vienna, there to undergo a similar treatment. Beust asked and received from his parliament a supplementary vote of £30,000,

"on behalf of expenses for political information that had become more than ever indispensable through the dangerous spread of the International all over Europe".

Since that time a true reign of terror against the working class has set in in Austria and Hungary. In its last agonies the Austrian Government seems still anxiously to cling to its old privilege of playing the Don Quixote of European reaction.

A few weeks after Jules Favre's circular, Dufaure proposed to his rurals a law which is now in force, and punishes as a crime the mere fact of belonging to the International Working Men's Association, or of sharing its principles.[174] As a witness before the rural committee of enquiry on Dufaure's Bill, Thiers boasted that it was the offspring of his own ingenious brains, and that he had been the first to discover the infallible panacea of treating the Internationals as the Spanish Inquisition had treated the heretics. But even on this point he can lay no claim to originality. Long before his appointment as saviour of society, the true law which the Internationals deserve at the hands of the ruling classes had been laid down by the Vienna courts.

---

[a] The leaflet and *Der Volksstaat* have "members" instead of "refugees".— *Ed.*

[*The International Herald*, No. 29, October 19, 1872]

On the 26th July, 1870, the most prominent men of the Austrian proletarian party were found guilty of high treason, and sentenced to years of penal servitude, with one fast day in every month.[175] The law laid down was this: —

> The prisoners, as they themselves confess, have accepted and acted according to the programme of the German Working Men's Congress of Eisenach (1869). This programme embodies the programme of the International. The International is established for the emancipation of the working class from the rule of the propertied class, and from political dependence. That emancipation is incompatible with the existing institutions of the Austrian state. Hence, whoever accepts and propagates the principles of the International programme, commits preparatory acts for the overthrow of the Austrian Government, and is consequently guilty of high treason.

On the 27th November, 1871, judgment was passed upon the members of the Brunswick Committee. They were sentenced to various periods of imprisonment. The court expressly referred, as to a precedent, to the law laid down at Vienna.

At Pesth, the prisoners belonging to the Working Men's Union, after having undergone for nearly a year a treatment as infamous as that inflicted upon the Fenians[176] by the British Government, were brought up for judgment on the 22nd April, 1872. The public prosecutor, here also, called upon the court to apply to them the law laid down at Vienna. They were, however, acquitted.

At Leipzig, on the 27th March, 1872, Bebel and Liebknecht were sentenced to two years imprisonment in a fortress for attempted high treason upon the strength of the law as laid down at Vienna. The only distinctive feature of this case is that the law laid down by a Vienna judge was sanctioned by a Saxon jury.

At Copenhagen the three members of the Central Committee of the International, Brix, Pio, and Geleff, were thrown into prison on the 5th of May[a] because they had declared their firm resolve to hold an open air meeting in the teeth of a police order forbidding it. Once in prison they were told that the accusation against them was extended, that the socialist ideas in themselves were incompatible with the existence of the Danish state, and that consequently the mere act of propagating them constituted a crime against the Danish constitution. Again the law as laid down in Vienna! The accused are still in prison awaiting their trial.[177]

The Belgian government, distinguished by its sympathetic reply to Jules Favre's demand of extradition, made haste to propose, through Malou, a hypocritical counterfeit of Dufaure's law.

___

[a] 1872.— *Ed.*

His Holiness Pope Pius IX gave vent to his feelings in an allocution to a deputation of Swiss Catholics.

"Your government," said he, "which is republican, thinks itself bound to make a heavy sacrifice for what is called liberty. It affords an asylum to a goodly number of individuals of the worst character. It tolerates that sect of the International which desires to treat all Europe as it has treated Paris. These gentlemen of the International who are no gentlemen, are to be feared because they work for the account of the everlasting enemy of God and mankind. What is to be gained by protecting them! One must pray for them."

Hang them first and pray for them afterwards!

Supported by Bismarck, Beust, and Stieber, the Prussian spy-in-chief, the Emperors of Austria and Germany met at Salzburg in the beginning of September, 1871, for the ostensible purpose of founding a holy alliance against the International Working Men's Association.[178]

"Such a European Alliance," declared the *North German Gazette*,[a] Bismarck's private *moniteur*,[b] "is the only possible salvation of state, church, property, civilisation, in one word, of everything that constitutes European states."

Bismarck's real object, of course, was to prepare alliances for an impending war with Russia and the International was held up to Austria as a piece of red cloth is held up to a bull.

Lanza suppressed the International in Italy by simple decree. Sagasta declared it an outlaw in Spain,[179] probably with a view to curry favour with the English stock exchange. The Russian government which, since the emancipation of the serfs, has been driven to the dangerous expedient of making timid concessions to popular claims today, and withdrawing them tomorrow, found in the general hue and cry against the International a pretext for a recrudescence of reaction at home. Abroad, with the intention of prying into the secrets of our Association, it succeeded in inducing a Swiss judge to search, in presence of a Russian spy, the house of Outine, a Russian International, and the editor of the Geneva *Égalité*, the organ of our Romance Federation.[180] The republican government of Switzerland has only been prevented by the agitation of the Swiss Internationals from handing up to Thiers refugees of the Commune.

Finally, the government of Mr. Gladstone, unable to act in Great Britain, at least set forth its good intentions by the police terrorism exercised in Ireland against our sections then in course

---

[a] *Norddeutsche Allgemeine Zeitung.—Ed.*
[b] Herald.— *Ed.*

of formation, and by ordering its representatives abroad to collect information with respect to the International Working Men's Association.

But all the measures of repression which the combined government intellect of Europe was capable of devising, vanish into nothing before the war of calumny undertaken by the lying power of the civilised world. Apocryphal histories and mysteries of the International, shameless forgeries of public documents and private letters, sensational telegrams, followed each other in rapid succession; all the sluices of slander at the disposal of the venal respectable press were opened at once to set free a deluge of infamy in which to drown the execrated foe. This war of calumny finds no parallel in history for the truly international area over which it has spread, and for the complete accord in which it has been carried on by all shades of ruling class opinion. When the great conflagration took place at Chicago, the telegraph round the world announced it as the infernal deed of the International; and it is really wonderful that to its demoniacal agency has not been attributed the hurricane ravaging the West Indies.

In its former annual reports, the General Council used to give a review of the progress of the Association since the meeting of the preceding Congress. You will appreciate, citizens,[a] the motives which induce us to abstain from that course upon this occasion. Moreover, the reports of the delegates from the various countries, who know best how far their discretion may extend, will in a measure make up for this deficiency. We confine ourselves to the statement that since the Congress at Basel, and chiefly since the London Conference of September 1871, the International has been extended to the Irish in England and to Ireland itself, to Holland, Denmark, and Portugal, that it has been firmly organised in the United States, and that it has established ramifications in Buenos Aires, Australia, and New Zealand.

The difference between a working class without an International, and a working class with an International, becomes most evident if we look back to the period of 1848. Years were required for the working class itself to recognise the Insurrection of June, 1848, as the work of its own vanguard. The Paris Commune was at once acclaimed by the universal proletariat.

You, the delegates of the working class, meet to strengthen the militant organisation of a society aiming at the emancipation of labour and the extinction of national feuds. Almost at the same

---

[a] The leaflet and *Der Volksstaat* have "working men" instead of "citizens".— *Ed.*

moment, there meet at Berlin the crowned dignitaries of the old world in order to forge new chains and to hatch new wars.[181]
Long life to the International Working Men's Association!

Written in late August 1872

First published as a leaflet: *Offizieller Bericht des Londoner Generalrats, verlesen in öffentlicher Sitzung des Internationalen Kongress*, Brunswick, 1872, and in the newspapers: *Der Volksstaat*, No. 75, September 18, 1872; *La Liberté*, No. 39, September 29, 1872; *L'Internationale*, No. 195, October 6, 1872; *La Emancipacion*, Nos. 68 and 69, October 5 and 13, 1872; *The International Herald*, Nos. 27, 28 and 29, October 5, 12 and 19, 1872

Reproduced from *The International Herald* checked with the leaflet and newspapers

Frederick Engels

REPORT ON THE ALLIANCE
OF SOCIALIST DEMOCRACY PRESENTED
IN THE NAME OF THE GENERAL COUNCIL
TO THE CONGRESS AT THE HAGUE[182]

The Alliance of Socialist Democracy was founded by M. Bakunin towards the end of 1868. It was an international society claiming to function, at the same time, both within and without the International Working Men's Association. Composed of members of the Association, who demanded the right to take part in all meetings of the International's members, this society, nevertheless, wished to retain the right to organise its own local groups, national federations and congresses alongside and in addition to the Congresses of the International. Thus, right from the onset, the Alliance claimed to form a kind of aristocracy within our Association, or élite with its own programme and possessing special privileges.

The letters which were exchanged between the Central Committee of the Alliance and our General Council at that time are reproduced on pp. 7-9 of the circular *Fictitious Splits in the International*[a] (appendix No. 1). The General Council refused to admit the Alliance as long as it retained its distinct international character; it promised to admit the Alliance only on the condition that the latter would dissolve its special international organisation, that its sections would become ordinary sections of our Association, and that the Council should be informed of the seat and numerical strength of each new section formed.

The following is the reply dated June 22, 1869, to these demands received from the Central Committee of the Alliance, which[b] has henceforth become known as the "Geneva Section of

---

a See this volume, pp. 86-89.— *Ed.*

b Further the following is crossed out in the manuscript: "changed its name for the occasion".— *Ed.*

the Alliance of Socialist Democracy" in its relations with the General Council.

"As agreed between your Council and the Central Committee of the Alliance of Socialist Democracy, we have consulted the various groups of the Alliance on the question of its dissolution as an organisation outside the International Working Men's Association... We are pleased to inform you that a great majority of the groups share the views of the Central Committee which intends to announce the dissolution of the International Alliance of Socialist Democracy. *The question of dissolution has today been decided.* In communicating this decision to the various groups of the Alliance, we have invited them to follow our example and constitute themselves into sections of the International Working Men's Association, and seek recognition as such either from you or from the Federal Councils of the Association in their respective countries. Confirming receipt of your letter addressed to the former Central Committee of the Alliance, we are sending today for your perusal the rules of our section, and hereby request your official recognition of it as a section of the International Working Men's Association..." (Signed) Acting Secretary, Ch. Perron (appendix No. 2).

A copy of these rules of the Alliance may be found among appendices *No. 3.*

The Geneva section proved to be the only one to request admission to the International. Nothing was heard about other allegedly existing sections of the Alliance. Nevertheless, in spite of the constant intrigues of the Alliancists who sought to impose their special programme on the entire International and gain control of our Association, one was bound to accept that the Alliance had kept its word and disbanded itself. The General Council, however,[a] has received fairly clear indications which forced it to conclude that the Alliance had never dissolved and that, in spite of its solemn undertaking, it existed and was continuing to function as a secret society, using this underground organisation to realise its original aim—that of domination. Its existence, particularly in Spain, became increasingly apparent as a result of discord within the Alliance itself, an account of which is given below. For the moment, suffice it to say that a circular drawn up by members of the old Spanish Federal Council, who were at the same time members of the Central Committee of the Alliance in Spain (see *Emancipacion*, No. 61, p. 3, column 2, appendix No. 4),[183] exposed the existence of the Alliance.[b] The circular, dated June 2, 1872[c]

---

[a] Further the words "from May of this year" are crossed out in the manuscript.— *Ed.*

[b] Further the following is crossed out in the manuscript: "finding it impossible to reconcile their duties within the International with their position as members of a secret society within its ranks, on June 2 they addressed".— *Ed.*

[c] Error in the rough manuscript. As is evident from what follows the circular in question was published a fortnight after that of June 2, 1872.— *Ed.*

and published in the *Emancipacion* (No. 59, appendix No. 5), informed all the sections of the Alliance in Spain that the signatories had dissolved themselves as a section of the Alliance and invited other sections to follow their example.[184]

The publication of this circular caused the Alliance newspaper, the Barcelona *Federacion* (No. 155, August 4, 1872), to publish the rules of the Alliance (*appendix No. 6*), thus putting the existence of this society beyond question.

A comparison of the rules of the secret society with the rules presented by the Geneva section of the Alliance to the General Council shows, firstly, that the introductory programme to the first document is identical to that of the second. There are merely a few changes in wording, as a result of which Bakunin's special programme is given more succinct expression in the secret rules. Below is an exact table of:

Geneva rules		Secret rules
Art. 1	corresponds literally to	Art. 5
Art. 2	corresponds generally to	Art. 1
Art. 3	corresponds literally to	Art. 2
Arts. 4. & 5	correspond generally to	Art. 3
Art. 6	corresponds generally to	Art. 4

The secret rules themselves are based on the Geneva rules. Thus, Article 4 of the secret rules corresponds literally to Article 3 of the Geneva rules; Articles 8 and 9 in the Geneva rules correspond in abbreviated form to Article 10 of the secret rules, as do the Geneva Articles 15-20 to Article 3 of the secret rules.

Contrary to the actual practice of the Alliancists, the Geneva Article 7 advocates the "*strong* organisation" of the International and binds all members of the Alliance to "uphold ... the decisions of the Congresses and *the authority of the General Council*". This article is not to be found in the secret rules, but evidence of its original inclusion in these rules is provided by the fact that it is reproduced almost word for word in Article 15 of the regulations of the Madrid *sección de oficios varios*^a (appendix No. 7) which also includes the programme of the Alliance.

It is, therefore, clear that we are dealing with one and the same society and not with two separate societies. At the same time as the

---

^a Section combining various types of professions.— *Ed.*

Geneva Central Committee was assuring the General Council that the Alliance had been disbanded, and was admitted as a section of the International on the basis of this assurance, the ringleaders of this Central Committee led by M. Bakunin were strengthening the organisation of this same Alliance, turning it into a secret society and preserving that very international character which they had undertaken to abolish. The good faith of the General Council and of the whole International, to whom the correspondence had been submitted, was betrayed in a most disgraceful manner. Having once committed such a deception, these men were no longer held back by any scruples from their machinations to subordinate the International, or, if this were unsuccessful, to disorganise it.

Below we quote the main articles of the secret rules:

"1) The Alliance of Socialist Democracy *shall consist of members of the International Working Men's Association* and has as its aim the propaganda and development of the principles of *its* programme, and the study of all means suited to advance direct and *immediate* emancipation of the working class.

"2) In order to achieve the best possible results and not to compromise the development of social organisation, the Alliance shall be *entirely secret.*

"4) No person shall be admitted to membership if he has not accepted beforehand the principles of the programme completely and sincerely, etc.

"5) The Alliance shall do its utmost *to exert from within its influence on the local workers' federation* in order to prevent the latter from embarking on a reactionary or anti-revolutionary course.

"6)ª Any member *may be dismissed from membership of the Alliance* on a majority decision *without any reason being given.*"

Thus, the Alliance is a secret society formed within the International itself, having a programme of its own differing widely from that of the International, a society which has as its aim the propaganda of that programme which it considers to be the only true revolutionary one. The society binds its members to act in such a way inside their local federation of the International as to prevent it from embarking on a reactionary or anti-revolutionary course, i.e., from the slightest deviation from the programme of the Alliance. In other words, the aim of the Alliance is to impose its sectarian programme on the whole International by means of its secret organisation. This can be most effectively achieved by taking over the local and Federal Councils and the General Council, using the power of a secret organisation to elect members of the Alliance to these bodies. This was precisely what the Alliance did in cases where it felt that it had a good chance of success, as we shall see below.

ª In the manuscript mistakenly: "9".— *Ed.*

Clearly no one would wish to hold it against the Alliancists for propagating[a] their own programme. The International is composed of socialists of the most various shades of opinion. Its programme is sufficiently broad to accommodate all of them; the Bakuninist sect was admitted on the same conditions as all the others. The charge levelled against it is precisely its violation of these conditions.

The secret nature of the Alliance, however, is an entirely different matter. The International cannot ignore the fact that in many countries, Poland, France and Ireland among them, secret organisations are a legitimate means of defence against government terrorism. However, at its London Conference the International stated that it wished to remain completely dissociated from these societies and would not, consequently, recognise them as sections. Moreover, and this is the crucial point, we are dealing here with a secret society created for the purpose of combatting not a government, but the International itself.

The organisation of a secret society of this kind is a blatant violation, not only of the contractual obligations to the International, but also of the letter and spirit of our General Rules.[b] Our Rules know only one kind of members of the International with equal rights and duties for all. The Alliance separates them into two castes: the initiated and the uninitiated, the aristocracy and the plebs, the latter destined to be led by the first by means of an organisation whose very existence is unknown to them. The International demands of its members that they should acknowledge Truth, Justice and Morality as the basis of their conduct; the Alliance imposes upon its adepts, as their first duty, mendacity, dissimulation and imposture, by ordering them to deceive the uninitiated members of the International as to the existence of the secret organisation and to the motives and aims of their words and actions. The founders of the Alliance knew only too well that the vast majority of uninitiated members of the International would never consciously submit to such an organisation were they aware of its existence. This is why they made it "entirely secret". For it is essential to emphasise that the secret nature of this Alliance is not aimed at eluding government vigilance, otherwise it would not have begun its existence as a public society; this secret nature[c] had as its sole aim the deception of the uninitiated members of the

---

[a] Further the word "openly" is crossed out in the manuscript.— Ed.

[b] Further the words "and Regulations" are crossed out in the manuscript.— Ed.

[c] Further the following is crossed out in the manuscript: "as the facts have shown".— Ed.

International, proof of which is the base way in which the Alliance deceived the General Council. Thus we are dealing with a genuine conspiracy against the International. For the first time in the history of the working-class struggle, we stumble upon a secret conspiracy plotted in the midst of the working class, and intended to undermine, not the existing exploiting regime, but the very Association in which that regime finds its fiercest opponent.

Moreover, it would be ludicrous to assert that a society has made itself secret in order to protect itself from the persecution of existing governments, when that same society is everywhere advocating the emasculating doctrine of complete abstention from political action and states in its programme (Article 3, preamble to the secret rules) that it

"rejects any revolutionary action which does not have as its immediate and direct aim the triumph of the workers' cause over capital".

How then has this secret society acted within the International?

The reply to this question is already given in part in the private circular of the General Council entitled *Fictitious Splits etc.* But due to the fact that the General Council was not yet at that time aware of the actual size of the secret organisation, and in view of the many important events which have taken place subsequently, this reply can be regarded only as most incomplete.

Let it be said right from the start that the activities of the Alliance fall into two distinct phases. The first is characterised by the assumption that it would be successful in gaining control of the General Council and thereby securing supreme direction of our Association. It was at this stage that the Alliance urged its adherents to uphold the "strong organisation" of the International and, above all,

"the *authority* of the General Council and of the Federal Council and Central Committee";

and it was at this stage that gentlemen of the Alliance demanded at the Basle Congress that the General Council be invested with those wide powers which they later rejected with such horror as being *authoritarian.*

The Basle Congress destroyed, for the time being at least, the hopes nourished by the Alliance.[a] Since that time it has carried on

---

[a] Further the following is crossed out in the manuscript: "whose activities were reduced to local intrigue (described in detail in the private circular *Fictitious Splits*). It remained fairly quiet until the point ... when the London Conference re-affirmed the original programme of the International as opposed to that of the Alliance with its resolutions on working-class policy and sectarian sections." — *Ed.*

the intrigues referred to in the *Fictitious Splits*; in the Jura district of Switzerland, in Italy and in Spain it has not ceased to push forward its special programme in place of that of the International. The London Conference put an end to this misunderstanding with its resolutions on working-class policy and sectarian sections. The Alliance immediately went into action again. The Jura Federation, the stronghold of the Alliance in Switzerland, issued its Sonvillier circular[a] against the General Council, in which the strong organisation, the authority of the General Council and the Basle resolutions, both proposed and voted for by the very people who were signatories to the circular, were denounced as *authoritarian*—a definition that, apparently, sufficed to condemn them out of hand; in which mention was made of "war, the open war that has broken out in our ranks"; in which it was demanded that the International should assume the form of an organisation adapted, not to the struggle in hand, but to some vague ideal of a future society, etc. From this point onwards tactics changed. An order was issued. Wherever the Alliance had its branches, in Italy and particularly in Spain, the authoritarian resolutions of the Basle Congress and the London Conference, as also the authoritarianism of the General Council, were subjected to the most violent attacks. Now there was nothing but talk of the autonomy of sections, free federated groups, anarchy, etc. This is quite understandable. The influence of the secret society within the International would naturally increase as the public organisation of the International weakened. The most serious obstacle in the path of the Alliance was the General Council, and this was consequently the body which came in for the most bitter attacks, although, as we shall see, the Federal Councils also received the same treatment whenever a suitable opportunity presented itself.

The Jura circular had no effect whatsoever, except in those countries where the International was more or less influenced by the Alliance, namely, in Italy and Spain. In the latter the Alliance and the International were founded simultaneously, immediately after the Basle Congress. Even the most devoted members of the International in Spain were led to believe that the programme of the Alliance was identical to that of the International, that this secret organisation existed everywhere and that it was almost the duty of all to belong to it. This illusion was destroyed by the London Conference, where the Spanish delegate,[b] himself a

---

[a] *Circulaire à toutes les fédérations de l'Association Internationale des Travailleurs. Sonvillier, le 12 novembre 1871*, Geneva, 1871.— *Ed.*

[b] Anselmo Lorenzo.— *Ed.*

member of the Central Committee of the Alliance in his country, could convince himself that the contrary was the fact, and also by the Jura circular itself, whose bitter attacks and lies against the Conference and the General Council were immediately taken up by all the organs of the Alliance. The first result of the Jura circular in Spain was the emergence of disagreements within the Spanish Alliance itself between those who were first and foremost members of the International and those who would not recognise it, since it had not come under Alliance control. The struggle, at first carried on in private, soon flared up in public at meetings of the International. When the Federal Council which had been elected by the Valencia Conference (September 1871)[185] demonstrated by its actions that it preferred the International to the Alliance, the majority of its members was expelled from the local Madrid Federation, where the Alliance was in control.[186] They were reinstated by the Saragossa Congress and two of them,[a] Mora and Lorenzo, were re-elected to the new Federal Council,[b] in spite of the fact that all the members of the old Council had previously announced that they would not recognise it.[c]

The Saragossa Congress[187] gave rise to fears on the part of the ringleaders of the Alliance that Spain might slip out of their hands. The Alliance immediately began a campaign against the authority of the Spanish Federal Council, similar to that which the Jura circular had directed against the so-called authoritarian powers of the General Council. A thoroughly democratic and at the same time coherent form of organisation had been worked out in Spain by the Barcelona Congress[188] and the Valencia Conference. Thanks to the activity of the Federal Council elected in Valencia (activity which was approved by a special vote of the Congress), this organisation achieved the outstanding successes referred to in the general report.[d] Morago, the leading light of the Alliance in Spain, declared at Saragossa that the powers conferred on the Federal Council in the Spanish organisation were *au-*

---

[a] Further the following is crossed out in the manuscript: "its most active members".— *Ed.*

[b] Further the following is crossed out in the manuscript: "meeting in Valencia".— *Ed.*

[c] Further the following is crossed out in the manuscript: "The Congress had chosen Valencia for the seat of the Federal Council in the hope that it would prove to be neutral territory and that these disagreements would not break out afresh. However, three of the five members of the new Federal Council were henchmen of the Alliance and, as a result of co-option, their number increased to at least five. On the other hand, the Alliance, fearing lest the leadership [...]".— *Ed.*

[d] See this volume, pp. 219-27.— *Ed.*

thoritarian, that it was essential to restrict them, and to deprive the Council of the right to accept or reject new sections and decide whether their rules were in accordance with the rules of the federation, in short, to reduce its role to that of a mere correspondence and statistics bureau. After rejecting Morago's proposals, the Congress resolved to preserve the existing authoritarian form of organisation (see *Estracto de las actas del segundo congreso obrero,* etc.,[a] pp. 109 and 110, appendix No. 8.[189] The relevant evidence given by Citizen Lafargue, a delegate to the Saragossa Congress, will be of great importance).

In order to isolate the new Federal Council from the disagreements, which had arisen in Madrid, the Congress transferred it to Valencia. However, the cause of the disagreements, namely, the antagonism, which had begun to develop between the Alliance and the International, was not of a local nature. Unaware even of the existence of the Alliance, the Congress set up a new Council composed entirely of members of that society; two of them, Mora and Lorenzo, opposed it and Mora refused a seat on the Council. The General Council's circular *Fictitious Splits,* which was a reply to the Jura circular, obliged all members of the International to make an open statement of their allegiance either to the International or to the Alliance. The polemics between *Emancipacion* on the one hand and the Alliance newspapers, the Barcelona *Federacion* and the Seville *Razon,* on the other, became increasingly virulent. Finally, on June 2 the members of the former Federal Council—the editors of the *Emancipacion* and members of the Spanish Central Committee of the Alliance—decided to address a circular to all the Spanish sections of the Alliance, in which they announced their dissolution as a section of the secret society and called on other sections to follow their example. Vengeance followed swiftly. They were immediately expelled again from the local Madrid Federation in flagrant violation of the existing regulations. Following this, they reorganised themselves into a New Madrid Federation and requested recognition from the Federal Council.

However, in the meantime the Alliancist element in the Council, strengthened by co-option, had gained complete control, causing Lorenzo to resign. The request of the New Madrid Federation met with a blank refusal on the part of the Federal Council, which was already concentrating all its efforts on ensuring the election of

---

[a] *Estracto de las actas del segundo Congreso Obrero de la Federacion regional Española, celebrado en Zaragoza en los dias 4 al 11 de abril de 1872, segun las actas y las notas tomadas por la comisión nombrada al efecto en el mismo,* Valencia, 1872.— *Ed.*

Alliance candidates to the Congress at The Hague. To this end the Council sent a private circular to local federations dated July 7, in which, repeating the slanderous remarks of the *Federacion* concerning the General Council, it proposed that the federations should send to the Congress a single delegation from the whole of Spain elected by a majority vote, the list of those elected to be drawn up by the Council itself. (Appendix No. 9.) It is obvious to anyone familiar with the secret society existing within the International in Spain that such a procedure would have meant the election of Alliance men to attend the Congress on funds provided by members of the International. As soon as the General Council, which was not sent a copy of the circular, got to know of these facts,[a] it addressed a letter dated July 24 to the Spanish Federal Council, which is attached as an appendix (No. 10).[b] The Federal Council[c] replied on August 1 to the effect that it would require time in order to translate our letter which had been written in French, and on August 3 it addressed an evasive reply to the General Council published in the *Federacion* (appendix No. 11). In this reply it sided with the Alliance. On receipt of the letter of August 1, the General Council had already published the correspondence in the *Emancipacion*.

It must be added that as soon as the secret organisation was discovered it was claimed that the Alliance had already been dissolved at the Saragossa Congress. The Central Committee had not, however, been informed to this effect (appendix No. 4).

The New Madrid Federation denies this, and it should have known. In general, the claim that the Spanish section of an international society such as the Alliance could dissolve itself without first consulting the other national sections is patently absurd.

Immediately after this the Alliance attempted a coup d'état. Realising that it would not be able to secure itself an artificial majority at the Hague Congress by means of the same manoeuvres employed at Basle and La Chaux-de-Fonds,[190] the Alliance took advantage of the Conference held at Rimini[d] by the self-styled Italian Federation in order to make a public announcement of the

---

[a] Further the following is crossed out in the manuscript: "this was the very moment when it received the first irrefutable evidence of the existence of the secret organisation".— *Ed.*

[b] See this volume, pp. 211-13.— *Ed.*

[c] Further the following is crossed out in the manuscript: "at first trying to gain time under the pretext that the translation".— *Ed.*

[d] See this volume, p. 216.— *Ed.*

split. The Conference delegates passed a unanimous resolution (see appendix No. 12). Thus the Congress of the Alliance stood in opposition to that of the International. However, it was soon realised that this plan had no chance of success. It was abandoned, and the decision was taken to go to The Hague, with the very same Italian sections, of which *only one* out of twenty-one belongs to our Association, having the audacity to send their delegates to the Hague Congress which they had already rejected!

Considering:

1) That the Alliance (the main organ of which is the Central Committee of the Jura Federation), founded and led by M. Bakunin, is a society hostile to the International, insofar as it aims at dominating or disorganising the latter;

2) That as a consequence of the foregoing the International and the Alliance are incompatible;

The Congress resolves:

1) That M. Bakunin and all the present members of the Alliance of Socialist Democracy be expelled from the International Working Men's Association and be granted readmission to it only after a public renunciation of all connections with this secret society;

2) That the Jura Federation be expelled as such from the International.

Written in late August 1872

First published in: Marx and Engels, *Works*, First Russian Edition, Vol. XIII, Part II, Moscow, 1940

Printed according to the rough manuscript

Translated from the French

Frederick Engels

[MOTION FOR THE PROCEDURE OF DEBATE ON THE GENERAL RULES AND ADMINISTRATIVE REGULATIONS] [191]

I propose to begin discussion of the second chapter of the Administrative Regulations concerning the General Council and, after that, of Articles 3, 4, 5 and 6 of the Rules dealing with the same subject.

F. Engels

Submitted to the Hague Congress on September 6, 1872

First published, in Russian, in *Gaagsky kongress Pervogo Internatsionala. 2-7 sentyabrya 1872. Protokoly i dokumenty,* Moscow, 1970

Printed according to the manuscript

Translated from the French

Karl Marx and Frederick Engels

[PROPOSAL ON THE TRANSFER OF THE SEAT AND ON THE COMPOSITION OF THE GENERAL COUNCIL FOR 1872-1873] [192]

We propose that the General Council for 1872-1873 be transferred to New York and be composed of the following members of the North American Federal Council: *Kavanagh, Saint Clair, Cetti, Levièle, Laurel, F. J. Bertrand, F. Bolte*, and *C. Carl.* It shall have the right to co-opt new members, but its total membership shall not exceed 15.

> *Karl Marx, F. Engels, Geo. Sexton, Walery Wróblewski, Ch. Longuet, A. Serraillier, J. P. MacDonnell, Eugène Dupont, F. Lessner, Le Moussu, M. Maltman Barry*[a]

The Hague, September 6, 1872

Submitted to the Hague Congress on September 6, 1872

First published in [E. Vaillant,] *Internationale et révolution. À propos du congrès de La Haye*, London, 1872

Printed according to the manuscript written by Marx

Translated from the French

---

[a] All the signatures are handwritten.— *Ed.*

Nous proposons que pour l'an 1872–73 le siège du Conseil Général soit transféré à New York et qu'il soit composé des ... membres suivants du Conseil Fédéral pour l'Amérique du Nord: Kavanagh, M. Clair, Laddi, Lawiele, Lawrel, F.J Bertrand, E. Bolte, et ... Carl ... Ils auront le droit d'adjonction (trois voix) des ... membres total ... Des membres du Conseil Général réescadera jusqu'au ... 15. —

La Haye
6 Sept., 1872

Karl Marx   F. Engels
Maurice Wickersheim   Geo. Eccarius
A. Serraillier   Ch. Longuet
                J.P. M'Donnell
                Le Moussu
Eugène Dupont
                M. Maltman Barry

Facsimile of Marx's manuscript with a proposal to transfer the seat of the General Council to New York

Karl Marx and Frederick Engels

RESOLUTIONS OF THE GENERAL CONGRESS HELD AT THE HAGUE

FROM THE 2nd TO THE 7th SEPTEMBER, 1872 [193]

I

RESOLUTION RELATIVE TO THE GENERAL RULES

The following article which resumes the contents of Resolution IX of the Conference of London (September 1871) to be inserted in the Rules after Article 7, viz.: —

Article 7a.—In its struggle against the collective power of the propertied classes, the working class cannot act as a class except by constituting itself into a political party, distinct from, and opposed to, all old parties formed by the propertied classes.

This constitution of the working class into a political party is indispensable in order to insure the triumph of the social revolution, and of its ultimate end, the abolition of classes.

The combination of forces which the working class has already effected by its economical struggles ought, at the same time, to serve as a lever for its struggles against the political power of landlords and capitalists.[a]

The lords of land and the lords of capital will always use their political privileges for the defence and perpetuation of their economical monopolies, and for the enslavement of labour. The conquest of political power has therefore become the great duty of the working class.

Adopted by 29 votes against 5, and 8 abstentions.[b]

---

[a] The French edition has here "its exploiters" instead of "landlords and capitalists".— *Ed.*

[b] The French text of the resolutions continues as follows:

"Voted for: Arnaud, J. Ph. Becker, B. Becker, Cournet, Dereure, Dumont, Dupont, Duval, Eccarius, Engels, Farkas, Friedländer, Frankel, Hepner, Heim, Johannard, Kugelmann, Lafargue, Longuet, Le Moussu, Mottershead, Pihl, Ranvier, Serraillier, Sorge, Swarm, Vaillant, Wilmot, MacDonnel.

"Voted against: Brismée, Coenen, Gerhard, Schwitzguébel, Van der Hout.

II

RESOLUTIONS RELATING
TO THE ADMINISTRATIVE REGULATIONS

1. Powers of the General Council.

Articles II, 2 and 6 have been replaced by the following articles:—

"*Article 2.*—The General Council is bound to execute the Congress Resolutions, and to take care that in every country the principles and the General Rules and Regulations of the International are strictly observed.

"*Article 6.*—The General Council has also the right to suspend Branches, Sections, Federal Councils or committees, and federations of the International, till the meeting of the next Congress.

"Nevertheless, in the case of sections belonging to a federation, the General Council will exercise this right only after having consulted the respective Federal Council.

"In the case of the dissolution of a Federal Council, the General Council shall, at the same time, call upon the Sections of the respective Federation to elect a new Federal Council within 30 days at most.

"In the case of the suspension of an entire federation, the General Council shall immediately inform thereof the whole of the federations. If the majority of them demand it, the General Council shall convoke an extraordinary conference, composed of one delegate for each nationality, which shall meet within one month and finally decide upon the question.

"Nevertheless, it is well understood that the countries where the International is prohibited shall exercise the same rights as the regular federations."

Article 2 was adopted by 40 votes against 4; abstentions, 11.[a]

"Abstained: Van den Abeele, Dave, Eberhardt, Fluse, Guillaume, Herman, Sauva, Marselau.

"The Congress officially decided to recognise as valid the votes of the delegates who could not attend the sitting because of their work in commissions. The following delegates voted for: Cuno, Lucain, Marx, Vichard, Walter, Wróblewski; 6 in all. Not a vote against."

In Engels' manuscript the following passage is crossed out: "As the resolution obtained more than two-thirds of the votes, according to Article 12 of the General Rules, it henceforth becomes part of the General Rules."—*Ed.*

[a] The French text of the resolutions continues as follows:

"Voted for: Arnaud, Barry, J. Ph. Becker, B. Becker, Cournet, Cuno, Dereure, Dumont, Dupont, Duval, Engels, Farkas, Frankel, Friedländer, Hepner, Heim, Johannard, Kugelmann, Lafargue, Lessner, Le Moussu, Longuet, Lucain, MacDon-

2. Contributions to be paid to the General Council:—With regard to the proposal, on the one hand to raise, on the other to reduce, the amount of their contributions, the Congress had to decide whether the actual amount of 1d.[a] per annum, should be altered or not. The Congress maintained the penny by 17 votes against 12, and 8 abstentions.[b]

III

RESOLUTIONS RELATING TO THE INTERNATIONALISATION OF TRADES' SOCIETIES[c]

The new General Council is entrusted with the special mission to establish International trades unions.

For this purpose it will, within the month following this Congress, draw up a circular which shall be translated and published in all languages, and forwarded to all trades' societies whose addresses are known, whether they are affiliated to the International or not.

---

nell, Marx, Milke, Pihl, Ranvier, Roach, Sauva, Scheu, Serraillier, Sexton, Sorge, Swarm, Schumacher, Vaillant, Vichard, Walter, Wróblewski.

"Voted against: Fluse, Gerhard, Splingard, Van der Hout.

"Abstained: Alerini, Coenen, Dave, Eberhardt, Guillaume, Herman, Morago, Marselau, Farga Pellicer, Schwitzguébel, Van den Abeele.

"Article 6—adopted by 36 votes against 6, abstentions, 16.

"Voted for: Arnaud, Barry, J. Ph. Becker, B. Becker, Cournet, Cuno, Dereure, Dupont, Duval, Engels, Farkas, Frankel, Friedländer, Hepner, Heim, Johannard, Kugelmann, Lafargue, Lessner, Le Moussu, Longuet, Ludwig, MacDonnell, Marx, Milke, Pihl, Ranvier, Serraillier, Schumacher, Sexton, Sorge, Swarm, Vaillant, Vichard, Walter, Wróblewski.

"Voted against: Brismée, Coenen, Fluse, Herman, Sauva, Splingard.

"Abstained: Alerini, Cyrille, Dave, Dumont, Eberhardt, Guillaume, Lucain, Marselau, Morago, Mottershead, Farga Pellicer, Roach, Schwitzguébel, Van den Abeele, Van der Hout, Wilmot."—Ed.

a The French text has "10 centimes" here and below.—Ed.

b The French text of the resolutions continues as follows:

"Voted against the contribution being altered: J. Ph. Becker, Brismée, Coenen, Cyrille, Dupont, Duval, Eberhardt, Eccarius, Farkas, Fluse, Gerhard, Herman, Hepner, Serraillier, Sorge, Swarm, Wilmot.

"Voted for the contribution being altered: Dumont, Engels, Frankel, Heim, Johannard, Lafargue, Le Moussu, Longuet, Lucain, MacDonnell, Pihl, Sauva.

"Abstained: Alerini, Dave, Dereure, Guillaume, Marselau, Morago, Farga Pellicer, Schwitzguébel.

"The following delegates, obliged to leave The Hague before this question was discussed, handed in their vote in writing for the raising of the contribution: Arnaud, Cournet, Ranvier, Vaillant."—Ed.

c The French text has here "societies of resistance" instead of "trades' societies".—Ed.

In this circular every Union[a] shall be called upon to enter into an International union of its respective trade.

Every Union[a] shall be invited to fix itself the conditions under which it proposes to enter the International Union of its trade.

The General Council shall, from the conditions fixed by the Unions,[b] adopting the idea of International union, draw up a general plan, and submit it to the provisional acceptance of the Societies.[c]

The next Congress will finally settle the fundamental treaty for the International trades unions.

(Voted unanimously minus a few abstentions, the number of which has not been stated in the minutes.)

IV

RESOLUTIONS RELATING
TO THE ADMISSION OF SECTIONS[d]

1. *Section 2* (New York, French) *of the North American Federation.*—This Section had been excluded by the American Federal Council. On the other hand, it had not been recognised as an independent Section by the General Council. It was not admitted by the Congress. Voted against the admission, 38; for, 9; abstained, 11.

2. *Section 12* (New York, American) *of the North American Federation.*—Suspended by the General Council.[e]

In the course of the debate on the credentials of Section 12, the following resolution was adopted by 47 votes against 0; abstentions, 9:

"The International Working Men's Association, based upon the principle of the abolition of classes, cannot admit any middle class Sections."[f]

---

[a] The French text has here "trades' society" instead of "Union".—*Ed.*

[b] The French text has here "societies" instead of "Unions".—*Ed.*

[c] The French text adds here: "which would wish to enter the International trades unions".—*Ed.*

[d] In the French edition, item 1 is preceded by the following text:

"The Mandate Commission was composed as follows: Gerhard (50 votes), Ranvier (44), Roach (41), Marx (41), MacDonnell (39), Dereure (36), Frankel (22)."—*Ed.*

[e] See this volume, p. 125.—*Ed.*

[f] After this the French text of the resolutions has:

"Voted for: Arnaud, J. Ph. Becker, Barry, Brismée, Cournet, Cuno, Coenen, Dave, Dereure, Dietzgen, Dupont, Duval, Eberhardt, Fluse, Farkas, Frankel,

Section 12 was excluded by 49 votes against 0; abstentions, 9.[a]

3. *Section of Marseilles.*—This Section, quite unknown to the General Council, and to the French Sections in correspondence with the latter, is not admitted. Against the admission, 38; for, 0; abstentions, 14.

4. *Section of Propaganda and Revolutionary Action, at Geneva.*— This Section, which is but the resurrection of the (public) "Alliance de la Démocratie Socialiste", of Geneva, dissolved in August 1871, had been recognised neither by the Romance Federal Committee nor by the General Council, which, indeed, had returned its contributions when sent by the Jurassian Federal Committee. The Congress resolved to suspend it till after the debate on the second[b] *Alliance.* The suspension was voted unanimously, less a few abstentions not counted.

5. *New Federation of Madrid.*—The new Federation of Madrid was formed by the members of the previous Spanish Federal Council, after the old Federation of Madrid, in flagrant breach of the rules then in force, had expelled them for having denounced the conspiracy of the secret alliance against the International Working Men's Association. They addressed themselves, in the first instance, to the Spanish Federal Council, which refused to affiliate the new Federation. They then addressed themselves to the General Council,[c] which took upon itself the responsibility of

---

Friedländer, Guillaume, Gerhard, Heim, Hepner, Herman, Johannard, Kugelmann, Lafargue, Le Moussu, Lessner, Lucain, Marx, Milke, Mottershead, Pihl, Ranvier, Sauva, Scheu, Schumacher, Serraillier, Sexton, Sorge, Splingard, Swarm, Vaillant, Vichard, Wilmot, Wróblewski, Walter, Van den Abeele.

"Abstained: Alerini, Eccarius, Harcourt, Marselau, Morago, Farga Pellicer, Roach, Schwitzguébel, Van der Hout."— *Ed.*

[a] After this the French text of the resolutions has:

"Voted for the exclusion: Arnaud, Barry, J. Ph. Becker, Brismée, Cournet, Coenen, Cuno, Dave, Dereure, Dietzgen, Dumont, Dupont, Duval, Eberhardt, Fluse, Farkas, Frankel, Friedländer, Gerhard, Heim, Hepner, Herman, Johannard, Kugelmann, Lafargue, Le Moussu, Lessner, Lucain, MacDonnell, Marx, Milke, Pihl, Ranvier, Roach, Sauva, Scheu, Schumacher, Serraillier, Sexton, Sorge, Splingard, Swarm, Vaillant, Van den Abeele, Van der Hout, Vichard, Wilmot, Wróblewski, Walter.

"Abstained: Alerini, Eccarius, Guillaume, Harcourt, Marselau, Morago, Farga Pellicer, Mottershead, Schwitzguébel."— *Ed.*

[b] The French text has "secret" instead of "second". Further the following passage is crossed out in Engels' manuscript: "Forced to stop its work right after this discussion, the Congress has not decided this question."— *Ed.*

[c] In Engels' manuscript the following passage is crossed out: "which recognised it without first asking the Spanish Federal Council, as is laid down in the Administrative Rules. In this case, the General Council was acting on its own

recognising it[a] without consulting the Spanish Council, amongst whose eight members not less than five belonged to the Alliance.

The Congress admitted this Federation by 40 votes against 0; the few abstentions were not counted.

V

AUDIT OF THE ACCOUNTS OF THE GENERAL COUNCIL

The Committee appointed by the Congress for the auditing of the accounts of the General Council for the year 1871-72, was composed of the following citizens:—Dumont, for France; Alerini, for Spain; Farkas, for Austria and Hungary; Brismée, for Belgium; Lafargue, for the new Federation of Madrid and for Portugal; Pihl, for Denmark; J. Ph. Becker, for German Switzerland; Duval, for the Romance Swiss Federation; Schwitzguébel, for the Jurassian Swiss Federation; Dave, for Holland; Dereure, for America; and Cuno, for Germany.

The accounts submitted to this Committee were approved and signed by all its members excepting Dave, absent.

The accounts having been read, the Congress approved of them by a unanimous vote.

VI

POWERS ISSUED BY THE GENERAL COUNCIL, AND BY FEDERAL COUNCILS

The Congress resolved, "To annul all powers issued, as well by the General Council as by any of the Federal Councils, to members of the International in such countries where the Association is prohibited, and to reserve to the new General Council the exclusive right of appointing, in those countries, the plenipotentiaries of the International Working Men's Association."

Adopted unanimously, less a few abstentions not specially counted.

---

responsibility and despite of the Regulations, because the Spanish Federal Council had at least 5 secret Alliance members amongst its 8 members. It was for disclosing this conspiracy against the International Working Men's Association that they wanted to ban the New Madrid Federation."— Ed.

[a] See this volume, p. 215.— Ed.

VII

RESOLUTIONS RELATING TO THE ALLIANCE

The Committee charged with the inquiry regarding the (second[a]) Alliance of Socialist Democracy, consisted of the citizens— Cuno (33 votes), Lucain (24), Splingard (31), Vichard (30), and Walter (29).

In its report to the Congress, the majority of this Committee declared that "the secret Alliance was established with rules entirely opposed to those of the International". It proposed:—

"To exclude from the International Michael Bakounine, as founder of the Alliance, and for a personal affair.

"To exclude Guillaume and Schwitzguébel, as members of the Alliance.

"To exclude B. Malon, Bousquet* (Secretary of Police at Béziers, France), and Louis Marchand, as convicted of acts aiming at the disorganisation of the International Working Men's Association.

"To withdraw the charges against Alerini, Marselau, Morago, Farga Pellicer, and Joukowski, upon their formal declaration that they no longer belong to the Alliance.

"To authorise the Committee to publish the documents upon which their conclusions were based."

The Congress resolved—

"1. To exclude Michael Bakounine. Voted for, 27; against, 6; abstentions, 7.[b]

"2. To exclude Guillaume. 25 for, 9 against, 8 abstentions.[c]

---

* The Committee was not acquainted with the fact that M. Bousquet, upon the demands of his Section, had already been excluded by a formal vote of the General Council.

---

[a] The French text has here "secret" instead of "second".— Ed.

[b] The French text of the resolutions continues as follows:

"Voted for: J. Ph. Becker, Cuno, Dereure, Dumont, Dupont, Duval, Engels, Farkas, Frankel, Heim, Hepner, Johannard, Kugelmann, Lafargue, Le Moussu, Longuet, Lucain, MacDonnell, Marx, Pihl, Serraillier, Sorge, Swarm, Vichard, Wilmot, Walter, Wróblewski.

"Voted against: Brismée, Dave, Fluse, Herman, Coenen, Van den Abeele.

"Abstained: Alerini, Guillaume, Marselau, Morago, Sauva, Splingard, Schwitzguébel."— Ed.

[c] The French text of the resolutions continues as follows:

"Voted for: J. Ph. Becker, Cuno, Dumont, Dupont, Duval, Engels, Farkas, Frankel, Heim, Hepner, Johannard, Kugelmann, Lafargue, Le Moussu, Longuet, Lucain, Marx, Pihl, Serraillier, Sorge, Swarm, Vichard, Walter, Wilmot, Wróblewski.

"Voted against: Brismée, Cyrille, Dave, Fluse, Herman, Coenen, Sauva, Splingard, Van den Abeele.

"3. Not to exclude Schwitzguébel. For exclusion 15; against 16; abstentions, 7.[a]

"4. To refrain from voting upon the other exclusions proposed by the Committee. Adopted unanimously, minus some few abstentions.

"5. To publish the documents relating to the Alliance. Adopted unanimously, minus some few abstentions."

It is to be noted that these votes upon the Alliance were taken after a great number of French[b] and German delegates had been obliged to leave.

VIII

RESIDENCE AND COMPOSITION OF THE NEXT GENERAL COUNCIL

1. Vote upon the change of residence of the General Council. Voted for the change, 26; against, 23; abstentions, 9.[c]

2. The seat of the General Council has been transferred to New York, by 30 votes against 14, for London, and 12 abstentions.[d]

"Abstained: Alerini, Dereure, Friedländer, MacDonnell, Marselau, Morago, Farga Pellicer, Schwitzguébel."— Ed.

[a] The French text of the resolutions continues as follows:
"Voted for the exclusion: J. Ph. Becker, Cuno, Dumont, Engels, Farkas, Heim, Hepner, Kugelmann, Le Moussu, Marx, Pihl, Splingard, Walter, Vichard, Wróblewski.

"Voted against: Brismée, Coenen, Cyrille, Dave, Dereure, Dupont, Fluse, Frankel, Herman, Johannard, Longuet, Sauva, Serraillier, Swarm, Wilmot, Van den Abeele.

"Abstained: Duval, Lafargue, Lucain, MacDonnell, Marselau, Morago, Farga Pellicer."

In the French text the number of those who voted against is 17.— Ed.

[b] Engels' manuscript has here "French, English".— Ed.

[c] The French text of the resolutions continues as follows:
"Voted for: Barry, J. Ph. Becker, Brismée, Cuno, Dave, Dumont, Dupont, Engels, Harcourt, Johannard, Kugelmann, Lafargue, Lessner, Le Moussu, Longuet, MacDonnell, Marx, Roach, Sauva, Serraillier, Sexton, Sorge, Swarm, Vichard, Van den Abeele, Wróblewski.

"Voted against: Arnaud, B. Becker, Cournet, Dereure, Duval, Farkas, Frankel, Friedländer, Gerhard, Heim, Hepner, Herman, Lucain, Ludwig, Milke, Pihl, Ranvier, Schumacher, Splingard, Vaillant, Wilmot, Walter, Van der Hout.

"Abstained: Cyrille, Eberhardt, Fluse, Guillaume, Marselau, Morago, Farga Pellicer, Schwitzguébel, Alerini."— Ed.

[d] The French text of the resolutions continues as follows:
"Voted for New York: J. Ph. Becker, B. Becker, Brismée, Cuno, Coenen, Dave, Dumont, Dupont, Engels, Farkas, Fluse, Friedländer, Herman, Kugelmann, Lafargue, Lessner, Le Moussu, Longuet, Lucain, MacDonnell, Marx, Pihl, Roach, Serraillier, Sexton, Splingard, Swarm, Vichard, Van den Abeele, Wróblewski.

Page of the manuscript of the Hague Congress resolutions

3. The Congress resolved to appoint twelve members, residing in New York, to the General Council, with the faculty of adding them[a] to that number. The following were elected:—

	Votes		Votes
Bertrand (German)	29	Carl (German)	28
Bolte (German)	29	David (French)	26
Laurel (Swede)	29	Dereure (French)	26
Kavanagh (Irish)	29	Fornaccieri (Italian)	25
Saint Clair (Irish)	29	Speyer (German)	23
Levièle (French)	28	Ward (American)	22

IX

PLACE OF MEETING OF NEXT CONGRESS

The proposition that the new Congress should meet in Switzerland, and that the new General Council should determine in what town, was adopted. There voted for Switzerland 15, for London 5, for Chicago 1, and for Spain 1.

X

COMMITTEE TO DRAW UP THE MINUTES

The following were appointed, without opposition:— Dupont, Engels, Frankel, Le Moussu, Marx and Serraillier.

Committee { *E. Dupont, F. Engels, Leó Frankel, Le Moussu, Karl Marx, Auguste Serraillier*

London, 21st October, 1872

First published as a pamphlet: *Résolutions du congrès général tenu à la Haye du 2 au 7 septembre 1872*. London, 1872, and in the newspapers *La Emancipacion*, No. 72, November 2, 1872, and *The International Herald*, No. 37, December 14, 1872

Reproduced from the text of *The International Herald* checked with Engels' manuscript and the pamphlet

"Voted for London: Arnaud, Cournet, Dereure, Duval, Frankel, Heim, Hepner, Ludwig, Milke, Ranvier, Schumacher, Vaillant, Wilmot, Walter.

"Abstained: Cyrille, Eberhardt, Gerhard, Guillaume, Johannard, Alerini, Marselau, Morago, Farga Pellicer, Sorge, Schwitzguébel, Van der Hout."

In the French text the number of the abstained is 13.— *Ed.*

[a] The French text has here "three other members" instead of "them".— *Ed.*

Karl Marx

ON THE HAGUE CONGRESS

[A CORRESPONDENT'S REPORT OF A SPEECH MADE AT A MEETING IN AMSTERDAM ON SEPTEMBER 8, 1872] [194]

In the 18th century the kings and potentates were in the habit of assembling at The Hague to discuss the interests of their dynasties.

It is there that we decided to hold our workers' congress despite the attempts to intimidate us. In the midst of the most reactionary population we wanted to affirm the existence, the spreading and hopes for the future of our great Association.

When our decision became known, there was talk of emissaries we had sent to prepare the ground. Yes, we have emissaries everywhere, we do not deny it, but the majority of them are unknown to us. Our emissaries in The Hague were the workers, whose labour is so exhausting, just as in Amsterdam they are workers too, workers who toil for sixteen hours a day. Those are our emissaries, we have no others; and in all the countries in which we make an appearance we find them ready to welcome us, for they understand very quickly that the aim we pursue is the improvement of their lot.

The Hague Congress has achieved three main things:

It has proclaimed the necessity for the working classes to fight the old disintegrating society in the political as well as the social field; and we see with satisfaction that henceforth this resolution of the London Conference will be included in our Rules.[a]

A group has been formed in our midst which advocates that the workers should abstain from political activity.

We regard it as our duty to stress how dangerous and fatal we considered those principles to be for our cause.

---

[a] See this volume, p. 243.— *Ed.*

One day the worker will have to seize political supremacy to establish the new organisation of labour; he will have to overthrow the old policy which supports the old institutions if he wants to escape the fate of the early Christians who, neglecting and despising politics, never saw their kingdom on earth.

But we by no means claimed that the means for achieving this goal were identical everywhere.

We know that the institutions, customs and traditions in the different countries must be taken into account; and we do not deny the existence of countries like America, England, and if I knew your institutions better I might add Holland, where the workers may achieve their aims by peaceful means. That being true we must also admit that in most countries on the Continent it is force which must be the lever of our revolution; it is force which will have to be resorted to for a time in order to establish the rule of the workers.[a]

The Hague Congress has endowed the General Council with new and greater powers. Indeed, at a time when the kings are assembling in Berlin and when from this meeting of powerful representatives of feudalism and the past there must result new and more severe measures of repression against us [195]; at a time when persecution is being organised, the Hague Congress rightly believed that it was wise and necessary to increase the powers of its General Council and to centralise, in view of the impending struggle, activity which isolation would render impotent. And, by the way, who but our enemies could take alarm at the authority of the General Council? Has it a bureaucracy and an armed police to ensure that it is obeyed? Is not its authority solely moral, and does it not submit its decisions to the Federations which have to carry them out? In these conditions, kings, with no army, no police, no magistracy, and reduced to having to maintain their power by moral influence and authority, would be feeble obstacles to the progress of the revolution.

Finally, the Hague Congress transferred the seat of the General Council to New York. Many, even of our friends, seemed to be surprised at such a decision. Are they then forgetting that America is becoming the world of workers *par excellence*; that every year half a million men, workers, emigrate to that other continent, and that the International must vigorously take root in that soil where the worker predominates? Moreover, the decision

---

[a] In place of this sentence *Der Volksstaat* has: "But this is not the case in all countries." — *Ed.*

taken by the Congress gives the General Council the right to co-opt those members whom it judges necessary and useful for the good of the common cause. Let us rely on its wisdom to choose men equal to the task and able to carry with a steady hand the banner of our Association in Europe.

Citizens, let us bear in mind this fundamental principle of the International: solidarity! It is by establishing this life-giving principle on a reliable base among all the workers in all countries that we shall achieve the great aim which we pursue. The revolution must display solidarity, and we find a great example of this in the Paris Commune,[a] which fell because there did not appear in all the centres, in Berlin, Madrid, etc., a great revolutionary movement corresponding to this supreme uprising of the Paris proletariat.

For my part I will persist in my task and will constantly work to establish among the workers this solidarity which will bear fruit for the future. No, I am not withdrawing from the International, and the rest of my life will be devoted, like my efforts in the past, to the triumph of the social ideas which one day, be sure of it, will bring about the universal rule of the proletariat.

First published in *La Liberté*, No. 37, September 15, 1872; *La Emancipacion*, No. 66, September 21, 1872; *Der Volksstaat*, No. 79, October 2, 1872

Printed according to *La Liberté* checked with *Der Volksstaat*

Translated from the French

---

[a] In *Der Volksstaat* the end of the sentence reads as follows: "which only fell because precisely this solidarity was lacking in the workers of the other countries".— *Ed.*

Karl Marx

TO THE EDITOR OF *LE CORSAIRE*[196]

Dear Sir,

The *Figaro* of September 11 reproduces a conversation which I am alleged to have had with the correspondent of the *Soir*.[a] The *Figaro*-type press can allow itself any calumny without anybody taking the trouble to point it out, but when the mercenary imagination of a correspondent goes so far as to put in my mouth grave accusations against my friends of the ex-General Council, I feel bound to say that he has violated all the rules of truth in daring to claim to have exchanged a single word with me.

I profit by this opportunity to let our friends and enemies know that I never dreamed of resigning from the International and that the transfer of the General Council to New York was proposed by me and several other members of the previous General Council.

It is false to report that Bakunin and his acolyte Guillaume were expelled as heads of a so-called federalist party. The expulsion of Bakunin and Guillaume was motivated by the creation within our Association of a secret society, the *Alliance of Socialist Democracy*, which claimed to direct the International to aims contrary to its principles.

The resolution of the London Conference on the political action of the working class was approved by the great majority of the Congress, and its insertion in the General Rules was voted.[b]

---

[a] "On continue à ne pas voir...", *Le Figaro*, September 11, 1872. The article is signed ". ' .".— *Ed.*

[b] See this volume, p. 243.— *Ed.*

The working-class public of The Hague and Amsterdam were most sympathetic towards the Congress.

So much for the value of the reports in the reactionary press.

Yours sincerely,

Karl Marx

The Hague, September 12, 1872

First published in *Le Corsaire*, September 15, 1872; *Gazzettino Rosa*, No. 260, September 18, 1872; *La Emancipacion*, No. 66, September 21, 1872; *Il Popolino*, No. 19, September 22, 1872

Printed according to *Le Corsaire*

Translated from the French

Karl Marx

TO THE EDITOR OF *THE DAILY NEWS*

Sir,—On my return from The Hague, I find that your paper attributes to me the intention of removing to New York, in the wake of the General Council of the I.W.A.[a] In reply, I beg to state that I intend and always intended remaining in London. Months ago I communicated to my friends here in London, and to my correspondents on the Continent, my firm resolve not to remain a member of the General Council, or indeed of any administrative body whatsoever, as my scientific labours would not permit me to do so any longer. As to the distorted reports of the press about the proceedings of the Congress at The Hague, they will be set at rest by the impending publication of the official Congress Minutes.[197]

I am, Sir, your obedient servant,

Karl Marx

Modena Villas,
Maitland Park, N.W.
September 17

First published in *The Daily News,* No. 8235, September 18, 1872

Reproduced from the newspaper

---

[a] "The New Constitution of the International", *The Daily News*, No. 8230, September 12, 1872.—*Ed.*

Frederick Engels

ON THE HAGUE CONGRESS
OF THE INTERNATIONAL[198]

[*Der Volksstaat*, No. 78, September 28, 1872]

The Congress comprised 64 delegates, sixteen of whom represented France, ten Germany, seven Belgium, five England, five North America, four Holland, four Spain, three the Romance Federation of Switzerland, two the Jura Federation of Switzerland, one Ireland, one Portugal, one Poland, one Austria, one Hungary, one Australia, and two Denmark. A number of them held mandates from two or three countries, so that the distribution given above is not quite accurate. According to their country of origin twenty of them were French, sixteen Germans, eight Belgians, six English, three Dutch, three Spanish, two Swiss, two Hungarian, one Polish, one Irish, one Danish, one Corsican.[199] At no previous congress had so many nations been represented.

The verification of the mandates took nearly three days. The reason for this was that the affiliation of various Sections to the International was disputed. Thus No. 2 (French) Section of New York, which after taking part in the last congress of the American Federation subsequently opposed its decisions, was therefore expelled from the Federation by the American Federal Council. As it had not been recognised since then as an independent section by the General Council and its exclusion from the Congress had not been opposed, its delegate[a] could not be admitted or its mandate acknowledged. (Administrative Regulations II, Articles 5, 6; IV, Article 4.)[b]

The opposite was the case with the credentials of the New Madrid Federation. This comprised a number of workers who had

---

[a] A. Sauva.— *Ed.*
[b] Error in *Der Volksstaat*: "III, Article 4". See this volume, p. 12.— *Ed.*

been expelled from the old Madrid Federation under all sorts of pretexts and in flagrant violation of the local Rules. The real reason was that they had accused the secret society "The Alliance of Socialist Democracy" organised within the Spanish International of betraying the International. They consequently organised themselves into the New Madrid Federation and applied to the Spanish Federal Council for recognition. The Federal Council, adhering in the majority if not entirely to the Alliance, refused. The General Council, to whom they then applied, having recognised them as an independent Federation,[a] they sent their delegate,[b] whose credentials were disputed by the delegates of the Spanish Federation. In this case the General Council disregarded the prescriptions of the Administrative Regulations (II, 5), according to which it ought to have consulted the Spanish Federal Council before admitting the New Madrid Federation; it did not do this because, on the one hand, there was danger in delay, and secondly because the Spanish Federal Council had placed itself in rebellion against the International by openly siding with the Alliance.

The Congress approved the General Council's way of acting by a large majority, nobody voting against, and thus the New Madrid Federation was recognised.

A similar question arose in respect of the credentials of the Geneva "Section of Revolutionary Propaganda", which the General Council, on the request of the Geneva Romance Federal Committee, had not recognised. The credentials, and with them the whole section, remained suspended until the end of the Congress, and as the case could not be settled for lack of time, the section is still suspended.

The General Council's right to be represented by six delegates as at previous congresses was recognised after weak objections.

The four delegates of the Spanish Federation, who had not sent any subscriptions for the past accounting year, were not admitted until the subscriptions had been paid.

Finally, the delegate of the American Section No. 12,[c] the one which caused all the scandal in New York (as related earlier in *Der Volksstaat*[d]), was unanimously rejected after pleading a long time

---

[a] F. Engels, "The General Council to the New Madrid Federation", see this volume, p. 215.— *Ed*

[b] P. Lafargue.— *Ed*

[c] W. West.— *Ed*

[d] F. Engels, "The International in America", see this volume, pp. 177-83.— *Ed*

for Section No. 12, and accordingly Section No. 12 ultimately finds itself outside the International.

We see that under the form of verifying the mandates nearly all the practical questions which had occupied the International for a year were examined and settled. By a majority of from 38 to 45 against a minority of from 12 to 20, who mostly abstained altogether from voting, every single action of the General Council was approved by the Congress and it was given one vote of confidence after another.

An Italian delegate had also arrived, Signor Cafiero, chairman of the Rimini conference at which on August 6 [a] twenty-one sections (twenty of which have not fulfilled a single one of the conditions laid down by the Rules for their admission and hence do not belong to the International) adopted a decision to break off all solidarity with the General Council and to hold a congress of like-minded sections on September 2, not at The Hague, but at Neuchâtel in Switzerland.

They apparently changed their minds and Signor Cafiero came to The Hague, but he was reasonable enough to keep his mandate in his pocket and to attend the Congress as an onlooker, relying on his membership card.

At the very first vote—the election of the commission to verify the mandates—the assembly split into a majority and a minority which, with few exceptions, remained a solid body till the end. France, Germany, America, Poland, Denmark, Ireland, Austria, Hungary, Portugal, the Romance Federation of Switzerland, and Australia formed the majority. Belgium, the Spanish and the Jura Federation, Holland, one French and one American delegate formed the minority, which on most questions abstained entirely or in part from voting. The English delegates voted dividedly and unevenly. The core of the majority was formed by the Germans and the French, who held together as though the great military, government and state actions [200] of the year 1870 had never occurred. The unanimity of the German and French workers was sealed on the second anniversary of the capitulation at Sedan—a lesson for Bismarck no less than for Thiers!

When the matter of the mandates had been settled, came the first urgent question—the position of the General Council. The first debate at the public sitting on the Wednesday evening already proved that there could be no talk of its *abolition*. The

---

[a] Error in *Der Volksstaat*: "August 7".— *Ed.*

high-sounding phrases about free federation, autonomy of sections and so on died away ineffectively before the compact majority who were obviously determined not to let the International develop into a plaything. The delegates of those countries where the International has to wage a real struggle against the state power, that is to say those who take the International most seriously, the Germans, French, Austrians, Hungarians, Poles, Portuguese and Irish, were of the view that the General Council should have definite powers and should not be reduced to a mere "post-box", a "correspondence and statistics bureau" as the minority demanded.

Accordingly, to Article 2, Section II of the Administrative Regulations, which reads:

"The General Council is bound to execute the Congress Resolutions",

was added the following, adopted by 40 votes for to 5 against and 4 abstentions:

"and to take care that the basic principles and the General Rules and Regulations of the International are strictly observed".

And Article 6 of the same section:

"The General Council has also the right to suspend any Section from the International till the next Congress" will henceforth read:

"The General Council has the right to suspend a Section, a Federal Council, or a Federal Committee and a whole Federation.

"Nevertheless, in the case of Sections belonging to a Federation, the General Council shall consult the respective Federal Council.

"In the case of the dissolution of a Federal Council, the General Council shall arrange the election of a new Federal Council within 30 days at most.

"In the case of the suspension of an entire Federation, the General Council shall inform thereof the whole of the Federations. If the majority of them demand it, the General Council shall convoke an extraordinary conference, composed of one delegate for each nationality, which shall meet within one month and finally decide upon the question." (36 for, 11 against, 9 abstentions.)

Thus the position of the General Council, which according to the previous Rules and Congress resolutions could have been doubtful, was made sufficiently clear. The General Council is the Association's executive committee, and as such has definite powers in respect of the Sections and Federations. These powers have not been really extended by the above-quoted decisions, they have only been formulated better and provided with such guarantees as will never allow the General Council to lose awareness of its responsibility. After this resolution there can be less talk of dictatorship of the General Council than ever before.

The introduction of these two articles into the Administrative Regulations satisfied the most urgent requirement. Owing to the short time available a detailed revision of the General Rules was dispensed with. Nevertheless, in this respect there still remained an important point to be discussed. Serious differences had arisen over the programme as regards the political activity of the working class. In the Jura Federation of Switzerland, in Spain and in Italy the Bakuninist sect had preached absolute abstention from all political activity, in particular from all elections, as a principle of the International. This misunderstanding had been removed by Resolution IX of the London Conference in September 1871; on the other hand, the Bakuninists had decried this resolution too, as exceeding the powers of the conference. The Congress clarified the matter once more by adopting the London[a] Conference resolution by a two-thirds majority in the following formulation:

"In its struggle against the collective power of the propertied classes, the proletariat cannot act as a class except by constituting itself into a political party, distinct from, and opposed to, all old parties formed by the propertied classes. This constitution of the proletariat into a political party is indispensable in order to insure the triumph of the social revolution, and of its ultimate end, the abolition of classes.

"The combination of forces which the working class has already effected by its economical struggles ought, at the same time, to serve as a lever for its struggles against the political power of its exploiters.

"The lords of land and the lords of capital will always use their political privileges for the defence and perpetuation of their economical monopolies, and for the enslavement of labour. The conquest of political power has therefore become the great duty of the proletariat."

This resolution was adopted by 28 votes to 13 (including abstentions). Moreover, four French and six German delegates who had had to leave earlier had handed in their votes in writing *for* the new articles of the General Rules, so that the real majority amounted to 38.

This resolution has made it impossible for the abstentionists to

---

[a] Error in *Der Volksstaat*: "English".— *Ed.*

spread the delusion that abstention from all elections and all political activity is a principle of the International. If this sect, the same one which from the very beginning has caused all the discords in the International, now finds it compatible with its principles to remain in the International, that is its business; certainly nobody will try to keep it in.

The next point was the election of the new General Council. The majority of the previous General Council[201]—Marx, Engels, Serraillier, Dupont, Wróblewski, MacDonnell and others—moved that the General Council should be transferred to New York and the eight members of the American Federal Council appointed to it and that the American Federation should add another seven. The reason for this proposal was that most active members of the previous General Council had been obliged recently to devote all their time to the International, but were no longer in a position to do so. Marx and Engels had already informed their friends months earlier that it was possible for them to pursue their scientific work only on the condition that they retired from the General Council.

Others had similar motives. As a result, the General Council, if it were to remain in London, would be deprived of those very members who had so far been doing all the actual work, both the correspondence and the literary work. And then there were two elements in London both striving to gain the upper hand in the General Council, and in such conditions they would probably have done so.

One of these elements consisted of the French Blanquists (who, it is true, had never been recognised by Blanqui), a small coterie who replaced discernment of the real course of the movement with revolutionary talk, and propaganda activity with petty spurious conspiracy leading only to useless arrests. To hand over the leadership of the International in France to these people would mean senselessly throwing our people there into prison and disorganising again the thirty *départements* in which the International is flourishing. There were enough opportunities at the Congress itself for people to become convinced that the Internationals in France would put up with anything rather than the domination of these gentlemen.

The second dangerous element in London comprised those English working-class leaders in whose face Marx at the Congress had flung the words: it is a disgrace to be among these English working-class leaders, for almost all of them have sold themselves to Sir Charles Dilke, Samuel Morley, or even Gladstone. These men, who have so far been kept down or outside by the compact Franco-German majority in the General Council, would now play quite a different role, and the activity of the International in England would not only come under the control of the bourgeois radicals, but probably even under the control of the government.

A transfer was therefore necessary, and once this was recognised, New York was the only place which combined the two necessary conditions: security for the Association's archives and an international composition of the General Council itself. It took some pains to carry this transfer through; this time the Belgians separated from the minority and voted for London, and the Germans in particular insisted on London. Nevertheless, after several votings the transfer to New York was decided and the following twelve members of the General Council were appointed, with the right to increase the number to fifteen: Kavanagh and Saint Clair (Irishmen), Laurel (a Swede), Fornaccieri (an Italian), David, Levièle, Dereure (Frenchmen), Bolte, Bertrand, Carl, Speyer (Germans), and Ward (an American).

It was further decided to hold the next Congress in Switzerland and to leave it to the General Council to determine the place.

[*Der Volksstaat*, No. 81, October 9, 1872]

After the election of the new General Council, Lafargue, in the name of the two Federations he represented, the Portuguese and the New Madrid Federation, tabled the following motion, which was adopted unanimously:

"The new General Council is entrusted with the special mission to establish International trades unions.

"For this purpose it will, within the month following this Congress, draw up a circular which it shall have printed and send to all the working-men's societies whose addresses it possesses, whether they are affiliated to the International or not.

"In this circular it shall call upon the working-men's societies to establish an International trades union for their respective trades.

"Every society shall also be invited to fix itself the conditions under which it wishes to enter the International Union of its trade.

"The General Council is directed to collect all the conditions proposed by the working-men's societies which have accepted the idea and to work them up into general draft Rules which will be submitted for provisional acceptance to all the societies wishing to join.

"The next Congress will finally confirm this agreement in due form."

In this way from the very beginning the new General Council was set an important task in practical organisation the solution of which might well alone suffice to give the allegedly dead International a hitherto unknown upswing.

Finally came the question of the "*Alliance*". After working for a long time the commission which had to prepare this point for the Congress at last had its report ready on Saturday[a] at 9 p.m. The report declared that the Rules and the aims of the Alliance were in contradiction with those of the International and demanded the expulsion of its founder, Bakunin, of the two leaders of the Jura Federation, Guillaume and Schwitzguébel, as the chief agents of the Alliance, and moreover of B. Malon and two others besides. It was proved to the majority of the commission that the Alliance was a secret society founded for conspiracy not against the government, but against the International. At the Basle Congress the Bakuninists had still hoped they would be able to seize the leadership in the International. That was why they themselves at the time proposed the famous Basle resolutions by which the General Council's powers were extended. Disappointed and again deprived of the fulfilment of their hopes by the London Conference, up to the time of which they had won considerable ground in Spain and Italy, they changed their tactics. The Jura Federation, which was entirely under the control of the Alliance, issued its Sonvillier circular in which the Basle resolutions once proposed by their own delegates were suddenly attacked as the source of all evil, as inspired by the evil spirit, the spirit of "authoritarianism", and in which complete autonomy, a free alliance of independent factions was put forward as the only aim for the International. Naturally. When a secret society formed for the purpose of exercising leadership over a bigger open society cannot directly achieve supreme leadership, the best means for it to achieve its purpose is to disorganise the open society. When there is no central authority and no national central agencies or only such as are deprived of all powers, conspiring intriguers can best ensure themselves the leadership of the whole indirectly, by their concerted action. The members of the Alliance of the Jura, Spain and Italy acted with great unanimity according to this plan and the disorganisation was to be carried so far at the Hague Congress that not only the General Council, but *all* central

---

[a] September 7, 1872.— *Ed.*

agencies, all the Congress resolutions and even the General Rules, with the exception of the Preamble, were to be abolished. The Italians had already included this in their Rules, and the Jura delegates had received definite instructions to propose this to the Congress and to withdraw in the event of its not being adopted. But they were grossly mistaken. Original documents were laid before the commission proving the link between all these intrigues in Spain, Italy and Switzerland, making it clear that the secret link lay precisely in the "*Alliance*" itself, whose slogan was provided by Bakunin and to which Guillaume and Schwitzguébel belonged. In Spain, where the Alliance had long been an open secret, it had been dissolved, as the delegates from that country belonging to it assured, and on these repeated assurances they were not subjected to disciplinary measures.

The debate on this question was heated. The members of the "Alliance" did all they could to draw out the matter, for at midnight the lease of the hall expired and the Congress had to be closed. The behaviour of the members of the Alliance could not but dispel all doubt as to the existence and the ultimate aim of their conspiracy. Finally the majority succeeded in having the two main accused who were present—Guillaume and Schwitzguébel—take the floor; immediately after their defence the voting took place. Bakunin and Cuillaume were expelled from the International, Schwitzguébel escaped this fate, owing to his personal popularity, by a small majority; then it was decided to amnesty the others.

These expulsions constitute an open declaration of war by the International to the "Alliance" and the whole of Mr. Bakunin's sect. Like every other shade of proletarian socialism Bakunin's sect was admitted in the International on the general condition of maintaining peace and observing the Rules and the Congress resolutions. Instead of doing so, this sect led by dogmatic members of the bourgeoisie having more ambition than ability tried to impose its own narrow-minded programme on the whole of the International, violated the Rules and the Congress resolutions and finally declared them to be authoritarian trash which no true revolutionary need be bound by. The almost incomprehensible patience with which the General Council put up with the intrigues and calumny of the small band of mischief-makers was rewarded only with the reproach of dictatorial behaviour. Now at last the Congress has spoken out, and clearly enough at that. Just as clear will be the language of the documents concerning the Alliance and Mr. Bakunin's doings in general which the Commission will publish in accordance with the Congress decision.[a] Then people will see what villainies the International was to be misused for.

Immediately after the voting a statement of the minority was read out, signed jointly by the Jura, Belgian, Dutch and four Spanish delegates, and also by one French and one American delegate, declaring that after the rejection of all their proposals they were still willing to remain in touch with the General Council as regards statistics and correspondence and the payment of subscriptions, but would suffer no interference by the General Council in the internal life of the Federations. In the event of such interference by the General Council all the undersigned Federations would declare their solidarity with the Federation concerned, such interference being justifiable only in blatant violation of the Rules adopted by the Geneva Congress.

The signatories of this statement thus declare themselves to be bound only by the Geneva Rules of 1866, but not by the subsequent alterations and Congress decisions. But they are forgetting that the Geneva Rules themselves acknowledge the binding force of all Congress decisions and thus the whole of their reservation falls to pieces. For the rest, this document signifies absolutely nothing and was received by the Congress with the indifference it deserves. The signatories exceeded their powers inasmuch as they wish

1. to oblige their respective Federations to set up a separate alliance[202] within the International and

2. to oblige these Federations to acknowledge only the Geneva Rules as being valid and to invalidate all other, subsequent Congress decisions.

The whole document, apparently forced on the duped minority only by the Alliance blusterers, is therefore worthless. And if a Section or a Federation were to try to contest the validity of the International's Congress decisions collected in our Rules and Administrative Regulations, the new General Council will not hesitate to do its duty as the old one did in respect of American Section No. 12. That is still a long way off for the separate alliance.

We note further that in the course of the same afternoon (Saturday) the General Council's accounts for the past financial year were audited, found correct and approved.

After yet another address from the Hague Section to the

---

[a] K. Marx, F. Engels, "The Alliance of Socialist Democracy and the International Working Men's Association" (see this volume, pp. 454-580).—*Ed.*

Congress had been read out the Congress was closed at half-past
midnight with shouts of: "Long live the International Working
Men's Association!"

Written after September 17, 1872

First published in *Der Volksstaat*, Nos. 78
and 81, September 28 and October 9,
1872

Printed according to the newspaper

Frederick Engels

THE CONGRESS AT THE HAGUE

(LETTER TO ENRICO BIGNAMI)[203]

London, October 1, 1872

Dear Bignami,

From September 2 to 7, the 64 delegates of the International Working Men's Association held their sittings at The Hague. Of these delegates 16 represented France; 10, Germany; 7, Belgium; 5, England; 5, America; 4, Holland; 4, Spain; 3, the Romance Federation (Switzerland); 2, the Jura Federation (idem); 1, Ireland; 1, Austria; 1, Hungary; 1, Poland; 1, Portugal; 1, Australia; and 2, Denmark. According to nationalities there were: 20 Frenchmen, 16 Germans, 8 Belgians, 6 Englishmen, 1 Pole, 1 Irishman, 1 Corsican, and 1 Dane.

The verification of the mandates took more than two days. In this form, all the internal questions which had occupied the International since the last Congress were examined, and in almost every case it was a question of the General Council's activity.

Of the three mandates held by Citizen Lafargue, representing Portugal and two Spanish local federations, one, that of the New Madrid Federation, was contested by the other Spanish delegates. The New Madrid Federation, formed by members of the International arbitrarily expelled from the old federation in violation of the General Rules, had not been recognised by the Spanish Federal Council; it had then applied directly to the General Council in London, which had recognised it.[a]

The Congress unanimously confirmed that decision.

The six delegates whom the General Council had sent, basing itself on the action of previous congresses, and who, by the way, with one exception, were also provided with other mandates, were

---

[a] See this volume, p. 215.— *Ed.*

admitted. The mandate of the delegate sent by the Section of Propaganda and Revolutionary Action of Geneva,[a] a section not recognised by the General Council, was suspended for the whole duration of the Congress, and the section was not recognised. The four delegates of the Spanish Federation were not admitted until they had paid the subscriptions they were owing to the General Council for the year 1871-1872. And finally, the delegate of Section No. 12 of New York,[b] which had been suspended by the General Council, was not admitted to the Congress, despite a speech which lasted more than an hour. All these decisions, adopted by a majority of three quarters of the votes, were at the same time expressions of confidence in the General Council, whose "authoritarian" action (as some are pleased to call it) was entirely approved by the immense majority of the Congress.

After these discussions, which smoothed out many differences which had arisen within the International, and which were therefore by no means without profit, the question of the General Council was posed. Was it necessary to abolish it? In the event of its being preserved, was it to retain its powers, or was it to be reduced to a mere correspondence and statistics bureau, a *boîte aux lettres*,[c] so to speak? The answer of the Congress left no doubt on this score: Article 2, Section II of the Administrative Regulations was formulated as follows:

"The General Council is bound to execute the Congress resolutions."

To this the Congress at The Hague added:

"and to take care that in every country the principles and the General Rules and Regulations of the International are strictly observed" (40 votes for this addition, 5 against, and 11 abstentions).

Article 6 of the same section, which confers on the General Council the right to suspend a section, was formulated as follows:

"*Article 6.* The General Council has also the right to suspend sections, federal councils or committees, and federations of the International, till the meeting of the next Congress.

"Nevertheless, in the case of sections belonging to a federation, the General Council will exercise this right only after having consulted the respective Federal Council [...][d]

---

a N. Zhukovsky.— *Ed.*

b W. West.— *Ed.*

c Letter-box.— *Ed.*

d Engels omits one paragraph from the Hague Congress Resolution on Article 6, Section II of the Administrative Regulations (cf. this volume, p. 244).— *Ed.*

"In the case of the suspension of an entire federation, the General Council shall immediately inform thereof all federations. If the majority of them demand it, the General Council shall convoke an extraordinary conference, composed of one delegate for each nationality, which shall meet within one month and finally decide upon the question.

"Nevertheless, it is well understood that the countries where the International is prohibited shall exercise the same rights as the regular federations."

It is clear that this new article of the Regulations defining with great clarity the powers of the General Council, contains the necessary guarantees against their abuse.

The Congress declared its will that the General Council should be invested with authority, but responsible. This article was adopted by a majority of 36 votes to 11 with 9 abstentions.

Then came the question of the new General Council. If the General Council, whose powers were on the point of expiring, wished to be re-elected as a whole or partially, it was sure of an almost unanimous vote, since the Belgians and the Dutch had separated from the minority on this question and voted for London. A proof that Marx, Engels, Serraillier, Wróblewski, Dupont, and the other members of the previous Council had by no means demanded wider and better defined powers of the General Council for themselves personally was their motion that the General Council should be transferred to New York, this being the only place, besides London, where the principal conditions were ensured, namely safety of the archives and the international character of the Council's composition. Of all the proposals moved by the previous Council, this was the only one which encountered any difficulty, since all the delegates, with the exception of the Jura Federation representatives and the Spaniards, agreed to leave the direction of the International in the same hands as it had been before. Only after the most active and well-known members of the previous Council had stated that they declined to be re-elected, was the transfer to New York adopted by a majority vote. The Congress went on to the election of the New Council, which was composed of 2 Irishmen, 1 Swede, 1 Italian, 3 Frenchmen, 1 American, and 4 Germans, with the right to co-opt three other members.

It is known that Resolution IX of the London Conference (September 1871) on the political action of the working class was vigorously opposed as being allegedly contrary to the principles of the International by the Jurassians, some of the Spaniards and the

majority of the Italians. Nevertheless, that resolution now constitutes Article 8[a] of the General Rules of the International, which is
as follows:

"*Article 8.* In its struggle against the collective power of the
propertied classes, the proletariat cannot act as a class except by
constituting itself into a political party, distinct from, and opposed
to, all old parties formed by the propertied classes.

"This constitution of the proletariat into a political party is
indispensable in order to insure the triumph of the social
revolution, and of its ultimate end, the abolition of classes. The
combination of forces which the working class has already effected
by its economical struggles ought, at the same time, to serve as a
lever for its struggles against the political power of its exploiters.
The lords of land and the lords of capital will always use their
political privileges for the defence and perpetuation of their economical monopolies, and for the enslavement of labour. The conquest of political power has therefore become the great duty of
the proletariat."[b]

This resolution was adopted by 28 votes to 13 (counting the
abstentions), and as the majority exceeded two-thirds, this
resolution has been included in the General Rules. To this
majority we must also add the votes of 6 German and 4 French
delegates who were obliged to leave The Hague and had left their
vote in writing for the resolution; thus abstention from politics was
condemned by a majority of three-quarters of the votes to one
quarter.

There remained only one important question. The General
Council had denounced to the Congress the existence within the
International of a secret society directed not against the existing
governments, but against our Association itself. The members of
this secret society, headed by its founder, Mikhail Bakunin, were
divided into three categories according to the degree of their
initiation. It set itself the aim of seizing the central leadership of
the International, or, failing that, to disorganise it in order thus
the better to ensure their own influence. With this objective,
slogans on the *autonomy* of sections and *resistance* to the
"authoritarian" tendencies of the General Council were spread.

---

[a] Under this number the article entered the draft of the General Rules and
Administrative Regulations formulated by the General Council in the summer
of 1872 (cf. this volume, p. 201). The Hague Congress included it into the General
Rules under No. 7a.— *Ed*

[b] Cf. this volume, p. 243.— *Ed*

The Congress appointed a commission to investigate the question of this society, and its report was read out at the closing sitting. The report contained proof of the existence of this secret society and of its hostile character. The report ended with a motion to expel from the International Bakunin, Guillaume, Schwitzguébel, Malon and two others.

The conclusions of this report concerning the Alliance were accepted by the Congress; as for the individuals, Bakunin and Guillaume were expelled, Schwitzguébel was saved by a small minority, and the others were amnestied.

These were the principal decisions of the Hague Congress; they are definite enough, and at the same time extremely moderate. The General Council, supported by a majority of three to one, did its utmost to ensure for the new Council a clear and well defined position, to establish with clarity the political programme of the International which had been placed in doubt by a sectarian minority and to eliminate a secret society which, instead of conspiring against the existing governments, conspired against the International itself. Then the General Council refused to have itself re-elected and had to go to great trouble for its resignation to be accepted.

The majority at the Congress was composed mainly of French, German, Hungarian, Danish, Polish, Portuguese, Irish, Australian and American delegates and the delegates of Romance Switzerland; the minority consisted of Belgians, Dutchmen, Spaniards, the delegates of the Jura Federation, and one American. The English delegates were divided in various ways at the voting. Not once did the minority (including the abstainers) exceed 20 out of 64 delegates; generally it numbered between 12 and 16.

There was one Italian delegate present, the chairman of the federation established at Rimini,[a] but he did not submit his mandate; the Congress would certainly not have accepted it. He attended the sittings as a spectator.

On my return from The Hague, I found in the Mantua *Favilla* an article signed Atheist which disputed the correctness of the assertion that out of the 21 sections whose delegates signed the Rimini resolution, only one (that of Naples) belonged to the *International.*

"In saying further that only the Naples section is in order, the Big Council is lying. The Milan workers' circle, the Girgenti society, that of Ravenna, that of

---

[a] Carlo Cafiero.— *Ed.*

Rome, and the Turin section, which was the initiator, have long since paid the ten centesimi fixed by the General Rules." [a]

In order to make sure who is lying, the General Council or Mr. Atheist, it is sufficient to note that neither the Milan section nor that of Girgenti, nor that of Turin appear among the signatories of the Rimini resolution, and that the Rome section did not apply to the General Council until after that conference (and I believe it was not the same section which was represented at Rimini).

The Italian Internationals may rest assured that as long as an *International*, a *Congress*, a *General Council*, *General Rules* and *Regulations* exist, no section will be recognised by the Congress or by the Council so long as it refuses to recognise the conditions fixed by the General Rules and Regulations, which are the same for all.

Frederick Engels

First published in *La Plebe*, No. 106, October 5, 1872

Printed according to the newspaper

Translated from the Italian

---

[a] [C. Terzaghi,] "Correspondence from Turin", *La Favilla*, No. 184, September 3, 1872. Signed: "Ateo".— *Ed.*

Frederick Engels

IMPERATIVE MANDATES
AT THE HAGUE CONGRESS [204]

The betrayals of their electors committed recently by many deputies to parliament have caused the return to fashion of the old imperative mandates of the Middle Ages which had been abolished by the Revolution of 1789. We shall not discuss here the principle of such mandates. We shall only note that if all electors gave their delegates imperative mandates concerning all points on the agenda, meetings and debates of the delegates would be superfluous. It would be sufficient to send the mandates to a central counting office which would count up the votes and announce the results. This would be much cheaper.

What is important for us to show is the most unusual situation in which imperative mandates place their holders at the Hague Congress—a situation which can serve as a very good lesson to the enthusiastic supporters of such mandates.

The delegates of the Spanish Federation, elected, as we know, owing to the influence of the Federal Council,[a] had an imperative mandate to ask

"that the votes be counted according to the number of those represented by the delegates holding an imperative mandate; that the votes of those represented by delegates not provided with an imperative mandate will not count until the sections or federations which they represent have discussed and voted on the questions debated at the Congress... In case the Congress persists in the traditional system of

---

a See this volume, p. 208. The mandate for the delegates of the Spanish Federation quoted below was published as a separate leaflet (*Mandato Imperativo*. In: *Asociacion Internacional de los Trabajadores. Federacion Regional Española*. Circular. Valencía. August 22, 1872).— *Ed.*

voting, our delegates will take part in the discussion, but will abstain from voting." *

This mandate therefore demands that the Congress, before dealing with anything else, should adopt the following three decisions:

1. To change the articles of the Administrative Regulations dealing with the mode of voting.

2. To decree that delegates not holding an imperative mandate should not have the right to vote.

3. To declare that these changes would apply immediately to the present Congress.

It was immediately pointed out to the delegates of the Spanish Federation that even if the Congress adopted their petitions Nos. 1 and 2, petition No. 3 would be inadmissible. The Hague Congress had been called on the basis of certain of the Association's organisational rules. It certainly had the right to change them, but if it did change them, it would at the same time have destroyed the basis of its own existence and would have placed itself in the absolute necessity to dissolve itself immediately, after convoking a new congress, whose delegates would be elected on the basis of the new organisational rules. To apply these new rules to the present Congress would be to make them retroactive and to violate every principle of justice. Consequently, whether or not the Congress adopted proposals Nos. 1 and 2, it could by no means adopt proposal No. 3; and if the Spanish delegates had received and accepted a mandate which was in flagrant contradiction with itself, a mandate which made it impossible for them to vote at any session of the Congress, whose fault was it?

The case was so clear that neither the minority, nor even the delegates of our region, found words to contest it. Consequently they remained present at the Congress without voting, and this ultimately so much exasperated the Dutch that one of them[b] asked:

---

* The Jura *Bulletin*, which is known to be the organ of the Alliance leaders, published in its latest issue a short account of the sessions of the Hague Congress, the authenticity of which can be judged by the following, which we translate word for word: "The Spaniards, who are supported by the Belgians and the Jurassians, demanded that the voting should be conducted not by individuals, but by *federations.*"[a] Is this what the mandate of the Spanish Federation demanded?

---

[a] [J. Guillaume,] "Le Congrès de la Haye", *Bulletin de la Fédération jurassienne...*, No. 17-18, September 15-October 1, 1872.— *Ed.*

[b] Isaac Salomon Van der Hout.— *Ed.*

"Why didn't you stay at home if you have a mandate which forbids you to vote and deprives the minority of four votes every time a vote is taken?"

But for a real Alliance mandate and an Alliance way of using it, the *Jura* Federation had no peers.

Here is the mandate of its delegates [a]:

"The delegates of the Jura Federation are given an imperative mandate to present to the Congress of The Hague the following principles as the basis of the organisation of the International:

"Any group of workers which accepts the programme of the International as it has been formulated by the preamble to the General Rules voted at the Geneva Congress, and which undertakes to observe economic solidarity in respect of all the workers and groups of workers in the struggle against monopoly capital shall be a section of the International enjoying full rights."

Here, indeed, the General Rules and Regulations are abolished. If the preamble is allowed to remain, that is only because, no conclusions being drawn from it, it is simply lacking in common sense.

"The federal principle being the basis of the organisation of the International," the mandate continues, "the sections federate freely among themselves and the federations federate freely among themselves, and do so with full autonomy, setting up, in accordance with their needs, all the organs of correspondence, statistics bureaux etc., which they deem suitable.

"The Jura Federation sees as a consequence of the above-mentioned principles the suppression of the General Council and of all authority in the International."

Thus, the General Council, the federal councils, the local councils, and various kinds of rules and regulations which possess "authority" are to be abolished. Each one will act as he thinks fit, "with full autonomy".

"The Jura delegates must act in complete solidarity with the Spanish, Italian and French delegates and all those who openly protest against the authoritarian principle. Consequently, refusal to admit a delegate of these federations must lead to the *immediate withdrawal* of the Jura delegates. Similarly, if the Congress does not accept the organisational principles of the International set forth above, the delegates will have to *withdraw* in agreement with the delegates of the anti-authoritarian federations."

Let us now see what use the Jura delegates made of this imperative mandate. In the first place, there were no French anti-authoritarian delegates at the Congress except one,[b] a madman, who did, in fact, "withdraw" very noisily many times, but

---

[a] The mandate for the delegates of the Jura Federation to the Hague Congress was published in the *Bulletin de la Fédération jurassienne...*, No. 15-16, August 15-September 1, 1872.— *Ed.*

[b] Victor Cyrille.— *Ed.*

always returned because he could never get a single other anti-authoritarian delegate to follow him. The mandate of Sauva of Section No. 2 (anti-authoritarian) of New York was annulled,[a] but the *Jurassians* remained at the Congress. That of the Section of *Propaganda and Revolutionary Socialist Action in Geneva*—a section which belonged directly to the Jura Federation—remained suspended until the end of the Congress,[b] and the *Jurassians* behaved as though nothing had happened. The mandate of Section No. 12 of New York which they themselves had encouraged to resist the General Council, was annulled,[c] and the *Jurassians* remained undisturbed. As for the mandate of the Italian delegate[d] that was present, they did not even attempt to present it.

But were the principles of organisation—or rather disorganisation—proposed by the Jurassians, adopted by the Congress? Not at all; exactly the opposite: the Congress decided to strengthen the organisation, that is, according to them, the authority. Did they withdraw after this? Nothing of the sort. They merely declared that they would abstain from voting in future.

So this was the proper way to use an imperative mandate. The delegate complies with it if it suits him and if not, he pleads unforeseen circumstances and ultimately does what is to his advantage. After all, is it not a duty for the anti-authoritarians to disregard the *authority* of imperative mandates just as all other authority? The radically Alliancist spirit which was so well revealed in the imperative mandate of the Jurassians was supplemented by the really anarchist manner in which they ignored that mandate. Does it not follow from this that these delegates are more initiated members of the Alliance than their Spanish counterparts?

The *Jura* mandate gives occasion for other reflections too. This mandate reveals on the whole the activities taking place in the Alliance, where, despite all the talk about *anarchy, autonomy, free federation* etc., there are in reality only two things: *authority* and *obedience*. A few weeks before Schwitzguébel and Guillaume wrote their own mandates, abolishing the General Rules except for the preamble, their friends, delegates, who did not belong to the International, at the Rimini Conference, drew up the rules of the self-styled Italian Federation, consisting of the preamble to the general rules and the regulations of the federation. Thus the

---

[a] See this volume, p. 246.— *Ed.*
[b] Ibid, p. 247.— *Ed.*
[c] Ibid, pp. 246-47.— *Ed.*
[d] Carlo Cafiero.— *Ed.*

organisation whose creation had been voted by the Rimini Conference *rejected* the General Rules. It is obvious that in their activities the men of the Alliance always obey secret and uniform orders. It was such secret orders that were undoubtedly obeyed by the Barcelona *Federacion* too, when it unexpectedly started preaching the disorganisation of the International. This was because the strong organisation of our Association in Spain was becoming a threat to the secret leaders of the Alliance. This organisation gives the working class too much strength and creates thereby difficulties to the secret rule of the gentlemen of the Alliance, who know perfectly well that fish are best caught in troubled waters.

Destroy the organisation, and the waters will be as troubled as you can wish. Destroy above all the trade unions, declare war on strikes, reduce working-class solidarity to empty words and you will have complete freedom for your pompous but empty and doctrinarian phrases. That is, if the workers of our region allow you to destroy the result of their four years of work, the organisation, which is, beyond doubt, the best in the whole of the International.

Returning to the imperative mandates, we still have one question to solve: Why do the Alliancists, who are inveterate enemies of the principle of authority in any form, so obstinately insist on the authority of imperative mandates? Because for a secret society like theirs, one existing within a public organisation like the International, there is nothing more convenient than the imperative mandate. The mandates of the Alliance members will all be identical, while the mandates of the sections not influenced by the Alliance or opposing it will contradict one another, so that very often the absolute majority, and always the relative majority, will belong to the secret society; whereas at a congress where there are no imperative mandates, the common sense of the independent delegates will swiftly unite them in a common party against the party of the secret society. This is an extremely effective means of domination, which is why the Alliance, despite all its *anarchism*, supports its authority.

Before finishing we must say that for the Spanish Federal Council, consisting of Alliancists, the most convenient form of action was the creation of a *collective* imperative mandate, a fact which was bound to lead to this mandate being the mandate of the Federal Council, or, what is the same, an Alliance mandate. All federations of our region that accepted the proposal of the Council contrary to the Regulations, sent extraordinary subscriptions to Valencia to pay the travelling expenses of the delegates, and together with these subscriptions the results of the voting in each local federation, and together with the results of the voting—the imperative mandate of the federation, in order to "unite all the mandates and create a *collective imperative mandate*". We readily admit that given a *loyal attitude* and *good will*, the Regional Council would have been able to count the votes of all the local federations, but to join in one the different opinions of all the federations, the Regional Council needed either supreme intelligence or a miraculous crucible in which it would probably have fused the various imperative mandates. And what came out of this new sort of crucible? What was bound to come out—the opinion of the Regional Council. We defy all the Alliancists to point out to us a chemico-electoral procedure which could produce another result.

The Spanish Federal Council, so anti-authoritarian, so anarchistic etc., thus *centralised* subscriptions in its hands so as to send delegates to The Hague; it *conducted* the elections of those delegates itself, and did it so skilfully that only Alliancists were elected, and, to crown it all, it composed the *collective imperative mandate*, which, it maintained, expressed the will of the members of the International in Spain.

Greater respect cannot be paid to autonomy.

Written before October 4, 1872   Printed according to the newspaper

First published in *La Emancipacion*,   Translated from the Spanish
No. 69, October 13, 1872

Frederick Engels

LETTERS FROM LONDON

II

[MORE ABOUT THE HAGUE CONGRESS] [205]

London, October 5, 1872

I hope that the outcome of the Hague Congress will make our Italian "autonomous" friends think. They ought to know that wherever there is an organisation, some autonomy is sacrificed for the sake of unity of action. If they do not realise that the *International* is a society organised for struggle, and not for fine theories, I am very sorry, but one thing is certain: the great *International* will leave Italy to act on its own until it agrees to accept the conditions common to all.

In the secret Alliance of Socialist Democracy there are three grades: international brethren (a tiny number), national brethren, and mere Alliancists. C.[a] is an *international* brother, just as Guillaume (chief of Bakunin's general staff) and one or two Spaniards.

Among the French delegates, five came from France under fictitious names, the others are refugees of the Commune. I attach the list, in which the names and localities of the French sections are not given so as not to betray them to the police.[b] But we have re-organised in more than thirty of the French *départements* and the *International* there is stronger and more active than ever.

It was gratifying to see the French and the Germans always voting in agreement at The Hague: it was obvious that all the wars, the conquests, the national hatred did not exist for the *International*. It was this union of the French and the Germans that led to all the resolutions without exception being adopted.

The reason for the transfer of the General Council to New York was: 1. The firm determination of Marx, Serraillier, Dupont and

---

[a] Carlo Cafiero.— *Ed.*

[b] *Liste nominale des délégués composant le 5-me Congrès universel, tenu à la Haye (Hollande), du 2 au 7 Septembre 1872*, Amsterdam [1872].— *Ed.*

Engels not to accept a new mandate. Marx and Engels have scientific works to complete and have not had time for this in the past two years; 2. The certainty that in the event of their resignation a General Council in London would be composed as far as the French were concerned of *Blanquists* who, with their *simulation* of conspiracy, would lead to the arrest of the majority of our members in France—if they were accepted by these at all; as far as the English were concerned, of corrupt men used to selling themselves to the liberal bourgeoisie and to Mr. Gladstone's *radical* agents; and as for all the other nationalities, they would not be represented at all, since Wróblewski, MacDonnell and Frankel did not want to remain on it without Marx and the others.

Whatever the bourgeois press may say, we were well received by the workers of The Hague. Once the reactionaries sent a handful of drunks to us to sing the Dutch national royal anthem after the ending of the sitting. We let them sing and, passing through them, replied with the *Marseillaise*. Even the minority at the Congress would have been sufficient to disperse them by force. At the last sitting, on the Saturday,[a] a numerous public gave the speakers a lot of applause.

First published in *La Plebe*, No. 107, October 8, 1872

Signed: *Federico Engels* "Our correspondence"

Printed according to the newspaper

Translated from the Italian

---

[a] September 7.— *Ed.*

Frederick Engels

TO THE BRITISH FEDERAL COUNCIL, INTERNATIONAL WORKING MEN'S ASSOCIATION

[CONCERNING PORTUGUESE STRIKES] [a]

122 Regent's Park Road. N.W.
London, 16th October, 1872

Citizens,

I had the honour of submitting to you, by citizen Dupont, at your meeting of September 26, a communication addressed to me by the Lisbon Federal Council regarding some trade matters of International Sections there, which required immediate action here.[206] I have seen this communication published in *The International Herald*[b] but have not had any intimation that the Federal Council has taken any further steps in the matter.

As I am bound to give an account to my Lisbon Correspondents of what I have done on behalf of the parties interested, I hope the Federal Council will be good enough to let me know whether anything, and what, has been done by the Council with regard to the subject in question.

I remain Citizens fraternally yours,

F. E.

First published in: Marx and Engels, *Works*, First Russian Edition, Vol. XXVI, Moscow, 1935

Reproduced from the rough manuscript

---

[a] The rough manuscript has Engels' note: "London, 16 October 72. To Brit. Fed. Council wegen [on account of] Portug. Strikes."—*Ed.*

[b] E. Hill, "International Working Men's Association. Federal Council", *The International Herald*, No. 27, October 5, 1872.—*Ed.*

Karl Marx

TO THE EDITORS OF *DER VOLKSSTAAT*[207]

The leading article in No. 84 of the *Volksstaat*—"Vom Haager Kongress. III"[a]—contains a factual error concerning me which I consider it necessary to rectify, and that, be it noted, only because it has slipped into the *Volksstaat* If I considered it worth the trouble to rectify the lies, calumnies, infamy and even involuntary "errors" of the press which is hostile to me, I would not have a minute left for actual work!

The article cited says:

"Lafargue, far from being Marx's 'adjutant', *abstained from voting* when it was a question of expelling Schwitzguébel, Guillaume's comrade, although the motion for expulsion [208] was tabled by *Marx.*"

That motion was tabled by the commission of inquiry appointed by the Congress, not by me. What I proposed at the Congress was the *expulsion of the Alliance* and the appointment of a commission of inquiry for that purpose. I appeared in front of this commission, just like others, as a witness for the prosecution. Only towards the end of the inquiry, at the last moment, and indeed during a sitting of the Congress, was I called upon. Previously, one of the members of the commission had desired a private meeting with me to elucidate purely factual questions. I refused, in order to avoid even the appearance of any personal influence on the commission.

When I was questioned by the commission I did not say a word about Schwitzguébel or his bell-wether, Guillaume. I mentioned

---

[a] Of October 19, 1872; the article was written by A. Hepner.— *Ed.*

only *one* of the Alliancists[a] attending the Congress and expressed my conviction that either he was not a member of the "secret" Alliance or that in any case he had for a long time been excluded from it.

I voted at the last Congress sitting *for* Schwitzguébel's expulsion because the proofs of his membership of the "secret" Alliance were exactly the same as those of Guillaume's. In these circumstances, Schwitzguébel's emotional poor-sinner speech could not shake my conviction. Let it be noted in passing that Mr. Guillaume *lies*—as incidentally every member of a "secret" society is obliged to do—intentionally in the *Bulletin jurassienne* when he avers that Schwitzguébel had declared solidarity with him.[b] On the contrary. Guillaume stated with great emphasis that Schwitzguébel would stand or fall with him, but Schwitzguébel turned a deaf ear to this cry *in extremis*[c]! His poor-sinner speech made no mention of Guillaume, and it was this poor-sinner speech that bribed the majority. As a member of the commission for publication of the Congress proceedings I naturally had to go very carefully into the official Minutes of the Congress.

In respect of Lafargue it must be noted that the honest Biedermann[d] is lying when he designates him as delegate for Barcelona.[209] Lafargue was delegated by the Portuguese Federal Council, the New Madrid Federation and also by a Spanish Section.

Karl Marx

London, October 20, 1872

First published in *Der Volksstaat*, No. 86, October 26, 1872

Printed according to the newspaper

---

[a] Tomás Morago.— *Ed.*

[b] [J. Guillaume,] "Le Congrès de la Haye", *Bulletin de la Fédération jurassienne...*, No. 17-18, September 15-October 1, 1872.— *Ed*

[c] At the point of death.— *Ed.*

[d] A pun on Biedermann, which means "honest man" and was also the name of the editor of the *Deutsche Allgemeine Zeitung.*— *Ed.*

Frederick Engels

REPORT TO THE GENERAL COUNCIL OF THE I.W.M.A. UPON THE SITUATION IN SPAIN, PORTUGAL AND ITALY[210]

1. SPAIN

In Spain the International was originally founded as a mere appendix to Bakounine's secret society, the *Alliance*, to which it was to serve as a kind of recruiting ground and at the same time as the lever by which to control the whole proletarian movement. You will see by and by that their Alliance intends openly to restore the Spanish International, at the present time, to this same subordinate position.

In consequence of this dependance, the special doctrines of the Alliance: immediate abolition of the state, anarchy, anti-authoritarism, abstention from all political action etc. were preached in Spain as *the doctrines* of the International. At the same time, every prominent member of the International was at once received into the secret organization and made to believe that this system of controlling the public association by the secret society existed everywhere and was a matter of course.

This took place in 1869 and the first man who introduced the International into Spain, along with the Alliance, was the Italian *Fanelli* who now, in spite of his abstentional convictions, is a member of the Italian parliament. In June 1870 took place the first Congress of the Spanish International at Barcelona and here the plan of organization was adopted which, afterwards fully developed by the Conference of Valencia (September 1871),[211] is now in force and has given the most excellent results.

As everywhere else, the part taken by (and also that ascribed to) our Association in the revolution of the Paris Commune, brought the International into prominence in Spain also. This prominence and the first attempted Government prosecutions following immediately afterwards, swelled our ranks in Spain very much.

Still, at the time of the Valencia Conference there existed only 13 local federations in Spain, besides single isolated Sections in various places.

The Conference of Valencia had left the Federal Council in Madrid where it had been placed by the Barcelona Congress, and had left its composition much the same as before; one important individual however, Tomas Gonzalez Moràgo (delegate at the Hague) had not been reelected. When, during the first Government prosecutions in June 1871, the Federal Council had for a time to seek a refuge in Lisbon, Moràgo abandoned his post at the moment of danger and this was the cause of his exclusion from the new Federal Council. From that moment began the secret war, which ended in an open split.

Immediately after the Valencia Conference, the Conference of London (September 1871) took place.[212] The Spaniards sent a delegate, Anselmo Lorenzo, who for the first time brought the news back to Spain that the secret "Alliance" was *not* an understood thing throughout our Association and that on the contrary the General Council and the majority of the Federations were directly opposed to the Alliance, as far as its existence was then known.

Shortly afterwards *Sagasta* began his prosecutions against the International which he declared was outside the law.[213] Moràgo, then still member of the Local Council of Madrid, again deserted his post and resigned. But the government threats were not followed up by any serious action; the right of *public* meeting was indeed denied to the International, but the sections and councils continued to hold their meetings undisturbed. The only effect of this government interference was an immense increase in the number of adherents to the International. At the Congress of Saragossa, April 1872,[214] the Association numbered 70 local federations regularly constituted, while in 100 other localities the work of organization and propaganda was actively pursued. There were moreover 8 Trades organized in Unions all over the country and under the control of the International, and the great union of all the mill-hands in Spain (mechanics, spinners and weavers) was upon the point of being constituted.

In the interval the secret war within the International had been carried on and it now commenced to take another and more important turn. The personal spite of Moràgo (who exercised great local influence in Madrid, his repeated desertions notwithstanding) against the members of the new Federal Council appointed at Valencia, was no longer the sole motive power of this war. The resolutions of the London Conference on the public branch of the Alliance and on the political action of the working class had aroused the fury of the leaders of the secret Alliance, and especially of the men in the higher degrees of secret initiation who received their instructions direct from Bakounine, and of whom Moràgo was one. This fury was expressed in the Sonvillier circular of the Jura Federation demanding the immediate convocation of an extraordinary Congress. In this question, the Federal Council of Spain, in accordance with many of the sections, hesitated to take part against the General Council and the London Conference, and this constituted a new crime. Moreover in January 1872 Paul Lafargue came to Madrid, and having entered into friendly relations with the members of the Federal Council, soon convinced them, by numerous facts, that the whole Jurassian affair was an intrigue, based upon calumny, to disorganize the International. From that moment their fate was doomed. The members of the Federal Council being at the same time editors of the *Emancipacion,* the Local Council picked a quarrel with that paper and then had them expelled from the Local Federation of Madrid. This expulsion was annulled by the Congress of Saragossa, but the immediate end was attained: to render the continuance of the Federal Council at Madrid impossible by personal squabbles. The Federal Council was indeed removed to Valencia and its composition entirely changed. Of the members of the previous Council, who were reelected, Mora declined at once and Lorenzo resigned very soon on the account of differences which ensued. The members who remained, were mostly members of the secret Alliance.[a]

After the Congress of Saragossa the split between the men of the Alliance and those who preferred the International to the Alliance became more and more apparent. At last, on June 2d 1872, the members of the previous Federal Council (Mesa, Mora, Pauly, Pagés and others), who formed at the same time the majority of the Madrid section of the Alliance, issued a circular to all the sections of the same secret Society, announcing their dissolution as such section and inviting them to follow their example.[215] The next day, they were under a false pretence, and by an open breach of the rules, expelled from the Local Federation of the Madrid International. Out of 130 members only

---

[a] Then follows the sentence crossed out in the manuscript: "As the International Congress of September 1872 approached, the manoeuvres of the Alliance to secure to itself a majority at the Congress, became more evident."—*Ed.*

15 had been present at this vote. They then formed a new Federation,[a] but the Federal Council refused to recognise them; the General Council, upon application, recognised them without consulting the Spanish Federal Council, and this act was sanctioned by the Congress at the Hague.

The reason why the late General Council did not consult the Spanish Council on this occasion, was this. The General Council, having at last received sufficient evidence of the existence and action of the Alliance in Spain and of the fact that a majority, if not all, of the members of the Spanish Council belonged to it, had written to that council, demanding explications and informations regarding the secret society.[b] In its reply, dated 3d August 1872, the Spanish Council openly took sides with the Alliance, stating moreover that the Alliance was dissolved. To refer to a Council which, in a collision between the International and a secret society within its ranks, had already taken the part of that secret society, would have evidently been more than superfluous, and the Hague Congress has fully sanctioned the action of the General Council.

To insure the election of men of the Alliance as delegates to the Hague, the Federal Council, by a private circular, never communicated by them to the General Council, resorted to manoeuvres, exposed at the Congress, manoeuvres which, had it not been for the uncommon leniency of the majority at the Hague, might have sufficed to invalidate the credentials of the four delegates[c] sent by the Spanish Federation.

Thus, the state of things in Spain now is as follows:

There exist in Spain only two local federations which openly and thoroughly acknowledge the resolutions of the Hague Congress and the new General Council: the new federation of Madrid and the federation of Alcalá de Henares. Unless they can succeed in drawing over to their side the bulk of the Spanish International, they will form the nucleus of a new Spanish Federation.

The great bulk of the Spanish International are still under the leadership of the Alliance which predominates in the Federal Council as well as in the most important Local Councils. But there are plenty of symptoms to show that the Congress resolutions have not been without great effect upon the masses in Spain. There the name of the International has a great weight, and its official expression, the Congress, a great moral influence. Thus, the men

---

[a] New Madrid Federation.— *Ed.*
[b] See this volume, pp. 211-13.— *Ed.*
[c] Moràgo, Alerini, Farga Pellicer, Marselau.— *Ed.*

of the Alliance have a hard struggle to convince the masses that they are in the right. The opposition begins to become serious. The factory workers of Catalonia, with a Trades Union, counting 40 000 members, are taking the lead and demand the convocation of an extraordinary Spanish Congress to hear the reports of the delegates to the Hague and to examine into the conduct of the Federal Council. The organ of the New Madrid Federation, *La Emancipacion*, perhaps the best paper the International now possesses anywhere, exposes the Alliance every week, and from the numbers I have sent over to cit. Sorge, the General Council can convince themselves, with what energy, good sense, and theoretical insight into the principles of our Association it carries on the struggle. Its present editor, José Mesa, is without doubt by far the most superior man we have in Spain, both as to character and talent and indeed one of the best men we have anywhere.

I have taken upon myself to advise our Spanish friends not to be in too great a hurry to force on the extraordinary Congress, but to prepare for it as much as possible. In the meantime I have contributed to the *Emancipacion* both Congress reports and other articles[a] and continue to do so, because Mesa, the only one now at Madrid who can use the pen with effect, cannot do everything, in spite of the wonderful energy, he displays. And I have no doubt that, if our friends in Spain are seconded well by the action of the General Council, we shall there overcome every obstacle and rescue from the influence of the Alliance humbugs one of the finest organizations within the International.

Fred. Engels,
Ex-Secretary for Spain

London, October 31, 1872

First published, in English, in *Briefe und Auszüge aus Briefen von Joh. Phil. Becker, Jos. Dietzgen, Friedrich Engels, Karl Marx u.A. an F. A. Sorge und Andere*, Stuttgart, 1906

Reproduced from the manuscript

---

[a] See this volume, pp. 277-82.— *Ed.*

Frederick Engels

TO THE WORKERS' AND PEASANTS' ASSOCIATION OF LOWER LOMBARDY (SECTION OF THE INTERNATIONAL) IN LODI[216]

London, November 13, 1872

Citizens,

It is with great pleasure that I have received the news of your formation as a section of the International, and I have immediately informed the new General Council in New York. I append below the address for direct correspondence with the General Council, while I remain always at your disposal for any information, clarification or service you may desire.

Fraternal greetings,

Frederick Engels

First published in *La Plebe*, No. 117, November 17, 1872

Printed according to the newspaper

Translated from the Italian

Published in English for the first time

Frederick Engels

LETTERS FROM LONDON [217]

III

[MEETING IN HYDE PARK]

London, November 14, 1872

The *Liberal* English Government has at the moment no less than 42 Irish political prisoners in its prisons and treats them with quite exceptional cruelty, far worse than thieves and murderers. In the good old days of King Bomba,[a] the head of the present *Liberal* cabinet, Mr. Gladstone, travelled to Italy and visited political prisoners in Naples; on his return to England he published a pamphlet [b] which disgraced the Neapolitan government before Europe for its unworthy treatment of political prisoners.

This does not prevent this selfsame Mr. Gladstone from treating in the very same way the Irish political prisoners, whom he continues to keep under lock and key. The Irish members of the International in London decided to organise a *giant* demonstration in Hyde Park (the largest public park in London, where all the big popular meetings take place during political campaigns) to demand a general amnesty. They contacted all London's democratic organisations and formed a committee which included McDonnell (an Irishman), Murray (an Englishman) and Lessner (a German)—all members of the last General Council of the *International.*

A difficulty arose: at the last session of Parliament the government passed a law which gave it the right to regulate public meetings in London's parks. It made use of this and had the regulation posted up to warn those who wanted to hold such a

---

a Ferdinand II; further on *La Plebe* has "son".— *Ed.*

b W. Gladstone, *Two Letters to the Earl of Aberdeen on the State Persecutions of the Neapolitan Government,* London, 1851.— *Ed.*

public meeting that they must give a written notification to the
police two days prior to calling it, indicating the names of the
speakers.[a] This regulation carefully kept hidden from the London
press destroyed with one stroke of the pen one of the most
precious rights of London's working people—the right to hold
meetings in parks when and how they please. To submit to this
regulation would be to sacrifice one of the people's rights.

The Irish, who represent the most revolutionary element of the
population, were not men to display such weakness. The
committee unanimously decided to act as if it did not know of the
existence of this regulation and to hold their meeting in defiance
of the government's decree.

Last Sunday[b] at about three o'clock in the afternoon two
enormous processions with bands and banners marched towards
Hyde Park. The bands played Irish songs and the *Marseillaise*;
almost all the banners were Irish (green with a gold harp in the
middle) or red. There were only a few police agents at the
entrances to the park and the columns of demonstrators marched
in without meeting with any resistance. They assembled at the
appointed place and the speeches began.

The spectators numbered at least thirty thousand and at least
half had a green ribbon or a green leaf in their buttonhole to
show they were Irish; the rest were English, German and French.
The crowd was too large for all to be able to hear the speeches
and so a second MEETING was organised nearby with other orators
speaking on the same theme. Forceful resolutions were adopted
demanding a general amnesty and the repeal of the coercion laws
which keep Ireland under a permanent state of siege. At about
five o'clock the demonstrators formed up into files again and left
the park, thus having flouted the regulation of Gladstone's
government.

This is the first time an Irish demonstration has been held in
Hyde Park; it was very successful and even the London bourgeois
press cannot deny this. It is also the first time the English and
Irish sections of our population have united in friendship. These
two elements of the working class, whose enmity towards each
other was so much in the interests of the government and wealthy
classes, are now offering one another the hand of friendship; this
gratifying fact is due principally to the influence of the last

---

[a] This refers to the Act for the Regulation of the Royal Parks and Gardens of
June 27, 1872.— *Ed.*

[b] November 3, 1872.— *Ed.*

General Council of the International, which has always directed all its efforts to unite the workers of both nations on a basis of complete equality. This meeting, of November 3, will usher in a new era in the history of London's working-class movement.

You might ask: "What is the government doing? Can it be that it is willing to reconcile itself to this slight? Will it allow its regulation to be flouted with impunity?"

Well, this is what it has done: it placed two police inspectors and two agents by the platforms in Hyde Park and they took down the names of the speakers. On the following day, these two inspectors brought a suit against the speakers before the *justice of the peace*. The justice sent them a summons and they have to appear before him next Saturday. This course of action makes it quite clear that they don't intend to undertake extensive proceedings against them. The government seems to have admitted that the Irish or, as they say here, the Fenians have beaten it and will be satisfied with a small fine. The debate in court will certainly be interesting and I shall inform you of it in my next letter.[a] Of one thing there can be no doubt: the Irish, thanks to their energetic efforts, have saved the right of the people of London to hold meetings in parks when and how they please.

First published in *La Plebe*, No. 117, November 17, 1872

Signed: *F. Engels*

Printed according to the newspaper

Translated from the Italian

---

[a] See this volume, pp. 298-300.— *Ed.*

Frederick Engels

MANDATE TO E. LARROQUE [218]

[*Draft*]
[London,] December 9, 72
122, Regent's Park Road

A. Serraillier

I, the undersigned, charged by the G. C. of the Assoc. with the receipt and payment, through its hands, of sums of money which may be remitted to me for it, by virtue of powers dated the 27/10/72

Authorise Citizen E. Larroque of Bordeaux to collect and forward to me all sums of money due, either to the preceding G. C. or to the present C., for subscriptions, stamps, printed matter, etc., in the Midi of France.

This authorisation is subject to the confirmation of the G. C. to which it has been communicated.

Signed *F. E.*

For the signature of the G. C.

A. Serraillier

First published in: Marx and Engels, *Works,* First Russian Edition, Vol. XXIX, Moscow, 1946

Printed according to the manuscript

Translated from the French

Published in English for the first time

Frederick Engels

LETTERS FROM LONDON

IV

[MEETING IN HYDE PARK.—SITUATION IN SPAIN]

London, December 11, 1872

The trial by the British government of speakers at the Irish MEETING in Hyde Park[a] has brought a storm on its head. It is true that the justice of the peace made the accused pay a fine of five pounds. But the trial has completely proved the illegality in several respects of the new regulation on public parks, such that the Court of Appeal, which is now handling the case, will have to absolve the accused.

And this is not all: after this first MEETING, not a Sunday goes by without public assemblies in Hyde Park; and the government dare not disturb a single orator. On one occasion there was a meeting there in support of policemen, who had come out on strike; on another a MEETING was held simply to reaffirm the right of assembly in parks.

A strike by policemen? I hear you say. Yes indeed; England is a devil of a country in which strikes penetrate everywhere. I remember that fifteen years ago the POLICEMEN of Manchester went on strike for a wage increase and were completely successful after just two days. A few weeks ago the policemen of the capital threatened to strike because a wage increase of about 20 per cent had been refused them. At the last moment the government deemed it expedient to comply with all their demands. By way of reprisal, however, it punished the secretary of the *resistance society* which the policemen had formed; and as he did not agree to submit to the punishment inflicted on him he was removed from office. A re-action then broke out in the ranks of the police and the Hyde Park meeting was announced. The government gave

---

[a] See this volume, pp. 294-96.— *Ed.*

way once again, granting the rebels an amnesty before the meeting took place—with the exception of the aforementioned secretary. This goes to show that in England—beneath its utterly aristocratic appearance—the spirit of the bourgeoisie has penetrated everywhere. What other nation is so bourgeois as to be able to permit itself *resistance societies* and strikes among policemen?

The news that has reached us of the attitude of the various federations of the *International* to the resolutions of the Hague Congress is most satisfying. In Holland (where that country's delegates had voted with the minority) a regional congress deliberated in conformity with the spirit of the great Association.[219] It was agreed that the Rules and Regulations of the General Council in New York should be followed, while reserving the right to make observations which are considered necessary at the Universal Congress, to be held in September 1873, and not to recognise the right of any other Congress to make decrees on the general interests of the Association.

In Spain too, where the leaders of the Hague minority thought they held absolute sway, the good sense of the workers is making headway. The partisans of the *Alliance*, who are at the head of the Federal Council, have called a regional Congress for December 25 in Cordova. This Congress, following the agenda voted at the previous one in Saragossa, should deal with the matter of bringing the Spanish federal organisation into line with the resolutions to be adopted by the international general Congress.[220] And yet the Federal Council has put on the agenda a choice between the resolutions of the international Congress at The Hague and the anti-international Congress at Saint-Imier.[221] This constitutes a flagrant violation of the General Rules. The New Federation of Madrid has consequently launched an appeal to all the truly international federations (namely those which recognise the General Rules and resolutions of Congresses) to elect a new provisional Federal Council.[a] Important federations and sections, such as those of Lérida, Badalona, Denia and Pont de Vilumara, have already responded with their support. In addition, the federations of Gracia, Toledo, Alcalá and a large number of those in Cádiz and Valencia have declared themselves against the present Federal Council. In Gracia, a manufacturing suburb of Barcelona, after three nights of discussions sustained by the

---

[a] "La Nueva Federacion Madrileña á todas las federaciones, secciones é individuos de la Asociacion Internacional en España", *La Emancipacion*, No. 73, November 9, 1872.— *Ed.*

Alliancists of Barcelona, the local federation—500 members strong—unanimously deliberated all the Hague resolutions and agreed to rebuke the Spanish delegates for their conduct at the last General Congress. In Valencia the Federal Council itself, seeing that it was in danger of being beaten in plenary session, blocked a vote which might have gone against it—a step which provoked splits.[222] And this is just the beginning of the movement in Spain. In a few weeks it will be strong enough to prove that the Spanish workers are not going to let the *International* be thrown into disarray for the profit of the leaders of a handful of secret societies.

The Hague Congress dealt with a certain Bousquet, secretary of the police commissariat at Béziers, who had infiltrated the ranks of the *International,* but who had in fact already been expelled at his section's request by the last General Council.[a] This gentleman, who was subsequently promoted by M. Thiers to the rank of chief of the police brigade in his town, found a defender in issue No. 21 of the *Bulletin jurassien.*[b] Hardly surprising, given that from the ranks of the Jura Federation have emerged two gentlemen—Albert Richard and Gaspard Blanc—who are currently collaborating with M. Louis Napoleon.

First published in *La Plebe*, No. 122, December 14, 1872

Signed: *F. Engels*

Printed according to the newspaper

Translated from the Italian

Published in English for the first time

---

[a] See this volume, p. 249.—*Ed.*

[b] J. Montels, "Compagnons rédacteurs...", *Bulletin de la Fédération jurassienne...*, No. 20/21, November 10, 1872.—*Ed.*

Karl Marx and Frederick Engels

TO THE EDITOR OF *THE INTERNATIONAL HERALD*[223]

Dear Citizen,—We have hitherto considered it superfluous to reply to the slanders and lies which the "autonomous" Mr. John Hales never tires spreading, with reference to us. But when such calumnies are bandied about under the name, and with the pretended authority of the British Federal Council, they are calculated to do harm to the International generally, and we are compelled to break our silence.

This Mr. Hales, who all at once turns up as the champion of the "autonomy" of sections and federations, practically interprets that autonomy as his own personal autocracy. He has got himself appointed, firstly, minute secretary; secondly, corresponding secretary (at home and abroad); thirdly, treasurer of the British Federal Council; but as he cannot fulfil all these duties at once, he, fourthly, appoints other members of that Council to do so in the capacity of his servants. And fifthly, he writes letters to all parts of the world in the name, but without the knowledge or sanction of the British Federal Council.

Thus, we find in No. 23 of the *Bulletin jurassien,* an official letter of the secessionist Jurassien Committee addressed to the British Federal Council,[a] in reply to a letter, also published, of Mr. John Hales.[b] The existence of this letter, we are sure, was quite unknown to the British Federal Council.

He asserts therein:

---

[a] "Le Comité fédéral jurassien a adressé la réponse suivante au Conseil fédéral anglais".— *Ed.*

[b] J. Hales, "Au Comité fédéral de la Fédération jurassienne. Londres, le 6 novembre 1872".— *Ed.*

"This Congress" (at the Hague) "has ... unmasked the hypocrisy of the men of the late General Council, who attempted to organise a vast secret society within our association, and that under the pretext of destroying another secret society, the existence of which they invented for their own purposes."

Mr. Hales is an admirable logician. The exclusion from the International, by Congress, of the *alliance*, proves to him the hypocrisy of the late General Council in disowning that body. As to the *alliance* invented, and the secret conspiracy organised by the General Council, citizen Jung, now a member of the Federal Council, is best adapted to give it all the information required. As former secretary for Switzerland, he knows the doings of the "Alliance", and as member of the Executive Committee of the late General Council[224] he knows all about the "Conspiracy" invented by John Hales. The performances of the public "Alliance" have been already publicly exposed in the circular of the late General Council, *Les prétendues scissions,* etc.[a] The secret action of that society will be brought to daylight by the publication, now preparing, of the documents in the hands of the committee of inquiry appointed by the Hague Congress.[b]

Mr. Hales complains that

"while I was General Secretary of the Council, I never knew, and never could obtain, the addresses of the Continental Federations".

When secretary to the General Council, and its only paid officer, Mr. Hales had no other duties than to prepare the minutes, to send an extract of them to the press, and to correspond with English Sections and Trades' Unions.

The correspondence with other federations, continental or otherwise, was entrusted to unpaid secretaries with whose action he had no business to meddle. How he fulfilled his duty of correspondence within his own department, is shown by a special resolution of the General Council transferring that duty to Citizen Milner.[225]

Mr. Hales states further:

"One day the British Federal Council received a very important letter from the Spanish Federal Council, but the writer, Citizen Anselmo Lorenzo, had forgotten to give his address; the British Federal Council requested Citizen Engels, then corresponding secretary for Spain, to give them the address of Lorenzo; Citizen Engels refused formally. Lately, he gave us the same refusal with regard to the Lisbon Federal Council."

---

a See this volume, pp. 79-123.— *Ed.*
b Ibid., pp. 454-580.— *Ed.*

All that Citizen Engels knows about the matter is, that the Spanish letter in question was sent to him by Citizen Jung with the simple request to translate it, which he did. Of a request of the British Federal Council to have Lorenzo's address, he knows nothing, and would be thankful for an extract of its minutes to that effect.

As to the Lisbon affair, the Portuguese Council applied to Engels for his assistance in a strike,[226] and the very first thing Engels did was to request the co-operation of the British Federal Council, while at the same time he took such other measures as were in his power. After repeated verbal applications, through members of the Federal Council, and after one written application,[a] Engels received, about two months later, a letter from Mr. Hales, stating that the Council had taken some action in the matter, and applying for the Lisbon address. To this letter Engels sent no reply, being then fully aware that Hales wanted such addresses merely for the purpose of his own personal intrigues. As to other members of the British Federal Council, no such reserve was ever thought of. When Jung, in the name of the Federal Council, demanded the addresses in Berlin, Leipzig, and Vienna, they were at once forwarded to him.

The publication of extracts from the minutes of the late General Council, mostly written by Mr. Hales himself, will lay bare the motives of his rancour against that body. To speak in the words of his own letter to the Jurassien Committee, it will then be seen that

"whoever has not been closely acquainted with the defunct General Council, cannot form an idea of the way in which facts are distorted"

by Mr. John Hales.

Yours fraternally,

F. Engels,
Karl Marx

Written on December 19-20, 1872

First published in *The International Herald,* No. 38, December 21, 1872 and in *La Emancipacion,* No. 80, December 28, 1872

Reproduced from *The International Herald*

---

a See this volume, p. 285.— *Ed.*

12*

Frederick Engels

THE MANCHESTER FOREIGN SECTION
TO ALL SECTIONS AND MEMBERS
OF THE BRITISH FEDERATION [227]

Fellow Working Men,

We feel compelled to address you in reply to a circular issued by those who call themselves the majority of the British Federal Council, and appealing to you to join them in open rebellion against the fundamental compact of our association.[a]

In that circular the majority of the Federal Council asserts that the minority have rendered all work impossible, and brought matters to a deadlock, owing to the last meeting having been dissolved by the chairman[b] in the midst of business in order to prevent discussion.[228]

It appears strange, at the first glance, that a majority should be brought to a deadlock by a minority, when a simple vote would have sufficed to silence that minority. Hitherto *minorities* have seceded often enough. This is the first instance of a *majority* seceding; and this fact alone is sufficient to render the whole proceeding more than suspicious. As to the pretence of the action of the chairman at one solitary meeting, we are credibly informed that, on that occasion, the chairman dissolved the meeting half an hour after the time for breaking up, at half past eleven, because members of the majority insisted upon interrupting the order of the day.

The Federal Council is divided, according to the circular, upon the question whether the resolutions of the General Congress of

---

[a] *To the Branches, Sections and Members of the British Federation of the International Working Men's Association.* [Signed:] Hales, J., Bennett, G. [London,] December 10, 1872.— *Ed.*

[b] Samuel Vickery.— *Ed.*

our Association, held at The Hague in September last, are to be considered valid or not. Now, for members of the International, this is not a question at all. According to its General Rules, Article 3, the duty of the General Congress is to "take the measures required for the successful working of our Association".[a] The Congress is its legislative power. Its resolutions are binding upon all. Those who do not like them may either leave the Association, or try to reverse them at the next Congress. But no individual member, no section, no Federal Council, no local or national congress, has the right to declare them null and void, while pretending to remain within the International.

The signataries of the circular pretend that the Hague Congress was not fairly constituted, and in no way represented the majority of the members of the Association. That Congress was regularly convoked by the General Council, in accordance with Art. 4 of the General Rules. It was attended by 64 delegates, representing 15 different nationalities, and belonging, individually, to 12 different nationalities. No previous Congress could boast of such a truly international composition. That the resolutions taken were penetrated by the true spirit of internationalism is proved by the fact that they were almost all taken by majorities of three to one, and that the delegates of the two nations lately involved in fratricidal war—the French and the Germans—almost always voted for them to a man. If England, through its own fault, was not very numerously represented, is that a reason to invalidate the Congress?

The circular complains of the Congress resolution as to the political action of the working class.[b] They say it was taken after the majority of the delegates had left. The official report published in No. 37 of *The International Herald* (December 14th), shows that 48 delegates out of 64 voted on the question, out of which 35 voted in favour of the resolution. Among these 35 we find the name of Mr. Mottershead, who now signs a circular repudiating it.

Now what is this resolution? It is the same in substance, and mostly in words too, as that adopted at the General Conference held in London in September, 1871, and published officially, along with the rest of the resolutions, on the 17th October of that year by the General Council,[c] and has the signatures, among

---

[a] Cf. this volume, p. 4.— *Ed.*
[b] See ibid., p. 243.— *Ed.*
[c] K. Marx and F. Engels, *Resolutions of the Conference of Delegates of the*

others, of John Hales, Th. Mottershead, H. Jung, F. Bradnick, H. Mayo, and John Roach! The General Council being bound to enforce the Conference resolutions, how is it that none of these citizens then thought fit to resign his seat on the General Council, and to protest against this resolution, now found out, all at once, to be so dangerous?

The circular totally falsifies the purport of this resolution, as will be easily seen by referring to its text as published in No. 37 of *The International Herald.* The resolution does not, as is pretended, make political action obligatory upon Trades' Unions and other politically neutral bodies. It merely demands the formation, in every country, of a distinct working class party, opposed to all middle class parties. That is to say, it calls here in England upon the working class to refuse any longer to serve as the fag-end of the "great Liberal party", and to form an independent party of their own, as they did in the glorious times of the great Chartist movement.

Thus the alleged breach of faith towards the Trades' Unions turns out to be a pure invention. But, we may be allowed to ask, *where are* the Trades' Unions *now* that at one time had affiliated themselves to the International? The cash accounts of last year show that they had almost every one disappeared during Citizen Hales' secretaryship.

The next complaint is that the General Council has been removed to New York, and that there are neither English nor Americans upon it. The new General Council is composed of men of five different nationalities, and if the English in New York keep aloof from the International, they have but themselves to blame, if they are not represented at the Council. While that Council was in London, the English were always far more strongly represented than any other nation, and very often formed the absolute majority; while the French, for instance, at one time were not represented at all. But the English cannot claim this as a vested right. The Hague Congress, when, in virtue of the duty and right conferred upon it by Art. 3 of the General Rules, it elected the new General Council, chose what was in its opinion the best locality, and in that locality the best men. The signataries of the Circular may be of a different opinion, but that does not affect the right of the Congress.

The Circular pretends that, by this action, the sections and

International Working Men's Association Assembled at London from 17th to 23rd September 1871.—Ed.

federations are deprived of the right they possessed, of deciding upon the policy to be pursued in their respective countries. This is again untrue. Whether the General Council sit in London, in New York, or anywhere else, the rights of the sections and federations remain the same. But, says the Circular, to prevent disobedience upon this point,

"the Congress armed this General Council with the power of suspending any section, federation, or federal council whenever it pleased, without assigning any reason for so doing".

Untrue, again. The right of suspending any section had been already conferred upon the General Council by the Basel Congress (1869). The official publication of the Hague Congress Resolutions, resolution II, art. 1, (*The International Herald*, No. 37) shows that, if the powers of the General Council have been increased, or rather better defined, they have also been surrounded by safeguards previously not existing.[a] Thus, if the General Council dissolve a Federal Council, it has to provide *within 30 days*, for the election of a new one; and thus, after all, the federation itself remains the ultimate judge. If the General Council suspend a whole federation, it has, if the rest of the federations demand it, to submit its decision *within one month* to the final judgment of a conference of delegates of all federations. And this is what the circular calls: the power of suspension without assigning any reason!

Fellow working men! whether you individually approve or disapprove of the resolutions passed at the Hague, they are at this moment *the law of the International*. If there are those among you who disapprove of them, they have their remedy at the next Congress. But neither any section, nor the British Federal Council, nor any national Congress called by it, has the right to repudiate resolutions of a General Congress lawfully convoked. Whoever attempts such a thing, places himself virtually outside the pale of the International, and that, in effect, the signataries of the circular have done. To allow such action to rule the International would be tantamount to its dissolution.

Even in the countries whose delegates formed the minority at the Hague, a strong re-action has set in against the secessionist tendencies fostered by those delegates. While in America, in France, in Germany, in Poland, in Austria, in Hungary, in Portugal, and in the whole of Switzerland, with the exception of a little knot of scarcely 200 men, the Hague resolutions are gladly

---

[a] See this volume, p. 244.— *Ed.*

accepted, the Dutch Internationals, in Congress assembled, have resolved to stand by the New York General Council, and to lay any grievances they may have before the next lawful General Congress of September, 1873, and before no other.[229] In Spain, where a secessionist movement similar to that inaugurated by the circular in question, was attempted by the Federal Council, the resistance against it is growing stronger every day, and section after section adheres to the Hague resolutions.

Fellow working men! for all these reasons, we protest against the convocation of any British Congress which is to sit in judgment upon the law of the Association as established by the delegates of all nations represented in it.

We protest against any Congress convoked at such a short notice as that called for the 5th January.[230]

We urge upon all sections to submit the foregoing to the consideration of their members, remembering that the future of our Association in England rests upon their action in the present crisis.

It is necessary that we recognise as legitimate delegates to the Federal Council only those who will uphold the authority of the Congress of the Hague, and endeavour to carry out the resolutions passed there.

Adopted at the general meeting of the Manchester Foreign Section, held on Saturday, 21st December, 1872.

Fraternal greeting to all members of our Association.

> *P. Zürcher*, Chairman of the Meeting
> *F. Kupper*, General and German Secretary
> *O. Wyss*, French Secretary

Written on about December 20, 1872   Reproduced from the leaflet

First published as a leaflet on December 23, 1872

Karl Marx

ADDRESS OF THE BRITISH FEDERAL COUNCIL TO THE SECTIONS, BRANCHES, AFFILIATED SOCIETIES AND MEMBERS OF THE INTERNATIONAL WORKING MEN'S ASSOCIATION [231]

Citizens,

At our sitting of December 19th, 1872, our attention was called to a Manifesto issued by the representatives of the party of secession in England.[a] We at once took the resolution to forward to every section a notice calling upon them to suspend their judgment thereon until they had our reply before them, which we promised to get out at once, and at a special meeting of the British Federal Council, held on Monday evening, December 23rd, the following was unanimously adopted in reply to the allegations made in the above mentioned Manifesto.

(1). The dead-lock has been caused by the constant introduction of Hales' personal matter; both he and Mottershead have already, on the General Council, by their mutual charges of corruption, attempted to cause a similar dead-lock there. The dead-lock at the meeting alluded to was caused by Mottershead, being drunk, rendering the dissolution of the meeting necessary, at half-past eleven, by constantly repeating violent personal charges against the Chairman[b]; such dissolution being demanded by none more than by Hales. The members will long ago have seen in *The International Herald* that the South Lambeth Section withdrew its delegate because the majority obstructed all real business.

(2). The real reason of this circular is an understanding between the secessionist minority of the Hague Congress to call all sorts of

---

[a] *To the Branches, Sections and Members of the British Federation of the International Working Men's Association*. [Signed:] Hales, J., Bennett, G. [London,] December 10, 1872.— *Ed.*

[b] Samuel Vickery (see also the previous document, pp. 304-06).— *Ed.*

congresses in all countries about Christmas and to get them to confirm their secessionist action. Thus similar congresses have been called in Belgium and in Spain for the 25th December (against which in Spain there is a strong opposition, getting stronger every day).[232] The English Sections are to be now bamboozled into assisting the plot without knowing what is going on.

(3). The circular now before us has not been laid before the Federal Council. Nothing shows better how its authors feared discussion, than that they concocted it, behind the back of the Council, in a hole and corner meeting. Has it ever been seen before that a majority, instead of outvoting a minority seceded from it? What do the majority want a special Congress for, when a simple vote of the Council which they profess to command, will decide the question in their favour?

(4). The signataries of this circular dare not yet go the full length of the continental secessionists, who plainly state that they repudiate the authority of every Congress except the first held at Geneva. In the mean time, they begin by impugning the validity of the Congress of the Hague, the most International and indeed the first really International Congress of the Association, because it was the first where the majority was not national or even merely local. If that congress was not fairly constituted, why did Citizen Roach who was a member of the Committee for examination of credentials, sign the report of that Committee? Yet he now signs the circular protesting against the Congress.

(5). They say they will stand by the General Rules as they existed prior to the Congress of the Hague. These Rules say, art. 3. "The Congress will have to take the measures required for the successful working of the Association and appoint the General Council of the Society." Art. 12. "The present Rules may be revised by each Congress provided that two-thirds of the delegates present are in favour of such revision." [a] The General Rules give no right whatever to any Local or Federal Congresses to revise the resolutions of any General Congress. Therefore the signataries of this circular declare themselves in open revolt not only against the Constitution of the International as fixed by the Congress of the Hague, but also against those General Rules which they declare they will stand by.

Now which are the resolutions of the Hague Congress which are so distasteful to the signataries of the circular?

---

[a] Cf. this volume, pp. 4 and 8.— Ed.

The first is the resolution about the political action of the Working Class[a] which, they assert, has been passed after the majority of the Delegates had left. This is so far from true, that out of the 64 Delegates who took part in the Congress, 48 took part in the vote on this resolution, and out of these 35, or more than two-thirds, voted for it, amongst whom Citizen Mottershead, who has nevertheless signed the present circular. Moreover, most of the Delegates who had left, had also left with the chairman a written declaration that they were in favour of the resolution.

The resolution itself is nothing but an extract from the resolution No. IX. of the Conference of London, September, 1871, published, along with the other resolutions, by the General Council on the 17th October, 1871,[b] and to which are appended the names of Citizens Bradnick, Mayo, Mottershead, Jung, Roach, and Hales, the latter as general Secretary. This resolution of the Conference quotes the general rules, the Inaugural Address, a Resolution of the Congress of Lausanne, and all the action of the General Council from the beginning, to prove that what it asserts is merely an explanation, in the same sense, of what has always been the officially adopted policy of the Association. Before the Hague Congress, the General Council resolved unanimously to propose to that Congress the introduction of this very resolution into the General Rules; Citizen Jung was acting as secretary that evening, Hales having been suspended.[233] And even the Nottingham Congress, to the resolutions of which the circular refers, as to a precedent, adopted a resolution virtually the same.[234]

As to the pretended turning adrift of Trades Unions by this resolution, the Congress, quite on the contrary, has even gone further than the General Rules or any previous Congress in favour of Trades Unions. It charged the New General Council to constitute an International Bond between the Trades Unions, to admit to it even Trades Unions that do not belong to the International, to invite every Trades Union to state itself the terms upon which it will enter such bond, and to draw up a general plan to be submitted to the provisional acceptance of all Trades Unions adhering, previous to its final sanction by the next Congress.

The next complaint is the removal of the General Council to New York. This amounts simply to the assertion that no General

---

[a] See this volume, p. 243.—*Ed.*

[b] K. Marx and F. Engels, *Resolutions of the Conference of Delegates of the International Working Men's Association Assembled at London from 17th to 23rd September 1871.—Ed.*

Council upon which Messrs Hales, Mottershead, Jung, Bradnick, Mayo and Roach do not sit, can pretend to represent the International.

Another complaint is that the powers of this General Council have been increased. Now the first resolution to that effect taken at the Hague was the following. "The General Council is bound to execute the Congress Resolutions, and to take care that in every country the principles and the General Rules and Regulations of the International are strictly observed."[a] This resolution was proposed to the Congress in consequence of a unanimous vote of the late General Council.[235] How could it be put in force if the General Council had not the power to suspend bodies acting within the International, against the International? Besides, the Hague resolutions relating to the right of suspension of Sections, Federal Councils and Federations, have in reality limited the power given by the Congress of Basle (see Administrative Regulation 2, article 6 & 7),[b] and subjected in every case the action of the General Council to a counter check.

Everywhere on the Continent, the governments and the middle-class press are supporting the attempts of the men who try to provoke a secession in the ranks of the Association, while those who cling to the International are everywhere arrested, and their newspapers prosecuted by the police. While the secessionists glory in the assertion, that the International by their exertions is everywhere in a state of dissolution, and in rebellion against the Hague resolutions, the fact is that the Association is stronger than ever, and that the Hague resolutions are fully endorsed in France, Germany, Austria, Hungary, Portugal, America, Denmark, Poland, and Switzerland, excepting, in the latter country, some 150 secessionists. In Holland, although the delegates of that country voted at the Hague with the minority, a Congress has been held which resolved to remain faithful to the General Council, and to recognise no other General Congress but the regular one of September, 1873, to be held in Switzerland.[236] In Spain where the secessionists expected to carry everything before them, because they had the Federal Council on their side, the opposition against them is growing stronger every day. Even in Italy Sections are continuing to send in their adhesion to the New General Council, and this New English Congress dodge is the last resource the secessionists are driven to.

---

[a] See this volume, p. 244.— *Ed.*
[b] Ibid., pp. 244 and 10.— *Ed.*

In reply to the propositions of the circular, we have to submit the following: —

(1). We declare any Congress held in England for the purpose of revising the resolutions passed at the Congress of the Hague to be illegal, because every Federation has the right of objecting at the next General Congress. Further the only legal Congress of the British Federation is the one to be held in Manchester at Whitsuntide next,[237] in accordance with the resolution passed at the Nottingham Congress of July, 1872.

(2). We call upon the Sections to revoke the powers given to the subscribers of the circular and to send new delegates to represent them on the Federal Council.

(3). We call upon the Sections to appoint a Committee to which the minutes of the Federal Council will be submitted and who will draw its own conclusions as to who obstructed and who forwarded the work of the Association, and who acted in the interest of the enemies of the working classes.

(4). We call upon the Sections to appoint a commission to inquire into the organisation, number of members and date of establishment of the Sections, and particularly the respective number of delegates they used to send to the Federal Council.

The Sections now being in possession of both Manifestoes, we leave the matter in their hands and only ask that their decision may be communicated to us at once.

But we unhesitatingly affirm that we are acting in accordance with the rules and constitution of the Association, and in the real interest of the working classes.

Long life to the International Working Men's Association.

> F. *Hurry*, South Lambeth Section, Chairman
> E. *Hills*, West End Section
> F. *Lessner*, Nottingham Congress, ex-member of the General Council, Founder of the I.W.M.A.
> W. H. *Riley*, Nottingham Congress
> Ch. *Murray*, Normanby Section, ex-member of the General Council
> G. *Milner*, National Reform League, ex-member of the General Council
> J. *Mitchell*, Hinckley Section, Leicestershire
> G. A. *Weiler,* London German Section

S. Vickery, Birkenhead Section
Eugène Dupont, Manchester Section,
ex-member of the General Council, Founder of the I.W.M.A.

All communications to be sent to Citizen *Riley,* Editor of *The International Herald,* 7, Red Lion Court, Fleet Street, London.

London, December 23rd, 1872

Drawn up on December 20, 1872   Reproduced from the leaflet

First published as a leaflet on
December 30-31, 1872

Zur Wohnungsfrage.

Von

Friedrich Engels.

Separatabdruck aus dem „Volksstaat".

Leipzig, 1872.

Verlag der Expedition des „Volksstaat".

Title page of the separate reprint of Engels' *The Housing Question*, Part I,
with the author's dedication to Laura Lafargue

Frederick Engels

THE HOUSING QUESTION [238]

Part I

HOW PROUDHON SOLVES
THE HOUSING QUESTION

In No. 10 and the following issues of the *Volksstaat* may be found a series of six articles on the housing question.[a] These articles are worthy of attention only because, apart from some long-forgotten would-be literary writings of the forties, they are the first attempt to transplant the Proudhonist school to Germany. This represents such an enormous step backward in comparison with the whole course of development of German socialism, which delivered a decisive blow precisely to the Proudhonist ideas as far back as twenty-five years ago,* that it is worth while answering this attempt immediately.

The so-called housing shortage, which plays such a great role in the press nowadays, does not consist in the fact that the working class generally lives in bad, overcrowded and unhealthy dwellings. *This* shortage is not something peculiar to the present; it is not even one of the sufferings peculiar to the modern proletariat in contradistinction to all earlier oppressed classes. On the contrary, all oppressed classes in all periods suffered rather uniformly from it. In order to put an end to *this* housing shortage there is only *one* means: to abolish altogether the exploitation and oppression of the working class by the ruling class.—What is meant today by housing shortage is the peculiar intensification of the bad housing conditions of the workers as a result of the sudden rush of population to the big cities; a colossal increase in rents, still greater

---

* In Marx: *Misère de la philosophie etc.*, Brussels and Paris, 1847.

---

[a] [A. Mülberger,] "Die Wohnungsfrage", *Der Volksstaat*, Nos. 10-13, 15, 19, February 3, 7, 10, 14, 21, March 6, 1872.—*Ed.*

congestion in the separate houses, and, for some, the impossibility of finding a place to live in at all. And *this* housing shortage gets talked of so much only because it is not confined to the working class but has affected the petty bourgeoisie as well.

The housing shortage from which the workers and part of the petty bourgeoisie suffer in our modern big cities is one of the innumerable *smaller,* secondary evils which result from the present-day capitalist mode of production. It is not at all a direct result of the exploitation of the worker *as* worker by the capitalist. This exploitation is the basic evil which the social revolution wants to abolish by abolishing the capitalist mode of production. The cornerstone of the capitalist mode of production is, however, the fact that our present social order enables the capitalist to buy the labour power of the worker at its value, but to extract from it much more than its value by making the worker work longer than is necessary to reproduce the price paid for the labour power. The surplus value produced in this fashion is divided among the whole class of capitalists and landowners, together with their paid servants, from the Pope and the Emperor down to the night watchman and below. We are not concerned here with how this distribution comes about, but this much is certain: that all those who do not work can live only on the pickings from this surplus value, which reach them in one way or another. (Compare *Marx's "Capital"*, where this was propounded for the first time.)

The distribution of this surplus value, produced by the working class and taken from it without payment, among the non-working classes proceeds amid extremely edifying squabblings and mutual swindling. In so far as this distribution takes place by means of buying and selling, one of its chief methods is the cheating of the buyer by the seller; and in retail trade, particularly in the big cities, this has become an absolute condition of existence for the seller. When, however, the worker is cheated by his grocer or his baker, either in regard to the price or the quality of the merchandise, this does not happen to him in his specific capacity as a worker. On the contrary, as soon as a certain average measure of cheating has become the social rule in any place, it must in the long run be adjusted by a corresponding increase in wages. The worker appears before the shopkeeper as a buyer, that is, as the owner of money or credit, and hence not at all in his capacity as a worker, that is, as a seller of labour power. The cheating may hit him, and the poorer class as a whole, harder than it hits the richer social classes, but it is not an evil which hits him exclusively, which is peculiar to his class.

And it is just the same with the housing shortage. The expansion of the big modern cities gives the land in certain sections of them, particularly in those which are centrally situated, an artificial and often enormously increasing value; the buildings erected in these areas depress this value, instead of increasing it, because they no longer correspond to the changed circumstances; they are pulled down and replaced by others. This takes place above all with centrally located workers' houses, whose rents, even with the greatest overcrowding, can never, or only very slowly, increase above a certain maximum. They are pulled down and in their stead shops, warehouses and public buildings are erected. Through its Haussmann in Paris,[a] Bonapartism exploited this tendency tremendously for swindling and private enrichment. But the spirit of Haussmann has also been abroad in London, Manchester and Liverpool, and seems to feel itself just as much at home in Berlin and Vienna. The result is that the workers are forced out of the centre of the towns towards the outskirts; that workers' dwellings, and small dwellings in general, become rare and expensive and often altogether unobtainable, for under these circumstances the building industry, which is offered a much better field for speculation by more expensive dwelling houses, builds workers' dwellings only by way of exception.

This housing shortage, therefore, certainly hits the worker harder than it hits any more prosperous class, but it is just as little an evil which burdens the working class exclusively as is the cheating of the shopkeeper, and, as far as the working class is concerned, when this evil reaches a certain level and attains a certain permanency, it must similarly find a certain economic adjustment.

It is largely with just such sufferings as these, which the working class endures in common with other classes, and particularly the petty bourgeoisie, that petty-bourgeois socialism, to which Proudhon belongs, prefers to occupy itself. And thus it is not at all accidental that our German Proudhonist seizes chiefly upon the housing question, which, as we have seen, is by no means exclusively a working-class question; and that he declares it to be, on the contrary, a true, exclusively working-class question.

"The *tenant* is in the same position in relation to the *house-owner* as the *wage-worker* in relation to the *capitalist*."[b]

---

[a] The words "in Paris" were added by Engels in the 1887 edition.— *Ed.*
[b] [A. Mülberger,] op. cit., *Der Volksstaat*, No. 12, February 10, 1872.— *Ed.*

This is totally untrue.

In the housing question we have two parties confronting each other: the tenant and the landlord, or house-owner. The former wishes to purchase from the latter the temporary use of a dwelling; he has money or credit, even if he has to buy this credit from the house-owner himself at a usurious price in the shape of an addition to the rent. It is a simple commodity sale; it is not a transaction between proletarian and bourgeois, between worker and capitalist. The tenant—even if he is a worker—appears as *a man with money*; he must already have sold his commodity, a commodity peculiarly his own, his labour power, to be able to appear with the proceeds as the buyer of the use of a dwelling or he must be in a position to give a guarantee of the impending sale of this labour power. The peculiar results which attend the sale of labour power to the capitalist are completely absent here. The capitalist causes the purchased labour power first to produce its own value but secondly to produce a surplus value, which remains in his hands for the time being, subject to distribution among the capitalist class. In this case, therefore, an excess value is produced, the sum total of the existing value is increased. In a renting transaction the situation is quite different. No matter how much the landlord may overreach the tenant it is still only a transfer of already *existing*, previously *produced* value, and the total sum of values possessed by the landlord and the tenant *together* remains the same after as it was before. The worker is always cheated of a part of the product of his labour, whether that labour is paid for by the capitalist below, above or at its value; the tenant, only when he is compelled to pay for the dwelling above its value. It is therefore a complete misrepresentation of the relation between landlord and tenant to attempt to make it equivalent to the relation between worker and capitalist. On the contrary, we are dealing here with a quite ordinary commodity transaction between two citizens, and this transaction proceeds according to the economic laws which govern the sale of commodities in general, and in particular the sale of the commodity "landed property". The building and maintenance costs of the house or of the part of the house in question enter first into the calculation; the value of the land, determined by the more or less favourable situation of the house, comes next; the relation between supply and demand existing at the moment decides in the end. This simple economic relation expresses itself in the mind of our Proudhonist as follows:

"The house, once it has been built, serves as a *perpetual legal title* to a definite fraction of social labour although the real value of the house has been paid to the owner long ago more than adequately in the form of rent. Thus it comes about that a house which, for instance, was built fifty years ago, during this period covers the original cost price two, three, five, ten and more times over in its rent yield." [a]

Here we have at once Proudhon in his entirety. First, it is forgotten that the rent must not only pay the interest on the building costs, but must also cover repairs and the average amount of bad debts and unpaid rents as well as the occasional periods when the house is untenanted,[b] and finally must pay off in annual instalments the building capital which has been invested in a house, which is perishable and which in time becomes uninhabitable and worthless. Secondly, it is forgotten that the house rent must also pay interest on the increased value of the land upon which the building is erected and that, therefore, a part of it consists of ground rent. Our Proudhonist immediately declares, it is true, that since this increment is brought about without the landowner having contributed anything, it does not equitably belong to him but to society as a whole. However, he overlooks the fact that he is thereby in reality demanding the abolition of landed property, a point which would lead us too far if we went into it here. And finally he overlooks the fact that the whole transaction is not at all one of buying the house from its owner, but of buying only its use for a certain time. Proudhon, who never bothered himself about the real, the actual conditions under which any economic phenomenon occurs, is naturally also unable to explain how the original cost price of a house is under certain circumstances paid back ten times over in the course of fifty years in the form of rent. Instead of examining this not at all difficult question economically and establishing whether it is really in contradiction to economic laws, and if so how, Proudhon resorts to a bold leap from economics into jurisprudence: "The house, once it has been built, serves as a *perpetual legal title*" to a certain annual payment. How this comes about, *how* the house *becomes* a legal title, on this Proudhon is silent. And yet that is just what he should have explained. Had he examined this question he would have found that all the legal titles in the world, no matter how perpetual, could not give a house the power of obtaining its cost price back ten times, over the course of fifty years, in the form of rent, but that only economic conditions (which may have obtained social recognition in the form of legal titles) can accomplish this. And with this he would again be where he started from.

---

[a] [A. Mülberger,] op. cit., *Der Volksstaat*, No. 10, February 3, 1872.— *Ed.*

[b] The rest of the sentence was added by Engels in the 1887 edition.— *Ed.*

The whole Proudhonist teaching rests on this saving leap from economic reality into legal phraseology. Every time our good Proudhon loses the economic hang of things—and this happens to him with every serious problem—he takes refuge in the sphere of law and appeals to *eternal justice*.

"Proudhon begins by taking his ideal of justice, of *'justice éternelle'*, from the juridical relations that correspond to the production of commodities; thereby, it may be noted, he proves, to the consolation of all good citizens, that the production of commodities is a form of production as everlasting as justice. Then he turns round and seeks to reform the actual production of commodities, and the actual legal system corresponding thereto, in accordance with this ideal. What opinion should we have of a chemist, who, instead of studying the actual laws of the molecular changes in the composition and decomposition of matter, and on that foundation solving definite problems, claimed to regulate the composition and decomposition of matter by means of the 'eternal ideas', of *'naturalité* and *affinité'*? Do we really know any more about 'usury', when we say it contradicts *'justice éternelle'*, *'équité éternelle'*, *'mutualité éternelle'*, and other *'vérités éternelles'*, than the fathers of the church did when they said it was incompatible with *'grâce éternelle'*, *'foi éternelle'*, and *'la volonté éternelle de Dieu'*?" (Marx, *Capital*, p. 45[a]).

Our Proudhonist does not fare any better than his lord and master:

"The rent agreement is one of the thousand exchanges which are as necessary in the life of modern society as the circulation of the blood in the bodies of animals. Naturally, it would be in the interest of this society if all these exchanges were pervaded by a *conception of right,* that is to say, if they were carried out everywhere according to the strict demands of justice. In a word, the economic life of society must, as Proudhon says, raise itself to the heights of *economic right.* In reality, as we know, exactly the opposite takes place."[b]

Is it credible that five years after Marx had characterised Proudhonism so summarily and convincingly precisely from this decisive angle, one can still print such confused stuff in the German language? What does this rigmarole mean? Nothing more than that the practical effects of the economic laws which govern present-day society run contrary to the author's sense of justice and that he cherishes the pious wish that the matter might be so

---

[a] Engels quotes from the first (1867) German edition of Volume One of *Capital*; see also the English edition which was edited by Engels (*Capital*, Vol. I, London, 1887, p. 56).— *Ed.*

[b] [A. Mülberger,] op. cit., *Der Volksstaat*, No. 11, February 7, 1872.— *Ed.*

arranged as to remedy this situation.—Yes, if toads had tails they would no longer be toads! And is then the capitalist mode of production not "pervaded by a conception of right", namely, that of its own right to exploit the workers? And if the author tells us this is not *his* conception of right, are we one step further?

But let us go back to the housing question. Our Proudhonist now gives his "conception of right" free rein and treats us to the following moving declamation:

> "We do not hesitate to assert that there is no more terrible mockery of the whole culture of our lauded century than the fact that in the big cities 90 per cent and more of the population have no place that they can call their own. The real nodal point of moral and family existence, hearth and home, is being swept away by the social whirlpool... In this respect we are far below the savages. The troglodyte has his cave, the Australian his clay hut, the Indian his own hearth, but the modern proletarian is practically suspended in mid-air," etc.[a]

In this jeremiad we have Proudhonism in its whole reactionary form. In order to create the modern revolutionary class of the proletariat it was absolutely necessary to cut the umbilical cord which still bound the worker of the past to the land. The hand weaver who had his little house, garden and field along with his loom was a quiet, contented man, "godly and honourable" despite all misery and despite all political pressure; he doffed his cap to the rich, to the priest and to the officials of the state and inwardly was altogether a slave. It is precisely modern large-scale industry which has turned the worker, formerly chained to the land, into a completely propertyless proletarian, liberated from all traditional fetters,[b] *a free outlaw*; it is precisely this economic revolution which has created the sole conditions under which the exploitation of the working class in its final form, in capitalist production, can be overthrown. And now comes this tearful Proudhonist and bewails the driving of the workers from hearth and home as though it were a great retrogression instead of being the very first condition of their intellectual emancipation.

Twenty-seven years ago I described, in *The Condition of the Working-Class in England*, the main features of just this process of driving the workers from hearth and home, as it took place in the eighteenth century in England.[c] The infamies of which the land and factory owners were guilty in so doing, and the deleterious effects, material and moral, which this expulsion inevitably had on the workers concerned in the first place, are there also described

---

[a] Ibid.—*Ed.*

[b] *Der Volksstaat* has "culture" instead of "fetters".—*Ed.*

[c] See present edition, Vol. 4, pp. 307-27.—*Ed.*

as they deserve. But could it enter my head to regard this, which was in the circumstances an absolutely necessary historical process of development, as a retrogression "below the savages"? Impossible! The English proletarian of 1872 is on an infinitely higher level than the rural weaver of 1772 with his "hearth and home". And will the troglodyte with his cave, the Australian with his clay hut or the Indian with his own hearth ever accomplish a June insurrection [239] or a Paris Commune?

That the situation of the workers has on the whole become materially worse since the introduction of capitalist production on a large scale is doubted only by the bourgeois. But should we therefore look backward longingly to the (likewise very meagre) fleshpots of Egypt,[240] to rural small-scale industry, which produced only servile souls, or to "the savages"? On the contrary. Only the proletariat created by modern large-scale industry, liberated from all inherited fetters including those which chained it to the land, and herded together in the big cities, is in a position to accomplish the great social transformation which will put an end to all class exploitation and all class rule. The old rural hand weavers with hearth and home would never have been able to do it; they would never have been able to conceive such an idea, not to speak of desiring to carry it out.

For Proudhon, on the other hand, the whole industrial revolution of the last hundred years, the introduction of steam power and large-scale factory production which substitutes machinery for hand labour and increases the productivity of labour a thousandfold, is a highly repugnant occurrence, something which really ought never to have taken place. The petty bourgeois Proudhon aspires to a world in which each person turns out a separate and independent product that is immediately consumable and exchangeable in the market. Then, as long as each person receives back the full value of his labour in the form of another product, "eternal justice" is satisfied and the best possible world created. But this best possible world of Proudhon has already been nipped in the bud and trodden underfoot by the advance of industrial development, which long ago destroyed individual labour in all the big branches of industry and which is destroying it daily more and more in the smaller and even smallest branches, which is setting social labour supported by machinery and the harnessed forces of nature in its place, and whose finished product, immediately exchangeable or consumable, is the joint work of the many individuals through whose hands it has had to pass. And it is precisely this industrial revolution which has raised

the productive power of human labour to such a high level
that—for the first time in the history of mankind—the possibility
exists, given a rational division of labour among all, of producing
not only enough for the plentiful consumption of all members of
society and for an abundant reserve fund, but also of leaving each
individual sufficient leisure so that what is really worth preserving
in historically inherited culture—science, art, forms of intercourse,
etc.—may not only be preserved but converted from a monopoly
of the ruling class into the common property of the whole of
society, and may be further developed. And here is the decisive
point: as soon as the productive power of human labour has risen
to this height, every excuse disappears for the existence of a ruling
class. After all, the ultimate basis on which class differences were
defended was always: there must be a class which need not plague
itself with the production of its daily subsistence, in order that it
may have time to look after the intellectual work of society. This
talk, which up to now had its great historical justification, has been
cut off at the root once and for all by the industrial revolution of
the last hundred years. The existence of a ruling class is becoming
daily more and more a hindrance to the development of industrial
productive power, and equally so to that of science, art and
especially of forms of cultural intercourse. There never were
greater boors than our modern bourgeois.

All this is nothing to friend Proudhon. He wants "eternal
justice" and nothing else. Each shall receive in exchange for his
product the full proceeds of his labour, the full value of his
labour. But to calculate this in a product of modern industry is a
complicated matter. For modern industry obscures the particular
share of the individual in the total product, which in the old
individual handicraft was obviously represented by the finished
product. Further, modern industry eliminates more and more
individual exchange, on which Proudhon's whole system is built
up,[a] namely, direct exchange between two producers each of
whom takes the product of the other in order to consume it.
Consequently a reactionary streak runs through the whole of
Proudhonism; an aversion to the industrial revolution and the
desire, sometimes overtly, sometimes covertly expressed, to drive
the whole of modern industry out of the temple—steam engines,
mechanical looms and the rest of the business—and to return to
old, respectable hand labour. That we would then lose nine
hundred and ninety-nine thousandths of our productive power,

---

[a] The rest of the sentence was added by Engels in the 1887 edition.— Ed.

that the whole of humanity would be condemned to the worst possible labour slavery, that starvation would become the general rule—what does all that matter if only we succeed in organising exchange in such a fashion that each receives "the full proceeds of his labour", and that "eternal justice" is realised? *Fiat justitia, pereat mundus!*[a]

Let justice be done though the whole world perish!

And the world would perish in this Proudhonist counter-revolution if it were at all possible to carry it out.

It is, however, self-evident that, even with social production conditioned by modern large-scale industry, it is possible to assure each person "the full proceeds of his labour", so far as this phrase has any meaning at all.[b] And it has a meaning only if it is extended to purport not that each individual worker becomes the possessor of "the full proceeds of his labour", but that the whole of society, consisting entirely of workers, becomes the possessor of the total product of their labour, which product it partly distributes among its members for consumption, partly uses for replacing and increasing its means of production, and partly stores up as a reserve fund for production and consumption.

After what has been said above, we already know in advance how our Proudhonist will solve the great housing question. On the one hand, we have the demand that each worker have and own his own home in order that we may no longer be *below the savages.* On the other hand, we have the assurance that the two, three, five or tenfold repayment of the original cost price of a house in the form of rent, as it actually takes place, is based on a *legal title,* and that this legal title is in contradiction to *"eternal justice".* The solution is simple: we abolish the legal title and by virtue of eternal justice declare the rent paid to be a payment on account of the cost of the dwelling itself. If one has so arranged one's premises that they already contain the conclusion, then of course it requires no greater skill than any charlatan possesses to produce the result, prepared beforehand, from the bag and proudly point to unshakeable logic whose result it is.

And so it happens here. The abolition of rented dwellings is proclaimed a necessity, and couched in the form of a demand that every tenant be turned into the owner of his dwelling. How are we to do that? Very simply:

---

a The motto of Ferdinand I, emperor of the Holy Roman Empire.— *Ed.*
b The next sentence was added by Engels in the 1887 edition.— *Ed.*

"Rented dwellings will be redeemed... The previous house-owner will be paid the value of his house to the last farthing. Hitherto the tenant has paid rent as his tribute to the perpetual title of capital, now, from the day when the redemption of rented dwellings is proclaimed, the exactly fixed sum paid by the tenant will become the annual instalment paid for the dwelling which has passed into his possession... Society ... transforms itself in this way into a totality of free and independent owners of dwellings."[a]

The Proudhonist finds it a crime against eternal justice that the house-owner can without working obtain ground rent and interest[b] out of the capital he has invested in the house. He decrees that this must cease, that capital invested in houses shall no longer yield interest; nor ground rent either, so far as it represents purchased landed property. Now we have seen that the capitalist mode of production, the basis of present-day society, is in no way affected hereby. The pivot on which the exploitation of the worker turns is the sale of his labour power to the capitalist and the use which the capitalist makes of this transaction, the fact that he compels the worker to produce far more than the paid value of his labour power amounts to. It is this transaction between capitalist and worker which produces all the surplus value afterwards divided in the form of ground rent, commercial profit, interest on capital,[c] taxes, etc., among the diverse varieties of capitalists and their servitors. And now our Proudhonist comes along and believes that if we were to prohibit *one single variety* of capitalists, and at that of capitalists who purchase no labour power directly and therefore also cause no surplus value to be produced, from making profit or receiving interest,[d] it would be a step forward! The mass of unpaid labour taken from the working class would remain exactly the same even if house-owners were to be deprived tomorrow of the possibility of receiving ground rent and interest.[e] However, this does not prevent our Proudhonist from declaring:

"The abolition of rented dwellings is thus one of the *most fruitful and magnificent aspirations* which have ever sprung from the womb of the revolutionary idea and it must become one of the *primary demands* of the Social-Democracy."[f]

---

[a] [A. Mülberger,] op. cit., *Der Volksstaat*, No. 12, February 10, 1872.— *Ed.*

[b] *Der Volksstaat* has "profit" instead of "interest".— *Ed.*

[c] The words "interest on capital" were added by Engels in the 1887 edition.— *Ed.*

[d] The words "or receiving interest" were added by Engels in the 1887 edition.— *Ed.*

[e] *Der Volksstaat* has "profit" instead of "interest".— *Ed.*

[f] [A. Mülberger,] op. cit., *Der Volksstaat*, No. 12, February 10, 1872.— *Ed.*

This is exactly the type of market cry of the master Proudhon himself, whose cackling was always in inverse ratio to the size of the eggs laid.

And now imagine the fine state of things if each worker, petty bourgeois and bourgeois were compelled by paying annual instalments to become first part owner and then full owner of his dwelling! In the industrial districts in England, where there is large-scale industry but small workers' houses and each married worker occupies a little house of his own, there might possibly be some sense in it. But the small-scale industry in Paris and in most of the big cities on the Continent is supplemented by large houses in each of which ten, twenty or thirty families live together. Supposing that on the day of the world-delivering decree, when the redemption of rent dwellings is proclaimed, Peter is working in an engineering works in Berlin. A year later he is owner of, if you like, the fifteenth part of his flat consisting of a little room on the fifth floor of a house somewhere in the neighbourhood of the Hamburger Tor. He then loses his job and soon afterwards finds himself in a similar flat on the third floor of a house in the Pothof in Hanover with a wonderful view of the courtyard. After five months' stay there he has just acquired $^1/_{36}$ part of this property when a strike sends him to Munich and compels him by a stay of eleven months to assume ownership of exactly $^{11}/_{180}$ of a rather gloomy abode on the street level behind the Ober-Angergasse. Subsequent removals, such as nowadays are so frequent with workers, saddle him further with $^7/_{360}$ of a no less desirable residence in Saint Gall, $^{23}/_{180}$ of another one in Leeds, and $^{347}/_{56223}$, figured out exactly in order that "eternal justice" may have nothing to complain about, of a third flat in Seraing. And now, of what use are all these shares in flats to our Peter? Who is to give him the real value of these shares? Where is he to find the owner or owners of the remaining shares in his various one-time flats? And what exactly are the property relations regarding any big house whose floors hold, let us say, twenty flats and which, when the redemption period has elapsed and rented flats are abolished, belongs to perhaps three hundred part owners who are scattered all over the world? Our Proudhonist will answer that by that time the Proudhonist exchange bank [241] will exist, which will pay to anyone at any time the full labour proceeds for any labour product, and will therefore pay out also the full value of a share in a flat. But in the first place we are not at all concerned here with the Proudhonist exchange bank since it is nowhere mentioned in the articles on the housing question; secondly it rests on the peculiar error that if someone wants to sell a commodity he will necessarily always find a buyer for its full value, and thirdly it went bankrupt in England more than once under the name of LABOUR EXCHANGE BAZAAR,[242] before Proudhon invented it.

The whole conception that the worker should *buy* his dwelling rests again on the reactionary basic outlook, already emphasised, of Proudhonism, according to which the conditions created by modern large-scale industry are morbid excrescences, and society must be brought forcibly, that is, against the trend which it has been following for a hundred years, to a condition in which the old stable handicraft of the individual is the rule, and which, generally speaking, is nothing but an idealised restoration of small-scale enterprise, which has gone and is still going to rack and ruin. Once the workers are flung back into these stable conditions and the "social whirlpool" has been happily removed, the worker can naturally again make use of property in "hearth and home", and the above redemption theory appears less absurd. Proudhon only forgets that in order to accomplish all this he must first of all put back the clock of world history a hundred years, and that if he did he would turn the present-day workers into just such narrow-minded, crawling, sneaking servile souls as their great-great-grandfathers were.

As far, however, as this Proudhonist solution of the housing question contains any rational and practically applicable content it is already being carried out today, but this realisation does not spring from "the womb of the revolutionary idea", but from—the big bourgeois themselves. Let us listen to an excellent Spanish newspaper, *La Emancipacion*, of Madrid, of March 16, 1872[a]:

"There is still another means of solving the housing question, the way proposed by Proudhon, which dazzles at first glance, but on closer examination reveals its utter impotence. Proudhon proposed that tenants should be converted into buyers on the instalment plan, that the rent paid annually be booked as an instalment on the redemption payment of the value of the particular dwelling, so that after a certain time the tenant would become its owner.[243] This method, which Proudhon considered very revolutionary, is being put into operation in all countries by companies of speculators who thus secure double and treble the value of the houses by raising the rents. M. Dollfus and other big manufacturers in North-Eastern France have carried out this system not only in order to make money but, in addition, with a political idea at the back of their minds.

"The cleverest leaders of the ruling class have always directed their efforts towards increasing the number of small owners in order to build an army for themselves against the proletariat. The bourgeois revolutions of the last century

---

[a] [P. Lafargue,] "Articulos de primera necesidad. II. La Habitacion", *La Emancipacion*, No. 40, March 16, 1872.— *Ed.*

divided up the big estates of the nobility and the church into small allotments, just as the Spanish republicans propose to do today with the still existing large estates, and created thereby a class of small landowners which has since become the most reactionary element in society and a permanent hindrance to the revolutionary movement of the urban proletariat. Napoleon III aimed at creating a similar class in the towns by reducing the denominations of the individual bonds of the public debt, and M. Dollfus and his colleagues sought to stifle all revolutionary spirit in their workers by selling them small dwellings to be paid for in annual instalments, and at the same time to chain the workers by this property to the factory once they worked in it.[244] Thus the Proudhon plan, far from bringing the working class any relief, even turned directly against it." *

How is the housing question to be settled, then? In present-day society, just as any other social question is settled: by the gradual economic levelling of demand and supply, a settlement which reproduces the question itself again and again and therefore is no settlement. How a social revolution would settle this question not only depends on the circumstances in each particular case, but is also connected with much more far-reaching questions, one of the most fundamental of which is the abolition of the antithesis between town and country. As it is not our task to create utopian systems for the organisation of the future society, it would be more than idle to go into the question here. But one thing is certain: there is already a sufficient quantity of houses in the big cities to remedy immediately all real "housing *shortage*", provided they are used judiciously. This can naturally only occur through the expropriation of the present owners by quartering in their houses homeless workers or workers overcrowded in their present homes. As soon as the proletariat has won political power, such a measure prompted by concern for the common good will be just as easy to carry out as are other expropriations and billetings by the present-day state.

However, our Proudhonist is not satisfied with his previous achievements in the housing question. He must raise the question

---

* How this solution of the housing question by means of chaining the worker to his own "home" is arising spontaneously in the neighbourhood of big or rapidly rising American towns can be seen from the following passage of a letter by Eleanor Marx-Aveling, Indianapolis, November 28, 1886: "In, or rather near, Kansas City we saw some miserable little wooden shacks, containing about three rooms each, still in the wilds; the land cost 600 dollars and was just big enough to put the little house on it; the latter cost a further 600 dollars, that is, together, 4,800 marks, for a miserable little thing, an hour away from the town, in a muddy desert." In this way the workers must shoulder heavy mortgage debts in order to obtain even these dwellings, and now indeed become the slaves of their employers. They are tied to their houses, they cannot go away, and must put up with whatever working conditions are offered them. [*Note by Engels to the 1887 edition.*]

from the level ground into the sphere of higher socialism in order that it may prove there also an essential "fractional part of the social question":

> "Let us now assume that the productivity of capital is really taken by the horns, as it must be sooner or later, for instance, by a transitional law which *fixes the interest on all capitals at one per cent,* but mark you, with the tendency to make even this rate of interest approximate more and more to the zero point, so that finally nothing more will be paid than *the labour necessary to turn over the capital.* Like all other products, houses and dwellings are naturally also included within the purview of this law... The owner himself will be the first one to agree to a sale because otherwise his house would be unused and the capital invested in it simply useless." [a]

This passage contains one of the chief articles of faith of the Proudhonist catechism and offers a striking example of the confusion prevailing in it.

The "productivity of capital" is an absurdity that Proudhon takes over uncritically from the bourgeois economists. The bourgeois economists, it is true, also begin with the proposition that labour is the source of all wealth and the measure of value of all commodities; but they likewise have to explain how it comes about that the capitalist who advances capital for an industrial or handicraft business receives back at the end of it not only the capital which he advanced but also a profit over and above it. In consequence they are compelled to entangle themselves in all sorts of contradictions and to ascribe also to capital a certain productivity. Nothing proves more clearly how completely Proudhon remains enmeshed in bourgeois thinking than the fact that he has taken over this phrase about the productivity of capital. We have seen at the very beginning that the so-called "productivity of capital" is nothing but the quality inherent in it (under present-day social relations, without which it would not be capital at all) of being able to appropriate the unpaid labour of wage-workers.

However, Proudhon differs from the bourgeois economists in that he does not approve of this "productivity of capital," but on the contrary, discovers in it a violation of "eternal justice". It is this productivity which prevents the worker from receiving the full proceeds of his labour. It must therefore be abolished. But how? By lowering the *rate of interest* by compulsory legislation and finally reducing it to zero. Then, according to our Proudhonist, capital will cease to be productive.

The interest on loaned *money* capital is only a part of profit; profit, whether on industrial or commercial capital, is only a part

---

[a] [A. Mülberger,] op. cit., *Der Volksstaat,* No. 13, February 14, 1872.— *Ed.*

of the surplus value taken by the capitalist class from the working class in the form of unpaid labour. The economic laws which govern the rate of interest are as independent of those which govern the rate of surplus value as could possibly be the case with laws of one and the same form of society. But as far as the distribution of this surplus value among the individual capitalists is concerned, it is clear that for industrialists and merchants who have in their businesses large amounts of capital advanced by other capitalists the rate of profit must rise—all other things being equal—to the same extent as the rate of interest falls. The reduction and final abolition of interest would, therefore, by no means really take the so-called "productivity of capital" "by the horns". It would do no more than re-arrange the distribution among the individual capitalists of the unpaid surplus value taken from the working class. It would not give an advantage to the worker as against the industrial capitalist, but to the industrial capitalist as against the rentier.

Proudhon, from his legal standpoint, explains the rate of interest, as he does all economic facts, not by the conditions of social production, but by the state laws in which these conditions receive their general expression. From this point of view, which lacks any inkling of the interconnection between the state laws and the conditions of production in society, these state laws necessarily appear as purely arbitrary orders which at any moment could be replaced just as well by their exact opposites. Nothing is, therefore, easier for Proudhon than to issue a decree—as soon as he has the power to do so—reducing the rate of interest to one per cent. And if all the other social conditions remain as they were, this Proudhonist decree will simply exist on paper only. The rate of interest will continue to be governed by the economic laws to which it is subject today, all decrees notwithstanding. Persons possessing credit will continue to borrow money at two, three, four and more per cent, according to circumstances, just as before, and the only difference will be that rentiers will be very careful to advance money only to persons with whom no litigation is to be expected. Moreover, this great plan to deprive capital of its "productivity" is as old as the hills; it is as old as—the *usury laws* which aim at nothing else but limiting the rate of interest, and which have since been abolished everywhere because in practice they were continually broken or circumvented, and the state was compelled to admit its impotence against the laws of social production. And the re-introduction of these medieval and unworkable laws is "to take the productivity of capital by the horns"? One sees that the closer Proudhonism is examined the more reactionary it appears.

And when thereupon the rate of interest has been reduced to zero in this fashion, and interest on capital therefore abolished, then "nothing more will be paid than the labour necessary to turn over the capital". This is supposed to mean that the abolition of the rate of interest is equivalent to the abolition of profit and even of surplus value. But if it were possible *really* to abolish interest by decree, what would be the consequence? The class of *rentiers* would no longer have any inducement to loan out their capital in the form of advances, but would invest it industrially, either on their own or through joint-stock companies. The mass of surplus value extracted from the working class by the capitalist class would remain the same; only its distribution would be altered, and even that not much.

In fact, our Proudhonist fails to see that already now, in commodity purchase in bourgeois society, no more is paid on the average than "the labour necessary to turn over the capital" (it should read, necessary for the production of the commodity in question). Labour is the measure of value of all commodities, and in present-day society—apart from fluctuations of the market—it is absolutely impossible that in the aggregate more should be paid on the average for commodities than the labour necessary for their production. No, no, my dear Proudhonist, the difficulty lies elsewhere. It is contained in the fact that "the labour necessary to turn over the capital" (to use your confused terminology) is simply *not fully paid for!* How this comes about you can look up in Marx (*Capital*, pp. 128-60 [a]).

But that is not enough. If interest *on capital* is abolished, *house rent* is abolished with it; for, "like all other products, houses and dwellings are naturally also included within the purview of this law". This is quite in the spirit of the old Major who summoned his one-year volunteer recruit and declared:

"I say, I hear you are a doctor; you might report from time to time at my quarters; when one has a wife and seven children there is always something to patch up."

Recruit: "Excuse me, Major, but I am a doctor of philosophy."

Major: "That's all the same to me; one sawbones is the same as another."

Our Proudhonist behaves the same way: house rent or interest

---

[a] Cf. the English edition of *Capital*, Vol. I, London, 1887, pp. 143-78.— *Ed.*

on capital, it is all the same to him. Interest is interest[a]; sawbones
is sawbones.

We have seen above that the rent price, commonly called house
rent, is composed as follows: 1) a part which is ground rent; 2) a
part which is interest on the building capital, including the profit
of the builder; 3) a part which goes for repairs and insurance; 4) a
part which has to amortise the building capital inclusive of profit
in annual deductions according to the rate at which the house
gradually depreciates.

And now it must have become clear even to the blindest that

"the owner himself will be the first one to agree to a sale because otherwise his
house would be unused and the capital invested in it simply useless".

Of course. If the interest on loaned capital is abolished, no
house-owner can thereafter obtain a penny piece in rent for his
house, simply because house rent may also be spoken of as rent
interest and because such rent interest contains a part which is really
interest on capital. Sawbones is sawbones. Whereas the usury
laws relating to ordinary interest on capital could be made ineffective
only by circumventing them, yet they never touched the rate of
house rent even remotely. It was reserved for Proudhon to imagine
that his new usury law would without more ado regulate and
gradually abolish not only simple interest on capital but also the
complicated house rent for dwellings.[b] Why then the "simply
useless" house should be purchased for good money from the
house-owner, and how it is that under such circumstances the

---

[a] The original has "Zins ist Zins"; a pun on "Mietzins" (house rent) and
"Kapitalzins" (interest on capital).— *Ed.*

[b] The passage "We have seen above ... house rent for dwellings" was edited by
Engels for the 1887 edition; in *Der Volksstaat* No. 53 of July 3, 1872 it runs as
follows:

"We have seen above that the rent price, commonly called house rent, is
composed as follows: 1) a part which is ground rent, 2) a part which is profit, not
interest, on the building capital, 3) a part which is the cost of repairs, maintenance,
and insurance. It contains no part which is interest on capital, unless the house is
encumbered with a mortgage debt.

"And now it must have become clear even to the blindest that 'the owner
himself will be the first one to agree to a sale because otherwise his house would be
unused and the capital invested in it simply useless'. Of course. If the interest on
loaned capital is abolished, no house-owner can thereafter obtain a penny piece in rent
for his house, simply because house rent may also be spoken of as rent *interest*.
Sawbones is sawbones."

After the sentence "It contains no part which is interest on capital, unless the
house is encumbered with a mortgage debt" in the 1872 separate reprint of Part I
of *The Housing Question* Engels made the following note, omitted in the 1887
edition:

house-owner would not pay money himself to get rid of this "simply useless" house in order to save himself the cost of repairs—about this we are left in the dark.

After this triumphant achievement in the sphere of higher socialism (Master Proudhon called it suprasocialism[a]) our Proudhonist considers himself justified in flying still higher:

"All that still has to be done now is to draw some conclusions in order to cast complete light from all sides on our so important subject."[b]

And what are these conclusions? Things which follow as little from what has been said before as the worthlessness of dwelling houses from the abolition of interest. Stripped of the pompous and solemn phraseology of our author, they mean nothing more than that, in order to facilitate the business of redemption of rented dwellings, the following is desirable: 1) exact statistics on the subject; 2) a good sanitary inspection force; 3) co-operatives of building workers to undertake the building of new houses. All these things are certainly very fine and good, but, despite all the vociferous phrases in which they are enveloped, they by no means cast "complete light" into the obscurity of Proudhonist mental confusion.

One who has achieved such great things has the right to address a serious exhortation to the German workers:

"Such and similar questions, it would seem to us, are well worth the attention of the Social-Democracy.... Let it seek to clarify its mind, as here on the housing question, so also on other and equally important questions, such as *credit, state debts, private debts, taxes*," etc.[c]

Thus, our Proudhonist here confronts us with the prospect of a whole series of articles on "similar questions", and if he deals with them all as thoroughly as with the present "so important subject", the *Volksstaat* will have copy enough for a year. But we are in a position to anticipate—it all amounts to what has already been said: interest on capital is to be abolished and with that the interest

---

"*For the capitalist* who buys a ready-built house, part of the rent price, which is not composed of ground rents and overhead expenses, may *appear* in the form of interest on capital. But this alters nothing because it does not matter whether the builder of the house lets it himself or sells it for that purpose to another capitalist."— *Ed.*

[a] P. J. Proudhon, *Système des contradictions économiques, ou Philosophie de la misère*, Vol. 1, Paris, 1846, p. III (Proudhon has "suprasocial").— *Ed.*

[b] [A. Mülberger,] op. cit., *Der Volksstaat*, No. 13, February 14, 1872.— *Ed.*

[c] Ibid.— *Ed.*

on public and private debts disappears, credit will be gratis, etc.
The same magic formula is applied to any and every subject and
in each particular case the same astonishing result is obtained with
inexorable logic, namely, that when interest on capital has been
abolished no more interest will have to be paid on borrowed
money.

They are fine questions, by the way, with which our Proudhonist
threatens us: *Credit!* What credit does the worker need besides that
from week to week, or the credit he obtains at the pawnshop?
Whether he gets this credit free or at interest, even at the usurious
interest charged by the pawnshop, how much difference does that
make to him? And if he did, generally speaking, obtain some
advantage from it, that is to say, if the cost of production of
labour power were reduced, would not the price of labour power
be bound to fall?—But to the bourgeois, and in particular to the
petty bourgeois, credit is an important matter, and it would be a
very fine thing for the petty bourgeois in particular if credit could
be obtained at any time, and besides without payment of interest.
"State debts!" The working class knows that it did not make them,
and when it comes to power it will leave the payment of them to
those who contracted them. "Private debts!"—see credit. "Taxes!"
A matter that interests the bourgeoisie very much but the worker
only very little. What the worker pays in taxes goes in the long run
into the cost of production of labour power and must therefore be
compensated for by the capitalist. All these things which are held
up to us here as highly important questions for the working class
are in reality of essential interest only to the bourgeois, and still
more so to the petty bourgeois; and, despite Proudhon, we
maintain that the working class is not called upon to safeguard the
interests of these classes.

Our Proudhonist has not a word to say about the great question
which really concerns the workers, that of the relation between
capitalist and wage-worker, the question of how it comes about
that the capitalist can enrich himself by the labour of his workers.
True enough, his lord and master did occupy himself with it, but
introduced absolutely no clearness into the matter. Even in his
latest writings he has got essentially no farther than he was in his
Philosophie de la misère, which Marx so strikingly reduced to
nothingness in 1847.[a]

---

[a] K. Marx, *The Poverty of Philosophy. Answer to the "Philosophy of Poverty" by
M. Proudhon.—Ed.*

It was bad enough that for twenty-five years the workers speaking Romance languages had almost no other socialist mental pabulum than the writings of this "socialist of the Second Empire", and it would be a double misfortune if the Proudhonist theory were now to inundate Germany too. However, there need be no fear of this. The theoretical standpoint of the German workers is fifty years ahead of that of Proudhonism, and it will be sufficient to make an example of this *one* question, the housing question, to save further trouble in this respect.

Part II

HOW THE BOURGEOISIE SOLVES THE HOUSING QUESTION

I

In the section on the *Proudhonist* solution of the housing question it was shown how greatly the petty bourgeoisie is directly interested in this question. However, the big bourgeoisie is also very much interested in it, even if indirectly. Modern natural science has proved that the so-called "bad districts", in which the workers are crowded together, are the breeding places of all those epidemics which from time to time afflict our towns. Cholera, typhus, typhoid fever, small-pox and other ravaging diseases spread their germs in the pestilential air and the poisoned water of these working-class quarters. Here the germs hardly ever die out completely, and as soon as circumstances permit they develop into epidemics and then spread beyond their breeding places into the more airy and healthy parts of the town inhabited by Messrs. the capitalists. Capitalist rule cannot allow itself the pleasure of generating epidemic diseases among the working class with impunity; the consequences fall back on it and the angel of death rages in the ranks of the capitalists as ruthlessly as in the ranks of the workers.

As soon as this fact had been scientifically established the philanthropic bourgeois became inflamed with a noble spirit of competition in their solicitude for the health of their workers. Societies were founded, books were written, proposals drawn up, laws debated and passed, in order to stop up the sources of the ever-recurring epidemics. The housing conditions of the workers were investigated and attempts made to remedy the most crying evils. In England particularly, where the largest number of big towns existed and where the bourgeoisie itself was, therefore, running the greatest risk, extensive activity began. Government commissions were appointed to inquire into the hygienic conditions of the working classes. Their reports, honourably distinguished from all continental sources by their accuracy, completeness and impartiality, provided the basis for new, more or less thoroughgoing laws. Imperfect as these laws are, they are still infinitely superior to everything that has been done in this direction up to the present on the Continent. Nevertheless, the capitalist order of society reproduces again and again the evils to be remedied, and does so with such inevitable necessity that even in England the remedying of them has hardly advanced a single step.

Germany, as usual, needed a much longer time before the chronic sources of infection existing there also reached the acute stage necessary to arouse the somnolent big bourgeoisie. But he who goes slowly goes surely, and so among us too there finally has arisen a bourgeois literature on public health and the housing question, a watery extract of its foreign, and in particular its English, predecessors, to which it is sought fraudulently to impart a semblance of higher conception by means of fine-sounding and unctuous phrases. *Die Wohnungszustände der arbeitenden Classen und ihre Reform*, by Dr. *Emil Sax*, Vienna, 1869, belongs to this literature.

I have selected this book for a presentation of the bourgeois treatment of the housing question only because it makes the attempt to summarise as far as possible the bourgeois literature on the subject. And a fine literature it is which serves our author as his "sources"! Of the English parliamentary reports, the real main sources, only three, the very oldest,[a] are mentioned by name; the whole book proves that its author has *never glanced at even a single one of them.* On the other hand, a whole series of banal bourgeois, well-meaning philistine and hypocritical philanthropic writings are enumerated: Ducpétiaux, Roberts, Hole, Huber,[245] the proceedings of the English social science (or rather social bosh) congresses,[b] the *Zeitschrift des Vereins für das Wohl der arbeitenden Klassen* in Prussia, the official Austrian report on the World Exhibition in Paris,[c] the official Bonapartist reports on the same

---

a For 1837, 1839 and 1842.— *Ed.*

b *Transactions of the National Association for the Promotion of Social Science*, London, 1859-1865.— *Ed.*

c *Bericht über die Welt-Ausstellung zu Paris im Jahre 1867*, Vienna, 1869.— *Ed.*

subject,[a] *The Illustrated London News*,[b] *Über Land und Meer*,[c] and finally "a recognised authority", a man of "acute practical perception", of "convincing impressiveness of speech", namely— *Julius Faucher*[d]! All that is missing in this list of sources is the *Gartenlaube*, *Kladderadatsch* and the Fusilier Kutschke.[e]

In order that no misunderstanding may arise concerning the standpoint of Herr Sax, he declares on page 22:

> "By social economy we mean the doctrine of national economy in its application to social questions; or to put it more precisely, the totality of the ways and means which this science offers us *for raising the so-called*" (!) "*propertyless classes to the level of the propertied classes, on the basis of its 'iron' laws within the framework of the order of society at present prevailing.*"

We shall not go into the confused idea that generally speaking "the doctrine of national economy", or political economy, deals with other than "social" questions. We shall get down to the main point immediately. Dr. Sax demands that the "iron laws" of bourgeois economics, the "framework of the order of society at present prevailing", in other words, the capitalist mode of production, must continue to exist unchanged, but nevertheless the "so-called propertyless classes" are to be raised "to the level of the propertied classes". Now, it is an unavoidable preliminary condition of the capitalist mode of production that a really, and not a so-called, propertyless class, should exist, a class which has nothing to sell but its labour power and which is therefore compelled to sell its labour power to the industrial capitalists. The task of the new science of social economy invented by Herr Sax is, therefore, to find ways and means—in a state of society founded on the antagonism of capitalists, owners of all raw materials, instruments of production and means of subsistence, on the one hand, and of propertyless wage-workers, who call only their labour power and nothing else their own, on the other hand—by which,

---

[a] *L'Enquête du dixième groupe*, Paris, 1867.—*Ed.*

[b] Ed. Chadwick, "Report on Dwellings Characterised by Cheapness Combined with the Conditions Necessary for Health and Comfort", *The Illustrated London News*, Vol. 51, No. 1434/1435, July 6, 1867.—*Ed.*

[c] L. Walesrode, "Eine Arbeiter-Heimstätte in Schwaben", *Über Land und Meer*, Nos. 35, 36, 44 and 45, 1868.—*Ed.*

[d] J. Faucher, "Die Bewegung für Wohnungsreform", *Vierteljahrschrift für Volkswirthschaft und Kulturgeschichte*, Vol. 4, 1865 and Vol. 3, 1866; "Bericht über die Verhandlungen des neunten Kongresses deutscher Volkswirthe zu Hamburg am 26., 27., 28. und 29. August 1867", ibid., Vol. 3, 1867.—*Ed.*

[e] Pseudonym of Gotthelf Hoffmann, author of nationalist soldier songs.—*Ed.*

under this state of society, all wage-workers can be turned into capitalists without ceasing to be wage-workers. Herr Sax thinks he has solved this question. Perhaps he would be so good as to show us how all the soldiers of the French army, each of whom carries a marshal's baton in his knapsack since the days of the old Napoleon, can be turned into field marshals without at the same time ceasing to be privates. Or how it could be brought about that all the forty million subjects of the German Empire could be made German emperors.

It is the essence of bourgeois socialism to want to maintain the basis of all the evils of present-day society and at same time to want to abolish the evils themselves. As already pointed out in the *Communist Manifesto*, the bourgeois socialists are desirous of "redressing social grievances, in order to secure the continued existence of bourgeois society"; they want *"a bourgeoisie without a proletariat"*.[a] We have seen that Herr Sax formulates the problem in exactly the same fashion. Its solution he finds in the solution of the housing problem. He is of the opinion that

"by improving the housing of the labouring classes it would be possible successfully to remedy the material and spiritual misery which has been described, and thereby"—by a radical improvement of the housing conditions *alone*—"to raise the greater part of these classes out of the morass of their often hardly human conditions of existence to the pure heights of material and spiritual well-being" (page 14).

Incidentally, it is in the interest of the bourgeoisie to gloss over the fact of the existence of a proletariat created by the bourgeois relations of production and determining the continued existence of these relations. Therefore Herr Sax tells us (page 21) that the expression labouring classes is to be understood as including all "impecunious social classes", "and, in general, people in a small way, such as handicraftsmen, widows, pensioners" (!), "subordinate officials, etc." as well as actual workers. Bourgeois socialism extends its hand to the petty-bourgeois variety.

Whence the housing shortage then? How did it arise? As a good bourgeois, Herr Sax is not supposed to know that it is a necessary product of the bourgeois social order; that it cannot fail to be present in a society in which the great labouring masses are exclusively dependent upon wages, that is to say, upon the quantity of means of subsistence necessary for their existence and for the propagation of their kind; in which improvements of the machinery, etc., continually throw masses of workers out of

---

[a] See present edition, Vol. 6, p. 513.— *Ed.*

employment; in which violent and regularly recurring industrial fluctuations determine on the one hand the existence of a large reserve army of unemployed workers, and on the other hand drive the mass of the workers from time to time on to the streets unemployed; in which the workers are crowded together in masses in the big towns at a quicker rate than dwellings come into existence for them under the prevailing conditions, in which, therefore, there must always be tenants even for the most infamous pigsties; and in which finally the house-owner in his capacity as capitalist has not only the right but, by reason of competition, to a certain extent also the duty of ruthlessly making as much out of his property in house rent as he possibly can. In such a society the housing shortage is no accident; it is a necessary institution and can be abolished together with all its effects on health, etc., only if the whole social order from which it springs is fundamentally refashioned. That, however, bourgeois socialism dare not know. It *dare* not explain the housing shortage as arising from the existing conditions. And therefore it has no other way but to explain the housing shortage by moralising that it is the result of the wickedness of man, the result of original sin, so to speak.

"And here we cannot fail to recognise—and in consequence we cannot deny" (daring conclusion!)—"that the blame ... rests partly *with the workers themselves,* those who want dwellings, and partly, the much greater part, it is true, with those who undertake to supply the need or those who, although they have sufficient means at their command, make no attempt to supply the need, namely, *the propertied, higher social classes.* The latter are to be blamed ... because they do not make it their business to provide for a sufficient supply of good dwellings." [Page 25.]

Just as Proudhon takes us from the sphere of economics into the sphere of legal phrases, so our bourgeois socialist takes us here from the economic sphere into the moral sphere. And nothing is more natural. Whoever declares that the capitalist mode of production, the "iron laws" of present-day bourgeois society, are inviolable, and yet at the same time would like to abolish their unpleasant but necessary consequences, has no other recourse but to deliver moral sermons to the capitalists, moral sermons whose emotional effects immediately evaporate under the influence of private interest and, if necessary, of competition. These moral sermons are in effect exactly the same as those of the hen at the edge of the pond in which she sees the brood of ducklings she has hatched out gaily swimming. Ducklings take to the water although it has no beams, and capitalists pounce on profit although it is heartless. "There is no room for sentiment in money matters," was already said by old Hansemann,[a] who knew more about it than Herr Sax.

"Good dwellings are so expensive that *it is absolutely impossible* for the greater part of the workers to make use of them. Big capital ... is shy of investing in houses for the working classes ... and as a result these classes and their housing needs fall mostly a prey to the speculators." [Page 27.]

Disgusting speculation—big capital naturally never speculates! But it is not ill will, it is only ignorance which prevents big capital from speculating in workers' houses:

"House-owners do not *know* at all what a great and important role ... is played by a normal satisfaction of housing needs; *they do not know what they are doing to the people* when they offer them, as a general rule so irresponsibly, bad and harmful dwellings, and, finally, they do not *know* how they damage themselves thereby." (Page 27.)

However, the ignorance of the capitalists must be supplemented by the ignorance of the workers before a housing shortage can be created. After Herr Sax has admitted that "the very lowest sections" of the workers "are obliged" (!) "to seek a night's lodging wherever and however they can find it in order not to remain altogether without shelter and in this connection are absolutely defenceless and helpless", he tells us:

"For it is a well-known fact that many among them" (the workers) "from carelessness, but chiefly from ignorance, deprive their bodies, one is almost inclined to say, with virtuosity, of the conditions of natural development and healthy existence, in that they *have not the faintest idea* of rational hygiene and, in particular, of the enormous importance that attaches to the dwelling in this hygiene." (Page 27.)

Here however the bourgeois donkey's ears protrude. Where the capitalists are concerned "blame" evaporates into ignorance, but where the workers are concerned ignorance is made the cause of their guilt. Listen:

"Thus it comes" (namely, through ignorance) "that if they can only save something on the rent they will move into dark, damp and inadequate dwellings, which are in short a mockery of all the demands of hygiene ... that often several families together rent a single dwelling, and even a single room—all this in order to spend as little as possible on rent, while on the other hand they *squander* their income *in truly sinful fashion on drink and all sorts of idle pleasures*"

The money which the workers "waste on spirits and tobacco" (page 28), the "life in the pubs with all its regrettable consequen-

---

[a] D. Hansemann's speech at the 34th sitting of the First United Diet, June 8, 1847. *Preussens Erster Reichstag*, Part 7, Berlin, 1847, p. 55.— *Ed.*

ces, which drags the workers again and again like a dead weight back into the mire", lies indeed like a dead weight in Herr Sax's stomach. The fact that under the existing circumstances drunkenness among the workers is a necessary product of their living conditions, just as necessary as typhus, crime, vermin, bailiff and other social ills, so necessary in fact that the average figures of those who succumb to inebriety can be calculated in advance, is again something that Herr Sax cannot allow himself to know. My old primary school teacher used to say, by the way: "The common people go to the pubs and the people of quality go to the clubs," and as I have been in both I am in a position to confirm it.

The whole talk about the "ignorance" of both parties amounts to nothing but the old phrases about the harmony of interests of labour and capital. If the capitalists knew their true interests, they would give the workers good houses and improve their position in general; and if the workers understood their true interests, they would not go on strike, they would not go in for Social-Democracy, they would not play politics, but would be nice and follow their betters, the capitalists. Unfortunately, both sides find their interests altogether elsewhere than in the sermons of Herr Sax and his countless predecessors. The gospel of harmony between capital and labour has been preached for almost fifty years now, and bourgeois philanthropy has expended large sums of money to prove this harmony by building model institutions; yet, as we shall see later, we are today exactly where we were fifty years ago.

Our author now proceeds to the practical solution of the problem. How little revolutionary Proudhon's proposal to make the workers *owners* of their dwellings was can be seen from the fact that bourgeois socialism even before him tried to carry this proposal out in practice and is still trying to do so. Herr Sax also declares that the housing problem can be completely solved only by transferring property in dwellings to the workers. (Pages 58 and 59.) More than that, he goes into poetic raptures at the idea, giving vent to his feelings in the following outburst of enthusiasm:

"There is something peculiar about the longing inherent in man to own land; it is an urge which not even the *feverishly pulsating business life* of the present day has been able to abate. It is the unconscious appreciation of the significance of the economic achievement represented by landownership. With it the individual obtains a secure hold; he is rooted firmly in the earth, as it were, and every enterprise" (!) "has its most permanent basis in it. However, the blessings of landownership extend far beyond these material advantages. Whoever is fortunate enough to call a piece of land his own has *reached the highest conceivable stage of economic independence*; he has a territory on which he can rule with *sovereign* power; he is *his own master*; he has a certain power and a *sure support* in time of need; his self-confidence develops and with this his moral strength. Hence the deep significance of property in the question before us... The worker, today helplessly exposed to all the vicissitudes of economic life and in constant dependence on his employer, would thereby be saved to a certain extent from this precarious situation; *he would become a capitalist* and be safeguarded against the dangers of unemployment or incapacitation as a result of the credit which his real estate would open to him. *He would thus be raised from the ranks of the propertyless into the propertied class.*" (Page 63.)

Herr Sax seems to assume that man is essentially a peasant, otherwise he would not falsely impute to the workers of our big cities a longing to own land, a longing which no one else has discovered in them. For our workers in the big cities freedom of movement is the prime condition of existence, and landownership can only be a fetter to them. Give them their own houses, chain them once again to the soil and you break their power of resistance to the wage cutting of the factory owners. The individual worker might be able to sell his house on occasion, but during a big strike or a general industrial crisis[a] all the houses belonging to the workers affected would have to be put up for sale and would therefore find no purchasers or be sold off far below their cost price. And even if they all found purchasers, Herr Sax's whole grand housing reform would have come to nothing and he would have to start from the beginning again. However, poets live in a world of fantasy, and so does Herr Sax, who imagines that a landowner has "reached the highest stage of economic independence", that he has "a sure support", that "he *would become a capitalist* and be safeguarded against the dangers of unemployment or incapacitation as a result of the credit which his real estate would open to him", etc. Herr Sax should take a look at the French and our own Rhenish small peasants. Their houses and fields are loaded down with mortgages, their harvests belong to their creditors before they are reaped, and it is not they who rule with sovereign power on their "territory" but the usurer, the lawyer and the bailiff. That certainly represents the highest conceivable stage of economic independence—for the usurer! And in order that the workers may bring their little houses as quickly as possible under the same sovereignty of the usurer, our well-meaning Herr Sax carefully points to the *credit* which their *real estate* can secure them in times of unemployment or incapacitation instead of their becoming a burden on the poor rate.

[a] The words "or a general industrial crisis" were added by Engels in the 1887 edition.— *Ed.*

In any case, Herr Sax has solved the question raised in the beginning: the worker "*becomes a capitalist*" by acquiring his own little house.

Capital is the command over the unpaid labour of others. The little house of the worker can therefore become capital only if he rents it to a third person and appropriates a part of the labour product of this third person in the form of rent. But the house is prevented from becoming capital precisely by the fact that the worker lives in it himself, just as a coat ceases to be capital the moment I buy it from the tailor and put it on. The worker who owns a little house to the value of a thousand thalers is, true enough, no longer a proletarian, but it takes Herr Sax to call him a capitalist.

However, this capitalist streak of our worker has still another side. Let us assume that in a given industrial area it has become the rule that each worker owns his own little house. In that case *the working class of that area lives rent-free*; housing expenses no longer enter into the value of its labour power. Every reduction in the cost of production of labour power, that is to say, every permanent price reduction in the worker's necessities of life is equivalent "on the basis of the iron laws of the doctrine of national economy" to a depression of the value of labour power and will therefore finally result in a corresponding drop in wages. Wages would thus fall on an average as much as the average sum saved on rent, that is, the worker would pay for his own house, but not, as formerly, in money to the house-owner, but in unpaid labour to the factory owner for whom he works. In this way the savings of the worker invested in his little house would in a certain sense become capital, however not capital for him but for the capitalist employing him.

Herr Sax thus lacks the ability to turn his worker into a capitalist even on paper.

Incidentally, what has been said above applies to all so-called social reforms which can be reduced to saving schemes or to cheapening the means of subsistence of the worker. Either they become general and then they are followed by a corresponding reduction of wages or they remain quite isolated experiments and then their very existence as isolated exceptions proves that their realisation on an extensive scale is incompatible with the existing capitalist mode of production. Let us assume that in a certain area a general introduction of consumers' co-operatives succeeds in reducing the cost of the means of subsistence for the workers by 20 per cent. Hence in the long run wages would fall in that area by approximately 20 per cent, that is to say, in the same proportion as the means of subsistence in question enter into the budget of the workers. If the worker, for example, spends three-quarters of his weekly wage on these means of subsistence, wages would in the end fall by $^3/_4 \times 20 = 15$ per cent. In short, as soon as any such saving reform has become general, the worker's wages diminish by as much as his savings permit him to live cheaper. Give *every* worker an independent income of 52 thalers, achieved by saving, and his weekly wage must finally fall one thaler. Therefore, the more he saves the less he will receive in wages. He saves, therefore, not in his own interest but in the interest of the capitalist. What else is needed to "stimulate" in him "in the most powerful fashion ... the primary economic virtue, thrift"? (Page 64.)

Incidentally, Herr Sax tells us immediately afterwards that the workers are to become house-owners not so much in their own interest as in the interest of the capitalists:

"However, not only the working class but society as a whole has the greatest interest in seeing as many of its members as possible bound" (!) "to the land" (I should like to see Herr Sax himself even for once in this posture).[a] "...All the secret forces which set on fire the volcano called the social question which glows under our feet, the proletarian bitterness, the hatred, ... the dangerous confusion of ideas, ... must all disappear like mist before the morning sun when ... the workers themselves enter in this fashion into the ranks of the propertied class." (Page 65.)

In other words, Herr Sax hopes that by a shift in their proletarian status, such as would be brought about by the acquisition of a house, the workers would also lose their proletarian character and become once again obedient toadies like their forefathers, who were also house-owners. The Proudhonists should lay this thing to heart.

Herr Sax believes he has thereby solved the social question:

"*A juster distribution of goods*, the riddle of the Sphinx which so many have already tried in vain to solve, does it not now lie before us as a tangible fact, has it not thereby been taken from the regions of ideals and brought into the realm of reality? And if it is carried out, does this not mean the achievement of one of the highest aims, one which even the *socialists of the most extreme tendency present as the culminating point of their theories?*" (Page 66.)

It is really lucky that we have worked our way through as far as this, because this shout of triumph is the "summit" of the Saxian book. From now on we once more gently descend from "the

---

[a] In the 1887 edition, Engels made the quotation shorter by deleting here the following sentence: "Landownership ... diminishes the number of those who struggle against the rule of the propertied class."— *Ed.*

regions of ideals" to flat reality, and when we get down we shall find that nothing, nothing at all, has changed in our absence.

Our guide takes us the first step down by informing us that there are two systems of workers' dwellings: the COTTAGE SYSTEM, in which each working-class family has its own little house and if possible a little garden as well, as in England; and the barrack system of the large tenement houses containing numerous workers' dwellings, as in Paris, Vienna, etc. Between the two is the system prevailing in Northern Germany. Now it is true, he tells us, that the COTTAGE SYSTEM is the only correct one, and the *only one* whereby the worker can acquire the ownership of his own house; besides, he argues, the barrack system has very great disadvantages with regard to hygiene, morality and domestic peace. But, alas and alack! says he, the COTTAGE SYSTEM is not realisable in the centres of the housing shortage, in the big cities, on account of the high cost of land, and one should, therefore, be glad if houses were built containing from four to six flats instead of big barracks, or if the main disadvantages of the barrack system were alleviated by various ingenious building devices. (Pages 71-92.)

We have come down quite a bit already, haven't we? The transformation of the workers into capitalists, the solution of the social question, a house of his own for each worker—all these things have been left behind, up above in "the regions of ideals". All that remains for us to do is to introduce the COTTAGE SYSTEM into the countryside and to make the workers' barracks in the cities as tolerable as possible.

On its own admission, therefore, the bourgeois solution of the housing question has come to grief—it has come to grief owing to the *antithesis between town and country*. And with this we have arrived at the kernel of the problem. The housing question can be solved only when society has been sufficiently transformed for a start to be made towards abolishing the antithesis between town and country, which has been brought to its extreme point by present-day capitalist society. Far from being able to abolish this antithesis, capitalist society on the contrary is compelled to intensify it day by day. On the other hand, already the first modern utopian socialists, Owen and Fourier, correctly recognised this. In their model structures the antithesis between town and country no longer exists. Consequently there takes place exactly the opposite of what Herr Sax contends: it is not that the solution of the housing question simultaneously solves the social question, but that only by the solution of the social question, that is, by the abolition of the capitalist mode of production, is the solution of the housing question made possible. To want to solve the housing question while at the same time desiring to maintain the modern big cities is an absurdity. The modern big cities, however, will be abolished only by the abolition of the capitalist mode of production, and when this is once set going there will be quite other issues than supplying each worker with a little house of his own.

In the beginning, however, each social revolution will have to take things as it finds them and do its best to get rid of the most crying evils with the means at its disposal. And we have already seen that the housing *shortage* can be remedied immediately by expropriating a part of the luxury dwellings belonging to the propertied classes and by compulsory quartering in the remaining part.

If now Herr Sax, continuing, once more leaves the big cities and delivers a verbose discourse on working-class colonies to be established *near* the towns, if he describes all the beauties of such colonies with their common "water supply, gas lighting, air or hot-water heating, laundries, drying-rooms, bath-rooms, etc.", each with ist "nursery, school, prayer hall" (!), "reading-room, library, ... wine and bear hall, dancing and concert hall in all respectability", with steam power fitted to all the houses so that "to a certain extent production can be transferred back from the factory to the domestic workshop"—this does not alter the situation at all. The colony he describes has been directly borrowed by Herr Huber[a] from the socialists Owen and Fourier and merely made entirely bourgeois by discarding everything socialist about it. Thereby, however, it has become really utopian. No capitalist has any interest in establishing such colonies, and in fact none such exists anywhere in the world, except in Guise in France, and that was built by a follower of Fourier,[246] not as profitable speculation but as a socialist experiment.* Herr Sax might just as well have quoted in support of his bourgeois project-spinning the example of the communist colony HARMONY HALL[247] founded by Owen in Hampshire at the beginning of the forties and long since defunct.

---

* And this one also has finally become a mere site of working-class exploitation. See the Paris *Socialiste* of 1886.[b] [*Note by Engels to the 1887 edition.*]

---

a V. A. Huber, "Ueber innere Colonisation", *Janus*, 1846, Parts 7 and 8.— *Ed.*
b "Le Familistère de Guise" and "Le programme de M. Godin", *Le Socialiste*, Nos. 45 and 48, July 3 and 24, 1886.— *Ed.*

In any case, all this talk about building colonies is nothing more than a lame attempt to soar again into "the regions of ideals" and it is immediately afterwards again abandoned. We descend rapidly again. The simplest solution now is

"that the employers, the factory owners, should assist the workers to obtain suitable dwellings, whether they do so by building such themselves or by encouraging and assisting the workers to do their own building, providing them with land, advancing them building capital, etc." (Page 106.)

With this we are once again out of the big towns, where there can be no question of anything of the sort, and back in the country. Herr Sax now proves that here it is in the interest of the factory owners themselves that they should assist their workers to obtain tolerable dwellings, on the one hand because it is a good investment, and on the other hand because the inevitably

"resulting uplift of the workers ... must entail an increase of their mental and physical working capacity, which naturally is of ... no less ... advantage to the employers. With this, however, the right point of view for the participation of the latter in the solution of the housing question is given. It appears as the outcome of a *latent association*, as the outcome of the care of the employers for the physical and economic, mental and moral well-being of their workers, which is concealed for the most part under the cloak of humanitarian endeavours and which is its own pecuniary reward because of its successful results: the producing and maintaining of a diligent, skilled, willing, contented and *devoted* working class." (Page 108.)

The phrase "latent association" with which Huber attempts to endow this bourgeois philanthropic drivel with a "loftier significance",[a] does not alter the situation at all. Even without this phrase the big rural factory owners, particularly in England, have long ago realised that the building of workers' dwellings is not only a necessity, a part of the factory equipment itself, but also that it pays very well. In England whole villages have grown up in this way, and some of them have later developed into towns. The workers, however, instead of being thankful to the philanthropic capitalists, have always raised very considerable objections to this "COTTAGE SYSTEM". Not only are they compelled to pay monopoly prices for these houses because the factory owner has no competitors, but immediately a strike breaks out they are homeless because the factory owner throws them out of his houses without any more ado and thus renders any resistance very difficult. Details can be studied in my *Condition of the Working-Class in England*, pp. 224 and 228.[b] Herr Sax, however, thinks that these

---

[a] V. A. Huber, *Sociale Fragen. IV. Die latente Association*, Nordhausen, 1866.— Ed.

[b] See present edition, Vol. 4, pp. 471-72, 477.— Ed.

objections "hardly deserve refutation" (page 111). But does he not want to make the worker the owner of his little house? Certainly, but as

> "the employers must always be in a position to dispose of the dwelling in order that when they dismiss a worker they may have room for the one who replaces him", well then, there is nothing for it but "to make provision for such cases *by agreeing that the ownership shall be revocable.*" (Page 113.)*

This time we have stepped down with unexpected suddenness. First it was said the worker must own his own little house. Then we were informed that this was impossible in the towns and could be carried out only in the country. And now we are told that ownership even in the country is to be "*revocable* by agreement"! With this new sort of property for the workers discovered by Herr Sax, with this transformation of the workers into capitalists "revocable by agreement", we have safely arrived again on level ground, and have here to examine what the capitalists and other philanthropists have *actually* done to solve the housing question.

II

If we are to believe our Dr. Sax, much has already been done by these gentlemen, the capitalists, to remedy the housing shortage, and the proof has been provided that the housing problem can be solved on the basis of the capitalist mode of production.

First of all, Herr Sax cites to us the example of—Bonapartist France! As is known, Louis Bonaparte appointed a commission at the time of the Paris World Exhibition ostensibly to report upon the situation of the working classes in France, but in reality to describe their situation as blissful in the extreme, to the greater glory of the Empire. And it is to the report of *this* commission,

---

* In this respect too the English capitalists have long ago not only fulfilled but far exceeded all the cherished wishes of Herr Sax. On Monday, October 14, 1872, the court in Morpeth for the establishment of the lists of parliamentary electors had to adjudicate a petition on behalf of 2,000 miners to have their names enrolled on the list of parliamentary voters. It transpired that the greater number of these men, according to the regulations of the mine at which they were employed, were *not* to be regarded *as lessees* of the dwellings in which they lived but as occupying these dwellings *on sufferance,* and could be thrown out of them at any moment without notice. (The mine-owner and house-owner were naturally one and the same person.) The judge decided that these men were not lessees but *servants,* and as such not entitled to be included in the list of voters. (["The Miners' Right to Vote",] *The Daily News,* [No. 8258,] October 15, 1872.)

composed of the corruptest tools of Bonapartism,[a] that Herr Sax refers, particularly because the results of its work are, "according to the authorised committee's *own statement*, fairly complete for France". And what are these results? Of eighty-nine big industrialists or joint-stock companies which gave information, thirty-one had built *no* workers' dwellings at all. According to Sax's own estimate the dwellings that were built house at the most from 50,000 to 60,000 people and consist almost exclusively of no more than two rooms for each family!

It is obvious that every capitalist who is tied down to a particular rural locality by the conditions of his industry—water power, the location of coal mines, iron-ore deposits and other mines, etc.—must build dwellings for his workers if none are available. To see in this a proof of "latent association", "an eloquent testimony to a growing understanding of the question and its wide import", a "very promising beginning" (page 115), requires a highly developed habit of self-deception. For the rest, the industrialists of the various countries differ from each other in this respect also, according to their national character. For instance, Herr Sax informs us (page 117):

"In *England only quite recently* has increased activity on the part of employers in this direction been observable. This refers in particular to the out-of-the-way hamlets in the rural areas... The circumstance that otherwise the workers often have to walk a long way from the nearest village to the factory and arrive there so exhausted that they do not perform enough work is the employers' main *motive for building* dwellings for their workers. However, the number of those who have a *deeper understanding* of conditions and who combine with the cause of housing *reform* more or less all the other elements of latent association is also increasing, and it is these people to whom credit is due for the establishment of those flourishing colonies... The names of Ashton in Hyde, Ashworth in Turton, Grant in Bury, Greg in Bollington, Marshall in Leeds, Strutt in Belper, Salt in Saltaire, Ackroyd in Copley, and others are well known on this account throughout the United Kingdom."

Blessed simplicity, and still more blessed ignorance! The English rural factory owners have only "quite recently" been building workers' dwellings! No, my dear Herr Sax, the English capitalists are really big industrialists, not only as regards their purses but also as regards their brains. Long before Germany possessed a really large-scale industry they had realised that for factory production in the rural districts expenditure on workers' dwellings was a necessary part of the total investment of capital, and a very profitable one, both directly and indirectly. Long before the

---

[a] *L'Enquête du dixième groupe*, Paris, 1867.— *Ed.*

struggle between Bismarck and the German bourgeois had given the German workers freedom of association,[248] the English factory, mine and foundry owners had had practical experience of the pressure they can exert on striking workers if they are at the same time the landlords of those workers. "The flourishing colonies" of a Greg, an Ashton and an Ashworth are so "recent" that even forty years ago they were hailed by the bourgeoisie as models, as I myself wrote twenty-eight years ago. (*The Condition of the Working-Class in England*. Note on pp. 228-30.[a]) The colonies of Marshall and Akroyd (that is how the man spells his name) are about as old, and the colony of Strutt is even much older, its beginnings reaching back into the last century. Since in England the average duration of a worker's dwelling is reckoned as forty years, Herr Sax can calculate on his fingers the dilapidated condition in which these "flourishing colonies" are today. In addition, the majority of these colonies are now no longer in the countryside. The colossal expansion of industry has surrounded most of them with factories and houses to such an extent that they are now situated in the middle of dirty, smoky towns with 20,000, 30,000 and more inhabitants. But all this does not prevent German bourgeois science, as represented by Herr Sax, from devoutly repeating today the old English paeans of praise of 1840, which no longer have any application.

And to give us old Akroyd as an example![b] This worthy was certainly a philanthropist of the first water. He loved his workers, and in particular his female employees, to such an extent that his less philanthropic competitors in Yorkshire used to say of him that he ran his factories exclusively with his own children! True, Herr Sax contends that "illegitimate children are becoming more and more rare" in these flourishing colonies (page 118). Yes, illegitimate children *born out of wedlock*, for in the English industrial districts the pretty girls marry very young.

In England the establishment of workers' dwellings close to each big rural factory and simultaneously *with* the factory has been the rule for sixty years and more. As already mentioned, many of these factory villages have become the nucleus around which later on a whole factory town has grown up with all the evils which a factory town brings with it. These colonies have therefore not

---

[a] See present edition, Vol. 4, p. 477.— *Ed.*

[b] Engels changed this sentence in the 1887 edition; earlier it read as follows: "And to give us old A. as an example—I do not wish to name him since he is long dead and buried."— *Ed.*

solved the housing question; on the contrary, they *first really created* it in their localities.

On the other hand, in countries which in the sphere of large-scale industry have only limped along behind England, and which really got to know what large-scale industry is only after 1848, in France and particularly[a] in Germany, the situation is quite different. Here it was only colossal foundries and factories which decided after much hesitation to build a certain number of workers' dwellings—for instance, the Schneider works in Creusot and the Krupp works in Essen. The great majority of the rural industrialists let their workers trudge miles through the heat, snow and rain every morning to the factories, and back again every evening to their homes. This is particularly the case in mountainous districts, in the French and Alsatian Vosges districts, in the valleys of the Wupper, Sieg, Agger, Lenne and other Rhineland-Westphalian rivers. In the Erzgebirge the situation is probably no better. The same petty niggardliness occurs among both Germans and French.

Herr Sax knows very well that the very promising beginning as well as the flourishing colonies mean less than nothing. Therefore, he tries now to prove to the capitalists that they can obtain magnificent rents by building workers' dwellings. In other words, he seeks to show them a new way of cheating the workers.

First of all, he holds up to them the example of a number of London building societies, partly philanthropic and partly speculative, which have shown a net profit of from four to six per cent and more. It is not at all necessary for Herr Sax to prove to us that capital invested in workers' houses yields a good profit. The reason why the capitalists do not invest still more than they do in workers' dwellings is that more expensive dwellings bring in still greater profits for their owners. Herr Sax's exhortation to the capitalists, therefore, amounts once again to nothing but a moral sermon.

Now, as far as these London building societies are concerned, whose brilliant successes Herr Sax so loudly trumpets forth, they have, according to his own figures—and every sort of building speculation is included here—provided housing for a total of 2,132 families and 706 single men, that is, for less than 15,000 persons! And is it presumed seriously to present in Germany this sort of childishness as a great success, although in the East End of London alone a million workers live under the

---

[a] The word was added by Engels in the 1887 edition.— *Ed.*

most miserable housing conditions? The whole of these philanthropic efforts are in fact so miserably futile that the English
parliamentary reports dealing with the condition of the workers
never even mention them.

We will not speak here of the ludicrous ignorance of London
displayed throughout this whole section. Just one point, however.
Herr Sax is of the opinion that the Lodging House for Single Men
in Soho went out of business because there "was no hope of
obtaining a large clientele" in this neighbourhood. Herr Sax
imagines that the whole of the West End of London is one big
luxury town, and does not know that right behind the most
elegant streets the dirtiest workers' quarters are to be found, of
which, for example, Soho is one. The model lodging house in
Soho, which he mentions and which I already knew twenty-three
years ago, was much frequented in the beginning, but closed down
because no one could stand it there, and yet it was one of the best.

But the workers' town of Mulhouse in Alsace—that is surely a
success, is it not?

The Workers' City in Mulhouse is the great show-piece of the
continental bourgeois, just as the one-time flourishing colonies of
Ashton, Ashworth, Greg and Co. are of the English bourgeois.
Unfortunately, the Mulhouse example is not a product of
"latent" association but of the open association between the
Second French Empire and the capitalists of Alsace. It was one of
Louis Bonaparte's socialist experiments, for which the state
advanced one-third of the capital. In fourteen years (up to 1867) it
built 800 small houses according to a defective system, an
impossible one in England where they understand these things
better, and these houses are handed over to the workers to
become their own property after thirteen to fifteen years of
monthly payments of an increased rental. It was not necessary for
the Bonapartists of Alsace to invent this mode of acquiring
property; as we shall see, it had been introduced by the English
co-operative building societies long before. Compared with that in
England, the extra rent paid for the purchase of these houses is
rather high. For instance, after having paid 4,500 francs in
instalments during fifteen years, the worker receives a house
which was worth 3,300 francs fifteen years before. If the worker
wants to go away or if he is in arrears with only a single monthly
instalment (in which case he can be evicted), six and two-thirds per
cent of the original value of the house is charged as the annual
rent (for instance, 17 francs a month for a house worth
3,000 francs) and the rest is paid out to him, but *without a penny of*

interest. It is quite clear that under such circumstances the society is able to grow fat, quite apart from "state assistance". It is just as clear that the houses provided under these circumstances are better than the old tenement houses in the town itself, if only because they are built outside the town in a semi-rural neighbourhood.

We need not say a word about the few miserable experiments which have been made in Germany; even Herr Sax, on page 157, admits their woefulness.

What, then, exactly do all these examples prove? Simply that the building of workers' dwellings is profitable from the capitalist point of view, even when not all the laws of hygiene are trodden underfoot. But that has never been denied; we all knew that long ago. *Any* investment of capital which satisfies an existing need is profitable if conducted rationally. The question, however, is precisely, why the housing shortage continues to exist *all the same*, why the capitalists all the same do not provide sufficient healthy dwellings for the workers. And here Herr Sax has again nothing but exhortations to make to capital and fails to provide us with an answer. The real answer to this question we have already given above.

Capital does not *want* to abolish the housing shortage even if it could; this has now been finally established. There remain, therefore, only two other expedients: self-help on the part of the workers, and state assistance.

Herr Sax, an enthusiastic worshipper of self-help, is able to report miraculous things about it also in regard to the housing question. Unfortunately he is compelled to admit right at the beginning that self-help can only effect anything where the COTTAGE SYSTEM either already exists or where it is feasible, that is, once again only in the rural areas. In the big cities, even in England, it can be effective only in a very limited measure. Herr Sax then sighs:

"Reform in this way" (by self-help) "can be effected only in a *roundabout way* and therefore *always* only imperfectly, namely, only in so far as the principle of private ownership is so strengthened as to react on the quality of the dwelling." [Page 170.]

This too could be doubted; in any case, "the principle of private ownership" has not exercised any reforming influence on the "quality" of the author's style. Despite all this, self-help in England has achieved such wonders

"that thereby everything done there along other lines to solve the housing problem has been *far exceeded*".

Herr Sax is referring to the English BUILDING SOCIETIES and he deals with them at great length particularly because

"very inadequate or erroneous ideas are current about their character and activities in general. The English BUILDING SOCIETIES are by no means ... associations for building houses or building co-operatives; they can be described ... in German rather as something like 'Hauserwerbvereine' [associations for the acquisition of houses]. They are associations whose object it is to accumulate funds from the periodical contributions of their members in order then, out of these funds and according to their size, to grant loans to their members for the purchase of a house.... The BUILDING SOCIETY is thus a savings bank for one section of its members, and a loan bank for the other section. The BUILDING SOCIETIES are, therefore, mortgage credit institutions designed to meet the requirements of the workers which, in the main ... use the savings of the workers ... to assist persons of the same social standing as the depositors to purchase or build a house. As may be supposed, such loans are granted by mortgaging the real estate in question, and on condition that they must be paid back at short intervals in instalments which combine both interest and amortisation.... The interest is not paid out to the depositors but always *placed to their credit and compounded*.... The members can demand the return of the sums they have paid in, plus interest ... at any time by giving a month's notice." (Pages 170 to 172.) "There are over 2,000 such societies in England; ... the total capital they have accumulated amounts to about £15,000,000. In this way about 100,000 *working-class* families have already obtained possession of their own hearth and home—a social achievement which it would certainly be difficult to parallel." (Page 174.)

Unfortunately here too the "but" comes limping along immediately after:

"But a perfect solution of the problem has *by no means been achieved* in this way, for the reason, if for no other, that the acquisition of a house is something only the *better situated* workers ... can afford.... In particular, sanitary conditions are often not sufficiently taken into consideration." (Page 176.)

On the Continent "such associations ... find only little scope for development". They presuppose the existence of the COTTAGE SYSTEM, which here exists only in the countryside; and in the countryside the workers are not yet sufficiently developed for self-help. On the other hand, in the towns where real building co-operatives could be formed they are faced with "very considerable and serious difficulties of all sorts". (Page 179.) They could build only COTTAGES and that will not do in the big cities. In short, "this form of co-operative self-help" cannot "in the present circumstances—and hardly in the near future either—play the chief role in the solution of the problem before us". These building societies, you see, are still "in their initial, undeveloped stage". "This is true even of England." (Page 181.)

Hence, the capitalists *will* not and the workers *cannot*. And with this we could close this section if it were not absolutely necessary to provide a little information about the English BUILDING SOCIETIES, which the bourgeois of the Schulze-Delitzsch type always hold up to our workers as models.[249]

These BUILDING SOCIETIES are not workers' societies, nor is it their main aim to provide workers with their own houses. On the contrary, we shall see that this happens only very exceptionally. The BUILDING SOCIETIES are essentially of a speculative nature, the small ones, which were the original societies, not less so than their big imitators. In a public house, usually at the instigation of the proprietor, on whose premises the weekly meetings then take place, a number of regular customers and their friends, shopkeepers, office clerks, commercial travellers, master artisans and other petty bourgeois—with here and there perhaps a mechanic or some other worker belonging to the aristocracy of his class—get together and found a building co-operative. The immediate occasion is usually that the proprietor has discovered a comparatively cheap plot of land in the neighbourhood or somewhere else. Most of the members are not bound by their occupations to any particular locality. Even many of the shopkeepers and craftsmen have only business premises in the town but no living quarters. Everyone in a position to do so prefers to live in the suburbs rather than in the centre of the smoky town. The building plot is purchased and as many COTTAGES as possible erected on it. The credit of the more substantial members makes the purchase possible, and the weekly contributions together with a few small loans cover the weekly costs of building. Those members who aim at getting a house of their own receive COTTAGES by lot as they are completed, and the appropriate extra rent serves for the amortisation of the purchase price. The remaining COTTAGES are then either let or sold. The building society, however, if it does good business, accumulates a more or less considerable sum. This remains the property of the members, provided they keep up their contributions, and is distributed among them from time to time, or when the society is dissolved. Such is the life history of nine out of ten of the English building societies. The others are bigger associations, sometimes formed under political or philanthropic pretexts, but in the end their chief aim is always to provide a more profitable mortgage investment for the savings of the *petty bourgeoisie*, at a good rate of interest and the prospect of dividends from speculation in real estate.

The sort of clients these societies speculate on can be seen from the prospectus of one of the largest, if not the largest, of them. The BIRKBECK BUILDING SOCIETY, 29 AND 30, SOUTHAMPTON BUILDINGS,

CHANCERY LANE, LONDON, whose gross receipts since its foundation total over £10,500,000 (70,000,000 thalers), which has over £416,000 in the bank or invested in government securities, and which at present has 21,441 members and depositors, introduces itself to the public in the following fashion:

"Most people are acquainted with the so-called three-year system of the piano manufacturers, under which anyone renting a piano for three years becomes the owner of the piano after the expiration of that period. Prior to the introduction of this system it was almost as difficult for people of limited income to acquire a good piano as it was for them to acquire their own house. Year after year such people had paid the rent for the piano and spent two or three times the money the piano was worth. What applies to a piano applies also to a house... However, as a house costs more than a piano, ... it takes longer to pay off the purchase price in rent. In consequence the directors have entered into an arrangement with house-owners in various parts of London and its suburbs which enables them to offer the members of the BIRKBECK BUILDING SOCIETY and others a great selection of houses in the most diverse parts of the town. The system which the Board of Directors intends to put into operation is as follows: it will let these houses for twelve and a half years and at the end of this period, providing that the rent has been paid regularly, the tenant will become the absolute owner of the house without any further payment of any kind... The tenant can also contract for a shorter space of time with a higher rental, or for a longer space of time with a lower rental... *People of limited income, clerks, shop assistants,* and others can make themselves independent of landlords immediately by becoming members of the BIRKBECK BUILDING SOCIETY."

That is clear enough. There is no mention of workers, but there is of people of limited income, clerks and shop assistants, etc., and in addition it is assumed that, as a rule, the applicants *already possess a piano.* In fact we do not have to do here with workers at all but with petty bourgeois and those who would like *and are able* to become such; people whose incomes gradually rise as a rule, even if within certain limits, such as clerks and similar employees. The income of the worker, on the contrary, at best remains the same in amount, and in reality falls in proportion to the increase of his family and its growing needs. In fact only a few workers can, by way of exception, belong to such societies. On the one hand their income is too low, and on the other hand it is of too uncertain a character for them to be able to undertake responsibilities for twelve and a half years in advance. The few exceptions where this is not valid are either the best-paid workers or foremen.*

* We add here a little contribution on the way in which these building associations, and in particular the London building associations, are managed. As is known, almost the whole of the land on which London is built belongs to about a dozen aristocrats, including the most eminent, the Duke of Westminster, the Duke of Bedford, the Duke of Portland, etc. They originally leased out the separate building sites for a period of ninety-nine years, and at the end of that period took

For the rest, it is clear to everyone that the Bonapartists of the workers' town of Mulhouse are nothing more than miserable apers of these petty-bourgeois English building societies. The sole difference is that the former, in spite of the state assistance granted to them, swindle their clients far more than the building societies do. On the whole their terms are less liberal than the average existing in England, and while in England interest and compound interest are calculated on each deposit and can be withdrawn at a month's notice, the factory owners of Mulhouse put both interest and compound interest into their own pockets and repay no more than the amount paid in by the workers in hard five-franc pieces. And no one will be more astonished at this difference than Herr Sax who has it all in his book without knowing it.

Thus, workers' self-help is also no good. There remains state assistance. What can Herr Sax offer us in this regard? Three things:

"First of all, the state must take care that in its legislation and administration all those things which in any way result in accentuating the housing shortage among the working classes are abolished or appropriately remedied." (Page 187.)

Consequently, revision of building legislation and freedom for the building trades in order that building shall be cheaper. But in England building legislation is reduced to a minimum, the building trades are as free as the birds in the air; nevertheless, the housing shortage exists. In addition building is now done so cheaply in England that the houses shake when a cart goes by and every day some of them collapse. Only yesterday (October 25, 1872) six of them collapsed simultaneously in Manchester and

possession of the land with everything on it. They then let the houses on shorter leases, thirty-nine years for example, on a so-called REPAIRING LEASE, according to which the leaseholder must put the house in good repair and maintain it in such condition. As soon as the contract has progressed thus far, the landlord sends his architect and the district SURVEYOR to inspect the house and determine the repairs necessary. These repairs are often very considerable and may include the renewal of the whole frontage, or of the roof, etc. The leaseholder now deposits his lease as security with a building association and receives from this society a loan of the necessary money—up to £1,000 and more in the case of an annual rental of from £130 to £150—for the building repairs to be made at *his* expense. These building associations have thus become an important intermediate link in a system which aims at securing the continual renewal and maintenance in habitable condition of London's houses belonging to the landed aristocracy without any trouble to the latter and at the cost of the public. And this is supposed to be a solution of the housing question for the workers! [*Note by Engels to the 1887 edition.*]

seriously injured six workers.[a] Therefore, that is also no remedy.

"Secondly, the state power must prevent individuals in their narrow-minded individualism from spreading the evil or calling it forth anew." [Page 187.]

Consequently, sanitary and building-police inspection of workers' dwellings; transference to the authorities of power to forbid the occupancy of dilapidated and unhygienic houses, as has been the case in England since 1857. But how did it come about there? The first law, that of 1855 (the NUISANCES REMOVAL ACT), was "a dead letter", as Herr Sax admits himself, as was the second, the law of 1858 (the LOCAL GOVERNMENT ACT) (page 197). On the other hand Herr Sax believes that the third law, the ARTISANS' DWELLINGS ACT, which applies only to towns with a population of over 10,000, "certainly offers favourable testimony of the great understanding of the British Parliament in social matters" (page 199). But as a matter of fact this assertion does no more than "offer favourable testimony" of the utter ignorance of Herr Sax in English "matters". That England in general is far in advance of the Continent "in social matters" is a matter of course. England is the motherland of modern large-scale industry; the capitalist mode of production has developed there most freely and extensively of all, its consequences show themselves there most glaringly of all and therefore it is likewise there that they first produced a reaction in the sphere of legislation. The best proof of this is factory legislation. If however Herr Sax thinks that an Act of Parliament only requires to become legally effective in order to be carried immediately into practice as well, he is grievously mistaken. And this is true of the LOCAL GOVERNMENT ACT more than of any other act (with the exception, of course, of the WORKSHOPS ACT). The administration of this law was entrusted to the urban authorities, which almost everywhere in England are recognised centres of corruption of every kind, of nepotism and JOBBERY.* The agents of

---

* JOBBERY is the use of a public office to the private advantage of the official or his family. If, for instance, the director of the state telegraph of a country becomes a silent partner in a paper factory, provides this factory with timber from his forests and then gives the factory orders for supplying paper for the telegraph offices, that is, true, a fairly small but still quite a pretty "JOB", inasmuch as it demonstrates a complete understanding of the principles of JOBBERY[b]; such as, by the way, in the days of Bismarck was a matter of course and to be expected.

---

[a] "Fall of Six Houses in Manchester", *The Daily News*, No. 8268, October 26, 1872.— *Ed.*

[b] The rest of the sentence was added by Engels in the 1887 edition.— *Ed.*

these urban authorities, who owe their positions to all sorts of family considerations, are either incapable of carrying into effect such social laws or disinclined to do so. On the other hand it is precisely in England that the state officials entrusted with the preparation and execution of social legislation are usually distinguished by a strict sense of duty—although in a lesser degree today than twenty or thirty years ago. In the town councils the owners of unsound and dilapidated dwellings are almost everywhere strongly represented either directly or indirectly. The system of electing these town councils by small wards makes the elected members dependent on the pettiest local interests and influences; no town councillor who desires to be re-elected dare vote for the application of this law in his constituency. It is comprehensible, therefore, with what aversion this law was received almost everywhere by the local authorities, and that up to the present it has been applied only in the most scandalous cases—and even then, as a general rule, only as the result of the outbreak of some epidemic, such as in the case of the small-pox epidemic last year in Manchester and Salford. Appeals to the Home Secretary have up to the present been effective only in such cases, for it is the principle of every *Liberal* government in England to propose social reform laws only when compelled to do so and, if at all possible, to avoid carrying into effect those already existing. The law in question, like many others in England, is of importance only because in the hands of a government dominated by or under the pressure of the workers, a government which would at last really administer it, it will be a powerful weapon for making a breach in the existing social state of things.

"Thirdly," the state power ought, according to Herr Sax, "to make the most extensive use possible of all the positive means at its disposal to allay the existing housing shortage." [Page 187.]

That is to say, it should build barracks, "truly model buildings", for its "subordinate officials and servants" (but then these are not workers!), and "grant loans ... to municipalities, societies and also to private persons for the purpose of improving the housing conditions of the working classes" (page 203), as is done in England under the PUBLIC WORKS LOAN ACT, and as Louis Bonaparte has done in Paris and Mulhouse. But the PUBLIC WORKS LOAN ACT also exists only on paper. The government places at the disposal of the commissioners a maximum sum of £50,000, that is, sufficient to build at the utmost 400 COTTAGES, or in forty years a total of 16,000 COTTAGES or dwellings for at the most 80,000 persons—a drop in the bucket! Even if we assume that after twenty years the funds at the disposal of the commission were to double as a result of repayments, that therefore during the past twenty years dwellings for a further 40,000 persons have been built, it still is only a drop in the bucket. And as the COTTAGES last on the average only forty years, after forty years the liquid assets of £50,000 or £100,000 must be used every year to replace the most dilapidated, the oldest of the COTTAGES. This, Herr Sax declares on page 203, is carrying the principle into practice correctly "and to an unlimited extent"! And with this confession that even in England the state, "to an unlimited extent", has achieved next to nothing, Herr Sax concludes his book, but not without having first delivered another homily to all concerned.*

It is perfectly clear that the state as it exists today is neither able nor willing to do anything to remedy the housing calamity. The state is nothing but the organised collective power of the possessing classes, the landowners and the capitalists, as against the exploited classes, the peasants and the workers. What the individual capitalists (and it is here only a question of these because in this matter the landowner, who is concerned, also acts primarily in his capacity as a capitalist) do not want, their state also does not want. If therefore the *individual* capitalists deplore the housing shortage, but can hardly be moved to palliate even superficially its most terrifying consequences, the *collective* capitalist, the state, will not do much more. At most it will see to it that that measure of superficial palliation which has become customary is carried into execution everywhere uniformly. And we have seen that this is the case.

But, one might object, in Germany the bourgeois do not rule as yet; in Germany the state is still to a certain extent a power hovering independently over society, which for that very reason

---

* In recent English Acts of Parliament giving the London building authorities the right of expropriation for the purpose of new street construction, a certain amount of consideration is given to the workers thus turned out of their homes. A provision has been inserted that the new buildings to be erected must be suitable for housing those classes of the population previously living there. Big five or six storey tenement houses are therefore erected for the workers on the least valuable sites and in this way the letter of the law is complied with. It remains to be seen how this arrangement will work, for the workers are quite unaccustomed to it and in the midst of the old conditions in London these buildings represent a completely foreign development. At best, however, they will provide new dwellings for hardly a quarter of the workers actually evicted by the building operations. [*Note by Engels to the 1887 edition.*]

represents the collective interests of society and not those of a single class. *Such* a state can certainly do much that a bourgeois state cannot do, and one ought to expect from it something quite different in the social field also.

That is the language of reactionaries. In reality however the state as it exists in Germany is likewise the necessary product of the social basis out of which it has developed. In Prussia—and Prussia is now decisive—there exists side by side with a landowning aristocracy, which is still powerful, a comparatively young and extremely cowardly bourgeoisie, which up to the present has not won either direct political domination, as in France, or more or less indirect domination as in England. Side by side with these two classes, however, there exists a rapidly increasing proletariat which is intellectually highly developed and which is becoming more and more organised every day. We therefore find here, alongside of the basic condition of the old absolute monarchy—an equilibrium between the landed aristocracy and the bourgeoisie—the basic condition of modern Bonapartism—an equilibrium between the bourgeoisie and the proletariat. But both in the old absolute monarchy and in the modern Bonapartist monarchy the real governmental authority lies in the hands of a special caste of army officers and state officials. In Prussia this caste is replenished partly from its own ranks, partly from the lesser primogenitary aristocracy, more rarely from the higher aristocracy, and least of all from the bourgeoisie. The independence of this caste, which appears to occupy a position outside and, so to speak, above society, gives the state the semblance of independence in relation to society.

The form of state which has developed with the necessary consistency in Prussia (and, following the Prussian example, in the new Imperial constitution of Germany) out of these contradictory social conditions is pseudo-constitutionalism, a form which is at once both the present-day form of the dissolution of the old absolute monarchy and the form of existence of the Bonapartist monarchy. In Prussia pseudo-constitutionalism from 1848 to 1866 only concealed and facilitated the slow decay of the absolute monarchy. However, since 1866, and still more since 1870, the upheaval in social conditions, and with it the dissolution of the old state, has proceeded in the sight of all and on a tremendously increasing scale. The rapid development of industry, and in particular of stock-exchange swindling, has dragged all the ruling classes into the whirlpool of speculation. The wholesale corruption imported from France in 1870 is developing at an unprecedented rate. Strousberg and Péreire take off their hats to each other. Ministers, generals, princes and counts gamble in stocks in competition with the most cunning stock-exchange wolves, and the state recognises their equality by conferring baronetcies wholesale on these stock-exchange wolves. The rural nobility, who have been industrialists for a long time as manufacturers of beet sugar and distillers of brandy, have long left the old respectable days behind and their names now swell the lists of directors of all sorts of sound and unsound joint-stock companies. The bureaucracy is beginning more and more to despise embezzlement as the sole means of improving its income; it is turning its back on the state and beginning to hunt after the far more lucrative posts on the administration of industrial enterprises. Those who still remain in office follow the example of their superiors and speculate in stocks, or "acquire interests" in railways, etc. One is even justified in assuming that the lieutenants also have their hands in certain speculations. In short, the decomposition of all the elements of the old state and the transition from the absolute monarchy to the Bonapartist monarchy is in full swing. With the next big business and industrial crisis not only will the present swindle collapse, but the old Prussian state as well.*

And this state, in which the non-bourgeois elements are becoming more bourgeois every day, is it to solve "the social question", or even only the housing question? On the contrary. In all economic questions the Prussian state increasingly comes under the control of the bourgeoisie. And if legislation in the economic field since 1866 has not been adapted even more to the interests of the bourgeoisie than has actually been the case, whose fault is that? The bourgeoisie itself is chiefly responsible, first because it is too cowardly to press its own demands energetically, and secondly because it resists every concession if the latter simultaneously provides the menacing proletariat with new weapons. And if the political power, that is, Bismarck, is attempting to organise the proletariat for its own needs to keep the political activity of the bourgeoisie in check, what else is that if not a necessary and quite familiar Bonapartist recipe which pledges the state to nothing more, as far as the workers are concerned, than a few benevolent phrases and at the utmost to a minimum of state assistance for building societies à la Louis Bonaparte?

* Even today, in 1886, the only thing that holds together the old Prussian state and its basis, the alliance of big landownership and industrial capital sealed by the protective tariffs, is fear of the proletariat, which has grown tremendously in numbers and class-consciousness since 1872. [*Note by Engels to the 1887 edition.*]

The best proof of what the workers have to expect from the Prussian state lies in the utilisation of the French milliards[250] which have given a new, short reprieve to the independence of the Prussian state machine in regard to society. Has even a single thaler of all these milliards been used to provide shelter for those Berlin working-class families which have been thrown on to the streets? On the contrary. As autumn approached, the state caused to be pulled down even those few miserable hovels which had given them a temporary roof over their heads during the summer. The five milliards are going rapidly enough the way of all flesh: for fortresses, cannon and soldiers; and despite Wagner's asininities, and despite Stieber's conferences with Austria,[251] less will be allotted to the German workers out of those milliards than was allotted to the French workers out of the millions which Louis Bonaparte stole from France.

III

In reality the bourgeoisie has only one method of settling the housing question after *its* fashion—that is to say, of settling it in such a way that the solution continually poses the question anew. This method is called "*Haussmann*".

By the term "Haussmann" I do not mean merely the specifically Bonapartist manner of the Parisian Haussmann—breaking long, straight and broad streets right through the closely-built workers' quarters and lining them on both sides with big luxurious buildings, the intention having been, apart from the strategic aim of making barricade fighting more difficult, to develop a specifically Bonapartist building trades' proletariat dependent on the government and to turn the city into a luxury city pure and simple. By "Haussmann" I mean the practice, which has now become general, of making breaches in the working-class quarters of our big cities, particularly in those which are centrally situated, irrespective of whether this practice is occasioned by considerations of public health and beautification or by the demand for big centrally located business premises or by traffic requirements, such as the laying down of railways, streets, etc. No matter how different the reasons may be, the result is everywhere the same: the most scandalous alleys and lanes disappear to the accompaniment of lavish self-glorification by the bourgeoisie on account of this tremendous success, but—they appear again at once somewhere else, and often in the immediate neighbourhood.

In *The Condition of the Working-Class in England* I gave a picture of Manchester as it looked in 1843 and 1844.[a] Since then the construction of railways through the centre of the city, the laying out of new streets and the erection of great public and private buildings have broken through, laid bare and improved some of the worst districts described there, others have been abolished altogether; although, apart from the fact that sanitary-police inspection has since become stricter, many of them are still in the same state or in an even worse state of dilapidation than they were then. On the other hand, thanks to the enormous extension of the town, whose population has since increased by more than a half, districts which were at that time still airy and clean are now just as overbuilt, just as dirty and congested as the most ill-famed parts of the town formerly were. Here is but one example: On page 80 et seq. of my book I described a group of houses situated in the valley bottom of the Medlock River, which under the name of LITTLE IRELAND was for years the disgrace of Manchester.[b] Little Ireland has long ago disappeared and on its site there now stands a railway station built on a high foundation. The bourgeoisie pointed with pride to the happy and final abolition of Little Ireland as to a great triumph. Now last summer a great inundation took place, as in general the rivers embanked in our big cities cause more and more extensive floods year after year for reasons that can be easily explained. And it was then revealed that Little Ireland had not been abolished at all, but had simply been shifted from the south side of Oxford Road to the north side, and that it still continues to flourish. Let us hear what *The Manchester Weekly Times*, the organ of the radical bourgeoisie of Manchester, has to say in its issue of July 20, 1872[c]:

> "The *one* good result which we may hope to obtain from the calamity which befell the inhabitants of the property built on the low lying ground near the banks of the Medlock on Saturday last, is that public attention will be concentrated on the palpable violation of sanitary laws which has been permitted so long to exist under the noses of the Corporation officers and the sanitary committee of the City Council. A correspondent in yesterday's paper, in a pithy letter, indicated only too feebly the shameful condition of some of the cellar dwelling houses in the neighbourhood of Charles-street and Brook-street, which were inundated by the flood. A minute investigation of one of the courts named in our correspondent's letter, which was made yesterday by our reporter, enables us fully to confirm all his statements, and to endorse his opinion that the cellar dwellings contained in it ought to have been closed long ago, or rather that their habitation ought never to

---

a See present edition, Vol. 4, p. 347 et seq.— *Ed.*

b Ibid., p. 361.— *Ed.*

c "The Floods in the Medlock. Charles-Street Pit", *The Manchester Weekly Times*, No. 763, July 20, 1872.— *Ed.*

have been allowed. Squire's Court consists of a group of seven or eight dwelling houses at the junction of Charles-street and Brook-street, over which the passenger, who reached the lowest step in the dip of Brook-street under the railway arches, may pass daily, unconscious of the knowledge that human beings burrow in the depths beneath him. It is hidden from public view, and is only accessible to those whom misery compels to seek a shelter in its grave-like seclusion. Even when the ordinary sluggish weir-pent waters of the Medlock are at their ordinary height, the floors of these dwellings can only be a few inches above their level, and are liable after any heavy shower to have their 'soughs' or drainpipes surcharged with filthy water and their dwellings poisoned by the pestiferous vapours which flood water invariably leaves as its souvenir... Squire's Court lies at even a lower level than these cellars ... 20 feet below the level of the street, and the foul water forced up the 'soughs' by the rising flood in the river on Saturday reached to the roofs. Knowing so much as this, we had expected on our visit yesterday to find the court deserted, or occupied only by the officers of the health committee, engaged in flushing the foetid walls and distributing disinfectants. The only thing we did observe, ... was a labouring man engaged, under the superintendence of a tenant (who had been so far fortunate that he possessed an upper storey to his cellar dwelling, in which he officiates as a barber, and carries on a miscellaneous business), in digging into a heap of mud and putrid matter collected in a corner, from which he was filling a wheelbarrow... The barber's cellar had been pretty well set to rights, but he directed us to a lower depth, where were a series of dwellings, regarding which he said if he were a scholar he should write to the newspapers, insisting that they should be shut up. Guided at last to Squire's Court proper, we found a buxom and healthy-looking Irishwoman busily engaged in her washtub. With her husband, a night watchman, she had lived in the court for six years, and had brought up a large family... Inside the house the water-mark had risen to within a few inches of the roof, the windows had been broken in, the furniture remaining in the house was a confused heap of broken and sodden timber... The tenant said that he had kept the place sweet by whitewashing its damp walls once in two months... This discovery made, our reporter on entering found three houses standing back to back, with those in the outer square. Two of these were occupied. The smell arising from them was so sickening that a few minutes' stay within their foetid portals was sufficient to upset the stomach of a healthy man ... this dismal dwelling place was occupied by a family of seven in all, everyone of whom had slept in the house on Thursday night" (the day of the beginning of the flood). "The woman who gave our reporter this information instantly corrected herself. Neither she nor her husband had slept at all. They had lain on the bare boards, but the smell of the place was so offensive that they had been vomiting during a great part of the night... On Saturday she ... had been obliged to wade breast-high through the flood, bearing two children in her arms... She agreed that the place was not fit for a pig to live in, but had been induced against her will to accept it, because of the cheapness of the rent (only 1s. 6d." (15 groschen) "a week), and because her husband, a labourer, had of late been much out of work through illness. The reflections raised in one's mind by the contemplation of this wretched court, and the poor creatures whom poverty has forced into it as into a premature grave, is one of almost utter hopelessness... In the public interest, however, we are forced to say a word. Observation during the past few days assures us that Squire's Court is a type, though perhaps an extreme one, of many other places in the neighbourhood which it is a reflection upon the health committee to have permitted so long to exist; if their further occupation under existing circumstances be allowed, the committee will incur a responsibility and the neighbourhood a danger of infectious visitation the seriousness of which we have no desire to prognosticate."

This is a striking example of how the bourgeoisie settles the housing question in practice. The breeding places of disease, the infamous holes and cellars in which the capitalist mode of production confines our workers night after night, are not abolished; they are merely *shifted elsewhere*! The same economic necessity which produced them in the first place produces them in the next place also. As long as the capitalist mode of production continues to exist it is folly to hope for an isolated settlement of the housing question or of any other social question affecting the lot of the workers. The solution lies in the abolition of the capitalist mode of production and the appropriation of all the means of subsistence and instruments of labour by the working class itself.

Part III

SUPPLEMENT ON PROUDHON AND THE HOUSING QUESTION

I

In No. 86 of the *Volksstaat*, A. Mülberger[a] reveals himself as the author of the articles criticised by me in No. 51 and subsequent numbers of the paper.[b] In his answer he overwhelms me with such a series of reproaches, and at the same time confuses all the issues to such an extent that willy-nilly I am compelled to reply to him. I shall attempt to give my reply, which to my regret must be made to a large extent in the field of personal polemics enjoined upon me by Mülberger himself, a general interest by presenting the chief points once again and if possible more clearly than before, even at the risk of being told once more by Mülberger that all this "contains nothing essentially new either for him or for the other readers of the *Volksstaat*".

Mülberger complains of the form and content of my criticism. As far as the form is concerned it will be sufficient to reply that at the time I did not even know who had written the articles in question. There can, therefore, be no question of any personal "prejudice" against their author; against the solution of the

---

[a] A. Mülberger, "Zur Wohnungsfrage", *Der Volksstaat*, No. 86, October 26, 1872.— *Ed.*

[b] See this volume, pp. 317-37.— *Ed.*

housing problem put forward in the articles I was of course in so far "prejudiced" as I was long ago acquainted with it from Proudhon and my opinion on it was firmly fixed.

I am not going to quarrel with friend Mülberger about the "tone" of my criticism. When one has been so long in the movement as I have, one develops a fairly thick skin against attacks, and therefore one easily presumes the existence of the same in others. In order to compensate Mülberger I shall endeavour this time to bring my "tone" into the right relation to the sensitiveness of his epidermis (outer layer of the skin).

Mülberger complains with particular bitterness that I said he was a Proudhonist, and he protests that he is not. Naturally I must believe him, but I shall adduce proof that the articles in question—and I had to do with them alone—contain nothing but undiluted Proudhonism.

But according to Mülberger I have also criticised Proudhon "frivolously" and have done him a serious injustice.

"The doctrine of the petty bourgeois Proudhon has become an accepted dogma in Germany, which is even proclaimed by many who have never read a line of him."

When I express regret that for twenty years the workers speaking Romance languages have had no other mental pabulum than the works of Proudhon, Mülberger answers that as far as the Latin workers are concerned, "the principles formulated by Proudhon are almost everywhere the driving spirit of the movement". This I must deny. First of all, the "driving spirit" of the working-class movement nowhere lies in "principles", but everywhere in the development of large-scale industry and its effects, the accumulation and concentration of capital, on the one hand, and of the proletariat, on the other. Secondly, it is not correct to say that in the Latin countries Proudhon's so-called "principles" play the decisive role ascribed to them by Mülberger; that "the principles of anarchism, of the *Organisation des forces économiques*, of the *liquidation sociale*, etc., have there ... become the true bearers of the revolutionary movement". Not to speak of Spain and Italy, where the Proudhonist panacea has gained some influence only in the still more botched form presented by Bakunin, it is a notorious fact for anyone who knows the international working-class movement that in France the Proudhonists form a numerically rather insignificant sect, while the mass of the French workers refuses to have anything to do with the social reform plan drawn up by Proudhon under the titles of *Liquidation sociale* and *Organisation des forces économiques.*[a] This was shown, among other things, in the Commune. Although the Proudhonists were strongly represented in the Commune, not the slightest attempt was made to liquidate the old society or to organise the economic forces according to Proudhon's proposals. On the contrary, it does the Commune the greatest honour that in all its economic measures the "driving spirit" was not any set of "principles", but simple, practical needs. And therefore these measures—abolition of night work in the bakeries, prohibition of monetary fines in the factories, confiscation of shut-down factories and workshops and handing them over to workers' associations—were not at all in accordance with the spirit of Proudhonism, but certainly in accordance with the spirit of German scientific socialism. The only social measure which the Proudhonists put through was the decision *not* to confiscate the Bank of France, and this was partly responsible for the downfall of the Commune. In the same way, when the so-called Blanquists made an attempt to transform themselves from mere political revolutionists into a socialist workers' faction with a definite programme—as was done by the Blanquist fugitives in London in their manifesto, *Internationale et révolution*—they did not proclaim the "principles" of the Proudhonist plan for the salvation of society, but adopted, and almost literally at that, the views of German scientific socialism on the necessity of political action by the proletariat and of its dictatorship as the transition to the abolition of classes and, with them, of the state—views such as had already been expressed in the *Communist Manifesto*[b] and since then on innumerable occasions. And if Mülberger even draws the conclusion from the Germans' disdain of Proudhon that there has been a lack of understanding of the movement in the Latin countries "down to the Paris Commune", let him as proof of this lack tell us what work from the Latin side has understood and described the Commune even approximately as correctly as has the *Address of the General Council of the International on the Civil War in France,* written by the German Marx.

The only country where the working-class movement is directly under the influence of Proudhonist "principles" is Belgium, and precisely as a result of this the Belgian movement comes, as Hegel would say, "from nothing through nothing to nothing".[c]

a P. J. Proudhon, *Idée générale de la révolution au XIXe siècle*, Paris, 1868.— *Ed.*

b See present edition, Vol. 6, pp. 504-06.— *Ed.*

c G. W. F. Hegel, *Wissenschaft der Logik*, *Werke*, Vol. 4, Berlin, 1834, Part 1, Section 2, pp. 15, 75, 145.— *Ed.*

When I consider it a misfortune that for twenty years the workers of the Latin countries fed intellectually, directly or indirectly, exclusively on Proudhon, I do not mean that thoroughly mythical dominance of Proudhon's reform recipe—termed by Mülberger the "principles"—but the fact that their economic criticism of existing society was contaminated with absolutely false Proudhonist phrases and that their political actions were bungled by Proudhonist influence. Whether thus the "Proudhonised workers of the Latin countries" "stand more in the revolution" than the German workers, who in any case understand the meaning of scientific German socialism infinitely better than the Latins understand their Proudhon, we shall be able to answer only after we have learnt what "to *stand* in the revolution" really means. We have heard talk of people who "stand in Christianity, in the true faith, in the grace of God", etc. But "standing" in the revolution, in the most violent of all movements? Is, then, "the revolution" a dogmatic religion in which one must believe?

Mülberger further reproaches me with having asserted, in defiance of the express wording of his articles, that he had declared the housing question to be an exclusively working-class question.

This time Mülberger is really right. I overlooked the passage in question. It was irresponsible of me to overlook it, for it is one most characteristic of the whole tendency of his disquisition. Mülberger actually writes in plain words:

"As we have been so frequently and largely exposed to the *absurd* charge of pursuing a *class policy*, of striving for *class domination,* and such like, we wish to stress first of all and expressly that the housing question is by no means a question which affects the proletariat exclusively, but that, *on the contrary*, it interests *to a quite prominent extent the middle classes proper*, the small tradesmen, the petty bourgeoisie, the whole bureaucracy... The housing question is precisely that point of social reform which more than any other seems appropriate to reveal the *absolute inner identity of the interests of the proletariat*, on the one hand, and the interests of the *middle classes proper* of society, on the other. The middle classes suffer just as much as, and *perhaps even more* than, the proletariat under the oppressive fetters of the rented dwelling... Today the middle classes proper of society are faced with the question of whether they ... can summon sufficient strength ... to participate in the process of the transformation of society in alliance with the youthful, vigorous and energetic workers' party, a transformation *whose blessings will be enjoyed above all by them.*" [a]

Friend Mülberger thus makes the following points here:
1. "We" do not pursue any "class policy" and do not strive for

---

[a] A. Mülberger, *Die Wohnungsfrage. Eine sociale Skizze. Separat-Abdruck aus dem "Volksstaat"* (The Housing Question. A Social Study. Separate Reprint from the *Volksstaat*), Leipzig, 1872.— *Ed.*

"class domination". But the German Social-Democratic Workers' Party, just *because* it is a *workers' party*, necessarily pursues a "class policy", the policy of the working class. Since each political party sets out to establish its rule in the state, so the German Social-Democratic Workers' Party is necessarily striving to establish *its* rule, the rule of the working class, hence "class domination". Moreover, *every* real proletarian party, from the English Chartists onward, has put forward a class policy, the organisation of the proletariat as an independent political party, as the primary condition of its struggle, and the dictatorship of the proletariat as the immediate aim of the struggle. By declaring this to be "absurd", Mülberger puts himself outside the proletarian movement and inside the camp of petty-bourgeois socialism.

2. The housing question has the advantage that it is not an exclusively working-class question, but a question which "interests to a quite prominent extent" the petty bourgeoisie, in that "the middle classes proper" suffer from it "just as much as, and perhaps even more than", the proletariat. If anyone declares that the petty bourgeoisie suffers, even if in one respect only, "perhaps even more than the proletariat", he can hardly complain if one counts him among the petty-bourgeois socialists. Has Mülberger therefore any grounds for complaint when I say:

"It is largely with just such sufferings as these, which the working class endures in common with other classes, and particularly the petty bourgeoisie, that petty-bourgeois socialism, to which Proudhon belongs, prefers to occupy itself. And thus it is not at all accidental that our German Proudhonist seizes chiefly upon the housing question, which, as we have seen, is by no means exclusively a working-class question." [a]

3. There is an "absolute inner identity" between the interests of the "middle classes proper of society" and the interests of the proletariat, and it is not the proletariat, but these middle classes proper which will "enjoy above all" the "blessings" of the coming process of transformation of society.

The workers, therefore, are going to make the coming social revolution "above all" in the interests of the petty bourgeoisie. And furthermore, there is an absolute inner identity of the interests of the petty bourgeoisie and those of the proletariat. If the interests of the petty bourgeoisie have an inner identity with those of the workers, then those of the workers have an inner identity with those of the petty bourgeoisie. The petty-bourgeois

---

standpoint has thus as much right to exist in the movement as the proletarian standpoint, and it is precisely the assertion of this equality of right that is called petty-bourgeois socialism.

It is therefore perfectly consistent when, on page 25 of the separate reprint, Mülberger extols "petty industry" as the "actual *buttress* of society", "because in accordance with its very nature it combines within itself the three factors: labour—acquisition—possession, and because in the combination of these three factors it places no bounds to the capacity for development of the individual"; and when he reproaches modern industry in particular with destroying this nursery for the production of normal human beings and "making out of a virile *class* continually reproducing itself an unconscious *heap* of humans who do not know whither to direct their anxious gaze". The petty bourgeois is thus Mülberger's model human being and petty industry is Mülberger's model mode of production. Did I defame him, therefore, when I classed him among the petty-bourgeois socialists?

As Mülberger rejects all responsibility for Proudhon, it would be superfluous to discuss here any further how Proudhon's reform plans aim at transforming all members of society into petty bourgeois and small peasants. It will be just as unnecessary to deal with the alleged identity of interests of the petty bourgeoisie and the workers. What is necessary is to be found already in the *Communist Manifesto*. (Leipzig edition, 1872, pp. 12 and 21.[a])

The result of our examination is, therefore, that side by side with the "myth of the petty bourgeois Proudhon" appears the reality of the petty bourgeois Mülberger.

II

We now come to one of the main points. I accused Mülberger's articles of falsifying economic relationships after the manner of Proudhon by translating them into legal terminology. As an example of this, I picked the following statement by Mülberger:

"The house, once it has been built, serves as a *perpetual legal title* to a definite fraction of social labour although the real value of the house has been paid to the owner long ago more than adequately in the form of rent. *Thus it comes about* that a house which, for instance, was built fifty years ago, during this period covers the original cost price two, three, five, ten and more times over in its rent yield."[b]

---

[a] See present edition, Vol. 6, pp. 494 and 509-10.— *Ed.*
[b] See this volume, pp. 320-21.— *Ed.*

Mülberger now complains as follows:

"This *simple, sober statement of fact* causes Engels to enlighten me to the effect that I should have explained *how* the house became a 'legal title'—something which was quite beyond the scope of my task.... A *description* is one thing, an *explanation* another. When I say with Proudhon that the economic life of society should be pervaded by a *conception of right*, I am *describing* present-day society as one in which, true, not every conception of right is absent, but in which the *conception of right of the revolution* is absent, a fact which Engels himself will admit." [a]

Let us keep for the moment to the house which has been built. The house, once it has been let, yields its builder ground rent, repairing costs, and interest on the building capital invested, including as well the profit made thereon in the form of rent [b]; and, according to the circumstances, the rent, paid gradually, can amount to twice, thrice, five times or ten times as much as the original cost price. This, friend Mülberger, is the "simple, sober statement" of "fact", an *economic* fact; and if we want to know "how it comes" that it exists, we must conduct our examination in the economic field. Let us therefore look a little closer at this fact so that not even a child may misunderstand it any longer. As is known, the sale of a commodity consists in the fact that its owner relinquishes its use-value and pockets its exchange-value. The use-values of commodities differ from one another among other things in the different periods of time required for their consumption. A loaf of bread is consumed in a day, a pair of trousers will be worn out in a year, and a house, if you like, in a hundred years. Hence, in the case of durable commodities, the possibility arises of selling their use-value piecemeal and each time for a definite period, that is to say, to *let* it. The piecemeal sale therefore realises the exchange-value only gradually. As a compensation for his renouncing the immediate repayment of the capital advanced and the profit accrued on it, the seller receives an increased price, interest, whose rate is determined by the laws of political economy and not by any means in an arbitrary fashion. At the end of the hundred years the house is used up, worn out and no longer habitable. If we then deduct from the total rent paid for the house the following: 1) the ground rent together with any increase it may have experienced during the period in question, and 2) the sums expended for current repairs, we shall find that the

---

[a] A. Mülberger, "Zur Wohnungsfrage", *Der Volksstaat*, No. 86, October 26, 1872.— *Ed.*

[b] In *Der Volksstaat* this part of the sentence reads as follows: "The house, once it has been let, yields its builder ground rent, repairing costs, and profit on the building capital invested in the form of rent".— *Ed.*

remainder is composed on an average as follows: 1) the building capital originally invested in the house, 2) the profit on this, and 3) the interest on the gradually maturing capital and profit.[a] Now it is true that at the end of this period the tenant has no house, but neither has the house-owner. The latter has only the lot (provided that it belongs to him) and the building material on it, which, however, is no longer a house. And although in the meantime the house may have brought in a sum "which covers the original cost price five or ten times over", we shall see that this is solely due to an increase of the ground rent. This is no secret to anyone in such cities as London where the landowner and the house-owner are in most cases two different persons. Such tremendous rent increases occur in rapidly growing towns,[b] but not in a farming village, where the ground rent for building sites remains practically unchanged. It is indeed a notorious fact that, apart from increases in the ground rent, house rents produce on an average no more than seven per cent per annum on the invested capital (including profit) for the house-owner, and out of this sum repair costs, etc., must be paid. In short, a rent agreement is quite an ordinary commodity transaction which theoretically is of no greater and no lesser interest to the worker than any other commodity transaction, with the exception of that which concerns the buying and selling of labour power, while practically the worker faces the rent agreement as one of the thousand forms of bourgeois cheating, which I dealt with on page 4 of the separate reprint.[c] But, as I proved there, this form is also subject to economic regulation.

Mülberger, on the other hand, regards the rent agreement as nothing but pure "arbitrariness" (page 19 of the separate reprint) and when I prove the contrary to him he complains that I am telling him "solely things which to his regret he already knew himself".

But all the economic investigations into house rent will not enable us to turn the abolition of the rented dwelling into "one of the most fruitful and magnificent aspirations which have ever sprung from the womb of the revolutionary idea".[d] In order to accomplish this we must translate the simple fact from sober economics into the really far more ideological sphere of jurispru-

---

[a] The words "and profit" were added by Engels in the 1887 edition.— Ed.

[b] Der Volksstaat has "in rapidly growing big towns".— Ed.

[c] The reference is to the separate reprint of F. Engels' Zur Wohnungsfrage, Part I, Leipzig, 1872 (see this volume, p. 318).— Ed.

[d] See this volume, p. 327.— Ed.

dence. "The house serves as a perpetual legal title" to house rent, and "*thus it comes*" that the value of a house can be paid back in rent two, three, five or ten times. The "legal title" does not help us a jot to discover how it really "does come", and therefore I said that Mülberger would have been able to find out *how* it really "does come" only by inquiring how the house becomes a legal title. We discover this only after we have examined, as I did, the *economic* nature of house rent, instead of quarrelling with the legal expression under which the ruling class sanctions it.—Anyone who proposes the taking of economic steps to abolish rent surely ought to know a little more about house rent than that it "represents the tribute which the tenant pays to the perpetual title of capital".[a] To this Mülberger answers, "A description is one thing, an explanation another."

We have thus converted the house, although it is by no means everlasting, into a perpetual legal title to house rent. We find, no matter how "it comes", that by virtue of this legal title, the house brings in its original value several times over in the form of rent. By the translation into legal phraseology we are happily so far removed from economics that we now can see no more than the phenomenon that a house can gradually get paid for in gross rent several times over. As we are thinking and talking in legal terms, we apply to this phenomenon the measuring stick of right, of justice, and find that it is *unjust*, that it is not in accordance with the "conception of right of the revolution", whatever that may be, and that therefore the legal title is no good. We find further that the same holds good for interest-bearing capital and leased agricultural land, and we now have the excuse for separating these classes of property from the others and subjecting them to exceptional treatment. This consists in the demands: 1) to deprive the owner of the right to give notice to quit, the right to demand the return of his property; 2) to give the lessee, borrower or tenant the gratuitous use of the object transferred to him but not belonging to him; and 3) to pay off the owner in instalments over a long period without interest. And with this we have exhausted the Proudhonist "principles" from this angle. This is Proudhon's "social liquidation".

Incidentally, it is obvious that this whole reform plan is to benefit almost exclusively the petty bourgeois and the small peasants, in that it *consolidates* them in their position as petty bourgeois and small peasants. Thus "the petty bourgeois

---

[a] Cf. this volume, p. 327.— *Ed.*

Proudhon", who, according to Mülberger, is a mythical figure, suddenly takes on here a very tangible historical existence. Mülberger continues:

"When I say with Proudhon that the economic life of society should be pervaded by a *conception of right*, I am *describing* present-day society as one in which, true, not every conception of right is absent, but in which the conception of right of the revolution is absent, a fact which Engels himself will admit." [a]

Unfortunately I am not in a position to do Mülberger this favour. Mülberger demands that society *should* be pervaded by a conception of right and calls that a description. If a court sends a bailiff to me with a summons demanding the payment of a debt, then, according to Mülberger, it does no more than *describe* me as a man who does not pay his debts! A description is one thing, and a presumptuous demand is another. And precisely herein lies the essential difference between German scientific socialism and Proudhon. We describe—and despite Mülberger every real description of a thing is at the same time an explanation of it—economic relationships as they are and as they are developing, and we provide the proof, strictly economically, that their development is at the same time the development of the elements of a social revolution: the development, on the one hand, of a class whose conditions of life necessarily drive it to social revolution, the proletariat, and, on the other hand, of productive forces which, having grown beyond the framework of capitalist society, must necessarily burst that framework, and which at the same time offer the means of abolishing class distinctions once and for all in the interest of social progress itself. Proudhon, on the contrary, demands of present-day society that it shall transform itself not according to the laws of its own economic development, but according to the precepts of justice (the "*conception* of right" does not belong to him, but to Mülberger). Where we prove, Proudhon, and with him Mülberger, *preaches* and laments.

What kind of thing "the conception of right of the revolution" is I am absolutely unable to guess. Proudhon, it is true, makes a sort of goddess out of "*the* Revolution", the bearer and executrix of his "Justice", in doing which he then falls into the peculiar error of mixing up the bourgeois revolution of 1789-94 with the coming proletarian revolution. He does this in almost all his works, particularly since 1848; I shall quote only one as an example, namely, the *Idée générale de la révolution*, pages 39 and 40

---

[a] Here and below Engels quotes from: A. Mülberger, "Zur Wohnungsfrage", *Der Volksstaat*, No. 86, October 26, 1872.— *Ed.*

of the 1868 edition. As, however, Mülberger rejects all and every responsibility for Proudhon, I am not allowed to explain "the conception of right of the revolution" from Proudhon and remain therefore in Egyptian darkness.

Mülberger says further:

"But neither Proudhon nor I appeal to an 'eternal justice' in order thereby to *explain* the existing unjust conditions, or even expect, as Engels imputes to me, the improvement of these conditions from an appeal to this justice."

Mülberger must be banking on the idea that "in Germany Proudhon is, in general, as good as unknown". In all his works Proudhon measures all social, legal, political and religious propositions[a] with the rod of "justice", and rejects or recognises them according to whether they conform or do not conform to what he calls "justice". In the *Contradictions économiques*[b] this justice is still called "eternal justice", *justice éternelle*. Later on, nothing more is said about eternity, but the idea remains in essence. For instance, in *De la justice dans la révolution et dans l'église*, 1858 edition, the following passage is the text of the whole three-volume sermon (Vol. 1, page 42):

"What is the basic principle, the organic, regulating, sovereign principle of societies, the principle which subordinates all others to itself, which rules, protects, represses, punishes, and in case of need even suppresses all rebellious elements? Is it religion, the ideal or *interest*? ... In my opinion this principle is *justice.*—What is justice? *It is the very essence of humanity.* What has it been since the beginning of the world? Nothing.—What ought it to be? Everything."

Justice which is the very essence of humanity, what is that if not *eternal* justice? Justice which is the organic, regulating, sovereign basic principle of societies, which has nevertheless been nothing up to present, but which ought to be everything—what is that if not the stick with which to measure all human affairs, if not the final arbiter to be appealed to in all conflicts? And did I assert anything else but that Proudhon cloaks his economic ignorance and helplessness by judging all economic relations not according to economic laws, but according to whether they conform or do not conform to his conception of this eternal justice? And what is the difference between Mülberger and Proudhon if Mülberger demands that "all these exchanges in the life of modern society" should be "pervaded by a *conception of right*, that is to say", should

---

[a] *Der Volksstaat* has "all social, legal, and political conditions, all theoretical, philosophical, and religious propositions".— *Ed.*

[b] This refers to P. J. Proudhon, *Système des contradictions économiques, ou Philosophie de la misère.— Ed.*

"everywhere be carried out according to the *strict demands of justice*"[a]? Is it that I can't read, or that Mülberger can't write?

Mülberger says further:

"Proudhon knows as well as Marx and Engels that the actual driving spirit in human society is the economic and not the juridical relations; he also knows that the given conceptions of right among a people are only the expression, the imprint, the product of the economic relations—and in particular the relations of production... In a word, for Proudhon right is a historically evolved economic product."

If Proudhon knows all this (I am prepared to let the unclear expressions used by Mülberger pass and take his good intentions for the deed), if Proudhon knows it all "as well as Marx and Engels", what is there left to quarrel about? The trouble is that the situation with regard to Proudhon's knowledge is somewhat different. The economic relations of a given society present themselves in the first place as *interests*. Now, in the passage which has just been quoted from his opus Proudhon says in so many words that the "regulating, organic, sovereign basic principle of societies, the principle which subordinates all others to itself", is not *interest* but *justice*. And he repeats the same thing in all the decisive passages of all his works, which does not prevent Mülberger from continuing:

"...The idea of economic right, as it was developed by Proudhon most profoundly of all in *La guerre et la paix*, completely coincides with the basic ideas of Lassalle so excellently expressed by him in his foreword to the *System der erworbenen Rechte*."

La guerre et la paix is perhaps the most schoolboyish of all the many schoolboyish works of Proudhon, but I could not have expected it to be put forward as proof of Proudhon's alleged understanding of the German materialist conception of history, which explains all historical events and ideas, all politics, philosophy and religion, from the material, economic conditions of life of the historical period in question. The book is so little materialistic that it cannot even construct its conception of war without calling in the help of the *creator*:

"However, the creator, who chose this form of life for us, had his own purposes." (Vol. II, page 100, 1869 edition.)

On what historical knowledge the book is based can be judged from the fact that it believes in the historical existence of the Golden Age:

---

[a] Cf. this volume, p. 322.—*Ed.*

"In the beginning, when the human race was still sparsely spread over the earth's surface, nature supplied its needs without difficulty. It was the Golden Age, the age of peace and plenty." (Ibid., page 102.)

Its economic standpoint is that of the crassest Malthusianism:

"When production is doubled, the population will soon be doubled also" (page 106).[252]

In what does the materialism of this book consist, then? In that it declares the cause of war to have always been and still to be: "pauperism" (for instance, page 143). Uncle Bräsig was just such an accomplished materialist when in his 1848 speech he placidly uttered these grand words: "The cause of the great poverty is the great *pauvreté*"

Lassalle's *System der erworbenen Rechte* bears the imprint of the illusions of not only the jurist, but also the Old Hegelian. On page VII, Lassalle declares expressly that also "in *economics* the conception of acquired right is the driving force of all further development", and he seeks to prove (page XI) that "right is a rational organism developing *out of itself*" (and not, therefore, out of economic prerequisites). For Lassalle it is a question of deriving right not from economic relations, but from

"the concept of the will itself, of which the philosophy of law [right—Rechtsphilosophie] is only the development and exposition" (page XII).

So, where does this book come in here? The only difference between Proudhon and Lassalle is that the latter was a real jurist and Hegelian, while in both jurisprudence and philosophy, as in all other matters, Proudhon was merely a dilettante.

I know perfectly well that this man Proudhon, who notoriously continually contradicts himself, occasionally makes an utterance which looks as though he explained ideas on the basis of facts. But such utterances are devoid of any significance when contrasted with the basic tendency of his thought, and where they do occur they are, besides, extremely confused and inherently inconsistent.

At a certain, very primitive stage of the development of society, the need arises to bring under a common rule the daily recurring acts of production, distribution and exchange of products to see to it that the individual subordinates himself to the common conditions of production and exchange. This rule, which at first is custom, soon becomes *law*. With law, organs necessarily arise which are entrusted with its maintenance—public authority, the state. With further social development, law develops into a more or less comprehensive legal system. The more intricate this legal system becomes, the more is its mode of expression removed from that in which the usual economic conditions of the life of society are expressed. It appears as an independent element which derives the justification for its existence and the substantiation of its further development not from the economic relations but from its own inner foundations or, if you like, from "the concept of the will". People forget that their right derives from their economic conditions of life, just as they have forgotten that they themselves derive from the animal world. With the development of the legal system into an intricate, comprehensive whole a new social division of labour becomes necessary; an order of professional jurists develops and with these legal science comes into being. In its further development this science compares the legal systems of various peoples and various times not as a reflection of the given economic relationships, but as systems which find their substantiations in themselves. The comparison presupposes points in common, and these are found by the jurists compiling what is more or less common to all these legal systems and calling it *natural right*. And the stick used to measure what is natural right and what is not is the most abstract expression of right itself, namely, *justice*. Henceforth, therefore, the development of right for the jurists, and for those who take their word for everything, is nothing more than a striving to bring human conditions, so far as they are expressed in legal terms, ever closer to the ideal of justice, *eternal* justice. And always this justice is but the ideologised, idealised expression of the existing economic relations, now from their conservative, and now from their revolutionary angle. The justice of the Greeks and Romans held slavery to be just; the justice of the bourgeois of 1789 demanded the abolition of feudalism on the ground that it was unjust. For the Prussian Junker even the miserable district regulations are a violation of eternal justice.[253] The conception of eternal justice, therefore, varies not only with time and place, but also with the persons concerned, and belongs among those things of which Mülberger correctly says, "everyone understands something different". While in everyday life, in view of the simplicity of the relations discussed, expressions like right, wrong, justice, and sense of right are accepted without misunderstanding even with reference to social matters, they create, as we have seen, the same hopeless confusion in any scientific investigation of economic relations as would be created, for instance, in modern chemistry if the terminology of the phlogiston theory were to be retained. The confusion becomes still worse if one, like Proudhon, believes in this social phlogiston, "justice", or if one, like Mülberger, avers that the phlogiston theory is as correct as the oxygen theory.*

III

Mülberger further complains that I called his "emphatic" utterance,

"that there is no more terrible mockery of the whole culture of our lauded century than the fact that in the big cities 90 per cent and more of the population have no place that they can call their own" [a]

— a reactionary jeremiad. To be sure. If Mülberger had confined himself, as he pretends, to describing "the horrors of the present time" I should certainly not have said one ill word about "him and his modest words". In fact, however, he does something quite different. He describes these "horrors" as the *result* of the fact that the workers *"have no place that they can call their own"*. Whether one laments "the horrors of the present time" for the reason that the ownership of houses by the workers has been abolished or, as the Junkers do, for the reason that feudalism and the guilds have been abolished, in either case nothing can come of it but a reactionary jeremiad, a song of sorrow at the coming of the inevitable, of the historically necessary. Its reactionary character lies precisely in the fact that Mülberger wishes to re-establish individual house ownership for the workers—a matter which history has long ago put an end to; that he can conceive of the emancipation of the workers in no other way than by making everyone once again the owner of his own house.

And further:

"I declare most emphatically, the real struggle is to be waged against the capitalist mode of production; only *from its transformation* is an improvement of housing conditions to be hoped for. Engels sees nothing of all this ... I presuppose

* Before the discovery of oxygen chemists explained the burning of substances in atmospheric air by assuming the existence of a special igneous substance, phlogiston, which escaped during the process of combustion. Since they found that simple substances on combustion weighed more after having been burned than they did before, they declared that phlogiston had a negative weight so that a substance without its phlogiston weighed more than one with it. In this way all the main properties of oxygen were gradually ascribed to phlogiston, but all in an *inverted* form. The discovery that combustion consists in a combination of the burning substance with another substance, oxygen, and the discovery of this oxygen disposed of the original assumption, but only after long resistance on the part of the older chemists.

[a] See this volume, p. 323.— *Ed.*

the complete settlement of the social question in order to be able to proceed to the abolition of the rented dwelling."ᵃ

Unfortunately, I still see nothing of all this even now. It surely is impossible for me to know what someone whose name I never heard presupposes in the secret recesses of his mind. All I could do was to stick to the printed articles of Mülberger. And there I find even today (pages 15 and 16 of the reprint) that Mülberger, in order to be able to proceed to the abolition of the rented dwelling, presupposes nothing except—the rented dwelling. Only on page 17 he takes "the productivity of capital by the horns", to which we shall come back later. Even in his answer he confirms this when he says:

"It was rather a question of showing how, *from existing conditions*, a complete transformation in the housing question could be achieved."

From existing conditions, and from the transformation (read: abolition) of the capitalist mode of production, are surely diametrically opposite things.

No wonder Mülberger complains when I regard the philanthropic efforts of M. Dollfus and other manufacturers to assist the workers to obtain houses of their own as the only possible practical realisation of his Proudhonist projects. If he were to realise that Proudhon's plan for the salvation of society is a fantasy resting completely on the basis of *bourgeois* society, he would naturally not believe in it. I have never at any time called his good intentions in question. But why then does he praise Dr. Reschauer ᵇ for proposing to the Vienna City Council that it should imitate Dollfus' projects?

Mülberger further declares:

"As far as the antithesis between town and country is particularly concerned, it is utopian to want to abolish it. This antithesis is a natural one, or more correctly, one that has arisen historically.... The question is not one of *abolishing* this antithesis, but of finding political and social forms in which it would be *harmless*, indeed even *fruitful*. In this way it would be possible to expect a peaceful adjustment, a gradual balancing of interests."

So the abolition of the antithesis between town and country is utopian, *because* this antithesis is a natural one, or more correctly, one that has arisen historically. Let us apply this same logic to other contrasts in modern society and see where we land. For instance:

ᵃ Here and below Engels quotes from: A. Mülberger, "Zur Wohnungsfrage", *Der Volksstaat*, No. 86, October 26, 1872.—*Ed.*

ᵇ H. Reschauer, *Die Wohnungsnoth und ihr schädlicher Einfluß auf die Kleingewerbetreibenden und Lohnarbeiter*, Vienna, 1871.—*Ed.*

"As far as the antithesis between" the capitalists and the wage-workers "is particularly concerned, it is utopian to want to abolish it. This antithesis is a natural one, or more correctly, one that has arisen historically. The question is not one of *abolishing* this antithesis, but of finding political and social forms in which it would be *harmless*, indeed even *fruitful*. In this way it would be possible to expect a peaceful adjustment, a gradual balancing of interests."

And with this we have once again arrived at Schulze-Delitzsch.

The abolition of the antithesis between town and country is no more and no less utopian than the abolition of the antithesis between capitalists and wage-workers. From day to day it is becoming more and more a practical demand of both industrial and agricultural production. No one has demanded this more energetically than Liebig in his writings on the chemistry of agriculture, in which his first demand has always been that man shall give back to the land what he receives from it, and in which he proves that only the existence of the towns, and in particular the big towns, prevents this.[a] When one observes how here in London alone a greater quantity of manure than is produced by the whole kingdom of Saxony is poured away every day into the sea with an expenditure of enormous sums, and what colossal structures are necessary in order to prevent this manure from poisoning the whole of London, then the utopia of abolishing the antithesis between town and country is given a remarkably practical basis. And even comparatively unimportant Berlin has been suffocating in the malodours of its own filth for at least thirty years. On the other hand, it is completely utopian to want, like Proudhon, to upheave present-day bourgeois society while maintaining the peasant as such. Only as uniform a distribution as possible of the population over the whole country, only an intimate connection between industrial and agricultural production together with the extension of the means of communication made necessary thereby—granted the abolition of the capitalist mode of production—will be able to deliver the rural population from the isolation and stupor in which it has vegetated almost unchanged for thousands of years. To be utopian does not mean to maintain that the emancipation of humanity from the chains which its historic past has forged will be complete only when the antithesis between town and country has been abolished; the utopia begins

---

[a] Justus von Liebig, *Die Chemie in ihrer Anwendung auf Agricultur und Physiologie*, Part 1, Brunswick, 1862, pp. 128-29 et seq.—*Ed.*

only when one ventures, "from existing conditions", to prescribe the *form* in which this or any other antithesis of present-day society is to be resolved. And this is what Mülberger does by adopting the Proudhonist formula for the settlement of the housing question.

Mülberger then complains that I have made him to a certain extent co-responsible for "Proudhon's monstrous views on capital and interest", and declares:

> "I presuppose the alteration of the relations of production *as an accomplished fact*, and the transitional law regulating the rate of interest does not deal with relations of production but with the social turnover, the relations of circulation... The alteration of the relations of production, or, as the German school says more accurately, the abolition of the capitalist mode of production, certainly does not result, as Engels *tries to make me say*, from a transitional law abolishing interest, but from the *actual seizure of all the instruments of labour*, from the seizure of industry as a whole by the working people. Whether the working people will in that event worship" (!) "redemption sooner than immediate expropriation is not for either Engels or me to decide."

I rub my eyes in astonishment. I am reading Mülberger's disquisition through once again from beginning to end in order to find the passage where he says his redemption of the rented dwelling presupposes as an accomplished fact "the actual seizure of all the instruments of labour, the seizure of industry as a whole by the working people", but I am unable to find any such passage. It does not exist. There is nowhere mention of "actual seizure", etc., but there is the following on page 17:

> "Let us now assume that the productivity of capital *is really taken by the horns*, as it must be sooner or later, for instance, *by a transitional law which fixes the interest on all capitals at one per cent*, but mark you, with the tendency to make even this rate of interest approximate more and more to the zero point... Like all other products, houses and dwellings are naturally also included within the purview of this law... We see, therefore, from this angle that the redemption of the rented dwelling *is a necessary consequence of the abolition of the productivity of capital in general*." [a]

Thus it is said here in plain words, quite contrary to Mülberger's latest about-face, that the productivity of capital, by which confused phrase he admittedly means the capitalist mode of production is really "taken by the horns" by a law abolishing interest, and that precisely as a result of such a law "the redemption of the rented dwelling is a necessary consequence of the abolition of the productivity of capital in general". Not at all, says Mülberger now. That transitional law "does not deal with relations of *production* but with relations of *circulation*". In view of

---

[a] A. Mülberger, *Die Wohnungsfrage* (see this volume, p. 331).—*Ed.*

this crass contradiction, "equally mysterious for wise men as for
fools", as Goethe would say,[a] all that is left for me to do is to
assume that I am dealing with two separate and distinct
Mülbergers, one of whom rightly complains that I "tried to make
him say" what the other caused to be printed.

It is certainly true that the working people will ask neither me
nor Mülberger whether in the actual seizure they will "worship
redemption sooner than immediate expropriation". In all probability they will prefer not to "worship" at all. However, there
never was any question of the actual seizure of all the instruments
of labour by the working people, but only of Mülberger's assertion
(page 17) that "the whole content of the solution of the housing
question is comprised in the word *redemption*". If he now declares
this redemption to be extremely doubtful, what was the sense in
giving the two of us and our readers all this unnecessary trouble?

Moreover, it must be pointed out that the "actual seizure" of all
the instruments of labour, the taking possession of industry as a
whole by the working people, is the exact opposite of the
Proudhonist "redemption". In the latter case the *individual worker*
becomes the owner of dwelling, the peasant farm, the instruments
of labour; in the former case, the "working people" remain the
collective owner of the houses, factories and instruments of
labour, and will hardly permit their use, at least during a
transitional period, by individuals or associations without compensation for the cost. In the same way, the abolition of property in
land is not the abolition of ground rent but its transfer, if in a
modified form, to society. The actual seizure of all the instruments
of labour by the working people, therefore, does not at all
preclude the retention of rent relations.

In general, the question is not whether the proletariat when it
comes to power will simply seize by force the instruments of
production, the raw materials and means of subsistence, whether it
will pay immediate compensation for them or whether it will
redeem the property therein by small instalment payments. To
attempt to answer such a question in advance and for all cases
would be utopia-making, and that I leave to others.

IV

There was need to consume so much ink and paper in order to
bore a way through Mülberger's diverse twists and turns to the

---

[a] Cf. Goethe, *Faust*, Part I, Scene 6 ("Hexenküche").— *Ed.*

real point at issue, a point which Mülberger carefully evades in his answer.

What were Mülberger's positive statements in his article?

First: that "the difference between the original cost price of a house, building site, etc., and its present value" belongs by right to society.[a] In the language of economics, this difference is called ground rent. Proudhon too wants to appropriate this for society, as one may read in his *Idée générale de la révolution*, page 219 of the 1868 edition.

Secondly: that the solution of the housing problem consists in everyone becoming the owner instead of the tenant of his dwelling.

Thirdly: that this solution shall be put into effect by passing a law turning rent payments into instalment payments on the purchase price of the dwelling.—Points 2 and 3 are both borrowed from Proudhon, as anyone can see in the *Idée générale de la révolution*, page 199 et seq., where on page 203 a project of the law in question is to be found already drafted.

Fourthly: that the productivity of capital is taken by the horns by a transitional law reducing the rate of interest provisionally to one per cent, subject to further reduction later on. This point has also been taken from Proudhon, as may be read in detail on pages 182 to 186 of the *Idée générale*.

With regard to each of these points I have cited the passage in Proudhon where the original of the Mülberger copy is to be found, and I ask now whether I was justified in calling the author of an article containing completely Proudhonist and nothing but Proudhonist views a Proudhonist or not? Nevertheless, Mülberger complains about nothing more bitterly than that I call him a Proudhonist because I "came upon a few *expressions* that are peculiar to Proudhon"! On the contrary. The "*expressions*" all belong to Mülberger, their *content* belongs to Proudhon. And when I then supplement this Proudhonist disquisition with Proudhon, Mülberger complains that I am ascribing to him the "monstrous views" of Proudhon!

What did I reply to this Proudhonist plan?

First: that the transfer of ground rent to the state is tantamount to the abolition of individual property in land.

Secondly: that the redemption of the rented dwelling and the transfer of property in the dwelling to the party who was the tenant hitherto does not at all affect the capitalist mode of production.

---

[a] A. Mülberger, *Die Wohnungsfrage*, p. 8.— *Ed.*

Thirdly: that with the present development of large-scale industry and towns this proposal is as absurd as it is reactionary, and that the reintroduction of the individual ownership of his dwelling by each individual would be a step backward.

Fourthly: that the compulsory reduction of the rate of interest on capital would by no means attack the capitalist mode of production[a]; and that, on the contrary, as the usury laws prove, it is as old as it is impossible.

Fifthly: that the abolition of interest on capital by no means abolishes the payment of rent for houses.

Mülberger has now admitted points 2 and 4. To the other points he makes no reply whatever. And yet these are just the points around which the whole debate centres. Mülberger's answer, however, is not a refutation: it carefully avoids dealing with all economic points, which after all are the decisive ones. It is a personal complaint, nothing more. For instance, he complains when I anticipate his announced solution of other questions, for example, state debts, private debts and credit, and say that his solution will everywhere be the same, namely, that, as in the housing question, the abolition of interest, the conversion of interest payments into instalment payments on the capital sum, and free credit. Nevertheless, I am still ready to bet that if these articles of Mülberger see the light of day, their essential content will coincide with Proudhon's *Idée générale*: credit, page 182; state debts, page 186; private debts, page 196—just as much as his articles on the housing question coincided with the passages I quoted from the same book.

Mülberger takes this opportunity to inform me that questions such as taxation, state debts, private debts and credit, to which is now added the question of communal autonomy, are of the greatest importance to the peasant and for propaganda in the countryside. To a great extent I agree, but 1) up to the moment there has been no discussion of the peasant, and 2) the Proudhonian "solutions" of all these problems are just as absurd economically and just as essentially bourgeois as his solution of the housing problem. *I* need hardly defend myself against Mülberger's suggestion that I fail to appreciate the necessity of drawing the peasants into the movement. However, I certainly consider it folly to recommend the Proudhonian quackery to them for this purpose. There is still very much big landed property in Germany. According to Proudhon's theory all this ought to be

---

[a] *Der Volksstaat* has "capitalist production".—*Ed.*

divided up into small peasant farms, which, in the present state of scientific agriculture and after the experience with small land allotments in France and Western Germany, would be positively reactionary. The big landed estates which still exist will rather afford us a welcome basis for the carrying on of agriculture on a large scale—the only system of farming which can utilise all modern facilities, machinery, etc.—by associated workers, and thus demonstrating to the small peasants the advantages of large-scale operation by means of association. The Danish socialists, who in this respect are ahead of all others, saw this long ago.[a]

It is equally unnecessary for me to defend myself against the suggestion that I regard the existing infamous housing conditions of the workers as "an insignificant detail". As far as I know, I was the first to describe in German these conditions in their classical form as they exist in England; not, as Mülberger opines, because they "violated my *sense of justice*"—anyone who insisted on writing books about all the facts which violated his sense of justice would have a lot to do—but, as can be read in the Preface to my book,[b] in order to provide a factual basis, by describing the social conditions created by modern large-scale industry, for German socialism, which was then arising and expending itself in empty phrases. However, it never entered my head to try to settle the so-called housing *question* any more than to occupy myself with the details of the still more important *food question*. I am satisfied if I can prove that the production of our modern society is sufficient to provide all its members with enough to eat, and that there are houses enough in existence to provide the working masses for the time being with roomy and healthy living accommodation. To speculate on how a future society might organise the distribution of food and dwellings leads directly to *utopia*. The utmost we can do is to state from our understanding of the basic conditions of all modes of production up to now that with the downfall of the capitalist mode of production certain forms of appropriation which existed in society hitherto will become impossible. Even the transitional measures will everywhere have to be in accordance with the relations existing at the moment. In countries of small landed property they will be substantially different from those in countries where big landed property prevails, etc. Mülberger himself shows us better than anyone else where one arrives at if

---

a F. Engels, "The Position of the Danish Members of the International on the Agrarian Question" (see this volume, pp. 57-58).— *Ed.*

b F. Engels, *The Condition of the Working-Class in England* (see present edition, Vol. 4, pp. 302-04).— *Ed.*

one attempts to find separate solutions for so-called practical problems like the housing question, etc. He first took 28 pages to explain[a] that "the whole content of the solution of the housing question is comprised in the word *redemption*", and then, when hard pressed, begins to stammer in embarrassment that it is really very doubtful whether, on actually taking possession of the houses, "the working people will worship redemption" sooner than some other form of expropriation.[b]

Mülberger demands that we should become *practical,* that we should not "come forward merely with dead and abstract formulas" when "faced with real practical relations", that we should "proceed beyond abstract socialism and *come close to the definite concrete relations of society*". If Mülberger had done this he might perhaps have rendered great service to the movement. The first step in coming close to the definite concrete relations of society is surely that one should learn what they are, that one should examine them according to their existing economic interconnections. But what do we find in Mülberger's articles? Two whole sentences, namely:

1. "The tenant is in the same position in relation to the house-owner as the wage-worker in relation to the capitalist." [Page 13.]

I have proved on page 6 of the reprint that this is totally wrong,[c] and Mülberger has not a word to say in reply.

2. "However, the bull which" (in the social reform) "must be taken by the horns is *the productivity of capital,* as the liberal school of political economy calls it, a thing which *in reality does not exist,* but which in *its seeming existence* serves as a cloak for all the inequality which burdens present-day society."[d]

Thus, the bull which has to be taken by the horns "*in reality does not*" exist, and therefore also has no "horns". Not the bull itself is the evil, but his *seeming existence.* Despite this, "the so-called productivity" (of capital) "is able to conjure up houses and towns" whose existence is anything but "seeming". (Page 12.) And a man who, although Marx's *Capital* "is familiar also to him", jabbers in this hopelessly confused fashion about the relation of capital and labour, undertakes to show the German workers a new and better path, and presents himself as the "master builder" who is

"clear about the architectural structure of the future society, at least in its main outlines"! [Page 13.]

---

a *Der Volksstaat* has "to explain in detail".— *Ed.*
b See this volume, p. 385.— *Ed.*
c Ibid., p. 320.— *Ed.*
d A. Mülberger, *Die Wohnungsfrage,* p. 7 (cf. this volume, p. 331).— *Ed.*

No one has come closer "to the definite concrete relations of society" than Marx in *Capital*. He spent twenty-five years investigating them from all angles, and the results of his criticism contain throughout also the germs of so-called solutions, in so far as they are possible at all today. But that is not enough for friend Mülberger. That is all abstract socialism, dead and abstract formulas. Instead of studying the "definite concrete relations of society", friend Mülberger contents himself with reading through a few volumes of Proudhon which, although they offer him next to nothing concerning the definite concrete relations of society, offer him, on the contrary, very definite concrete miraculous remedies for all social evils. He then presents this ready-made plan for social salvation, this Proudhonian *system*, to the German workers under the pretext that *he* wants "to say good-bye to the *systems*", while I "choose the opposite path"! In order to grasp this I must assume that I am blind and Mülberger deaf so that any understanding between us is utterly impossible.

But enough. If this polemic serves for nothing else it has in any case the value of having given proof of what there really is to the practice of these self-styled "practical" socialists. These practical proposals for the abolition of all social evils, these universal social panaceas, have always and everywhere been the work of founders of sects who appeared at a time when the proletarian movement was still in its infancy. Proudhon too belongs to them. The development of the proletariat soon casts aside these swaddling-clothes and engenders in the working class itself the realisation that nothing is less practical than these "practical solutions", concocted in advance and universally applicable, and that practical socialism consists rather in a correct knowledge of the capitalist mode of production from its various aspects. A working class which knows what's what in this regard will *never* be in doubt in any case as to which social institutions should be the objects of its main attacks, and in what manner these attacks should be executed.

Written in May 1872-January 1873

First published in *Der Volksstaat*, Nos. 51, 52, 53, 103 and 104, June 26 and 29, July 3, December 25 and 28, 1872; Nos. 2, 3, 12, 13, 15 and 16, January 4 and 8, February 8, 12, 19 and 22, 1873; and in three separate reprints in Leipzig in 1872-73

Printed according to the 1887 edition checked with the newspaper text

Karl Marx

POLITICAL INDIFFERENTISM [254]

"The working class must not constitute itself as a political party; it must not, under any pretext, engage in political action, for to combat the State is to recognise the State: and this is contrary to eternal principles. Workers must not go on strike; for to struggle to increase one's wages or to prevent their decrease is like recognising *Wages*: and this is contrary to the eternal principles of the emancipation of the working class!

"If in the political struggle against the bourgeois State the workers succeed only in extracting concessions, then they are guilty of compromise; and this is contrary to eternal principles. All peaceful movements, such as those in which English and American workers have the bad habit of engaging, are therefore to be despised. Workers must not struggle to establish a legal limit to the working day, because this is to compromise with the masters, who can then only exploit them for 10 or 12 hours, instead of 14 or 16. They must not even exert themselves in order legally to prohibit the employment in factories of children under the age of ten, because by such means they do not bring to an end the exploitation of children under ten: they thus commit a new compromise, which stains the purity of the eternal principles.

"Workers should even less desire that, as happens in the United States of America, the State whose BUDGET is swollen by what is taken from the working class should be obliged to give primary education to the workers' children; for primary education is not complete education. It is better that working men and working women should not be able to read or write or do sums than that they should receive education from a teacher in a school run by the State. It is far better that ignorance and a working day of 16 hours should debase the working classes than that eternal principles should be violated!

"If the political struggle of the working class assumes violent forms and if the workers replace the dictatorship of the bourgeois class with their own revolutionary dictatorship, then they are guilty of the terrible crime of *lèse-principe*; for, in order to satisfy their miserable profane daily needs and to crush the resistance of the bourgeois class, they, instead of laying down their arms and abolishing the State, give to the State a revolutionary and transitory form. Workers must not even form single unions for every trade, for by so doing they perpetuate the social division of labour as they find it in bourgeois society; this division, which fragments the working class, is the true basis of their present enslavement.

"In a word, the workers should fold their arms and stop wasting time in political and economic movements. These movements can never produce anything more than short-term results. As truly religious men they should scorn daily needs and cry out with voices full of faith: 'May our class be crucified, may our race perish, but let the eternal principles remain immaculate!' As pious Christians they must believe the words of their pastor, despise the good things of this world and think only of going to Paradise. In place of Paradise read the *social liquidation* which is going to take place one day in some or other corner of the globe, no one knows how, or through whom, and the mystification is identical in all respects.

"In expectation, therefore, of this famous social liquidation, the working class must behave itself in a respectable manner, like a flock of well-fed sheep; it must leave the government in peace, fear the police, respect the law and offer itself up uncomplaining as cannon-fodder.

"In practical everyday life, workers must be the most obedient servants of the State; but in their hearts they must protest energetically against its very existence, and give proof of their profound theoretical contempt for it by acquiring and reading literary treatises on its abolition; they must further scrupulously refrain from putting up any resistance to the capitalist regime apart from declamations on the society of the future, when this hated regime will have ceased to exist!"

It cannot be denied that if the apostles of political indifferentism were to express themselves with such clarity, the working class would make short shrift of them and would resent being insulted by these doctrinaire bourgeois and displaced gentlemen, who are so stupid or so naive as to attempt to deny to the working class any real means of struggle. For all arms with which to fight must be drawn from society as it is and the fatal conditions of this struggle have the misfortune of not being easily adapted to the idealistic fantasies which these doctors in *social science* have exalted as divinities, under the names of *Freedom, Autonomy, Anarchy*. However, the working-class movement is today so powerful that these philanthropic sectarians dare not repeat for the economic struggle those *great truths* which they used incessantly to proclaim on the subject of the political struggle. They are simply too cowardly to apply them any longer to strikes, combinations, single-craft unions, laws on the labour of women and children, on the limitation of the working day, etc., etc.

Now let us see whether they are still able to be brought back to the good old traditions, to modesty, good faith and eternal principles.

The first socialists (Fourier, Owen, Saint-Simon, etc.), since social conditions were not sufficiently developed to allow the working class to constitute itself as a militant class, were necessarily obliged to limit themselves to dreams about the *model society* of the future and were led thus to condemn all the attempts such as strikes, combinations or political movements set in train by the workers to improve their lot. But while we cannot repudiate these patriarchs of socialism, just as chemists cannot repudiate their forebears the alchemists, we must at least avoid lapsing into their mistakes, which, if we were to commit them, would be inexcusable.

Later, however, in 1839, when the political and economic struggle of the working class in England had taken on a fairly marked character, Bray, one of Owen's disciples and one of the many who long before Proudhon hit upon the idea of *mutualism,* published a book entitled *Labour's Wrongs and Labour's Remedy.*[a]

In one of the chapters on the inefficacy *of all the remedies aimed for by the present struggle,* he makes a savage critique of all the activities, political or economic, of the English working class, condemns the political movement, strikes, the limitation of the working day, the restriction of the work of women and children in factories, since all this—or so he claims—instead of taking us out of the present state of society, keeps us there and does nothing but render the antagonisms more intense.

---

[a] The title of the book is in English in the original with the Italian translation in brackets.— *Ed.*

This brings us to the oracle of these doctors of social science, M. Proudhon. While the master had the courage to declare himself energetically opposed to all economic activities (combinations, strikes, etc.) which contradicted his redemptive theories of *mutualism*, at the same time by his writings and personal participation, he encouraged the working-class political movement, and his disciples do not dare to declare themselves openly against it. As early as 1847, when the master's great work, *Système des contradictions économiques*,[a] had just appeared, I refuted his sophisms against the working-class movement.* None the less, in 1864, after the Ollivier law, which granted the French workers, in a very restrictive fashion, a certain right of combination,[255] Proudhon returned to the charge in a book, *De la capacité politique des classes ouvrières*, published a few days after his death.

The master's strictures were so much to the taste of the bourgeoisie that *The Times*, on the occasion of the great tailors' strike in London in 1866, did Proudhon the honour of translating him and of condemning the strikers with the master's very words. Here are some selections.

The miners of Rive-de-Gier went on strike; the soldiers were called in to bring them back to reason.[256]

Proudhon cries: "The authority which had the miners of Rive-de-Gier shot acted disgracefully. But it was acting like Brutus of old caught between his paternal love and his consular duty: it was necessary to sacrifice his sons to save the Republic. Brutus did not hesitate, and posterity dare not condemn him."**

In all the memory of the proletariat there is no record of a bourgeois who has hesitated to sacrifice his workers to save his interests. What Brutuses the bourgeois must then be!

"Well, no: there is no right of combination, just as there is no right to defraud or steal or to commit incest or adultery."***

There is however all too clearly a right to *stupidity*.

What then are the eternal principles, in whose name the master fulminates his mystic anathema?

* See in the book *The Poverty of Philosophy. Answer to the "Philosophy of Poverty" by M. Proudhon* (Paris, 1847, published by A. Frank, Chapter II, para. 5, "Strikes and Combinations of Workers"[b]).

** P. J. Proudhon, *De la capacité politique des classes ouvrières*, Paris, 1868, published by Lacroix and Co., p. 327.

*** Op. cit., p. 333.

---

[a] Here and below the titles of Proudhon's works are given in Italian.— *Ed.*

[b] See present edition, Vol. 6, pp. 206-12.— *Ed.*

First eternal principle:

"Wage rates determine the price of commodities" [p. 340].

Even those who have no knowledge of political economy and who are unaware that the great bourgeois economist Ricardo in his *On the Principles of Political Economy*,[a] published in 1817, has refuted this long-standing error once and for all, are however aware of the remarkable fact that British industry can sell its products at a price far lower than that of any other nation, although wages are relatively higher in England than in any other European country.

Second eternal principle:

"The law which authorises combinations is highly anti-juridical, anti-economic and contrary to any society and order" [p. 335].

In a word, "contrary to the economic *Right* of free competition" [p. 334].

If the master had been a little less *chauvin*, he might have asked himself how it happened that forty years ago a law, thus contrary to the *economic rights of free competition*, was promulgated in England,[257] and that as industry develops, and alongside it *free competition*, this law—so contrary to *any society and order*—imposes itself as a necessity even to bourgeois states themselves. He might perhaps have discovered that this right (with a capital R) exists only in the *Economic Manuals* written by the Brothers Ignoramus of bourgeois political economy, in which manuals are contained such pearls as this: *Property is the fruit of labour ... of others,* they neglect to add.

Third eternal principle:

"Therefore, under the pretext of raising the working class from its condition of so-called social inferiority, it will be necessary to start by denouncing a whole class of citizens, the class of bosses, entrepreneurs, masters and bourgeois; it will be necessary to rouse workers' democracy to despise and to hate these unworthy members of the middle class; it will be necessary to prefer mercantile and industrial war to legal repression, and class antagonism to the State police." *

The master, in order to prevent the working class from escaping from its condition of so-called *social inferiority*, condemns the combinations that constitute the working class as a class antagonistic to the respectable *category of masters, entrepreneurs and bourgeois*,

---

* Op. cit., pp. 337-38.

---

[a] In the original the title of Ricardo's book is given in Italian.— *Ed.*

who for their part certainly prefer, as does Proudhon, *the State police to class antagonism*. To avoid any offence to this respectable class, the good M. Proudhon recommends to the workers (up to the coming of the *mutualist regime*, and despite its serious disadvantages) "freedom or competition, our only guarantee".*

The master preached indifferentism in matters of economics— *so as to protect freedom or bourgeois competition*, our only guarantee. His disciples preach indifferentism in matters of politics—so as to protect bourgeois freedom, their only guarantee. If the early Christians, who also preached political indifferentism, needed an emperor's arm to transform themselves from oppressed into oppressors, so the modern apostles of political indifferentism do not believe that their own eternal principles impose on them abstinence from worldly pleasures and the temporal privileges of bourgeois society. However we must recognise that they display a stoicism worthy of the early Christian martyrs in supporting those 14 or 16 working hours such as overburden the workers in the factories.

London, January 1873

Written in December 1872-early January 1873

First published in December 1873 in the collection *Almanacco Repubblicano per l'anno 1874*

Signed: *Karl Marx*

Printed according to the collection

Translated from the Italian

---

* Op. cit., p. 334.

Karl Marx

TO THE EDITOR OF *THE TIMES*

Sir,—My attention is called to a paragraph in *The Times* of to-day[a] headed "Karl Marx and the International". It is there asserted that the General Council of the International Working Men's Association, while calling upon the different federations and sections to propose themselves the plenipotentiaries to be appointed by the General Council, has declared it

"imperatively necessary that an exact copy should be simultaneously forwarded to Karl Marx in London. The drift of this is that none will receive credentials but those acceptable to and approved by Karl Marx in London, and as these agents will, as a matter of course, have to be in constant communication with him, he will be virtually the autocrat of the movement".

The circular in question is published, among others, in the Leipsic *Volksstaat* of the 25th of December.[b] It calls upon the German members of the Association to send a copy of their proposals to the late corresponding secretary for Germany (that is to say, to me) for the purpose of authentication. It is evident that the new General Council cannot know either the persons or their handwriting. The service demanded from me appeared to the New York General Council so much a matter of course that I was not even previously communicated with upon the subject. With the authentication of agents for the other countries, where the free organization of the International meets with legal impediments, I have nothing whatever to do.

---

[a] No. 27576, January 2, 1873.— *Ed.*

[b] "Der Generalrath der Internationalen Arbeiter-Assoziation an alle Föderationen, Sektionen, Comites und Mitglieder der Internationalen Arbeiter-Assoziation in Deutschland. New-York, den 1. Dez. 1872". [Signed:] F. A. Sorge, *Der Volksstaat*, No. 103, December 25, 1872.— *Ed.*

The paragraph further states,

"In France these agents expel members without a hearing, and dissolve sections, committees, and federations at pleasure."

Your correspondent will have to explain how these agents can commit all these horrors before a single one of them has been appointed. If in France individuals have been expelled from the International,[a] it has been by the local sections, and not at all by the New York General Council.

I remain, Sir, your obedient servant,

Karl Marx

January 2

First published in *The Times,* No. 27577, January 3, 1873

Reproduced from the newspaper

---

[a] The reference is to Louis Marchand, Abel Bousquet and Paul Brousse.— *Ed.*

15*

Frederick Engels

THE "CRISIS" IN PRUSSIA

The "great nation" of France has, indeed, been ousted by the "great nation" of Germany, and rightly so. In Versailles, a political crisis arises because the French rural squirearchy are conspiring to replace the existing republic with the monarchy[258]; at the same time, a crisis breaks out in Berlin because the rural squirearchy of Prussia are unwilling to sacrifice the old feudal estate-police, to which they are still entitled, eighty years after the French Revolution. Can anyone doubt for a moment longer the superiority of German "culture" over French civilisation? With their customary superficiality, the French squabble about mere *forms*, such as republic and monarchy. The thorough Prussians get to the bottom of the matter by safeguarding, not a day too early, in 1872—the last in Europe to do so except for Mecklenburg and Russia—the foundation of society, the peasants' backsides, from the squires' flogging—or may be not!

Nothing is more indicative of the wretched attitude of the Prussian bourgeoisie than this entire farce about district regulations.[259] In 1848, Prussia had its revolution; the bourgeoisie held power in its hands; an oath of loyalty from the army to the constitution—no matter what kind of constitution—would have sufficed to secure power to the bourgeoisie. The feudal elements and the bureaucrats were so terrified that, at the time, the abolition of the remnants of feudalism seemed to be a matter of course. The first draft constitutions of 1848 and even 1849 did, in fact, contain all the essentials for this development, if only in the usual miserable form. The very slightest resistance from the bourgeoisie would have sufficed to make a return of the feudal rights impossible; for, apart from the few rural squires, nobody had any interest in this happening, except for the romantic Frederick William IV. Yet hardly had European reaction triumphed when the Prussian bourgeoisie crawled to the feet of Manteuffel, responding to every cut from his whip with grateful tail-wagging. Not only did it return the estate-police and all sorts of other feudal rubbish to the landed nobility east of the Elbe; it chastised itself for its sinful liberalism by destroying, on its own, even the liberty to exercise trades instituted in 1808, and by restoring the guilds in the middle of the nineteenth century.[260]

The bourgeoisie is, at best, an unheroic class. Even its most brilliant achievements, those in England in the seventeenth century and those in France in the eighteenth, were not gained in battle by the bourgeoisie itself, but won for it by the popular masses, the workers and peasants. In France, too, the bourgeoisie rescued itself from the terror of the June days of 1848[261] by throwing itself at the feet of a play-actor[a]; in England, too, 1848 was followed by a long period of reaction; but in both countries this reaction was based on the pretext of protecting the foundations of *bourgeois* society from attacks by the proletariat. In Prussia, the result of the revolution was to permit the romantic Frederick William IV finally to fulfil the medieval desires of his heart, as triumphant reaction swept away a multitude of anti-romantic institutions that had smuggled their way into the Prussian state in the period from Frederick II until Stein and Hardenberg. On the pretext of protecting it from the proletariat, bourgeois society was once again placed under the rule of feudalism. No bourgeoisie in the world can boast of such a period of ignominy as that experienced by the Prussian bourgeoisie under Manteuffel. In what other country would it have been possible to hail a man like Hinckeldey a champion and martyr of liberty?[262]

Finally, as a result of conflicting palace intrigues, along comes the *New Era*.[263] An old-style liberal ministry unexpectedly falls into the lap of the bourgeoisie, and the latter, the most cowardly of all bourgeoisies, not having raised a finger to bring it into being, suddenly imagines that it is at the helm of the state, that the old Prussian military and police state has vanished, that it can appoint and depose ministers and impose its will on the Court. If the Manteuffel period had proved the cowardliness of the bourgeoisie, the New Era exposed its political incompetence.

---

[a] Louis Bonaparte.— *Ed.*

The price at which the old-liberal ministry was admitted was the re-organisation of the army. The Italian war[264] provided the desired opportunity to demand this of the Diet. On the one hand, the mobilisation of 1859 had proved that the old army organisation had become totally obsolete. On the other, the indifference with which the annexation of Savoy and Nice was greeted in France proved that French chauvinism could only be effectively set in motion by the prospect of conquests on the Rhine, i.e., by a war against Prussia. It was thus evident that, as soon as Louis Bonaparte's position as emperor was again placed in jeopardy by internal developments in France, this danger could only be warded off by a war against Prussia, which, without alliances, could only result in the defeat of the old Prussian army. On the other hand, although itself essentially a military state, Prussia had not created the necessity for the large armies of nowadays. It was too weak for this. Yet all the less could it steer clear of the common continental necessity since its ambiguous "policy of having a free hand" had cut it off from all reliable alliances. Finally, whatever the nature of the re-organisation of the army, the Prussian bourgeoisie must have realised *it* could not prevent it. Its one correct plan of action could, therefore, only be to barter the approval of the inevitable re-organisation for as many political concessions as possible. But the Prussian bourgeoisie, though still black and blue from the trampling it had received from the Manteuffel regime, all at once started getting above itself. It suddenly imagined itself to be the decisive power in the state; it rejected the re-organisation of the army. With that, the dream was again over. Bismarck came to teach them that their paper constitution and their votes in the Chambers were nothing but dead wood, that in Prussia it was the King who ruled and the Chambers were only there to say Yes. The army re-organisation was carried out despite the constitution and the deputies were treated once again *à la* Manteuffel.[265] After a brief sham resistance, of which it tired sooner than its adversary Bismarck did, the bourgeoisie found in the Danish war[266] the first pretext for making bashful attempts at a reconciliation; and after Sadowa[267] it no longer showed any embarrassment at all, falling enthusiastically at Bismarck's feet, to figure from now on only in his retinue; after the French war[a] its enthusiasm no longer knew any bounds. From then on it belonged to Bismarck body and soul, and was virtually absorbed by him.

---

[a] The Franco-Prussian war of 1870-71.— *Ed.*

There is, however, a thing in this world that Hegel discovered and called "the irony of history".[268] This irony of history has played its game with greater men than Bismarck, and the Prussian state and Bismarck also succumbed to it. From the moment the long-desired goals of Prussian policy were, one by one, attained— from that moment, the foundations of the Prussian state began to shake. Old Prussia is essentially based on the Junkerdom, from which officers and bureaucracy are chiefly recruited. The Junkers exist in their most flourishing form only in the six eastern provinces, and need, their estates being mostly limited, certain feudal privileges in order to exist. Without these, most Junkers would soon sink to the level of ordinary landowners. As long as there were only the two western provinces[a] to compete with it, the Junkerdom was in no danger. But the annexations of 1866[269] had already strengthened the bourgeois and peasant element in the state to a tremendous degree. It was not merely legitimist humbug, but rather the justified awareness of its own position being endangered that provoked the resistance of the Stahl-Gerlach party[270] to these annexations. The incorporation of the petty states in the North German Confederation, the transfer of the decisive state functions to this Confederation, the consequent mediatisation of the Prussian Upper House, the final accession of the southern states[271]—all these events were just so many hard blows to the Junkerdom, which only formed a tiny minority in the Empire. Yet this is not all. Every government, even the most despotic, is compelled to govern with due regard for the existing conditions, or else it breaks its neck. Prussia could subjugate Little Germany, but it could not impose its Junkerdom on the twenty-five million Germans west of the Elbe. On the contrary: the Junkers, a necessity for old Prussia, became a fetter on the "Empire". Just as Bismarck had been compelled, against his earlier intentions, to introduce freedom to pursue trades, freedom of movement between the individual states and other bourgeois reforms— admittedly in a bureaucratically mutilated form—the irony of history finally condemned him, the Junker *par excellence*, to use the axe on the Junkers by having recourse to district regulations.

These district regulations are some of the most woe-begone laws ever made. Their content may be summarised in two words. They deprive the *individual* Junker of the power appertaining to him by virtue of feudal prerogative, in order, in the guise of district

---

[a] Westphalia and the Rhine Province.— *Ed.*

self-administration, to give it back to the Junker *class*. As before, medium-size and big landed property will dominate in the agricultural districts of the eastern provinces; it will even receive a new accretion of power through having been allocated rights hitherto belonging to the state. The individual Junker, however, loses the privileged position he used to enjoy as a feudal lord. He descends to the level of an ordinary modern landowner—thus ceasing to be a Junker. But thereby the foundations of old Prussia are undermined and, therefore, the Upper House was quite right, from its own point of view, to resist the district regulations. With the district regulations—no Junkerdom, and without Junkerdom—no more Prussia as such.

The Prussian bourgeoisie remained worthy of itself in this affair. At first, it was claimed that the district regulations were merely an instalment on self-administration; they had to be accepted because, at the time, nothing better could be achieved; they were a compromise with the government, but in future not another inch should be conceded. The Upper House rejects the district regulations. Although already bound by the compromise vis-à-vis the House of Deputies, the government demands new concessions from it. The House is brave enough to grant them without any further ado; in return, the bourgeois are promised a wholesale creation of new peers[272] and are presented with the prospect of a reform of the Upper House. The new peers are created—twenty-five generals and bureaucrats—and the Upper House accepts. The compromise is saved, but—the reform of the Upper House has been shelved. Comfort is taken in the idea that the district regulations are still a quite enormous step forward—and along comes the news of the ministerial crisis. Roon, Selchow, Itzenplitz wish to resign—a sweeping victory for the Liberals—inevitability of a liberal...?—no, not precisely!—of a *united* ministry! Our bourgeois are so modest. In fact, they are content with even less. Bismarck vacates the premiership; Roon, the opponent of the district regulations, succeeds him; yet another general[a] enters the ministry; Selchow and Itzenplitz remain; the united ministry is less united than ever, with the feudal elements in it strengthened, while the bourgeois calmly continues to swill down his beer in the proud awareness that, when all is said and done, Bismarck is still the soul of the whole affair.

This example describes exactly the position of the Prussian bourgeoisie. It claims the credit for the fact that Bismarck is

---

[a] A. K. G. von Kameke.— *Ed.*

forced, by the historical situation in which he has placed Prussia and by the industrial progress of the last twenty years, to do what it itself was too cowardly to push through between 1848 and 1850. It does not even have the courage to force its Bismarck to carry out these small reforms in a straightforward, openly bourgeois way without police-state bungling; it loudly rejoices that Bismarck is compelled to—castrate—its own demands of 1846.[273] And, mark well, only its economic demands—which not even a thousand Bismarcks could prevent being put into effect, even if they wanted to. The *political* demands, the transfer of political power to the bourgeoisie, are now only mentioned for decency's sake, if at all. The Prussian bourgeoisie does not *want* political dominance; rotten without having reached maturity, as official Russia already was in the age of Voltaire, it has already arrived, without ever having ruled, at the same stage of degeneration that the French bourgeoisie has attained after eighty years of struggles and a long period of dominance. *Panem et circenses*, bread and circuses, the degenerate Roman plebs demanded of their emperors; *panem et circenses*, soaring profits and brute luxury, are what the Prussian bourgeoisie, not the Prussian people, demand of theirs. The Roman plebeians were swept away, along with their emperors, by the Germanic barbarians; behind the Prussian bourgeoisie, the German workers loom up menacingly.

Written at the beginning of January 1873

First published in *Der Volksstaat*, No. 5, January 15, 1873

Printed according to the newspaper

Published in English for the first time

Karl Marx

[REPLY TO THE SECOND CIRCULAR
OF THE SELF-STYLED MAJORITY
OF THE BRITISH FEDERAL COUNCIL][274]

The new circular of the self-styled majority of the B.F.C.[a] pretends to be a reply to the two circulars of the B.F.C. and of the Manchester Foreign Section.[b] In reality it does not refute one single point raised in these circulars. It merely attempts to throw dust into the eyes of its readers by personal gossip, slander, and lies, relying upon the unavoidable want of acquaintance, on the part of the newly-formed Sections, with the history of the International.

It is very characteristic, that of six members of the Executive Committee whose signatures figure at the bottom of that circular,[c] two, Messers. Jung and Pape, have no longer any *locus standi*[d] on the B.F.C. They were delegates, the first for Middlesbro', the second for Nottingham, and one of the above Sections has withdrawn the credential, while the other unanimously repudiated the manifesto. We shall quote some instances only of the impudence of assertion which distinguishes the document in question.

As to the so-called official reports, it says,

"No list of delegates to the Hague has been given, though the Circulars glibly speak of '64'."

---

[a] *Address of the British Federal Council to the Branches, Sections, Affiliated Societies, and Members of the Federation. British Federation of the International Working Men's Association,* London [1873].— *Ed.*

[b] See this volume, pp. 304-14.— *Ed.*

[c] H. Jung, H. Mayo, F. Pape, R. Foster, J. Grout and J. Hales.— *Ed.*

[d] Recognised position.— *Ed.*

The report here mentioned is merely an official edition of the *resolutions passed by the Congress,*[a] and the list of delegates, already printed at the Hague, and reprinted in most continental papers, International or Middle-class, would have been out of place. Besides, the report gives for every vote, the numbers voting, and where a division took place, the names too.

"Resolutions have been suppressed, or cooked—for instance—the resolution relative to the contribution to the General Council was to raise the contribution to the General Council to 1s. per year for every member of the Association, Trades Unions included."

The official report states 2nd, under the heading "Contributions to be paid to the General Council". With regard to the demands, on the one hand to raise, on the other to diminish the rate of contributions, the Congress maintained the 1d. by 17 votes against 12, and 8 abstentions.[b] What is there suppressed?

As to the "cooking" of resolutions, let them dare to point out one resolution of the Report which is not in strict accordance with the minutes.

What, on the other hand, the authors of this circular are capable of in the line of "cooking", is shown by their assertions regarding the Congress resolutions on political action. In the first instance the phrase, "The conquest of political power has become the great duty of the working class", has been literally inserted in Resolution IX of the London conference from the Inaugural Address of the International (1864) although they pretend that it had been invented by the Hague Congress.

Secondly, the authors of the Circular maintain that it is a mis-translation to render the French "*doit* servir" by the English "*ought* to serve".[c] If a mistake had been made, it would have been made by the late General Council in the official English translation of the original French text of the Conference Resolutions. But there is no mistake. As the authors of the Circular do not appear to be on the best terms with either their English or their French, we must refer them to any common dictionary, for instance, Boyer's English-French dictionary, Paris, Baudry, 1854, under *ought* "It ought to be so, cela doit être ainsi."

In order to disprove the statement that the Hague resolutions are fully endorsed in France, Germany, Austria, Hungary, Portugal, America, Denmark, Poland and Switzerland, the circular

---

a See this volume, pp. 243-53.— *Ed.*

b Ibid., p. 245.— *Ed.*

c Ibid., p. 243.— *Ed.*

of John Hales demands the addresses of the secretaries of these different countries. As to Germany, he has only to look to the *Volksstaat* and half a dozen other working men's papers; as to Austria and Hungary, to the *Volkswille*; as to Portugal, to the *Pensamento Social*; as to Denmark, to the *Socialist*; as to Spain, to the *Emancipacion*; as to Holland, to *De Werkman*; as to Italy, to the *Plebe*; as to Switzerland, to the *Égalité* and the *Tagwacht.* With regard to America, the only working-men's federation there existing appointed last year for its Federal Council, the very men now forming the General Council.[275] With regard to Poland and France, the addresses of the respective correspondents will certainly not be entrusted to the discretion of John Hales and Co.

As to the "spontaneous" character of the secession movement, the simple fact is that the Secessionist Congress held in September last, in opposition to the International Hague Congress, at St. Imier,[276] passed a formal resolution to organize that movement everywhere by "coming to an immediate agreement with all Sections and Federations" favourable to Secession so as to be able to hold a secessionist "International Congress within six months at latest".[a]

Written in mid-January 1873

First published in *The International Herald,* No. 43, January 25, 1873

Reproduced from the newspaper checked with Marx's partly extant manuscript

---

[a] "Les deux Congrès de Saint-Imier", *Bulletin de la Fédération jurassienne...*, No. 17-18, September 15-October 1, 1872, p. 14.— *Ed.*

Frederick Engels

[NEWS ON THE ACTIVITIES OF THE INTERNATIONAL ON THE CONTINENT] [277]

I

[*The International Herald*, No. 41, January 11, 1873]

From the Continent we receive the following information:—
From the Italian International newspaper *La Plebe*,[a] it appeared
that the Italian Government, which nowhere interferes with the
Secessionist Sections, had opened a campaign of violent prosecutions against the Lodi Section, which had recognised the new
General Council, and adhered to the Hague resolutions. The
Section was dissolved and warrants of arrest launched against all
the members of the Committee, three of whom were actually
thrown into prison, while the six others escaped. Amongst those
arrested is Bignami, the editor of the *Plebe*. The number of that
paper containing the address of the General Council (published in
No. 34 of *The International Herald*)[b] was also seized on that
account, while the most violent manifestoes of the Secessionists are
freely allowed to circulate. The prisoners are to be tried for high
treason.

Our Madrid paper *La Emancipacion*, states that the movement of
resistance to the secessionist action of the Spanish Federal Council
is growing daily.[c] The moment that Council convoked a Congress

---

[a] This refers to the articles "Sequestro LIX", "Uno post unum", "Jeri é stato",
and to Petrus, "Ai lettori!" in *La Plebe*, Nos. 119-121, December 4, 8 and 12,
1872.— *Ed.*

[b] The reference is to the General Council address of October 20, 1872, "To the
Federations, Affiliated Societies, Sections and All Members of the International
Working Men's Association" published by *The International Herald*, No. 34,
November 23, 1872; the Italian translation appeared in *La Plebe*, No. 118,
November 27, 1872.— *Ed.*

[c] "La Nueva Federacion Madrileña á todas las federaciones y secciones de la
Asociacion Internacional en España", *La Emancipacion*, No. 76, November 30,
1872.— *Ed.*

to meet at Cordova on the 26th December,[278] in order to accept or
reject the Hague resolutions, the New Federation of Madrid
declared that by this action the Council had placed itself outside
the pale of the International, and called upon all Sections and
Local Federations not to send delegates to the Secession Congress,
but to appoint a new provisional Federal Council.[a] To this
proposition have adhered the local Federations of Lérida, Toledo,
Saragossa, Vitoria, Alcalá de Henares, the New Federation of
Cadiz, and important Sections of Valencia, Denia, Pont de
Vilumara, and other places. Besides these the Federation of Gracia
(manufacturing suburb of Barcelona) has adhered to the Hague
resolutions, and blamed the conduct of the Spanish delegates at
that Congress, while the Federation of Granada has resolved to
send a delegate[b] to the Secession Congress at Cordova, but has
elected for that purpose a staunch anti-secessionist.[279] No doubt
the Spanish Federal Council will have it all their own way at
Cordova, but that will only bring the crisis to a head.

From a letter from Portugal,[280] it appeared that the working-
class movement there, organised by the International, was growing
to extraordinary dimensions. In Lisbon and neighbourhood alone,
above fifteen thousand working men had been organised in
Trades' Unions, and the organisation was spreading to Oporto
and the North. The whole of these societies have been formed by,
and continue under the direct influence of the International,
which, however, is prevented by the laws of the country to
organise itself with full liberty. The International paper, *O Pensamento Social*, is now self-supporting. We may add that in
Portugal there are no secessionists. The Hague resolutions have
been not only unanimously endorsed, but received with enthusiasm. The *Pensamento*, in its No. 25, contains an article
declaring the Hague Congress to be the most important one ever
held since the foundation of the International, and hailing its
resolutions as establishing an immense progress in the development of the Association.[c]

It will be seen by the above statements that the late majority of
the British Federal Council have, in their action, imitated to the
letter that of the Spanish Secessionist Council. It is thus evident

---

  a "La Nueva Federacion Madrileña á todas las federaciones, secciones é individuos
de la Asociacion Internacional en España", *La Emancipacion*, No. 73, November 9,
1872.— *Ed.*

  b Mariano Rodriguez.— *Ed.*

  c "O Congreso da Internacional na Haya", *O Pensamento Social*, No. 25,
October 6, 1872.— *Ed.*

that they have been acting upon the same plan here and in Spain, and have been led by the same wire-pullers. Unfortunately in Spain a number of true Internationals have joined the late insurrection, and this may give the Secessionists a momentary advantage.[281]

II

[*The International Herald*, No. 44, February 1, 1873]

A letter from the Spanish Federal Council invited our attention to the fact that the engine-drivers and stokers are now on strike in Spain, and that the railway companies are sending to England, Belgium, and other countries for men to use in defeating the attempts of their employees to improve their position. Our Council appointed a committee to draw up a paragraph containing a statement of the case, and to send it to the newspapers.[282] The committee attended to its duty, as proved by the appearance of the paragraph in the papers published the following Saturday.[a] Other steps for making the Spanish strike known to the engine-drivers and stokers of England were adopted.

III

[*The International Herald*, No. 45, February 8, 1873]

The news we have from the Continent is interesting.

The report from Germany brought intelligence of a great victory. The International deputy to the German Parliament, Bebel, who had been sentenced by a Saxon Law-court for offences committed in a speech, to be imprisoned for nine months, and to lose all rights derived from public election, has just been re-elected on the 20th January, by the majority of 10,470 votes [283] against 4,420 given to the government candidate.[b] This is the third time that Bebel has been elected in his district, and by 2,500 more votes than he had at any previous election. Thus, Bismarck will again have to face the only man who, in the present parliament, dares openly to oppose him in the interest of the working class, and

---

[a] February 1, 1873.— *Ed.*
[b] Ernst Petzold.— *Ed.*

the only man of whom he is really afraid. Everything has been done to prevent Bebel's re-election; intimidation, dissolution, by the police, of meetings of electors, etc.; the candidate opposed to him was about the decentest man they could find, but in spite of all these efforts, the working men of Glauchau and neighbourhood gave Bebel nearly three votes out of every four votes polled, and that without any Samuel Morley to pay expences.

Further details have arrived respecting the Secessionist Congress in Spain. It appears that it was to all intents and purposes a Minority Congress. Out of 101 local federations, counting altogether 398 Sections, only 41 local federations, or 57 Sections, were represented; so that the votes passed at that Congress have been taken by delegates representing less than one sixth of the Sections existing in Spain. The above statistics being taken from the secessionist paper "*La Federacion*",[a] will not be disputed. To act by surprise, and to get a minority vote to sanction their acts, is everywhere the policy of the Secessionists; another proof that they are everywhere acting under the same secret instructions.

In France, numerous arrests of pretended members of the International have taken place in almost all the large towns. It is of course impossible to know whether the real members of the Association have been found out, and even if it were known, it could not be published, in the interests of the parties arrested, as it is now punishable in France to belong to the International. All that is known is, that the few secessionists in France have gone scot-free. They, on the contrary, are on such excellent terms with M. Thiers's government, that, for instance, at Béziers they are represented by a superintendent of police, a certain Bousquet, for whose honesty the gospel of the secession party, the *Bulletin jurassien*, has lately vouched in the most enthusiastic manner.[284]

IV

[The International Herald, No. 46, February 15, 1873]

From Portugal we hear that the Portuguese Federation, on learning that the so-called Spanish congress at Cordova had declared for secession, immediately wrote to the new federation of

---

[a] "Tercer Congreso Regional de la Federacion Española" and "Movimento obrero universal. España", *La Federacion*, Nos. 177 and 178, January 4 and 11, 1873.— *Ed.*

Madrid (International) to declare that Portugal, to a man, stood by the Association against the Secessionists; that attempts had been made to introduce into their ranks the secret "Alliance", and that Bakounine, himself, had written to one of them,[a] persuading them to push that secret society; but that they unanimously resolved to express to Bakounine their formal disapprobation of the acts of the Alliance. This letter to the New Federation of Madrid is written and signed by the Secretary, Franca, by order, and in the name of the delegates of the sections, and published in the Madrid *Emancipacion* of the first of February. The Portuguese Federation now counts more than 15,000 members; it has, in Lisbon alone, 48 sections of trades, each forming a Trade's Union. So much for the assertion of the Secessionists, that all the organized federations are with them!

Written in January-mid-February 1873   Reproduced from the newspaper

First published in *The International Herald*, Nos. 41, 44, 45 and 46, January 11, February 1, 8 and 15, 1873

---

[a] This refers to M. Bakunin's letter to F. Mora of April 5, 1872 (see this volume, pp. 578-80).—*Ed.*

Frederick Engels

NOTES FOR THE GENERAL COUNCIL [285]

1. *The International Herald* and the *Emancipacion* sent regularly, hope they have arrived.

2. The Hales gang actually did hold their congress on January 26, all 10 of them; they dare not even say which sections they claim to represent. A wretched fiasco. Naturally decided not to recognise the Hague decisions or the General Council. Report—first half—in *The Eastern Post*, February 1; today's contains no continuation! [286] The Federal Council will send you the things officially. These people have lost almost all their support, apart from Hales' personal following in the East End of London. One of the signatories of Hales' first circular,[a] Bennett, has returned to our people with strict orders from his section (Halifax) to stand by them and the LAWFUL Association. He was only re-admitted after much EATING OF HUMBLE PIE. (See today's *International Herald*.[b])

3. In *Lodi*, the *Plebe* is remaining loyal, though not breaking openly with the others, which they would not be able to do for the time being anyway. But the others themselves are carrying things to the limit. They are convening an Italian congress for March 15, but only intend to admit sections that have recognised the Rimini resolutions [287] or recognise them by the deadline! So much for autonomy and free federations. It is all right to trample the Rules of the International underfoot, but the Rimini resolutions are sacrosanct.

---

[a] *To the Branches, Sections and Members of the British Federation of the International Working Men's Association,* [London,] December 10, 1872.— *Ed.*

[b] J. Mitchell, S. Vickery, "International Working Men's Association. British Federal Council", *The International Herald,* No. 45, February 8, 1873.— *Ed.*

4. We greatly regret that the G.C., instead of simply stating that the Jurassians have *resigned* by rejecting the Hague resolutions and forming a separate league [Sonderbund], has merely suspended them.[288] First, it is always possible that a conference will be demanded. Second, the issue now comes before Congress in a quite different form: their delegates must be admitted provisionally, until their mandate has been put to the vote. Third, the G.C. must take the same steps against the Belgians and the Spaniards, ditto against the Hales gang, and these successive suspensions make a much worse impression than if the G.C. had waited a few more weeks, until it knew the results of the Belgian and Spanish congresses, and then issued one general proclamation setting out the formal reasons and also explaining in simple terms that one cannot be both inside and outside the International, cannot claim to belong to it and simultaneously declare its rules invalid, and then *purement et simplement* stating that those in question had placed themselves outside the International.

5. I hope the relevant resolution has been sent to Sonvillier and Geneva from there, as I have received no instruction to this effect. As far as Serraillier is concerned, he cannot send anything there at the moment, with arrests raining down and all correspondence with France cut.

6. Your authorised representative *Larroque* has collected his authorisation here himself—as a refugee. From here he went to San Sebastián, where he will get the thing moving again.

7. In *Portugal* all is well, as the *Emancipacion* sent today shows. We also have private letters from there; the people are working very hard on the TRADE UNIONS.

8. In Lodi only Bignami is left. The party[a] committee in Hamburg has sent them 20 thalers and Oberwinder 50 guldens from Vienna, which has not failed to have an effect.

9. Cuno's manoeuvre, to disguise himself as Capestro, has already been exposed in the Brussels *Internationale*.[289]

10. If the G.C. is not already receiving the secessionist sheets, some unknown name will have to take out a subscription to them. Here, with the greatest difficulty and by roundabout ways, we obtain *one* copy of each, and not always that—we still have not received the last three issues of the *Bulletin jurassien*. So, with the best will in the world, we cannot procure them for you. Anyway, they are only *L'Internationale* (Brussels), the *Bulletin de la Fédération jurassienne.* (Sonvillier) and *La Federacion* (Barcelona).

---

[a] Social-Democratic Workers' Party.— *Ed.*

11. I have spoken to Le Moussu about the STAMPS; he will procure them, just as last year.[290] Yet it is odd that this could not be done in New York.

12. What has become of MacDonnell? He must have arrived long since. I have neither seen nor heard anything of him.

Must catch the post.

Best wishes,

F. Engels

London, February 8, 1873 [a]

First published in: Marx and Engels, *Works*, First Russian Edition, Vol. XXVI, Moscow, 1935

Printed according to the manuscript

Published in English for the first time

---

[a] In the manuscript mistakenly: "1872".— *Ed.*

Frederick Engels

THE REPUBLIC IN SPAIN[291]

It is hard to say which has sunk lower in the last three years, the monarchy or the republic. The monarchy—on the continent of Europe, at least—is everywhere assuming its final form, Caesarism, at an increasing pace. Everywhere sham constitutionalism with universal suffrage, an overgrown army as the buttress of government, bribery and corruption as the chief means of government, and enrichment through corruption and fraud as the sole end of government, are irresistibly undermining all the splendid constitutional guarantees, the artificial balance of forces, of which our bourgeois dreamt in the idyllic days of Louis Philippe, when even the most corrupt were still angels of innocence compared with the "great men" of today. As the bourgeoisie daily loses the character of a class temporarily indispensable in the social organism, shedding its specific social functions to become a mere gang of swindlers, its state turns into an institution for the protection, not of production, but of the overt theft of products. Not only does this state carry its own condemnation within itself; it has actually already been condemned by history in Louis Napoleon. Yet it is also the last possible form of monarchy. All other forms of monarchy are worn out and obsolete. After it, the only possible type of state left is the republic.

The republic, however, is not faring any better. From 1789 to 1869, it was the ideal of enthusiastic freedom fighters, always aspired to, attained after a hard, bloody struggle, and scarcely attained—fleeing again. Since a King of Prussia[a] succeeded in

---

[a] William I.— *Ed.*

setting up a French republic all that has changed. From 1870—and this is the progress attained—republics are no longer made by republicans, precisely because there are no pure republicans left, but by royalists despairing of the monarchy. To avoid civil war, the monarchist-minded bourgeois are consolidating the republic in France and proclaiming it in Spain [292]—in France, because there are too many pretenders; in Spain, because the last possible king [a] is on strike.

Herein lies a twofold advance.

First, the magic that hitherto surrounded the name of the republic has been dispelled. After the events in France and in Spain, only a Karl Blind can cling to the superstitious belief in the miraculous effects of a republic. The republic is finally seen in Europe, too, for what it is in essence, and in America in actual fact—*as the consummate form of the rule of the bourgeoisie.* I say "finally in Europe, too", because republics like Switzerland, Hamburg, Bremen, Lübeck and the ex-free city of Frankfort— God rest her soul—are irrelevant here. The modern republic, with which alone we are concerned at this point, is the political organisation of a great people, not the provincial political institution of a city, a canton or a club of cantons that has been historically handed down from the Middle Ages, assuming more or less democratic forms, and, at best, replacing patrician rule with a peasant rule that is scarcely any better. Switzerland exists partly through the indulgence and partly through the jealousy of its great neighbours; whenever these are united, it is forced to swallow its republican phrases and obey orders. Such countries exist only as long as they do not attempt to intervene in the course of history, which is why they are neutralised and thus prevented from doing so. The era of the *true* European republics dates from September 4, or rather from the day of Sedan, [293] even if a brief Caesarist setback (under no matter which pretender) might be possible. And in this sense, it might be said that the Thiers republic is the final realisation of the republic of 1792; the republic of the Jacobins without the self-deception of the Jacobins. From now on, the working class can no longer have any illusions about the nature of the modern republic: the type of state in which the rule of the bourgeoisie achieves its final, consummate expression. In the modern republic political equality, which is still subject to certain exceptions in all monarchies, is at last fully implemented. And this political equality—what is it but the

---

[a] Amadeo I.— *Ed.*

declaration that class differences do not concern the state, that the bourgeois have as much right to be bourgeois as the workers to be proletarians?

Yet this final, consummate form of bourgeois rule, the republic, is only introduced by the bourgeois themselves with the utmost reluctance; it forces itself on them. Why this curious contradiction? Because the introduction of the republic means breaking with all political tradition; because it requires every political institution to justify its existence; because, therefore, all the traditional influences that support the powers that be under the monarchy fall away. In other words: if the modern republic is the consummate form of bourgeois rule, it is also the type of state that frees the class struggle from its last fetters and prepares the battleground for it. The modern republic is, in fact, nothing but this battleground. And this is the second advance. On the one hand, the bourgeoisie feels that its end is near as soon as the ground of the monarchy is whipped away from under its feet and, with it, all the conservative power that resided in the superstitious belief of the uneducated masses, particularly in the countryside, in the traditional supremacy of the royal houses—no matter whether this superstition worships the kingdom of God's grace, as in Prussia, or the legendary peasant emperor Napoleon, as in France. On the other hand, the proletariat feels that the funeral dirge of the monarchy is simultaneously the clarion call for the decisive battle with the bourgeoisie. The modern republic is nothing but the stage cleared for the last great class struggle in world history—and this is what gives it its tremendous significance.

In order, however, for this class struggle between bourgeoisie and proletariat to be decided, these two classes must be sufficiently developed in the countries concerned, at least in the large towns. In Spain this is only the case in individual parts of the country. In Catalonia, large-scale industry is relatively highly developed. In Andalusia and some other areas big landed property and large-scale agriculture—landowners and wage-labourers—prevail; in most of the country small farmers prevail in rural areas, small industry in the towns. The conditions for a proletarian revolution are thus relatively poorly developed, and, for precisely this reason, there still remains a great deal to be done in Spain for a bourgeois republic; above all, its mission here is to clear the stage for the imminent class struggle.

A primary necessity is the *abolition of the army* and the introduction of a *people's militia.* Geographically, Spain is so favourably situated that it can only be seriously attacked by one neighbour, and even then only along the short front of the Pyrenees; a front that does not even comprise an eighth of its total perimeter. Moreover, the conditions of the terrain in the country are such that they complicate mobile warfare by large armies in the same measure as they facilitate irregular popular warfare. We saw this under Napoleon, who at times despatched up to 300,000 men to Spain, but they were always defeated by the people's dour resistance; we have seen this countless times since then and see it to this day in the impotence of the Spanish army in the face of the few gangs of Carlists in the mountains.[294] A country like this has no pretext for an army. Furthermore, since 1830 the army in Spain has merely been the lever of all those generals' plots which have brought down the government every few years with a military revolt, in order to replace old thieves with new. To dissolve the Spanish army is to release Spain from civil war. This, then, would be the first demand the Spanish workers should make on the new government.

Once the army is abolished, the main reason that the Catalans, in particular, are demanding a federal state organisation disappears. Revolutionary Catalonia, the great working-class suburb of Spain, as it were, has hitherto been kept down by heavy concentrations of troops, just as Bonaparte and Thiers kept Paris and Lyons down. This is why the Catalans demanded the division of Spain into federal states with independent administration. If the army goes, so does the main reason for this demand; it will be possible to achieve independence in principle without the reactionary destruction of national unity, and without reproducing a larger Switzerland.

The financial legislation of Spain, as regards both internal taxes and border tariffs, is nonsensical from start to finish. A bourgeois republic can do a great deal about this. The same applies to the confiscation of the landed property of the Church, which has often been confiscated but has always been amassed once again, and, last but not least, the provision of highways, which are nowhere in a worse state than here.

A few years of peaceful bourgeois republic would prepare the ground in Spain for a proletarian revolution in a way that would surprise even the most advanced Spanish workers. Instead of repeating the bloody farce of the previous revolution,[a] instead of staging isolated, easily crushed rebellions, it is to be hoped that the

---

[a] Engels means the earlier stages of the Spanish bourgeois revolution of 1868-74.— Ed.

Spanish workers will make use of the republic in order to join together more firmly and organise themselves with a view to an approaching revolution, a revolution *they* will command. The bourgeois government of the new republic is merely seeking an excuse to suppress the revolutionary movement and shoot down the workers, as the republicans Favre and consorts did in Paris. May the Spanish workers not give them the excuse!

Written in the latter half of February 1873

First published in *Der Volksstaat*, No. 18, March 1, 1873; *La Emancipacion*, March 7, 1873; *O Pensamento Social*, March 23, 1873

Printed according to *Der Volksstaat*

Published in English for the first time

Frederick Engels

ON AUTHORITY [295]

A number of socialists have latterly launched a regular crusade against what they call the *principle of authority*. It is sufficient for them to say that this or that act is *authoritarian* for it to be condemned. This summary mode of procedure is being abused to such an extent that it has become necessary to look into the matter somewhat more closely. Authority, in the sense in which the word is used here, means: the imposition of the will of another upon ours; on the other hand, authority presupposes subordination. Now, since these two words sound bad and the relationship which they represent is disagreeable to the subordinated party, the question is to ascertain whether there is any way of dispensing with it, whether—given the conditions of present-day society—we could not create another social system, in which this authority would be given no scope any longer and would consequently have to disappear. On examining the economic, industrial and agricultural conditions which form the basis of present-day bourgeois society, we find that they tend more and more to replace isolated action by combined action of individuals. Modern industry with its big factories and mills, where hundreds of workers supervise complicated machines driven by steam, has superseded the small workshops of the separate producers; the carriages and wagons of the highways have been substituted by railway trains, just as the small schooners and sailing feluccas have been by steam-boats. Even agriculture falls increasingly under the dominion of the machine and of steam, which slowly but relentlessly put in the place of the small proprietors big capitalists, who with the aid of hired workers cultivate vast stretches of land. Everywhere combined action, the complication of processes dependent upon each other, displaces independent action by individuals. But whoever mentions combined action speaks of organisation; now, is it possible to have organisation without authority?

Supposing a social revolution dethroned the capitalists, who now exercise their authority over the production and circulation of wealth. Supposing, to adopt entirely the point of view of the anti-authoritarians, that the land and the instruments of labour had become the collective property of the workers who use them. Will authority have disappeared or will it only have changed its form? Let us see.

Let us take by way of example a cotton spinning mill. The cotton must pass through at least six successive operations before it is reduced to the state of thread, and these operations take place for the most part in different rooms. Furthermore, keeping the machines going requires an engineer to look after the steam engine, mechanics to make the current repairs, and many other labourers whose business it is to transfer the products from one room to another, and so forth. All these workers, men, women and children, are obliged to begin and finish their work at the hours fixed by the authority of the steam, which cares nothing for individual autonomy. The workers must, therefore, first come to an understanding on the hours of work; and these hours, once they are fixed, must be observed by all, without any exception. Thereafter particular questions arise in each room and at every moment concerning the mode of production, distribution of materials, etc., which must be settled at once on pain of seeing all production immediately stopped; whether they are settled by decision of a delegate placed at the head of each branch of labour or, if possible, by a majority vote, the will of the single individual will always have to subordinate itself, which means that questions are settled in an authoritarian way. The automatic machinery of a big factory is much more despotic than the small capitalists who employ workers ever have been. At least with regard to the hours of work one may write upon the portals of these factories: *Lasciate ogni autonomia, voi che entrate!*[a] If man, by dint of his knowledge and inventive genius, has subdued the forces of nature, the latter avenge themselves upon him by subjecting him, in so far as he employs them, to a veritable despotism independent of all social organisation. Wanting to abolish authority in large-scale industry is

---

[a] "Leave, ye that enter in, all autonomy behind!" (Dante, *The Divine Comedy,* Hell, Canto III, Verse 3—paraphrased).— *Ed.*

tantamount to wanting to abolish industry itself, to destroy the power loom in order to return to the spinning wheel.

Let us take another example—the railway. Here, too, the co-operation of an infinite number of individuals is absolutely necessary, and this co-operation must be practised during precisely fixed hours so that no accidents may happen. Here, too, the first condition of the job is a dominant will that settles all subordinate questions, whether this will is represented by a single delegate or a committee charged with the execution of the resolutions of the majority of persons interested. In either case there is very pronounced authority. Moreover, what would happen to the first train despatched if the authority of the railway employees over the Hon. passengers were abolished?

But the necessity of authority, and of imperious authority at that, will nowhere be found more evident than on board a ship on the high seas. There, in time of danger, the lives of all depend on the instantaneous and absolute obedience of all to the will of one.

When I submitted arguments like these to the most rabid anti-authoritarians the only answer they were able to give me was the following: Yes, that's true, but here it is not a case of authority which we confer on our delegates, *but of a commission entrusted*! These gentlemen think that when they have changed the names of things they have changed the things themselves. This is how these profound thinkers mock at the whole world.

We have thus seen that, on the one hand, a certain authority, no matter how delegated, and, on the other hand, a certain subordination, are things which, independently of all social organisation, are imposed upon us together with the material conditions under which we produce and make products circulate.

We have seen, besides, that the material conditions of production and circulation inevitably develop with large-scale industry and large-scale agriculture, and increasingly tend to enlarge the scope of this authority. Hence it is absurd to speak of the principle of authority as being absolutely evil, and of the principle of autonomy as being absolutely good. Authority and autonomy are relative things whose spheres vary with the various phases of the development of society. If the autonomists confined themselves to saying that the social organisation of the future would restrict authority solely to the limits within which the conditions of production render it inevitable, we could understand each other; but they are blind to all facts that make the thing necessary and they passionately fight the word.

Why do the anti-authoritarians not confine themselves to crying out against political authority, the state? All socialists are agreed that the political state, and with it political authority, will disappear as a result of the coming social revolution, that is, that public functions will lose their political character and be transformed into the simple administrative functions of watching over the true interests of society. But the anti-authoritarians demand that the authoritarian political state be abolished at one stroke, even before the social conditions that gave birth to it have been destroyed. They demand that the first act of the social revolution shall be the abolition of authority. Have these gentlemen ever seen a revolution? A revolution is certainly the most authoritarian thing there is; it is the act whereby one part of the population imposes its will upon the other part by means of rifles, bayonets and cannon—authoritarian means, if such there be at all; and if the victorious party does not want to have fought in vain, it must maintain this rule by means of the terror which its arms inspire in the reactionaries. Would the Paris Commune have lasted a single day if it had not made use of this authority of the armed people against the bourgeois? Should we not, on the contrary, reproach it for not having used it freely enough?

Therefore, either one of two things: either the anti-authoritarians don't know what they are talking about, in which case they are creating nothing but confusion; or they do know, and in that case they are betraying the movement of the proletariat. In either case they serve the reaction.

Written in October 1872 and in March 1873

First published in December 1873 in the collection *Almanacco Repubblicano per l'anno 1874*

Signed: *Federico Engels*

Printed according to the collection

Translated from the Italian

Frederick Engels

[NEWS
ON THE INTERNATIONAL LABOUR MOVEMENT][296]

[I]

[*The International Herald*, No. 51, March 22, 1873]

Spain

The strike of the engineers and stokers on the Northern Railway still continues.[a] The middle class papers state that the engineers and stokers, on strike of the Valencia Railway, have given in, but this is about the third time this assertion is made by them, and we shall not believe it until we see it confirmed in the Spanish International papers.

The demand of the International factory workers of Barcelona and neighbourhood for a reduction of the hours of work to ten, appears to have been complied with, as the factories keep working, and the respectable papers are ominously silent on this point. The hours of work, heretofore, were from 12 to 13. It is to be observed that this point has been carried principally by the men of Gracia, the manufactory suburb of Barcelona, and that they, as early as November last, had unanimously declared for the Hague Resolutions.

The letter-press compositors of Madrid have compelled the masters, without strike, to agree to the new terms proposed by them.

Germany

The type-compositors of Germany are engaged in a struggle which threatens to become very severe. They have a Trades Union which numbers about 4,000, out of 7,000 type-compositors in all Germany. On the other hand, the master printers have a society

---

[a] See this volume, p. 411.— *Ed.*

also, by the rules of which, the masters bind themselves upon an appeal on behalf of the Committee in case of a serious strike, to discharge at once any Union men in their employ. Now, the type-compositors of Leipzig, a short time ago, went on strike for higher wages, and the masters' committee finding themselves beaten in Leipzig, have called upon the masters all over Germany to give notice to all Union men. This has been done in Leipzig, Berlin, Breslau,[a] Frankfort, Munich and most other large towns of Germany, so that unless an agreement is come to within a few days, the great mass of the compositors will be locked out by next Sunday week, and the whole German press and book trade completely disorganised. While thus the printing offices of the masters are completely paralyzed, the co-operative printing establishment of Leipzig is flourishing to such a degree that the orders on hand cannot be executed.

Dresden.—A Co-operative Carpenters and Joiners Association has been started.

Switzerland

The strike of the jewellers of Geneva for the nine hours' working day still continues; at the same time the great majority of the masters have given in, and reopened their shops on the nine hours' system, so that with a little continued assistance to the men, the final victory cannot be doubtful.

This is the second great strike in Geneva which has been won through the intercession of the International.[297]

[II]

[*The International Herald*, No. 52, March 29, 1873]

Spain

The strike of the engineers and stokers on the railway from Valencia to Tarragona and Almansa has ended by the complete triumph of the men who have obtained all their demands. That on the Northern Railway of Spain, on the other hand, appears to have broken down for want of a proper organization.

---

[a] Wrocław.— *Ed.*

At Barcelona, the coalheavers of the port have gained, in consequence of a short and successful strike, an advance of wages averaging 10d. a day—instead of 3s. 9d. they now get 4s. 7d. for every working day of eight hours.

Switzerland

There will be held shortly a Swiss Working Men's Congress at Olten; the date has not yet been fixed.[298] A Swiss Shoemaker's Congress is preparing.

Germany

The type-compositors' strike, alluded to in our last, appears to take a very favourable turn for the men. The masters had played out their great trump card, by calling upon all members of their society all over Germany to give notice to all members of the men's union that might be in their employ. But this appeal, though perfectly justified by the rules of the masters' society, does not appear to have been met everywhere with the necessary alacrity; indeed the Hamburg master printers declared it to be uncalled for, and left the society altogether rather than obey. In consequence the masters' committee has been obliged to eat humble pie and to apply to the men's committee—hitherto ignored and repudiated by them—to re-open negotiations for an amicable settlement of the dispute.

At Dresden, the International Trades Union of house painters, japanners, gilders, etc., has its central seat. This society established only a year ago, has not only compelled the masters to do away with Sunday obnoxious regulations, but also established a co-operative workshop in which numerous members of the associated trades find employment.

At Regensburg (Bavaria) the shoemakers, headed by the members of the International Shoemaker's Union, have gone on strike for a rise of wages.

At Mayence, a shoemakers' strike has been going on for a full month, without a prospect of being brought soon to a close; most of the unmarried men have left.

The Berlin coopers published an appeal to their colleagues in the north of Germany to form a Trades Union; they state that they have just carried a strike to a victorious end and wish to expand the organisation which has so far been locally successful.

In Hamburg the 350 workmen of a large piano-factory are on strike for an advance of wages.

In Görlitz (Silesia) the tailors have struck, on the 17th of March, for an advance of wages of 30 per cent; the masters offered 10 per cent which was refused.

The Berlin joiners and cabinet-makers are asking an advance of 33 per cent, and are determined to go on strike if not successful by peaceable means.

United States

In New York, a German Working Men's paper [a] has been started under the auspices of the International. It exposes the shameful tricks by which the American manufactories coin money out of the sweat and the starvation of their workpeople. The Singer Sewing Machine Co., is chosen for a first example. Thus, the company's manager gives out the work, to the overlookers in every room in the shape of contracts; they again employ sub-contractors, these parcel out their jobs to other sub-sub-contractors, until finally the last understrapping contractor makes his own contract with the workpeople that have to do the real work. It is impossible to drive the "sweating system" any further; here we see it in its perfection. Not only the capitalist, but a whole hierarchy of understrappers are here directly interested in sweating a profit out of the workman's labour—no wonder that he, the workman, scarcely receives the pittance without which life and work become an impossibility.

[III]

[*The International Herald*, No. 54, April 12, 1873]

Germany

The letter-press printers' and compositors' strike continues. The masters' proposals, being unacceptable, have been refused by the men. In the meantime one master after another, especially in the smaller towns, have to give in, so that the prospects are very favourable for the men.

---

[a] *Arbeiter-Zeitung.—Ed.*

At Hanover, the bookbinders' strike has ended in the complete victory of the men. Their demands, a ten hours' working day and an advance of wages of 25 per cent, have been accorded to in full by the masters. The bookbinders of Germany will hold a General Congress at Nuremberg on Easter Sunday.

At Chemnitz, the tailors demanded from their employers an advance of wages of 33 per cent, and the complete cessation of Sunday labour. These demands having been refused, the men went on strike on the 30th of March.

The shoemakers' strike at Mayence continues. Another strike in the same trade has broken out at Pforzheim; at Würzburg and at Erfurt strikes of that trade appear impending, the men asking an advance of wages.

The German Bricklayers Union announces a strike of bricklayers and masons at Flensburg for shorter hours of work. The basket makers at Hamburg are on strike for the same reason, as also the workpeople of a large cotton mill near Hanover.

Austria

The Vienna tailors having demanded from their employers an advance of wages and a reduction of the hours of work, which was refused, the men of more than forty shops, including the principal ones, went on strike.

The same has occurred with the tailors at Graz.

Belgium

A General European Tailors' Congress has just taken place at Brussels, at which the provisional Rules of a European Tailors' Union were adopted, to which all democratic socialist tailors' societies are invited to accede; all societies wishing to go on strike, to obtain, before striking, the approval of the rest, if they intend to claim the support of the European Union. An annual Congress of the Union is to take place.

Switzerland

The Geneva Jewellers' strike is now finally brought to a close. The nine hours' working day has been victoriously carried.

At Zurich the carpenters and joiners, at Winterthur the tailors, are on strike for the usual reasons, shorter hours and higher wages.

At Neuchâtel, the shoemakers have gained an advance without resorting to a strike.

America

The servant girls of Ottawa (Canada) have formed a Trades Union.

[IV]

[*The International Herald*, No. 56, April 26, 1873]

Germany

Berlin.—The gardeners' journeymen are on strike for ten hours and an advance of wages.—A strike of the pianoforte makers for $33^1/_2$ per cent advance of wages and 8 hours a day is impending.

Munich.—The working class movement here is very active. Almost all trades have their unions; a central Trades' Council is being formed. The jewellers have carried an advance of wages of 25 per cent; the tailors, without a strike, 15 per cent.

Augsburg.—A portion of the carpenters—those employed by the seven largest masters of the town, about 90 in all—are locked out, because they will not accept the new tariff of wages offered by the masters.

Leipzig.—The great struggle between the master printers and the type-compositors, which from here spread all over Germany, has ended in the complete victory of the men. The haughty masters have had to accept all the conditions imposed by the latter, namely, withdrawal of the general notice given to all union men, and settlement of a new scale of wages by a mixed committee of men and masters. These conditions being agreed to, the men's committee declared the strike at an end.

Danzig.[a]—The ships' carpenters' strike has ended in a defeat, owing to the direct interference of the government in favour of the masters, by threatening with dismissal every man employed in

---

[a] Gdansk.— *Ed.*

16*

the navy yards who should support the strike, and other similar measures.

Hamburg.—A strike of the shoemakers of Hamburg, Altona, and neighbourhood is impending, as the masters seem determined to resist the demands of the men.

Of smaller strikes we noticed those of the ships' carpenters at Kiel (Holstein); the moulders at Itzehoe (Holstein); the cork cutters at Delmenhorst, about 900; the joiners and cabinet-makers at Bremerhaven, etc., principally caused by insufficient wages. All over Germany the organization of Trades Unions, local and national, and even international (comprising the workmen of each trade in Germany, Austria, and Switzerland) is progressing very actively, and wages are more and more approaching the English level.

Austria

Vienna.—The tailors' strike continues. That of the engineers in a large machine shop, begun inconsiderately, has broken down completely. On the other hand, that of the file cutters has been triumphant; the whole of the masters have agreed to the 20 per cent advance asked by the men.

Graz.—The cabinet-makers and joiners went on strike on the 21st April for shorter hours and 20 per cent advance of wages. The shoemakers in a large shoe shop have struck for 11 hours a day, which is now the usual time in Vienna.

Hungary

Pesth.—The Hungarian Working Men's Organization suppressed after the defeat of the Paris Commune, has now been re-established at a large meeting held on the 23rd March.[299] The Organization possesses two newspapers, one in the Hungarian, the other in the German language.[a] The committee is composed of old Internationals, amongst whom we find the name of C. Farkas,[b] delegate at the Hague Congress as treasurer.

---

[a] The reference is to the weekly published in Hungarian (*Munkás-Heti-Krónika*) and German (*Arbeiter-Wochen-Chronik*).— *Ed.*

[b] In the newspaper mistakenly: O. Farkas.— *Ed.*

Switzerland

The Geneva jewellers' strike is now completely ended; the nine hours have been completely carried by the men. At Zurich the carpenters are out; six masters, so far, have given in. The tailors' strike at Winterthur continues. The tailors' demands at Lausanne have been acceded to by the employers to avoid a strike.

Belgium

At Écaussinnes 200 quarrymen turned out, but the strike appears to have come to an end very soon. Particulars are wanting.

[V]

[*The International Herald*, No. 57, May 3, 1873]

Switzerland

The tailors' strike at Winterthur has been successful. All employers but one have acceded to the demands of the men.

The shoemakers of Zurich intend striking for higher wages and request the men of the trade to refrain from seeking work there.

Roumania

The workpeople on the railway workshop at the Bucharest Station are on the point of striking unless the directors accede to their demands.

Germany

The International Metal Workers' Union (Germany, Austria, and Switzerland) has convoked its annual Congress at Dresden for Whit-Sunday, June 1st.

Hamburg.—The Saddlers are on strike since the 19th April, the masters having declined acceding to the men's demands. The shoemakers' strike, of which we spoke as impending in our last week's issue, has now broken out. The men are asking an advance of wages of 25 per cent. The ships' carpenters' strikes in various places of the North of Germany, of which we have already spoken, are principally caused by the masters' resistance to the newly formed German ships' carpenters' union which it is intended to nip in the bud; but the men stood out valiantly. As a matter of course, the Imperial German Navy Yard authorities at Kiel and elsewhere give all the support in their power to the masters.

Munich.—The shoemakers are on strike for 30 per cent advance of wages and 12 hours maximum daily labour. Masters employing 250 men have given in; 150 unmarried men have left the place, so that victory appears certain.

Berlin.—The shoemakers, about 3,000 in number, have struck for an advance of wages of 33 per cent. All unmarried men are leaving. The strike of the gardeners' assistants appears to have broken down, for want of a proper organization. This however is now being prepared. The men have formed a union with a view to speedy action.

Pforzheim.—The shoemakers' strike is at an end. The men asked for an advance of 20 per cent, and have got 15 per cent.

Mayence.—The strike in Wolfs' shoe-factory has been brought to a close by the employers withdrawing the notice of 15 per cent reduction of wages and paying to the men about £20 *towards the expenses of the strike.*

At Cologne the joiners, at Trier the tanners, were on the point of striking for higher wages.

Austria

Workers in wood visiting the Vienna Exhibition are informed that the Committee of the Vienna Union of the trade meets at the Florian Tavern, Stumpergasse, Mariahilf, Vienna.

[VI]

[*The International Herald*, No. 60, May 24, 1873]

America

The Gasmen of the New York Gas Company went on strike on April 5th for the restoration of the eight hours working day, which had been conceded to them some time ago, but soon lengthened again to 12 and 15 hours for night and day work respectively. The Republican police of the City of New York took at once the part of the Company, and sent strong detachments of constables to the different Gas Works: while the Charity Committee for Emigrants at once sent thither 200 Italians, just landed at Ward's Island,[a] to take the places of the men on strike. These Italians, marched to the works under a strong escort of police, and there compelled by brute force to perform a kind of work they were utterly unused to, and incompetent to perform, very soon demanded to be brought back to the Island. This was refused point blank and they were kept to work by the intervention of the police. Two of them tried to escape by climbing over the wall, but fell into the East River and were drowned; several others who tried the same experiment were recaptured by the police in the water; since then the Gas Works are surrounded, both on the land-side and on the water-side, by a cordon of police to prevent escapes from this new kind of prison. These Italians, moreover, are utterly incompetent for the work they are expected to perform.

This is the way in which the *Model Republic* proceeds, as soon as the working class, in demanding its rights, interferes with the interests of the comforts of the capitalist class.

Austria

Vienna.—The File-cutters' strike continues. The Tailors' strike is at an end—the men have gained considerable advantages if they could not carry all their points; their wages have been raised and their hours of labour reduced.

Graz.—Great agitation among the journeymen Bakers in order to reduce the working hours, hitherto *from 18 to 20 a day!*—The Joiners' strike continues.

The working men's agitation in Austria is everywhere proceeding in a most satisfactory manner.

Hungary

A general congress of the Hungarian Shoemakers is going to take place on the 1st June at Pesth. The Austrian Shoemakers

---

[a] Where the emigrants were placed in quarantine.— *Ed.*

intend to send delegates too. Amongst the questions to be discussed is the establishment of a normal working day of equal length all over the country, the establishment of a Hungarian Shoemaker's Union, and of co-operative workshops, etc.

Switzerland

The Jewellers' strike just closed by the victory of the men, has again proved what fools the masters are to themselves when they resist the just demands of the workmen. Barely one fourth of the strikers have returned to work; the rest have found employment elsewhere, and the masters now have the greatest difficulty in finding the sufficient number of men. Serves them right.

Germany

Halle.—A strike of Miners has been successful, it lasted only a few days, when the masters gave in.

Hamburg.—The Shoemakers' strike continues.

Altenburg.—The Tailors, after a short strike, obtained an advance of $16^2/_3$ per cent.

Numerous strikes are in preparation, among others, those of the Brushmakers of Berlin for 25 per cent advance; of the Saddlers of Stuttgart for 10 hours a day and 25 per cent advance, together with the abolition of compulsory boarding and lodging in the master's house.

A lock out has taken place among the Stonemasons of Zeitz and neighbourhood, but as this trade is internationally united in Germany, Austria, and Switzerland, success is pretty safe. The same association has a strike on its hands at Hamburg.

The annual general congress of the German Building Trades, will take place at Chemnitz (Saxony) in June.

Written in March-May 1873   Reproduced from the newspaper

First published in *The International Herald*, Nos. 51, 52, 54, 56, 57, 60, March 22 and 29, April 12 and 26, May 3 and 24, 1873

Frederick Engels

TO THE GENERAL COUNCIL
OF THE INTERNATIONAL
WORKING MEN'S ASSOCIATION

122 Regent's Park Road N. W.
London 15-th April 1873

Citizens,

I have received your letter of the 21-st March along with Bill
£8.-6 for Lodi. At the same time I received a letter from
Bignami stating that he was again hiding in order to avoid being
dragged to prison to undergo a sentence of imprisonment which
he prefers doing later on after having been restored to better
health. The money could therefore not have arrived at a more
favourable moment. I got it changed for 200 francs in *French*
banknotes which I sent to him immediately.

Le Moussu has undertaken to do the stamps[300] and I have
repeatedly reminded him of it, but as far as I know they are not
much advanced yet.

The *Arbeiter-Zeitung* has come to hand regularly.

The cost of printing of the Rules[a] in English and French was
about £15 each, those in German were much cheaper as they were
first printed in the *Volksstaat* and nothing charged for composition, but only for paper, printing and binding.[301] This of course
could not be repeated now.

The report on the Alliance[b] is now being drawn up, and
Lafargue & I work at it daily, no time is being lost. The
documents were kept by Lucain at Brussels until after Christmas,[c]
and he has some still.

German Rules are still here, several hundreds which are at the

---

a See this volume, pp. 3-20.— *Ed.*

b Ibid., pp. 454-580.— *Ed.*

c This refers to the papers of the Commission to investigate the Bakuninist
Alliance appointed at the Hague Congress.— *Ed.*

Council's[a] disposal. English none. French have all been sent to France, but not arrived. Perhaps we can recover some. We are trying.

As soon as the Alliance is put into shape, we shall do the Congress minutes.[302]

The *Emancipacion* of Madrid is dying if not dead. We have sent them £15.-, but as scarcely anybody paid for the copies received, it appears impossible to keep it up.[303] I am in correspondence with Mesa with regard to another paper to be started but cannot say what will be the result.

The *Pensamento Social* of Lisbon, an excellent paper which in its last number had a very good reply to the Spanish federal Commission of Alcoy on the Alliance question,[b] will also have to suspend its publication for a short time, but will reappear.

The International Herald, as you will have seen, also is on its last legs. We may try to keep it alive till the next English Congress (Whit-week)[304] after which it may be possible to start something else. The *Herald* is not worth much except as an organ of publicity for the B.F.C., but, as such, for the moment almost indispensable.

You will have seen from the French papers that Walter (Heddeghem) comes out as a downright spy. He is said to have been a Bonapartist *mouchard*.[c] At Toulouse, Swarm (Dentraygues) has not behaved much better, but not having read the full report, I cannot speak with certainty; at all events he was no *mouchard* before, but seems weak & capricious.

Fraternal Greeting

F. Engels

So far, no money has been received by me for the Council. No news either from Italy, except that temporarily the *Plebe* appears to be suspended too. The arrest of the Alliancists at Bologna & Mirandola will not last long, they will soon be liberated; if some of them are now and then arrested by mistake, they never suffer seriously.

First published in an abridged form, in   Reproduced from the manuscript
English, in: *Briefe und Auszüge aus Briefen
von Joh. Phil. Becker, Jos. Dietzgen, Friedrich
Engels, Karl Marx u. A. an F. A. Sorge und
Andere*, Stuttgart, 1906

---

[a] British Federal Council.— *Ed.*

[b] "Da commissao de correspondencia...", *O Pensamento Social*, No. 51, April 5, 1873.— *Ed.*

[c] Police agent.— *Ed.*

Frederick Engels

[ON THE ARTICLES
IN THE *NEUER SOCIAL-DEMOKRAT*
(FROM A LETTER TO A. HEPNER)] [305]

For your further information about the *Neuer*'s notorious article,[a] we wish to draw your attention—and, in part, not for the first time—to the following: a) to the absurdity of maintaining that Bakunin is against conspiracies, when he has instigated a general conspiracy—the Alliance—within the International, admittedly not against the government, but against the International; b) the notion that the International in France could lead any kind of existence *other than* a "secret" one after the Dufaure Law [306]; that, however, a secret propaganda society and a conspiracy are two different things; c) the fact that the Hague Congress came out so energetically against the Blanquists, who wanted to make the International a vehicle for conspiracies, that they withdrew from the International and openly declared that they were against it because it lacked "revolutionary energy"; d) the fact that Heddeghem (Walter), the tall quiet man in The Hague with red hair—accompanied by a small woman dressed in mourning with a Mary Magdalene face, allegedly his "wife"—who has now been unmasked as an old police agent, was only put forward to the old General Council by Serraillier for admittance, along with his branch, after he [Heddeghem] had referred to the Blanquist *Ranvier*, a member of the General Council, and was acknowledged by the latter as *thoroughly reliable*; e) the fact that both Heddeghem and Dentraygues had the mandates of their sections[b] as laid down in the Rules, and thus *had* to be admitted to the Congress, so long

---

[a] "Internationale Arbeiterassoziation", *Neuer Social-Demokrat*, No. 49, April 27, 1873.— *Ed.*

[b] Of the Paris and Toulouse sections respectively.— *Ed.*

as no charge was brought against them, which did not occur to any member of the minority; f) the fact that the *Neuer* cannot be considered anything but a police organ as it reiterates the catchphrase, disseminated by police agents and Bonapartists such as Vogt & Co., that Marx is attempting to act as an "international leader of conspirators"[a] and has already had "a dozen Communist trials", when the very actions of the Hague Congress, with whose majority Marx is identified, against the Blanquists prove the opposite, and the police lies about the *one* Communist trial of 1852 were exposed long ago by Marx's *Revelations Concerning the Communist Trial in Cologne*; g) the fact that if anyone from the *Neuer Social-Demokrat* is now, for once, sentenced to imprisonment, we know what we are to think, since the *Neuer* has itself drawn attention to the police manoeuvre of having police agents sentenced along with the others, but allowing them to lead a more comfortable life in prison. "*May the workers always keep their eyes open!*"[b]

Incidentally, Dentraygues was no spy, but a down-at-heel character, who only became an informer in *cachot*[c] and then soon became an out-and-out creature of the police. On the other hand, Heddeghem was already a *mouchard*[d] under Bonaparte; we have *only* the Blanquists to thank for him. The "grand old freedom fighter" Bakunin, however, has always had *mouchards* in his ranks—for example, Albert Richard, who has been his right-hand-man for France since 1868, since the foundation of the Alliance. And as the Jurassians claim that they *also* have secret sections in France[e] (the trials prove the converse[307]), where then is the difference affected by the *Neuer?*

As far as the article in No. 45[f] is concerned, a few things still need to be said about the claims made in it. Opposition to the Hague Congress has been voiced by: 1. The so-called Italian Federation, which has never belonged to the International because it refuses to recognise the General Rules, and for this reason can

---

[a] C. Vogt, *Mein Prozess gegen die Allgemeine Zeitung*, Geneva, December 1859.— *Ed.*

[b] Engels ironically quotes from the article in the *Neuer Social-Demokrat* under discussion.— *Ed.*

[c] Gaol.— *Ed.*

[d] Police agent.— *Ed.*

[e] "Les proconsuls marxistes en France", *Bulletin de la Fédération jurassienne...*, No. 8, April 15, 1873.— *Ed.*

[f] "Internationale Arbeiterassoziation", *Neuer Social-Demokrat*, No. 45, April 18, 1873.— *Ed.*

never belong to the International until it falls in line.—On the other hand, a number of genuine Italian sections have recognised them, and are in regular contact with the General Council. 2. The Jura Federation, 150 men, as against 4,000-5,000 in French Switzerland alone; it has, therefore, been suspended. 3. The Belgians. 4. Some of the Spaniards, while others have set up the Federal Council in Valencia, which is in regular contact with the General Council in New York. 5. In England all of ten men, who have not got a single real section behind them, while the English Federal Council, supported by numerous sections, several of which are 500 or more strong, and which are increasing week by week, makes recognition of the Hague resolutions a basic condition for admission. 6. The fact that, in France, "*insofar as any organisation survives there*", it has remained loyal to The Hague and the General Council is demonstrated *precisely* by the trials that are the pretext for the article in No. 49. The "*refugees of the Commune*", neither as such nor in their "majority", have ever had occasion for "turning energetically against, etc." since the faction never existed. The Blanquists, all five of them, including four members of the Commune,[a] have withdrawn because the International would not allow itself to become the *tool* of their conspiracy. Otherwise *nothing* whatsoever has occurred to provide the remotest pretext for this lie.

Written in late April 1873

First published in *Der Volksstaat*, No. 37, May 7, 1873

Printed according to the newspaper

Published in English for the first time

---

[a] The four Communards were, apparently, A. Arnaud, M. E. Vaillant, F. É. Cournet and G. Ranvier. The fifth Blanquist was Walter (L. Van-Heddeghem).— *Ed.*

Frederick Engels

THE INTERNATIONAL AND THE *NEUER*

London, May 2, 1873

No. 49 of the *Neuer* carries a mendacious article[a] about the latest trials of the International in France,[308] which will probably have earned its author an extra *douceur*[b] from the reptile funds,[309] so thickly does he lay on the lies. For the trial in Toulouse the *Neuer* refers to an article in the Brussels *Internationale*[c]; this article was itself borrowed from the *Liberté* and emanates from Mr. Jules Guesde,[d] a French refugee who, since his arrival in Geneva, has been blowing the Bakunist trumpet fit to burst, along with the other panjandrums in exile there, and was one of the signatories of the famous circular of the Jura Federation at the Jura Congress at Sonvillier (November 1871), in which the secret Alliance of Mr. Bakunin declared war on the public International.[e] We shall see presently what part Mr. Guesde played in the French International. He calls Mr. Dentraygues, who at this trial had denounced his co-defendants as members of the International, the general authorised representative of Marx and wants to transfer the blame for this betrayal and the subsequent sentences on Marx, the General Council, and the "authoritarian organisation from above".

Here are the facts.

On December 24, 1871, Mr. Dentraygues, a draughtsman at the railway office at Pézenas (Département Hérault), contacted the

---

[a] "Internationale Arbeiterassoziation", *Neuer Social-Demokrat*, No. 49, April 27, 1873.— *Ed.*

[b] Consideration.— *Ed.*

[c] "Nous extrayons les lignes suivantes...", *L'Internationale*, No. 223, April 20, 1873.— *Ed.*

[d] J. Guesde, "Les arrestations continuent...", *La Liberté*, No. 15, April 13, 1873.— *Ed.*

[e] See this volume, pp. 64-70, 102-05 and 116-22.— *Ed.*

General Council to announce that a radical democratic committee representing seven trade unions, whose president he was, was seeking admission to the International. On January 4, the secretary for France[a] wrote to Pézenas to Calas (now sentenced to one year), who was fully accredited by a reference from the affiliated Social-Democratic committee in Béziers (Hérault)—its members were also sentenced and were, moreover, known to be trustworthy by several members of the Commune present in London. On January 14, Calas gave Dentraygues a declaration of trustworthiness, saying that he had reached agreement with him: "we will play into each other's hands". In March, Dentraygues moved to Toulouse; thus, at the time of his arrest, he had been active there for a full nine months, and far from complaining about him, the Toulouse Internationals had always lived in harmony with him, and confirmed this on August 18, by selecting him *unanimously* in all four—large—sections as their delegate to the Hague Congress. The four mandates, signed only by the members of the committee and the group leaders, bear a total of 67 signatures. If, then, the General Council appointed this man as its authorised representative for Toulouse and area, it was merely expressing the wishes of the Toulouse members themselves.

Now for Mr. Guesde.

On August 18, 1872, the Montpellier section informed the General Council that Mr. Paul Brousse, a correspondent and friend of Mr. Guesde, was trying to bring about a split in the section; he was demanding that the members refuse to pay the agreed contributions to the travel expenses of the Toulouse delegate, in fact do nothing at all until the Hague Congress had decided. Mr. Brousse, it was said, had been expelled from the section for this; it requested the General Council to expel him from the International. The letter was signed by Calas and three others. The General Council knew that Mr. Brousse was engaged in intrigues on behalf of the secessionists of the Jura Federation, but considered it unnecessary to attribute any further importance to the young man—he was a medical student—and let him go. Mr. Guesde, then in Rome, wrote in early October to the *Liberté*[b] branding the quite natural steps of the Montpellier section as "authoritarian"; but while he designated his friend Brousse by his initial only, he had the name "Calas in Montpellier" *printed in full.* The French police needed no further prompting. A letter

a A. Serraillier.— *Ed.*

b J. Guesde, "Rien ou presque rien...", *La Liberté*, No. 42, October 20, 1872.— *Ed.*

despatched about this time from the secretary of the General Council[a] to Calas was immediately intercepted at the post office; in it there was much talk of Dentraygues; Dentraygues was immediately arrested and, shortly afterwards, so was Calas.

Who, then, was the informer—Dentraygues or Guesde?

When Mr. Guesde further says that the despatch of *missi dominici*[b] by the General Council, that the coming and going of delegates from outside, whose description is well known to the police, is the best way to betray the International in France,[c] he is forgetting:

1. that the three authorised representatives of the General Council in France[d] were not benefactors who had arrived from outside, but people resident at the places that had authorised them, who enjoyed the trust of the sections themselves;

2. that the only international "delegates from outside" who figured in Southern France last autumn and winter had not been sent by the General Council, but by the secessionists of the Jura Federation. These gentlemen were so loudmouthed in public cafés in Toulouse, etc., shortly before the arrests, that the attention of the police was thereby directed to our Association; and only the real Internationals were seized, as always and everywhere, while the anarchistic braggarts enjoy the special protection of the upper police echelons.

Although Mr. Dentraygues has made certain revelations for personal reasons and from weakness, there are sufficient grounds for proving he was not a police spy up to his conviction. In any event, the gentlemen of the Alliance, whose co-founder was the present Bonapartist agent Albert Richard of Lyons, have no cause whatsoever to throw stones at others, still less has the *Neuer*, whose political past and present constitute the worst blemish on the German labour movement.

As far as the Paris trial is concerned, it is now established that Heddeghem was a police spy. This man, appointed secretary by his section in Paris, gave as his reference the Communard and member of the General Council *Ranvier*, who gave him a splendid

[a] Engels apparently refers to A. Serraillier's letter to Calas of December 18, 1872, written on behalf of the New York General Council; it was intercepted by the French police.— *Ed.*

[b] Plenipotentiaries (in the Carolingian state, the appellation of officials exercising control over local administration).— *Ed.*

[c] [J. Guesde,] "Le Congrès de Mirandola...", *La Liberté*, No. 13, March 30, 1873.— *Ed.*

[d] Ch. Larroque, F. Argaing and L. Van-Heddeghem.— *Ed.*

testimonial with regard to his reliability and activity; Heddeghem was admitted on its basis. In this case, as in the first, the General Council had thus observed all the precautions at its disposal.

What is new is the assertion that Bakunin was expelled at The Hague because he wished to "eliminate the reprehensible engagement in secret conspiracies". The commission of the Hague Congress on the Alliance to which the rules of this Bakuninist secret conspiracy—not against the government but against the International—were submitted, came to a quite different result.

Just as new is the assertion that Marx has "experienced more than a dozen Communist trials of his followers". History knows of only one Communist trial, that in Cologne in 1852; but the *Neuer* is not paid for telling the truth. In any event, we shall bear in mind its final warning:

"The manoeuvre of the police force, when they bring about a political trial, of formally convicting their secret agents, too, but ensuring that they have a comfortable life in prison thereafter."

We should give heed to this passage taken from the "Life" of Herr von Schweitzer.

"So may the workers always keep their eyes open", if one day the gentlemen of the *Neuer* should happen to be "formally convicted"!

First published in *Der Volksstaat*, No. 38, May 10, 1873

Printed according to the newspaper

Published in English for the first time

Frederick Engels

[COMMUNICATION FROM THE CONTINENT] [310]

Communications from the Continent reported that the Secession movement, which had been set on foot in some places, had been followed by the usual result—Anarchy. Certain individuals, envying the cheap importance that the mere act of secession had given some of their fellows had resolved to learn the trick themselves, and had, of course, found no difficulty in setting up a very ready pretext in order to become Seceders from Secession. The attempt which had been made to remedy this state of things by inducing the erratic Sections to affiliate to the Jurassian Federation, though doubtless pleasing enough to M. M. Bakounin and Guillaume, whom it would have elevated to virtual dictatorship and to the national susceptibilities of a prime mover of the pernicious agitation in England,[a] had not been found so acceptable to the denizens of those other countries whose "Institutions" had escaped the blotting of a co-operative pennyworth of foggy elucidation.[311] Hence the anticipated result, the Secessionist fractions were rapidly thinning out into mere isolated groups, without a common understanding, except to quarrel with each other and to keep the peace towards the enemies of Labour—a situation which, though possibly not without its *charme* for a Morley, could only gain its full need of appreciation at the hands of a Thiers or a Bismarck.

Written on about May 22, 1873

First published in *The International Herald*, No. 60, May 24, 1873

Reproduced from the newspaper

---

[a] J. Hales.— *Ed.*

Frederick Engels

TO THE GENERAL COUNCIL OF THE INTERNATIONAL WORKING MEN'S ASSOCIATION

122 Regents Park Road N.W.
London, June 14th, 1873

Citoyens,

I have to reply to your two letters of the 11th April and 14th May. As communicated before,[a] the whole of the money for Lodi (fr. 200) was forwarded by me on April 10th to Bignami, new persecutions having arisen. The money was acknowledged by Bignami whose receipt I hold.— About 10 days ago, the *Plebe* has re-appeared and brought your address to the Spaniards and also, in a very prominent place, your declaration about the self-exclusion, from our Association, of the Secessionists.[312]

The documents in question have been sent to the Spanish Federal Council.

My copy of the alterations of rules as prepared for the late General Council[313] has disappeared, I have however been promised another which shall be forwarded as soon as received.

As the *Plebe* is alive again I shall report about Italian Emigration and Gas strike etc. in my first correspondence to that paper. I could not act before, my only correspondent Bignami being out of the way and not having given me another address.

Le Moussu has been reminded of the stamps.[b]

The £4.-3 are to hand and shall be used and directed as soon as a safe address in Paris can be found.

Fraternally yours,
F. Engels

First published in: Marx and Engels, *Works*, First Russian Edition, Vol. XXVI, Moscow, 1935

Reproduced from the manuscript

---

[a] See this volume, p. 437.— *Ed.*
[b] Ibid.— *Ed.*

Frederick Engels

FROM THE INTERNATIONAL[314]

For a long time, the *Volksstaat* has published nothing about the state of affairs in the International Working Men's Association except the official documents of the General Council in New York. It acted in the same way as all the other international papers and the greater part of the members of the Association itself. While the organs of the Hague minority led by the Bakuninist secret Alliance moved heaven and earth to present themselves as representatives of the real majority of the International, to defame and slander in every way the majority of the Congress, the old General Council and especially Marx, and to rally the unrecognised geniuses of all nations,—those attacked by them contented themselves with stating once and for all the real facts about the Hague Congress and to contrast the worst of the slanders against the facts. For the rest, they relied on the good sense of the workers and the actions of the General Council, which showed itself quite equal to the tasks of its position.

The following will show that this mode of action spontaneously adhered to without any further arrangements has borne fruit.

In *England*, several English members of the last General Council, in whose faces Marx threw in The Hague the accusation of corruption—on the basis of documentary proofs and their own admissions, without any of them daring to raise any objections—caused a split in the British Federal Council last December. They left and convened a secessionist congress, which consisted of *eleven* persons altogether, of whom no one even dared to say which sections they represented or whether they represented any at all.[315] The eleven persons spoke out in indignation against the Hague decisions and rallied under the banner of the secessionists, foremost among them two foreigners, *Eccarius* and *Jung*. From that moment, there were two federal councils, with the difference, however, that one of them, the international one, had almost all sections behind it, while the other, the secessionist one, represented no one but its own members. The latter played out this comedy for several months, but has finally passed away. One cannot play this sort of farce before the English workers, schooled by a fifty-year-old movement. On the other hand, the British Federation of the International held a congress at Manchester on June 1 and 2,[316] which was undoubtedly an epoch-making event in the English labour movement. It was attended by 26 delegates who represented the main centres of English industry as well as several smaller towns. The report of the Federal Council differed from all previous documents of this kind by the fact that—in a country with a tradition of legality—it asserted the right of the working class to *use force in order to realise* its demands.[a]

The congress approved the report and decided that the red flag is to be the flag of the British adherents of the International; the working class demands not only the return of all landed property to the working people but also of all means of production; it calls for the eight-hour working day as a preliminary measure; it sends congratulations to the Spanish workers who have succeeded in establishing a republic and in electing ten workers to the Cortes; and requests the English Government immediately to release all Irish Fenians[317] still imprisoned.—Anyone familiar with the history of the English labour movement will admit that no English workers' congress has ever advanced such far-reaching demands. In any case, this congress and the miserable end of the separatist, self-appointed Federal Council has determined the attitude of the British Section of the International.

In *Switzerland*, the secessionists have it just as tough. It is known that the Jura Federation was, from time immemorial, the soul of all secessionism [Sonderbündlerei] in the International.[318] Already at the Hague Congress its delegates declared that they represented the true majority of the International and would prove it at the next congress. But time is the best adviser, even to those who blow their own trumpet. On April 27 and 28, the Jura Federation held its congress in Neuchâtel. It transpires from the proceedings that

---

[a] "Report of the British Federal Congress, held at Manchester, June 1 and 2, 1873 ", *General and British Federative Rules of the International Working Men's Association, together with a Report of the Second Annual Congress of the British Federation, held at Manchester, June 1st & 2nd, 1873* [London, 1873]. The resolutions of the congress mentioned below were also published in that volume.— *Ed.*

the federation has *eleven* Swiss sections, out of which *nine* were represented. The report of the committee does not say a single word on the situation in these eleven sections, on their strength, etc.; on the other hand it declares that the whole International is, so to speak, solidly behind their secessionism.[a] Now, will this enormous majority come out at the next general congress and overturn the decisions of the Hague Congress? No, not exactly. On the contrary, the same committee proposes—and these "autonomous" delegates immediately accept the proposal: Lest the new congress should again fall in the dangerous errors of the Hague Congress, the secessionist federations should hold their own congress in some Swiss city and recognise no congress that might be convened by the New York General Council.

The Hague Congress expressly instructed the General Council to select a Swiss city in which to hold the next congress.[b] The decision of the Jura Federation thus signifies nothing but yet another climb-down hiding behind loud phrases.

In fact, it was time for these gentlemen to cover their rear. On June 1 and 2—fatal days for the secessionists—the congress of Swiss workers was held at Olten. Out of 80 delegates, there were *five* (!) Jurassians. It was proposed to found a centralised Swiss workers' union.

The five delegates from Jura[c] countered with a proposal for an artificial federal system limited by all sorts of provisos which would have made the whole organisation ineffective. As they were in a hopeless minority, they set to the work of wasting other people's time, just as in The Hague. The congress lost the whole Sunday debating this so-called "fundamental issue". Finally, the majority found itself compelled, just as in The Hague, to shut these tiresome talkers up, in order to get to work. On Monday it was simply decided to found a centralised union, whereupon the five preachers read out a meaningless statement, left the hall and went home. And these people, these complete nothings in their own land, have for years proclaimed their vocation to reorganise the International!

Well, it never rains but it pours. In Italy, where the anarchists of the secessionist variety are lording it for the present, one of them, Crescio of Piacenza, sent his new paper *L'Avvenire Sociale* (The

---

[a] "Le Congrès Jurassien, des 27 et 28 avril 1873", *Bulletin de la Fédération jurassienne...*, No. 9, May 1, 1873.— *Ed.*

[b] See this volume, p. 253.— *Ed.*

[c] J. L. Pindy, J. Guillaume, L. Schwitzguébel, Ch. Gameter, H. Wenker.— *Ed.*

Social Future) to Garibaldi, who, as these gentlemen constantly claim, is one of them. The paper was full of angry invective against what they call "the authoritarian principle", which in their view is at the root of all evil. Garibaldi replied:

"Dear Crescio, hearty thanks, etc. You intend, in your paper, to make war upon untruth and slavery. That is a very fine programme, but I believe that the International, in fighting against the principle of authority, makes a mistake and obstructs its own progress. *The Paris Commune fell because there was in Paris no authority but only anarchy.*"[a]

This veteran fighter for freedom who achieved more in one year—i.e., 1860—than all the anarchists will ever attempt in the course of their life, places a great value on discipline because he himself had to discipline his troops, and he did it not like the official soldiers, by drill and the threat of the firing-squad, but when facing the enemy.

Unfortunately we have not yet come to the end of the list of mishaps which the secessionists had to endure. Only one thing was still missing and that too took place. The *Neuer*, whose police nose had long since caught the peculiar smell of these arch mischief-makers of the International, now supports them whole-heartedly. In issue 68 the paper states[b] that the rules drafted by the Belgians[319]—who had in fact left the International—completely correspond to its views and holds out the prospect of its joining the secessionists. Thus all our wishes have been fulfilled. When Hasselmann and Hasenclever appear at the secessionist congress, this separatist organisation will acquire its true character. On the right Bakunin, on the left Hasenclever and in the middle the hapless Belgians, who are led by the nose of their Proudhonist phrases!

Written on June 19-20, 1873

First published in *Der Volksstaat*, No. 53, July 2, 1873

Printed according to the newspaper

Published in English in full for the first time

---

a G. Garibaldi, "Caro Crescio", *La Favilla*, No. 134, June 5, 1873 (cf. this volume, pp. 453 and 504).— *Ed.*

b "Internationale Arbeiterassoziation", *Neuer Social-Demokrat*, No. 68, June 18, 1873.— *Ed.*

Frederick Engels

[NOTE ON A REVIEW
OF E. RENAN'S *L'ANTÉCHRIST*][320]

I heard Renan's alleged discoveries, e.g., with regard to the exact dating, to the month, of the composition of the so-called Revelation of St. John, the solution of the mystical number 666=Νέρων Καῖσαρ and its confirmation by the variant 616=Nero Caesar, etc., etc.,[a] in Berlin in the winter term of 1841-42 at Professor Ferdinand Benary's lecture on the Apocalypse. Only Benary, the real solver of the mystical number, was honest enough to admit how much he owed to his predecessors,[b] while Mr. Renan, here as elsewhere, simply appropriates for himself the results of a protracted development in German science.

Written between July 5 and mid-July 1873	Printed according to the newspaper
First published in *Kölnische Zeitung*, No. 197 (First Instalment), July 18, 1873	Published in English for the first time

---

[a] E. Renan, *L'Antéchrist*, Paris, 1873.— *Ed.*
[b] F. Benary, "Erklärung der Zahl 666 <χζσ'> in der Apocalypse <13, 18.> und ihrer Variante 616 <χισ'>", *Zeitschrift für spekulative Theologie...*, Vol. 1, Part 2, Berlin, 1836, pp. 205-06.— *Ed.*

Frederick Engels

[COMMENT UPON GIUSEPPE GARIBALDI'S LETTER TO PROSPERO CRESCIO][321]

My dear Crescio,

Hearty thanks for sending to me your *Avvenire Sociale* which I shall read with interest.

You intend, in your paper, to make war upon untruth and slavery. That is a very fine programme, but I believe that the International, in fighting against the principle of authority, makes a mistake and obstructs its own progress. The Paris Commune fell because there was in Paris no authority but only anarchy. Spain and France are suffering from the same evil.

I wish success to the *Avvenire*, and,

Remain yours,

G. Garibaldi.[a]

It is necessary to explain that "the International" which Garibaldi evidently has in mind's eye is the Italian portion of the Association, the majority of which is, upon this very question of authority, in rebellion against the General Council. Garibaldi's censure of the "anti-authoritists" as they call themselves, is, therefore, a justification of the attitude which the Association generally, holds on this question.

Written between July 7 and 12, 1873

First published in *The Eastern Post*, No. 250, July 13, 1873

Reproduced from the newspaper

---

[a] G. Garibaldi, "Caro Crescio", *La Favilla*, No. 134, June 5, 1873.— *Ed.*

Karl Marx and Frederick Engels

THE ALLIANCE OF SOCIALIST DEMOCRACY AND THE INTERNATIONAL WORKING MEN'S ASSOCIATION [322]

REPORT AND DOCUMENTS PUBLISHED BY DECISION
OF THE HAGUE CONGRESS OF THE INTERNATIONAL

I

INTRODUCTION

The International Working Men's Association, in setting itself the aim of rallying under one banner the scattered forces of the world proletariat and thus becoming the living representative of the community of interests that unites the workers, was bound to open its doors to socialists of all shades. Its founders and the representatives of the workers' organisations of the Old and New worlds who at international congresses sanctioned the General Rules of the Association, forgot that the very scope of its programme would allow the declassed elements* to worm their way in and establish, at its very heart, secret organisations whose efforts, instead of being directed against the bourgeoisie and the existing governments, would be turned against the International itself. Such has been the case with the *Alliance of Socialist Democracy.*

At the Hague Congress, the General Council demanded an inquiry into this secret organisation. The Congress entrusted the

---

* In French the *déclassés* are people of the propertied classes who were ousted or who broke away from that class without thereby becoming proletarians, such as business adventurers, rogues and gamblers, most of them professional literati or politicians, etc. The proletariat, too, has its *déclassé* elements; they make up the lumpenproletariat. [*Engels's note to the 1874 German edition.*]

L'ALLIANCE

DE LA

DÉMOCRATIE SOCIALISTE

ET

L'ASSOCIATION INTERNATIONALE
DES TRAVAILLEURS.

RAPPORT ET DOCUMENTS PUBLIÉS PAR ORDRE DU
CONGRÈS INTERNATIONAL DE LA HAYE.

LONDRES :
A. DARSON, SUCCESSEUR DE FOUCAULT,
46B, RATHBONE PLACE, OXFORD ST.

HAMBOURG :
EN VENTE CHEZ OTTO MEISSNER.

1873.

PRICE TWO SHILLINGS.

Title page of Marx and Engels' pamphlet *The Alliance of Socialist Democracy and the International Working Men's Association*

task to a commission of five (citizens Cuno, Lucain, Splingard, Vichard and Walter, who resigned), which delivered its report at the session of September 7. The Congress passed the following resolution:

1. To expel from the International Mikhail Bakunin, as founder of the Alliance and also for an act committed on his own behalf;
2. To expel James Guillaume, as a member of the Alliance;
3. To publish the documents relating to the Alliance.

Since its members are scattered over various countries, the Commission of Inquiry into the Alliance was unable to publish the documents which were the basis of its report, and so Citizen Vichart, the only member resident in London, sent them to the protocol commission,[323] which is now publishing them, on its own responsibility, in the ensuing report.

The file on the Alliance was so voluminous that the commission sitting during the Congress only had time to familiarise itself with the most important documents in order to arrive at a practical conclusion; thus, most of the Russian material could not be submitted to it; and the report presented by it to the Congress,[a] since it only covered part of the question, can no longer be considered adequate. We have therefore been obliged to give a history of the Alliance so that the reader will be able to understand the meaning and importance of these documents.

The documents published by us belong to several categories. Some have already been published separately and mostly in French, but to understand the spirit of the Alliance properly, they must be compared with others, since, collated in this way, they appear in a new light. One of them is the programme of the public Alliance.[b] Other documents belong to the International and are being published for the first time; still others belong to the Spanish branch of the secret Alliance, whose existence was publicly disclosed in the spring of 1872[c] by members of the Alliance. Anyone who has followed the Spanish movement during this period will only find more detailed information on facts which have already been made more or less public. These documents are important, not because they are being published for the first time, but because it is the first time that they have been compared in such a manner as to reveal the common secret action from which

---

[a] "Rapport de la commission d'enquête sur la Société l'Alliance", La Liberté, No. 37, September 15, 1872.— Ed.

[b] See this volume, pp. 577-78.— Ed.

[c] The original mistakenly has: "1871".— Ed.

they originated, and above all because we are comparing them with the two categories of documents which follow. The first consists of documents published in Russian which disclose the true programme and methods of the Alliance. These documents, thanks to the language which protected them, remained hitherto unknown in the West, and this circumstance made it possible for the authors to give free rein to their imagination and their language. The faithful translations furnished by us will allow the reader to gauge the intellectual, moral, political and economic worth of the Alliance's leaders.

The second category consists of a single document: the Alliance's secret statutes; it is the only document of any substantial length that is being published, for the first time, in this report. It may be asked whether revolutionaries are permitted to publish the statutes of a secret society, of a supposed conspiracy. First, these secret statutes were expressly named among the documents whose publication was demanded at the Hague Congress by the Alliance commission and none of the delegates, not even the member constituting the minority of the commission,[a] voted against this. This publication has therefore been formally ordered by the Congress, whose instructions we must carry out; but it is essential to point out the following:

Here we have a society which, under the mask of the most extreme anarchism, directs its blows not against the existing governments but against the revolutionaries who accept neither its dogma nor its leadership. Founded by a minority at a bourgeois congress,[324] it infiltrates the ranks of the international organisation of the working class, at first attempts to dominate it and, when this plan fails, sets to work to disorganise it. It brazenly substitutes its sectarian programme and narrow ideas for the broad programme and great aspirations of our Association; it organises within the public sections of the International its own little secret sections which obey the same instructions and in a good many instances succeed in gaining control of the public sections by prearranged action; in its newspapers it publicly attacks all those who refuse to submit to its will, and by its own avowal provokes open warfare within our ranks. It resorts to any means, any disloyalty to achieve its ends; lies, slander, intimidation, the stab in the back—it finds them all equally suitable. Finally, in Russia it substitutes itself entirely for the International and commits, in its name, crimes against the common law, acts of fraud and an assassination for

---

[a] Splingard.— Ed.

which the government and bourgeois press has blamed our Association. And the International must remain silent about all these acts because the society responsible for them is secret! The International has in its possession the statutes of this society, which is its mortal enemy; statutes in which it openly proclaims itself a modern Society of Jesus and declares that it has the right and the duty to practise all the methods employed by the Jesuits; statutes that explain in a flash the whole series of hostile acts to which the International has been subjected from this quarter; but the International must not make use of these statutes—that would be denouncing a secret society!

There is only one means of combating all these intrigues, but it will prove astonishingly effective; this means is complete publicity. Exposure of all these schemings in their entirety will render them utterly powerless. To protect them with our silence would be not only an act of naïveté that the leaders of the Alliance would be the first to ridicule; it would be sheer cowardice. What is more, it would be an act of treachery towards those Spanish members of the International who, while belonging to the secret Alliance, have not hesitated to divulge its existence and its mode of action, since it has set itself up in open hostility to the International. Besides, all that is contained in the secret statutes is to be found, in much more emphatic form, in the documents published in Russian by Bakunin and Nechayev themselves. The statutes are but their confirmation.

Let the ringleaders of the Alliance cry out that they have been denounced. We deliver them up to the scorn of the workers and the benevolence of the governments whom they have served so well in disorganising the proletarian movement. The Zurich *Tagwacht,* in a reply to Bakunin, had every right to say:

"If you are not a paid agent, the one thing quite certain is that a paid agent would never have succeeded in doing as much harm as you." [a]

II

THE SECRET ALLIANCE

The Alliance of Socialist Democracy is entirely bourgeois in origin. It did not emerge from the International; it is the

---

[a] "Diese Anmerkungen...", an editorial note to Bakunin's letter "An die Redaktion der *Tagwacht* in Zürich" of February 14, 1872, *Die Tagwacht,* No. 11, March 16, 1872.— *Ed.*

offspring of the League of Peace and Freedom, a still-born bourgeois republican society. The International was already firmly established when Mikhail Bakunin took it into his head to play the part of the proletariat's emancipator. The International only offered him a field of activity common to all its members. In order to secure advancement there, he would have had to win his spurs by dint of hard and dedicated work; he thought he would find a better opportunity and an easier path on the side of the bourgeois members of the League.

Thus, in September 1867, he had himself elected member of the Permanent Committee of the League of Peace, and he took his part seriously; it could even be said that he and Barni, now a deputy at Versailles, were the life and soul of this committee. Posing as theoretician of the League, Bakunin was to have published under its auspices a work entitled *Le fédéralisme, le socialisme et l'anti-théologisme.** However, he soon realised that the League was still an insignificant society and that the liberals of which it was composed only saw in its congresses a means of combining pleasure trips with high-flown harangues, while the International, in contrast, was growing from day to day. He now dreamed of grafting the League onto the International. To put this plan into practice, Bakunin, on Elpidin's introduction, had himself accepted in July 1868 as member of the Geneva Central Section[a]; on the other hand, he got the League Committee to adopt a proposal suggesting that the International Congress of Brussels should form a pact of offensive and defensive alliance between the two societies; and in order that the League's Congress should sanction this fiery initiative, he drew up, and then made the Committee endorse and distribute, a confidential circular to the "Gentlemen" of the League.[325] In it, he admitted frankly that the League, hitherto a hopeless farce, could not gain in importance except by opposing the alliance of the oppressors with

"the alliance of the peoples, the alliance of the workers ... we will not become anything unless we wish to be the sincere and serious representatives of millions of workers."

The providential mission of the holy League was to present a bourgeois parliament, nominated by itself, to the working class, which was invited to entrust this body with its political management.

---

* This bible of *isms* was discontinued by the third sheet owing to lack of copy.

---

a Of the International.— *Ed.*

"In order to become a beneficial and real power," concludes the circular, "our League must become *the pure political expression* of the great economic and social interests and principles which are triumphantly developed and propagated today by the great International Association of the Working Men of Europe and America."

The Congress of Brussels had the temerity to reject the League's proposition.[326] Bakunin's disappointment and fury knew no bounds. On the one hand, the International was slipping out of his protection. On the other, the League's chairman, Professor Gustav Vogt, read him a stern lecture.

"Either you were not sure," he wrote to Bakunin, "of the effect of our invitation, in which case you have compromised our League; or you knew what a surprise your friends of the International had in store for us, in which case you have most infamously deceived us. I ask you what we are going to tell our Congress..." [327]

Bakunin replied in a letter which anyone was invited to read.

"I could not have foreseen," he said, "that the Congress of the International would reply with an insult as gross as it was pretentious, but this is due to the intrigues of a certain clique of Germans who detest the Russians" (verbally, he explained to his audience that this clique was Marx's). "You ask me what we are going to do. I earnestly request the honour of replying to this gross insult on behalf of the Committee, from the platform of our Congress."

Instead of keeping his word, Bakunin changed his tune. He proposed to the League's Berne Congress a programme of fantasy socialism in which he called for equalisation of classes and individuals,[a] in order to outdo the ladies of the League who had hitherto only demanded equalisation of the sexes. Defeated again, he left the Congress with an insignificant minority and went to Geneva.*

The alliance of bourgeois and workers dreamed of by Bakunin was not to be limited to a public alliance. The secret statutes of the Alliance of Socialist Democracy (see Documents, No. 1[b]) contain indications which make it clear that, in the very heart of the League, Bakunin had laid the foundations for the secret society which was to control it. Not only are the names of the governing

---

* Among the secessionists, we find the names of Albert Richard from Lyons, now an agent of the Bonapartist police; Gambuzzi, a Neapolitan lawyer (see the chapter on Italy); Zhukovsky, later secretary of the public Alliance; and a certain Buttner, a Geneva tinsmith, who now belongs to the ultra-reactionary party.

[a] *Discours de Bakounine et de Mroczkowski au deuxième Congrès de la Paix, à Berne, Kolokol,* No. 14/15, December 1, 1868.— *Ed.*

[b] See this volume, p. 571.— *Ed.*

bodies identical to those of the League (Permanent Central Committee, Central Bureau, National Committees), but the secret statutes declare that the "majority of the founder members of the Alliance" are "former members of the Berne Congress". In order to win recognition for himself as head of the International, he had to present himself as head of another army whose absolute devotion to him was to be ensured by a secret organisation. After having openly planted his society in the International, he counted on extending its ramifications into all sections and on taking over absolute control by this means. With this aim, he founded the (public) Alliance of Socialist Democracy in Geneva. Ostensibly, this was only a public society which, although entirely absorbed by the International, was, however, to have a separate international organisation, a central committee, national bureaux, and sections independent of our Association; alongside our annual Congress, the Alliance was to hold its own publicly. But this public Alliance covered another which, in its turn, was controlled by the even more secret Alliance of the international brethren, the Bodyguard Hundred of the dictator Bakunin.

The secret statutes of the "organisation of the Alliance of the international brethren" indicate that in this Alliance there were "three grades: I. *The international brethren*; II. *the national brethren*; III. the half-secret, half-public organisation of the *International Alliance of Socialist Democracy*".

I. The international brethren, whose number is limited to a "hundred", form the college of cardinals. They are subordinate to a central committee and to national committees organised into executive bureaux and supervisory committees. These committees are themselves responsible to the "constituent", or general, assembly of at least two-thirds of the international brethren. These members of the Alliance

"have no homeland other than the world revolution, no foreign land and no enemy other than the reaction. They reject any policy of negotiation and concession, and regard as reactionary any political movement which does not have as its immediate and direct goal the triumph of their principles".

But since this article relegates to the Greek Calends the political action of the Hundred, and since these irreconcilable ones do not intend to renounce the advantages attached to public functions, Article 8 reads:

"No brother shall accept a public post except with the consent of the Committee to which he belongs."

We shall see, when we come to discuss Spain and Italy, how the leaders of the Alliance hastened to implement this article in practice. The international brethren

"are brethren ... each of whom must be sacred to all the others, more sacred than a blood brother. Each brother shall be helped and protected by all the others *to the limits of the possible.*"

The Nechayev affair will show us what this mysterious limit of the possible is.

"All the international brethren know one another. *No political secret must ever exist among them.* None may take part in any secret society whatever without the positive consent of his Committee and, if necessary, should the latter so demand, without that of the Central Committee. And he may take part only on condition that he reveals to them all the secrets that could interest them directly or indirectly."

The Pietris and the Stiebers only use inferior or lost people as informers; but by sending their false brethren into secret societies to betray secrets of the latter, the Alliance imposes the role of spy on the very men who, according to its plan, should take control of the "world revolution".—Moreover, the revolutionary buffoon crowns the ignoble with the grotesque.

"Only he may become an international brother who has sincerely accepted all the programme in all its consequences, theoretical and practical, and who adds revolutionary passion to intelligence, energy, honesty" (!) "and discretion—he *who has the devil in his flesh.*"

II. The national brethren are organised in each country as a national association by the international brethren and under the same plan, but in no case should they suspect even the existence of an international organisation.

III. The Secret International Alliance of Socialist Democracy, whose members are recruited everywhere, has a legislative body in the *Permanent Central Committee* which, when it meets, christens itself the General Secret Assembly of the Alliance. This meeting takes place once a year during the Congress of the International, or, in special cases, when convoked by the Central Bureau or else by the Geneva Central Section.

The *Geneva Central Section* is the "permanent delegation of the permanent Central Committee", and the "Executive Council of the Alliance". It is subdivided into the *Central Bureau* and the *Supervisory Committee.* The Central Bureau, consisting of 3 to 7 members, is the real executive power of the Alliance:

"it will receive its guidance from the Geneva Central Section and will pass on its communications, *not to say its secret orders,* to all the National Committees, from which it will receive secret reports at least once a month."

This Central Bureau has found a way of having its cake and eating it, of being secret and public at the same time; for, as part of the

"secret central section, the Central Bureau shall be a secret organisation ... as the executive directorate of the public Alliance, it shall be a public organisation".

And so it can be seen that Bakunin had already organised all the secret and public direction of his "dear Alliance" even before it existed, and that the members who took part in any election were only puppets in a play staged by himself. Moreover, he did not hesitate to say so, as we shall soon see.—The Geneva Central Section, whose task was to guide the Central Bureau, was itself only part of the comedy; for its decisions, although settled by majority vote, were only binding on the Bureau if the majority of its members did not wish to appeal against them to the general assembly, which it must convoke at three weeks' notice.

"To be regular, the General Assembly, when thus convoked, must be composed of two-thirds of all its members."

It can be seen that the Central Bureau had surrounded itself with all the constitutional guarantees necessary to ensure its independence.

One might be naive enough to believe that this autonomous Central Bureau had at least been freely elected by the Geneva Central Section. Nothing of the kind. The provisional Central Bureau had been

"presented to the Geneva initiating group as provisionally elected by all the founder members of the Alliance, of whom the majority, as former members of the Berne Congress, have returned to their countries" (except for Bakunin) "*after having delegated their powers to Citizen B.*"

The founder members of the Alliance were thus nothing more than a few bourgeois secessionists from the League of Peace.

In this way, the Permanent Central Committee, which had annexed the constituent and legislative power over the whole Alliance, was nominated by itself. The permanent executive delegation of this Permanent Central Committee, the Geneva Central Section, was nominated by itself and not by this Committee. The Central Executive Bureau of this Geneva Central Section, instead of being elected by it, was imposed on it by a group of individuals who had all "delegated their powers to Citizen B."

And so "Citizen B." is the pivot of the Alliance. To retain his pivotal function, the secret statutes of the Alliance say literally:

"Its ostensible form of government will be that of a presidency in a federative republic",—

a presidency prior to which the president already existed in permanent "Citizen B."

Since the Alliance is an international society, each country is to have a National Committee formed

"of all the members of the Permanent Central Committee who belong to the same nation".

It only requires three members to constitute a National Committee. To ensure the regularity of the hierarchical ladder,

"the National Committees will serve as the *sole* intermediaries between the Central Bureau and all the local groups of their country".

The National Committees

"shall have the task of organising the Alliance in their countries so that it shall *always be dominated* and represented at the Congresses by members of the Permanent Central Committee".

This is what is known in the language of the Alliance as organising from the bottom to the top. These local groups only have the right to approach the National Committees with their programmes and rules so that they might be submitted

"for confirmation by the Central Bureau, without which the local groups cannot belong to the Alliance".

Once this despotic and hierarchic secret organisation had been injected into the International, all that remained to finish matters was to disorganise it. All it needed for this was to anarchise and autonomise its sections and transform its central organs into simple letter-boxes—"correspondence and statistical bureaus"—as was, indeed, attempted later.

The list of revolutionary services rendered by permanent "Citizen B." was not so glorious that he could hope to make permanent in the secret Alliance, much less in the public one, the dictatorship which he had appropriated for his own convenience. He therefore had to hide it under democratic-sounding humbug. And so the secret statutes prescribe that the provisional Central Bureau (for which read the permanent citizen) will function until the Alliance's first public general assembly, which would nominate the members of the new Permanent Central Bureau. But "as it is urgent that the Central Bureau should always consist of members of the Permanent Central Committee, this latter, through the organ of its National Committees, will take care to organise and *direct* all the local groups in such a way that they will *delegate* to this assembly *only members of the Permanent Central Committee* or, failing them, men *absolutely devoted to the leadership* of their respective National Committees, so that the Permanent Central Committee *should always have the upper hand* in the entire organisation of the Alliance".

These instructions were not given by a Bonapartist minister or prefect on the eve of the elections, but, in order to ensure his permanence, by the anti-authoritarian, quintessential, immense anarchist, the archpriest of the organisation from bottom to top, the Bayard of the autonomy of sections and the free federation of autonomous groups—Saint-Michael Bakunin.

So far we have analysed the secret organisation designed to perpetuate the dictatorship of "Citizen B."; now let us deal with his programme.

"The association of international brethren aims for a universal revolution, simultaneously social, philosophical, economic and political, so that of the present order of things—based on private property, exploitation, and the principle of authority, whether religious, metaphysical, bourgeois-doctrinaire, or even Jacobin-revolutionary—not a stone shall remain standing, first in all Europe and then throughout the rest of the world. With the cry of peace for the workers, liberty for all the oppressed and death to the rulers, exploiters and guardians of all kinds, we seek to destroy all states and all churches along with all their institutions and laws, religious, political, juridical, financial, police, university, economic and social, so that all these millions of poor human beings, deceived, enslaved, tormented and exploited, delivered from all their directors and benefactors, official and officious, collective and individual, may breathe at last with complete freedom."

Here indeed we have revolutionary revolutionism! The first condition for the achievement of this astounding goal is to refuse to fight the existing states and governments with the means employed by ordinary revolutionaries, but on the contrary to hurl resounding, grandiloquent phrases at

"the institution of the State and that which is both its consequence and basis—i.e., private property".

Thus it is not the Bonapartist State, the Prussian or Russian State that has to be overthrown, but an abstract State, the State as such, a State that nowhere exists. But while the international brethren in their desperate struggle against this State that is situated somewhere in the clouds know how to avoid the truncheons, the prison and the bullets that real states deal out to ordinary revolutionaries, we see on the other hand that they have reserved themselves the right, subject only to papal dispensation, to profit by all the advantages offered by these real bourgeois states. Fanelli, an Italian deputy, Soriano, an employee of the government of Amadeus of Savoy, and perhaps Albert Richard and Gaspard Blanc, Bonapartist police agents, show how amenable the Pope is in this respect... That is why the police shows so little concern over "the Alliance or, to put it frankly, the conspiracy" of Citizen B. against the abstract idea of the state.

The first act of the revolution, then, must be to decree the abolition of the state, as Bakunin did on September 28 in Lyons,[328] despite the fact that this abolition of the state is of necessity an authoritarian act. By the state he means all political power, revolutionary or reactionary,

"for it matters little to us that this authority calls itself church, monarchy, constitutional state, bourgeois republic, or even revolutionary dictatorship. We detest them and we reject them all alike as infallible sources of exploitation and despotism".

And he goes on to declare that all the revolutionaries who, on the day after the revolution, want "construction of a revolutionary state" are far more dangerous than all the existing governments put together, and that

"we, the international brethren, are the natural enemies of these revolutionaries"

because to disorganise the revolution is the first duty of the international brethren.

The reply to this bragging about the immediate abolition of the state and the establishment of anarchy has already been given in the last General Council's private circular on "Fictitious Splits in the International", of March 1872, page 37 [a]:

"Anarchy, then, is the great war-horse of their master Bakunin, who has taken nothing from the socialist systems except a set of labels. All socialists see anarchy as the following programme: once the aim of the proletarian movement, i.e., abolition of classes, is attained, the power of the State, which serves to keep the great majority of producers in bondage to a very small exploiter minority, disappears, and the functions of government become simple administrative functions. The Alliance reverses the whole process. It proclaims anarchy in proletarian ranks as the most infallible means of breaking the powerful concentration of social and political forces in the hands of the exploiters. Under this pretext, it asks the International, at a time when the old world is seeking a way of crushing it, to replace its organisation with anarchy."

[a] See this volume, pp. 121-22.— Ed.

Let us see, however, just what the consequences of the anarchist gospel are; let us suppose the state has been abolished by decree. According to Article 6,[a] the consequences of this act will be: the bankruptcy of the state, an end to the payment of private debts by the intervention of the state, an end to the payment of all taxes and all contributions, the dissolution of the army, the magistrature, the bureaucracy, the police and the clergy (!); the abolition of official justice, accompanied by an auto-da-fé of all title-deeds and all judicial and civil junk, the confiscation of all productive capital and instruments of labour for the benefit of the workers' associations and an alliance of these associations, which "will form the Commune". This Commune will give individuals thus dispossessed the strict necessaries of life, while granting them freedom to earn more by their own labour.

What happened at Lyons has proved that merely decreeing the abolition of the state is far from sufficient to accomplish all these fine promises. Two companies of the bourgeois National Guards proved quite sufficient, on the other hand, to shatter this splendid dream and send Bakunin hurrying back to Geneva with the miraculous decree in his pocket. Naturally he could not imagine his supporters to be so stupid that they need not be given some sort of plan of organisation that would put his decree into practical effect. Here is the plan:

"For the organisation of the Commune—a federation of permanently acting barricades and the functioning of a Council of the Revolutionary Commune by the delegation of one or two deputies from each barricade, and one per street, or per block, these deputies being invested with imperative mandates and always responsible and revocable at any time" (odd barricades, these barricades of the Alliance, where instead of fighting they spend their time writing mandates). "The *Commune Council*, thus organised, will be able to elect from its membership special *Executive Committees* for each branch of the revolutionary administration of the Commune."

The insurgent capital, thus constituted as a Commune, then proclaims to the other communes of the country that it renounces all claim to govern them; it invites them to reorganise themselves in a revolutionary way and then to send their responsible and recallable deputies, vested with their imperative mandates, to an agreed place where they will set up a federation of insurgent associations, communes and provinces and organise a revolutionary *force* capable of triumphing over reaction. This organisation will not be confined to the communes of the insurgent country; other provinces or countries will be able to take part in it, while

---

[a] See pp. 575-76 of this volume.— *Ed.*

"the provinces, communes, associations and individuals that side with the reaction *shall be debarred from it*".

So the abolition of frontiers goes hand in hand with the most benevolent tolerance towards the reactionary provinces, which would not hesitate to resume the civil war.

Thus in this anarchistic organisation of the tribune-barricades we have first the Commune Council, then the executive committees which, to be able to be anything at all, must be vested with some power and supported by a public force; this is to be followed by nothing short of a federal *parliament*, whose principal object will be to organise this *public force*. Like the Commune Council, this parliament will have to assign *executive power* to one or more *committees* which by this act alone will be given an authoritarian character that the demands of the struggle will increasingly accentuate. We are thus confronted with a perfect reconstruction of all the elements of the "authoritarian State"; and the fact that we call this machine a "revolutionary Commune organised from bottom to top", makes little difference. The name changes nothing of the substance; organisation from bottom to top exists in any bourgeois republic and imperative mandates date from the Middle Ages. Indeed Bakunin himself admits as much when (in Article 8 [a]) he describes his organisation as a "new revolutionary State".

As for the practical value of this plan of revolution with its talking instead of fighting, we shall say nothing.

Now we shall reveal the secret of all the Alliance's double and triple-bottomed boxes. To make sure that the orthodox programme is adhered to and that anarchy behaves itself properly,

"it is necessary that in the midst of popular anarchy, which will constitute the very life and energy of the revolution, *unity of revolutionary idea and action should find an organ*. This organ must be the *secret and world association of the international brethren*.

"This association proceeds from the conviction that revolutions are never made either by individuals or by secret societies. They come about, as it were, of their own accord, produced by the force of things, by the course of events and facts. They are prepared over a long time deep in the instinctive consciousness of the popular masses, and then they flare up.... All that a well-organised secret society can do is, first, to assist in the birth of the revolution by spreading among the masses ideas corresponding to their instincts, and to organise, not the army of the revolution—the army must always be the people" (cannon fodder), "but *a revolutionary General Staff* composed of devoted, energetic, intelligent and above all sincere friends of the people, who are not ambitious or vain, and who are capable of serving as intermediaries between the revolutionary idea" (monopolised by them) "and the popular instincts."

---

[a] See p. 576 of this volume.— *Ed.*

"The number of these individuals should not, therefore, be too large. For the international organisation in the whole of Europe *a hundred firmly and seriously united revolutionaries would be sufficient.* Two or three hundred revolutionaries would be enough for the organisation of the biggest country."

So everything changes. Anarchy, the "unleashing of popular life", of "evil passions" and all the rest is no longer enough. To assure the success of the revolution one must have *unity of thought and action.* The members of the International are trying to create this unity by propaganda, by discussion and the public organisation of the proletariat. But all Bakunin needs is a secret organisation of one hundred people, the privileged representatives of the *revolutionary idea,* the general staff in the background, self-appointed and commanded by the permanent "Citizen B". Unity of thought and action means nothing but orthodoxy and blind obedience. *Perinde ac cadaver.*[a] We are indeed confronted with a veritable Society of Jesus.

To say that the hundred international brethren must "serve as intermediaries between the revolutionary idea and the popular instincts", is to create an unbridgeable gulf between the Alliance's revolutionary idea and the proletarian masses; it means proclaiming that these hundred guardsmen cannot be recruited anywhere but from among the privileged classes.

III

THE ALLIANCE IN SWITZERLAND

The Alliance, like Falstaff, found that "the better part of valour is discretion".[b] Also, the "devil in the flesh" of the international brethren did not prevent them from deferring humbly in every way to the power of the existing States, while protesting vigorously against the institution of the abstract State; but he directed their attacks solely against the International. First, they wanted to dominate it. Having failed to do so, they tried to disorganise it. We shall now show their activities in the different countries.

The international brethren were merely a general staff in the reserve: they lacked an army. They considered the International created to that end. If they were to be allowed to take command

---

[a] "Be like unto a corpse." The phrase used by St. Ignatius of Loyola, founder of the Society of Jesus, to formulate the Jesuit principle imposing unquestioning obedience on the junior members of the Society.— *Ed.*

[b] W. Shakespeare, *King Henry IV,* Part I, Act 5, Scene 4.— *Ed.*

of an army, they had to insinuate the public Alliance into the International. Fearing that the former might lose face if they applied to the General Council for admission, which would be tantamount to recognising its authority, they approached the Belgian and Paris Federal Councils several times and without success. These repeated refusals forced the Alliance to ask the General Council, on December 15, 1868, for affiliation.[a] They sent their statutes and their programme in which they openly announced their intentions (Documents, No. 2[b]). Although the Alliance declared itself "entirely absorbed by the International" it aspired to form a second international corps within the International. Alongside the International's General Council, elected by the Congresses, there was to be the Alliance's Central Committee, which would sit at Geneva and would be self-nominated; alongside the International's local groups, there would be the Alliance's local groups which, through the intermediary of their national bureaux, functioning outside the national bureaux of the International, "would apply to the Alliance's Central Bureau for their admission into the International". The Central Bureau of the Alliance was, then, appropriating the right of admittance to the International. Alongside the Congresses of the International, there were to be the Congresses of the Alliance, for "during the annual working men's Congresses, the Alliance's delegation" aspired to hold "its public sittings in separate premises".

On December 22, the General Council (in a letter published in its circular: *Fictitious Splits in the International,* p. 7[c]) stating that these aspirations were in flagrant contradiction to the International's rules, flatly rejected the affiliation of the Alliance. Several months later, the Alliance again applied to the General Council and demanded to know whether its principles were acceptable or not. In case of an affirmative answer, it declared itself prepared to dissolve and break up into simple sections of the International. On March 9, 1869, the General Council (see *Fictitious Splits in the International,* p. 8[d]) replied that for it to pronounce on the scientific value of the Alliance's programme would be to exceed its functions, and that if "equalisation of classes" was replaced by "abolition of classes", there would be no obstacle to converting the sections of the Alliance into sections of the International. It added:

---

[a] The Alliance's address was dated November 29, 1868; on December 15 it was discussed in the General Council of the International.— *Ed.*

[b] See this volume, pp. 577-78.— *Ed.*

[c] Ibid., pp. 86-87.— *Ed.*

[d] Ibid., pp. 88-89.— *Ed.*

"*The dissolution of the Alliance and the entrance of its sections into the International* once settled, it would, according to our Regulations, become necessary *to inform the Council of the seat and the numerical strength of each new section.*"

On June 22, 1869, the Geneva section of the Alliance announced to the General Council as a *fait accompli* the dissolution of the International Alliance of Socialist Democracy, all of whose sections had been invited "to transform themselves into the International sections". After this explicit declaration, and misled by some signatures on the programme which gave the impression that the Alliance had been recognised by the Romance Federal Committee, the General Council admitted it. It should be added that not one of the conditions accepted had ever been fulfilled. Far from it: the secret organisation hidden behind the public Alliance now went into full action. Behind the International's Geneva section was the Central Bureau of the secret Alliance; behind the International's sections of Naples, Barcelona, Lyons and Jura hid the secret sections of the Alliance. Relying on this free-masonry, whose existence was suspected neither by the mass of the International's membership nor by their administrative centres, Bakunin hoped to win control of the International at the Basle Congress in September 1869. At this Congress, thanks to its dishonest methods, the secret Alliance found itself represented by at least ten delegates, including the famous Albert Richard and Bakunin himself. They had brought with them a number of blank mandates which could not be used owing to the lack of reliable people, although they were offered to the Basle members of the International. Even this numerical strength, however, was not enough to make Congress sanction the abolition of the right of inheritance, that relic of Saint-Simon which Bakunin wanted to use as the practical point of departure for socialism[329]; much less was it able to impose on the Congress his dream of transferring the General Council from London to Geneva.

Meanwhile, there was open war in Geneva between the Romance Federal Committee, almost unanimously supported by the Geneva members of the International, and the Alliance. The latter's allies in this war were *Le Progrès* of Locle edited by James Guillaume, and *L'Égalité* of Geneva which, although an official organ of the Romance Federal Committee, was edited by a committee which mainly consisted of the Alliance members and attacked the Romance Federal Committee at every possible opportunity. Without losing sight of its great aim—the transfer of the seat of the General Council to Geneva—the editorial board of

L'Égalité launched a campaign against the existing General Council and invited *Le Travail* of Paris to lend its support. In its circular of January 1, 1870, the General Council declared that it considered it unnecessary to enter into controversy with these newspapers.[a] Meanwhile, the Romance Federal Committee had already removed the Alliance members from the editorial board of *L'Égalité*.

At this stage, the sect had not yet donned its anti-authoritarian mask. Believing that it would be able to take over the General Council, it was the first, at the Basle Congress, to put forward and edit the administrative resolutions conceding to the latter the "authoritarian powers" which it was to attack so violently two years later. Nothing gives a clearer picture of its idea of the General Council's authoritarian role than the following extract from *Le Progrès* of Locle edited by James Guillaume (December 4, 1869)[b] concerning the conflict between the *Social-Demokrat* and *Der Volksstaat*[330]:

> "It seems to us that it should be the *duty* of our Association's General Council to *intervene*, to open an inquiry into what is happening in Germany, to *decide* between Schweitzer and Liebknecht, and *thereby put a stop to the uncertainty* into which we are thrown by this strange situation."

Is it possible to believe that this is the same Guillaume who, in a circular from Sonvillier on November 12, 1871, reproached this same General Council, which had not been authoritarian enough previously, for having "wanted to introduce the *principle of authority* into the International"?[c]

Ever since they began to appear, the Alliance's newspapers had not confined themselves to propagating its special programme, in which no one could have seen any harm; but they insisted on creating and interposing a premeditated confusion between its own programme and that of the International. This occurred wherever the Alliance was running, or collaborating with, a newspaper—in Spain, in Switzerland, in Italy; but it was in the Russian publications that the system reached perfection.

The sect struck a decisive blow during the Congress of the Romance Federation at La Chaux-de-Fonds (April 4, 1870). It was a matter of forcing the Geneva sections to recognise the public Alliance of Geneva as being part of the federation and of

---

[a] K. Marx, *The General Council to the Federal Council of Romance Switzerland.—Ed.*
[b] "On sait que la presque totalité", *Le Progrès*, No. 25, December 4, 1869.— *Ed.*
[c] *Circulaire à toutes les fédérations de l'Association Internationale des Travailleurs, Sonvillier, le 12 novembre, 1871.—Ed.*

transferring the Federal Committee and its organ to a locality in Jura where the secret Alliance was in control.

When the Congress opened, two delegates from the "Alliance section" asked to be admitted. The Geneva delegates proposed the deferment of this matter until the end of the Congress and the immediate discussion of the programme as more important. They declared that their imperative mandate ordered them to resign rather than admit this section to their group

"in view of the intrigues and domineering tendencies of the Alliance people, and because to vote for the admission of the Alliance would be to vote for a split in the Romance Federation".[331]

But the Alliance did not want to miss this opportunity. The proximity of the little Jura sections had enabled them to obtain a feeble fictitious majority, since Geneva and the big centres of the International were only very weakly represented. On the insistence of Guillaume and Schwitzguébel, the section was admitted by a majority contested by only one or two votes. The Geneva delegates received from all the sections, which were immediately consulted by telegraph, the order to withdraw from the Congress. With the International's members at La Chaux-de-Fonds supporting the Genevans, the members of the Alliance had to leave the premises of the Congress, since they belonged to the local sections. Although, according to their own organ (see La Solidarité for May 7, 1870), they only represented fifteen sections, whereas Geneva alone had thirty, they usurped the name of the Romance Congress, nominated a new Romance Federal Committee, in which Chevalley and Cagnon * distinguished themselves, and promoted Guillaume's La Solidarité to the rank of the Romance Federation's organ. This young schoolmaster had the special mission of decrying "the factory workers"[332] of Geneva, those odious "bourgeois", of making war on L'Égalité, the newspaper of the Romance Federation, and of preaching absolute abstention in political matters. The most notable articles on this latter subject were written by Bastelica at Marseilles, and by the two pillars of the Alliance at Lyons, Albert Richard and Gaspard Blanc.[a]

___

* Two months later, the organ of that same Committee, La Solidarité for July 9 warned that these two persons were *thieves*. They had in fact proved their anarchic revolutionism by robbing the Co-operative Association of Tailors at La Chaux-de-Fonds.

___

[a] A. Bastelica, "Mon cher Guillaume...", La Solidarité, No. 5, May 7, 1870 and [A. Richard, G. Blanc], "La Commission fédérale", La Solidarité, Nos. 3 and 5, April 23 and May 7, 1870.— Ed.

Incidentally, the short-lived and fictitious majority of the Congress at La Chaux-de-Fonds had acted in flagrant violation of the statutes of the Romance Federation which it claimed to represent; and it should be noted that the Alliance's leaders had played an important part in compiling these statutes.[a] Under articles 53 and 55, any important decision by the Congress, to acquire force of law, had to be sanctioned by two-thirds of the federal sections. Now the sections of Geneva and La Chaux-de-Fonds alone, which had declared themselves opposed to the Alliance, constituted over two-thirds of the total number. At two big general meetings,[b] the International's Geneva members, in spite of opposition from Bakunin and his friends, almost unanimously approved the conduct of their delegates who, to general applause, suggested to the Alliance that it should stay where it belonged and give up its ambitions of entering the Romance Federation; on this condition, reconciliation could be achieved. Later, some disillusioned members of the Alliance proposed its dissolution, but Bakunin and his acolytes opposed this with all their might. Nevertheless, the Alliance continued to insist on joining the Romance Federation, which was then forced to decide on the expulsion of Bakunin and the other ringleaders.

And so there were now two Romance Federal committees, one at Geneva, the other at La Chaux-de-Fonds. The vast majority of the sections remained loyal to the former, while the latter had a following of only fifteen sections, many of which, as we shall see later, ceased to exist one by one.

Hardly had the Romance Congress closed, when the new Committee at La Chaux-de-Fonds in a letter signed by F. Robert, secretary, and Henri Chevalley, chairman (see note above, p. 474), called for the intervention of the General Council. After examining the documents submitted by both sides, the General Council decided, on June 28, 1870, to let the Geneva Committee retain its old functions, and to invite the new Federal Committee of La Chaux-de-Fonds to adopt a local name.[c] Disappointed in its hopes by this decision, the Committee of La Chaux-de-Fonds denounced the General Council for authoritarianism, forgetting that it had

---

[a] *Statuts pour la Fédération des Sections Romandes adoptés par le Congrès Romand, tenu à Genève au Cercle international des Quatre-Saisons, les 2, 3 et 4 janvier 1869*, Geneva, pp. 15-16.— *Ed.*

[b] Of April 9 and 10, 1870.— *Ed.*

[c] K. Marx, *General Council Resolution on the Federal Committee of Romance Switzerland.—Ed.*

been the first to ask for the latter's intervention.[a] The trouble caused to the Swiss Federation by this persistence in trying to usurp the name of the Romance Federal Committee forced the General Council to suspend all official relations with the Committee of La Chaux-de-Fonds.

On September 4, 1870, the Republic was proclaimed in Paris. The Alliance felt that the hour had come to "unchain the revolutionary hydra in Switzerland" (Guillaume's style). *La Solidarité* launched a manifesto[b] demanding the formation of Swiss volunteers to fight the Prussians. This manifesto, if we are to believe the pedagogue Guillaume, although "in no way *anonymous*", was nevertheless "unsigned". Unfortunately, all the Alliance's belligerent fervour evaporated after the seizure of the newspaper and the manifesto. "But I," exclaimed the seething Guillaume, who was burning to "risk his neck", "I have remained at my post ... by the newspaper's printing press" (*Bulletin jurassien*, June 15, 1872).[c]

The revolutionary movement in Lyons was just flaring up. Bakunin hastened to rejoin his lieutenant, Albert Richard, and his sergeants, Bastelica and Gaspard Blanc. On September 28, the day of his arrival, the people had occupied the Town Hall. Bakunin installed himself there. And then came the critical moment, moment anticipated for many years, when Bakunin could at last accomplish the most revolutionary act that the world had ever seen: he decreed the *Abolition of the State*. But the State, in the shape and form of two companies of bourgeois National Guards, made an entry through a door which had inadvertently been left unguarded, cleared the hall, and forced Bakunin to beat a hasty retreat to Geneva.

At the very moment when the belligerent Guillaume was defending the September Republic "at his post", his faithful Achates, Robin, fled from this Republic and sought refuge in London. Although aware that he was one of the Alliance's most fanatic supporters and, moreover, the author of the attacks launched against it in *L'Égalité*, and in spite of the reports from the Brest sections on Robin's far from courageous conduct, the General Council accepted him owing to the absence of its French

---

[a] [J. Guillaume,] "Le Conseil général...", *La Solidarité*, No. 16, July 23, 1870.— *Ed.*

[b] [J. Guillaume, G. Blanc,] "Manifeste aux sections de l'Internationale", *La Solidarité*, No. 22, supplement, September 5, 1870.— *Ed.*

[c] J. Guillaume, "Au Comité fédéral jurassien", *Bulletin de la Fédération jurassienne...*, No. 10/11, June 15, 1872.— *Ed.*

members. From that moment on, Robin never ceased to act as the officious correspondent of the Committee of La Chaux-de-Fonds. On March 14, 1871, he proposed convoking a private conference of the International to clear up the Swiss dispute. The Council, realising in advance that great events were brewing in Paris, flatly refused. Robin made several more attempts and even proposed that the Council should make a definite decision on the dispute. On July 25, the General Council decided that this matter should be one of the questions submitted to the Conference which was to be convoked in September 1871.

On August 10, the Alliance, little desirous of seeing its activities scrutinised by a conference, announced that it had been dissolved as from the sixth of that month. However, reinforced by a few French refugees, it soon reappeared under other names, such as the "Section of Socialist Atheists" and the "Section of Propaganda and Revolutionary Socialist Action". In conformity with Resolution V of the Basle Congress and by agreement with the Romance Federal Committee, the General Council refused to recognise these sections, which were new hotbeds of intrigue.[333]

The London Conference (September 1871) confirmed the General Council's decision of June 28, 1870 concerning the Jura dissidents.

La Solidarité had ceased to exist, and the new adherents of the Alliance founded La Révolution Sociale, one of whose contributors was Mme. André Léo. At the Congress of the League of Peace in Lausanne,[a] when Ferré was in prison waiting for the time when he would go to Satory, she had declared that

Raoul Rigault and Ferré were the two sinister figures of the Commune who, until then" (the execution of the hostages)[334] "had not ceased to demand bloody measures, though always unsuccessfully".[b]

From its first issue, this newspaper had striven to put itself on the same level as Le Figaro, Le Gaulois, and Le Paris-Journal and other filthy rags by republishing their scurrilous attacks on the General Council. It now considered the time ripe for fanning the flames of national hatred even within the International itself. According to it, the General Council was a German committee master-minded by a Bismarck.

With its three resolutions concerning the Swiss dispute, the political action of the working class, and the public disowning of

---

[a] On September 26, 1871.— Ed.

[b] A. Léo, La guerre sociale. Discours prononcé au Congrès de la Paix à Lausanne. Neuchâtel 1871.— Ed.

Nechayev, the Conference had hit the Alliance hard. The first of these resolutions placed the blame directly on the pseudo-Romance Committee at La Chaux-de-Fonds and approved the action of the General Council.[a] It advised the Jura sections to join the Romance Federation, and in the event of this union not proving possible, it decided that the sections representing the mountains should take the name of the Jura Federation. It was stated that if their committee continued its newspaper war in front of the bourgeois public, these papers would be disowned by the General Council.—The second resolution, on the political action of the working class,[b] nullified the confusion which Bakunin had wished to cause in the International by inserting into his programme the doctrine of absolute abstention in political matters.—The third resolution, on Nechayev,[c] was a direct threat to Bakunin. It will be seen later, when we discuss Russia, to what extent Bakunin was personally interested in hiding the nefarious deeds of the Alliance from Western Europe.

The Alliance rightly saw this as a declaration of war, and immediately went into action. The Jura sections which supported the pseudo-Romance committee met in Congress on November 12, 1871 at Sonvillier. There were sixteen delegates present who claimed to represent nine sections. In accordance with the report by the Federal Committee,[d] the Courtelary section, represented by two delegates, "had suspended its activities"; the central section of Locle "had ended by dissolving itself", but had temporarily reconstituted itself in order to send two delegates to the Congress of sixteen; the section representing the engravers and guillocheurs of Courtelary (two delegates) "formed as a resistance society" outside the International; the propaganda section of La Chaux-de-Fonds (one delegate) "is in a critical situation, and its position, far from improving, tends rather to deteriorate". The central section of Neuchâtel (two delegates, one of them Guillaume) "has suffered considerably, and would have inevitably fallen, but for the dedication of several members". The two social study circles of Sonvillier and Saint-Imier (four delegates) in the district of

---

[a] K. Marx and F. Engels, *Resolutions of the London Conference.* "Split in the French-Speaking Part of Switzerland". See present edition, Vol. 22, p. 430.— *Ed.*

[b] K. Marx and F. Engels, *Resolutions of the Conference of Delegates of the International Working Men's Association.* Assembled at London from 17th to 23rd September 1871. See also this volume, pp. 105-06.— *Ed.*

[c] See this volume, p. 23.— *Ed.*

[d] *Rapport du Comité Fédéral Romand.* [Signed:] A. Schwitzguébel. *La Révolution Sociale*, No. 5, November 23, 1871.— *Ed.*

Courtelary were formed, according to the report, due to the dissolution of the Courtelary central section; now, the few members of this district had themselves represented three times, and by six delegates! The Moutier section (one delegate) seemed only to consist of its Committee. And so of sixteen delegates, fourteen represented dead or moribund sections. But to gain some idea of the damage done to this federation by the preaching of anarchy, one must read this report a little further. Of twenty-two sections, only nine were represented at the Congress; seven had never replied to any of the Committee's communications, and four were declared well and truly defunct. And this is the federation which believed itself called to shake the International to its very foundations!

The Congress of Sonvillier began, however, by submitting to the London Conference, which had imposed on it the name of the Jura Federation; but at the same time, as proof of anarchism, it declared that the whole of the Romance Federation was dissolved. (The latter restored autonomy to the Jurassians by driving them out of the sections.) The Congress then put out its bombastic circular with the principal aim of protesting against the legality of the Conference and of appealing to a general Congress which should be convoked as soon as possible.[a]

The circular accused the International of having deviated from its spirit, which was no less than "an immense protest against authority". Until the Congress of Brussels, everything had been for the best in the best of all possible societies; but at Basle, the delegates lost their heads and, prey to "blind trust", they "violated the spirit and the letter of the general statutes" in which the autonomy of each section and each group of sections had been so clearly proclaimed. Now the International had written the word authority on its banners, but the Jura Federation, that puppet of the Alliance, had written autonomy of the sections. We have already seen how the Alliance means to put this autonomy into practice.

The sins of the Basle Congress were exceeded even more by those of the London Conference, whose resolutions

"tend to turn the International, a free federation of autonomous sections, into an hierarchic and authoritarian organisation of disciplined sections placed entirely under the control of the General Council which can arbitrarily either refuse to admit them or suspend their work".

---

[a] *Circulaire à toutes les fédérations de l'Association Internationale des Travailleurs.*— Ed.

The members of the Alliance who drew up this circular evidently forgot that their secret rules were only made to consolidate an "hierarchic and authoritarian organisation" dominated by permanent "Citizen B.", and that instructions were being given in it to "discipline" the sections and place them not only "in the hands", but under "the *high* hand", of that same "citizen".

If the sins of the Conference were mortal, then the sin of sins, the sin against the holy spirit, was committed by the General Council. There were "several individuals" in it who considered their

"mandate" (as Council members) "to be their own private property, and London seemed to them the immutable capital of our Association.... Some went so far ... as to make their particular programme, their personal tenets the predominant ones in the International ... as the only official theory acknowledged in the Association ... and in this way an orthodoxy gradually formed with its seat at London and the members of the General Council as its representatives."

In short, they wanted to establish the unity of the International by "centralisation and dictatorship".—In this same circular, the Alliance aspired to dominate the International "with its own particular programme", declaring it to be "an immense protest against authority" and proclaiming that the emancipation of the workers by the workers themselves must be achieved "without any controlling authority, even though this authority has been elected and sanctioned by the workers". We shall see that wherever the Alliance had any influence, it did exactly what it falsely accused the General Council of doing—it tried to impose its ridiculous travesty of a theory as "the only official theory acknowledged in the Association".*—This only affected the Alliance's public and

---

* Mazzini, for example, held the entire International responsible for the grotesque inventions of pope Bakunin.[a] The General Council felt itself obliged to declare publicly in the Italian newspapers that it "has always opposed the repeated attempts to substitute for the broad, comprehensive programme of the International Working Men's Association (which has made membership open to Bakunin's followers) Bakunin's narrow and sectarian programme, the adoption of which would automatically entail the exclusion of the vast majority of members of the International".[b] Jules Favre's circular, the report of the Rural Sacase on our Association, the reactionary discussions during the debates by the Spanish Cortès on the International,[335] and, finally, all the public attacks launched against it, are riddled with quotations of ultra-anarchist phrases that originated in the Bakuninist camp.

---

[a] G. Mazzini. "Documenti sull'Internazionale", *La Roma del Popolo*, No. 38, November 16, 1871.—*Ed.*

[b] F. Engels, *Declaration Sent by the General Council to the Editors of Italian Newspapers Concerning Mazzini's Articles about the International* (see this volume, pp. 60-61).—*Ed.*

open activities. As for its secret activities, "the spirit and the letter" of the secret statutes have already enlightened us concerning the degree of "orthodoxy", of "personal doctrine", of "centralisation" and of "dictatorship" which reigned in this "free federation of autonomous groups". We fully realise that the Alliance wanted to prevent the working class from creating for itself a common leadership, since Bakunin's providence had already foreseen this when setting up his *Alliance* as the general staff of the revolution.

Far from wanting to impose an orthodoxy on the International, the General Council had proposed at the London Conference that the sectarian names of certain sections should be abolished, and this proposition was accepted unanimously.*

Here is the General Council's statement on sects in its private circular (*Fictitious Splits*, p. 24 ª).

"The first phase of the proletariat's struggle against the bourgeoisie is marked by a sectarian movement. That is logical at a time when the proletariat has not yet developed sufficiently to act as a class. Certain thinkers criticise social antagonisms and suggest fantastic solutions thereof, which the mass of workers is left to accept, preach and put into practice. The sects formed by these initiators are abstentionist by their very nature, i.e., alien to all real action, politics, strikes, coalitions, or, in a word, to any united movement. The mass of the proletariat always remains indifferent or even hostile to their propaganda. The Paris and Lyons workers did not want the Saint-Simonians, the Fourierists, the Icarians, any more than the Chartists and the English trades unionists wanted the Owenists. These sects act as levers of the movement in the beginning, but become an obstruction as soon as the movement outgrows them; after which they become reactionary. Witness the sects in France and England, and lately the Lassalleans in Germany who, after having hindered the proletariat's organisation for several years, ended by becoming simple instruments of the

---

* Resolution II of the Conference, Art. 2: "All local branches, sections, groups and their committees are henceforth to designate and constitute themselves simply and exclusively as branches, sections, groups and committees of the International Working Men's Association, with the names of their respective localities attached." Art. 3: "Consequently, no branches, sections or groups will henceforth be allowed to designate themselves by sectarian names, such as Positivists, Mutualists, Collectivists, Communists, etc., or to form separatist bodies under the name of *sections of propaganda*, etc., pretending to accomplish special missions distinct from the common purposes of the Association."

ª See this volume, p. 106-07.— *Ed.*

police. To sum up, we have here the infancy of the proletarian movement, just as astrology and alchemy are the infancy of science. If the International were to be founded it was necessary that the proletariat would go through this phase.

"Contrary to the sectarian organisations with their vagaries and rivalries, the International is a genuine and militant organisation of the proletarian class of all countries united in their common struggle against the capitalists and the landowners, against their class power organised in the state. The International's Rules, therefore, speak of only simple 'working men's societies', all following the same goal and accepting the same programme, which presents a general outline of the proletarian movement, while leaving its theoretical elaboration to be guided by the needs of the practical struggle and the exchange of ideas in the sections, unrestrictedly admitting all shades of socialist convictions in their organs and Congresses."

The Alliance did not want the International to be a militant society. The circular demanded that it should be the faithful image of the future society:

"We must therefore try to bring this organisation as close as possible to our ideal.... The International, embryo of the future human society, must henceforth be the faithful image of our principles of liberty and federation, and must reject any principle leading to authoritarianism, to dictatorship."

If the Jura Federation had succeeded in its plan to transform the International into the faithful image of a society which did not yet exist, and to forbid it any means of concerted action, with the secret aim of subjecting it to the "authoritarianism and dictatorship" of the Alliance and its permanent dictator, "Citizen B.", this would have gratified the desires of the European police, who wanted nothing more than to see the International forced to retreat.

To prove to their former colleagues of the League of Peace and to the radical bourgeoisie that the campaign which they had just launched was directed against the International and not against the bourgeoisie, the men of the Alliance sent their circular to all the radical newspapers. M. Gambetta's *La République française* hastened to acknowledge their services with an article full of encouragement for the Jurassians and attacks on the London Conference.[a] The *Bulletin jurassien*, happy to have found this support in the bourgeois press, reproduced *in extenso* this article in

---

[a] "Questions ouvrières", *La République française*, No. 125, March 11, 1872.— *Ed.*

its issue No. 3,[a] thus showing that the ultra-revolutionary members of the Alliance and the Gambettists of Versailles were united by an *entente* that was indeed *cordiale.* To spread more widely among the bourgeoisie the welcome tidings of an incipient split in the International, the Sonvillier circular was sold in the streets of several French cities, notably Montpellier, on market day. It is known that the sale of printed matter on the streets, in France, must be authorised by the police.*

This circular was distributed by the bale wherever the Alliance thought it could recruit friends and malcontents against the General Council. The result was almost negligible. The Spanish members of the Alliance declared themselves opposed to the convocation of the Congress as demanded by the circular and even had the audacity to send reprimands to the Pope.[337] In Italy, only one person, Terzaghi, declared himself in favour of the Congress for a while. In Belgium, where there were no known members of the Alliance, but where the International's entire movement was floundering in a morass of bourgeois phrases about political abstention, autonomy, liberty, federation, and decentralisation and was stuck fast in its own petty parochial interests, the circular had some success. Although the Belgian Federal Council abstained from supporting the convocation of an extraordinary General Congress—which, incidentally, would have been absurd, since Belgium had been represented by six delegates at the Conference—it drew up draft general statutes which simply suppressed the General Council. When this proposition was discussed at the Belgian Congress, the delegate for Lodelinsart[b] observed that the best criterion, for the workers, was the mood of their employers. To judge solely by the joy which the idea of suppressing the General Council engendered among the employers, it could be claimed that it was impossible to

"commit a bigger blunder than to decree this suppression".[c]

The proposition was consequently rejected.[338] In Switzerland, the Romance Federation protested vigorously,[339] but everywhere else the circular was merely received with the silence of contempt.

* The Toulouse Trial. See *La Réforme* (of Toulouse), March 18, 1873.[336]

---

a "Les socialistes n'ayant plus d'organes...", *Bulletin de la Fédération jurassienne...*, No. 3, March 15, 1872, p. 3.— *Ed.*

b Joseph Hubert.— *Ed.*

c "Congrès Ouvrier Belge du 14 juillet", *L'Internationale*, No. 184, July 21, 1872.— *Ed.*

The General Council replied to the Sonvillier Circular and to the Alliance's continual manoeuvrings with a ´ private circular: *Fictitious Splits in the International* dated March 5, 1872. A large part of this circular has been summarised above. The Hague Congress effectively dealt with these intrigues and with the intriguers themselves.

Indeed, these men who made a noise out of all proportion to their importance, met with indisputable success. The whole of the liberal and police press openly sided with them; in their personal defamation of the General Council and their impotent attacks on the International, they were backed by self-styled reformers from all countries: in England, by the bourgeois republicans whose intrigues were foiled by the General Council[a]; in Italy, by the dogmatic free-thinkers who, under Stefanoni's banner, proposed to found a "universal society of rationalists".[340] with an obligatory seat at Rome, an "authoritarian" and "hierarchic" organisation, atheist monasteries and convents, etc., and whose statutes award a marble bust to be installed in the Congress hall for every bourgeois who donates ten thousand francs; finally, in Germany, by the Bismarckian socialists who, apart from their police newspaper, the *Neuer Social-Demokrat,* act as whiteshirts[341] for the Prusso-German Empire.

When *La Révolution Sociale* ceased publication, the Alliance used as its official press organ the *Bulletin jurassien* which, under the pretext of protecting the autonomous sections against the authoritarianism of the General Council and against the usurpations of the London Conference, was working to disorganise the International. Its issue of March 20, 1872 frankly averred that

"by International it does not mean this or that organisation embracing part of the proletariat today. Organisations are secondary and transitory.... The International is, to put it more generally, the feeling of solidarity among the exploited which dominates the modern world".[b]

The International reduced to a pure "feeling of solidarity" will be even more platonic than Christian charity. To give proof of the honest methods applied by the *Bulletin,* we quote the following passage from a letter by Tokarzewicz, editor-in-chief of the Polish newspaper *Wolność* in Zurich:

---

[a] K. Marx, *Declaration of the General Council Concerning the Universal Federalist Council* (see this volume, pp. 157-59).— *Ed.*

[b] "Le 18 mars", *Bulletin de la Fédération jurassienne...*, No. 4, March 20, 1872.— *Ed.*

"In the *Bulletin jurassien* No. 13, there is a *programme of the Polish Socialist Society of Zurich* which will publish its newspaper *Wolność* in a few days. We authorise you, three days after the receipt of this letter, to inform the International's General Council that the programme is *false.*" [342]

The issue of this *Bulletin* for June 15 contains the answers from the Alliance members (Bakunin, Malon, Claris, Guillaume, etc.) [a] to the General Council's private circular. Their answers do not answer any of the accusations which the General Council brought against the Alliance and its leaders. The pope, [b] at a loss for explanations, decided to close the debate by calling the circular "a pile of filth".

"Moreover," he declared, "I have always reserved the right to bring all my calumniators before a jury of honour, which the next Congress will doubtless not refuse me. *And as soon as this jury* OFFERS ME *all the guarantees of an impartial and serious trial,* I will be able to reveal to it, with all the necessary details, all the facts, both political and personal, without fearing the inconveniences and dangers of an indiscreet disclosure."

Needless to say, Citizen B. risked his neck—as usual. He did not appear at The Hague.

The Congress was drawing near, and the Alliance knew that before it was held, a report was to be published on the Nechayev affair. Citizen Utin had been commissioned by the Conference to compile it. It was of vital importance that this report should not be published before the Congress, so that the members would not be fully informed about it. Citizen Utin went to Zurich to carry out his task. Hardly had he settled there, when he was the victim of an assassination attempt which we unhesitatingly ascribe to the Alliance. In Zurich, Utin had no enemies apart from a few Slavs of the Alliance under the "high hand" of Bakunin. Moreover, the organisation of ambushes and assassinations is one of the methods of struggle recognised and employed by this society; we shall see other examples in Spain and Russia. Eight persons who spoke a Slavonic language lay in wait for Utin in an isolated spot near a canal. When he drew near them, they attacked him from behind, hit him repeatedly on the head with large stones, inflicted a dangerous wound on one of his eyes, and would have killed him and thrown him into the canal after first beating him up, had it

---

[a] M. Bakunin, "Aux compagnons rédacteurs..."; B. Malon, "Je n'accorde pas..."; A. Claris, "La bonne foi..."; J. Guillaume, "Au Comité fédéral jurassien", *Bulletin de la fédération jurassienne...*, No. 10/11, June 15, 1872.— *Ed.*

[b] M. Bakunin.— *Ed.*

not been for the arrival of four German students.[a] On seeing
them, the assassins fled. This attempt did not prevent Citizen Utin
from finishing his work and sending it to the Congress.[b]

IV

THE ALLIANCE IN SPAIN

After the Congress of the *League of Peace* held at Berne in
September 1868,[c] Fanelli, one of the Alliance's founders and a
member of the Italian parliament, went to Madrid. He had been
furnished with references by Bakunin for Garrido, deputy at
Cortès, who put him in touch with republican circles, bourgeois
and working-class alike. A short while after, in November of that
year, Alliance membership cards were sent from Geneva to
Morago, Cordova y Lopez (republican with ambitions of becoming
a deputy and the editor of the *Combate*, a bourgeois newspaper), and
to Rubau Donadeu (unsuccessful candidate for Barcelona, founder
of a pseudo-socialist party). The knowledge of the arrival of these
membership cards threw the young international section of
Madrid into confusion. President Jalvo withdrew, not wanting to
belong to an association which harboured a secret society composed of bourgeois and which allowed itself to be ruled by that
society.

As early as the Basle Congress, the Spanish International had
been represented by two Alliance members, Farga Pellicer and
Sentiñon, the latter being featured on the official list of delegates
as "delegate for the Alliance".[d] After the Congress of the Spanish
International in Barcelona (June[e] 1870),[343] the Alliance established
itself at Palma, Valencia, Malaga and Cadiz. In 1871, sections were
founded at Seville and Cordoba. At the beginning of 1871,
Morago and Viñas, delegates of the Barcelona Alliance, suggested
to members of the Federal Council (Francisco Mora, Angel Mora,
Anselmo Lorenzo, Borrell, etc.) ... the foundation of an Alliance
section in Madrid; but the latter objected, saying that the Alliance

---

[a] This assault took place on June 18, 1872.— *Ed.*

[b] N. Outine, *Au Vme Congrès de l'Association Internationale des Travailleurs à La
Haye*, manuscript (see English translation in *The Hague Congress of the First
International, September 2-7, 1872. Minutes and Documents,* Moscow, 1976.— *Ed.*

[c] The original mistakenly has: "1869".— *Ed.*

[d] *Compte-rendu du IVe Congrès international, tenu à Bâle, en septembre 1869,*
Brussels, 1869.— *Ed.*

[e] The original mistakenly has: "July".— *Ed.*

was a dangerous society if it was secret, and useless if it was public. For the second time, the mere mention of the name was enough to sow the seeds of discord in the heart of the Federal Council; Borrell even uttered these prophetic words:

"From now on, all trust between us is dead." [a]

But when government persecution forced the members of the Federal Council to emigrate to Portugal, it was there that Morago succeeded in convincing them of the usefulness of this secret association, and it was there that the Alliance section of Madrid was founded at their initiative. At Lisbon, a few Portuguese, who were members of the International, were affiliated to the Alliance by Morago. Finding, however, that these newcomers did not offer him enough guarantees, he founded, without their knowledge, another Alliance group consisting of the worst elements among the bourgeois and the workers, recruited from the freemasons. This new group, which included an unfrocked curate named Bonança, attempted to organise the International by sections of ten members who, under its direction, were to help carry out the schemes of the Comte de Péniche, and whom this political intriguer managed to drag into a dangerous venture of which the sole aim was to put him in power. In view of the Alliance intrigues in Portugal and Spain, the Portuguese members of the International withdrew from this secret society and at the Hague Congress they pressed for its expulsion from the International as a public safety measure.

At the Conference of the Spanish International at Valencia (September 1871),[344] the Alliance delegates, also delegates of the International as always, gave their secret society a complete organisation for the Iberian peninsula. The majority of them, believing that the Alliance programme was identical to that of the International, that this secret organisation existed everywhere, that it was almost a duty to join it, and that the Alliance was striving to develop and not dominate the International, decided that all the members of the Federal Council should be initiated. As soon as Morago, who until then had not dared to return to Spain, heard about this fact, he came to Madrid in all haste and accused Mora of "wanting to subordinate the Alliance to the International", which was contrary to the Alliance's intentions. And to give weight to this opinion, he let Mesa read, the following January, a letter

---

[a] The quotation is from the pamphlet by P. Lafargue, *A los Internacionales de la region Española*, Madrid, 1872.— *Ed.*

from Bakunin in which the latter evolved a Machiavellian plan for domination over the working class. This plan was as follows:

"The Alliance must appear to exist within the International, but in reality at a certain distance from it, in order better to observe and control it. For this reason, members who belong to Councils and Committees of International sections must *always be in the minority in the Alliance sections.*" (Statement by José Mesa, dated September 1, 1872, addressed to the Hague Congress).[345]

At a meeting of the Alliance, Morago accused Mesa of having betrayed Bakunin's society by initiating all the members of the Federal Council, which gave them a majority in the Alliance section and established, in fact, the domination of the International over the Alliance. To avoid this domination, the secret instructions prescribed that only one or two Alliance members should infiltrate into the councils or committees of the International and control them under the direction and with the support of the Alliance section where all resolutions were passed which the International ought to adopt.—From that moment, Morago declared war on the Federal Council and, as in Portugal, founded a new Alliance section which remained unknown to those under suspicion. The initiates at various points in Spain backed him up and began to accuse the Federal Council of neglecting its duties to the Alliance, as is proved by a circular from the Valencia Alliance section (January 30, 1872) signed "Damon", Montoro's Alliance pseudonym.[346]

When the Sonvillier circular arrived, the Spanish Alliance took care not to side with Jura. Even the mother section of Barcelona, in an official letter of November 14, 1871, treated pope Michael, whom it suspected of personal rivalry with Karl Marx,* very curtly and in an altogether heretic manner.

* Copies of this letter, addressed by Alerini "on behalf of the Barcelona group" of the Alliance to "my dear Bastelica and dear friends", were sent to all the sections of the Spanish Alliance. Here are some extracts:
"The present General Council cannot last beyond next year's Congress, and its baneful activities can only be temporary.... A public rupture, on the contrary, would deal our cause a blow from which it would only recover with difficulty, assuming it resisted. We cannot, then, encourage in any way your *separatist tendencies...* Some of us have wondered if, apart from the question of principle, there might not also be in it, or alongside it, *personal problems—problems of rivalry, for instance, between our friend Michael and Karl Marx, between the members of the old A. and the General Council..* We have been distressed to see, in *La Révolution Sociale,* the attacks on the General Council and Karl Marx [a] ... When we know the opinion

---

[a] The reference is to the anonymous articles [written by A. Léo] "Comment les socialistes honnêtes" and "L'esprit de l'Association internationale", *La Révolution Sociale,* Nos. 2 and 3, November 2 and 9, 1871.—*Ed.*

The Federal Council supported this letter, which shows how little influence the Swiss centre had in Spain at the time. But afterwards it was noticeable that grace had fallen on the recalcitrant hearts. At a meeting of the Madrid Federation of the International (January 7, 1872), at which the Sonvillier circular was discussed, the new group, headed by Morago, prevented the reading of the Romance Federation's counter-circular[a] and suppressed the discussion. On February 24, Rafar (Alliance pseudonym of Rafael Farga) wrote to the Alliance's Madrid section:

"It is essential to kill the reactionary influences and authoritarian tendencies of the General Council."

However, it was only at Palma in Majorca that the Alliance was able to achieve the public adherence of the International's members to the Jura circular. It can be seen that ecclesiastical discipline was beginning to break the last attempts at resistance to the infallibility of the pope.

Faced with all this underground work, the Spanish Federal Council realised that it must get rid of the Alliance as soon as possible. The government persecutions furnished it with a pretext. In the event of the International's dissolution, it proposed to form secret groups of "defenders of the International" into which the Alliance sections would imperceptibly merge. The introduction of numerous members was bound to change the character of the sections, and they would finally disappear with these groups on the day when the persecutions ceased. But the Alliance guessed at the hidden purpose of this plan and foiled it, although without this organisation, the International's existence in Spain would have been in jeopardy if the government had carried out its threats. The Alliance, on the contrary, made the following proposal:

"If we are outlawed, it would be useful to give the International an external form which *could be allowed by the government*; the local councils would be like secret cells which, under the Alliance's influence, would impose on the sections a wholly revolutionary direction." (Circular of the Alliance's Seville section, October 25, 1871.[347])

of our friends on the peninsula, *who are influencing the local councils*, then this might change our attitude towards a general decision, to which we shall conform in every respect, etc., etc."

The old A. is the public Alliance nipped in the bud by the General Council. The copy of the letter from which we have taken these passages is in Alerini's handwriting.

---

[a] "Réponse du Comité Fédéral Romand à la circulaire des 16 signataires membres du Congrès de Sonvilliers", *L'Égalité*, No. 24, December 24, 1871.— *Ed.*

Cowardly in action, bold in words—such was the Alliance in Spain, as elsewhere.

The London Conference's resolution on working-class politics [a] forced the Alliance into open hostilities with the International and gave the Federal Council an opportunity to state its perfect agreement with the great majority of the International's membership. Furthermore, it suggested the idea of forming a big working men's party in Spain. To achieve this aim, the working class would first have to be completely isolated from all the bourgeois parties, especially the Republican party which recruited most of its voters and active supporters from the workers. The Federal Council advised abstention in all elections of deputies, whether monarchist or republican. To rid the people of all illusions about the pseudo-socialist phraseology of the Republicans, the editors of *La Emancipacion*, who were also members of the Federal Council, sent a letter to the representatives of the Federalist Republican party, who were holding a congress in Madrid, in which they asked them for practical measures and called on them to state their attitude to the International's programme.[348] This meant delivering a serious blow to the Republican party. The Alliance undertook to soften it, since it was, on the contrary, in league with the Republicans.[349] In Madrid, it founded a newspaper, *El Condenado*, which adopted as its programme the three cardinal virtues of the Alliance: *Atheism*, *Anarchy*, and *Collectivism*, but which preached to the workers that they should not demand a reduction in working hours. "Brother" Morago had a fellow contributor in Estévanez, one of the three members of the Republican party's Directing Committee and lately governor of Madrid and Minister for War. At Malaga, Pino, a member of the Federal Commission of the pseudo-International, and, at Madrid, Felipe Martin, now the Alliance's commercial traveller, were serving the Republican party as electoral agents. And in order to have its Fanelli in the Spanish Cortès, the Alliance proposed backing Morago's candidature.

The Alliance already had two serious grudges against the Federal Council: 1) the latter had abstained on the Jura question; 2) it had also attempted to infringe its [the Alliance's] inviolability. After the Council adopted a position over the Republican party which wrecked all the Alliance's plans, the latter decided to destroy it. The letter to the Republican Congress was taken by the Alliance as a declaration of war. *La Igualdad*, the party's most

---

[a] See present edition, Vol. 22, pp. 426-27.— *Ed.*

influential organ, violently attacked the editors of *La Emancipacion* and accused them of having sold themselves to Sagasta.[a] The *Condenado* encouraged this disgraceful charge by maintaining a stubborn silence. The Alliance did more for the Republican party. As a result of this letter, it had the editors of *La Emancipacion* expelled from the International's Madrid Federation, which it dominated.

In spite of government persecution, the Federal Council, during its six-month period of administration after the Conference of Valencia, had raised the number of local federations from 13 to 70; it had, in 100 other localities, prepared the setting up of local federations and had organised eight trades into national resistance societies; moreover, the great association of Catalan factory workers was being formed under its auspices. These services had given the members of the Council such moral influence that Bakunin felt it necessary to bring them back on to the path of truth with a long fatherly admonition sent to Mora, the Council's general secretary, on April 5, 1872 (see Documents, No. 3 [b]). The Congress of Saragossa (April 4-11, 1872),[350] despite the efforts of the Alliance, which was represented by at least twelve delegates, annulled the expulsion and renominated two of the expelled members for the new Federal Council,[c] ignoring their repeated refusals to accept their candidatures.

During the Congress of Saragossa, as always, the Alliance was holding secret meetings on the side. The members of the Federal Council proposed dissolving the Alliance. To prevent the proposal being rejected, it was neatly circumvented. Two months later, on June 2, those same citizens, in their capacity as leaders of the Spanish Alliance and on behalf of its Madrid section, sent the other sections a circular [351] in which they renewed their proposal, giving the following reason:

"The Alliance has deviated from the path which it should, in our opinion, have taken in this region; it has falsified the idea which brought it into being and, instead of being an integral part of our great Association, an active element which would have given impetus to the different organisations of the International by helping and encouraging them in their development, it has broken away completely from the rest of the Association and has become an organisation apart and, as it were, superior, with tendencies towards domination, introducing mistrust, discord

---

[a] "Segun dice el combate...", "No quieron acabas...", *La Igualdad,* Nos. 1069 and 1074, March 19 and 24, 1872.— *Ed.*

[b] See this volume, pp. 578-80.— *Ed.*

[c] Francisco Mora and Anselmo Lorenzo.— *Ed.*

and division among us.... At Saragossa, instead of bringing solutions and ideas, it has, on the contrary, only put impediments and obstacles in the way of the important work of the Congress."[a]

Of all the Spanish Alliance sections, only the one at Cadiz responded by announcing its dissolution. On the very next day, the Alliance again had the signatories of the June 2 circular expelled from the International's Madrid Federation. It used as its pretext an article in *La Emancipacion* of June 1 which demanded an enquiry into

"the sources of the wealth acquired by ministers, generals, magistrates, public officials, mayors, etc. ... and by all those in politics who, without having exercised any public functions, have lived under the wing of the governments, lending them their support in the Cortès and hiding their iniquities under a mask of false opposition ... and whose property should have been confiscated as a first measure on the day after a revolution".[b]

The Alliance saw this as a direct attack on its friends in the Republican party and accused the editors of *La Emancipacion* of having betrayed the cause of the proletariat under the pretext that in demanding the confiscation of property stolen from the State, they implicitly recognised private property. Nothing demonstrates more clearly the reactionary spirit which was hidden under the Alliance's revolutionary charlatanism and which it wanted to inject into the working class. Nothing proves more clearly the bad faith of the Alliance members than the expulsion, as defenders of private property, of the very men whom they had anathematised for their communist ideas.

This new expulsion was made in violation of the rules in force prescribing the formation of a jury of honour for which the accused could nominate two out of the seven jurors, against whose verdict he could appeal to the section's general assembly.[c] Instead of all this, the Alliance, in order to avoid any restriction of its autonomy, had the expulsion decreed at the same sitting at which it made the accusation. Out of the section's total membership of 130, only 15 were present, and these were in league with one another. The expelled members appealed to the Federal Council.[d]

This Council, thanks to the Alliance's intrigues, had been transferred to Valencia. Of the two members of the old Federal

---

[a] Circular "Seccion de la A... de Madrid. 2 de junio de 1872", *La Emancipacion*, No. 59, July 27, 1872, p. 3.— *Ed.*

[b] "Informacion revolucionaria", *La Emancipacion*, No. 51, June 1, 1872.— *Ed.*

[c] *Estatutos de la Federacion Regional Española de la Asociacion Internacional de los Trabajadores.—Ed.*

[d] See "Nueva Federacion Madrileña. Circular. Madrid 22 de julio de 1872", *La Emancipacion*, No. 59, July 27, 1872.— *Ed.*

Council who were re-elected at the Congress of Saragossa, Mora had not accepted and Lorenzo had tendered his resignation shortly afterwards. From that moment, the Federal Council belonged body and soul to the Alliance. And so it responded to the appeal of the expelled members with a declaration of its incompetence, although Article 7 of the Spanish Federation's rules imposed on it the duty of suspending, with the right of appeal to the next Congress, any local federation which violated the statutes. The expelled members then formed a "new federation" and demanded recognition from the Council which, in deference to the autonomy of the sections, formally refused. The New Madrid Federation then approached the General Council, which accepted it in conformity with Articles II, 7 and IV, 4 of the Administrative Regulations.[a] The Hague General Congress approved this act and *unanimously* admitted the delegate from the New Madrid Federation.[b]

The Alliance realised the full importance of this first rebellious move. It realised that, unless it were nipped in the bud, the Spanish International, so docile hitherto, would slip out of its hands; and so it set in motion all the means at its disposal, honest and otherwise. It began with defamation. It announced in the newspapers and posted up in the section halls the names of the expelled members: Angel and Francisco Mora, José Mesa, Victor Pagés, Iglesias, Saenz, Calleja, Pauly and Lafargue were dubbed traitors. Mora, who, to carry out his duties as general secretary, had given up his job and for long months had been maintained by his brother, since there were no funds out of which to pay him, was accused of having lived at the International's expense. Mesa, who was editing a fashion magazine to earn his living and had just translated an article for an illustrated journal, was alleged to have sold himself to the bourgeoisie. Lafargue was charged with the mortal sin of having, by a gargantuan dinner, submitted to the temptations of St. Anthony the weak flesh of Martinez and Montoro, two members of the new Federal Council of the Alliance, as if they carried their consciences in their paunches. We are only mentioning here the public and published libels. These measures failing to yield the results desired, the next move was intimidation. In Valencia, Mora was lured into an ambush by members of the Federal Council who were waiting for him armed with clubs. He was rescued by the members of the local federation

---

[a] See this volume, pp. 10, 12.— *Ed.*

[b] Paul Lafargue.— *Ed.*

who knew the ways of these gentlemen and asserted that it was in the face of arguments equally striking that Lorenzo had tendered his resignation. At Madrid, a similar attempt was made shortly afterwards on Iglesias. The Alliance congregation of the Index marked out *La Emancipacion* for the censure of the faithful. At Cadiz, to instil a salutary fear into the hearts of the sinful, it was stated that any person selling *La Emancipacion* would be expelled from the International as a traitor. The Alliance's anarchy takes the form of inquisitorial practice.

As was its custom, the Alliance tried to have all the representation of the Spanish International at the Hague Congress made up of its own members. To this end, the Federal Council passed round the sections a private circular[a] whose existence was carefully kept secret from the New Madrid Federation. It proposed to send to the Congress a collective representation elected by the votes of all members of the International, and to raise a general contribution of 25 centimos per head to defray the expenses. Since the local federations had no time to arrive at an agreement on the candidatures, it was clear, as the facts proved, that the Alliance's official candidates, delegated to the Congress at the International's expense, would be elected. However, this circular fell into the hands of the New Madrid Federation and was forwarded to the General Council which, knowing that the Federal Council was subordinate to the Alliance, saw that the moment for action had arrived and sent a letter to the Spanish Federal Council, in which it was stated:

"Citizens,

"We hold proof that within the International, and particularly in Spain, there exists a secret society called the Alliance of Socialist Democracy. This society, whose centre is in Switzerland, considers it its special mission to guide our great Association in keeping with its own particular tendencies and lead it towards goals unknown to the vast majority of International members. Moreover, we know from the Seville *Razon* that at least three members of your Council belong to the Alliance...

"If the organisation and character of this society were already contrary to the spirit and the letter of our Rules, when it was still public, its secret existence within the International, in spite of its promise, represents no less than treason against our Association.

---

[a] *Asociación Internacional de los Trabajadores. Federación Regional Española. Circular reservada.* "Compañeros: uno de los actos más trascendentales de nuestra gran Asociación...", Valencia, July 7, 1872.— *Ed.*

The International knows but one type of members, all with equal rights and duties; the Alliance divides them into two classes, the initiated and the uninitiated, the latter doomed to be led by the former by means of an organisation of whose very existence they are unaware. The International demands that its adherents should acknowledge *Truth, Justice and Morality* as the basis of their conduct; the Alliance obliges its supporters to hide from the uninitiated members of the International the existence of the secret organisation, the motives and even the aim of their words and deeds." [a]

The General Council also asked them to provide certain material for the inquiry into the Alliance which it intended to present to the Hague Congress, and an explanation of how they reconciled their duties to the International with the presence in the heart of the Federal Council of at least three notorious members of the Alliance.

The Federal Council replied with an evasive letter in which, however, it recognised the Alliance's existence.

Since the manoeuvres which we have been discussing seemed inadequate to guarantee the success of the election, the Alliance went so far in its newspapers as to nominate Farga, Alerini, Soriano, Marselau, Mendez and Morago as official candidates. The result of the voting was: Marselau—3,568; Morago—3,442; Mendez—2,850; Soriano—2,751. Of the other candidates, Lostau obtained 2,430 votes in four Catalan towns which were clearly not yet properly disciplined; Fusté scored 1,053 votes at Sans in Catalonia. None of the other candidates gained more than 250 votes. To ensure the election of Farga and Alerini, the Federal Council gave the city of Barcelona, where the Alliance predominated, the privilege of nominating its own delegates, who were, naturally, Alerini and Farga.—The same official circular stated that the four Catalan towns which had nominated Lostau and Fusté, thus rejecting the Alliance's official candidates, paid 2,654 reales (663 frs. 50 c.) for the delegation's expenses whereas the other Spanish cities, on which the Alliance had foisted its own candidates, since the workers were little accustomed to managing their own affairs, only paid a total of 2,799 reales (699 frs. 75 c.). The New Madrid Federation had good reason to say that the money of the International's members was being used to send the Alliance's delegates to the Hague.[b] Furthermore, the Alliance's

---

[a] See this volume, pp. 211-12.— *Ed.*

[b] "Compañeros ... Madrid, 21 de julio de 1872", *La Emancipacion*, No. 59, July 27, 1872.— *Ed.*

Federal Council did not pay in full the subscriptions due to the General Council.

All this was not enough for the Alliance. It had to have an Alliance imperative mandate for its delegates, and this is how it was wangled. Through its circular of July 7, the Federal Council demanded, and obtained, the authorisation to lump together in one collective mandate the imperative mandates issued by the local federations. This manoeuvre, worse than any Bonapartist plebiscite,[352] allowed the Alliance to draw up for its delegation a mandate which it intended to impose on the Congress, while forbidding its own delegates to take part in the voting unless an immediate change was made in the manner of voting as prescribed to the International in its Administrative Regulations. That this was mere mystification is proved by the fact that the Spanish delegates at the Congress of Saint-Imier,[353] despite their mandate, took part in the voting which was being carried out by federations, the manner so much praised by Castelar and practised by the League of Peace.*

---

* *Sentiñon*, a doctor of medicine in Barcelona, a personal friend of Bakunin, and one of the founders of the Spanish Alliance, advised members of the International well before the Hague Congress not to pay their subscriptions to the General Council because it would use them to buy rifles. He tried to prevent the Spanish International from defending the cause of the defeated Commune. Imprisoned for a press offence, he launched a manifesto in which he courageously renounced the International, which was being persecuted at the time. Shunned for this by the whole of the working class in Barcelona, he nevertheless continued to be one of the Alliance's secret leaders, for in a letter of August 14, 1871, three months after the collapse of the Commune, Montoro, a member of the Alliance, referred an Alliance correspondent to Sentiñon who, he said, could recommend him and confirm his Alliance membership.

Viñas, a medical student, whom Sentiñon, in a letter of January 26, 1872, recommended to Liebknecht as "the soul of the International in Barcelona", left the International during the persecution so as not to compromise his family, although the police did not even bother to imprison him.

Farga Pellicer, another Alliance leader, was accused in the same letter from Sentiñon of having absconded during the persecution, leaving the others to take the legal responsibility for his articles. The rabbit-like courage of the Alliance members boldly asserts, at all times and in all places, their anti-authoritarian autonomy. Their way of protesting against the authority of the bourgeois state is to take flight.

Soriano, another leader, and a professor of ... occult sciences, withdrew from the International at the height of the persecution. At the Congress of Saragossa, he opposed, with pathetic courage, the public holding of the Congress demanded by Lafargue and other delegates, because he considered it imprudent to provoke the anger of the authorities. Recently, under Amadeus, Soriano accepted a government post.

V

THE ALLIANCE IN ITALY

In Italy, the Alliance preceded the International. Pope Michael stayed there and built up numerous contacts among the young radical elements of the bourgeoisie. The first section of the Italian International, the one at Naples, was, since the time of its foundation, controlled by these bourgeois and Alliance elements. Gambuzzi,* a lawyer and one of the founders of the Alliance, raised his "model worker" Caporusso to the chairmanship of the section. At the Basle Congress, Bakunin, arm in arm with his faithful Caporusso, represented the Neapolitan members of the International, whereas Fanelli,** the Antonelli of the Alliance and a delegate for workers' associations formed outside the International, was delayed *en route* owing to illness.

Morago, shopkeeper and frequenter of taverns, preserved his autonomy as a professional gambler by living on the earnings of his wife and his apprentices. When the Federal Council emigrated to Lisbon, he deserted his post as member of the Council and suggested throwing the International's papers into the sea. When Sagasta outlawed the International, he again deserted his post as member of the Madrid local Council and sheltered from the storm in the haven of the Alliance. Although lacking a Christ, the Alliance abounded in St. Peters.

Clementé Bové, as Chairman of the Catalan Factory Workers' Association (las tres clases de vapor[354]), was discharged and expelled for his excessively autonomous handling of funds.

Dionisio Garcia Fraile, called "our dear colleague" by *La Federacion,* an Alliance organ, in its issue of July 28, 1872, where he published a long letter full of attacks on the New Madrid Federation, worked for the police at Saint-Sebastien and embezzled funds belonging to sections of the International.

* "One of Caporusso's most fervent partisans was the lawyer Carlo Gambuzzi, who thought he had found in him the ideal chairman for an International section. It was Gambuzzi who furnished him with the necessary means to go to the Basle Congress. When Caporusso's expulsion was decided upon in the general assembly of the section, Gambuzzi protested vigorously against the publication of this fact in the *Bulletin,* and also persuaded his friends not to insist on the insertion in the bulletin of the other shameful fact, the embezzlement of 300 frs." (Letter from Cafiero, July 12, 1871).[355]

** Fanelli had long been a member of the Italian parliament. On being questioned about this matter, Gambuzzi stated that it was an excellent thing to be a deputy; that it made you immune to the police and allowed you to travel free of charge on all the Italian railways. The Alliance forbade the workers all political action, since to demand of the State any regulation of working hours for women and children was to recognise the State and to acknowledge the principle of evil; but the Alliance's bourgeois leaders had papal dispensations which allowed them to sit in parliament and enjoy the privileges offered by bourgeois States. Fanelli's atheistic and anarchistic activities in the Italian parliament had been limited, so far, to a high-flown eulogy of the authoritarian Mazzini, the man of "Dio e popolo".

His close friendship with the Holy Father went to our brave Caporusso's head. On returning to Naples, he thought himself superior to the other Alliance members; he behaved as if he were the boss of the section.

"His trip to Basle changed Caporusso completely... He came back from the Congress with strange ideas and pretensions entirely contrary to our association's principles. He spoke, at first quietly, then openly in an imperious manner, of powers which he did not, and could not, have; he affirmed that the General Council had confidence in no one but himself, and that if the section did not bow to his will, he had been empowered to dissolve it and found another." (Official report from the Naples section to the General Council, November a 1871, drawn up and signed by Carmelo Palladino, Alliance lawyer.) b

Caporusso's powers must have come from the Alliance's Central Committee, for the International never issued any of the kind. The good Caporusso, who only saw the International as a source of personal profit, nominated his son-in-law, an ex-Jesuit and an unfrocked priest,c

"professor of the International, and compelled the unfortunate workers to swallow his tirades on respect for private property and other fatuities of bourgeois political economy" (letter from Cafiero).*

He then sold himself to the capitalists, who were disturbed about the progress being made by the International in Naples. On their orders, he dragged the Neapolitan furriers into a completely hopeless strike. Imprisoned with three other members, he pocketed the sum of 300 frs. sent by the section for the maintenance of the four prisoners. These noble deeds led to his expulsion from the section, which continued to exist until it was forcibly dissolved (August 20, 1871). But the Alliance, on escaping from police persecution, profited by this to take the International's place. When sending the official report quoted above, Carmelo

---

* Rebuffed at Naples, Caporusso had the nerve, two years later, to try and inflict this same individual on the General Council with the following testimonial: "Citizen Chairman of the International, the great problem of labour and capital, which was dealt with at the Working Men's Congress of Basle and which is today taxing the minds of all classes, has now been solved. The man who has been studying the complex problem of the social question is my son-in-law, my daughter's husband, who, examining the decisions of this Congress and invoking the favours of science, has picked up the thread of the difficult knot wherewith to put into perfect equilibrium the working-class family and the bourgeoisie, each in its own right", etc. (signed: Stefano Caporusso).356

---

a The original has: "July".— Ed.

b Carmelo Palladino, Relazione Sulla Sezione Napoletana dell'Associazione Internazionale dei Lavoratori. Napoli, November 13, 1871 (manuscript).— Ed.

c Michelangelo Statuti.— Ed.

Palladino protested on November 13, 1871 against the London Conference in the very terms and with the very arguments used in the Sonvillier circular dated one day earlier.

In November 1871, a section consisting of various elements was formed in Milan.[357] It included workers, mainly mechanics brought by Cuno, alongside students, journalists from the small newspapers, and clerks, all completely under the influence of the Alliance. Owing to his pan-Germanic origins, Cuno was debarred from these mysteries. However, he made sure that after a pilgrimage to Locarno, the Rome of the Alliance, these young bourgeois were organised into a section of the secret society. Shortly afterwards (February 1872), Cuno was arrested and deported by the Italian police.[a] Thanks to this heavenly providence, the Alliance now had a free field, and gradually gained control over the Milan section of the International.

On October 8, 1871, the *Working Men's Federation* was formed in Turin.[358] It asked the General Council for admission to the International. Its secretary, Carlo Terzaghi, wrote literally: "*Attendiamo i vostri ordini*" (we await your *orders*). To prove that the International in Italy, from its first steps, must work its way through the bureaucratic channels of the Alliance, he announced that [359]

"the Council will receive through Bakunin a letter from the Working Men's Association in Ravenna declaring itself a section of the International".[b]

On December 4, Carlo Terzaghi informed the General Council that the *Working Men's Federation* was divided, since the majority were Mazzinists and the minority had formed a section called *Emancipation of the Proletarian*. He profited by the occasion to ask the Council for money for his newspaper *Il Proletario*. It was not the General Council's business to provide for the needs of the press; but there was in London a committee which was engaged in collecting funds to assist the International's press. The committee was about to send a subsidy of 150 frs., when the *Gazzettino Rosa* announced that the Turin section had openly sided with Jura and had decided to send a delegate to a world congress convoked by the Jura Federation.[c] Two months later, Terzaghi boasted to Regis that he had taken this resolution after having received Bakunin's instructions personally, at Locarno. In view of this hostile attitude to the International, the committee did not send the money.

---

[a] See this volume, pp. 151-52.— *Ed.*
[b] C. Terzaghi's letter to the General Council of October 10, 1871.— *Ed.*
[c] "Movimento operajo", *Gazzettino Rosa*, No. 360, December 28, 1871.— *Ed.*

Although Terzaghi was the Alliance's right arm at Turin, the true papal nuncio there was a certain Jacobi, a self-styled Polish physician. In order to explain the hatred which he felt for the so-called pan-Germanism of the General Council, this doctor member of the Alliance accused it of

> "negligence and inertia in the Franco-Prussian war; it should be blamed for the failure of the Commune, in that it did not use its immense power to support the movement in Paris, and its Germanic tendencies are conspicuous when one considers that, at the walls of Paris, in the German army, there were 40,000 members of the International" (!), "and the General Council could not, or would not, use its influence to prevent the continuation of the war" (!!—Report from Regis to the General Council, March 1, 1872).[360]

Confusing the General Council with the Press Committee, he accused it of "following the theory of corrupt and corrupting governments" by refusing the 150 francs to Terzaghi of the Alliance. To prove that this complaint came from the bottom of the Alliance's heart, Guillaume considered it his duty to repeat it at the Hague Congress.

While Terzaghi was publicly beating the big anti-authoritarian drum of the Alliance in his newspaper, he was secretly writing to the General Council and asking it to refuse authoritatively the subscriptions of the *Working Men's Federation* of Turin and demanding the formal excommunication of the journalist Beghelli, who was not even a member of the International. This same Terzaghi, the "friend (*amicone*) of the Turin prefect of police, who used to offer him vermouth when they met" (official report of the Federal Council of Turin, April 5, 1872[a]), denounced at a public meeting the presence of the refugee Regis, sent to Turin by the General Council. Given these leads, the police went in pursuit of Regis, who only managed to cross the frontier thanks to the section's help.

Terzaghi ended his Alliance assignment in Turin as follows. When serious charges were levelled against him, he

> "threatened to burn the section's books if he were not re-elected secretary, if they refused to submit to his authority, or if they censured him in any way. In any one of these cases, he would take his revenge by becoming a police agent, (*questurino*)" (report of the Turin Federal Council, quoted above).

Terzaghi had good reason for wanting to intimidate the section. In his capacity as treasurer and secretary, he had helped himself to the funds far too liberally in the truly Alliance fashion. Despite the

---

[a] C. Bert, *Associazione Internazionale dei Lavoratori. Società l'Emancipazione del Proletario Regione Piemontese*, Turin, April 5, 1872.— *Ed.*

Council's official ban, he had allotted himself an allowance of 90 frs.; he had entered in the books, as paid, sums which had not been paid and which had disappeared from the funds. The balance sheet personally drawn up by him showed 56 frs. in hand which could not be found and which he refused to make good, as well as declined to pay for 200 subscription stamps received from the General Council. The General Assembly unanimously threw him out (*scaccio*) (see report quoted above). The Alliance, which always respected the autonomy of sections, ratified this expulsion by immediately nominating Terzaghi honorary member of the Florentine section and, later, as delegate for that section to the Conference of Rimini.[361]

In a letter of March 10 a few days later, Terzaghi explained his expulsion to the General Council as follows: he had tendered his resignation as member and secretary of that section of riff-raff and spies (*canaglia et mardocheria*) because it was "composed of government agents and Mazzinists", and they had tried to pin the blame on him "do you know what for? For preaching war on capital!" (a war which he had been practising on the section's funds). The letter was intended to prove that the General Council had been strangely misled about the character of this brave Terzaghi who asked for nothing better than to be its humble servant. After all, he had "always declared that, to be a member of the International, it was necessary to pay one's subscriptions to the General Council"—contrary to the secret orders of the Alliance.

"If we joined the Congress of Jura, it was not to make war on you, dear friends; we were merely swimming with the stream. Our aim was to bring a word of peace into the conflict. As for the centralisation of the sections, without depriving them, however, of some of their own autonomy, I find it very useful".—"I hope that the higher Council will refuse to admit the Mazzinist *Working Men's Federation*. You may be sure that no one will dare tax you with authoritarianism. Myself, I assume all the responsibility... If it were available, I would like to have an accurate biography of Karl Marx. We haven't an authentic one in Italy, and I would like to be the first to have this honour."

And what was behind all this toadying?

"Not for myself, but for the cause, so as not to give way to my numerous enemies and to show them that the International is united, I earnestly beg you, if there is still time, to allow me the subsidy of 150 frs. which was decreed to me by the higher Council."

Imagining himself to be immune, Terzaghi seems to have made himself so impossible in Florence with new escapades that even *Fascio Operaio*[a] was forced to disown him. Let us hope that the Jura Committee will better appreciate his services.

---

[a] Workers' Union.— *Ed.*

If in Terzaghi the Alliance had found its true representative, it was in Romagna that it found its real territory, where it formed its group of so-called International sections whose first rule of conduct was not to observe the General Rules, not to announce their own formation, and not to pay subscriptions to the General Council. They were true autonomous sections. They adopted the name of *Fascio Operaio* and served as centres for various working men's associations. Their first Congress, held at Bologna on March 17, 1872, was asked:

"In the general interest, and to guarantee the complete autonomy of the *Fascio Operaio*, should we subject it to the direction of the General Committee in London or to the one in Jura, or should it remain entirely independent, while keeping up relations with both committees?"

The reply was in the form of the following resolution:

"The Congress does not recognise the General Committee of London or that of Jura as anything other than mere correspondence and statistical bureaux, and instructs the local representation in Bologna to establish relations with both of them and to report back to the sections."[a]

The *Fascio Operaio* committed a great blunder in disclosing the mysterious existence of the Alliance's secret centre to the profane. The Jura Committee felt obliged to make a public denial of its secret existence.—As for the General Council, the representation at Bologna never once informed it of its own existence.

As soon as the Alliance heard about the convocation of the Hague Congress, it pushed to the fore its *Fascio Operaio* which, in the name of its autonomous authority, or its authoritarian autonomy, grabbed the title of Italian Federation and convoked a conference at Rimini on August 5. Of the 21 sections represented there, only one, that of Naples, belonged to the International, whereas none of the really active sections of the International was represented, not even that of Milan. This Conference disclosed the Alliance's plan of campaign in the following resolution:

"Considering that the London Conference (September 1871) has tried to impose, with its resolution IX, on the whole International Working Men's Association an authoritarian doctrine which is that of the *German Communist Party*;

"that the General Council is the promoter and supporter of this fact;

"that the doctrine of the *authoritarian communists* is the negation of the revolutionary sentiment of the Italian proletariat;

"that the General Council has employed highly unworthy methods, such as

---

[a] "Associazione Internazionale dei Lavoratori. Fascio Operaio. Federazione Italiana—Regione di Bologna. Primo Congresso Regionale. Sunto del Processo Verbale", *Il Fascio Operaio*, No. 13, March 24, 1872.— *Ed.*

calumny and mystification, with the sole aim of imposing its special *communist authoritarian* doctrine on entire International Association;

"that the General Council has reached the height of unworthiness with its private circular, dated London, March 5, 1872, in which, pursuing its work of calumny and mystification, it reveals all its craving for authority, particularly in the two remarkable passages following:

"'It would be difficult to carry out orders without enjoying moral "authority", in the absence of any other "freely recognised authority"'. (Private circular, p. 27 [a]).

"'The General Council intends to demand at the next Congress an investigation of this secret organisation and its promoters in certain countries, such as Spain, for example (p. 31 [b]);

"that the reactionary spirit of the General Council has provoked the revolutionary resentment of the Belgians, the French, the Spaniards, the Slavs, the Italians, and some of the Swiss, and has also provoked the proposition for the suppression of the Council and likewise the reform of the General Rules;

"that the General Council, not without reason, has convoked the General Congress at The Hague, the place furthest removed from these revolutionary countries;

"FOR THESE REASONS,

"The Conference solemnly declares to all the workers of the world that from this moment the Italian Federation of the International Working Men's Association breaks off all solidarity with the General Council of London, affirming at the same time economic solidarity with all the workers and proposing to all sections which do not share the authoritarian principles of the General Council that they send their representatives on September 2, 1872 not to The Hague, but to Neuchâtel (Switzerland) for the opening of the general anti-authoritarian Congress on the same day.

"Rimini, August 6, 1872. For the Conference: Carlo Cafiero, chairman, Andrea Costa, secretary".[c]

The attempt to substitute the *Fascio Operaio* for the General Council was a total failure. Even the Spanish Federal Council, a mere branch of the Alliance, did not dare to submit the Rimini resolution to the vote of the International's Spanish members. The Alliance, to make amends for its blunder, went to the Hague Congress without cancelling the convocation of its anti-authoritarian Congress at Saint-Imier.

Italy had only become the promised land of the Alliance by special act of grace. Pope Michael unveils this mystery for us in his letter to Mora (Documents, No. 3 [d]):

"Italy has what other countries lack: a youth which is passionate, energetic, *completely at a loss, with no prospects, with no way out,* and which, despite its bourgeois origins, is not morally and intellectually exhausted like the bourgeois youth of other countries. Today it is throwing itself headlong into revolutionary socialism,

---

[a] See this volume, p. 110.— *Ed.*

[b] Ibid., p. 115.— *Ed.*

[c] *Associazione Internazionale dei Lavoratori. Federazione Italiana. Prima Conferenza. Risoluzione,* Rimini, August 6, 1872.— *Ed.*

[d] See this volume, pp. 578-80.— *Ed.*

accepting *our entire programme*, the programme of the Alliance. Mazzini, our mighty antagonist *of genius" (sic)* "is dead, and the Mazzinist party is completely disorganised, and Garibaldi is letting himself be carried away more and more by that youth which bears his name, but is going, or rather running, infinitely further ahead of him." *

The Holy Father is right. The Alliance in Italy is not a "workers' union", but a rabble of *déclassés*. All the · so-called sections of the Italian International are run by lawyers without clients, doctors with neither patients nor medical knowledge, students of billiards, commercial travellers and other tradespeople, and principally journalists from small papers with a more or less dubious reputation. Italy is the only country where the International press—or what calls itself such—has acquired the typical characteristics of *Le Figaro*. One need only glance at the writing of the secretaries of these so-called sections to realise that it is the work of clerks or professional authors. By taking over all the official posts in the sections in this way, the Alliance managed to compel the Italian workers, every time they wanted to enter into relations with one another or with the other councils of the International, to resort to the services of *déclassé* members of the Alliance who found in the International a "career" and a "way out".

VI

THE ALLIANCE IN FRANCE

The French members were not very numerous but they were more keen. At Lyons, the Alliance was led by Albert Richard and Gaspard Blanc, and at Marseilles by Bastelica—all three of whom were active contributors to the newspapers run by Guillaume. It is thanks to them that the Alliance succeeded in disorganising the movement at Lyons in September 1870. This movement, for them,

* Here is what Garibaldi himself says about this: "My dear Crescio—hearty thanks for sending to me your *Avvenire Sociale* which I shall read with interest. You intend, in your paper, to make war upon untruth and slavery. That is a very fine programme, but I believe that the International, in fighting against the principle of authority, makes a mistake and obstructs its own progress. The Paris Commune fell because there was in Paris no authority but only anarchy, Spain and France are suffering from the same evil. I wish success to the *Avvenire*, and, remain yours, G. Garibaldi.»[a]

---

[a] *La Favilla*, No. 134, June 5, 1873 (cf. this volume, p. 453).— *Ed.*

was only important in that it allowed Bakunin to launch his unforgettable decree on the abolition of the State.—The activities of the Alliance after the failure of the Lyons insurrection are neatly summed up in the following passage from a letter by Bastelica (Marseilles, December 13, 1870[a]):

"Our real power among the workers is enormous; but our section has not been reorganised since the last persecutions. We dare not do this for fear that *in the absence of the leaders, the elements may disintegrate.* We are biding our time."

That Bastelica, then in a foot regiment, could at any moment be sent away from Marseilles, was sufficient reason for him to hinder the reorganisation of the International section, so essential to its autonomy did he consider the presence of Alliance leaders.—The most evident result of the Alliance's activities was to discredit in the eyes of the workers of Lyons and Marseilles the International, which, as always and everywhere, it claimed to represent.

The end of Richard and Blanc is known. In the autumn of 1871, they turned up in London and attempted to recruit from among the French refugees auxiliaries for a Bonapartist restoration. In January 1872, they published a brochure: L'EMPIRE ET LA FRANCE NOUVELLE. *Appel du peuple et de la jeunesse a la conscience française,* by Albert Richard and Gaspard Blanc, Brussels, 1872.

With the usual modesty of the Alliance's quacks, they trotted out their patter as follows:

"We, who have formed the great army of the French proletariat ... we, the most influential leaders of the International in France ... happily, we have not been shot, and we are here to raise before them (*ambitious parliamentarians, bloated republicans, self-styled democrats of all kinds*) the standard under which we fight, and to fling forth to an astounded Europe—despite the calumnies, despite the threats, despite the attacks of every kind in store for us—this cry which issues from the depths of our conscience and which shall resound ere long in the hearts of all the French: — LONG LIVE THE EMPEROR!"

We shall refrain from investigating whether these two members of the Alliance who had become imperialists owing to the "normal progression of their ideas", were mere "riff-raff", as they were called by their old friend Guillaume at The Hague, or whether the pope of the Alliance had given them the special mission of joining the ranks of the Bonapartist agents. The documents of the Russian Alliance which, according to the secret statutes, will unveil the mystery of mysteries of this mysterious society and from which

---

[a] The letter was addressed to Paul Lafargue.— *Ed.*

we shall be citing extracts further on, state expressly that the international brethren must infiltrate everywhere and may even receive orders to enrol in the police force. Incidentally, the veneration of these two brethren for their emperor of the peasants does not exceed that in which Bakunin held his own tsar of the peasants in 1862.[a]

After the fall of the Commune, the International grew rapidly in all the French cities which had not been infiltrated by the Alliance. At the Hague Congress, the Secretary for France[b] was able to announce that the International had its organisations in over thirty departments. The two principal Alliance correspondents for France, Benoît Malon and Jules Guesde (the latter was a signatory of the Sonvillier circular) who knew about this rapid development of our Association, tried to disorganise it in the Alliance's favour. When their letters failed to have the desired effect, emissaries were sent, including a Russian named Mechnikov; but their efforts came to nothing. These same individuals who impudently accused the General Council of preventing the workers from

"organising themselves in each country freely, spontaneously, and according to their own spirit, and particular customs" (letter from Guesde, September 22, 1872)[362]

told the workers—as soon as they began to organise themselves freely, spontaneously, etc., but in complete harmony with the General Council—that the Germans in the Council were oppressing them and that there was no salvation outside their orthodox anti-authoritarian church. The French workers, who were aware only of the oppression from the Versailles, sent these letters to the General Council and asked them what it all signified.

This move by the Alliance in France is the best proof that, as soon as it began to lose hope of dominating the International, it began to fight it. Every section which was not brought under its domination was regarded as an enemy more hostile even than the bourgeoisie. *He who is not for us, is against us* is the rule which it openly avowed in its Russian manifestos.[c] For the Alliance, the success of the general movement was a misfortune if that movement did not bow under the yoke of its sectarianism. And at

---

[a] An allusion to the estimation of Alexander II in Bakunin's pamphlet *Народное Дѣло. Романовъ, Пугачевъ или Пестель?* (see this volume, pp. 562-63).— *Ed.*

[b] Auguste Serraillier.— *Ed.*

[c] «Кто не за насъ, тотъ противъ насъ», *Изданія Общества «Народной Расправы»*, No. 2; М. Бакунинъ, *Къ офицерамъ русской арміи*. Geneva, 1870.— *Ed.*

the very time when the French working class needed above all some kind of organisation, the Alliance went to the aid of Thiers and the Rurals[363] by declaring war on the International.

Now let us see who were the Alliance's agents during its campaign in favour of the Versailles.

At Montpellier, M. Guesde had for confidant a man named Paul Brousse, a medical student, who was attempting to carry out Alliance propaganda through the whole department of Hérault, where Guesde had formerly been editor of the *Droits de l'Homme*. Shortly before the Hague Congress, when members of the International for the South of France met to subscribe for a common delegate to the Congress, Brousse tried to persuade the Montpellier section not to pay its share and not to say anything until the Congress had settled matters under discussion. The Committee for the South—the Montpellier section, decided to ask the Congress to exclude Brousse from the International for having "acted disloyally in provoking a split in the heart of the section."[364] His friend Guesde, in a communication sent in October from Rome to the *Liberté* of Brussels,[a] denounced this authoritarian move against Brousse and cited Calas of Montpellier as the instigator, writing out his name in full, whereas he referred to Brousse by his initials. Alerted by this denunciation, the police kept watch on Calas, and immediately afterwards confiscated a letter in the post from Serraillier to Calas in which much was said about Dentraygues of Toulouse. On December 24, Dentraygues was arrested.

The Alliance's most active helpers at Narbonne were: Gondres, unmasked as a police informer; Bacave who, at Narbonne and Perpignan, was carrying out the duties of police agent; and de Saint-Martin, a lawyer and a correspondent of Malon's. In 1866, M. de Saint-Martin had applied for a post in the Ministry of the Imperial Court and the Fine Arts. When he was sentenced in 1869 to pay fine of 800 frs. for a press offence, republicans collected money to pay his fine; but Saint-Martin, instead of using the funds for this purpose, went on a little trip to Paris at the expense of the workers who, to avoid a scandal, had to contribute all over again. Shortly after the May days in 1871,[365] the same Saint-Martin applied to the Versailles government for the post of sub-prefect.

Here is another Alliance agent: in November 1871, Calas wrote to Serraillier:

---

a J. Guesde, "Rien ou presque rien...", *La Liberté*, No. 42, October 20, 1872.— *Ed.*

"You may count on Citizen Abel Bousquet's absolute devotion to the social cause, he is ... chairman of the Socialist Committee of Béziers."

Two days later, on November 13, Serraillier received the following statement:

"Convinced that our mutual friend, Citizen Calas, has been badly let down in that this citizen relied on M. Bousquet, Chairman of the Electoral Committee of Béziers, and the latter is most unworthy of this, since he is secretary to the Central Police Commissioner for Béziers ... in agreement with Citizen Calas, who has recognised the mistake of which he was the victim, we shall ask Citizen Serraillier to regard as cancelled the last letter sent to him by Citizen Calas and, moreover, we shall ask him, if it can be done, to have M. Bousquet expelled from the International. By authority of the socialist democracy of Béziers and Pézénas" (here follow the signatures).

Serraillier profited by this statement to denounce, in *L'Emancipation* of Toulouse (December 19, 1871), this M. Bousquet as a police agent.[a]—A letter dated Narbonne, July 24, 1872, says that M. Bousquet

"is combining the functions of brigadier chief of police with those of travelling agent for the Genevan dissidents".[366]

It is therefore only natural that the *Bulletin jurassien* of November 10, 1872 should have come out in his defence.[b]

VII

THE ALLIANCE AFTER THE HAGUE CONGRESS

It is known that at the last sitting of the Hague Congress, the fourteen delegates of the minority tabled a declaration of protest against the resolutions adopted.[c] This minority consisted of the following delegates: four Spanish, five Belgian, two Jurassian, two Dutch, and one American.

After having agreed at Brussels with the Belgians on the principles for common action against the new General Council, the Jurassians and the Spaniards left for Saint-Imier in Switzerland to hold the anti-authoritarian Congress which the Alliance had arranged to have convoked by its acolytes in Rimini.

This Congress was preceded by that of the Jura Federation,

---

[a] A. Serraillier, "A la rédaction de *L'Émancipation* de Toulouse", *L'Emancipation*, No. 1243, December 19, 1871.— *Ed.*

[b] J. Montels, "Compagnons rédacteurs...", *Bulletin de la Fédération jurassienne...*, No. 20/21, November 10, 1872 (see also this volume, p. 300).— *Ed.*

[c] "Déclaration de la minorité", *La Liberté*, No. 37, September 15, 1872.— *Ed.*

which rejected the resolutions of The Hague, notably the one expelling Bakunin and Guillaume. As a result, the Federation was suspended by the General Council.[367]

The Alliance was fully represented at the anti-authoritarian congress. Beside the Spaniards and the Jurassians, there were six Italian delegates, including Costa, Cafiero, Fanelli, and Bakunin in person; two delegates claimed to represent "several French sections", and another delegate—two American ones. In all, fifteen "allies". This Congress finally offered Bakunin "all the guarantees of an impartial and serious trial"[a]; and here, too, complete unanimity prevailed. These men, of whom at least half did not belong to the International, appointed themselves members of a supreme tribunal called upon to pronounce the final sentence upon the acts of a General Congress of our Association. They announced their absolute rejection of all resolutions passed by the Hague Congress and refused to recognise in any way the powers of the new General Council elected by it. Finally, they formed, on behalf of their federations and without any form of mandate to that effect, an offensive and defensive alliance, a "pact of friendship, of solidarity, and of mutual defence", against the General Council and all those who recognised the resolutions of the Hague Congress. They defined their abstentionist anarchism in the following resolution, which was a direct condemnation of the Paris Commune:

"The Congress declares 1) that the destruction of all political power is the first duty of the proletariat; 2) that *any organisation of supposedly provisional and revolutionary political power aiming to bring about this destruction can only be yet another hoax* and will be as dangerous to the proletariat as *all* governments in existence today."[b]

Finally, it was decided to invite the other autonomist federations to join the new *pact* and to hold a second anti-authoritarian Congress six months later.

The split within the International was thus proclaimed. From that moment, the Jura Committee openly took over the management of the dissidents' affairs. The part of the International which followed it was no more than the old public Alliance reconstituted and serving as a cover and tool for the secret Alliance.

On returning to Spain, the four Aymon sons, members of the

---

[a] See this volume, p. 485.— *Ed.*

[b] "Les deux congrès de Saint-Imier", *Bulletin de la Fédération jurassienne...*, No. 17/18, September 15-October 1, 1872, p. 12.— *Ed.*

Spanish Alliance,[a] published a manifesto full of calumnies against the Congress at The Hague and flattery for the one at Saint-Imier.[b] The Federal Council supported this libel and, on the orders of the Swiss centre, convoked at Cordoba for December 25, 1872 the regional Congress which was not to have taken place until April 1873. The Swiss centre, for its part, hastened to disclose to everybody the subordinate position which the Council had been occupying beside it. Over the head of the Spanish Council, the Jura Committee sent the Saint-Imier resolutions to all the local federations in Spain.

At the Congress of Cordoba, there were only 36 federations represented out of 101 (the official number given by the Federal Council); and so this was a minority Congress if ever there was one. The newly formed federations were represented by numerous delegates; Alcoy had six, and yet this federation had never been represented before in a regional Congress. Even during the time of the Hague Congress, it had not yet existed, since it had not provided one vote or one centime to the Spanish delegation. The important and active federations, such as Gracia (500 members), Badalona (500), Sabadell (125), Sans (1,061), were conspicuous by their absence. In a list of forty-eight delegates, there were fourteen notorious Alliance members, of whom ten represented federations of which they were not members and which probably did not even know them. Sure of the majority which it had engineered, the Alliance gave itself a free hand. The regional federation's statutes, drawn up at Valencia and sanctioned at Saragossa, were scrapped, the Spanish Federation decapitated, and its Federal Council replaced by a simple correspondence and statistical commission which did not even retain the function of sending in the Spanish subscriptions to the General Council. Finally, the Alliance broke with the International, rejecting the resolutions of the Hague Congress and adopting the Saint-Imier pact. It went so far in its anarchy as to repudiate in advance the next General Congress and to substitute for it a new *anti-authoritarian* Congress

"*in case the first one does not restore the dignity and independence of the International by repudiating the Hague Congress*".[c]

At The Hague, the Alliance wanted to impose, by means of the Spanish imperative mandate, the manner of voting which best suited it at the time. At Cordoba, it went so far as to prescribe,

a Alerini, Farga Pellicer, Morago and Marselau.— *Ed.*
b "Memoria. A todos los Internacionales Españoles", Valencia, 1872.— *Ed.*
c "El Congreso de Córdoba", *La Federacion,* No. 179, January 18, 1873.— *Ed.*

nine months in advance, the resolutions which must be adopted by the next General Congress. It must be admitted that the autonomy of sections and federations could not be pushed any further.

In expelling the Alliance and its leaders from the International, the Hague Congress gave fresh impetus to the anti-Alliance movement in Spain. The New Madrid Federation was supported in its newly launched campaign by the federations of Saragossa, Vitoria, Alcalá de Henares, Gracia, Lerida, Denia, Pont de Vilumara, Toledo, Valencia, the new federation of Cadiz, etc. The Federal Council's circular convoking the Congress of Cordoba asked it to set itself up in judgment on the resolutions passed at the Hague General Congress.[a] This was in flagrant violation not only of the General Rules, but also of the Spanish regional statutes, which stated in Article 13:

"The Federal Council will implement, and will cause to be implemented, the resolutions of the regional and *international* Congresses."

The New Madrid Federation reacted with a circular to the other local federations[b] in which it declared that by this act the Federal Council had put itself outside the International, and asked them to replace it with a new provisional council whose mission would be strict observance of the Rules and not passive obedience to the Alliance's orders. This proposal was accepted; a new Federal Council was appointed with its seat at Valencia. In its first circular (February 2, 1873), it declared itself to be "the faithful guardian of the International's Rules as drawn up and sanctioned at the international and regional Congresses", and protested vigorously against those who wished to sow

"anarchy within the International, anarchy before revolution, disarmament before triumph! What a joy to the bourgeoisie!"[c]

The Belgians held their Congress at the same time as the Spaniards and likewise rejected the Hague resolutions. The General Council replied to them, as to the Spanish secessionists,

---

[a] "Asociacion Internacional de los Trabajadores. Federacion Regional Española. Consejo Federal. Circular á todas las federaciones locales". [November 14, 1872]. [Signed:] Vicente Rossell, Vicente Torres. *La Federacion*, No. 171, November 23, 1872.— *Ed.*

[b] "La Nueva Federacion Madrileña. Á todas las federaciones... Madrid, 1° de noviembre de 1872", *La Emancipacion*, No. 73, November 9, 1872.— *Ed.*

[c] "Asociacion Internacional de los Trabajadores. Consejo Federal de la Region Española. Compañeros..., Valencia, 2 de febrero de 1873", *La Emancipacion*, No. 85, February 8, 1873.— *Ed.*

with the resolution of January 26, 1873, which declared that "all societies or individuals refusing to acknowledge the Congress resolutions, or wilfully neglecting to perform the duties imposed by the rules and administrative regulations—place themselves outside of, and cease to belong to the International Working Men's Association." On May 30, it finalised this declaration with the following resolution:

"Whereas the Congress of the Belgian federation, held at Brussels on the 25th & 26th day of December 1872, resolved to declare null & void the resolutions of the 5th General Congress;

"Whereas the Congress of a part of the Spanish federation, held at Cordoba from December 25th [1872] to January 2nd 1873, resolved: to repudiate the resolutions of the 5th General Congress & to adopt the resolutions of an anti-international meeting;

"Whereas a meeting, held at London January 26th 1873, resolved: to repudiate the action taken by the 5th General Congress;

"The General Council of the International Workingmen's Association in obedience to the statutes & administrative regulations & in accordance with its resolution of January 26th 1873, hereby declares:

"All regional & local federations, sections & individuals having participated in & recognising the resolutions of the above mentioned meetings & Congresses at Brussels, Cordoba & London,— *have placed themselves outside of & are no longer members of the International Workingmen's Association.*"

At the same time, it declared once more that no regional Italian federation of the International exists, since no organisation calling itself by this name has fulfilled the minimal conditions for admission and affiliation as imposed by the Rules and Administrative Regulations. In different parts of Italy, however, there are sections which are in order as far as the General Council is concerned and are in communication with it.

For their part, the Jurassians held another Congress on April 27 and 28 at Neuchâtel. There were nineteen delegates present from ten Swiss sections, and a so-called section from Alsace; two Swiss sections and one French section sent no delegates. The Jura Federation thus claimed to count twelve sections in Switzerland. But the delegate for Moutier[a] declared that he had only come to speak in favour of reconciliation with the International, and had an imperative mandate not to take part in the work of the

---

[a] Henri Favre.— *Ed.*

Congress. Moutier had, in fact, broken away from the Jura Federation after the Congress of Saint-Imier. This left *eleven* sections. The fact that the report from the Committee[a] scrupulously abstained from giving the slightest indication about their internal position and their strength gives us the right to assume that they had no more vitality than at the time of the Congress of Sonvillier. In compensation, the report draws up in battle order the external forces of the Jurassians, the allies whom the Alliance gained after the Hague Congress. According to this report, they were nearly all federations of the International:

"Italy"—But we have seen that there is no Italian federation.

"Spain"—Although the majority of the Spanish International members have moved across into the secessionist camp, we have just seen that the Spanish Federation still exists and is in regular communication with the General Council.

"France, in what is seriously organised there", that is, the "section of France", which apologised to the Congress of Neuchâtel for not having sent a delegate. We are taking good care not to disclose to the Jurassians what is still "seriously organised" in France, despite the latest persecutions, which have demonstrated well enough on whose side this serious organisation was and which, as always, have solicitously spared the few Alliance members in France.

"The whole of Belgium"—is the dupe of the Alliance, whose principles she is far from sharing.

"Holland, except for one section"—that is to say, *two* Dutch sections supported not the Saint-Imier pact, but the anti-separatist declaration of the minority at The Hague.

"England, except for a few dissidents"!—The "dissidents", that is to say, the vast majority of the English sections of the International, held their Congress on June 1 and 2 at Manchester, where twenty-six delegates were present representing twenty-three sections[368]; whereas the "England" of the Jurassians had no sections or Federal Council, much less a Congress.

"America, apart from a few dissidents"!—The American Federation of the International exists and functions regularly in complete harmony with the General Council. It has its Federal Council and its Congresses. The "America" of the Jura Committee consists purely of those bourgeois dealers in free love, paper money, public appointments and bribes, who were represented so

---

[a] "Rapport du Comité Fédéral Jurassien...", *Bulletin de la Fédération jurassienne...*, No. 9, May 1, 1873.— *Ed.*

magnificently at the Hague Congress by Mr. West that even the
Jura delegates dared not speak or vote in his favour.

"The Slavs"—that is to say, the "Slav section of Zurich", which,
as always, figures as a whole race. The Poles, the Russians, and the
Austrian and Hungarian Slavs of the International, as open
enemies of the secessionists, do not count.

This is what the allies of the Alliance amounted to. If the eleven
Jura sections were no more real than the majority of these allies,
their committee had good reason to keep silent about them.

In this battle order of the Alliance, Switzerland was conspicuous
by her absence. There were very good reasons for this. A month
later, on June 1 and 2, a general Swiss Working Men's Congress
was held in Olten to organise resistance and strikes.[369] Five
Jurassians[a] there preached the gospel of absolute autonomy of the
sections; they made the Congress waste over half its time. Finally,
the matter had to be put to vote. The result was that of eighty
delegates, seventy-five voted against the five Jurassians who had
no alternative but to leave the hall.

At its secret gatherings, however, the Alliance apparently did
not subscribe, where its real forces were concerned, to the illusions
which it wanted to impose on the public. At that same Congress of
Neuchâtel, it had the following resolution adopted:

"Considering that, in accordance with the General Rules, the General Congress
of the International meets every year without need of convocation by the General
Council, the Jura Federation proposes to all the federations of the International
that they should meet for a General Congress on Monday, September 1, in a Swiss
town."

And to prevent this congress from repeating the "fatal errors of
The Hague", it was requested that the Alliance delegates and their
allies should meet, on August 28, for an anti-authoritarian
Congress. From the debate on this proposition, it emerges that

"for us, the only General Congress of the International will be the one
convoked directly by the federations themselves, and not the *one which the so-called
General Council of New York might attempt to convoke*".[b]

Here, then, is the split carried to extremes with all the attendant
consequences. The members of the International will go to the
congress which the preceding Congress has instructed the General
Council to convoke in a Swiss town of its own choosing. The

---

    [a] James Guillaume, J.-L. Pindy, Henri Wenker, Léon Schwitzguébel, Charles
Gameter.— *Ed.*

    [b] "Le Congrès jurassien, des 27 et 28 avril 1873", *L'Internationale*, No. 228, May
18, 1873.— *Ed.*

Alliance members and their suite of dupes will go to a congress convoked by themselves on the strength of their autonomy. We wish them a pleasant journey.

VIII

THE ALLIANCE IN RUSSIA

1. THE NECHAYEV TRIAL

The Alliance's activities in Russia were revealed to us by the political trial known as "the Nechayev affair" which took place in July 1871 before the Court of Justice in St. Petersburg. For the first time in Russia, a political trial took place before a jury and in public. All the accused, numbering over eighty men and women, belonged, with a few exceptions, to the student youth. From November 1869 to July 1871, they were kept in detention in the dungeons of the fortress[a] in St. Petersburg, with the result that two of them died and several others went insane. They were brought out of prison to be condemned to the Siberian mines, to penal servitude, and to imprisonment for fifteen, twelve, ten, seven and two years. And those acquitted by the public tribunal were then exiled as an "administrative measure".

Their crime was that they had belonged to a secret society which had usurped the name of the International Working Men's Association, to which they had been affiliated by an emissary of the international revolutionary committee who carried mandates stamped with a fake seal of the International; and this emissary had forced them to commit a series of frauds and had obliged several of them to help him in an assassination. It was this assassination which put the police on the trail of the secret society; but, as always, the emissary disappeared. The police showed such perspicacity in their investigations that it was possible to assume a detailed denunciation. Throughout the whole of this affair, the role of the emissary was highly ambiguous. This emissary was Nechayev, who carried a certificate-mandate to the following effect:

"The bearer of this certificate is one of the authorised representatives of the Russian branch of the World Revolutionary Alliance.—No. 2771."

---

[a] Peter and Paul Fortress.— *Ed.*

This certificate carried: 1) a stamp, in French: "European Revolutionary Alliance. General Committee"; 2) date—May 12, 1869; 3) signature—*Mikhail Bakunin.**

In 1861, as a result of the fiscal measures intended to deprive poor young people of a higher education, and as a result of disciplinary steps aimed at subjecting them to arbitrary police control, the students made a vigorous and unanimous protest which they took from their meetings out into the streets to be expressed in impressive demonstrations. St. Petersburg University was then closed for a time and the students were imprisoned or exiled. This government move drove the young people into secret societies which inevitably resulted in large numbers of the members being imprisoned, banished, or sent to Siberia. Others, to provide the necessary means for the poor students to continue their studies, founded mutual aid funds. The more serious of them decided not to give the government any further pretext for suppressing these funds, which were organised so that business matters could be discussed at small meetings. These business meetings provided the opportunity to discuss political and social questions at the same time. Socialist ideas had penetrated so deeply among the Russian student youth, who were mainly the sons of peasants and other poor people, that they already dreamed of putting them immediately into practice. Every day, this movement spread further in the educational institutions and injected into Russian society poor young people of plebeian origin who were instructed in, and permeated with, socialist ideas. The heart and soul of this movement's theoretical aspect was Chernyshevsky, now in Siberia.[370] It was at this point that Nechayev, profiting by the International's prestige and the enthusiasm of the young, tried to convince the students that the time had passed for concern with such trivialities, now that there existed a huge secret society affiliated to the International and occupied in fomenting world revolution and ready for immediate action in Russia. He managed to hoodwink a few young people and inveigle them into committing criminal acts, which gave the police the pretext for

---

* *St. Petersburg Gazette*[a], 1871, Nos. 180, 181, 187 and others.

---

[a] *С.-Петербургскія Вѣдомости.—Ed.*

crushing the whole of this student movement, so dangerous to official Russia.

In March 1869, there arrived at Geneva a young Russian who tried to ingratiate himself with all the Russian emigrants by posing as a delegate from the St. Petersburg students. He introduced himself under various names. Some of the emigrants knew positively that no delegate had been sent from that city; others, after talking to the supposed delegate, took him for a spy. In the end, he let himself be known by his real name, which was Nechayev. He said that he had escaped from the St. Petersburg fortress, where he had been incarcerated as one of the chief instigators of the disorders which had broken out in January 1869 in the capital's educational institutions. Several of the emigrants, who had suffered long spells of detention in this fortress, knew from experience that all escape was impossible, and so they were aware that on this point Nechayev was lying; on the other hand, since the newspapers and letters which they received with the names of wanted students never mentioned Nechayev, they regarded his alleged revolutionary activity as mere legend. But Bakunin took up Nechayev's cause and made a tremendous fuss about it. He proclaimed to all and sundry that this was the "envoy extraordinary of the great secret organisation existing and active in Russia". Bakunin was beseeched not to disclose to this person the names of his acquaintances whom he could compromise. Bakunin gave his word; how he kept it will be shown by the documents of the trial.

During an interview that Nechayev requested of a refugee,[a] he was forced to admit that he was not the delegate of any secret organisation, but he had, he said, comrades and acquaintances whom he wished to organise, adding that it was essential to gain control over the old emigrants in order to influence the young people with their prestige and to profit by their printing press and their money. Shortly afterwards, *Words* came out, addressed to the students by Nechayev and Bakunin.[b] In it, Nechayev repeated the legend of his escape and appealed to the young people to devote themselves to the revolutionary struggle. In the student unrest Bakunin discovers "an all-destroying spirit opposed to the State ...

---

[a] N. I. Utin.— *Ed.*

[b] The reference is to Bakunin's leaflet *Нѣсколько словъ къ молодымъ братьямъ въ Россіи* and Nechayev's *Студентамъ университета, академіи и тех[нологическаго] института въ Петербургѣ*, Geneva, 1869.— *Ed.*

which has emerged from the very depths of the people's life" *; he congratulates his "young brethren on their revolutionary tendencies.... This means that the end is in sight of this infamous Empire of all the Russias!" His anarchism served him as a pretext to take a swipe at the Poles, accusing them of only working

"for the restoration of their historic state" (!!).—"They dream, therefore, of a new enslavement of their people", and should they succeed "they would become our enemies as much as the oppressors of their own people. We shall fight them in the name of the social revolution and liberty for the whole world".

Bakunin is clearly in agreement with the tsar on this issue: The Poles must be prevented at all costs from managing their internal affairs as they think fit. During all Polish insurrections, the official Russian press has always accused the Polish insurgents of being "the oppressors of their own people". A touching point of agreement between the organs of the Third Department ** and the archanarchist of Locarno!

The Russian people, Bakunin continues, are at present living in conditions similar to those that forced them to rise under Tsar Alexei, father of Peter the Great. Then it was Stenka Razin, the Cossack brigand chief, who placed himself at their head and showed them "the road" to "freedom". In order to rise today the people are waiting only for a new Stenka Razin; but this time he

"will be replaced by the legion of *déclassé* young men who already live the life of the people... Stenka Razin, no longer an individual hero but a collective one" (!) "consequently they have an invincible hero behind them. Such a hero are all the magnificent young people over whom his spirit already soars."

To perform this role of a collective Stenka Razin, the young people must prepare themselves through ignorance:

"Friends, abandon with all speed this world doomed to destruction. Leave its universities, its academies, its schools [...] and go among the people," to become "the mid-wife of the people's self-emancipation, the uniter and organiser of their forces and efforts. Do not bother at this moment with learning, in the name of which they would bind you, castrate you... Such is the belief of the finest people in the West... The world of the workers of Europe and America calls you to join them in a fraternal alliance."

* It shall be noted that these *Words* were published at the very moment of the persecutions and sentences, when the young people were doing their utmost to moderate their movement which the police themselves found it so advantageous to exaggerate.

** The Third Department of the Imperial Russian Chancellory is the Central Bureau of the secret political police in Russia.

In its secret statutes, the Alliance tells its third-grade members that

"the principles of this organisation ... shall be even more explicitly exposed in the programme of the Russian socialist democracy".[a]

We have here the beginnings of this promise's fulfilment. In addition to the habitual anarchist phrases and the chauvinistic hatred of the Poles that Citizen B. has never been able to conceal, we see him here for the first time acclaiming the Russian brigand as the type of the true revolutionary and preaching to Russian young the cult of ignorance, under the pretext that modern science is merely official science (can one imagine an official mathematics, physics or chemistry?), and that this is the opinion of the finest people in the West. Finally he ends his leaflet by letting it be understood that through his mediation the International is proposing an alliance to these young people, whom he forbids even the *learning* of the Ignorantines.[371]

This evangelical *Word* played a great part in the Nechayev conspiracy. It was read secretly to every neophyte before his initiation.

At the same time as this *Word* (1869), anonymous Russian publications came out: 1) *The Setting of the Revolutionary Question*[b]; 2) *The Principles of Revolution*[c]; 3) *Publications of the "People's Judgment" Society* ("Narodnaya Rasprava") No. 1, summer 1869, Moscow.[d]— All these writings were printed in Geneva, as is proved by the fact that the type was identical with that used for other Russian publications in Geneva—furthermore, this fact was a matter of public notoriety among all the Russian emigrants,— which did not prevent these publications from carrying on their first page the stamp: "Printed in Russia—Gedruckt in Russland", to mislead the Russian students into thinking that the secret society possessed considerable resources in Russia itself.

The Setting of the Revolutionary Question gives away its authors at once. The same phrases, the same expressions as those used by Bakunin and Nechayev in their *Words*:

"Not only the state must be destroyed, but also revolutionaries of the State and the cabinet. We are certainly for the people."

---

[a] See this volume, p. 573.— *Ed.*

[b] [M. Бакунин,] *Постановка революціоннаго вопроса.* Here and below the titles of Bakunin's and Nechayev's works, as well as those of some other authors, are given in the original in French.—*Ed.*

[c] *Начала Революціи.* (Written by M. Bakunin or S. Nechayev), Geneva, 1869.— *Ed.*

[d] *Изданія Общества «Народной Расправы»,* No. 1.— *Ed.*

By the law of anarchist assimilation, Bakunin assimilates himself to the student youth:

"The government itself shows us the road *we* must follow to attain *our* goal, that is to say, the goal of the people. It drives *us* out of the universities, the academies, the schools. We are grateful to it for having thus put us on such glorious, such firm ground. Now we have ground under our feet, now we can do things. And what are we going to do? Teach the people? That would be stupid. The people know themselves, and better than we do, what they need" (compare the secret statutes which endow the masses with "popular instincts", and the initiates with "the revolutionary idea" a). "Our task is not to teach the people but to rouse them." Up to now "they have always rebelled in vain because they have rebelled separately... We can render them extremely valuable assistance, we can give them what they have lacked so far, what has been the principal cause of all their defeats. We can give them the unity of universal movement by rallying their own forces."

This is where the doctrine of the Alliance, anarchy at the bottom and discipline at the top, emerges in all its purity. First by rioting comes the "unleashing of what today are called the evil passions" but "in the midst of popular anarchy, which will constitute the very life and energy of the revolution, unity of revolutionary idea and action should find an organ". That organ will be the world Alliance, Russian section, the *Society of the People's Judgment.*

But Bakunin is not to be satisfied merely with youth. He calls all brigands to the banner of his Alliance, Russian section.

"Brigandage is one of the most honourable forms of the Russian people's life. The brigand is a hero, a protector, a people's avenger, the irreconcilable enemy of the state, and of all social and civil order established by the state, a fighter to the death against the whole civilisation of the civil servants, the nobles, the priests and the crown... He who fails to understand brigandage understands nothing of Russian popular history. He who is not in sympathy with it, cannot be in sympathy with Russian popular life, and has no heart for the measureless, age-long sufferings of the people; he belongs to the enemy camp, among the supporters of the state... Brigandage is the sole proof of the vitality, the passion and the strength of the people... The brigand in Russia is the true and only revolutionary—the revolutionary without phrases, without rhetoric culled from books, an indefatigable revolutionary, irreconcilable and irresistible in action, a popular and social revolutionary, not a political or class revolutionary... The brigands in the forests, in the towns and in the villages scattered all over Russia, and the brigands held in the countless gaols of the empire make up a single, indivisible, close-knit world—the world of the Russian revolution. It is here, and here alone, that the real revolutionary conspiracy has long existed. He who wants to undertake real conspiracy in Russia, who wants a people's revolution, must go into this world... Following the road pointed out to us now by the government, which drives us from the academies, the universities and schools, let us throw ourselves, brethren, among the people, into the people's movement, into the brigand and peasant rebellion

_____

a See this volume, p. 576.— *Ed.*

and, maintaining a true and firm friendship among ourselves, let us rally into a single mass all the scattered outbursts of the muzhiks" (peasants). "*Let us turn* them into a people's revolution, meaningful but ruthless." *

In the second leaflet, *The Principles of Revolution*, we find a development of the order given in the secret statutes that "not a stone shall remain standing" [b]. All must be destroyed in order to produce "complete amorphism", for if even "one of the old forms" be preserved, it will become the "embryo" from which all the other old social forms will be regenerated. The leaflet accuses the political revolutionaries who do not take this amorphism seriously of deceiving the people. It accuses them of having erected

"new gallows and scaffolds where the surviving brother revolutionaries have been done to death... So it is that the people have not yet known a real revolution... A real revolution does not need individuals standing at the head of the crowd and commanding it, but men hidden invisibly among the crowd and forming an invisible link between one crowd and another, and thus invisibly giving one and the same direction, one spirit and character to the movement. This is the sole purpose of bringing in a secret preparatory organisation and only to this extent is it necessary."

Here, then, the existence of the *international brethren,* so carefully concealed in the West, is exposed to the Russian public and the Russian police. Further the leaflet goes on to preach systematic assassination and declares that for people engaged in practical revolutionary work all argument about the future is

"criminal because it hinders *pure destruction* and hampers the advent of the beginning of the revolution. We believe only in those who show their devotion to the cause of revolution by deeds, without fear of torture or imprisonment, and we renounce all words that are not immediately followed by deeds. We have no further use for aimless propaganda that does not set itself a definite time and place for realisation of the aims of revolution. What is more, it stands in our way and we shall make every effort to combat it... We shall silence by force the chatterers who refuse to understand this."

* To mystify his readers Bakunin confuses the leaders of the popular uprisings of the 17th and 18th centuries with the brigands and thieves of the Russia of today. As regards the latter, the reading of Flerovsky's book *The Condition of the Working Class in Russia* [a] would disillusion the most romantic souls concerning these poor creatures from whom Bakunin proposes to form the sacred phalanx of the Russian revolution. The sole brigandage — apart from the governmental sphere, of course — still being carried out on a large scale in Russia is the stealing of horses, run as a commercial enterprise by the capitalists, of whom the "revolutionaries without phrases" are but the tools and victims.

---

[a] Н. Флеровскій, *Положеніе рабочаго класса въ Россіи. Наблюденія и изслѣдованія*, St. Petersburg, 1869.— *Ed.*

[b] See this volume, p. 573.— *Ed.*

These threats were addressed to the Russian emigrants who had not bowed to Bakunin's papal authority and whom he called doctrinaires.

"We break all ties with the political emigrants who refuse to return to their country to join our ranks, and until these ranks become evident, with all those who refuse to work for their public emergence on the scene of Russian life. *We make exception for the emigrants who have already declared themselves workers of the European revolution.* From now on we shall make no further repetitions or appeals... He who has ears and eyes will hear and see the men of action, and if he does not join them his destruction will be no fault of ours, just as it will be no fault of ours if all who hide behind the scenes are cold-bloodedly and pitilessly destroyed, along with the scenery that hides them."

At this point we can see right through Bakunin. While enjoining the emigrants on pain of death to return to Russia as agents of his secret society—like the Russian police-spies who would offer them passports and money to go there and join in conspiracies—he grants himself a papal dispensation to remain peacefully in Switzerland as "a worker of the European revolution", and to occupy himself composing manifestos that compromise the unfortunate students whom the police hold in their prisons.

"While not recognising any other activity but that of destruction, we acknowledge that the forms in which it manifests itself may be extremely varied: poison, dagger, noose, etc. The revolution sanctifies all without distinction. The field is open!—Let all young and healthy minds undertake at once the sacred work of destroying evil, purging and enlightening the Russian land by fire and sword, uniting fraternally with those who will do the same thing throughout Europe."

Let us add that in this sublime proclamation the inevitable brigand figures in the melodramatic person of Karl Moor (from Schiller's *Robbers*), and that No. 2 of *The People's Judgment*,[a] quoting a passage from this leaflet, calls it straight out "*a proclamation of Bakunin's*".

Number 1 of the *Publications of the "People's Judgment"** Society begins by proclaiming that the general uprising of the Russian people is imminent and close at hand.[b]

"We, that is to say, that part of the popular youth which have reached a certain stage of development, we must clear the way for it; in other words, we must

* Bakunin and Nechayev always translate this expression as "justice populaire", but the Russian word "rasprava" means not justice, but judgment, or rather revenge.

---

[a] «Кто не за насъ, тотъ противъ насъ», *Изданія Общества «Народной Расправы»*, No. 2, St. Petersburg, 1870.— *Ed.*

[b] «Всенародное возстаніе», *Изданія Общества «Народной Расправы»*, No. 1, Moscow, 1869.— *Ed.*

eliminate all the obstacles to its progress and prepare favourable conditions for it... In view of the imminence of the uprising, we deem it necessary to unite into a single indissoluble whole all revolutionary efforts scattered all over Russia. That is why we have decided to publish, *on behalf of the revolutionary centre,* leaflets in which every one of our coreligionaries scattered all over Russia, every one of the workers for the sacred cause of the Revolution, although unknown to us, will always see what we want and where we are going."

The leaflet then states:

"Thought has value for us only inasmuch as it serves the great cause of *universal pan-destruction.* The revolutionary who studies the revolution in books will never be good for anything... We have no more faith in words. The word has value for us only when it is followed by action; but not all is action which bears the name. For example, the modest and too circumspect organisation of secret societies which have no external manifestations is, in our view, nothing but ridiculous and disgusting child's play. By external manifestations, we mean only a series of acts positively destroying something, a person, a thing, an enchainment which hinders popular emancipation... Without sparing our lives, without stopping before any threat, any obstacle, any danger, etc., we must, by a series of audacious and, yes, arrogant attempts, burst into the life of the people and inspire them with faith [...] in their own powers, awaken them, rally them and urge them on to the triumph of their own cause."

But suddenly the revolutionary phrases of the *Judgment* turn into attacks on *The People's Cause,*[a] a Russian newspaper published in Geneva which defended the programme and organisation of the International. It was, as we see, of the greatest importance for the Alliance propaganda that Bakunin was carrying out in Russia in the name of the International, that a newspaper unmasking his fraud should be silenced.

"If this newspaper continues in the same fashion, we shall not hesitate to express and demonstrate to it what our relations with it must be... We are convinced that all serious men will now lay aside all theory, and the more so all doctrinairism. *We can prevent* the publication of writings which, though sincere, are nevertheless contrary to our banner, *by various practical means at our disposal.*"

After these threats to its dangerous rival, the *People's Judgment* continues:

"Among the leaflets lately published abroad, we recommend, almost without any reserve, *Bakunin's appeal to the déclassé student youth...* Bakunin is right when he advises to leave the academies, the universities, and the schools, and to go among the people."

Bakunin noticeably never lets slip the occasion to offer himself a swing of the censer.

---

[a] *Народное Дѣло. La Cause du Peuple.*—*Ed.*

The second article is entitled: "A glimpse at the past and present notions of the *cause*."[a] We have just seen Bakunin and Nechayev threatening the Russian organ of the International abroad. In this article, we shall see them descend on Chernyshevsky, the man who, in Russia, had done most to draw into the socialist movement the student youth whom they claimed to represent.

"Certainly, the peasants have never engaged in imagining forms of the future social order; nevertheless, after the elimination of all obstructions (that is, after the pan-destructive revolution, which is the first thing to be accomplished and consequently the most important one for us), they will be able to arrange their lives with more sense than can be found in the theories and projects of the doctrinarian socialists who want to impose themselves on the people as teachers and, even worse, directors. In the eyes of people not corrupted by the spectacles of civilisation, the tendencies of these unwanted teachers are only too obvious. They seek, under the pretext of science and art, etc., to prepare *cosy little niches* for themselves and their kind. Even if these tendencies were disinterested and naive, even if they were but the inevitable fruit of all order imbued with modern civilisation, the people would gain nothing by them. The ideal goal of social equality was incomparably better achieved in the Cossack society organised by Vasily Us in Astrakhan after the departure of Stenka Razin, than in Fourier's phalansteries, the institutions of Cabet, Louis Blanc and other socialist savants" (!), "or in the associations of Chernyshevsky."

Here follows a page of invective against the latter and his comrades.

The *cosy little niche* that Chernyshevsky was preparing for himself was presented to him by the Russian government in the form of a prison cell in Siberia, whereas Bakunin, relieved of this danger in his capacity as worker for the European revolution, limited himself to demonstrations *from without*. And it was at the very time when the government severely forbade the mere mention of Chernyshevsky's name in the press, that Messrs Bakunin and Nechayev attacked him.

Our "amorphous" revolutionaries continue:

"We undertake to demolish this rotten social edifice... We come from the people with our skins rent by the teeth of the existing order; we come guided by hatred for all that is not of the people, having no notion of moral obligations or of any kind of honesty towards this world which we hate and of which we expect nothing but evil. We have but one single invariable and negative plan: that of merciless destruction. We categorically renounce the elaboration of future conditions of life, this task being incompatible with our activities, and for that reason we regard as futile all purely theoretical brain work... We undertake exclusively the destruction of the existing social order."

---

[a] «Взглядъ на прежнее и нынѣшнее пониманіе дѣла», *Изданія Общества* «*Народной Расправы*», No. 1.— *Ed.*

These two demonstrators from without are insinuating that the attempted assassination of the tsar [a] in 1866 was one of a "series of pan-destructive acts" committed by their own secret society:

"It was Karakozov who began our sacred work on April 4, 1866. Only since that time has the consciousness of their revolutionary powers been stirring to life among the young people... It was an example, a deed! No propaganda can be of such great significance."

They then draw up a long list of "creatures" condemned by the committee to immediate death. Several "will have their tongues torn out" ... but

"*we shall not touch the tsar* ... we shall save him for the judgment of the people, of the peasants; this right belongs to all the people ... so let our executioner live until the moment of the popular storm... "

No one will venture to doubt that these Russian pamphlets, the secret statutes, and all the works published by Bakunin since 1869 in French,[b] come from one and the same source. On the contrary, all these three categories complement one another. They correspond to some extent to the three degrees of initiation into the famous organisation of pan-destruction. The French brochures of Citizen B. are written for the rank and file of the Alliance, whose prejudices are taken into account. They are told of nothing but pure anarchy, of anti-authoritarianism, of a free federation of autonomous groups and other equally harmless things: a mere jumble of words. The secret statutes are intended for the international brethren of the West; there anarchy becomes "the complete unleashing of people's life ... of evil passions", but underneath this anarchy there lies the secret directing element— the brothers themselves; they are given only a few vague indications on the morality of the Alliance, stolen from Loyola, and the necessity of leaving not a stone standing is mentioned only in passing, because these are Westerners brought up on philistine prejudices and some allowances have to be made for them. They are told that the truth, too blinding for eyes not yet accustomed to true anarchism, will be fully revealed in the programme of the Russian section. Only to the born anarchists, to the people elect, to his young people of Holy Russia does the prophet dare to speak out openly. There anarchy means universal pan-destruction;

---

[a] Alexander II.— *Ed.*

[b] The reference is to the following Bakunin's works: *Programme de la Section de l'Alliance de la Démocratie Socialiste; Quelques paroles—Á mes jeunes frères en Russie; Lettres à un Français sur la crise actuelle. Septembre 1870; L'Empire knouto-germanique et la révolution sociale.—Ed.*

the revolution, a series of assassinations, first individual and then *en masse*; the sole rule of action, the Jesuit morality intensified; the revolutionary type, the brigand. There, thought and learning are absolutely forbidden to the young as mundane occupations that could lead them to doubt the all-destructive orthodoxy. Those who persist in adhering to these theoretical heresies or who apply their vulgar criticism to the dogmas of universal amorphism are threatened with a holy inquisition. Before the youth of Russia the Pope need feel no restraint either in the form or substance of his utterances. He gives his tongue free play and the complete absence of ideas is expressed in such grandiloquent verbiage that it cannot be reproduced in French without weakening its comic effect. His language is not even real Russian. It is Tartar, so a native Russian has stated.[a] These small men with atrophied minds puff themselves up with horrific phrases in order to appear in their own eyes as giants of revolution. It is the fable of the frog and the ox.[b]

What terrible revolutionaries! They want to annihilate and amorphise everything, "absolutely everything". They draw up lists of proscribed persons, doomed to die by their daggers, their poison, their ropes, by the bullets from their revolvers; they "will tear out the tongues" of many, but they will bow before the majesty of the tsar. Indeed, the tsar, the officials, the nobility, the bourgeoisie may sleep in peace. The Alliance does not make war on the established states, but on the revolutionaries who do not stoop to the role of supernumeraries in this tragicomedy. Peace to the palaces, war on the cottages! Chernyshevsky was libelled; the editors of *The People's Cause* were warned that they would be silenced "by various practical means at our disposal"; the Alliance threatened to assassinate all revolutionaries who were not with it. This is the only part of their pan-destructive programme which they began to carry out. We shall now describe the first exploit of this nature.

After April 1869, Bakunin and Nechayev began preparing the ground for the revolution in Russia. They sent letters, proclamations and telegrams from Geneva to St. Petersburg, Kiev, and other cities. They knew, however, that they could not send letters and proclamations, much less telegrams, to Russia without the "Third Department" (the secret police) knowing about them. All

---

[a] N. I. Utin.— *Ed.*

[b] La Fontaine, "La grenouille qui se veut faire aussi grosse que le bœuf", Paris, 1779.— *Ed.*

this could have no purpose other than that of compromising others. These cowardly tricks of men who risked nothing in their fine city of Geneva resulted in the arrest of a great many persons in Russia. However, they were warned of the danger that they were causing. We have in our hands proof that the following passage in a letter from Russia was communicated to Bakunin:

"For mercy's sake, let Bakunin know that if he holds anything sacred in the revolution, he must stop sending his lunatic proclamations, which are leading to searches in several cities and to arrests, and are paralysing all serious work." [372]

Bakunin replied that it was all nonsense and that Nechayev had left for America. But, as will be seen later, Bakunin's clandestine code makes it obligatory to

"compromise completely ... the ambitious men and liberals of different shades ... so that retreat becomes impossible for them, and make use of them". (The Revolutionary Catechism,[373] § 19.) [a]

Here is one proof. On April 7, 1869, Nechayev wrote to Mme. Tomilova, wife of a colonel who later died of grief after the arrest of his wife, that "there is an enormous amount to be done in Geneva", and he urged her to send a reliable man for talks with him.

"The cause on which we must take counsel does not concern only *our trade*, but that of all Europe. Things are in ferment here. There's a soup boiling up that Europe will never manage to swallow. So make haste."

Then comes the Geneva address. This letter did not reach its destination; it was confiscated in the post by the secret police, and resulted in the arrest of Mme. Tomilova, who only learned about it during the investigation. (Report of the Nechayev trial, *St. Petersburg Gazette*, No. 187, 1871.*)

Here is another fact which demonstrates Bakunin's circumspection in organising a conspiracy. Mavritsky, a student at the Kiev Academy, received proclamations which had been sent to him from Geneva. He immediately handed them over to the government, which hastened to send to Geneva a trustworthy man, that is, a spy. Bakunin and Nechayev formed a close association with this delegate from the south of Russia, supplied him with

* All the facts cited by us in connection with the Nechayev conspiracy are extracts from the reports of the trial as published in the *St. Petersburg Gazette*. We shall quote the number of the issue from which they have been taken.

---

[a] See this volume, p. 547.— Ed.

19*

proclamations and the addresses of persons whom Nechayev claimed to know in Russia, and gave him what could only be taken as a letter of confidence and recommendation (*St. Petersburg Gazette*, No. 187).

On September 3 (September 15, new style), 1869, Nechayev introduced himself in Moscow to Uspensky, a young man he had known before going abroad, as emissary of the World Revolutionary Committee in Geneva, and showed him the mandate quoted above. He told Uspensky that emissaries from this European Committee would be coming to Moscow furnished with similar mandates, and that he, Nechayev, had been given the mission of

"organising a secret society among the student youth ... to provoke a popular uprising in Russia".

On Uspensky's recommendation, Nechayev, in order to find a safe refuge, went to the Agricultural Academy, which was some distance from the city, and contacted Ivanov, one of the students best known for their devotion to the interests of the young and the people. Henceforth, the Agricultural Academy was to be Nechayev's centre of activity. First, he introduced himself under a false name and told how he had travelled a great deal in Russia; that the people were ready to rise everywhere and would have done so long ago had not the revolutionaries advised them to wait patiently until the completion of their great and powerful organisation, which was going to combine all the revolutionary forces of Russia. He urged Ivanov and other students to join this secret society, headed by an all-powerful Committee in whose name everything was done, but whose composition and locale must remain unknown to its members. This Committee and this organisation constituted the *Russian Branch of World Union, of the Revolutionary Alliance, of the International Working Men's Association!* *

Nechayev began by distributing the above-mentioned *Words* among the students to show them that Bakunin, the celebrated revolutionary of 1848 who had escaped from Siberia, was playing an important role in Europe, that he was the chief plenipotentiary

---

* It should be noted that in Russian the words for association, union and alliance (*obshchestvo, soyuz, tovarishchestvo*) are more or less synonymous and can often be used indiscriminately. Similarly, the word for international is mostly rendered by "world" (*vsemirny*). In the Russian press, "International Association" is thus often translated by words which could equally well be rendered into French as "Alliance universelle". It was by making use of this confusion in terms that Bakunin and Nechayev succeeded in exploiting our Association's name and in ruining about a hundred young people.

of the workers, that he signed the mandates issued by the General Committee of the World Association, and that this hero advised them to give up their studies, etc. To give them a striking example of devotion unto death, he read them a poem by Ogarev, Bakunin's friend and the editor of Herzen's *Kolokol*; entitled *The Student*, it was dedicated to his "young friend Nechayev".[374] In it, Nechayev was represented as the ideal student, as the "indefatigable fighter since childhood". Ogarev sang of how Nechayev suffered in his early years for the sake of the living work of science; how his devotion to the people had grown; how, pursued by the vengeance of the tsar and by the fear of the Boyars, he took to a life of wandering (*skitanye*, or vagabondage); how he went on a pilgrimage to cry out to the peasants from east to west: "Assemble together, rise up courageously", etc. etc.; how he ended his life in penal servitude amid the snows of Siberia; how, being no hypocrite, he remained faithful all his life to the struggle; and how, till his last breath, he repeated: "All the people must conquer their land and their liberty!" This Alliance poem was published in the spring of 1869, when Nechayev was amusing himself in Geneva. Batches of it were sent to Russia along with the other proclamations. It would seem that the mere act of copying out this poem had the effect of inspiring a feeling of self-sacrifice in the neophytes, for, on the Committee's instructions, Nechayev had it copied out and distributed by each new initiate (statements by several of the defendants).

Music seems to be the only thing which was to escape the amorphism to which universal pan-destruction reduced all the arts and sciences. On behalf of the Committee, Nechayev ordained that propaganda should be carried out by means of *revolutionary music*, and tried hard to find a tune to which this poetic masterpiece could be sung by the young people (*St. Petersburg Gazette*, No. 190).

The mystic legend of his death did not prevent him from hinting that Nechayev might well be still alive, or from telling, under oath of secrecy, that Nechayev was in the Urals as a worker and that he had founded workers' associations there. (*St. Petersburg Gazette*, No. 202). He disclosed this mainly to those who were "good for nothing", that is, to those who dreamed of founding working men's associations, in order to inspire them with admiration for this fabulous hero. Finally, when the legends of his imaginary escape from the St. Petersburg Fortress[a] and of his

---

[a] Peter and Paul Fortress.— *Ed.*

poetic death in Siberia had sufficiently prepared their minds and he believed that the initiates were well enough versed in the catechism, he finally brought about his evangelical resurrection and announced that he was Nechayev in person! But it was no longer the Nechayev of old, ridiculed and despised by the students of St. Petersburg, as is affirmed by the witnesses and the defendants; this was the plenipotentiary of the World Revolutionary Committee. The miracle of his transformation had been engineered by Bakunin. Nechayev had complied with all the conditions demanded by the statutes of the organisation he preached; he had "distinguished himself by actions known and appreciated by the Committee"; he had, in Brussels, organised and directed an important strike by members of the International; the Belgian Committee had sent him as delegate to the Geneva International, where he had met Bakunin, and since, to use his own expression, "he disliked resting on his laurels", he had returned to Russia to begin "revolutionary activities". He gave an assurance that a whole general staff of sixteen Russian refugees had come with him.*

Uspensky, Ivanov, and four or six other young people appear to have been the only ones in Moscow who let themselves be taken in by this balderdash. Four of these initiates were ordered to recruit new adherents and to form circles or small sections. The plan of organisation is to be found in the documents of the trial; it conforms in almost every point to that of the secret Alliance. The "general rules of the organisation" were read out before the court, and not one of the principal initiates disputed their authenticity. Furthermore, issue No. 2 of *The People's Judgment* edited by Bakunin and Nechayev admitted the authenticity of the following articles:

"The organisation is based on *trust* in the individual.—No member knows to which grade he belongs, that is to say, whether he is far from or near the centre.— *Obedience to the Committee's orders must be absolute, without any objections.*— Renunciation of all property in favour of the Committee, which can dispose of it.—Any member who has recruited a certain number of proselytes to our cause and who has proved by his deeds the degree of his strength and abilities, may familiarise himself with these rules and, later, with the society's statutes to a greater or lesser extent. The degree of his strength and abilities is assessed by the Committee." [a]

* None of the Russian refugees re-entered Russia, and in any case there are no sixteen Russian political refugees to be found in the whole of Europe.

---

[a] «Извѣщеніе и предостереженіе отъ Комитета», *Изданія Общества «Народной Расправы»*, No. 2, St. Petersburg, 1870.— *Ed.*

To hoodwink the Moscow members, Nechayev told them that the organisation in St. Petersburg was already an enormous one, whereas in reality not a single circle or section existed there. In a moment of forgetfulness, he exclaimed to an initiate[a]: "In St. Petersburg, they have been faithless to me like women and have betrayed me like slaves." When in St. Petersburg, however, he said that the organisation was making admirable progress in Moscow.

When, in this latter city, they asked to see a member of the Committee, he invited a young St. Petersburg officer,[b] who was interested in the student movement, to come with him to Moscow and see the circles there. The young man agreed, and on the way Nechayev consecrated him "*delegate extraordinary of the Committee of the International Association of Geneva*".

"You could not," he said, "be admitted to our meetings if you were not a member, but here is a mandate certifying that you are a member of the International Association, and as such you will be admitted."

The mandate bore a French stamp and read: "The bearer of this mandate is the plenipotentiary representative of the International Association." The other defendants affirm that Nechayev assured them that this stranger was the "true agent of the Geneva Revolutionary Committee" (*St. Petersburg Gazette*, Nos. 225 and 226).

Dolgov, a friend of Ivanov, testifies that

"when speaking of the secret society organised with the aim of supporting the people in the event of an uprising and of directing the insurrection so as to ensure its success, Nechayev also spoke of the International Association and said that Bakunin was serving as a contact with it" (No. 198).

Ripman confirms that

"to divert him from his ideas on cooperative associations, Nechayev told him that there was an International Working Men's Association in Europe, and that to attain the goal pursued by the International, it was enough to join this Association, a section of which already existed in Moscow" (No. 198).

Further on, we see from the statements of the defendants that Nechayev was misrepresenting the International as a secret society and his own society as a branch of the International. He also assured the initiates that their Moscow section was going to proceed by strikes and associations on a large scale, just like the International. When the accused Ripman asked him for the society's programme, Nechayev read him several passages from a

---

[a] I. G. Pryzhov.— *Ed.*
[b] Shimanovsky.— *Ed.*

French leaflet on the aims of the society. The defendant understood that this leaflet was the International's programme and added:

"Since there had been a lot of talk about this society in the press, I did not see anything very criminal in Nechayev's proposition."

Kuznetsov,[a] one of the chief defendants, said that Nechayev had read the programme of the International Association (No. 181). His brother[b] stated that

"he had seen them at his brother's place copying out a French leaflet which must have been the society's programme" (No. 202).

The defendant Klimin declared that he had been read

"the programme of the International Association with a few lines written as a postscript by Bakunin ... but as far as I remember, this programme was couched in very vague terms and said nothing about the means of achieving the aim, but spoke only of equality in general" (No. 199).

The defendant Gavrishev explained that the

"French leaflet, insofar as it was possible to grasp its meaning, contained an exposition of the principles held by the representatives of socialism who had had their Congress at Geneva".

Finally, the deposition of the defendant Svyatsky completely clarifies for us the nature of this mysterious French leaflet: during the search, he was found in possession of a leaflet written in French and entitled: *Programme de l'Alliance internationale de la democratie socialiste.*

"Much had been said about the *International Association* in the newspapers," he said, "and I was interested to know *its* programme for purely theoretical purposes" (*St. Petersburg Gazette*, No. 230.)

These depositions prove that the secret programme of the Alliance had been passed off in manuscript as the International's programme. That the World Revolutionary Committee, of which Nechayev said he was an emissary, and the Central Bureau of the Alliance (Citizen B.) were identical is proved by the deposition of the chief defendant, Uspensky, who declared that he had collected together all the minutes of the circle's meetings "in order to send an account to Bakunin in Geneva". Pryzhov, one of the principal defendants, testified that Nechayev had ordered him to go to Geneva with a report for Bakunin.

---

[a] Alexei Kuznetsov.— *Ed.*
[b] Semyon Kuznetsov.— Ed.

Owing to lack of space, we are not going to mention here all the lies, stupidities, swindles, and acts of violence on the part of Bakunin's agent which were brought to light by the trial. We will only take note of the more striking examples.

Everything was a mystery in this organisation. Dolgov said that

"before joining this society, he would have liked to know its organisation and means. Nechayev had replied that that was a secret and he would get to know it later" (*St. Petersburg Gazette*, No. 198).

When the members ventured to ask questions, Nechayev shut them up, saying that in accordance with the statutes, no one had the right to know anything until he had distinguished himself by some act (No. 199).

"As soon as we had agreed to become members of the society," declared one of the accused,[a] "Nechayev began to terrorise us with the power and might of the Committee which, according to him, existed and directed us. He said that the Committee had its own police, and that if anybody broke his word or acted contrary to the orders of individuals who were more *highly placed* than our circle, the Committee would have recourse to vengeance." The defendant confessed that "having noticed Nechayev's swindles, he informed him that he intended to withdraw completely from this business and go to the Caucasus to recover his health. Nechayev told him that this was not allowed, and that the Committee could punish him with death if he dared to leave the society. He also ordered him to go to a meeting and speak there of the secret society in order to recruit new members, and to read the poem on Nechayev's death. When the defendant refused, Nechayev threatened him. 'You're not here to discuss matters,' he shouted. 'You're obliged to obey the Committee's orders without objection'" (No. 198).

If this were only an isolated instance, there might be grounds for doubt; but several of the defendants, who could not possibly have come to an understanding with one another, testify to exactly the same thing.—Another declared that the circle's members, on realising that they had been tricked, wanted to leave the society but did not dare do so for fear of the Committee's revenge (No. 198).

One witness, speaking of one of his accused friends, said: The accused Florinsky did not know how to shake off Nechayev, who was preventing him from getting on with his work. The witness advised him to leave Moscow and go to St. Petersburg, but Florinsky replied that Nechayev would find him in St. Petersburg just as he did in Moscow; that Nechayev was outraging the convictions of a great many young people by terrorising them, and that what Florinsky seemed to fear was a denunciation on Nechayev's part.

---

[a] F. F. Ripman.— *Ed.*

"It was said, and I heard it," testified Likhutin, "that Nechayev was sending very violent letters from abroad to his acquaintances to compromise them and get them arrested. This way of acting was one trait of his character" (No. 186).

Yenisherlov stated even that he was beginning to regard Nechayev as a government agent.

During the meeting of a small circle, one of the members, Klimin, in reply to a stranger who was present as emissary of the Committee and expressed his dissatisfaction with the conduct of the circle, said that

"they themselves were also dissatisfied; that at the beginning the recruits were told that each section could act more or less independently without passive obedience being demanded of its members; but subsequently things had been run quite differently and the Committee was reducing them to the state of slaves" (No. 199).

Nechayev used to issue his orders on pieces of paper stamped: "Russian Section of the World Revolutionary Alliance. Form for the public", and he formulated his instructions as follows: "The Committee orders you to..." carry out such-and-such, go to such-and-such a place, etc.

One young officer, who had become disillusioned, wanted to leave the society. Nechayev seemed to agree to this, but he demanded compensation. The officer had to obtain for him a bill for 6,000 rubles (nearly 20,000 frs.) signed by Kolachevsky. In 1866, Kolachevsky, after Karakozov's attempt to assassinate the tsar, had been detained with his two sisters [a] for a long period. At the time of the present incident, one of them was serving a second term in prison for a political offence. The whole family was under rigorous police surveillance and Kolachevsky could expect to be arrested at any moment. Nechayev made use of this situation. On his orders, the young officer mentioned above invited Kolachevsky to his own place under a false pretext, entered into conversation with him, and gave him some proclamations, which the other took out of curiosity. No sooner had Kolachevsky gone out into the street, than he was accosted by an officer who ordered the other to follow him, announcing that he was working for the Third Department (secret police), and that he knew that Kolachevsky had on his person proclamations of a seditious nature. Now the possession of these alone is enough to lead to years of detention and penal servitude for a man if he has had the misfortune already to have been compromised in a political matter. The self-styled agent of the Third Department invited Kolachevsky to

---

[a] Alla Nikolayevna and Lyudmila Nikolayevna Kolachevskaya.— Ed.

get into a carriage, and, once they were inside, offered him the chance to buy himself off by signing on the spot a bill for 6,000 rubles. Forced to choose between this offer and the prospect of going to Siberia, Kolachevsky signed. The next day, another young man, Negreskul, on learning of this business, suspected Nechayev of being involved, immediately sought out the supposed agent of the Third Department, and demanded an explanation of his swindle. The latter denied everything; the bill had been hidden and was not retrieved until later during the search. The discovery of the conspiracy and Nechayev's flight made it impossible for him to cash the note.—Negreskul had known Nechayev for a long time and had been the victim of one of his swindles in Geneva. Bakunin had then tried to recruit him. Later, they had extorted a hundred rubles from him (No. 230). He had ended up by being compromised by Nechayev, although he detested him and thought him capable of any villainy. He was arrested and died in prison.

We have seen that Ivanov had been one of Nechayev's first recruits. He was one of the most beloved and most influential students at the Moscow Agricultural Academy. He devoted himself to bettering the lot of his comrades and organised aid societies and dining rooms where poor students could eat free of charge and which served as a cover for meetings at which they discussed social questions. He devoted all his spare time to teaching the children of peasants living near the Academy. His comrades testify that he threw himself passionately into all these activities, giving away his last kopek and quite often sacrificing his own hot meals.

Ivanov was struck by the stupidity of the terrorist proclamations issued by Nechayev and Bakunin. He could not understand why the Committee kept ordering the distribution of *Words*, Ogarev's *Song of Death*, *The People's Judgment* and, finally, Bakunin's *Appeal to the Russian Nobility*, a purely aristocratic proclamation.* He

---

* Here are some extracts from the *Appeal to the Russian Nobility*,[375] a proclamation published by Bakunin: "What privileges have we received for having, during the first half of the 19th century, been the mainstay of the throne which has been shaken to its very foundations so many times; for having, in 1848, during the storms of popular madness unleashed over Europe, saved by our noble deeds the Russian empire from the socialist utopias that threatened to invade it?... What have we been accorded for having saved the Empire from dismemberment, for having extinguished in Poland the flames of the conflagration which threatened to set all Russia on fire, for having, to this very moment, worked with unsparing energy and with unparalleled courage to destroy the revolutionary elements in Russia? — Was it not from our midst that there came Mikhail Muravyov, that gallant man whom Alexander II himself, for all his feeble-mindedness, named the saviour of his country? — What have we gained from all this? For all these inestimable services,

began to lose patience and to ask where this Committee was, what
it was doing, and what sort of a Committee it was that invariably
put Nechayev in the right and the other members in the wrong.
He expressed a desire to see someone from this Committee. He
had acquired the right to this, since Nechayev himself had
promoted him to a rank equivalent to that of member of a
national committee of the secret Alliance. It was then that
Nechayev extricated himself from this predicament by staging the
comedy, as described above, of the emissary from the Geneva
International.

One day, Nechayev ordered the transfer to the Committee of
money intended for the students' mutual aid society. Ivanov
protested, and a quarrel ensued. Other comrades urged Ivanov to
submit to the Committee's decision, since they had accepted the
statutes which demanded this submission. Ivanov gave way to their
insistences and grudgingly complied. Nechayev then began thinking out a plan for getting rid of this man whom he probably
regarded as a doctrinaire revolutionary deserving death. He
engaged Uspensky in theoretical conversations on punishment, on
the elimination of disloyal members who, by their rebellion, could
compromise and ruin the whole vast secret organisation.

The manner in which Nechayev ran his secret society was such
as to engender doubts concerning the serious nature of the
organisation. The sections had to hold regular sittings to examine
the academic registers of the names of all the students, to mark
those who were considered likely recruits, and to investigate means
of procuring money. One such means was subscription lists for
"students who have suffered", that is, who had been administra-
tively banished. The proceeds from these lists went straight into
the Committee's pocket, that is to say, Nechayev's. The sections
had to obtain all kinds of clothes which were kept in a safe place
and were used by Nechayev as disguise during his flight. But the
principal occupation consisted in copying out the *Song of Death*
and the proclamations cited above. The members of the conspiracy had to write down as accurately as possible everything that was

we have been skinned of everything we possess... Our present appeal is a
declaration by a *vast majority of the Russian nobility* which has long been *ready and
organised*... We feel our strength in our right, we boldly throw down the gauntlet
before the despot, the German princeling Alexander II Saltykov-Romanov, and we
challenge him to a noble and knightly combat *which must be taken up in* 1870
between the descendants of Rurik and the party of the Russian independent
nobility."

"Muravyov, that gallant man", is nothing but the executioner of Poland.

said at their meetings, and Nechayev threatened them with the Committee, which had its spies everywhere, in the event of them daring to hide anything. Each had to bring to the circle written reports on everything that he had been doing in between meetings, and these reports had to be compiled into a summary for despatch to Bakunin.

All these puerile and inquisitorial practices made Ivanov doubt the very existence of the Committee and the much vaunted powers of this organisation. He began to suspect that it all boiled down to preposterous exploitation and a colossal hoax. He confided to his close friends that if things stayed as they were and if they were given nothing better to do than these silly tasks, he would break with Nechayev and would found a serious organisation himself.

It was then that Nechayev took a decisive step. He gave the order for his proclamations to be put up in the students' dining rooms. Ivanov realised that the posting up of these proclamations would lead to the closing of the dining rooms, the banning of meetings, and the dispersal of the best students. He therefore opposed the measure (this is, in fact, what happened: the students' dining room was closed down and all the delegates appointed to manage it were exiled). A quarrel flared up over this, during which Nechayev kept repeating his stereotyped statement: "It's the Committee's orders!"

Ivanov was in utter despair. On November 20, 1869, he approached a member of the section, Pryzhov, and informed him that he was quitting the society. Pryzhov communicated this statement to Uspensky who, in his turn, hastened to inform Nechayev and, a few hours later, these three met at Kuznetsov's place, where Nikolayev also had lodgings. Nechayev announced that Ivanov must be punished for rebelling against the Committee's orders, and that he must be eliminated to prevent him from doing them any more damage. Kuznetsov, Ivanov's close friend, apparently did not grasp Nechayev's intention, and so the latter declared that Ivanov must be killed. Pryzhov shouted to Kuznetsov: "Nechayev is mad, he wants to kill Ivanov, he must be prevented." Nechayev put a stop to their hesitation with his habitual statement: "Do you also want to rebel against the Committee's orders? If there's no other way of killing him, I'll go to his room tonight with Nikolayev and we'll strangle him." He then suggested luring Ivanov that night to a grotto in the Academy park under pretext of digging up a printing-press which had been hidden for a long time, and they would assassinate him there.

Thus, even at this supreme moment, Nechayev himself paid tribute to Ivanov's loyalty. He was sure that, in spite of his resignation, Ivanov would come and help to dig up the printing-press, and that he was incapable of betraying him since, if he had been harbouring any such intention, he would have carried it out before leaving the society or immediately afterwards. If Ivanov had wanted to denounce Nechayev to the police, he had the chance to get them caught in the act. Quite to the contrary, Ivanov was delighted to have positive proof at last that this organisation actually existed, a tangible sign that it possessed the means of action, even if it were only printer's type. Forgetting all the threats so often made by Nechayev to the unfaithful, he hastened to leave a friend with whom he was having tea and at whose place Nikolayev had called on Nechayev's orders, and off he went in obedience to the summons.

In the darkness of the night, Ivanov went unsuspectingly towards the grotto. Suddenly, a cry rang out. Someone had jumped on him from behind. A terrible struggle began, with nothing to be heard but the grunting of Nechayev and the groans of his victim, whom he was strangling with his bare hands. Then a shot rang out, and Ivanov fell down dead. Nechayev's revolver bullet had pierced Ivanov's skull. "Quick, rope and stones," shouted Nechayev, rummaging through the dead man's pockets for papers and money. They then threw him into a pond.

On returning to Kuznetsov's place, the assassins took measures to hide the traces of their crime. They burned Nechayev's blood-stained shirt. The accomplices were gloomy and uneasy. Suddenly, a second revolver shot rang out and a bullet whistled past Pryzhov's ear. Nechayev apologised for "having wanted to show Nikolayev how his revolver worked". The witnesses unanimously testified that this had been another assassination attempt. Nechayev had wanted to kill Pryzhov because the latter had dared in the morning to protest against the murder of Ivanov.

Immediately afterwards, Nechayev rushed from Moscow to Petersburg with Kuznetsov, leaving Uspensky to act in Moscow. At Petersburg, he made a pretence of always being busy with his organisation; but, to his great astonishment, Kuznetsov noted that there was even less of an organisation there than in Moscow. He dared to question Nechayev: "Where is the Committee, then? Would it be you, by any chance?"—Nechayev denied this again and assured him that the Committee existed. He returned to Moscow and admitted to Nikolayev that since Uspensky had already been arrested, the same would happen to all the others very soon, and that "he did not know what he ought to do any more". It was then that Nikolayev, his most faithful follower, decided to ask him if the famous Committee really existed, or if Nechayev himself was its sole embodiment.

"Without giving a positive reply to this question, he told me that all means were permissible for drawing people into such a cause, that this rule was also practised abroad, that this rule was *followed by Bakunin* just as by others, and that if such men submitted to this rule, it was entirely natural that he, Nechayev, should act in the same manner" (No. 181).

He then ordered Nikolayev to go with Pryzhov to Tula and fraudulently extort a passport from a worker who was an old friend of Nikolayev's. He later went to Tula himself, where he entreated a Mme. Alexandrovskaya to accompany him to Geneva; it was absolutely necessary for him.

Mme. Alexandrovskaya had been seriously compromised during the disturbances of 1861 and 1862. She even had been committed to prison, where her conduct had left much to be desired. In a fit of frankness, she had written a confession to her judges, and this confession had compromised many people. After all this, she was interned in a provincial town under police surveillance. As she was afraid of not being able to obtain a passport, Nechayev procured one for her, no one knows how. It might be asked why Nechayev had sought out for his travelling companion a woman whose company alone would be enough to get him arrested at the frontier. However, he arrived in Geneva safe and sound with Mme. Alexandrovskaya at his side and, while his wretched dupes were being thrown into prison cells, he and Bakunin set about preparing the second issue of *The People's Judgment.* Bakunin, unbelievably proud to see the *Journal de Genève*[a] mention the Nechayev conspiracy with himself as having played the principal part, forgot that his *The People's Judgment* claimed to be published in Moscow, and he inserted in it a whole page of the article from the *Journal de Genève* in French. As soon as the journal was ready, Mme. Alexandrovskaya was given the task of taking it into Russia with other proclamations. At the frontier, an agent of the Third Department, who was waiting for Mme. Alexandrovskaya, confiscated the parcel. After her arrest, she gave him a list of names which could not have been known except to Bakunin alone.—One

---

[a] "On s'occupe...", *Journal de Genève*, No. 3, January 5, 1870. Reprinted from *Изданія Общества «Народной Расправы»*, No. 2, the article «Въ послѣднихъ числахъ...» — *Ed.*

of the accused in the Nechayev affair, and one of his closest friends,[a] admitted to the tribunal that

"he had hitherto considered Bakunin an honest man, and he could not understand how he and others could have subjected this woman in such a craven fashion to the danger of arrest".

If Bakunin evaded the necessity of himself going to Russia in order to direct in person the great revolution whose imminent explosion he predicted, at least he worked in Europe as if he had "the devil in his flesh". Le Progrès of Locle, the organ of the Swiss Alliance, published long excerpts from The People's Judgment.[b] In it, Guillaume praised the great successes of the great Russian socialists,[c] and declared that his abstentionist programme was identical to that of the great Russian socialists.* At the Congress of La Chaux-de-Fonds, when Utin attempted to disclose Nechayev's nefarious deeds, Guillaume interrupted him by saying that to speak of these men was espionage.[d] As for Bakunin, he was writing in La Marseillaise as if he had just returned from "a long journey through distant lands which are not reached by free newspapers"[e] so as to create the impression that matters in Russia were taking such a revolutionary turn that he considered his presence there essential.

We now come to the dénouement of the tragi-comedy of the Russian Alliance. In 1859, Herzen had received a bequest of 25,000 frs. from a young Russian to carry on revolutionary propaganda in Russia.[377] Herzen, who had never wanted to release this sum to just anybody, nevertheless let himself be caught by Bakunin, who managed to relieve him of it by assuring him that Nechayev represented a vast and powerful secret organisation. Nechayev therefore thought himself entitled to demand his share. But the two international brethren, whom the assassination of

---

* In 1868, less than two years before the Congress of La Chaux-de-Fonds at which the Alliance members had their doctrine of political abstention sanctioned, Bakunin deploring, in La Démocratie of Chassin,[376] the political abstention of the French workers, wrote: "Political abstention is a stupidity invented by scoundrels to deceive idiots."

---

[a] Alexei Kuznetsov.— Ed.

[b] "Événements de Russie", Le Progrès, No. 6, February 5, 1870.— Ed.

[c] [J. Guillaume,] "Le congrès de la Chaux-de-Fonds", Le Progrès, No. 14, April 2, 1870.— Ed.

[d] "Procès-verbaux du Congrès Romand", L'Égalité, No. 18, April 30, 1870.— Ed.

[e] M. Bakounine, "Herzen", La Marseillaise, No. 72, March 2, 1870.— Ed.

Ivanov had failed to split, began quarrelling over a money matter. Bakunin refused. Nechayev left Geneva and published in London, in the spring of 1870, a Russian newspaper *The Commune* (*Obshchina*) in which he publicly claimed from Bakunin the rest of the capital which the latter had received from the then deceased Herzen.[a] Here, indeed, is proof that the international brethren

"never attack one another, nor settle their differences in public".[b]

The leading article in the second issue of *The People's Judgment* contains yet another funeral dirge in poetic prose on Nechayev, that hero always dead and always living.[c] This time, the hero had been strangled by the gendarmes who were taking him to Siberia. Disguised as a workman, he had been arrested at Tambov while drinking in a tavern. This arrest had led to extraordinary unrest in government circles. They could speak of nothing but "Nechayev in disguise ... denunciations ... secret societies ... Bakuninists ... revolution". On the occasion of Nechayev's death, the governor of Perm has sent a telegram to Petersburg. The text of this telegram is quoted in full. Another telegram, also quoted in full, was sent to the Third Department, and *The People's Judgment* knew that "having received this telegram, the chief of police jumped in his chair and smiled an evil smile all that evening". Thus it was that Nechayev died a second time.

Ivanov's murder is admitted in the article, which describes it as

"an act of vengeance by the society on a member for any deviation from his duties. The stern logic of true workers for the cause must not stop at any act leading to the success of the cause, much less at acts which may save the cause and avert its ruin".

For Bakunin, the "success of the cause" was the imprisonment of eighty young people.

The second article is entitled: "He who is not for us, is against us",[d] and contains an apologia for political assassination. The fate of Ivanov, who is not mentioned by name, is promised to all revolutionaries who do not adhere to the Alliance:

---

[a] С. Нечаевъ, «Письмо къ Огареву и Бакунину», *Община*, No. 1, London, 1870.— *Ed.*

[b] See this volume, p. 568.— *Ed.*

[c] «Въ послѣднихъ числахъ...», *Изданія Общества «Народной Расправы»*, St. Petersburg, 1870.— *Ed.*

[d] «Кто не за насъ, тотъ противъ насъ», *Изданія Общества «Народной Расправы»*, No. 2.— *Ed.*

"The critical moment has come ... military operations between the two camps have commenced ... it is no longer possible to remain neutral: to abide by the golden mean is out of the question, for this would mean being caught in the cross-fire between two hostile armies which have begun shooting at one another; this would mean exposing oneself pointlessly to death, it would mean falling under fire from both sides without a chance of defending oneself. It would mean suffering the lashes and tortures of the Third Department, or falling under the bullets of our revolvers."

Next come expressions of gratitude, apparently ironical, to the Russian government for its

"cooperation in the development and the rapid advance of our work, which is approaching its much-desired goal at a headlong speed".

At the very time when the two heroes were thanking the government for speedily bringing closer "the much-desired goal", all the members of the so-called secret organisation were under arrest.—Then the article makes a new appeal. It "welcomes with open arms all fresh and honest forces", but warns them that once they have submitted to these embraces, they must yield to all the exigencies of the society:

"Any renunciation, any withdrawal from the society, made knowingly through lack of faith in the truth and justice of certain principles, leads to removal from the list of the living".

And our two heroes ridicule those who have been arrested; they are nothing more than petty liberals; the true members of the organisation are protected by the secret society, which does not allow them to be apprehended.

The third article is entitled: *The Fundamental Principles of the Social Order of the Future*.[a] This article shows that if the ordinary mortal is punished like a criminal for even thinking about the social organisation of the future, this is because the leaders have arranged everything in advance.

"The ending of the existing social order and the renewal of life with the aid of the new principles can be accomplished *only by concentrating all the means of social existence in the hands of* OUR COMMITTEE, *and the proclamation of compulsory physical labour for everyone.*

"The committee, as soon as the present institutions have been overthrown, proclaims that everything is common property, orders the setting up of workers' societies" (*artels*) "and at the same time publishes statistical tables compiled by experts and pointing out what branches of labour are most needed in a certain locality and what branches may run into difficulties there.

---

a «Главныя основы будущаго общественнаго строя», *Изданія Общества «Народной Расправы»*, No. 2.— *Ed.*

"For a certain number of days assigned for the revolutionary upheaval and the disorders that are bound to follow, each person must join one or another of these *artels* according to his own choice... All those who remain isolated and unattached to workers' groups without sufficient reason will have no right of access either to the communal eating places or to the communal dormitories, or to any other buildings assigned to meet the various needs of the brother-workers or that contain the goods and materials, the victuals or tools reserved for all members of the established workers' society; in a word, he who without sufficient reason has not joined an *artel*, will be left without means of subsistence. All the roads, all the means of communication will be closed to him; he will have no other alternative but work or death."

Each *artel* will elect from its members an assessor ("*otsenshchik*"), who regulates the work, keeps the books on production and consumption and the productivity of every worker, and acts as a go-between with the general office of the given locality. The office, consisting of members elected from among the *artels* of the locality, conducts exchange between these *artels*, administers all the communal establishments (dormitories, canteens, schools, hospitals) and directs all public works:

"All general work is managed by the office, while all individual work requiring special skills and craftsmanship is performed by special *artels*."

Then comes a long set of rules on education, hours of work, feeding of children, freeing of inventors from work and so on.

"With full publicity, knowledge and activity on the part of everyone all ambition, as we now know it, all deception will disappear without a trace, will vanish forever... Everyone will endeavour to produce as much as possible for society and consume as little as possible; all the pride, all the ambition of the worker of those times will rest in the awareness of his usefulness to society."

What a beautiful model of barrack-room communism! Here you have it all: communal eating, communal sleeping, assessors and offices regulating education, production, consumption, in a word, all social activity, and to crown all, OUR COMMITTEE, anonymous and unknown to anyone, as the supreme director. This is indeed the purest anti-authoritarianism.

To give this absurd plan of practical organisation the semblance of a theoretical basis, a small note is attached to the very title of this article:

"Those who wish to know the complete theoretical development of *our* principal theses, will find them in the writing published by *us*: *Manifesto of the Communist Party*."

In fact, the Russian translation of the Manifesto (German) of the Communist Party, 1847,[378] was announced, price one franc, in every issue of the *Kolokol* in 1870, alongside Bakunin's *Appeal to the Officers of the Russian Army*[a] and the two issues of *The People's Judgment*. The very Bakunin who abused this Manifesto to lend weight to his Tartar fantasies in Russia, had it denounced by the Alliance in the West as an ultra-heretical writing preaching the baleful doctrines of German authoritarian communism (see the resolution of the Rimini Conference,[b] Guillaume's address at The Hague,[379] *Bulletin jurassien* No. 10-11,[c] the *Federacion* of Barcelona,[d] etc.)

Now that the common herd knows the role "our committee" is destined to perform, it is easy to understand this competitive hatred of the state and of any centralisation of the workers' forces. Assuredly, while the working class continues to have any representative bodies of its own, Messrs. Bakunin and Nechayev, revolutionising under the incognito of "our committee", will not be able to put themselves in possession of the public wealth or reap the benefit of this sublime ambition which they so ardently desire to inspire in others—that of working much to consume little!

2. *THE REVOLUTIONARY CATECHISM*

Nechayev took great care of a booklet written in cypher and called *The Revolutionary Catechism*. He claimed that the possession of this book was the special privilege of any emissary or agent of the International Association. According to all the depositions and the strong evidence provided by the lawyers, this catechism had been written by Bakunin, who never dared to deny paternity. Furthermore, the form and the content of this work clearly show that it came from the same source as the secret statutes, the *Words*, the proclamations, and *The People's Judgment*, which we have already mentioned. The revolutionary catechism was only a supplement to these. These pan-destructive anarchists, who want to reduce everything to amorphism in order to create anarchy in morality, push bourgeois immorality to the limit. We have already been able to assess, from a few examples, the worth of this Alliance morality whose dogmas, purely Christian in origin, were first drawn up

---

[a] М. Бакунинъ, *Къ офицерамъ русской арміи.— Ed.*

[b] See this volume, pp. 502-03.— *Ed.*

[c] "Réponse à M. Lafargue", *Bulletin de la Fédération jurasienne...*, No. 10/11, June 15, 1872.— *Ed.*

[d] "El Congreso de La Haya", *La Federacion,* No. 164, October 5, 1872.— *Ed.*

in meticulous detail by the Escobars of the 17th century.[380] The only difference being that the Alliance exaggerated the terms to the ridiculous and replaced the Holy Catholic Apostolic and Roman Church of the Jesuits with its arch-anarchist and pan-destructive "holy revolutionary cause". The revolutionary catechism is the official code of this morality, formulated systematically and quite openly this time. We are publishing it *in extenso*, just as it was read before the tribunal during the sitting of July 8, 1871.

The revolutionary's duties to himself

§ 1. The revolutionary is a dedicated man. He has neither personal interests, nor affairs, nor feelings, nor attachments, nor property, nor even a name. Every part of him is absorbed by one sole interest, one sole thought, one sole passion: the revolution.

§ 2. In the depths of his being, not only in words, but in deeds, he has severed all ties with civil order and with the entire civilised world, with laws, decencies, morality, and the conventions generally accepted in that world. He is its implacable enemy, and if he continues to live in it, it is only to destroy it more surely.

§ 3. A revolutionary despises all doctrinairism and renounces worldly science, leaving it for future generations. He only knows one science: that of destruction. For that purpose and none other, he studies mechanics, physics, chemistry, and perhaps medicine. With the same goal, he studies living science day and night—men, characters, positions, and all conditions of the existing social order in all possible spheres. The goal remains the same: the destruction, as quickly as possible and as certainly as possible, of this foul (*poganyi*) order.

§ 4. He despises public opinion. He despises and hates the existing social morality with all its instincts and in all its manifestations. For him, everything is moral that favours the triumph of the revolution, and everything is immoral and criminal that impedes it.

§ 5. The revolutionary is a dedicated man. He has no mercy for the State in general or for the entire civilised class of society, and he should no more expect mercy for himself. Between him and society there is a struggle, open or concealed, but always incessant, irreconcilable, and to the death. He must accustom himself to withstand torture.

§ 6. Strict with himself, he must be the same with others. All feelings of affection, all the softening feelings of kinship, friendship, love and gratitude must be stifled in him by a unique and cold passion for the revolutionary cause. For him, there is only one joy, one consolation, one reward and one satisfaction: the success of the revolution. Night and day, he must have only one thought and one goal—implacable destruction. Pursuing this goal coldly and without respite, he must himself be ready to perish and to destroy with his own hands all that which obstructs the achievement of this goal.

§ 7. The nature of the true revolutionary excludes all romanticism, all sensitivity, all enthusiasm, and all involvement; it even excludes personal hatred and vengeance. Revolutionary passion, having become with him a habit every day and every moment, must be combined with cold calculation. Everywhere and always he must obey not his personal impulses, but whatever is prescribed to him by the general interests of the revolution.

Duties of the revolutionary to his comrades in revolution

§ 8. The revolutionary can only have friendship and affection for the man who has proved by his deeds that he is, like him, a revolutionary agent. The degree of friendship, devotion, and other obligations towards such a comrade are only measured by the degree of his usefulness in the practical work of the pan-destructive (*vserazrushitelnaya*) revolution.

§ 9. It is superfluous to speak of solidarity among revolutionaries, for in it lies all the strength of the revolutionary cause. The revolutionary comrades who find themselves at the same level of revolutionary consciousness and passion must, as much as possible, deliberate in common on all important matters and make their decisions unanimously. In the execution of a matter thus decided, each must rely on himself as much as possible. In the execution of a series of destructive acts, each must act on his own and not have recourse to the assistance or advice of his comrades, unless it is indispensable for success.

§ 10. Each comrade should have at hand several revolutionaries from the second and third rank, that is, from those who have not been fully initiated. He must consider them as part of the general revolutionary capital placed at his disposal. He must expend his share of the capital economically and try to extract from it as much profit as possible. He regards himself as capital destined to be expended for the triumph of the revolutionary cause, but it is capital which he cannot dispose of alone and without the consent of all the fully initiated comrades.

§ 11. When a comrade finds himself in danger, then in order to decide whether or not he should be saved, the revolutionary must not consider any personal feeling, but solely the interest of the revolutionary cause. Consequently, he must calculate, on the one hand, the degree of usefulness furnished by his comrade and, on the other, the quantity of revolutionary forces necessary to rescue him; he must see which way the scales tip and he must act accordingly.

Duties of the revolutionary to society

§ 12. A new member, after having proved his worth, not by words, but by deeds, can only be accepted by the association unanimously.

§ 13. A revolutionary enters the world of the State, the world of the classes, the so-called civilised world, and lives in it solely because he has faith in its imminent and total destruction. He is not a revolutionary if he holds on to anything whatever in this world. *He must not hesitate before the destruction of any position, tie or man belonging to this world.* He must hate everything and everybody equally. So much the worse for him if he has in this world ties of kinship, friendship, or love; *he is not a revolutionary if these ties can stay his hand.*

§ 14. With the aim of implacable destruction, a revolutionary can, and often must, live in society, while pretending to be entirely different from what he really is. A revolutionary must penetrate everywhere, into the upper and the middle classes alike, into the merchant's shop, into the church, into the aristocratic palace, into the bureaucratic, military and literary world, into the *Third Department* (secret police), and even into the imperial palace.

§ 15. The whole of this foul society must be divided into several categories. The first consists of those who are condemned to death without delay. The comrades should draw up lists of these condemned men in the order of their relative harmfulness to the success of the revolutionary cause, so that the first numbers may be disposed of before the others.

§ 16. In drawing up these lists and in establishing these categories, no influence should be exerted by the personal villainy of a man, or even by the hatred which he inspires in the members of the organisation or in the people. This villainy and this hatred may even be useful to some extent in stirring up a popular revolt. The only consideration should be taken of the measure of profit for the revolutionary cause which may result from the death of a certain person. Consequently, the first to be destroyed must be those who are most dangerous to the revolutionary organisation and whose violent and sudden death can most frighten the government and break its strength by depriving it of energetic and intelligent agents.

§ 17. The second category should consist of people who are allowed to live provisionally (!) so that by a series of monstrous acts they will drive the people to the inevitable revolt.

§ 18. The third category covers a large number of highly placed brutes or individuals who are remarkable neither for their minds nor for their energy, but who, by virtue of their position, have wealth, connections, influence, and power. We must exploit them in every way possible, outwit them, confuse them, and, wherever possible, by *possessing ourselves of their filthy secrets*, make them our slaves. In this way, their power, connections, influence and wealth will become an inexhaustible treasure and an invaluable help in various enterprises.

§ 19. The fourth category is composed of various ambitious men in the State service, and liberals of different shades. We can conspire with these on their own programme, putting up an appearance of following them blindly. We must get them into our hands, *seize their secrets, compromise them completely*, so that retreat becomes impossible for them, and make use of them to cause trouble within the State.

§ 20. The fifth category consists of doctrinaires, conspirators, revolutionaries, all those who babble at meetings and on paper. They must be constantly encouraged and inveigled into practical and dangerous[a] demonstrations which will have the effect of eliminating the majority, while making true revolutionaries out of some.

§ 21. The sixth category is very important—the women, who must be divided into three classes: first, useless women without spirit or heart, who must be exploited in the same way as the third and fourth categories of men; second, fervent, devoted and capable women, who are nevertheless not with us because they have not yet arrived at a practical and phraseless revolutionary awareness; they must be used like the fifth category of men; finally, women who are entirely with us, that is to say, who have been fully initiated and who have accepted our programme in its entirety. We must treat them as the most valuable of our treasures, for without their help we can do nothing.

Duties of the Association to the people

§ 22. The Association has no goal other than the total emancipation and the happiness of the people, that is to say, manual workers (*chernorabochi lyud*). But, convinced that this emancipation and this happiness cannot be achieved except by means of a people's revolution which will destroy everything, *the Association will employ all its means and all its forces to magnify and increase the ills and evils* which must finally exhaust the patience of the people and stir them to a mass uprising.

§ 23. By a people's revolution, the Society does not mean a movement directed after the classic model of the West, which, always hesitating before property and

---

[a] In the Russian text: "golovolomnye" (lit. "breakneck").— *Ed.*

the traditional social system of so-called civilisation and morality, has hitherto restricted itself to the overthrow of one political form in order to replace it with another and to creating a so-called revolutionary State. The only revolution which can be beneficial to the people is that which will destroy from bottom to top the whole idea of the State and will turn upside-down all the traditions, state system, and classes in Russia.

§ 24. To this end, the Society has no intention of imposing on the people any kind of organisation from above. The future organisation will undoubtedly emerge from the movement and life of the people, but that is the concern of future generations. Our concern is terrifying, total, implacable and universal destruction.

§ 25. Consequently, in drawing closer to the people, we must above all join up with the elements of the people's life which, since the foundation of the Muscovite State, have not ceased to protest, not only with words, but with their deeds, against everything which is directly or indirectly tied up with the State, against the nobility, against the bureaucracy, against the clergy, against the business[a] world, and against petty tradesmen, the exploiters of the people.[b] We must join the adventurist world of the brigands, who are the true and unique revolutionaries in Russia.

§ 26. To concentrate this world into a single pan-destructive and invincible force—that is the whole meaning of our organisation, our conspiracy, and our task.

To criticise this masterpiece would be to weaken its comic impact. It would also mean taking too seriously this amorphous pan-destroyer who succeeded only in making a single personage of Rodolphe, Monte-Christo, Karl Moor and Robert Macaire. We shall limit ourselves to stating, with the aid of a few comparisons, that the spirit and even the terms of the catechism, without counting the laborious exaggerations, are identical to those of the secret statutes and other Russian works of the Alliance.

The three grades of initiation defined in the Alliance's secret statutes are reproduced in § 10 of the catechism, where mention is made of "revolutionaries from the second and third rank... who have not been fully initiated".—The duties of the international brethren as defined in Article 6 of the rules are the same as those enjoined by §§ 1 and 13 of the catechism.—The conditions under which the brethren can accept governmental posts as defined in Article 8 of the rules "are even more explicitly defined"[c] in § 14 of the catechism, where they are given to understand that they may join the police if so ordered.—The advice given to the brethren (Rules, Article 9) to consult one another, is reproduced in § 9 of the catechism.—Articles 2, 3 and 6 of the programme of the international brethren attribute to the revolution precisely the same character as §§ 22 and 23 of the catechism.—The Jacobins

---

[a] In the Russian text: "gildeiskogo" ("pertaining to a merchant guild or order").— Ed.

[b] In the Russian text: "kulaka-miroyeda" ("the bloodsucker kulak").— Ed.

[c] See this volume, p. 568.— Ed.

of Article 4 of the programme become, in § 20 of the catechism, a subdivision of "the fifth category of men", condemned to death in both documents.—The ideas expressed in Articles 5 and 8 of the programme on the progress of a truly anarchist revolution are the same as those in § 24 of the catechism.

The condemnation of science in § 3 of the catechism recurs in all the Russian publications. The idealisation of the brigand as the type of the revolutionary, which does not exist in the *Words* except in embryo, is openly affirmed and preached in all the other writings: The "fifth category" of § 20 of the catechism is applied, in *The Setting of the Revolutionary Question*, to "Revolutionaries of the State and the Cabinet". Here, as in §§ 25 and 26, it is stated that the first duty of the revolutionary is to throw himself into brigandage. It is only *The Principles of Revolution* and *The People's Judgment* that begin to preach the pan-destruction ordained by §§ 6, 8 and 26 of the catechism, and systematic assassination in §§ 13, 15, 16 and 17.

3. BAKUNIN'S APPEAL
TO THE OFFICERS OF THE RUSSIAN ARMY

Bakunin, however, tried to leave no room for doubt over his complicity in the so-called Nechayev conspiracy. He published a proclamation: *To the Officers of the Russian Army*, dated "Geneva, January 1870" and signed Mikhail Bakunin.[a] This proclamation, "price one franc", was announced as Bakunin's work in all the issues of the *Kolokol* for 1870. Here are some extracts.

It begins by declaring, as Nechayev had done in Russia, that

"the hour of the last struggle between the house of Romanov-Holstein-Gottorp and the Russian people is approaching, the struggle between the Tartar-German yoke and the broad liberty of the Slavs. Spring is on our threshold, and the battle will commence in the first days of spring ... the revolutionary force is ready and its triumph is assured in the presence of the profound and general mass discontent now reigning all over Russia".

An organisation exists to direct this imminent revolution, for a secret organisation is like the general staff of an army, and this army is the entire people.[b]

"In my appeal to the young Russian brothers, I said that Stenka Razin who will put himself at the head of the masses during the destruction, so clearly at hand, of the Russian Empire, will no longer be an individual hero, but a collective Stenka

---

[a] М. Бакунинъ, *Къ офицерамъ русской арміи.— Ed.*
[b] See this volume, p. 576.— *Ed.*

Razin.[a] Every man who is not a fool will easily understand that I was speaking of a secret organisation existing and acting already at this moment, strong in the discipline, devotion, and passionate self-sacrifice of its members and in their passive obedience to all the instructions of *an unique committee* which knows everything and is known by no one.

"The members of this committee have achieved total self-renunciation. This is what gives them the right to demand absolute renunciation from all the other members of the organisation. They have to such an extent renounced everything most coveted by vain, ambitious, and the power-seeking men, that, having finally renounced personal property, public or official power, and, in general, all fame in society, they have condemned themselves to eternal oblivion, ceding to others glory, external appearances, and the renown of the cause, and only keeping for themselves, and even then always collectively, the very essence of this cause.

"*Like the Jesuits*, only not with the aim of enslaving, but with that of liberating the people, each of them has even renounced his own will. In the committee, as in the whole organisation, it is not the individual who thinks, wishes and acts, but the collective. Such a renunciation of his own life, his own thought and his own will may seem impossible, even revolting, to many. It is, in fact, difficult to achieve, but it is indispensable. It will seem particularly difficult to the novices, to those who have only just joined the organisation, to men who have not yet lost the habit of wordy and futile bragging, to men who play at honour, personal dignity and right, to those who in general let themselves be diverted by the wretched phantoms of a supposed humanity, behind which can be seen, in Russian society, a general servility towards the most vile and abject realities of life. This renunciation will seem painful to those who seek in a great cause the satisfaction of their vanity and an occasion for phrase-making, and who love the cause not for its own sake, but for the drama which it confers on them personally."

"Each new member joins our organisation voluntarily, knowing in advance that once he has become a part of it, he belongs to it entirely and not to himself any more. *Entry into the organisation is voluntary, but to leave it is impossible,* since every member who resigns will undoubtedly endanger the very existence of the organisation, which must not depend on the irresponsibility, the whims or discretion, however great or small it may be, or on the honesty and the strength of one or several individuals... Consequently, whoever wishes to join must know in advance that he is giving himself to it entirely, with all that he possesses by way of strength, means, knowledge and life, *unreturnably*... This is clearly and precisely expressed in its programme, which has been published and is obligatory for all members of the committee and for all those who do not belong to it... If a member is truly inspired by" (revolutionary) "passion, everything that the organisation demands of him will seem easy. It is a known fact that passion acknowledges no difficulties; it recognises nothing as impossible, and the greater the obstacles are, the greater is the screwing up of the will, strength, and knowledge of the man moved by passion. There is no room for minor personal passions in a man possessed by this passion; he does not even need to sacrifice them, because they do not exist in him any more. A serious member of the association has stifled in himself all feeling of curiosity, and he remorselessly persecutes this failing in all others. Although he recognises himself as worthy of all confidence, and precisely because he is worthy of it, that is to say, because he is a serious man, he does not seek, and does not even want to know, more than is necessary for him to fulfil as well as possible the mission entrusted to him. He only discusses business with

---

[a] М. Бакунинъ, *Нѣсколько словъ къ молодымъ братьямъ въ Россiи,* Geneva, 1869, (see this volume, p. 518).— *Ed.*

persons who have been allocated to him, and he says nothing which has been forbidden by the orders he has received, and in general he conforms strictly and unconditionally to the orders and instructions which come down to him *from above*, without ever asking, or even wanting to ask about the position of the organisation to which he belongs, since he naturally wishes to be entrusted with as many tasks as possible, but he nevertheless waits patiently for the moment when it will be entrusted to him.

"So rigid and so absolute a discipline may astonish and even shock the novice; but it will neither astonish nor offend a serious member, a man truly strong and sensible. On the contrary, it will afford him pleasure and guarantee his security, provided that he is under the influence of that absorbing passion, which I have already mentioned: for the people's triumph. A serious member will realise that such discipline is an indispensable pledge of the relative impersonality of each member, a *sine qua non* of the common triumph; that this discipline alone is capable of forming a true organisation and of creating a collective revolutionary force which, basing itself on the elemental power of the people, will be in a condition to conquer the formidable force of the State organisation.

"You may ask: how can you submit to the *dictatorial* control of a Committee unknown to you? But the Committee is known to you: first, by its published programme, which has been drawn up with such clarity and precision, and which is explained in even greater detail to every member who joins the organisation. Secondly, it recommends itself to you by the blind confidence placed in it by persons whom you know and respect—the confidence which makes you give preference to this organisation rather than to any other. It makes itself known even still more fully to the active members of the organisation by its indefatigable and determined activity, which extends everywhere and always conforms to the programme and goal of the organisation. And everybody submits voluntarily to its *authority*, becoming more and more convinced, through practical experience, on the one hand, of its truly astonishing foresight, of its vigilance, of its energy so full of wisdom and of its ability to match its instructions to the sought-after goal; and, on the other hand, of the necessity and salutary effect of such discipline.

"I could be asked: if the identity of the personnel constituting the Committee remains an impenetrable mystery to everyone, how were you able to find out about it and convince yourself of its real worth?—I will answer this question frankly. I do not know a single member of this Committee, nor the number of its members, nor its place of residence. I know one thing: it is not abroad, but is in Russia itself, as is only right; for a Russian revolutionary committee abroad would be an absurdity, the very idea of which could only occur to those empty-headed and stupidly ambitious phrasemongers who belong to the emigration and who hide their conceited and evilly intriguing inactivity behind the sonorous name of *The People's Cause*.*

"After the Decembrist conspiracy of the nobility (1825),[381] the first serious attempt at organisation was made by Ishutin and his comrades.[382] The existing organisation is the first organisation of revolutionary forces in the whole of Russia which has truly succeeded. It has profited by all preparations and experience; no reaction will force it to dissolve; it will survive all governments, and it will not cease to act until its entire programme has become daily life in Russia and everywhere else in the world.

* The reader will remember that this was the title of a Russian newspaper of the International published in Geneva by a few young Russians who knew perfectly well the real worth of the so-called committee and Bakunin's organisation.

"About a year ago, the Committee thought it would be useful to inform me of its existence and it sent me its programme, together with an exposition of the general plan of revolutionary action in Russia. Completely in agreement with both of these, and having assured myself that the enterprise, like the men who had taken the initiative with it, was truly serious, I did what, in my opinion, every honest refugee ought to do: I submitted unconditionally to the authority of the Committee as the sole representative and controlling body of the revolution in Russia. If I am addressing you today, I am only obeying the Committee's orders. I cannot say more to you about this. I will add one more word on this subject. I know the organisation's plan sufficiently well to be convinced that no force is capable of destroying it. Even if, in the imminent struggle, the popular party has to suffer a new defeat—which none of us fears, since we all believe in the forthcoming triumph of the people—but even if our hopes should be dashed, in the midst of the most appalling reprisals, in the midst of the most savage reaction, the organisation will still remain safe and sound...

"The basis of the programme is the widest and most humanitarian possible: complete liberty and complete equality of all human beings, based on communal ownership and communal labour and equally obligatory to all except, of course, those who would rather die of hunger than work.

"This is the present programme of the working people in all countries, and it fully corresponds to the age-old demands and the instincts of our people... In submitting this programme to the lower orders[a] of the people, the members of our organisation are astounded to notice how immediate and broad is their grasp of it, and with what eagerness they accept it. This means that the programme is ready. It is unvarying. He who is for this programme will come with us. He who is against us is the friend of the people's enemies, the tsar's gendarme, the tsar's executioner, our own enemy...

"I have told you that our organisation is solidly built and now I add that it has taken root so strongly among the people that, even if we suffer a defeat, the reaction will be powerless to destroy it...

"The servile press, obedient to the orders of the Third Department, is trying to persuade the public that the government has managed to seize the conspiracy by its very roots. It has not seized anything whatever. The Committee and the organisation are intact and always will be, the government will soon be convinced of this, for the explosion of the people is near at hand. It is so near, that everyone must now decide if he wishes to be our friend, the friend of the people, or our enemy instead and that of the people. To all friends, to whatever place or position they belong, our ranks are open. But how are we to find you, you will ask? The organisation, *which surrounds you on all sides*, which counts among you its *numerous* adherents, will itself find him who seeks with sincere desire and strong will to serve the cause of the people. He who is not with us, is against us. Choose."

In this pamphlet signed with his name, Bakunin pretends not to know the place and composition of the Committee on whose behalf he speaks and on whose behalf Nechayev acted in Russia. However, the only authority which the latter had to act on the Committee's behalf was signed by Mikhail Bakunin, and the only man who received reports on the activity of the sections was, once again, Mikhail Bakunin. And so when Mikhail Bakunin vows

---

[a] The Russian text of Bakunin's appeal has "chernorabochemu lyudu" ("to unskilled workers") instead of "lower orders".— *Ed.*

passive obedience to the committee, it is to Mikhail Bakunin himself that he swears obedience.

We consider it useless to insist that the trend and even the language of this work signed by Bakunin are entirely identical with the other anonymous Russian documents. What we want to point out is the manner in which Bakunin applied the morality of the catechism here. He commences, first, by preaching it to the Russian officers. He tells them that he and the other initiates have simultaneously carried out a duty and filled a gap in setting themselves up as the Jesuits of the revolution and that, as far as the Committee is concerned, they have no more personal will than the celebrated "corpse" of the Society of Jesus. In order that the officers should not be shocked by the murder of Ivanov, he tries to make them understand the necessity of assassinating every member who would like to leave the secret society. He then applies this same morality to his own readers by lying flagrantly to them. Bakunin knew that the government had arrested not only all the initiates in Russia, but ten times more that number of persons who had been compromised by Nechayev for belonging to the famous "fifth category" of the catechism; that there was no longer so much as the shadow of an organisation in Russia; that its Committee no longer existed there and never had existed apart from Nechayev, then with him in Geneva; furthermore, that this pamphlet would not bring in a single recruit in Russia; that it could only furnish the Government with a pretext for fresh persecutions. Yet he proclaimed that the Government had seized nothing whatever; that the Committee was still holding sessions in Russia and was displaying indefatigable and determined activity that extended everywhere, truly astounding foresight, vigilance, energy full of wisdom, and staggering ingenuity (the statements made at the trial testify to this); that his secret organisation, the only serious one that had existed in Russia since 1825, was intact; that it had penetrated down to the lower orders of the people, who were eagerly accepting its programme; that the officers were surrounded by it; that the revolution was imminent and would break out in a few months, in the spring of 1870. It was purely to give himself the pleasure of the drama which it conferred on him personally in front of his false international brethren and in front of his mirror that Bakunin, who pretended to have "renounced his own life, his own thought, and his own will", to be superior to the "wordy and futile bragging" of "men who play at honour, personal dignity, and right", that he, Mikhail Bakunin, addressed the Russians with these lies and this bragging.

This same man who in 1870 preaches to the Russians passive, blind obedience to orders coming from above and from an anonymous and unknown committee; who declares that Jesuitical discipline is the condition *sine qua non* of victory, the only thing capable of defeating the formidable centralisation of the State— not just the Russian state but any state; who proclaims a communism more authoritarian than the most primitive communism—this same man, in 1871, weaves a separatist and disorganising movement into the fabric of the International under the pretext of combating the authoritarianism and centralisation of the German Communists, of introducing autonomy of the sections, a free federation of autonomous groups, and of making the International what it should be: the image of the future society. If the society of the future were modelled on the Alliance, Russian section, it would far surpass the Paraguay of the Reverend Jesuit Fathers,[383] so dear to Bakunin's heart.

IX

CONCLUSION

While granting the fullest freedom to the movements and aspirations of the working class in various countries, the International had nevertheless succeeded in uniting it into a single whole and making the ruling classes and their governments feel for the first time the worldwide power of the proletariat. The ruling classes and the governments recognised this fact by concentrating their attacks on the executive body of our whole Association, the General Council. These attacks became increasingly intense after the fall of the Commune. And this was the moment that the Alliancists, on their part, chose to declare open war on the General Council! They claimed that its influence, a powerful weapon in the hands of the International, was but a weapon directed against the International itself. It had been won in a struggle not against the enemies of the proletariat but against the International. According to them, the General Council's domineering tendencies had prevailed over the autonomy of the sections and the national federations. The only way of saving autonomy was to decapitate the International.

Indeed the men of the Alliance realised that if they did not seize this decisive moment, it would be all up with their plans for the secret direction of the proletarian movement of which Bakunin's hundred international brethren had dreamed. Their invective wakened approving echoes in the police press of all countries.

Their resounding phrases about autonomy and free federation, in a word, war-cries against the General Council, were thus nothing but a manoeuvre to conceal their true purpose—to disorganise the International and by doing so subordinate it to the secret, hierarchic and autocratic rule of the Alliance.

Autonomy of the sections, free federation of the autonomous groups, anti-authoritarianism, anarchy—these were convenient phrases for a society of the "declassed" "with no prospects and no way out", conspiring within the International to subject it to a secret dictatorship and impose upon it the programme of M. Bakunin!

Stripped of its melodramatic finery, this programme amounts to the following:

1. All the depravities in which the life of declassed persons ejected from the upper strata of society must inevitably become involved are proclaimed to be so many ultra-revolutionary virtues.

2. It is regarded as a matter of principle and necessity to debauch a small minority of carefully selected workers, who are enticed away from the masses by a mysterious initiation, by making them take part in the game of intrigues and deceit of the secret government, and by preaching to them that through giving free rein to their "evil passions" they can shake the old society to its foundations.

3. The chief means of propaganda is to attract young people by fantastic lies about the extent and power of the secret society, prophecies of the imminent revolution it has prepared and so on, and to compromise in government eyes the most progressive people from among the well-to-do classes with a view to exploiting them financially.

4. The economic and political struggle of the workers for their emancipation is replaced by the universal *pan-destructive* acts of heroes of the underworld—this latest incarnation of revolution. In a word, one must let loose the street hooligans suppressed by the workers themselves in "the revolutions on the Western classical model", and thus place gratuitously at the disposal of the reactionaries a well-disciplined gang of *agents provocateurs.*

It is hard to say what predominates in the theoretical elucubrations and practical endeavours of the Alliance—clowning or infamy. Nevertheless, it has succeeded in provoking within the International a muffled conflict which for two years has hindered the actions of our Association and has culminated in the secession of some of the sections and federations. The resolutions adopted by the Hague Congress against the Alliance were therefore merely a matter of duty: the Congress could not allow the International, that great creation of the proletariat, to fall into nets spread by the riff-raff of the exploiting classes. As for those who wish to deprive the General Council of the prerogatives without which the International would be nothing but a confused, disjointed and, to use the language of the Alliance, "amorphous" mass, we cannot regard them otherwise than as traitors or dupes.

London, July 21, 1873

The Commission: E. Dupont, F. Engels, Léo Frankel, C. Le Moussu, Karl Marx, Aug. Serraillier[a]

X

APPENDIX

1. BAKUNIN'S HEGIRA[384]

In 1857, Bakunin was sent to Siberia, not to forced labour, as his accounts would have us believe, but simply to live there in exile. At that period, the governor of Siberia was Count Muravyov-Amursky, Bakunin's cousin and a relative of the Muravyov who was the executioner of Poland. Thanks to this relationship and to the services which he had rendered to the government, Bakunin enjoyed exceptional position and favours in Siberia.

Petrashevsky, leader and organiser of the 1849 conspiracy,[385] was in Siberia at that time. Bakunin adopted an openly hostile attitude to him and tried to harm him in every way possible, which was easy for him as a cousin of the governor-general. His persecution of Petrashevsky gave Bakunin further grounds for governmental favours. A shady affair, which had considerable repercussions in Siberia and in Russia, put an end to this struggle between the two exiles. As a result of criticism levelled against the conduct of a highly-placed official who was playing at liberalism, a storm broke out in the governor-general's entourage and ended in a duel[b] to the death. Now this whole affair stank so much of personal intrigues and fraudulent dealings, that the whole population was disturbed and accused the chief officials of having

---

a See this volume, pp. 454-57.— *Ed.*

b Between F. A. Beklemishev and M. S. Neklyudov, who was killed.— *Ed.*

assassinated the victim of the duel, a young friend of Petrashevsky's. Unrest took on such proportions that the government became fearful of a popular riot. Bakunin sided with the high officials, Muravyov included. He used his influence to have Petrashevsky exiled to a remoter place and he defended Petrashevsky's persecutors in a long letter signed by him as witness and sent to Herzen.[386] The latter, when publishing it in the *Kolokol*,[a] suppressed all the attacks against Petrashevsky; but the manuscript copy made of this letter while on its way to St. Petersburg was circulated there, and so the original text reached the public.

The merchants of Siberia, who are generally more liberal than those in Russia, wanted to found a university there in order not to have to send their children any more to distant schools in Russia, and to create an intellectual centre in those parts. For this, they needed imperial authorisation.[b] Muravyov, advised and encouraged by Bakunin, opposed this project. Bakunin's hatred of science goes back a long way. This is perfectly well-known in Siberia. Challenged on this point several times by the Russians, Bakunin could not deny it, but always explained his conduct by saying that, *while preparing for his escape*, he sought to win the good graces of his cousin the governor.

Not only did Bakunin use and abuse governmental favours, but for trifling sums of money he obtained them in abundance for the capitalists, contractors and tax-farmers. Bakunin's proclamations, confiscated from Nechayev's victims and published by the government in 1869 and 1870, contained lists of proscribed persons, including the notorious Katkov, editor-in-chief of the *Moscow Gazette*.[c] The latter took his revenge by publishing the following disclosure in his newspaper: he had in his possession letters sent to him by Bakunin from London on his arrival from Siberia, in which he begged Katkov, as an old friend, to advance him several thousand rubles.[d] Bakunin admits that during his stay in Siberia he had been receiving an annuity from a vodka tax-farmer[e] who paid him for ensuring, by his intercession, the good graces of the

a [М. Бакунин,] «Письмо въ редакцію по поводу дуэли Беклемишева съ Неклюдовымъ», *Колоколъ*, приложеніе «Подъ судъ!», л.л. 6, 7, July 1 and 15, 1860.— *Ed.*
b By Alexander II.— *Ed.*
c *Московскія вѣдомости.— Ed.*
d [М. Н. Катков,] «Самое тяжелое впечатлѣніе...», *Московскія Вѣдомости*, No. 4, January 6, 1870. (Katkov referred to Bakunin's letter from Irkutsk of January 2, 1861.)— *Ed.*
e Dmitry Benardaki.— *Ed.*

governor. This dishonourable fee (Bakunin ceased to collect it after his escape) weighed on his conscience; he wanted to send back to the tax-farmer the money received from him. He asked his friend Katkov for an advance to enable him to perform this good deed. Katkov refused.

At the time when Bakunin sent this request to his old friend Katkov, the latter had long since won his spurs in the service of the Third Department, devoting his newspaper to denunciations of the Russian revolutionaries and particularly of Chernyshevsky, as well as of the Polish revolution. And so, in 1862, Bakunin requested money of a man whom he knew to be a denouncer and a literary bandit in the pay of the Russian Government. Bakunin has never dared to deny this grave charge.

Supplied with money obtained by the methods already known to us, and enjoying the high protection of the governor, Bakunin was able to escape with the greatest of ease. Not only did he procure a passport in his own name to travel in Siberia, he obtained the official assignment of inspecting the region as far as its eastern frontiers. Once he arrived at the port of Nikolayevsk, he crossed without difficulty to Japan, from where he was able calmly to embark for America and arrive in London at the end of 1861. Thus did this new Mohammed accomplish his miraculous hegira.

2. BAKUNIN'S PAN-SLAV MANIFESTO

On March 3, 1861, Alexander II proclaimed, to the tumultuous plaudits of all liberal Europe, the emancipation of the serfs. The efforts of Chernyshevsky and the revolutionary party to obtain the preservation of communal landownership had produced results, but in a manner so unsatisfactory that, even before the proclamation of the manifesto emancipating the serfs,[387] Chernyshevsky sadly admitted:

> "Had I known that the question raised by me was to receive such a solution, I would have preferred to suffer a defeat rather than win such a victory. I would rather they had acted as they had intended, without any regard for our claims."

And, indeed, the act of emancipation was nothing but a swindle. A large part of the land was taken away from its real owners, and a system was proclaimed whereby the peasants could buy back their land. This act of bad faith by the tsar gave Chernyshevsky and his party a new and irresistible argument against imperial reforms. The liberals, ranging themselves under Herzen's banner, bayed at the top of their voices: "Thou hast conquered,

O Galilean!"[a] By Galilean, they meant Alexander II.—From that moment, the liberal party, whose chief organ was Herzen's *Kolokol*, never ceased to sing the praises of the tsar-liberator and, to distract the public's attention from the complaints and claims which were stirred up by this anti-popular act, they asked the tsar to continue his emancipatory work and to launch a crusade for the liberation of the oppressed Slav peoples and for the achievement of pan-Slavism.

In the summer of 1861, Chernyshevsky, in the journal *Sovremennik*, denounced the manoeuvres of the pan-Slavists and told the Slav peoples the truth about the state of affairs in Russia and about the selfish obscurantism of their false friends, the pan-Slavists.[b] It was then that Bakunin, on his return from Siberia, judged that the moment had arrived for him to step forward. He wrote the first part of a long manifesto published as a supplement by *Kolokol* on February 15, 1862, and entitled: *To the Russian, Polish and All Slav Friends*.[c] The second part never appeared.

The manifesto begins with the following declaration:

"I have retained the audacity of all-conquering thought, and in heart, will and passion I have remained true to my friends, to the great common cause, to myself... I now appear before you, my old and tested friends, and you, my young friends, who live by one thought and one will with us, and I ask you: admit me to your midst again and may I be permitted, with you and in your midst, to devote all my remaining life to the struggle for Russian freedom, for Polish freedom, for the freedom and independence of all Slavs."

If Bakunin addresses this humble prayer to his old and young friends, it is because

"it is bad to be active in a foreign land. I experienced this in the revolutionary years: neither in France nor in Germany was I able to gain a foothold. And so, while preserving all my ardent sympathy of former years for the progressive movement of the whole world, in order not to waste the rest of my life I must henceforth limit my direct activity to Russia, Poland, and the Slavs. These three separate worlds are inseparable in my love and in my faith."

In 1862, eleven years ago, at the age of forty-seven,[d] the great

---

a А. И. Герценъ, «На канунѣ», *Колоколъ*, London, No. 93, March 1, 1861.— *Ed.*

b Н. Г. Чернышевскій, «Національная безтактность», *Современникъ*, No, 7, St. Petersburg, July 1861; *idem*, «Народная безтолковость», *Современникъ*, No. 9/10, St. Petersburg, September-October 1861.— *Ed.*

c М. А. Бакунинъ, «Русскимъ, польскимъ и всѣмъ славянскимъ друзьямъ», *Колоколъ*, No. 122/123, February 15, 1862, supplement.— *Ed.*

d The original mistakenly has: "51 years" (Bakunin was born in May 1814).— *Ed.*

anarchist Bakunin preached the cult of the state and pan-Slav patriotism.

"It might be said that the Great-Russian people has hitherto lived only the external life of the state. However burdensome its position may have been within, reduced to extreme ruin and slavery, it has nevertheless cherished the unity, strength and greatness of Russia, and has been ready to make any sacrifice for their sake. And so there has been a growing awareness among the Great-Russian people of the state and patriotism, not in words, but in deeds. And so it alone has survived as a people among the Slav tribes; it alone has held out in Europe and made itself felt by all as a force... Do not fear that it may lose its legitimate influence and the political force which it has acquired solely by struggles lasting three centuries and accomplished by martyr-like abnegation to safeguard its state integrity... Let us send the Tartars to Asia, the Germans to Germany, and let us be a free people, a purely Russian people..."

To lend more authority to this pan-Slav propaganda, which ends by calling for a crusade against the Tartars and the Germans, Bakunin refers the reader to the Emperor Nicholas:

"They say that Emperor Nicholas himself, not long before his death, when preparing to declare war on Austria, wanted to call all the Austrian and Turkish Slavs, Magyars and Italians to a general uprising. He had stirred up against himself an eastern storm and, to defend himself against it, he wanted to transform himself from a despotic emperor into a revolutionary emperor. They say that his proclamations to the Slavs as also an appeal to the Poles had already been signed by him. However much he hated Poland, he understood that, without it, a Slav uprising was impossible ... he overcame his aversion to such an extent that he was ready, it is said, to recognise the independent existence of Poland, but ... only beyond the Vistula."

The very man who, since 1868, has played the internationalist, preached, in 1862, a war of the races in the interests of the Russian Government. Pan-Slavism is an invention of the St. Petersburg cabinet and has no other goal but to extend Russia's European frontiers further west and south. But since one dare not announce to the Austrian, Prussian and Turkish Slavs that their destiny is to be absorbed into the great Russian Empire, one represents Russia to them as the power which will deliver them from the foreign yoke and which will reunite them in a great free federation. Thus, pan-Slavism is open to various shades of interpretation, from the pan-Slavism of Nicholas to that of Bakunin; but they all tend to the same end and all are, at bottom, in an *entente cordiale*, as is proved by the passage which we have just quoted. The manifesto[a] to which we now turn will leave us in no doubt on this score.

---

[a] М. А. Бакунинъ, *Народное Дѣло. Романовъ, Пугачевъ, или Пестель?* London, 1862.— *Ed.*

3. BAKUNIN AND THE TSAR

We have seen that, consequent upon the emancipation of the serfs, war broke out between the liberal and the revolutionary parties in Russia. Round Chernyshevsky, leader of the revolutionary party, there gathered a whole phalanx of journalists, a large group of officers, and the student youth. The liberal party was represented by Herzen, a few pan-Slavists, and a large number of peaceful reformers and admirers of Alexander II. The government lent its support to the liberals. In March 1861, the university students in Russia declared themselves vigorously in favour of the affranchisement of Poland. In the autumn of 1861, they tried to resist the "coup d'état" which wanted, by disciplinary and fiscal measures, to deprive the poor students (over two-thirds of the total number) of the chance to receive a higher education. The government declared this protest to be a riot, and in Petersburg, Moscow and Kazan, hundreds of young people were thrown into gaols, expelled from the universities, or banned from them after three months' detention. And for fear that these young people might aggravate the discontent of the peasants, a decree of the State Council forbade ex-students all access to public functions in the villages. But the persecutions did not stop there. Professors such as Pavlov were exiled; public courses organised by students who had been expelled from the universities, were shut down; fresh police hunts were undertaken on the most futile pretexts; the "student youth fund", only just authorised, was abruptly suppressed; newspapers were banned. All this brought the indignation and agitation of the radical party to a head and compelled it to resort to the underground press. At this point, a manifesto entitled *Young Russia* was published with an epigraph by Robert Owen.[388] This manifesto exposed clearly and in detail the internal situation of the country, the state of the various parties and of the press, and, in proclaiming communism, deduced the necessity for a social revolution. It called on all serious people to group round the radical banner.

Hardly had this manifesto issued from the underground press, when, by a fatal coincidence (unless the police had a hand in it), numerous fires broke out in St. Petersburg. The government and the reactionary press joyously seized on the occasion to accuse the young people and all the radical party of incendiarism. The prison cells filled up again, and the roads to exile were once more thronged with victims. Chernyshevsky was arrested and thrown into the St. Petersburg fortress, from where, after two

long years of intense suffering, he was sent to forced labour in
Siberia.

Before this catastrophe, Herzen and Gromeka, who later
contributed to the pacification of Poland as governor of one of its
provinces, delivered a series of furious attacks, the former in
London, the latter in Russia, on the radical party, and insinuated
that Chernyshevsky would perhaps end up by receiving a
decoration.[a]— In as moderate an article as possible, Chernyshevsky
called on Herzen to consider carefully the consequences of the
new role which the *Kolokol* was going to play in open hostility to
the Russian revolutionary party.[b] Herzen pompously declared that
he was ready to pronounce, in the presence of those he called
international democrats—Mazzini, Victor Hugo, Ledru-Rollin,
Louis Blanc, etc.—the famous toast to the health of the great
tsar-liberator[c] and, "whatever is said", he added, "by the
revolutionary *Daniels* of Petersburg, I know that despite all their
protests, this toast will find a favourable echo in the Winter
Palace" (the tsar's residence).[d] The revolutionary Daniels were
Chernyshevsky and his friends.[389]

Bakunin got the better of Herzen. It was when the revolutionary
party was completely routed and Chernyshevsky was in prison,
that Bakunin published, at the age of fifty-one,[e] his notorious
pamphlet to the peasant tsar: *Romanov, Pugachev or Pestel. The
People's Cause.* By Mikhail Bakunin, 1862.

"Many are still wondering whether there will be a revolution in Russia. It is
taking place gradually, it reigns everywhere, in everything, in all minds. It acts still
more successfully through the hands of the government than through the efforts
of its own adherents. It will not abate and will not cease until it has regenerated the
Russian world, until it has created a new Slav world.

"The dynasty is working to bring about its own destruction. It seeks its salvation
in wishing to stop the life of the people which is awakening instead of protecting it.
This life, if it were understood, could have raised the imperial house to hitherto
unknown heights of power and glory... It is a pity! Rarely has it fallen to the lot of
the tsar's house to play so majestic and so beneficent a role. Alexander II could so

---

a [А. И. Герцен,] "Very Dangerous!!!", *Колоколъ*, No. 44, June 1, 1859.— *Ed.*

b [Н. Г. Чернышевский,] «Политика. Похвала миру.— Сраженія при Мад-
женте и Сольферино.— Причины слабости австрійской арміи. Причина, по
которой былъ заключенъ миръ», *Современникъ*, No. 7, July 1859.— *Ed.*

c [А. И. Герцен,] «10 апрѣля 1861 и убійства въ Варшавѣ», *Колоколъ*, No. 96,
April 15, 1861.— *Ed.*

d [А. И. Герцен,] «Лишніе люди и желчевики», *Колоколъ*, No. 83, October 15,
1860.— *Ed.*

e Bakunin's age is given here according to Utin's report; in fact, Bakunin was
born on May 30, 1814.— *Ed.*

easily become the idol of the people, the first peasant tsar,* mighty not through fear, but through the love, liberty and prosperity of his people. Relying on that people, he could become the saviour and head of the entire Slav world...

"For that all that was necessary was a Russian heart, broad and strong in magnanimity and truth. All Russian and Slav living reality went to him with open arms, ready to serve as a pedestal for his historic greatness."

Bakunin then demands the abolition of the state of Peter the Great, of the *German* state, and the creation of the "new Russia". The fulfilment of this task is entrusted to Alexander II.

"His beginning was magnificent. He proclaimed freedom for the people, freedom and a new life after a thousand years of slavery. It seemed as if he wanted to organise the Russia of the peasants" (*zemskaya Rossiya*), "because in Peter's state a free people was unthinkable. On February 19, 1861, in spite of all the shortcomings and absurd contradictions in the Ukase on the Emancipation of the peasants, Alexander II was the greatest, most loved and most powerful tsar who ever existed in Russia."—However, "liberty is contrary to all the instincts of Alexander II", because he is German, and "a German will never understand and never love the Russia of the peasants ... he only dreamed of strengthening the edifice of Peter's state ... having undertaken a thing that is fatal and impossible, he is working to his own ruin and that of his house, and he is on the point of plunging Russia into a bloody revolution".

According to Bakunin, all the contradictions of the ukase on emancipation, all the shootings of peasants, the student disturbances, all the terror, in a word,

"is fully explained by the tsar's lack of a Russian spirit and of a heart loving the people, by his insane striving to preserve Peter's state at all costs ... and yet it is he, he alone who could accomplish in Russia the most serious and most beneficial revolution without shedding a drop of blood. He can still do so now. If we despair of the peaceful outcome, it is not because it would be too late, but because we have ended up by despairing of Alexander II and his ability to understand what is the only way of saving himself and Russia. To stop the movement of the people who are wakening up after a thousand years of sleep is impossible. But if the tsar were to put himself firmly and boldly at the head of the movement, his power for the good and the glory of Russia would be unlimited."

For this, he would only have to give the peasants land, liberty, and SELF-GOVERNMENT.

"Do not fear that regional SELF-GOVERNMENT might break the ties between the provinces, that the unity of the Russian land might be shaken; the autonomy of the provinces will be only administrative, internally legislative, juridical, but not political. And in no country, with the exception, perhaps, of France, is the people endowed to the same extent as in Russia with a sense of unity, of harmony, of integrity of the state, and of national greatness."

---

* The title of peasant tsar (*Zemsky Tsar*) conferred on Alexander II was invented by Bakunin and the *Kolokol.*

At that time, the convocation of a national assembly[a] was being demanded in Russia. Some wanted it to resolve the financial difficulties, others to put an end to the monarchy. Bakunin wanted it to express the unity of Russia and to consolidate the power and greatness of the tsar.

"Since the unity of Russia has hitherto found its expression only in the person of the tsar, it needs another representation, that of a national assembly... The question is not to know whether or not there will be a revolution, but whether it will be peaceful or bloody. It will be peaceful and beneficial if the tsar, putting himself at the head of the popular movement, undertakes, with the national assembly, broadly and resolutely to transform Russia radically in the spirit of freedom; but if he wishes to retreat, or stops at half-measures, the revolution will be frightful. It will then take on the character of a pitiless massacre in consequence of the uprising of the entire people... Alexander II can still save Russia from total ruin and from bloodshed."

Thus, in 1862, the revolution, for Bakunin, meant the total ruin of Russia, and he beseeched the tsar to save the country from it. For many Russian revolutionaries, the convocation of a national assembly would be equivalent to the collapse of the imperial house; but Bakunin puts an end to their hopes and announces to them that

"a national assembly will be against them and for the tsar. And if the national assembly should be hostile to the tsar? It is not possible; it is the people who will send their delegates, the people whose faith in the tsar is without limits to this day and who respect everything about him. Whence, then, would the hostility come?.. There is no doubt that if the tsar convoked the national assembly now" (February 1862), "he would, for the first time, find himself surrounded by men sincerely devoted to him. If the anarchy[b] lasts a few years longer, the attitudes of the people may change. Life moves fast in our times. But, at present the people are for the tsar and against the nobility, against the officials, against everything that wears German dress" (that is to say, European-style dress). "In the official Russian camp, all are enemies of the people, *all except the tsar*. Who, then, will try to speak to the people against the tsar? And even if someone should try to do so, would the people believe him? *Was it not the tsar who emancipated the peasants against the will of the nobility, against the general desire of the officials?*

"Through their delegates, the Russian people will meet *their* tsar face to face for the first time. It is a decisive moment, critical to the highest degree. Will they like one another? The whole future of the tsar and of Russia will depend on this meeting. The confidence and devotion of the delegates towards the tsar will be boundless. Relying on them, going to meet them with faith and love, he will elevate his throne to a height and a security which it has never attained before. But what if, instead of the tsar-emancipator, the people's[c] tsar, the delegates find in him a

---

[a] In the Russian text here and subsequently Bakunin uses the term "vsenarodny Zemsky Sobor" ("elective council of the whole people").— *Ed.*

[b] The Russian text has: "bezuryaditsa" ("lack of order").— *Ed.*

[c] The Russian text has: "zemsky". "Zemsky tzar"—tsar elected by all the people of the land, or by the Zemstvo.— *Ed.*

Petersburg emperor in Prussian uniform, a narrow-hearted German? What if, instead of the expected liberty, the tsar gives them nothing, or next to nothing?.. Then, woe to tsarism! At least it will be the end of the Petersburg, German, Holstein-Gottorp emperorship.

"If, at this fatal moment, when the question of life or death, of peace or blood, is about to be decided for the whole of Russia, if the tsar of the people were to appear before the national assembly as a *good and loyal tsar,* loving Russia, ready to give the people an organisation according to its will, what could he not do with such a people! Who would dare to rise up against him? Peace and confidence would be re-established as if by a miracle, money would be found, and everything would be arranged simply, naturally, without prejudice to anybody, and to the general satisfaction. *Guided by such a tsar,* the national assembly would create a new Russia. No malevolent attempt, no hostile force, would be in a state to fight against the reunited might of the tsar and the people... May one hope that this alliance will become fact? We have every reason to say No.

Whatever he might say, Bakunin does not despair of dragging his tsar along, and in order to persuade him, he threatens him with the revolutionary youth who, if the tsar does not make haste, will be able to accomplish its mission and find its way to the people.

"And why is this youth not for you, but against you? That is a great misfortune for you ... they need, above all, liberty and truth. But why has it abandoned the tsar? Why has it declared itself against him who first gave liberty to the people?... Has it perhaps let itself be carried away *by the abstract revolutionary ideal and the sonorous word 'republic'*? That may be partly so, but it is only a secondary and superficial cause. The majority of our progressive youth understands well that *Western abstractions,* whether conservative, bourgeois, liberal, and democratic, *are not applicable to the Russian movement...* The Russian people is not moved according to abstract principles ... the Western ideal is alien to it, and all attempts by conservative, liberal or even revolutionary doctrinairism to subject it to its own tendencies will be futile ... it has its own ideal ... it will bring new principles into history, will create another civilisation, *a new religion,* a new right, a new life.

"Faced with this great, serious, and even terrible figure of the people one dare not commit stupidities. Youth will abandon the ridiculous and disgusting role of impostrous schoolteachers... What could we teach the people? If one leaves aside the natural sciences and mathematics, the last word of our science will be the negation of the so-called immutable truths of the Western doctrine, the complete negation of the West."

Bakunin then descends on the authors of *Young Russia* accusing them of doctrinairism, of wanting to set themselves up as the people's teachers, of having compromised the cause, of being children who do not understand anything and who have drawn their ideas from a few Western books which they have read.— The government, which at that time arrested these same young people as incendiaries, hurled the same reproaches at them. And so to reassure his tsar, Bakunin announces that "the people do not support this revolutionary party ... the vast majority of our youth belongs to the people's party, to the party which has as its sole and single aim the triumph of the people's cause. This party has no prejudices either for or against the tsar, and if the tsar, having begun the great work, had not betrayed the people, it would never have abandoned him, and even now it is not too late for him; and even now that youth would follow him with joy provided he would march at the head of his people. It would not allow itself to be stopped *by any of the Western revolutionary prejudices.* It is time for the Germans to go to Germany. If the tsar had realised that henceforth he must be the head not of an enforced centralisation, but of *a free federation of free peoples,* then, relying on a solid and regenerated force, allying himself with Poland and the Ukraine, breaking all the detested German alliances, and boldly raising the pan-Slav banner, he would become *the saviour of the Slav world.*

"Yes, indeed, war on the Germans is a good and indispensable thing for the Slavs, at all events better than stifling the Poles to please the Germans. To rise and free the Slavs from the yoke of the Turks and the Germans will be a necessity and a sacred duty of the emancipated Russian people."

In the same pamphlet, he calls on the revolutionary party to rally under the banner of the people's cause. Here are some articles of faith from the programme of this popular cause *à la* tsar:

"Article 1. We" (Bakunin and Co.) "want popular SELF-GOVERNMENT in the commune, in the province,[a] in the region and, finally, in the state, with or without the tsar—it doesn't matter, according as the people wish.—Article 2. ...We are ready, and duty commands us, to come to the aid of Lithuania, Poland, and the Ukraine so as to prevent all violence, and to protect them against all their external enemies, especially the Germans.—Article 4. With Poland, Lithuania, and the Ukraine, we wish to lend a hand to all our Slav brothers now groaning under the yoke of the kingdom of Prussia and of the Austrian and Turkish empires, and we undertake not to sheathe the sword as long as a single Slav remains in German, Turkish, or any other slavery."

Article 6 prescribes an alliance with Italy, Hungary, Rumania and Greece. These were the very alliances then being sought by the Russian Government.

"Article 7. We shall strive, with all the other Slav tribes, to make the cherished dream of the Slavs come true, to establish a great and free pan-Slav federation, [...] so that there shall be but a sole indivisible pan-Slav power.

"This is the vast programme of the Slav cause, this is the last indispensable word of the Russian popular cause. To this cause we have devoted our whole life.

"And now, where shall we go, and with whom shall we march? We have said where we want to go; we have also said with whom we shall march—with none other than the people. It remains to be known whom we shall follow. Shall we

---

[a] "Volost", "uyezd" in the Russian text.—*Ed.*

follow Romanov, Pugachev, or a new Pestel, if one can be found?*

"Let us tell the truth. *We would prefer to follow Romanov,* if Romanov could, and would, transform himself from a Petersburg emperor into a peasant tsar. We would willingly rally under his banner, because the Russian people still recognises him, and because his power is already created, ready to act, and could become an invincible force if he gave it the popular baptism. We would follow him, moreover, because *he alone* can accomplish the great peaceful revolution without shedding a drop of Russian or Slav blood. Bloody revolutions sometimes become necessary owing to human stupidity; nevertheless they are a great evil and a great misfortune, not only as regards their victims, but as regards the purity and the fullness of the goal for which they are accomplished. We saw this during the French revolution.

"Thus, our attitude to Romanov is clear. *We are not his enemies,* any more than we are his friends. We are the friends of the Russian popular cause, of the Slav cause. If the tsar is at the head of this cause, we shall follow him; but if he opposes it, we shall be his enemies. Therefore, the whole question is to know whether he wishes to be the Russian tsar, the peasant tsar, Romanov, or the Petersburg, the Holstein-Gottorp emperor. Does he wish to serve Russia, the Slavs, or the Germans? This question will soon be settled, and then we shall know what we must do."

Unfortunately, the tsar did not deem it appropriate to convoke the national assembly for which Bakunin, in this pamphlet, was already proposing his own candidature. He gained nothing out of his electoral manifesto and his genuflexions before Romanov. Humiliatingly deceived in his frank confidence, he had no alternative but to throw himself headlong into pan-destructive anarchy.

After this lucubration of a teacher who prostrated himself before his peasant tsar, his pupils and friends, Albert Richard and Gaspard Blanc, had every right to cry at the top of their voices: "Long live Napoleon III, emperor of the peasants!"

XI

DOCUMENTS

1. THE SECRET STATUTES OF THE ALLIANCE

The copy of these statutes which is now in our possession is partly written in Bakunin's hand. He gave copies not only to his initiates, but to many more people whom he hoped to seduce with the disclosure of his splendid programme. The vanity of the author proved stronger than the sinister furtiveness of the mystifier.

* Romanov is the tsar's surname. Pugachev was the leader of a great Cossack uprising under Catherine II. Pestel was the leader of the 1825 conspiracy against Nicholas I. He was hanged.

ORGANISATION OF THE ALLIANCE OF THE INTERNATIONAL BRETHREN[a]

THREE GRADES:

I. *International brethren.*
II. *National brethren.*
III. The half-secret, half-public organisation of *the International Alliance of Socialist Democracy.*

I. RULES OF THE INTERNATIONAL BRETHREN

1. The International Brethren have no homeland other than the world Revolution, no foreign land and no enemy other than the Reaction.
2. They reject any policy of negotiation and concession, and regard as reactionary any political movement which does not have as its immediate and direct goal the triumph of their principles.
3. They are Brethren—they never attack one another, nor settle their differences in public or in front of the courts. Their only justice is a jury of arbitrators, elected from among the brethren by the two parties.
4. Each must be sacred to all the others, more sacred than a blood brother. Each brother shall be helped and protected by all the others to the limits of the possible.
5. Only he may become an international brother who has sincerely accepted all the programme in all its consequences, theoretical and practical, and who adds *revolutionary passion* to intelligence, energy, honesty and discretion, he who has the devil in his flesh. We impose neither duty nor sacrifice. But he who has this passion will do many things without even imagining that he is making sacrifices.
6. A brother must have neither business, interests, nor duties more serious and more sacred than the service of the revolution and of our secret Association, which must serve the revolution.
7. A brother always has the right to refuse to render the services demanded of him by the Central Committee or by his National Committee, but many successive refusals will lead to his being considered unconscientious or lazy, and he may be suspended by his National Committee and, on the representation of this latter, temporarily expelled by the Central Committee pending a final decision by the Constituent Committee.
8. No brother shall accept a public post except with the consent of the Committee to which he belongs.—None shall undertake public actions or appearances contrary or even foreign to the line of conduct determined by his Committee and without having consulted the latter. Every time that two or more brothers are together, they shall consult each other on all important public matters.
9. All the International Brethren know one another. *No political secret must ever exist among them.* None may take part in any secret society whatever without the positive consent of his Committee and, if necessary, should the latter so demand, without that of the Central Committee.—And he may take part only on condition that he reveals to them all the secrets that could interest them directly or indirectly.

---

[a] [M. A. Bakunin,] *Organisation de l'Alliance des Frères Internationaux,* manuscript.— *Ed.*

10. The organisation of International Brethren is subdivided as follows: A. *The General, or Constituent, Committee.* B. *The Central Committee.* C. *The National Committees.*

A. *The General Committee*

This is an assembly of all or at least two-thirds of the International Brethren convoked regularly either at stipulated intervals, or in extraordinary assembly by a majority of the Central Committee. It is the supreme constituent and executive power of our entire organisation, whose programme, rules and organic statutes it can modify.

B. *The Central Committee*

Consists of: a) the *Central Bureau,* and b) the *Central Supervisory Committee.* The latter's members are all the international brethren who, not belonging to the Bureau, are sufficiently near to be convoked at two days' notice, and, naturally, all brethren who happen to be passing through. For the rest, they are guided in all their mutual relationships by the Rules of the Alliance of Socialist Democracy (see Articles 2-4).[a]

C. *The National Committees*

Each National Committee shall consist of all the international brethren (irrespective of nationality) who are in or near the centre of the national organisation. Each National Committee is subdivided equally into: a) a *National Executive Bureau,* and b) a *National Supervisory Committee.* This latter will include all international brethren present who are not in the Bureau. The same relationships as in the Alliance of Socialist Democracy.

11. The admission of a new brother requires the *unanimity* of all members present (not less than three) of the National Committee and the *confirmation* by a two-thirds majority of the *Central Committee.* The *Central Committee* may admit a new member by the unanimous agreement of all its members.

12. Each National Committee is to meet at least once a week to control and activate the organisational, propaganda and administrative work of its Bureau.—It is the natural judge of the conduct of each member in everything affecting his revolutionary dignity or relations with society. Its verdicts must be presented to the Central Committee for confirmation. It will direct the activities and all the public appearances of all members. Either through its Bureau or through a brother designated by it, it must maintain regular correspondence with the *Central Bureau,* to which it must write at least once every fortnight.

13. The *National Committee* will organise a secret *Association* of the National Brethren in its country.

II. THE NATIONAL BRETHREN

14. The National Brethren must be organised in each country so that they can never deviate from the guidance of the general organisation of the International Brethren, and notably from that of the *General Committee* and of the *Central Committee.* Their programmes and their rules may only be finally put into operation after they have received the sanction of the *Central Committee.*

---

[a] See this volume, pp. 570-71.—*Ed.*

15. Each National Committee may, if it finds it useful, establish among them two categories: a) that of National Brethren who know one another all over the country, and b) that of Brethren who do not know one another except in small groups.—In no case will the National Brethren even suspect the existence of an international organisation.

16. The *provincial centres*, consisting entirely or partly of international brethren or national brethren of the first category, shall be established at all the principal points in the country, with the mission of promoting as thoroughly and as far as possible the secret organisation and the propaganda of its principles—not contenting themselves with acting in the cities, but also trying to propagate them in the villages and among the peasants.

17. The National Committees shall attempt to raise the necessary financial means as soon as possible, not only for the success of their own organisation, but also for the general needs of the whole Association. They will therefore send a part—half?—to the Central Bureau.

18. The National Bureaux must be very active, remembering that the principles, programmes and rules are of no worth unless the persons who have to put them into execution have the devil in their flesh.

SECRET ORGANISATION OF THE INTERNATIONAL ALLIANCE OF SOCIALIST DEMOCRACY

1. The *Permanent Central Committee* of the Alliance consists of all the members of the *Permanent National Committees* and of those of the *Geneva Central Section.*

When together, all these members constitute the *Secret General Assembly* of the Alliance, which is the constituent and supreme power of the Alliance and which will meet at least once a year at the Working Men's Congress as delegates of the Alliance's different national groups; it may also be convoked at any time equally by the *Central Bureau* or by the *Geneva Central Section.*

2. The Geneva Central Section is the permanent delegation of the permanent Central Committee. It is composed of all the members of the *Central Bureau* and of all those of the *Supervisory Committee,* who must always be members of the permanent Central Committee.—The *Central Section* will be the *Supreme Executive Council* of the Alliance, within the limits of the Constitution and of the line of conduct which can only be laid down and modified by the *General Assembly.* It will decide on all questions of execution (not of constitution and general policy) by a simple majority of votes, and its resolutions thus adopted shall be *binding* on the *Central Bureau,* unless the Bureau, by a majority of its members, wishes to appeal to the *General Assembly,* which it must convoke in this case at three weeks' notice.—To be regular, the *General Assembly,* when thus convoked, must be composed of two-thirds of all its members.

3. The *Central Bureau,* the executive power, will consist of 3 to 5 or even 7 members, who must always at the same time be *members of the Permanent Central Committee.* Like one of the two parts which make up the *Secret Central Section,* the *Central Bureau* shall be a secret organisation. As such, it will receive its guidance from the *Central Section* and will pass on its communications, not to say its secret orders, to all the *National Committees,* from which it will receive secret reports at least once a month. As the *Executive Directorate* of the public Alliance, it shall be a public organisation. As such, it shall be on more or less private or public terms, according to country and circumstances, with all the *National Bureaux,* from which it shall also receive reports once a month. Its ostensible form of government

will be that of a presidency in a federative republic. The *Central Bureau*, as the secret as well as public executive power of the Alliance, shall activate the society's secret and public propaganda and shall promote its development in all countries by all possible means. It shall administer the part of the finances which, in accordance with Article 6 of the public regulations,[a] are sent to it from all countries for general needs. It shall publish a newspaper and pamphlets, and shall send travelling agents to form Alliance groups in the countries where there are none. In all the measures which it adopts for the good of the Alliance, it shall moreover submit to the decisions of the majority of the *Secret Central Section*, to which, incidentally, all its members shall belong. As an organisation both secret and public, and since it must be composed entirely of members of the *Permanent Central Committee*, the *Central Bureau* must always be a direct representation of this *Committee*. The *Provisional Central Bureau* will now be presented to the *Geneva initiating group* as provisionally elected by *all the founder members of the Alliance*, of whom the majority, as former members of the Berne Congress,[b] have returned to their countries after having delegating their powers to Citizen B.[c] This Bureau will function until the first public General Assembly which, in accordance with Article 7 of the public Regulations,[d] must meet as a branch of the International Working Men's Association at the next Working Men's Congress. It follows that members of the *New Central Bureau* must be nominated by this Assembly. But as it is urgent that the *Central Bureau* should always consist solely of members of the *Permanent Central Committee*, this latter, through the organ of its national committees, will take care to organise and direct all the local groups in such a way that they will delegate to this Assembly only members of the Permanent Central Committee, or, failing them, men absolutely devoted to the leadership of their respective national committees, so that the Permanent Central Committee should always have the upper hand in the entire organisation of the Alliance.

4. The *Supervisory Committee* shall exercise control over all the actions of the Central Bureau.—It shall consist of all the members of the Permanent Central Committee resident either in the place itself, or near the residence of the *Central Bureau*, and also all the members temporarily present or just passing through, with the exception of the members who make up the Bureau. At the request of two members of the Supervisory Committee, all the members of the latter must at three days' notice meet with the members of the Central Bureau to constitute the *Assembly of the Central Section of the Supreme Executive Council*, whose rights are defined in Article 2.

5. The *National Committees* will be formed of all the members of the Permanent Central Committee who belong to the same nation.—As soon as there are three members of the Permanent Central Committee who belong to the same nation, they will be invited by the Bureau and, if necessary, by the Central Section, to form the National Committee of their country. Each National Committee may create a new member of the Central Committee of its country, but not otherwise than by the unanimous agreement of all the members. As soon as a new member has been appointed by a National Committee, the latter shall immediately inform the Central Bureau, which shall register this new member and shall thereby confer on him all the rights of a member of the Permanent Central Committee.—The Geneva *Central Section* is likewise invested with the power to create new members by the unanimous agreement of all its members.

---

[a] See this volume, p. 578.—*Ed.*
[b] The League of Peace and Freedom.—*Ed.*
[c] Mikhail Bakunin.—*Ed.*
[d] See this volume, p. 578.—*Ed.*

Each *National Committee* has, as its special mission, the foundation and organisation of the public as well as secret national group of the Alliance in its country. It shall be the group's supreme chief and administrator through its *National Bureau*, which it shall have the task of creating and forming entirely of Permanent Central Committee members. The *national committees* shall have the same relationship, rights and powers with regard to their respective Bureaux as the *central section* with regard to the *Central Bureau*.—The *national committees*, which shall be formed by combining their respective *bureaux* and *supervisory committees*, shall recognise no authority other than the *Central Bureau*, and shall serve as the sole intermediaries between this latter and all the *local groups* of their country for propaganda and administration, and likewise for the collecting and paying in of subscriptions. The *national committees*, through their respective bureaux, shall have the task of organising the Alliance in their countries so that it shall always be dominated and represented at the Congresses by members of the Permanent Central Committee.

As the national bureaux organise their local groups, they shall make it their concern to submit the regulations and programme to the central bureau for confirmation, without which the local groups cannot belong to the International Alliance of Socialist Democracy.

PROGRAMME
OF THE INTERNATIONAL SOCIALIST ALLIANCE

1. The International Alliance has been founded to promote the organisation and acceleration of the World Revolution on the basis of the principles proclaimed in our programme.

2. In conformity with these principles, the goal of the revolution cannot be other than: *a*) The destruction of all ruling powers and all religious, monarchic, aristocratic and bourgeois authority in Europe. Consequently, the destruction of all existing states with all their political, juridical, bureaucratic and financial institutions. *b*) The reconstitution of a new society on the sole basis of freely associated labour, taking collective ownership, equality and justice as the starting point.

3. The Revolution as we conceive it, or rather as the force of circumstances today inevitably presents it, is essentially international or universal in character. In view of the menacing coalition of all the privileged interests and all the reactionary powers in Europe, which have at their disposal all the formidable means given them by a cleverly organised organisation, and in view of the profound schism which reigns everywhere today between the bourgeoisie and the workers, no national revolution will succeed if it does not extend at once to all the other nations, and it will never cross the frontiers of a country and adopt this universal character unless it carries within itself all the elements of this universality—that is to say, unless it is an openly socialist revolution, destructive of the state, and creative of liberty through equality and justice; for nothing henceforth shall be able to reunite, electrify, and arouse the great and only true power of the century—the workers—except the total emancipation of labour on the ruins of all the institutions which protect hereditary landownership and capital.

4. Since the impending Revolution can only be universal, the Alliance, or, not to mince words, the conspiracy which must prepare, organise and accelerate it, must also be universal.

5. The Alliance will pursue a double aim: *a*) It will endeavour to disseminate among the masses of all countries the right ideas on politics, social economy, and all philosophical questions. It will carry out active propaganda by means of newspapers, pamphlets and books, and also by founding public associations. *b*) It will seek to affiliate to itself all intelligent, energetic, discreet and well-disposed men who are sincerely devoted to our ideas, in order to form all over Europe, and as far as possible in America, an invisible network of dedicated revolutionaries who have become more powerful through this very Alliance.

PROGRAMME AND OBJECTIVES
OF THE REVOLUTIONARY ORGANISATION
OF THE INTERNATIONAL BRETHREN

1. The principles of this organisation are the same as those of the programme of the International Alliance of Socialist Democracy. They are even more explicitly defined, as regards women, the family from the point of view of religion and law, and the state, in the programme of the *Russian Socialist Democracy*.

The Central Bureau moreover reserves the right to present shortly a more comprehensive theoretical and practical exposition of these principles.

2. The association of international brethren aims for a universal revolution, simultaneously social, philosophical, economic and political, so that of the present order of things—based on private property, exploitation, domination and the principle of authority, whether religious, metaphysical, bourgeois-doctrinaire, or even Jacobin-revolutionary—not a stone shall remain standing, first in all Europe and then throughout the rest of the world. With the cry of peace for the workers, liberty for all the oppressed, and death to the rulers, exploiters and guardians of all kinds, we seek to destroy all states and all churches along with all their institutions and laws, religious, political, juridical, financial, police, university, economic and social, so that all these millions of poor human beings, deceived, enslaved, tormented and exploited, delivered from all their directors and benefactors, official and officious, collective and individual, may breathe at last with complete freedom.

3. Convinced that individual and social evil resides far less in individuals than in the organisation of things and in social position, we shall be humane as much from a sense of justice as from considerations of utility, and we shall destroy positions and things without pity in order to be able to spare human beings without any danger to the Revolution. We deny to society *free will* and the supposed right to punish. Justice itself, taken in the most humane and broadest sense, is but a negative and transitional idea, as it were. It poses social problems, but it does not think them over, merely indicating the only possible way to human liberation, namely, the humanisation of society through liberty in equality; the positive solution can only be given through the increasingly rational organisation of society. This solution, which is so desirable and is the ideal that we all have in common ... is the liberty, morality, intelligence and well-being of each through the solidarity of all—human fraternity.

Every human individual is the involuntary product of the natural and social environment in which he is born and develops, and which continues to exert an influence upon him. The three great causes of all human immorality are: inequality, political, economic and social; the ignorance which is its natural result; and their inevitable consequence— *slavery*.

Since the organisation of society is always and everywhere the sole cause of the crimes committed by men, it is hypocritical or obviously absurd on society's part to punish criminals, when all punishment presumes culpability and the criminals are never culpable. The theory of culpability and punishment is a theological issue, that is to say, it is a combination of religious hypocrisy and the absurd.

The only right which can be allowed to society in its present state of transition is the natural right to *assassinate* the criminals, which it has itself produced, in the interests of its own protection, and not the right to judge and condemn them. This right will not even be one in the strictly accepted sense of the word; it will be rather a natural fact, distressing but unavoidable, a sign and product of the impotence and stupidity of the existing society; and the more society is able to avoid using it, the nearer it will be to its own actual liberation. All revolutionaries, all oppressed, all suffering victims of the existing organisation of society, whose hearts are naturally full of vengeance and hatred, would do well to remember that the kings, oppressors and exploiters of all kinds are as much to blame as the criminals who have emerged from the masses: they are malefactors, but they are not to blame, since they too are, like ordinary criminals, the involuntary products of the existing order of society. One should not be surprised if, at the first moment, the insurgent people kill a great many of them—this will be an inevitable calamity, perhaps, as futile as the damage caused by a tempest.

But this natural fact will be neither moral nor even useful. In this respect, history is full of lessons: the terrible guillotine of 1793, which could not be accused of idleness or tardiness, did not succeed in destroying the nobility in France. The aristocracy there was, if not completely destroyed, at least profoundly shaken, not by the guillotine, but by the confiscation and sale of its estates. And, in general, it may be said that political massacres have never killed parties; they have shown themselves above all impotent against the privileged classes, since power is rooted much less in men than in the positions which are given to the privileged by the organisation of things, that is to say, by the *institution of the state* and by its consequence and also by its natural basis, *private property*.

To carry out a radical revolution, one must therefore attack positions and things, one must destroy property and the state; then there will be no need to destroy men and to condemn oneself to the unfailing and inevitable reaction which has never failed and never will fail to produce the massacre of human beings in any society.

But in order to have the right to be humane to human beings without endangering the revolution, one must be ruthless with positions and things; it will be necessary to destroy everything, and, above all and before everything else, property and its inevitable corollary—the *State*. This is the whole secret of the revolution.

One should not be surprised at the Jacobins and the Blanquists who became socialists by necessity rather than by conviction, and for whom socialism is a means, not an end of the Revolution, since they want the dictatorship, that is to say, the centralisation of the state, and the state will lead them by a logical and inevitable necessity to the reconstitution of property—it is quite natural, we say, that, not wishing to carry out a radical revolution against things, they dream of a bloody revolution against men.—But this bloody revolution, founded on the construction of a powerfully centralised revolutionary state, would inevitably result, as we shall prove more fully later, in a military dictatorship under a new master. Consequently, the triumph of the Jacobins or the Blanquists would mean the death of the Revolution.

4. We are the natural enemies of those revolutionaries—future dictators, regulators and tutors of the revolution—who, even before the existing monarchic, aristocratic and bourgeois states have been destroyed, already dream of creating new revolutionary states as centralised as, and even more despotic than the existing states, and who have acquired so great a habit of order created from above

and so great a horror of what seems to them like disorder, but is nothing other than the frank and natural expression of the people's life, that even before a good and salutary disorder has been produced by the revolution, they already dream of putting an end to it and of muzzling it by the force of an authority which will have nothing of revolution but the name, but which will, in effect, be no more than a new reaction, since it will really be a new condemnation of the masses, governed by decrees, to obedience, stagnation and death, that is, to slavery and exploitation by a new quasi-revolutionary aristocracy.

5. We understand revolution to mean the unleashing of what today are called the evil passions and the destruction of what, in the same language, is called "public order".

We do not fear anarchy, and we invoke it, convinced that from this anarchy, that is to say, from the complete manifestation of the people's life unleashed, there must emerge liberty, equality, justice, a new order, and the very force of Revolution against Reaction. This new life—the people's revolution—will doubtless not delay in organising itself, but will create its revolutionary organisation from bottom to top and from the circumference to the centre—in conformity with the principle of liberty, and not from top to bottom, nor from the centre to the circumference after the manner of all authority—for it matters little to us that this authority calls itself Church, Monarchy, constitutional State, bourgeois Republic, or even revolutionary dictatorship. We detest them and we reject them all alike as infallible sources of exploitation and despotism.

6. The revolution, as we understand it, must from the very first day destroy, radically and totally, the state and all the state's institutions. The natural and necessary consequences of this destruction will be: *a*) the bankruptcy of the state; *b*) an end to the payment of private debts by the intervention of the state, leaving each debtor the right to pay if he wants; *c*) an end to the payment of all taxes and to the deduction of all contributions, direct or indirect; *d*) the dissolution of the army, the magistrature, the bureaucracy, the police and the clergy; *e*) the abolition of official justice, the withdrawal of everything which juridically called itself law, together with the exercise of those laws. Consequently, the abolition and *auto-da-fé* of all title-deeds, deeds of inheritance, purchase, gift, and all trials—in a word, of all juridical and civil red tape. Everywhere and in everything, revolutionary acts instead of the law created and guaranteed by the state; *f*) the confiscation of all productive capital and instruments of labour for the benefit of working men's associations, which should collectively use them for production; *g*) the confiscation of all church and state property, and likewise of individually owned precious metals for the benefit of the Federative Alliance of all the working men's associations, that is, the Alliance which will form the Commune.

In return for the confiscated goods, the Commune will give what is strictly necessary to all individuals thus deprived, who may later gain more by their own work if they are able and willing.—*h*) For the organisation of the Commune—a federation of permanently acting barricades and the functioning of a Council of the Revolutionary Commune by the delegation of one or two deputies from each barricade and one per street, or per block, these deputies being invested with imperative mandates and always responsible and revocable at any time. The Commune Council, thus organised, will be able to elect from its membership special executive committees for each branch of the revolutionary administration of the Commune. *i*) A declaration by the insurgent capital, once organised as a commune, that, having destroyed the authoritarian and tutelary state, which it was entitled to do since it had been the state's slave like all the other localities, it renounces its right, or rather all claims, to direct or dictate to the provinces. *k*) An appeal to all provinces, communes, and associations, while allowing them all to follow the example set by the capital, first *to reorganise themselves* in a revolutionary way, and then to delegate to an agreed place of assembly their deputies, all likewise empowered with imperative mandates and responsible and revocable, to constitute a federation of associations, communes and provinces which have risen in the name of the same principles, and to organise a revolutionary force capable of triumphing over the reaction. The sending, not of official revolutionary commissars with shoulder sashes, but of revolutionary propagandists into all the provinces and communes—above all among the peasants, who can be turned into revolutionaries neither by principles nor by the decrees of some dictatorship, but only by revolutionary action itself, that is to say, by the consequences which will infallibly be produced in all the communes by the complete cessation of the official juridical life of the state. Abolition of the national state also in the sense that any foreign country, province, commune, association, or even isolated individual that rises in the name of the same principles, shall be received into the revolutionary federation without regard for existing state frontiers, although they belong to different political or national systems; and in the sense that any of one's own provinces, communes, associations and individuals that side with the Reaction, shall be excluded from it. It is, then, by the very fact of the spreading and organisation of the revolution with a view to the mutual defence of the insurgent countries, that the universality of the revolution shall triumph, based on the abolition of frontiers and on the destruction of the states.

7. There can be no victorious political or national revolution henceforth unless the political revolution becomes a social revolution, and unless the national revolution, precisely because of its character, radically socialist and destructive of the state, becomes the universal revolution.

8. Since the revolution must be carried out everywhere by the people, and since the supreme direction of it must always remain with the people organised into a free federation of agricultural and industrial associations, the new and revolutionary state, organising itself from bottom to top by way of revolutionary delegation, and embracing all the countries that have risen in the name of the same principles without regard for the old frontiers and for differences in nationality, will have as its goal the administration of the public services and not the government of the peoples. It will constitute the *new homeland, the Alliance of the Universal Revolution* against the Alliance of all the reactionary forces.

9. This organisation excludes any idea of dictatorship and of tutelary ruling power. But for the very establishment of this revolutionary alliance and for the triumph of the revolution against the reaction, it is necessary that in the midst of popular anarchy which will constitute the very life and energy of the revolution, *unity of revolutionary idea and action should find an organ*. This organ must be the *secret and world Association of the international brethren*.

10. This association proceeds from the conviction that revolutions are never made either by individuals, or even by secret societies. They come about, as it were, of their own accord, produced by the force of things, by the course of events and facts. They are prepared over a long time deep in the instinctive consciousness of the popular masses, and then they flare up, often induced, apparently, by insignificant causes. All that a well-organised secret society can do is, first, to assist in the birth of the revolution by spreading among the masses ideas corresponding to their instincts, and to organise, not the army of the revolution—the army must always be the people—but a sort of revolutionary general staff composed of devoted, energetic, intelligent and above all sincere friends of the people, who are not ambitious or vain, and who are capable of serving as intermediaries between the revolutionary idea and the popular instincts.

11. The number of these individuals should not,therefore,be too large. For the

international organisation in the whole of Europe, a hundred firmly and seriously united revolutionaries would be sufficient. Two or three hundred revolutionaries would be enough for the organisation of the biggest country.

2. PROGRAMME AND REGULATIONS OF THE PUBLIC ALLIANCE[a]

The *socialist minority of the League of Peace and Freedom* having broken away from this league owing to the majority vote at the Berne Congress, which made a formal declaration opposing the fundamental principle of all the working men's associations, namely, the *economic and social equality of classes and individuals*, has thereby adhered to the principles proclaimed by the *Working Men's Congresses* held at Geneva, Lausanne and Brussels. Several members of this minority, who belong to different nations, have suggested to us that we organise a new *International Alliance of Socialist Democracy* wholly merged with the great *International Working Men's Association*, but adopting *as its special mission* the study of political and philosophical questions on the same basis of this great principle of the universal and real equality of all human beings on earth.

Convinced, for our part, of the *usefulness* of such an enterprise, which *will give* the sincere socialist democrats of Europe and America *a means of understanding one another and of affirming their ideas* without any pressure from the false socialism which bourgeois democracy now finds it useful to flaunt, we have thought it our duty to take the joint initiative with these friends in forming this new organisation.

Consequently, we have set ourselves up as the central section of the *International Alliance of Socialist Democracy*, and we are today publishing its *Programme* and *Regulations*.

PROGRAMME OF THE INTERNATIONAL ALLIANCE OF SOCIALIST DEMOCRACY

1) The *Alliance* declares itself to be atheist; it strives for the abolition of cults, the substitution of science for faith and of human justice for divine justice.

2) It seeks, above all, the *political, economic and social equalisation of classes* and of individuals of both sexes, commencing *with the abolition of the right of inheritance*, so that in future the enjoyment of the benefits should be equal to the production of each, and so that, in conformity with the decision taken by the last Congress of workers at Brussels, the land and instruments of labour, like all other capital, by becoming the collective property of society as a whole, may not be used except by the workers, that is to say, by agricultural and industrial associations.

3) It requires all children of both sexes, from the day of their birth, to have equality of the means of development, that is to say, maintenance, education and training at all levels in science, industry and the arts, being convinced that this equality, at first purely economic and social, will eventually lead to the increasing natural equality of individuals by eliminating all the artificial inequalities which are historical products of social organisation as false as it is iniquitous.

---

[a] [M. Bakounine,] *Programme et règlement de l'Alliance Internationale de la Démocratie Socialiste*, Geneva, 1868.—*Ed.*

4) As the enemy of all despotism, *recognising no political form other than the republican*, and rejecting outright all reactionary alliance, the Alliance also rejects all political action which does not have for its immediate and direct goal the triumph of the cause of the workers against Capital.

5) It recognises that all the political and authoritarian states now existing, *as they are reduced more and more to the simple administrative functions* of the public services in their respective countries, must disappear in the universal union of free Associations, agricultural and industrial alike.

6) Since the social question cannot find a definitive and practicable solution except on the basis of the international or universal solidarity of the workers of all countries, the *Alliance* rejects any policy founded on so-called patriotism and the rivalry of nations.

7) It wants the universal Association of all the local Associations through liberty.

REGULATIONS

1) The *International Alliance of Socialist Democracy* is constituted as a *branch* of the *International Working Men's Association*, all of whose General Rules it accepts.

2) The *founder-members of the Alliance* provisionally organise a *Central Bureau* at Geneva.

3) The founder-members belonging to the same country constitute the *National Bureau* of that country.

4) The National Bureaux have the mission of establishing, in all localities, *local groups* of the *Alliance of Socialist Democracy* which, through the intermediary of their respective National Bureaux, will apply to the Central Bureau of the *Alliance* for admission to the *International Working Men's Association*.

5) All the local groups will form their bureaux in accordance with the custom adopted by the local sections of the *International Working Men's Association*.

6) All members of the *Alliance* undertake to pay a subscription of *ten centimes* per month, of which half shall be retained for its own needs by each national group, and the other half shall be remitted to the funds of the Central Bureau for its general needs.

In countries where this sum is considered too high, the National Bureaux, in agreement with the Central Bureau, may reduce it.

7) During the annual Congress of Workers, the *Delegation of the Alliance of Socialist Democracy*, as a branch of the *International Working Men's Association*, shall hold its public sessions in a separate place.

3. LETTER FROM BAKUNIN TO FRANCISCO MORA IN MADRID

(Written in French)

"April 5, 1872, Locarno,

"Dear *Ally* and Comrade,

"As our friends at Barcelona have invited me to write to you, I do so with all the more pleasure since I have learned that I also, like my friends, *our allies* of the Jura Federation, have become, in Spain as much as in other countries, the target for the calumnies of the London General Council. It is indeed a sad thing that in this time of terrible crisis, when the fate of the proletariat of all Europe is being decided for many decades to come, and when all the friends of the proletariat, of humanity and justice, should unite fraternally to make a front against the common enemy, the world of the privileged which has been organised into a state—it is very sad, I say, that men who have, moreover, rendered great services to the International in the past, should be impelled today by evil authoritarian passions, should lower themselves to falsification and the sowing of discord, instead of creating everywhere the free union which alone can create strength.

"To give you a fair idea of the line which we are taking, I have only one thing to tell you. Our programme is yours; it is the very one which you proclaimed at your Congress last year,[a] and if you stay faithful to it, you are with us for the simple reason that we are with you. We detest the principle of dictatorship, governmentalism and authority, just as you detest them; we are convinced that all political power is an infallible source of depravity for those who govern, and a cause of servitude for those who are governed.—The state signifies domination, and human nature is so made that all domination becomes exploitation. As enemies of the state in all its manifestations anyway, we certainly do not wish to tolerate it within the International. We regard the London Conference and the resolutions which it passed as an ambitious intrigue and a coup d'état, and that is why we have protested, and shall continue protesting to the end. I am not touching on personal questions, alas! they will take up too much time at the next world Congress, if this Congress takes place, which I strongly doubt myself; for if things continue to proceed as they are doing, there will soon no longer be a single point on the continent of Europe where the delegates of the proletariat will be able to assemble in order to debate in freedom. All eyes are now fixed on Spain, and on the outcome of your Congress.[b] What will come of it? This letter will reach you, if it reaches you at all, after this Congress. Will it find you at the height of revolution or at the height of reaction? All our friends in Italy, France and Switzerland are waiting for news from your country with unbearable anxiety.

"You doubtless know that the International and *our dear Alliance* have progressed enormously in Italy of late. The people, in the country as much as in the towns, are now in an entirely revolutionary situation, that is to say, they are economically desperate; the masses are beginning to organise themselves in a most serious manner and their interests are beginning to become ideas.—Up to now, what was lacking in Italy was not instincts, but organisation and an idea. Both are coming into being, so that Italy, after Spain and with Spain, is perhaps the most revolutionary country at this moment. Italy has what other countries lack: a youth which is passionate, energetic, *completely at a loss, with no prospects, with no way out,* and which, despite its bourgeois origins, is not morally and intellectually exhausted like the bourgeois youth of other countries. Today, it is throwing itself headlong into revolutionary socialism *accepting our entire programme, the programme of the Alliance.* Mazzini, our mighty antagonist of genius, is dead, the Mazzinist party is completely disorganised, and Garibaldi is letting himself be carried away more and more by that youth which bears his name, but is going, or rather running, infinitely further ahead of him. I have sent to our friends in Barcelona an Italian address; I shall soon send them others. It is good and it is necessary that the *Alliancists* in Spain should enter into direct relations with those in Italy. Are you receiving the Italian socialist newspapers? I recommend above all: the *Eguaglianza* of Girgenti, Sicily; the

---

[a] The reference is apparently to the Spanish Federation Congress in Barcelona (June 1870).— *Ed.*

[b] Bakunin refers to the Spanish Federation Congress in Saragossa (April 4-11, 1872).— *Ed.*

Campana of Naples; the *Fascio Operaio* of Bologna; *Il Gazzettino Rosa*, and, above all, *Il Martello* of Milan—unfortunately the latter has been banned and all the editors imprisoned.

"In Switzerland, I recommend to you two *Alliancists*: James Guillaume (Switzerland, Neuchâtel, 5, rue de la Place d'Armes) and *Adhémar Schwitzguébel*, engraver (member and corresponding secretary of the Committee of the Jura Federation), Switzerland, Jura Bernois, Sonvillier, Mr. Adhémar Schwitzguébel, engraver." (Bakunin's address follows.)

"Alliance and fraternity.

M. Bakunin

"Please convey my greetings to *brother* Morago, and ask him to send me his newspaper.

"Are you receiving the *Bulletin de la Fédération jurassienne?*

"Please burn this letter, as it contains names."

The Hague Congress has expelled Bakunin from the International, not only as a founder of the Alliance, but also for a personal deed.[390] The authentic document in support of this deed is still in our hands, but political considerations oblige us to refrain from publishing it.

The End

Written between April and July 1873

First published as a pamphlet in London and Hamburg in August-September 1873

Printed according to the pamphlet

Translated from the French

Frederick Engels

THE BAKUNINISTS AT WORK

AN ACCOUNT OF THE SPANISH REVOLT
IN THE SUMMER OF 1873 [391]

I

The report just published by the Hague Commission on Mikhail Bakunin's secret Alliance* has revealed to the working world the underhand activities, the dirty tricks and phrase-mongery by which the proletarian movement was to be placed at the service of the inflated ambition and selfish ends of a few misunderstood geniuses. Meanwhile these would-be-great men have given us the opportunity in Spain to see something of their practical revolutionary activity. Let us see how they put into practice their ultra-revolutionary phrases about anarchy and autonomy, about the abolition of all authority, especially that of the state, and the immediate and complete emancipation of the workers. We are at last able to do this, since, apart from the newspaper reports about the events in Spain, we now have the report of the New Madrid Federation of the International[a] presented to the Geneva Congress.[393]

As we know, at the time the split in the International occurred the odds were in favour of the members of the secret Alliance in Spain; the great majority of Spanish workers followed their lead. When the Republic was proclaimed in February 1873, the Spanish members of the Alliance found themselves in a quandary. Spain is such a backward country industrially that there can be no question

---

* *L'Alliance de la Démocratie socialiste*, London, 1873. The German edition was published under the title: *Ein Komplott gegen die Internationale* (Bookshop of the *Vorwärts*).[392]

---

[a] *La Nueva Federación Madrileña á los delegados al sexto Congreso general.* Madrid 24 de agosto de 1873.— Ed.

there of *immediate* complete emancipation of the working class. Spain will first have to pass through various preliminary stages of development and remove quite a number of obstacles from its path. The Republic offered a chance of going through these stages in the shortest possible time and quickly surmounting the obstacles. But this chance could be taken only if the Spanish working class played an active *political* role. The labour masses felt this; they strove everywhere to participate in events, to take advantage of the opportunity for action, instead of leaving the propertied classes, as hitherto, a clear field for action and intrigues. The government announced that elections were to be held to the Constituent Cortes.[a] What was the attitude of the International to be? The leaders of the Bakuninists were in a predicament. Continued political inaction became more ridiculous and impossible with every passing day; the workers wanted "to see things done".[b] The members of the Alliance on the other hand had been preaching for years that no part should be taken in a revolution that did not have as its aim the immediate and complete emancipation of the working class, that political action of any kind implied recognition of the State, which was the root of all evil, and that therefore participation in any form of elections was a crime worthy of death. How they got out of this fix is recounted in the already mentioned Madrid report:

"The same people who rejected the Hague resolution on the political attitude of the working class and who trampled under foot the Rules of the [International Working Men's] Association, thus bringing division, conflict and confusion into the Spanish Section of the International; the same people who had the effrontery to depict us to the workers as ambitious place-hunters, who, under the pretext of establishing the rule of the working class, sought to establish their own rule; the same people who call themselves autonomists, anarchist revolutionaries, etc., have on this occasion flung themselves into politics, bourgeois politics of the worst kind. They have worked, not to give political power to the working class—on the contrary this idea is repugnant to them—but to help to power a bourgeois faction of adventurers, ambitious men and place-hunters who call themselves Intransigent (irreconcilable) Republicans.

"Already on the eve of the general election to the Constituent Cortes the workers of Barcelona, Alcoy and other towns wanted to know what political line they should adopt in the parliamentary struggle and other campaigns. Two big meetings were therefore held, one in Barcelona, the other in Alcoy; at both meetings the Alliance members went out of their way to prevent any decision being reached as to what political line was to be taken by the International" (nota bene: by their own International). "It was therefore decided that the *International, as an association, should not engage in any political activity whatever, but that its members, as*

---

[a] On May 10, 1873.— *Ed.*
[b] J. W. Goethe, *Zueignung.— Ed.*

individuals, could act on their own as they thought fit and join the party they chose, in accordance with their famous doctrine of autonomy! And what was the result of the application of this absurd doctrine? That most of the members of the International, including the anarchists, took part in the elections with no programme, no banner, and no candidates, thereby helping to bring about the election of almost exclusively bourgeois republicans. Only two or three workers got into the Chamber, and they represent absolutely nothing, their voice has not once been raised in defence of the interests of our class, and they cheerfully voted for all the reactionary motions tabled by the majority."

That is what Bakuninist "abstention from politics" leads to. At quiet times, when the proletariat knows beforehand that at best it can get only a few representatives to parliament and have no chance whatever of winning a parliamentary majority, the workers may sometimes be made to believe that it is a great revolutionary action to sit out the elections at home, and in general, not to attack the State in which they live and which oppresses them, but to attack the State as such which exists nowhere and which accordingly cannot defend itself. This is a splendid way of behaving in a revolutionary manner, especially for people who lose heart easily; and the extent to which the leaders of the Spanish Alliance belong to this category of people is shown in some detail in the aforementioned publication.[a]

As soon as events push the proletariat into the fore, however, abstention becomes a palpable absurdity and the active intervention of the working class an inevitable necessity. And this is what happened in Spain. The abdication of Amadeo ousted the radical monarchists[394] from power and deprived them of the possibility of recovering it in the near future; the Alfonsists[395] stood still less chance at the time; as for the Carlists, they, as usual, preferred civil war to an election campaign.[396] All these parties, according to the Spanish custom, abstained. Only the federalist Republicans, split into two wings, and the bulk of the workers took part in the elections. Given the enormous attraction which the name of the International still enjoyed at that time among the Spanish workers and given the excellent organisation of the Spanish Section which, at least for practical purposes, still existed at the time, it was certain that any candidate nominated and supported by the International would be brilliantly successful in the industrial districts of Catalonia, in Valencia, in the Andalusian towns and so on, and that a minority would be elected to the Cortes large enough to decide the issue whenever it came to a vote between the two wings of the Republicans. The workers were aware of this;

---

[a] See this volume, pp. 486-97.—*Ed.*

they felt that the time had come to bring their still powerful organisation into play. But the honourable leaders of the Bakuninist school had been preaching the gospel of unqualified abstention too long to be able suddenly to reverse their line; and so they invented that deplorable way out—that of having the International abstain as a body, but allowing its members as individuals to vote *as they liked.* The result of this declaration of political bankruptcy was that the workers, as always in such cases, voted for those who made the most radical speeches, that is, for the Intransigents, and considering themselves therefore more or less responsible for subsequent steps taken by their deputies, became involved in them.

II

The members of the Alliance could not possibly persist in the ridiculous position into which their cunning electoral policy had landed them; it would have meant the end of their control over the International in Spain. They had to act, if only for the sake of appearances. Salvation for them lay in a *general* STRIKE.

In the Bakuninist programme a general STRIKE is the lever employed by which the social revolution is started. One fine morning all the workers in all the industries of a country, or even of the whole world, stop work, thus forcing the propertied classes either humbly to submit within four weeks at the most, or to attack the workers, who would then have the right to defend themselves and use this opportunity to pull down the entire old society. The idea is far from new; this horse was since 1848 hard ridden by French, and later Belgian socialists; it is originally, however, an English breed. During the rapid and vigorous growth of Chartism among the English workers following the crisis of 1837, the "holy month", a strike on a national scale was advocated as early as 1839 (see Engels, *The Condition of the Working-Class in England,* Second Edition [1892], p. 234 [a]) and this had such a strong appeal that in July 1842 the industrial workers in northern England tried to put it into practice.—Great importance was also attached to the general STRIKE at the Geneva Congress of the Alliance held on September 1, 1873,[397] although it was universally admitted that this required a well-formed organisation of the

---

[a] See present edition, Vol. 4, p. 520; *Der Volksstaat* refers to the first German edition: *Die Lage der Arbeitenden Klasse in England,* Leipzig, 1845, p. 279.— *Ed.*

working class and plentiful funds. And there's the rub. On the one hand the governments, especially if encouraged by political abstention, will never allow the organisation or the funds of the workers to reach such a level; on the other hand, political events and oppressive acts by the ruling classes will lead to the liberation of the workers long before the proletariat is able to set up such an ideal organisation and this colossal reserve fund. But if it had them, there would be no need to use the roundabout way of a general STRIKE to achieve its goal.

No one with any knowledge of the secret springs of the Alliance can doubt that the idea of using this well-tried method originated in the Swiss centre. Be that as it may, the Spanish leaders saw in this a way of doing something without actually delving in "politics" and they gladly took it. The miraculous qualities of a general STRIKE were everywhere propounded and preparations were made to start it at Barcelona and Alcoy.

Meanwhile the political situation was steadily heading for a crisis. Castelar and his associates, the old federal republican braggarts, were frightened by the movement, which had outgrown them. They were obliged to hand over the reigns of government to Pi y Margall,[a] who sought a compromise with the Intransigents. Of all the official republicans, Pi was the only Socialist, the only one who realised that the republic had to depend on the support of the workers. He promptly produced a programme of social measures which could be carried out immediately and would not only benefit the workers directly but eventually lead to further steps, thus at least giving the first impetus to the social revolution. But the Bakuninist members of the International, who were obliged to reject even the most revolutionary measures if they emanated from the "State", preferred to support the most preposterous swindlers among the Intransigents rather than a minister. Pi's negotiations with the Intransigents dragged on. The Intransigents began to lose patience, and the most hot-headed of them started a cantonal uprising in Andalusia. The leaders of the Alliance now had to act too if they did not want to trail in the wake of the intransigent bourgeois. And so a general STRIKE was ordered.

Presently, among other things, a poster was issued in Barcelona stating:

"Workers! We are calling a general STRIKE to show the profound abhorrence we

---

[a] On June 11, 1873.—*Ed.*

feel on seeing the government using the army fight our brother workers, while neglecting the struggle against the Carlists", etc.[a]

The workers of Barcelona—Spain's largest industrial city, which has seen more barricade fighting than any other city in the world—were asked to oppose the armed government force not with arms in their hands, but with a general strike, that is, a measure directly involving only individual bourgeois, but not their collective representative—the State power. During the period of peacetime inaction, the workers of Barcelona had been able to listen to the inflammatory phrases of mild men like Alerini, Farga Pellicer and Viñas; but when the time came to act, when Alerini, Farga Pellicer and Viñas first announced their fine election programme, then proceeded to calm passions, and finally, instead of issuing a call to arms declared a general STRIKE, the workers actually despised them. Even the weakest Intransigent showed more energy than the strongest member of the Alliance. The Alliance and the International,which was hoodwinked by it,lost all influence and when these gentlemen called for a general STRIKE claiming that this would paralyse the government the workers simply ridiculed them. What the activities of the false International did achieve, however, was that Barcelona took no part in the cantonal uprising. Barcelona was the only town whose participation could have provided firm support for the working-class element, which was everywhere strongly represented in the movement, and thus held out the prospect of the workers ultimately controlling the entire movement. Furthermore, with the participation of Barcelona, victory would have been as good as won. But Barcelona did not raise a finger; the workers of Barcelona, who had seen through the Intransigents and been cheated by the Alliance, remained inactive, thus allowing the Madrid government to secure the final victory. All of which did not prevent Alerini and Brousse, members of the Alliance (the report on the Alliance contained further details about them[b]), from stating in their paper, the *Solidarité Révolutionnaire*:

"The revolutionary movement is spreading like wildfire throughout the peninsula ... *nothing has as yet happened* in Barcelona, *but the revolution is permanent in the market place!*"[c]

---

[a] Engels probably quotes from *La Solidarité Révolutionnaire*, No. 6, July 16, 1873.—*Ed.*

[b] See this volume, pp. 488, 495, 507-10.—*Ed.*

[c] "Le mouvement révolutionnaire...", *La Solidarité Révolutionnaire*, No. 6, July 16, 1873. Quotations below are taken from the same article.—*Ed.*

But it was the revolution of the Alliancists, which consists in beating the big drum and for this reason remains "permanently" in the same "place".

At the same time the general STRIKE became the order of the day in Alcoy. Alcoy is a new industrial town of some 30,000 inhabitants, where the International, in its Bakuninist form, gained a foothold only a year ago and spread rapidly. Socialism, in any form, went down well with these workers, who until then had known nothing of the movement; the same thing happens in Germany where occasionally in some backward town the General Association of German Workers[398] suddenly gains a large temporary following. Alcoy was therefore chosen as the seat of the Bakuninist Federal Commission for Spain,[399] and it is the work of this Federal Commission that we are going to see here.

On July 7, a workers' meeting voted for a general STRIKE and on the following day sent a deputation to the alcalde (the mayor) asking him to summon the manufacturers within 24 hours and present to them the workers' demands. Albors, the alcalde, a bourgeois Republican, stalled off the workers, sent to Alicante for troops and advised the manufacturers not to yield but to barricade themselves in their houses. He himself would remain at his post. After a meeting with the manufacturers—we are here following the official report of the Alliance Federal Commission dated July 14, 1873[a]—Albors, who had originally promised the workers to remain neutral, issued a proclamation in which he "insulted and slandered the workers and sided with the manufacturers thus destroying the rights and the freedom of the strikers and challenging them to fight". How the pious wishes of a mayor can destroy the rights and the freedom of the strikers is not made clear. Anyway, the workers led by the Alliance notified the municipal council through a committee that if it did not intend to remain neutral during the strike as it promised, it had better resign in order to avoid a conflict. The committee was turned away and as it was leaving the town hall, the police opened fire on the peaceful and unarmed people standing in the square. This is how the fight started, according to the report of the Alliance. The people armed themselves, and a battle began which was said to have lasted "twenty hours". On one side, the workers, whose number is given by the *Solidarité Révolutionnaire* as 5,000, on the other, 32 gendarmes in the town hall and a few armed men in four or five houses in the market place. These houses were burnt

---

[a] "Á los Trabajadores", *La Federacion*, No. 206, July 26, 1873.—*Ed.*

down by the people in the good Prussian manner. Eventually the gendarmes ran out of ammunition and had to surrender.

"There would have been less misfortunes to lament," says the report of the Alliance Commission, "if the Alcalde Albors had not deceived the people by pretending to surrender and then cowardly ordering the murder of those who entered the town hall relying on his word. And the Alcalde himself would not have been killed by the justly enraged population had he not fired his revolver point-blank at those who went to arrest him."

And what were the casualties in this battle?

"Although we cannot know exactly the number of dead and wounded" (on the people's side) "we can nevertheless say that they numbered *no less than ten*. On the side of provokers there were no less than *fifteen* dead and wounded."

This was the first street battle of the Alliance. For twenty hours, 5,000 men [a] fought against 32 gendarmes and a few armed bourgeois, and defeated them after they had run out of ammunition, losing *ten men* in all. The Alliance may well drum Falstaff's dictum into the heads of its adepts that "the better part of valour is discretion". [b]

Needless to say, all the horror stories carried by the bourgeois papers about factories senselessly burnt down, numerous gendarmes shot down, and of people having petrol poured over them and set on fire, are pure inventions. The victorious workers, even if led by members of the Alliance whose motto is, "to hell with ceremony!", always treat their defeated adversaries far too generously, and so the latter accuse them of all the misdeeds which *they themselves* never fail to perpetrate when they are victorious.

And so victory had been won.

The *Solidarité Révolutionnaire* writes jubilantly: "Our friends in Alcoy, numbering 5,000, are masters of the situation."

And what did these "masters" do with their "situation"?

Here the report of the Alliance and its newspaper leave us in the lurch and we have to rely on the ordinary newspaper reports. From these we learn that a "Committee of Public Safety", that is, a revolutionary government, was then set up in Alcoy. To be sure, at their Congress at Saint-Imier [400] (Switzerland), on September 15, 1872, the members of the Alliance decided that

---

a *Der Volksstaat* does not give the number of people.— *Ed.*
b W. Shakespeare, *The First Part of King Henry IV*, Act V, Scene 4.— *Ed.*

"any organisation of political, so-called provisional or revolutionary authority, can be nothing but a new fraud and would be just as dangerous for the proletariat as any of the now existing governments".[a]

The members of the Spanish Federal Commission, meeting at Alcoy, had moreover done everything they could to get this resolution adopted also by the Congress of the Spanish Section of the International. And yet we find that Severino Albarracin, a member of this Commission, and, according to some reports, also Francisco Tomas, its secretary, were members of this provisional and revolutionary government, the Committee of Public Safety, of Alcoy!

And what did this Committee of Public Safety do? What measures did it adopt to bring about "the immediate and complete emancipation of the workers"? It forbade any man to leave the city, although women were allowed to do so, provided they ... had a *pass*! The enemies of all authority re-introducing a pass! Everything else was utter confusion, inactivity and helplessness.

Meanwhile, General Velarde was coming up from Alicante with troops. The government had every reason for wishing to deal with the local insurrections in the provinces quietly. And the "masters of the situation" in Alcoy had every reason for wanting to extricate themselves from a situation which they did not know how to handle. Accordingly, Deputy Cervera, who acted as a go-between, had an easy task. The Committee of Public Safety resigned, and on July 12 the troops entered the town without meeting any resistance, the only promise made to the Committee of Public Safety for this being ... a general amnesty. The Alliance "masters of the situation" had once again extricated themselves from a tight spot. And there the Alcoy adventure ended.

The Alliance report tells us that at Sanlúcar de Barrameda, near Cádiz,

"the Alcalde closed down the premises of the International and his threats and his incessant attacks on the personal rights of the citizens incensed the workers. A commission demanded of the minister observance of the law and the re-opening of the premises which had been arbitrarily closed down. Mr. Pi agreed to this in principle ... but refused to comply in practice. It became clear to the workers that the Government was determined to outlaw their Association; they dismissed the local authorities and appointed others in their place, who re-opened the premises of the Association."[b]

---

[a] "Les deux Congrès de Saint-Imier", *Bulletin de la Fédération jurassienne...*, No. 17-18, September 15-October 1, 1872, p. 13.—*Ed.*

[b] "Á los Trabajadores", *La Federacion*, No. 206, July 26, 1873.—*Ed.*

"In Sanlúcar ... the people are masters of the situation!" the *Solidarité Révolutionnaire* writes triumphantly. The members of the Alliance, who here too, contrary to their anarchist principles, formed a revolutionary government, did not know what to do with their power. They wasted time in futile debates and paper resolutions, and when General Pavía, on August 5, after taking Seville and Cádiz, sent a few companies of the Soria brigade to Sanlúcar he encountered ... no resistance.

Such were the heroic deeds performed by the Alliance where it had no competition.

III

The street fighting in Alcoy was immediately followed by a revolt of the Intransigents in Andalusia. Pi y Margall was still at the helm, engaged in continuous negotiations with the leaders of this party with the object of forming a ministry with them; why then did they begin an uprising before the negotiations had failed? The reason for this rash action has never been properly explained; it is however certain, that the main concern of the Intransigents was the actual establishment of a federal republic as quickly as possible in order to seize power and the many new administrative posts that were to be created in the various cantons. The splitting up of Spain had been deferred too long by the Cortes in Madrid, and so they had to tackle the job themselves and proclaim sovereign cantons everywhere. The attitude hitherto maintained by the (Bakuninist) International, which since the elections was deeply involved in the actions of the Intransigents, gave grounds for counting on the Bakuninists' support: indeed, had not the Bakuninists just seized Alcoy by force and were thus in open conflict with the government? The Bakuninists moreover had for years been preaching that all revolutionary action from above was an evil, and everything should be organised and carried through from below. And now here was an opportunity to apply the famous principle of autonomy from below, at least in a few towns. Predictably, the Bakuninist workers fell into the trap and pulled the chestnuts out of the fire for the Intransigents, only to be rewarded later by their allies with the usual kicks and bullets.

What was the position of the members of the Bakuninist International in all this movement? They helped to evolve its federalist particularism; they put into practice as far as possible their anarchist ideal. The same Bakuninists who in Cordoba a few

months earlier had declared that to establish a revolutionary
government was to betray and cheat the workers, the same
Bakuninists now sat in all the revolutionary municipal governments of Andalusia, but always in a minority, so that the
Intransigents could do whatever they wished. While the latter
retained the political and military leadership, the workers were put
off with pompous phrases or resolutions purporting to introduce
social reforms of the crudest and most meaningless sort, which
moreover existed only on paper. As soon as the Bakuninist leaders
demanded real concessions, they were scornfully repulsed. When
talking to English newspaper correspondents, the Intransigent
leaders of the movement hastened to dissociate themselves from
these so-called "members of the International" and to renounce all
responsibility for them, declaring that their leaders and all fugitives
from the Paris Commune were being kept under strict police
supervision. Finally, as we shall see, the Intransigents in Seville,
during the battle with the government troops, fired also on their
Bakuninist allies.[a]

Thus it happened that within a few days the whole of Andalusia
was in the hands of the armed Intransigents. Seville, Málaga,
Granada, Cádiz, etc. were taken almost without resistance. Each
town proclaimed itself a sovereign canton and set up a revolutionary committee (junta). Murcia, Cartagena, and Valencia followed
suit. A similar attempt, but of a more peaceful nature, was made
in Salamanca. Thus, nearly all the large Spanish cities were held
by the insurgents, with the exception of Madrid, the capital, which
is purely a luxury city and hardly ever plays a decisive role, and of
Barcelona. If Barcelona had risen success would have been almost
assured, and in addition it would have provided powerful support
for the working-class element of the movement. But, as we have
seen, the Intransigents in Barcelona were comparatively powerless,
whereas the Bakuninists, who were still very strong there at the
time, used the general STRIKE only for *appeasement purposes*. Thus,
Barcelona this time was not at its post.

Nevertheless, the uprising, though started in a senseless way,
had a fair chance of success if conducted with some intelligence,
even if in the manner of the Spanish military revolts, in which the
garrison of one town rises, marches to the next town and wins
over the garrison there which had been propagandised in advance,

---

[a] *Der Volksstaat* (No. 106) printed the following three paragraphs, apparently
by mistake, at the end of Article III. Engels replaced them when preparing the
article for the 1894 collection *Internationales aus dem Volksstaat (1871-1875).— Ed.*

and, growing like an avalanche, advances on the capital, until a successful engagement or the desertion to its side of the troops sent out against it, decides the victory. This method was eminently suited to the occasion. The insurgents had long been organised everywhere into volunteer battalions, whose discipline, it is true, was poor, but certainly no worse than that of the remnants of the old Spanish army, which for the most part had been disbanded. The only reliable troops the government had were the gendarmes (*guardias civiles*), and these were scattered all over the country. The thing was to prevent the gendarmes from mustering, and this could only be done by boldly giving battle in the open field. No great risk was involved in this since the government could send against the volunteers only troops that were just as undisciplined as they themselves. And if they wanted to win, this was the only way to go about it.

But no. The federalism of the Intransigents and their Bakuninist tail consisted precisely in the fact that each town acted on its own, declaring that the important thing was not co-operation with other towns but separation from them, thus precluding any possibility of a combined attack. What was an unavoidable evil during the German Peasant War and the German insurrections of May 1849, namely, the fragmentation and isolation of the revolutionary forces which enabled the government troops to smash one revolt after the other,[401] was here proclaimed a principle of supreme revolutionary wisdom. Bakunin had that satisfaction. As early as September 1870 (in his *Lettres à un français*[a]) he had declared that the only way to drive the Prussians out of France by a revolutionary struggle was to do away with all forms of centralised leadership and leave each town, each village, each parish to wage war on its own. If one thus opposed the Prussian army under its centralised command with unfettered revolutionary passion victory would be ensured. Confronted with the collective mind of the French people, thrown at last on its own resources, the individual mind of Moltke would obviously sink into insignificance. The French then refused to see this, but in Spain Bakunin had won a brilliant victory, as we have already seen and shall yet see.

Meanwhile, this uprising, launched without reason like a bolt from the blue, had made it impossible for Pi y Margall to continue his negotiations with the Intransigents. He was compelled to

---

[a] [M. Bakounine,] *Lettres à un français sur la crise actuelle* [Neuchâtel, 1870].— *Ed.*

resign,[a] and was replaced by pure republicans like Castelar, undisguised bourgeois, whose primary aim was to crush the working-class movement, which they had previously used but which had now become a hindrance to them. One division under General Pavía was sent against Andalusia, another under General Campos against Valencia and Cartagena. The main body consisted of gendarmes drawn from all over Spain, all of them old soldiers whose discipline was still unshaken. Here too, as during the attacks of the Versailles army on Paris, the gendarmes were to bolster up the demoralised regulars and to form the spearhead of the attacking columns, a task which in both cases they fulfilled to the best of their abilities. Besides the gendarmes, the divisions contained a few rather diminished line regiments, so that each of them numbered some 3,000 men. This was all the Government was able to raise against the insurgents.

General Pavía took the field round about July 20. A detachment of gendarmes and line troops under Ripoll occupied Cordoba on the 24th. On the 29th Pavía attacked the barricaded Seville, which fell to him on the 30th or 31st, the dates are often not clearly stated in these telegrams. Leaving behind a flying column to put down the surrounding country, he marched against Cádiz, whose defenders only fought on the approaches to the city, and with little spirit at that, and then, on August 4, they allowed themselves to be disarmed without resistance. In the days that followed, Pavía disarmed, also without resistance, Sanlúcar de Barrameda, San Roque, Tarifa, Algeciras, and a great many other small towns, each of which had set itself up as a sovereign canton. At the same time he sent detachments against Málaga, which surrendered on August 3, and Granada, which surrendered on August 8, without offering any resistance. Thus by August 10, in less than a fortnight and almost without a struggle, the whole of Andalusia had been subdued.

On July 26, Martinez Campos began the attack on Valencia. The revolt there had been raised by the workers. When the split in the Spanish International occurred, the real International had the majority in Valencia, and the new Spanish Federal Council was transferred there.[402] Soon after the proclamation of the Republic, when revolutionary battles lay ahead, the Bakuninist workers of Valencia, mistrusting the Barcelona leaders who cloaked their appeasement policy with ultra-revolutionary phrases, offered the members of the real International their co-operation in all local

---

[a] On July 18, 1873.— *Ed.*

movements. When the cantonal movement started, both groups, making use of the Intransigents, immediately attacked and ejected the troops. Who formed the Valencian junta remains unknown, but from the reports of the English newspaper correspondents it appears that workers definitely predominated in the junta, just as they did among the Valencian Volunteers. The same correspondents spoke of the Valencian insurgents with a respect which they were far from showing towards the other rebels, who were mostly Intransigents; they praised their discipline and the order which prevailed in the city, and predicted a long resistance and a hard struggle. They were not mistaken. Valencia, an open city, withstood the attacks of Campos' division from July 26 to August 8, that is longer than the whole of Andalusia.

In the province of Murcia, the capital of the same name was occupied without a fight; after the fall of Valencia Campos moved against Cartagena, one of the strongest fortresses in Spain, protected on the landward side by a rampart and advanced forts on the commanding heights. The 3,000 government troops, who had no siege artillery whatsoever, and whose light field guns were of course powerless against the heavy artillery of the forts, had to confine themselves to laying siege to the city from the landward side. This was of little avail, however, as long as the people of Cartagena dominated the sea with the naval vessels they had captured in the harbour. The insurgents, who, while the fight had been going on in Valencia and Andalusia, were wholly preoccupied with their own affairs, began to think of the outside world after the other revolts had been quelled, when they themselves began to run short of money and provisions. Only then did they make an attempt to march on Madrid, which was at least 60 German miles [a] away, more than twice as far as, for instance, Valencia or Granada! The expedition ended in disaster not far from Cartagena. The siege precluded any possibility of further land sorties, so they attempted sorties with the aid of the fleet. And what sorties! There could be no question of raising revolts again with the aid of Cartagena warships in the coastal towns which had recently been subdued. The fleet of the Sovereign Canton of Cartagena therefore confined itself to threatening to shell the other coastal towns from Valencia to Málaga, which, according to the theory of the people of Cartagena, were likewise sovereign—and if need be to shell them in actual fact if they failed to deliver on board the required provisions and war

---

[a] The German mile is equal to 7,420,438 metres.— *Ed.*

contribution in hard cash. While these cities, as sovereign cantons, had been fighting the government, Cartagena adhered to the principle of "every man for himself". Now when they had been defeated the principle which was held to be valid was—"everyone for Cartagena!" That was how the Intransigents of Cartagena and their Bakuninist supporters interpreted the federalism of the sovereign cantons.

In order to reinforce the ranks of the fighters for liberty, the government of Cartagena released from the local jail about 1,800 convicts—Spain's worst robbers and murderers. After the disclosures made in the report on the Alliance there can no longer be any room for doubt that this revolutionary step was suggested to it by the Bakuninists. The report shows Bakunin enthusiastically advocating the "unleashing of all evil passions" and holding up the Russian brigand as a model for all true revolutionaries.[a] What is fair for the Russian is fair for the Spaniard. When the local government of Cartagena released the "evil passions" of the 1,800 jailed cut-throats, thereby carrying demoralisation among its troops to the extreme limit, it acted wholly in the spirit of Bakunin. And when, instead of battering down its own fortifications, the Spanish government awaited the fall of Cartagena through the internal disorganisation of its defenders, it was pursuing an entirely correct policy.

IV

Now let us hear what the report of the New Madrid Federation has to say about the whole movement.

"On the second Sunday in August a Congress was to be held in Valencia, which, among other things, was to determine the attitude the Spanish International Federation was to adopt towards the important political events taking place in Spain since February 11, the day the Republic was proclaimed. But this nonsensical" (descabellada, literally: dishevelled) "cantonal uprising, which was such an abject failure and in which members of the International eagerly took part in almost all the insurgent provinces, has not only brought the work of the Federal Council to a standstill by dispersing most of its members, but has almost completely disorganised the local federations and, what is worse, exposed their members to the full measure of hatred and persecution that an ignominiously started and defeated popular insurrection always entails....

"When the cantonal uprising started, when the juntas, i.e., the cantonal governments, were formed, these people" (the Bakuninists) "who had spoken so

---

[a] See this volume, pp. 520-21.—Ed.

violently against political power, and accused us of authoritarianism, lost no time in joining those governments. And in important cities such as Seville, Cádiz, Sanlúcar de Barrameda, Granada and Valencia, many members of the International who call themselves anti-authoritarians sat on the cantonal juntas with no programme other than that of autonomy for the provinces or cantons. This is officially established by the proclamations and other documents issued by those juntas over the signatures of well-known members of this International.

"Such a flagrant contradiction between theory and practice, between propaganda and action, would be of small account if our Association could have derived any benefit from it, or if it could have advanced the organisation of our forces, or in any way furthered the attainment of our main goal—the emancipation of the working class. Just the opposite took place, as it was bound to in the absence of the primary condition, namely, the active collaboration of the Spanish proletariat, which could have been so easily achieved by acting in the name of the International. There was no agreement between the local federations; the movement was abandoned to individual or local initiative without leadership (apart from that *which the mysterious Alliance was able to force upon it, and that Alliance to our shame still dominates the Spanish International*) and without any programme other than that of our natural enemies, the bourgeois republicans. Thus, the cantonal movement suffered the most ignominious defeat without offering hardly any resistance, and dragging down with it also the prestige and organisation of the International in Spain. For every excess, every crime, every outrage that takes place the republicans today blame the members of the International. We are even assured, that at Seville during the fighting the Intransigents fired at their own allies, the members of the" (Bakuninist) "International. Taking clever advantage of our follies, the reactionaries are inciting the republicans to persecute us and vilify us in the eyes of the indifferent masses; it seems that what they were unable to achieve in the days of Sagasta, i.e., to give the International a bad name among the great mass of Spanish workers, they may be able to achieve now.

"A number of workers' sections in Barcelona dissociated themselves from the International and publicly protested against the people of the newspaper *La Federación*" (the main organ of the Bakuninists) "and their inexplicable attitude. In Jérez, Puerto de Santa Maria and elsewhere the federations have decided to dissolve themselves. The few members of the International who lived in Loja (Granada province) were expelled by the population. In Madrid, where people still enjoy the greatest freedom, the old" (Bakuninist) "federation shows no sign of life, while ours is compelled to remain inactive and silent if it does not want to take the blame for other people's sins. In the northern cities the Carlist war, which is becoming more bitter day by day, precludes any activity on our part. Finally, in Valencia, where the government won the day after a struggle lasting a fortnight, the members of the International who have not fled are forced to remain in hiding, and the Federal Council has been dissolved."

So much for the Madrid report. As we see, it agrees in all particulars with the above historical account.

What then is the result of our whole investigation?

1. As soon as they were faced with a serious revolutionary situation, the Bakuninists had to throw the whole of their old programme overboard. First they sacrificed their doctrine of absolute abstention from political, and especially electoral, ac-

tivities. Then anarchy, the abolition of the State, shared the same fate. Instead of abolishing the State they tried, on the contrary, to set up a number of new, small states. They then dropped the principle that the workers must not take part in any revolution that did not have as its aim the immediate and complete emancipation of the proletariat, and they themselves took part in a movement that was notoriously bourgeois. Finally they went against the dogma they had only just proclaimed—that the establishment of a revolutionary government is but another fraud, another betrayal of the working class—for they sat quite comfortably in the juntas of the various towns, and moreover almost everywhere as an impotent minority outvoted and politically exploited by the bourgeoisie.

2. This renunciation of the principles they had always been preaching was made moreover in the most cowardly and deceitful manner and was prompted by a guilty conscience, so that neither the Bakuninists themselves nor the masses they led had any programme or knew what they wanted when they joined the movement. What was the natural consequence of this? It was that the Bakuninists either prevented any action from being taken, as in Barcelona, or drifted into sporadic, desultory and senseless uprisings, as in Alcoy and Sanlúcar de Barrameda; or that the leadership of the uprising was taken over by the intransigent bourgeois, as was the case in most of the revolts. Thus, when it came to doing things, the ultra-revolutionary rantings of the Bakuninists either turned into appeasement or into uprisings that were doomed to failure, or, led to their joining a bourgeois party which exploited the workers politically in the most disgraceful manner and treated them to kicks into the bargain.

3. Nothing remains of the so-called principles of anarchy, free federation of independent groups, etc., but the boundless, and senseless fragmentation of the revolutionary resources, which enabled the government to conquer one city after another with a handful of soldiers, practically unresisted.

4. The outcome of all this is that not only have the once so well organised and numerous Spanish sections of the International—both the false and the true ones—found themselves involved in the downfall of the Intransigents and are now actually dissolved, but are also having ascribed to them innumerable atrocities, without which the philistines of all nationalities cannot imagine a workers' uprising, and this may make impossible, perhaps for years to come, the international re-organisation of the Spanish proletariat.

5. In short, the Bakuninists in Spain have given us an unparalleled example of how a revolution should *not* be made.

Written in September-October 1873

First published in *Der Volksstaat*, Nos. 105-107, October 31, November 2 and 5, 1873

Printed according to F. Engels, *Internationales aus dem Volksstaat (1871-1875)*, Berlin, 1894, checked with the newspaper

Frederick Engels

VARIA ON GERMANY [403]

I. INTRODUCTION 1500-1789

1. Germany more and more fragmented and the centre weakened end of 15th century, with France and England already more or less centralised and the nation in the process of formation. This impossible in Germany because 1. feudalism developed later than in the countries that had suffered conquest [a]; 2. Germany had French and Slavonic constituents and saw Italy as belonging to it and Rome as its centre—thus no *national* complex; 3. because, and this is the main thing, the individual provinces and groups of provinces were still utterly isolated from one another, no traffic, etc. (vid. *Peasant War*).[b] The Hansa, the Rhenish League of Cities and Swabian League of Cities [404] represented natural, but separate groups.

Ad I, 1. Spain, France, England end 15th century grown together into constituted national states. This consolidation epoch-making for 15th century (Spain—unification of the Catalan and Castilian nationalities; Portugal, the Iberian Holland, had established its right to a separate existence through its navigation; France—through the dynasty-allodium, which gradually absorbed the nation.—England (England only reached this stage after being forced to renounce its Quixotic plans for conquest of France— similar to Germany's Roman campaigns—which would have bled it white, as the Roman campaigns had bled white Germany)—by the Wars of the Roses,[405] which destroyed the nobility.—Germany

---

[a] The allusion is to the conquest of Western Europe by the Germanic tribes in the 5th-6th centuries.— *Ed.*

[b] See F. Engels, *The Peasant War in Germany* (present edition, Vol. 10, p. 401).— *Ed.*

would still have been centralised despite its economic desultoriness, indeed earlier (e.g., under the Ottos), had it not been for the fact 1) that the Roman emperorship, with its claim to world domination, ruled out the establishment of a national state and dissipated its energies on the Italian campaigns of conquest (after-effects in Austria until 1866!), in which German interests were continually betrayed, and 2) that the system of elective monarchy never permitted a merging of the nation with the imperial allodium but always—and particularly in the 15th, decisive, century—changed dynasties as soon as their allodium grew too great for the princes.—In France and Spain, too, there was economic fragmentation, overcome by force.

The "Kulturkampf"[406] between the Emperor and the Pope in the Middle Ages split Germany and Italy (where the Pope was an obstacle to national unity and, at the same time, often apparently its champion, but in such a way that, e.g., Dante saw the saviour of Italy in the foreign Emperor[a]) and, by 1500, the Pope had positioned himself right across Italy as the prince possessing the middle of the country, and made unity physically impossible.

2. Nevertheless, Germany would have grown into a single entity through the natural development of trade, the Germanisation of the Slavs and the loss of the French provinces[407] and of Italy since the world trade route passed through Germany, had two decisive events not occurred to prevent this:

—1) The German burghers made their revolution—which, in accordance with the spirit of the age, appeared in a religious form—the Reformation. But how lousy! Impossible without the imperial knights and the peasants; but all 3 estates prevented by conflicting interests: knights often the robbers of the towns (vid. Mangold von Eberstein) and oppressors of the peasants, and towns also peasant-bashers (Council of Ulm and peasants![408]); imperial knights rise up first, are left in the lurch by the burghers, perish; peasants rise up, are *directly opposed* by the burghers. At the same time, the bourgeois religious revolution so castrated that it appeals to the *princes*, and the latter are given the leadership. Ad 2, 1: Specifically theological-theoretical character of the German revolution of the 16th century. Predominant interest in things not of this world, abstraction from wretched reality—basis of subsequent theoretical superiority of the Germans from Leibniz to Hegel.

—2) The world trade route removed from Germany, and

---

[a] Dante Alighieri, *De Monarchia.*—*Ed.*

Germany pushed into an isolated corner, whereby the power of the burghers broken, the Reformation *ditto.*

—3) Result that *cuius regio, eius religio,*[a] and that Germany actually disintegrated into a predominantly Protestant North, predominantly Catholic but very mixed Southwest, and exclusively Catholic Southeast. This already predetermined developments of 1740-1870 (Prussia, split between North and South, finally Little Germany[409] and Austria). Opposite of France. Suppression of the Huguenots (vid. "Varia" p. 2[b]).

3. Germany, once condemned industrially to passivity and setbacks, was bound to be more exposed to the influences of changing political factors than industrially active and progressive countries. (Develop this in general terms.) The split into 2 parties placed civil war on the agenda; enumeration of the wars up to 1648—civil war. French exploitation of the opportunity and the alliance with and *payment of the Protestant princes* and German mercenaries. Culminates in the Thirty Years War.[410] Thirty Years War—Irishmen in Germany, Germans in Ireland, 1693 and 1806.[411] Description of the devastation. Result: economically, socially, politically—losses to France; settlement by Sweden and Denmark in Germany; the guarantee-powers' right of intervention; total collapse of the central power; right of rebellion against the Emperor, civil war and treason *guaranteed by Europe* to the German princes.

4. 1648-1789

a. Political condition. The German princes exploit the Peace of Westphalia by trying to outdo one another in selling themselves to foreign countries, and these—France, and also the princes— exploit Germany's weakness in order gradually to appropriate all Germany's French possessions and encircle Alsace. Historical right of France, and Teutons' outcry about "robbery".[412] Unchanging nature of linguistic boundaries (vid. Menke[c]) since circa A.D. 1000, except for the districts left of the Vosges. This the general situation. In particular: Rise of a rival power to Austria and the empire in the North: Prussia. Beginning of the realisation of the division into North and South. Critique of Prussian history.

---

a The ruler of a country determines its religion (the underlying principle of the Augsburg Religious Peace of 1555; it ended a series of Catholic-Protestant wars in Germany by leaving it to the respective princes to lay down the religion for their subjects).— *Ed.*

b See this volume, pp. 607-08.— *Ed.*

c [K.] Spruner and [H. Th.] Menke, *Hand-Atlas für die Geschichte des Mittelalters und der neueren Zeit,* Gotha, [1871-]1880.— *Ed.*

Frederick II.—Rise of Russia and Frederick II's subjection to Russian policy.—Because of Prussia the civil wars now wars of rivalry between Austria and Prussia.

b. *Economic matters.* For all that, *slow recovery from the consequences of the Thirty Years War* and renewed crawling up of the burghers. Only the possession of *infamous* virtues made this revival possible in such circumstances. For all that, economic progress only made possible through political intervention—by the infamy of the princes and the money paid to them from abroad. This proves how deeply humiliated Germany was economically. This period the source of the patriarchal régime. After 1648, the state really called on to perform social functions and forced to assume them by financial embarrassment; where it failed to exercise them— stagnation (the Westphalian bishoprics). What a state of humiliation! And how lousy the state aid! In relation to the world market, purely passive; only as *neutrals* in great world wars (American and Revolutionary Wars until 1801)[413] was anything to be earned. On the other hand, powerless against the robber states. (Thanks to the French Revolution this European disgrace eliminated.)

c. Literature and language utterly degenerate; theology wooden dogmatism; in other sciences Germany also in a state of degradation, yet rays of hope: J. Böhme (again, a sign of the philosophers to come), Kepler, Leibniz—again abstraction from the existing, the real. *Bach.*

d. State of Germany in 1789. a) Agriculture—peasant conditions. Serfdom, corporal punishment, dues. b) Industry—a sheer starvation affair, essentially manual labour, but in England already the beginnings of large-scale industry, and German industry, before it was even fully developed, doomed to die. c) Trade— passive. d) Social status of the burghers vis-à-vis nobility and government.—e) Political obstacle to development: fragmentation. Description as in Menke. Tolls, prevention of river traffic. FREE TRADE along internal borders forced through by dismemberment. Tolls chiefly urban consumption dues.

These princes, powerless to do good, even when enlightened— as Schubart's patrons[414] and Karl August—all were happy to join the Confederation of the Rhine,[415] rather than fight a war. Invasion of 1806[a] the test, when it was a matter of life or death for them. Moreover, all of these 1,000 princes absolute monarchs, coarse, uneducated scoundrels, from whom no cooperation could

---

[a] Napoleon's army invaded Germany in the course of France's war against Prussia.— *Ed.*

be expected, moods always en masse (Schlözer[a]). Trade in soldiers during American War.—Yet their worst atrocity was their *mere existence.* And alongside them, on the eastern frontier, Prussia in the North, Austria in the South, both greedily stretching out their hands for the territories—the only two that could have saved the situation, if only one of them was there, but whose inevitable rivalry made any such solution impossible. A sheer blind-alley, only from outside could help come—the French Revolution brought it. Only 2 signs of life: military skill, and also literature and philosophy and conscientious, objective scientific investigation, whereas in France, as early as 18th century, mainly partisan writings, albeit first-class ones—in Germany all this was a flight from reality into ideal regions. "*Man*" and the development of the language; 1700 barbarism, 1750 Lessing and Kant, soon Goethe, Schiller, Wieland, Herder; Gluck, Händel, Mozart.

1789-1815

1. The German enclaves in Alsace-Lorraine, etc.—already half under French sovereignty—joined the French Revolution; thus an excuse for war.[416] Prussia and Austria *now suddenly united.* Valmy.[417] Defeat of linear tactics by massed artillery. Fleurus and Jemappes.[418] Defeat of the Austrian cordon tactics? Capture of the left bank of the Rhine. Rejoicing of the peasants and the liberal towns could not be dispelled even by odd cases of extortion, or Napoleon's bloodtaxes.—Peace of Amiens and the most important act of the Imperial Deputation—the dissolution of the Empire.[419] Confederation of the Rhine. The abolition of small states by Napoleon unfortunately failed to go far enough. He, always revolutionary vis-à-vis the princes, would have gone further if the petty princes had not humbled themselves so abjectly before him. 1806, Napoleon's error was not to have destroyed Prussia altogether.—Economic facts on Germany under the Continental Blockade.[420]—This period of the utmost humiliation from abroad coincides with the heyday of literature and philosophy and the culmination of music in Beethoven.

---

[a] A. L. Schlözer, *Briefwechsel meist historischen und politischen Inhalts*, Vols. 1-10, Göttingen, 1776-1782. *Staats-Anzeigen*, Vols. 1-18, Göttingen, 1782-1793.— *Ed.*

VARIA ON GERMANY 1789-1873

Prussia: und sint Weletabi so wir Wilzi heizzent etc.[a]
Prussian Army: hungry of old. Höpfner 1788-1806.[b]—Scarcity
of funds under Frederick William III. Embezzlement (1st
and 9th Guard Artillery Comp. coats, 1842). Old harness in the
armoury.—Frederick William III also peaceful, owing to need to
summon the *estates* in the event of war.—1st turning-point
1848.—Waldersee and needle (gun). 2nd turning-point the
mobilisation 1850 and finally the Italian War,[421] army reorganisation, rejection of the old ways. Since 1864 much self-criticism and
purely businesslike procedure. Nevertheless, total misunderstanding of the character of Prussian army organisation.—Tragi-comic
conflict: the state *must* wage political wars, for distant interests that
never arouse national enthusiasm, and to this end requires an
army that is only any good for national defence and the offensives
resulting immediately therefrom (1814 and 1870).—This conflict
will be the downfall of the Prussian state and the Prussian
army—probably in a war with Russia, which might last 4 years
and would yield nothing but disease and shattered bones.

Jewish element absolutely vital to Germany; the Jews a class that
stood even lower than the serfs, no homeland, no rights (cf.
Gülich on Frederick William II[c]), but free and because dependent
on trade, an element of the future in themselves; therefore able to
react while the mass unable to react to the pressure; also livelier
and more active by nature than the Germans, rise under
Napoleonic rule (Rothschild and the Elector of Hesse[422]); soon
after 1815 strong enough in North and West Germany to break
the ghetto law where it had been imposed (Frankfurt); Börne and
Heine; penetration into literature, especially the daily press;
character of the Jewish man of letters to aim at immediate
practical gain; character of the Jewish merchant, Polish and
German tradition of petty swindling, only disappearing in the 2nd

---

[a] And there are the Weletabi, whom we call Wilzi. Engels gives a free rendering
of a passage from Notker Laber's 11th-century translation of Martianus Capella's
De Nuptiis Mercurii et Philologiae. In: J. Grimm, *Deutsche Rechtsalterthümer*, Götting-
en, 1828, p. 488.— *Ed.*

[b] E. von Höpfner, *Der Krieg von 1806 und 1807. Ein Beitrag zur Geschichte der
Preussischen Armee nach den Quellen des Kriegsarchivs bearb,* Vol. 1, Berlin, 1850.— *Ed.*

[c] G. Gülich, *Geschichtliche Darstellung des Handels, der Gewerbe und des Ackerbaus
der bedeutendsten handeltreibenden Staaten unsrer Zeit,* Vol. 2, Jena, 1830, pp. 242-53,
530-33.— *Ed.*

Page of the manuscript *Varia on Germany*

or 3rd generation—finally merging more and more, the Germans become Jewish and the Jews German.

German trading colonies abroad even before 1789, but only significant after 1814. Only since 1848 real lever for Germany's entry into world trade, but then tremendously effective. Gradual growth. Character of the trading colonies until 1848—generally uneducated and ashamed of their country. (Mchr.[a] English in 10 German dialects.) Inadequate protection (Weerth's Mexican story and his experience with German diplomats in South America in general[423]); German world trade language through the colonies and the Jews in Eastern Europe (details of these) and through Hamburg posts in Scandinavia. The fact that in trade, outside Romance Europe and at most the Levant, German goes further than French, Italian, Spanish, Portuguese, in short all languages except English. Now rapid expansion of German colonies—cf. the fear of the English in London itself.

Epigonic literature—starting as early as Heine—its mission the polishing of the language, much needed. This achieved in poetry; prose worse than ever.

General feeling 1859-63 on the left bank of the Rhine they were becoming French again—not wished for, not opposed, but they submitted and would also have voted for the inevitable. How much better, then, the Alsatians!—Utter lack of trust in Prussia on account of its attitude and powerlessness [18]59. In addition, reaction among German chauvinists against Bonapartist Rhenish cravings, Alsace and Lorraine German!

Schleswig Holstein—England's eastern Ireland on account of cattle and butter imports, ruin of agriculture at the expense of cattle-raising, emigration, now still in its beginnings, the rest of North German marshlands facing the same fate.

Gold and silverware, jewellery considerable export from Hanau, Pforzheim, Gmünden, Berlin, etc. (K.Z.[b]).

Prussian Rules concerning servants[424]—not to be forgotten! And one-year volunteers in France.

---

[a] Thus in the manuscript. Presumably: Manchester.— *Ed.*
[b] *Kölnische Zeitung* (?).— *Ed.*

During *the Huguenot wars*[425] respect for the monarchy, as representing the nation, already so great that *only* the King was permitted, both legally and by public opinion, to make foreign alliances and engage foreign auxiliaries. The others always rebels and traitors. This never more evident than at the death of Henry III—when Henry IV, merely by virtue of the royal name, is able to achieve final victory.

The eventual suppression of Protestantism in France was no misfortune for France—*teste* Bayle, Voltaire and Diderot. Similarly, its suppression in Germany would not have been a disaster for Germany, but certainly *for the world*. It would have imposed the Catholic *form* of development of the Romance countries on Germany, and as the English form of development was also semi-Catholic and medieval (universities, etc., colleges, PUBLIC SCHOOLS are all Protestant monasteries), the entire Protestant German form of education (education at home or in private houses, students living out and choosing [courses of lectures]) would have been swept away and European intellectual development would have become infinitely uniform. France and England exploded prejudices of *fact*, Germany those of *form*, *pattern*. Hence, also, partly, the amorphous nature of everything German, till now still bound up with great drawbacks, such as the fragmentation into small states, but a tremendous gain for the nation's capacity for development, one that will bear its full fruits only in the future, when this one-sided stage has been passed.

Then: *German Protestantism the only modern form of Christianity worth criticising*. Catholicism, even in the 18th century, *beneath criticism*, object of *polemics* (what asses, therefore, are the Old Catholics![426]). The English having disintegrated into *x* sects, with no theological development, or one every step of which became fixed as a sect. The German alone has a theology and thus an object of criticism—historical, philological and philosophical. *This supplied by Germany*, impossible without German Protestantism and yet absolutely necessary. A religion such as Christianity is not destroyed by ridicule and invective *alone*; it also needs *to be overcome scientifically*, i.e., *explained historically*, which is beyond even the natural sciences.

Holland and Belgium, separated from Germany by the moors between the Rhine and North Sea, by the Ardennes and Venn in the South, play vis-à-vis Germany the role of Phoenicia vis-à-vis Palestine, and also the same lamentation as in the old prophets, customary in Germany.

Flanders from the partition of Verdun[427] until after 1500 a part

of France—hence the establishment of the French language—
promoted by Flemish trade in the Middle Ages, when the
merchants certainly spoke no Flemish with the Italian, etc.,
merchants. Now the Teutomaniacs are demanding the restoration
of the Flemish language, which even the Dutch do not recognise
as full-fledged; the Flemish movement of the priests! IT IS TIME the
Flemish finally had *one* language instead of 2, and that can only
be French.

After the discovery of America, Germany's agriculture, industry
and trade a perpetual patient experimentation—agriculture vid.
the many unsuccessful attempts in Langethal[a]—industry
everywhere and always things which, scarcely instituted, were
forced off the world market—most striking example linen; on a
small scale, e.g., the Wuppertal industry 1820-60—trade ditto.
This only now placed on a normal footing.

Even in 1848 Germany's main export still—*human beings.*
1) ordinary emigration. 2) prostitution: in East Prussia regular
establishments of higher and lower status for training girls to be
whores of every variety and FIT FOR ANYTHING—from the sailors'
brothel to the "educated" cavalier's mistress and, on all sorts of
false pretext, sent abroad where most of them first met their fate.
Many of those in a better position accepted their lot, even sending
their *maquerelle* tender letters of thanks, in which they always
concealed their prostituted position, figuring as governesses,
companions or as brilliantly married. Bergenroth was of the opinion
that all this was impossible without the authorities—FOR A CONSIDERA-
TION?—turning a blind eye; he says it was always very difficult to
get hold of any tangible evidence in judicial inquiries. From Petersburg and Stockholm to Antwerp the entire Baltic and North Sea
coast was supplied with East Prussian women.—3) the vagabond
girls from the Vogelsberg area of Hesse and Nassau, who travelled around the fairs in England as BROOMGIRLS[428] (the older ones
also with barrel organs), but particularly those shipped to America
as HURDY-GURDIES and making up the lowest stratum of prostitution
there. 4) the young merchants of the Hansa and the Rhenish factory towns, later from Saxony and Berlin, too, and 5) then just beginning, later developing strongly, the chemists (the Liebig school
in Giessen), with whores the chief export of the Grand Duchy of
Hesse.—Emigrants to Holland from Westphalia—now common
for Dutch to seek work in the Westphalian industrial areas.

---

[a] Chr. Ed. Langethal, *Geschichte der teutschen Landwirtschaft,* Part 2, Book 4,
Jena, 1856.—*Ed.*

The stinginess of the German governments, especially that of Prussia of 1815-70, apparent in everything: poor-quality dirty coinage; *ditto* banknotes; coarse office paper; writing-sand (all official documents a frightful sight); fat, clumsily carved stamps; everything coarse, not least the officials themselves. French, English, Belgian money, post-marks, banknotes, everything gave an impression of superiority from the outset.

The awkwardness of German for everyday use, together with its enormous facility in dealing with the most difficult topics is partly the cause—or a symptom?—of the fact that, in most disciplines, the Germans have the greatest men, whereas their mass production is unusually awful rubbish. Literature: the numerous solid second-rate poets in England, the brilliant mediocrity that fills almost all French literature, are almost entirely absent in Germany. Our second-rate writers hardly bear reading a generation later. *Ditto* philosophy: alongside Kant and Hegel—Herbart, Krug, Fries and finally Schopenhauer and Hartmann. The genius of the great ones finds its complement in the unthinking nature of the Educated Mass, thus no name is more spurious than that of the "*nation* of thinkers". *Ditto* military literature. Only in things that are more or less independent of language is it any different, and second-rate people, too, important in Germany: natural sciences and particularly music. Our historical works unreadable.

The present so-called German Empire: The setting of the Nibelungs is Germany's 2 greatest rivers, the Rhine and the Danube. It would seem unnatural to us if Worms, the home of Kriemhild and scene of Siegfrid's deeds, were French. But is it any less unnatural for the Danube region to lie outside the German Empire, for Rüdiger of Bechelaren once again to be, as it were, a vassal of the Magyar Etzel? And how did Walther von der Vogelweide describe Germany: "Von der Elbe unz an den Rîn und hinwider unz an Ungerlant"[a]—the Old German Austria is outside Germany, and the then non-German East Elbe region is the centre and focal point! And that calls itself a German Empire!

Written late 1873-early 1874

First published in: *Marx-Engels Archives*, Russian Edition, Vol. X, Moscow, 1948

Printed according to the manuscript

Published in English in full for the first time

---

[a] "From the Elbe to the Rhine and in the other direction as far as Hungary", *Die Gedichte Walthers von der Vogelweide*, 4th edition, Berlin, 1864, pp. 56-57.—*Ed.*

Frederick Engels

THE ENGLISH ELECTIONS[429]

London, February 22, 1874

The English parliamentary elections are now over. The brilliant Gladstone, who could not govern with a majority of sixty-six, suddenly dissolved Parliament, ordered elections within eight to fourteen days, and the result was—a majority of more than fifty *against* him. The second Parliament elected under the Reform Bill of 1867 and the first by secret ballot has yielded a *strong conservative majority.*[430] And it is particularly the big industrial cities and factory districts, where the workers are now absolutely in the majority, that send Conservatives to Parliament. How is this?

This is primarily the result of Gladstone's attempt to effect a *coup d'état* by means of the elections. The election writs were issued so soon after the dissolution that many towns had hardly five days, most of them hardly eight, and the Irish, Scotch and rural electoral districts at most fourteen days for reflection. Gladstone wanted to stampede the voters, but *coup d'état* simply won't work in England and attempts to stampede rebound upon those who engineer them. In consequence, the entire mass of apathetic and wavering voters voted solidly against Gladstone.

Moreover, Gladstone had ruled in a way that directly flouted John Bull's traditional usage. There is no denying that John Bull is dull-witted enough to consider his government to be not his lord and master, but his servant, and at that the only one of his servants whom he can discharge forthwith without giving any notice. Now, if the party in office time and again allows its ministry, for very practical reasons, to spring a big surprise with theatrical effect on occasions when taxes are reduced or other financial measures instituted, it permits this sort of thing only by

way of exception in case of important legislative measures. But
Gladstone had made these legislative stage tricks the rule. His
major measures were mostly as much of a surprise to his own
party as to his opponents. These measures were practically foisted
upon the Liberals, because if they did not vote for them they
would immediately put the opposition party in power. And if the
contents of many of these measures, e.g., the Irish Church Bill
and the Irish Land Bill,[431] were for all their wretchedness an
abomination to many old liberal-conservative Whigs, so to the
whole of the party was the manner in which these bills were
forced upon it. But this was not enough for Gladstone. He had
secured the abolition of the purchase of army commissions by
appealing without the slightest need to the authority of the Crown
instead of Parliament,[432] thereby offending his own party. In
addition he had surrounded himself with a number of importu-
nate mediocrities who possessed no other talent than the ability to
make themselves needlessly obnoxious. Particular mention must be
made here of Bruce, Home Secretary, and Ayrton, the real head of
the London local government. The former was distinguished for
his rudeness and arrogance towards workers' deputations;
the latter ruled London in a wholly Prussian manner, for instance,
in the case of the attempt to suppress the right to hold public
meetings in the parks. But since such things simply can't be
done here, as is shown by the fact that the Irish immediately
held a huge mass meeting in Hyde Park[a] right under Mr. Ayrton's
nose in spite of the parks regulations, the Government suffered a
number of minor defeats and increasing unpopularity in consequence.

Finally, the secret ballot has enabled a large number of workers
who usually were politically passive to vote with impunity against
their exploiters and against the party in which they rightly see that
of the big barons of industry, namely, the Liberal Party. This is
true even where most of these barons, following the prevailing
fashion, have gone over to the Conservatives. If the Liberal Party
in England does not represent large-scale industry as opposed to
big landed property and high finance, it represents nothing at all.

Already the previous Parliament ranked below the average in its
general intellectual level. It consisted mainly of the rural gentry
and the sons of big landed proprietors, on the one hand, and of
bankers, railway directors, brewers, manufacturers and sundry
other rich upstarts, on the other; in between, a few statesmen,

---

[a] On November 3, 1872 (see this volume, pp. 294-96).— *Ed.*

jurists and professors. Quite a number of the last-named representatives of the "intellect" failed to get elected this time, so that the new Parliament represents big landed property and the money-bags even more exclusively than the preceding one. It differs, however, from the preceding one in comprising two new elements: two workers[a] and about fifty Irish HOME RULERS.[433]

As regards the workers it must be stated, to begin with, that no separate political working-class party has existed in England since the downfall of the Chartist Party[434] in the fifties. This is understandable in a country in which the working class has shared more than anywhere else in the advantages of the immense expansion of its large-scale industry. Nor could it have been otherwise in an England that ruled the world market;, and certainly not in a country where the ruling classes have set themselves the task of carrying out, parallel with other concessions, one point of the Chartists' programme, the People's Charter, after another. Of the six points of the Charter two have already become law: the secret ballot and the abolition of property qualifications for the candidates. The third, universal suffrage, has been introduced, at least approximately; the last three points are still entirely unfulfilled: annual re-elections, payment of members, and, most important, equal electoral areas.

Whenever the workers lately took part in general politics in particular organisations they did so almost exclusively as the extreme left wing of the "great Liberal Party" and in this role they were duped at each election according to all the rules of the game by the great Liberal Party. Then all of a sudden came the Reform Bill which at one blow changed the political status of the workers. In all the big cities they now form the majority of the voters and in England the Government as well as the candidates for Parliament are accustomed to court the electorate. The chairmen and secretaries of TRADES UNIONS and political working men's societies, as well as other well-known labour spokesmen who might be expected to be influential in their class, had overnight become important people. They were visited by Members of Parliament, by lords and other well-born rabble, and sympathetic enquiry was suddenly made into the wishes and needs of the working class. Questions were discussed with these "labour leaders" which formerly evoked a supercilious smile or the mere posture of which used to be condemned; and one contributed to collections for working-class purposes. It thereupon quite naturally occurred to

---

[a] A. Macdonald and T. Burt.— *Ed.*

the "labour leaders" that they should get themselves elected to Parliament, to which their high-class friends gladly agreed in general, but of course only for the purpose of frustrating as far as possible the election of workers in each particular case. Thus the matter got no further.

Nobody holds it against the "labour leaders" that they would have liked to get into Parliament. The shortest way would have been to proceed at once to form anew a strong workers' party with a definite programme, and the best political programme they could wish for was the People's Charter. But the Chartists' name was in bad odour with the bourgeoisie precisely because theirs had been an outspokenly proletarian party, and so, rather than continue the glorious tradition of the Chartists, the "labour leaders" preferred to deal with their aristocratic friends and be "respectable", which in England means acting like a *bourgeois*. Whereas under the old franchise the workers had to a certain extent been compelled to figure as the tail of the radical bourgeoisie, it was inexcusable to make them go on playing that part after the Reform Bill had opened the door of Parliament to at least sixty working-class candidates.

This was the turning point. In order to get into Parliament the "labour leaders" had recourse, in the first place, to the votes and money of the bourgeoisie and only in the second place to the votes of the workers themselves. But by doing so they ceased to be workers' candidates and turned themselves into bourgeois candidates. They did not appeal to a working-class party that still had to be formed but to the bourgeois "great Liberal Party". Among themselves they organised a mutual election assurance society, the LABOUR REPRESENTATION LEAGUE,[435] whose very slender means were derived in the main from bourgeois sources. But this was not all. The radical bourgeois has sense enough to realise that the election of workers to Parliament is becoming more and more inevitable; it is therefore in their interest to keep the prospective working-class candidates under their control and thus postpone their actual election as long as possible. For that purpose they have their Mr. *Samuel Morley*, a London millionaire, who does not mind spending a couple of thousand pounds in order, on the one hand, to be able to act as the commanding general of this sham labour general staff and, on the other, with its assistance to let himself be hailed by the masses as a friend of labour, out of gratitude for his duping the workers. And then, about a year ago, when it became ever more likely that Parliament would be dissolved, Morley called his faithful together in the London Tavern. They all appeared, the

Potters, Howells, Odgers, Haleses, Mottersheads, Cremers, Eccariuses and the rest of them—a conclave of people every one of whom had served, or at least had offered to serve, during the previous parliamentary elections, in the pay of the bourgeoisie, as an agitator for the "great Liberal Party". Under Morley's chairmanship this conclave drew up a "labour programme" to which any bourgeois could subscribe and which was to form the foundation of a mighty movement to chain the workers politically still more firmly to the bourgeoisie and, as these gentlemen thought, to get the "founders" into Parliament. Besides, dangling before their lustful eyes these founders already saw a goodly number of Morley's five-pound notes with which they expected to line their pockets before the election campaign was over. But the whole movement fell through before it had fairly started. Mr. Morley locked his safe and the founders once more disappeared from the scene.

Four weeks ago Gladstone suddenly dissolved Parliament. The inevitable "labour leaders" began to breathe again: either they would get themselves elected or they would again become well-paid itinerant preachers of the cause of the "great Liberal Party". But alas! the day appointed for the elections was so close that they were cheated out of both chances. True enough, a few did stand for Parliament; but since in England every candidate, before he can be voted upon, must contribute two hundred pounds (1,240 thalers) towards the election expenses and the workers had almost nowhere been organised for this purpose, only such of them could stand as candidates seriously as obtained this sum from the bourgeoisie, i.e., as acted *with its gracious permission*. With this the bourgeoisie had done its duty and in the elections themselves allowed them all to suffer a complete fiasco.

Only two workers got in, both miners from coal pits. This trade is very strongly organised in three big TRADES UNIONS, has considerable means at its disposal, controls an indisputed majority of the voters in some constituencies and has worked systematically for direct representation in Parliament ever since the Reform Acts were passed. The candidates put up were the secretaries of the three TRADES UNIONS. The one, Halliday, lost out in Wales; the other two came out on top: *Macdonald* in *Stafford* and *Burt* in *Morpeth*. Burt is little known outside of his constituency. Macdonald, however, betrayed the workers of his trade when, during the negotiations on the last mining law,[a] which he attended as the

---

[a] This refers to "An Act to consolidate and amend the Act relating to the Regulation of Coal Mines and certain Miners" of August 10, 1872.—*Ed.*

representative of his trade, he sanctioned an amendment which was so grossly in the interests of the capitalists that even the Government had not dared to include it in the draft.

At any rate, the ice has been broken and two workers now have seats in the most fashionable debating club of Europe, among those who have declared themselves the first gentlemen of Europe.

Alongside of them sit at least fifty Irish HOME RULERS. When the Fenian (Irish-republican) rebellion of 1867[436] had been quelled and the military leaders of the Fenians had either gradually been caught or driven to emigrate to America, the remnants of the Fenian conspiracy soon lost all importance. Violent insurrection had no prospect of success for many years, at least until such time as England would again be involved in serious difficulties abroad. Hence a legal movement remained the only possibility, and such a movement was undertaken under the banner of the HOME RULERS, who wanted the Irish to be "masters in their own house". They made the definite demand that the Imperial Parliament in London should cede to a special Irish Parliament in Dublin the right to legislate on all purely Irish questions; very wisely nothing was said meanwhile about what was to be understood as a purely Irish question. This movement, at first scoffed at by the English press, has become so powerful that Irish M.P.s of the most diverse party complexions—Conservatives and Liberals, Protestants and Catholics (Butt, who leads the movement, is himself a Protestant) and even a native-born Englishman sitting for Galway—have had to join it. For the first time since the days of O'Connell, whose REPEAL movement[437] collapsed in the general reaction about the same time as the Chartist movement, as a result of the events of 1848—he had died in 1847—a well-knit Irish party once again has entered Parliament, but under circumstances that hardly permit it constantly to compromise à la O'Connell with the Liberals or to have individual members of it sell themselves retail to Liberal governments, as after him has become the fashion.

Thus both motive forces of English political development have now entered Parliament: on the one side the workers, on the other the Irish as a well-knit national party. And even if they may hardly be expected to play a big role in this Parliament—the workers will certainly not—the elections of 1874 have indisputably ushered in a new phase in English political development.

Written on February 22, 1874

First published in *Der Volksstaat*, No. 26, March 4, 1874

Printed according to the newspaper

Frederick Engels

THE IMPERIAL MILITARY LAW [438]

I

[*Der Volksstaat,* No. 28, March 8, 1874]

It is truly comical the way the National Liberals and the men of Progress [439] are acting in the Imperial Diet with respect to §1 of the Military Law:

"The effective strength of the army in peacetime in non-commissioned officers and soldiers shall, *until the issue of further legal regulations,* amount to 401,659 men." [a]

This paragraph, they cry, is unacceptable; it cancels out the Imperial Diet's budgetary rights and turns the approval of military estimates into a mere farce!

Quite right, gentlemen! And precisely *because* this is so, *because* the article is unacceptable, you will accept it in its essentials. Why make so much fuss because you are expected to bend your knees once again, as you have so often done before with such grace?

The root of the whole wretched business is the re-organisation of the Prussian army. It engendered the glorious conflict. [440] During the whole period of the conflict, the liberal opposition put into practice Manteuffel's principle: "He who is strong gives way bravely." [441] After the Danish War their braveness in giving way increased considerably. Yet when Bismarck returned in triumph from Sadowa in 1866 and went so far as to apply for an indemnity for his previous unauthorised expenditure—then their giving way no longer knew any bounds. [442] The military estimate was immediately approved, and in Prussia what has once been

---

[a] *Entwurf eines Reichs-Militär-Gesetzes.* Engels quotes from a newspaper. Cf. *Stenographische Berichte über die Verhandlungen des Deutschen Reichstags. 2. Legislatur-Periode. 1. Session. 1874,* Vol. 3, Berlin, 1874.—*Ed.*

approved is, according to the Prussian constitution, approved forever, for "the current" (once approved) "taxes shall continue to be raised"![a]

Then came the North German Imperial Diet, which debated the constitution of the Confederation.[443] There was much talk of budgetary rights, the government proposal was declared unacceptable on the grounds of inadequate control over finances; there was much twisting and turning this way and that, and finally they swallowed the bitter pill and transferred the regulations of the Prussian constitution on the military estimate to the North German Confederation on all major points. By this measure, the strength of the army in peacetime was already raised from 200,000 to 300,000 men.

Then came the glorious war of 1870, and with it the "German Empire". Another constituent (!) Imperial Diet and a new imperial constitution.[444] More high-minded speeches and countless reservations on account of the budgetary rights. And what did the gentlemen decide?

The Imperial Constitution §60:

"The strength of the German army in peacetime is set until December 31, 1871, at one per cent of the population of 1867 and shall be provided *pro rata* in respect of the same by the individual federal states. *After this date, the strength of the army in peacetime shall be laid down by means of imperial legislation.*"[b]

One per cent of the population of 1867 means 401,000 men. This effective strength has since been prolonged by decision of the Imperial Diet until December 31, 1874.

§62: "To meet the expenditure for the whole of the German army and the institutions appertaining to the same, the Emperor shall have 225 thalers multiplied by the number of men constituting the peacetime strength of the army according to §60 placed annually at his disposal until December 31, 1871. *After December 31, 1871, these amounts shall continue to be paid to the Imperial Exchequer by the individual states of the Confederation. For the purpose of calculating the same, the peacetime effective strength provisionally laid down in §60 shall be retained until changed by imperial law.*"

That was the third time our Nationals had knelt down before the inviolable military estimate. And when Bismarck now comes and demands that the happy *provisorium* be turned into an even happier *definitivum*, these gentlemen cry out at the infringement of the budgetary rights, which they themselves have sacrificed three times in a row!

---

a Engels quotes §109 of the 1850 Prussian constitution.—*Ed.*

b Here and below cf. "Verfassung des Deutschen Reichs", *Reichs-Gesetzblatt*, No. 628, Berlin, 1871.—*Ed.*

My dear Sirs, the Nationals! Go in for "practical politics"! Make allowances for "current circumstances"! Cast your "unattainable ideals" overboard and carry on bravely "on the basis of the realities"! You have not only said A, you have already said B and C, so do not hesitate to say D! Dithering and dathering is no use here. Now is the time for another of your glorious "compromises" whereby the government gets its own way entirely and you may be pleased to get off without being kicked. Leave budgetary rights to the English, bogged down in their materialism, to the decadent French and the backward Austrians and Italians; do not cling to "foreign models", do a "genuinely German job"! Yet *if* you absolutely insist on having budgetary rights, then there's only one thing to do: next time elect only Social-Democrats!

II

[Der Volksstaat, No. 29, March 11, 1874]

That the Nationals are stupid—despite all their smart little Laskers—we have known for a long time, and they know it themselves. Yet we would not have believed that they were as stupid as Moltke thinks they are. The Master of Silence spoke for a whole hour in the Imperial Diet and yet remained the Master of Silence; for he withheld from his audience virtually all of what he himself thinks. Only on two issues did he frankly speak his mind: first, that the fatal §1 is absolutely necessary, and second, with the splendid words:

"What we have conquered with arms in half a year, we must guard with arms for half a century, lest it be snatched away from us again. Since our successful wars we have gained respect everywhere, love nowhere." [a]

Habemus confitentem reum. Here we have the guilty party brought to confession. [b] When Prussia came out with its annexation demands after Sedan,[445] it claimed: the new border is determined solely by strategic necessity; we are only taking what we absolutely need to safeguard ourselves; within this new border and after the completion of our fortifications we shall be able to look forward to any attack with equanimity.—And this is certainly true, from a purely strategic point of view.

---

[a] Here and below Engels quotes Moltke's speech in the German Imperial Diet on February 16, 1874.—*Ed.*

[b] Engels quotes from Cicero's *Oratio pro Q. Ligario.*—*Ed.*

The fortified line along the Rhine, with its three major bases, Cologne, Coblenz and Mainz, had only two faults. First, it could be circumvented by way of Strasbourg; second, it lacked an advance line of fortified points giving depth to the whole position. The annexation of Alsace-Lorraine eliminated both of these drawbacks. Strasbourg and Metz now form the first line; Cologne, Coblenz and Mainz, the second; all of them are first-class strongholds, with well advanced forts and capable of resisting modern rifled artillery; moreover, they are situated at such distances from one another as best to afford the colossal armies of today freedom of movement, on terrain extremely well-suited to defence. As long as the neutrality of Belgium is respected, a French attack may be easily confined to the narrow strip of land between Metz and the Vosges; it is also possible, if deemed desirable, to retreat behind the Rhine at the outset, thus forcing the French to weaken themselves before the first major battle by despatching troops to Metz, Strasbourg, Coblenz and Mainz. It is a position unequalled in strength throughout Europe; the Venetian Quadrilateral[446] was child's play in comparison with this almost impregnable position.

Yet precisely the capture of this almost impregnable position forces Germany, according to Moltke, to defend its conquests by arms for half a century! The strongest position does not defend itself, it needs defending; defence requires soldiers; and so the stronger the positions the more soldiers are needed, and so on, in an eternal vicious circle. In addition, the newly recovered "lost brother-tribe" in Alsace-Lorraine[a] simply does not want anything to do with Mother Germania and the French are obliged, come what may, to attempt to liberate the Alsatians and Lorrainians from the Germanic embrace at the first opportunity. The strong position is thus outweighed by the fact that Germany has forced the French to side with anyone who wishes to attack her. In other words, this strong position *contains within it the seed of a European coalition against the German Empire*. No amount of three-Emperor or two-Emperor meetings[447] and toasts alters this in the slightest, and nobody knows this better than Moltke and Bismarck; as Moltke, in fact, discreetly puts it in this melancholy sentence:

"Since our successful wars we have gained respect everywhere, love nowhere!"

So much for the *truth* according to Moltke. Now for his *fictions*.[b]

---

[a] This may be an allusion to a passage in A. Wagner's pamphlet *Elsass und Lothringen und ihre Wiedergewinnung für Deutschland,* Leipzig, 1870, p. 36.— *Ed.*

[b] In the original: "Dichtung" (poetry, fiction)—an allusion to Goethe's autobiographical work *Dichtung und Wahrheit. Aus meinem Leben.* (Truth and Poetry. From My Life).— *Ed.*

We shall waste no time discussing the sentimental sigh with which the great strategist announces his sorrow that the army is unfortunately obliged to consume such colossal sums for the good of the people, posing, as it were, as a Prussian Cincinnatus who desires nothing more ardently than to be promoted from General Field-Marshal to cabbage-farmer. Still less shall we dwell on the hackneyed theory that, on account of the poor education given to the nation by the school-master, every German must be sent to spend three years at the high-school where the sergeant-major is the professor. We are not speaking to Nationals here, as poor Moltke was obliged to do. We shall pass on at once to the staggering military tall stories that, to the universal amusement of the great General Staff, he told his astonished audience.

It is again a matter of justifying the large German armaments by the allegedly even larger ones of the French. And so Moltke discloses to the Imperial Diet that the French Government already has the right to call 1,200,000 men to arms for the regular army and over a million for the territorial army. In order to place these men, "indeed only a part of them", the French had increased their cadres. They now had 152 infantry regiments (as against 116 before the war), 9 new battalions of fusiliers, 14 new cavalry regiments, 323 batteries instead of the former 164. And "these reinforcements have not yet stopped". The peacetime effective strength of the army amounts to 40,000 men more than in 1871, now being set at 471,170. Instead of the eight army corps with which the French faced us at the outbreak of the war, France will, in future, have 18, and a nineteenth for Algiers; the national assembly is virtually imposing money for armaments on the government, the local authorities provide free training grounds and officers' messes, and build barracks at their own expense, displaying an almost violent patriotism such as could only be wished for in Germany—in short, everyone is preparing for a great war of revenge.

Now, if the French government had done everything with which Moltke credits it, it would have been doing no more than its duty. After defeats such as those of 1870, it is the first duty of the government to build up the defences of the nation sufficiently to guard against a recurrence of such disasters. Precisely the same thing happened to the Prussians in 1806; their entire obsolete army was transported free of charge to France as prisoners of war. After the war, the Prussian government did its utmost to make the whole nation capable of bearing arms; the men were only given six months' training, and despite Moltke's aversion to the militia, we have Blücher's word for it that, after the first few engagements, these "militia patteljohns",[448] as he expressed himself, were every bit as good as the battalions of the line. If the French government did likewise, if it devoted all its energies to making the whole nation capable of bearing arms in five or six years—it would only be doing its duty. But the opposite is the case. With the exception of the newly-formed battalions, squadrons and batteries, which, up to now, have only reached the level of the German organisation *of the line*, everything else exists *solely on paper*, and France is militarily weaker than ever.

"France," says Moltke, "has faithfully copied all our military institutions... Above all, they have introduced universal compulsory military service, basing it on a 20-year commitment, whereas ours is for only 12 years."

If this were really so, what does the difference between 20 years and 12 years amount to? Where is the German who would really be relieved of his militia commitment after 12 years? Is it not generally said: the 12 years only come into effect when we have enough men; until then you will have to remain in the militia for 14, 15, 16 years? And why have we exhumed the extinct Landsturm,[449] if not to render every German who was ever in uniform liable to military service for the rest of his earthly life?

In fact, however, universal compulsory military service in France is of a rather special character. France lacks precisely the semi-feudal eastern provinces of Prussia that form the real basis of the Prussian state and the new German Empire; provinces providing recruits who obey without question, and never become much wiser afterwards, as militiamen, either. The extension of universal compulsory military service to the western provinces already showed in 1849 that one man's meat is another man's poison[450]; the extension now made to the whole of Germany will create men trained in arms who will put the Moltkes and Bismarcks out of business, at the very latest by the time the twelve years so dear to Moltke are up—should the whole little scheme last that long.

In France, then, not even the basis exists for universal compulsory military service to create soldiers obedient to reaction. In France the Prussian non-commissioned officer was an obsolete concept even before the Great Revolution. Minister of War Saint-Germain introduced Prussian flogging in 1776; but the flogged soldiers shot themselves, and flogging had to be abolished the very same year. Really introduce universal compulsory military service in France, train the mass of the population in the use of arms, and where would Thiers and Mac-Mahon be? But Thiers and Mac-Mahon, although far from geniuses, are not the schoolboys Moltke makes them out to be. On paper they have set up universal compulsory military service, certainly; in reality they have been insisting with the greatest obstinacy on *five-year* service under the colours.[451] Now, everyone knows that universal compulsory military service is quite incompatible even with the Prussian three-year term of service; either one must accept a peacetime effective strength for Germany of at least 600,000 men, or one must allow men to draw lots for exemption, as does happen. What peacetime effective strength would a five-year term of service yield in France under universal compulsory military service? Almost a million; but even Moltke cannot manage to impute even half this figure to the French.

The same day Moltke impressed his audience so astonishingly, the *Kölnische Zeitung* published a "military announcement" about the French army.[a] These military announcements come to the *Kölnische Zeitung* from a very good semi-official source, and the military "swineherd" concerned will have received a first-class ticking-off for dropping this clanger at such an eminently unsuitable juncture. For the man actually tells the truth. He states that the latest official French statistics prove

"that France would scarcely be able to carry out the military goal that she has set herself in the new defence law, even by stretching her powers to the utmost".

According to him, "the strength of the army for this year has been set at 442,014 men". First, however, the Republican Gendarmerie Guard of 27,500 must be deducted from this figure; "yet according to the budget figures given for the individual services the actual strength of the army, in fact, amounts to only 389,965 men". From this must be subtracted

"*recruited* troops (the Foreign Legion and native Algerian units), administrative troop bodies and cadres of non-commissioned officers and re-enlisted soldiers, which were fixed at 120,000 men, according to the earlier authentic French figures. However, even estimating the real effective strength of the same at only 80,000 men, there only remains—with regard to recruitment—an actual army strength of 309,000 men, *consisting of five annual intakes of the first contingent and one of the second* (reserve) *contingent.* The one annual intake of the second contingent consists of 30,000 men, and thus *the annual enlisted intake of the first contingent and annual recruit intake of the same may be calculated as 55,800 men each.* If we then add to this the 30,000 men of the second contingent, *the largest annual recruitment to the French army would still be only 99,714 men*".

---

a "Die französische Heer- und Flottenstärke für 1874", *Kölnische Zeitung*, No. 48, February 17, 1874, 1st supplement, p. 3.—*Ed.*

22*

Thus: the French call up about 60,000 men annually for five years' service, making 1,200,000 men in 20 years, and if we deduct such wastage as actually occurs in the Prussian militia, a maximum of 800,000 men. Further, 30,000 men for one year's service—worthless militiamen, according to Moltke—makes 600,000 men in 20 years, after deductions for wastage 400,000 men at the most. Thus, when the French have, undisturbed for 20 years, indulged the patriotism so praised by Moltke, they will eventually be able to confront the Germans, not with Moltke's 2,200,000 men, but at the most with 800,000 trained soldiers and 400,000 militiamen, whereas Moltke can already easily mobilise one and a half million fully trained German soldiers at any time. It is against these facts that one should weigh the amusement that Moltke's speech—greeted with astonishment by the Imperial Diet—produced among the General Staff.

One must allow this to Moltke: As long as he was dealing with naive adversaries like Benedek and Louis Napoleon, he engaged in thoroughly *honest* warfare. He followed the strategic rules discovered by Napoleon I to the letter, meticulously and scrupulously. No enemy could reproach him with ever having employed surprise, secrecy, or any other vulgar ruse of war. Consequently it could be doubted whether Moltke really was a genius. This doubt has been removed since Moltke has had to fight opponents who are his equals—the geniuses of the Imperial Diet. In confrontation with the latter he has demonstrated that he can outfool his opponents if necessary. There is no longer any doubt of it: Moltke is a genius.

But what may we suppose Moltke really thinks of the French armaments? Here, too, we have a number of indications to help us.—Moltke and Bismarck were under no illusions about the fact that, just as the victories of 1866 could not fail to elicit a cry for revenge for Sadowa from official circles in France, neither could the successes of 1870 fail to impose "revenge for Sedan" on official Russia. Hitherto the obedient servant of Russia, Prussia had suddenly revealed itself as the foremost military power of Europe; such an immense shift in the European situation to the detriment of Russia was tantamount to a defeat for Russian policy; the cry for revenge rang out loud enough in Russia. Under the circumstances, Berlin thought it better to settle the matter as soon and as rapidly as possible, without leaving the Russians any time to arm. The measures taken at the time by the Prussians to prepare for war against Russia we shall perhaps discuss on another occasion; suffice it to say that, in the summer of 1872, they were more or less ready, particularly with the plan of campaign, which this time did not aim to be a "blow to the heart".[a] Then Tsar Alexander of Russia came uninvited on an imperial visit to Berlin, presenting "in an authoritative place" certain documents that brought the little plan to nothing. The renewed Holy Alliance, directed, to begin with, against Turkey, replaced for the time being the ultimately inevitable war against Russia.

This little plan naturally also provided for the eventuality of France's allying herself with Russia against Prussia. In this event, it was decided to remain on the defensive against France. And how many men were then considered sufficient to repel all French attacks?

An army of two hundred and fifty thousand men!

Written in late February-early March 1874

First published as leaders in *Der Volksstaat*, Nos. 28 and 29, March 8 and 11, 1874

Printed according to the newspaper

Published in English for the first time

---

[a] This expression ("Stoss ins Herz") was used by the Prussian Ambassador to Italy Charles George Usedom in his despatch of June 17, 1866 concerning joint actions by Prussia and Italy in the war against Austria.— *Ed.*

Frederick Engels

[SUPPLEMENT TO THE PREFACE OF 1870 FOR *THE PEASANT WAR IN GERMANY*] [452]

The preceding passage [a] was written over four years ago. It is still valid today. What was true after Sadowa and the partition of Germany is being reconfirmed after Sedan and the establishment of the Holy German Empire of the Prussian nation. [453] So little do "world-shaking" grand performances of state [454] in the realm of so-called high politics change the direction of the historical movement.

What these grand performances of state are able to do, however, is to accelerate this movement. And in this respect, the authors of the above-mentioned "world-shaking events" have had involuntary successes, which they themselves surely find most undesirable but which, all the same, for better or for worse, they have to accept.

The war of 1866 shook the old Prussia to its foundations. After 1848 it had a hard time bringing the rebellious industrial element—bourgeois as well as proletarian—of the Western provinces, [b] under the old discipline again; still, this had been accomplished, and the interests of the Junkers of the Eastern provinces [c] again became, next to those of the army, the dominant interests in the state. In 1866 almost all Northwest Germany became Prussian. Apart from the irreparable moral injury the Prussian crown by the grace of God suffered owing to its having swallowed three other crowns by the grace of God, [455] the centre of

---

[a] F. Engels, "Preface to the Second Edition of 1870 of *The Peasant War in Germany*".— *Ed.*

[b] Rhine Province and Westphalia.— *Ed.*

[c] Prussia, Brandenburg, Pomerania, Poznan, Silesia and Saxony.— *Ed.*

gravity in the monarchy now shifted considerably to the west. The five million Rhinelanders and Westphalians were reinforced, first, by the four million Germans annexed directly, and then by the six million annexed indirectly, through the North German Confederation.[456] And in 1870 there were further added the eight million Southwest Germans,[457] so that in the "New Empire", the fourteen and a half million old Prussians (from the six East Elbian provinces, including, besides, two million Poles) were confronted by some twenty-five million who had long outgrown the old Prussian Junker-feudalism. In this way the very victories of the Prussian army shifted the entire basis of the Prussian state structure; the Junker domination was becoming increasingly intolerable even for the government. At the same time, however, the extremely rapid industrial development caused the struggle between bourgeois and worker to supersede the struggle between Junker and bourgeois, so that internally also the social foundations of the old state underwent a complete transformation. The basic condition for the monarchy, which had been slowly rotting since 1840, was the struggle between nobility and bourgeoisie, in which the monarchy held the balance. From the moment when it became necessary instead of protecting the nobility against the onrush of the bourgeoisie to protect all the propertied classes against the onrush of the working class, the old, absolute monarchy had to go over completely to the form of state expressly devised for this purpose: *the Bonapartist monarchy*. This transition of Prussia to Bonapartism I have already discussed elsewhere (*The Housing Question*, Part 2, pp. 26 et seq.[a]). What I did not have to stress there, but what is very essential here, is that this transition was the *greatest progress* made by Prussia since 1848, so much had Prussia lagged behind in modern development. It was, to be sure, still a semi-feudal state, whereas Bonapartism is, at any rate, a modern form of state which presupposes the abolition of feudalism. Hence, Prussia has had to begin to get rid of its numerous survivals of feudalism, to sacrifice Junkerdom as such. This, naturally, is being done in the mildest possible form and to the favourite tune of: *Immer langsam voran!*[b] Take the notorious district regulations.[458] It abolishes the feudal privileges of the individual Junker in relation to his estate only to restore them as privileges of the totality of big landowners in relation to the entire

---

a See this volume, pp. 363-64.— *Ed.*

b "Always slowly forward"—the refrain of the folk song *Die Krähwinkler Landwehr* ("Landwehr from the sleepy village") which appeared in 1813.— *Ed.*

district. The substance remains, being merely translated from the feudal into the bourgeois dialect. The old Prussian Junker is being forcibly transformed into something resembling an English SQUIRE, and need not have offered so much resistance because the one is as stupid as the other.

Thus it has been the peculiar fate of Prussia to complete its bourgeois revolution—began in 1808 to 1813 and advanced to some extent in 1848—in the pleasant form of Bonapartism at the end of this century. If all goes well and the world remains nice and quiet, and all of us live long enough, we may see—perhaps in 1900—that the government of Prussia will actually have abolished all feudal institutions and that Prussia will finally have arrived at the point where France stood in 1792.

The abolition of feudalism, expressed positively, means the establishment of bourgeois conditions. As the privileges of the nobility fall, legislation becomes more and more bourgeois. And here we come to the crux of the relation of the German bourgeoisie to the government. We have seen that the government is *compelled* to introduce these slow and petty reforms. However, in its dealings with the bourgeoisie it portrays each of these small concessions as a *sacrifice* made to the bourgeois, as a concession wrung from the crown with the greatest difficulty, for which they, the bourgeois, ought in return to concede something to the government. And the bourgeois, though the true state of affairs is fairly clear to them, allow themselves to be fooled. This is the origin of the tacit agreement that forms the mute basis of all Reichstag and Prussian Chamber debates in Berlin. On the one hand, the government reforms the laws at a snail's pace in the interest of the bourgeoisie, removes the feudal obstacles to industry as well as those which arose from the multiplicity of small states, establishes uniform coinage, weights and measures, freedom of occupation, etc., puts Germany's labour power at the unrestricted disposal of capital by granting freedom of movement, and favours trade and swindling. On the other hand, the bourgeoisie leaves all actual political power in the hands of the government, votes taxes, loans and soldiers, and helps to frame all new reform laws in a way as to sustain the full force and effect of the old police power over undesirable elements. The bourgeoisie buys gradual social emancipation at the price of the immediate renunciation of political power. Naturally, the chief reason why such an agreement is acceptable to the bourgeoisie is not fear of the government but fear of the proletariat.

However wretched a figure our bourgeoisie may cut in the

political field, it cannot be denied that as far as industry and commerce are concerned it is at last doing its duty. The impetuous growth of industry and commerce referred to in the preface to the second edition[a] has since proceeded with still greater vigour. What has taken place in this respect since 1869 in the Rhine-Westphalian industrial region is quite unprecedented for Germany and reminds one of the upsurge in the English manufacturing districts at the beginning of this century. The same thing holds true for Saxony and Upper Silesia, Berlin, Hanover and the seaports. At last we have world trade, a really big industry, a really modern bourgeoisie. But in return we have also had a real crash,[459] and have likewise got a real, powerful proletariat.

The future historian will attach much less importance in the history of Germany from 1869 to 1874 to the roar of battle at Spichern, Mars-la-Tour[460] and Sedan, and everything connected therewith, than to the unpretentious, quiet but constantly progressing development of the German proletariat. As early as 1870, the German workers were subjected to a severe test: the Bonapartist war provocation and its natural effect, the general national enthusiasm in Germany. The German socialist workers did not allow themselves to be confused for a single moment. They did not show any hint of national chauvinism. They kept their heads in the midst of the wildest jubilation over the victory, demanding "an equitable peace with the French republic and no annexations". Not even the state of siege could silence them. No battle glory, no talk of German "imperial magnificence", produced any effect on them; liberation of the entire European proletariat was still their sole aim. One may say with assurance that in no other country have the workers hitherto been put to so hard a test and acquitted themselves so splendidly.

The state of siege during the war was followed by trials for high treason, for *lèse majesté*, for insulting officials, and by the ever increasing police chicanery of peacetime. The *Volksstaat* usually had three or four editors in prison at one time and the other papers too. Every party speaker of any distinction had to stand trial at least once a year and was almost always convicted. Deportations, confiscations and the breaking-up of meetings proceeded in rapid succession, thick as hail. All in vain. The place of every man arrested or deported was at once filled by another; for every broken-up meeting two new ones were called, and thus the arbitrary power of the police was worn down in one place

---

[a] See present edition, Vol. 21, pp. 96-97.— *Ed.*

after the other by endurance and strict conformity to the law. All this persecution had the opposite effect to that intended. Far from breaking the workers' party or even bending it, it served only to enlist new recruits and consolidated the organisation. In their struggle with the authorities and also individual bourgeois, the workers showed themselves intellectually and morally superior, and proved, particularly in their conflicts with the so-called "providers of work", the employers, that they, the workers, were now the educated class and the capitalists were the ignoramuses. Moreover, they conduct the fight for the most part with a sense of humour, which is the best proof of how sure they are of their cause and how conscious of their superiority. A struggle thus conducted on historically prepared soil must yield good results. The successes of the January elections stand unique in the history of the modern workers' movement [461] and the astonishment they caused throughout Europe was fully justified.

The German workers have two important advantages over those of the rest of Europe. First, they belong to the most theoretical people of Europe, and have retained the sense of theory which the so-called "educated" classes of Germany have almost completely lost. Without German philosophy, particularly that of Hegel, German scientific socialism—the only scientific socialism that has ever existed—would never have come into being. Without the workers' sense of theory this scientific socialism would never have entered their flesh and blood as much as is the case. What an incalculable advantage this is may be seen, on the one hand, from the indifference to theory which is one of the main reasons why the English working-class movement crawls along so slowly in spite of the splendid organisation of the individual trades, and on the other hand, from the mischief and confusion wrought by Proudhonism in its original form among the French and Belgians, and in the form further caricatured by Bakunin among the Spaniards and Italians.

The second advantage is that, chronologically speaking, the Germans were about the last to come into the workers' movement. Just as German theoretical socialism will never forget that it rests on the shoulders of Saint-Simon, Fourier and Owen—three men who, in spite of all their fantastic notions and all their utopianism, stand among the most eminent thinkers of all time and whose genius anticipated innumerable things the correctness of which is now being scientifically proved by us—so the practical workers' movement in Germany ought never to forget that it developed on the shoulders of the English and French movements, that it was able simply to utilise their dearly paid experience and could now avoid their mistakes, which were then mostly unavoidable. Where would we be now without the precedent of the English TRADE UNIONS and French workers' political struggles, and especially without the gigantic impulse of the Paris Commune?

It must be said to the credit of the German workers that they have exploited the advantages of their situation with rare understanding. For the first time since a workers' movement has existed, the struggle is being waged pursuant to its three sides—the theoretical, the political and the economico-practical (resistance to the capitalists)—in harmony and in its interconnections, and in a systematic way. It is precisely in this, as it were concentric, attack that the strength and invincibility of the German movement lies.

Due to this advantageous situation, on the one hand, and to the insular peculiarities of the English and the forcible suppression of the French movement, on the other, the German workers stand for the moment in the vanguard of the proletarian struggle. How long events will allow them to occupy this place of honour, cannot be foretold. But let us hope that as long as they occupy it they will fill it fittingly. This demands redoubled efforts in every field of struggle and agitation. In particular, it will be the duty of the leaders to gain an ever clearer insight into all theoretical questions, to free themselves more and more from the influence of traditional phrases inherited from the old world outlook, and constantly to keep in mind that socialism, since it has become a science, demands that it be pursued as a science, that is, that it be studied. The task will be to spread with increased zeal among the masses of workers the ever more lucid understanding thus acquired and to knit together ever more strongly the organisation both of the party and of the trade unions. Even if the votes cast for the Socialists in January have formed quite a decent army, they are still far from constituting the majority of the German working class; encouraging as are the successes of propaganda among the rural population, infinitely more remains to be done in this field. Hence, we must make it a point not to slacken the struggle, and to wrest from the enemy one town, one constituency after the other; the main point, however, is to safeguard the true international spirit, which allows no patriotic chauvinism to arise and which readily welcomes every new advance of the proletarian movement, no matter from which nation it comes. If the German workers progress in this way, they will not be marching exactly at the head of the movement—it is not at all in the interest of this movement that the workers of any particular country should march at its head—but will occupy an honourable place in the battle line; they will stand armed for battle when either unexpectedly grave trials or momentous events demand of them added courage, added determination and energy.

Frederick Engels

London, July 1, 1874

First published in: Friedrich Engels, *Der Deutsche Bauernkrieg*, Leipzig, 1875   Printed according to the book

FROM THE PREPARATORY MATERIALS

Karl Marx

[NOTES ON THE CONDITION OF THE REFUGEES FROM THE COMMUNE] [462]

460 (foreigners) arrested on the fall of the Commune. 5 months on the pontoons. Order of nonsuit.

Disembarked at Newhaven; had not received any food on the boat. They were released scarcely clothed, without money, told to apply to their respective consuls for help in getting out of their plight.

Made their way, partly on foot, from Newhaven to London.

Written in early November 1871

First published, in Russian, in *Kommunist*, No. 2, Moscow, 1971

Printed according to the manuscript

Translated from the French

Published in English for the first time

Karl Marx

AMERICAN SPLIT[463]

MAY 1872[a]

15 October 1871 was published in the journal of *Woodhull* (a banker's woman, free-lover, and general humbug) and *Claflin* (her sister in the same line) an *Appeal of Section No. 12* (founded by *Woodhull,* and almost exclusively consisting of middle-class humbugs and worn-out Yankee swindlers in the Reform business; *Section IX* is founded by Miss Claflin).

An Appeal of Section XII (to the *English-speaking citizens* of the United States) (d.d. August 30, 1871, signed by *W. West*, Secretary of Section 12).*

The following are extracts from this APPEAL:

* "The object of the International is simply to emancipate the labourer, male and female, by the conquest of political power." "It involves, first, the *Political Equality* and *Social Freedom* of men and women alike." "*Political Equality* means the personal participation of each in the preparation, administration and execution of the laws by which all are governed." "*Social Freedom* means *absolute immunity* from impertinent intrusion in all affairs of exclusively personal concernment, such as religious belief, the *sexual relation, habits of dress*, etc."

"The proposition involves, secondly, the *establishment of a Universal Government*... Of course, the abolition of ... even *differences of language are embraced in the programme*." *[b]

* "Section No. 12" invites the formation of "English-speaking sections" in the United States upon this programme.*

That the whole organisation for PLACE-HUNTING and ELECTORAL PURPOSES:

* "If practicable, *for the convenience of political action*, there should be a section formed *in every primary election district.*"

---

a The heading was given by Engels on a separate sheet of paper.— *Ed.*

b *Woodhull & Claflin's Weekly*, No. 19 (71), September 23, 1871.— *Ed.*

"There must ultimately be instituted *in every town a Municipal Committee or Council*, corresponding with the Common Councils; in every State a State Committee or Council, corresponding with the State legislature, and in the Nation a National Committee or Council, corresponding with the United States National Congress."

"The work of the International includes nothing less than the institution, *within existing forms, of another form of Government*, which shall supersede them all."*

This APPEAL—and the formation thereupon OF ALL SORTS OF MIDDLE-CLASS HUMBUG SECTIONS, FREE-LOVERS, SPIRITISTS, SPIRITIST SHAKERS,[464] etc.—gave rise to a split in which SECTION I (German) of the OLD COUNCIL demanded the expulsion of SECTION 12, the non-admittance of sections in which at least two-thirds of the membership are not workers.

First, 5 dissidents set up, on *November 19, 1871*, a separate COUNCIL consisting of Yankees, Frenchmen, Germans, etc.

In "Woodhull's, etc., Journal" of 18 November 1871, SECTION 12 (West as SECRETARY) protests against SECTION I, and states there, among other things:

* "The simple truth is that Political Equality and Social Freedom for all alike, of all races, both sexes, and *every condition*, are necessary precursors of the more radical reforms demanded by the International."

"*The extension of equal citizenship to women, the world over, must **precede** any general change in the subsisting relations of capital and labour.*" "Section 12 would also remonstrate against the vain assumption, running all through the Protest (of Section I) under review, that the International Working Men's Association *is an organisation of the working classes...*"*

Previously, already in *"Woodhull's Journal" of October 21, 1871*, SECTION 12 ASSERTS

* "*the independent right of each section* to have, hold and *give expression to its own constructions of said proceedings of the several Congresses, and the Rules and Regulations* (!) of said General Council, *each section being alone responsible for its own action*".*

"Woodhull's, etc., Journal". 25 November 1871. Protest of SECTION 12 against *"ADDRESS OF SECTION I"* (the same address that you[a] have reprinted in Italian etc. papers).

* "It is not true that the 'common understanding or agreement' of the working men of all countries, of itself, standing alone, constitutes the Association... The statement that the emancipation of the working classes can only be conquered by themselves, cannot be denied, *yet it is true so far as it describes the fact that the working classes cannot be emancipated against their will.*"

3 December 1871. The new Federal Council for North America formally* constituted (Yankees, Germans, Frenchmen).

---

[a] Engels.— *Ed.*

4 DECEMBER. The OLD COUNCIL (10 Ward Hotel) denounces the swindlers in a CIRCULAR to all the Sections of the International in the UNITED STATES. It says, among other things:

"In the COMMITTEE (the old CENTRAL COMMITTEE), which is supposed to be a defence against all reformist swindles, the majority finally consisted of reformists and benefactors of the nation who had already almost sunk into oblivion... Thus it came about that the people who preached the gospel of free love sat most fraternally beside those who wanted to bless the whole world with one common language—supporters of LAND COOPERATIVES, *spiritualists*, atheists and deists—each trying to ride his own particular hobby-horse. Particularly Section 12 Woodhull... The first step that has to be taken here, in order to advance the movement, is to organise and, at the same time, to stimulate the revolutionary element, which lies in the conflict of interests of capitalist and worker...

"The delegates of sections 1, 4, 5, 7, 8, 11, 16, 21, 23, 24, 25 and other sections, having seen that all efforts to direct this nonsense were in vain, therefore decided, after the old CENTRAL COMMITTEE had been adjourned *sine die* (3 DECEMBER 1871) to found a new one, *which consists of actual workers* and from which all those who can only confuse matters must be excluded" (*"New-Yorker Demokrat", 9 DECEMBER 1871*).

West ELECTED AS DELEGATE for the new COUNCIL.

It should be noted that the new COUNCIL very quickly filled with delegates, mostly from new sections, founded by SECTION 9 (Claflin) and SECTION 12 (Woodhull), RIFFRAFF, besides mostly so weak that they were too few in numbers to nominate the necessary OFFICERS.

In the meantime the *Woodhull Journal* (West, etc.) lied shamelessly asserting that they were certain of the support of the GENERAL COUNCIL.

Both COUNCILS appealed to the General Council. Various sections, such as the French SECTION 10 (New York) and all the Irish sections recalled their delegates from both COUNCILS pending a decision of the General Council. About the lies of the *Woodhull Journal,* ARTICLE in the *issue of December 2* under the title "*Section 12 Sustained.— The Decision of the General Council*". (That was the decision of the General Council of November 5, 1871, in which the CENTRAL COMMITTEE, on the contrary, makes a stand against the ambition of SECTION 12, *as Yankees,* to replace it.)

Resolutions of the General Council of March 5 and 12, 1872.[a]

The fate of the Internationals in the UNITED STATES depended on that. (Incidentally, note the humbug cult of myself which the *Woodhull Journal* has boosted to date.)

As soon as the resolutions came to New York, the people of the

---

[a] A slip of the pen in Marx's manuscript: 1871. See this volume, pp. 124-26.— *Ed.*

COUNTER COMMITTEE took up their old policy. Previously they had discussed the original SPLIT in the most disreputable bourgeois papers of New York. Now they did the same against the General Council (presenting the whole thing as a struggle between the French and the Germans, between socialism and communism) amid jubilant cries of all organs hostile to the workers.

Very characteristic marginal notes in "*Woodhull's Journal*", *4 May, 1872* on the resolutions of the GENERAL COUNCIL.

Before that, "*Woodhull's Journal*", *16 DECEMBER 1871*:

* "No new test of membership, as that two-thirds or any part of a section shall be *wages-slaves, as if it were a crime to be free,* was required." *

(That is to say, in the composition of the COUNTER COUNCIL.) "*Woodhull's Journal*", *4 MAY 1872*.

* "...In this decree of the General Council its authors presume to recommend that in future no *American* section be admitted, of which two-thirds at least are not wages-slaves. *Must they be politically* slaves also? As well one thing as the other..."
"The intrusion into the International Working Men's Association of *bogus reformers, middle-class quacks* and *trading politicians* is mostly to be feared from *that class of citizens* who have nothing better to depend upon *than the proceeds of wages-slavery.*" *

Meanwhile, as the PRESIDENTIAL ELECTIONS approached, the cloven foot came into the open—namely that the International should assist in the ELECTION of—*Madame Woodhull!*

A propos. Before that: "*Woodhull's etc. Journal*", *2 MARCH 1872* in an ARTICLE SIGNED W. *West* one reads:

* "The issue of the 'Appeal' of Section 12 to the English-speaking citizens of the United States in August last, *was a new departure in the history of the International, and has resulted in the recognition by the General Council of Political Equality and Social Freedom of both sexes alike,* and of the essential *political* character of the work *before us.*" * a

"*Woodhull's etc. Journal*", *2 MARCH 1872*. Under the title "*The Coming Combination Convention*" it says:

* "There is a proposition under consideration by the representatives of the various reformatory elements of the country looking to a grand consolidated convention to be held in this city in May next, during Anniversary week... Indeed, if this convention in May acts wisely, who can say that *the fragments of the defunct* [...] *Democratic Party* [may not come to it ... that every individual who loves equality and justice, and who prices truth and principle more than the Republican or the Democratic party] b will come out from them and take part in the proposed convention... *Everybody of Radicals* everywhere in the United States should, as soon as the call is made public, take immediate steps to be represented in it." *

---

a W. West, *To the Members of Section Twelve of the I.W.A.*—*Ed.*

b Omission in the text. The text in square brackets restored from the newspaper.— *Ed.*

(A propos. The *Woodhull Journal*—I cannot find the date—comforts the SPIRITIST SECTIONS by arguing that they can tell the General Council to go to the devil.)

"Woodhull etc. Journal", April 6, 1872:

* "Every day the evidence, that the convention called for the 9 and 10 May, by representatives of the various reforms ... is to be a spontaneous uprising of the people, increases in volume." *

In addition, the NATIONAL WOMEN SUFFRAGE ASSOCIATION demands:

* "This Convention will ... *consider the nominations for President and Vice-President of the United States*." *

Ditto under the title:

* "*The Party of the People to secure and maintain human rights, to be inaugurated in the United States, in May, 1872*." *

The appeal SIGNED, first, by *Victoria C. Woodhull*, then *Theodore H. Banks, R. W. Hume* (FELLOWS, AND Banks one of the founders, of the COUNTER COUNCIL). In this appeal: The CONVENTION WILL CONSIDER "NOMINATIONS FOR PRESIDENT AND VICE-PRESIDENT OF THE UNITED STATES". Especially invited

* "Labor, Land, Peace and Temperance reformers, and *Internationals* and *Women Suffragists*—including all the various Suffrage Associations—as well as *all others*, who believe the time has come when the principles of eternal justice and human equality should be carried into our halls of legislation." *

"Woodhull etc. Weekly", 13 APRIL 1872. The presidency DODGE is becoming more and more obvious. This time for a change

* "*Internationals*, and other Labor Reformers—the friends of peace, temperance and education, and by all those who believe that the time has come to carry the principles of true morality *and religion* into the State House, the Court and the Market Place".*

Under the title: "*The Party of the People etc.*" a new appeal, as ever with *Victoria C. Woodhull* at the head; in the retinue, the chief scoundrels of the COUNTER COUNCIL, *Th. H. Banks, R. W. Hume, G. R. Allen, William West, G. W. Maddox* (later chairman of the Apollo meeting), *J. T. Elliott* (the English secretary of the COUNTER COUNCIL), *T. Millot* (delegate of the FRENCH SECTION II).

"Woodhull etc. Weekly" (it is not called a journal), 20 APRIL, 1872. Continuation of the same DODGE.

The lists grow, the *duce*, as always, V. C. Woodhull (there are "HONORABLES"[a] among them).

---

[a] Members of the US Congress.— *Ed.*

"*Woodhull etc. Weekly*", *27 April, 1872.* Continuation of the same advertising. (Begins to publish lists of delegates.)

"*Woodhull etc. Weekly*", MAY *4, 1872.* Continuation of the DODGE. (Continual printing of the same and larger lists.)

"*Woodhull etc. Weekly*", *25* MAY, *1872.* At last (9, 10, 11 MAY APOLLO HALL SCANDAL) Woodhull FOR PRESIDENT OF UNITED STATES, F. Douglass FOR VICE-president. (*Maddox* OF COUNTER COUNCIL, chairman of the CONVENTION, FIRST DAY.) LAUGHING-STOCK OF NEW YORK AND UNITED STATES.

Other officials of the COUNTER COUNCIL: *John T. Elliott*, VICE-president, *G. R. Allen*, SECRETARY (and MEMBER OF COMMITTEE ON RESOLUTIONS AND PLATFORM). In the latter COMMITTEE: *Th. H. Banks* (one of the 5 founders of the COUNTER COUNCIL of November 19, 1871). MRS. *Maria Huleck* also on a COMMITTEE. In CENTRAL NATIONAL COMMITTEE AT *New York* for the UNITED STATES figured *G. R. Allen, Th. H. Banks* (next to COLONEL Blood, MEMBER of SECTION 12, and junior husband of Victoria), *I. B. Davis.*

BREAK-UP OF THE COUNTER COUNCIL.

SECTION 2 (FRENCH) removes *Laugrand* as DELEGATE (previously FRENCH SECRETARY of the COUNTER COUNCIL). Accuse the fellows

* "of using the organisation for political purposes, and as a sort of adjunct to the free-love branch of the women's rights' party... Citizen *Millot* stated * (he proposed the WITHDRAWAL of SECTION 2 from the COUNTER COUNCIL, [the proposal] WAS accepted) *upon the introduction of the Resolution that only 3 sections—9 (Claflin), 12 (Woodhull) and 35—were represented in the Apollo Hall 'odds and ends' Convention, by scheming men for political purposes, and that the delegation in the said convention pretending to act for the Federal Council was a spurious one and self-appointed." *

(*But the* FEDERAL COUNTER COUNCIL *DID NOT REPUDIATE THEM.*) ("*The World*", MAY *13, 1872*).

SECTION *6* (German) recalls its delegate E. Grosse (ex-private secretary of H. von Schweitzer) and declares that it will withdraw unless the COUNTER COUNCIL accepts all the resolutions of the GENERAL COUNCIL.

Le Socialiste (New York), May 18, 1872.

Section 2, of New York, at a sitting on Sunday, May 12, passed the following resolutions:

"Considering, etc., etc.,

"That Section 2 has reason to believe that the Jewellers' Union refuses to affiliate with the International, and that in the meantime a delegate continues to represent it at the Federal Council;

"That Section 2 has reasons to believe that other delegates represent *fictitious sections or sections consisting* of 6 or 8 members;

"Section 2 declares: An enquiry is necessary etc..."

"Considering that, *rightly or wrongly*, Section 12 has been suspended by the General Council acting in virtue of the power vested in it by the Basle Congress; Section 2 protests against keeping at the Federal Council of a delegate from Section 12 with a deciding vote.

"Finally, considering that the International is *an Association of workers having for its goal the liberation of workers by the workers themselves*:

"Section 2 protests against *the admission of sections composed mostly of non-workers*." [a]

Another resolution of SECTION *2.*

"Section 2,

"Fully recognising in principle the electoral rights for women, *in the face of insinuations of citizen Woodhull*, at a meeting in the Apollo Hall, *leading the public to believe that the International supports the candidates of that Assembly,*

"Declares:

"That, for the present, the International neither can nor has any right to be taken in tow by any political party in America; for not one of them represents the aspirations of workers, and not one of them has the economic emancipation of workers as its programme and goal.

"Section 2 thinks:

"That our sole object must be, for the present, the organisation and greater solidarity of the working class in America."

Under the title "Internationaux, prenez garde à vous!", the same issue of the *Socialiste* has this to say, among other things:

"The International is not and cannot be persecuted in America; the politicians, far from aiming at its destruction, only think of using it as a lever or point of support for the triumph of their personal views. Once the International lets itself be drawn to that path, it will cease to be *an Association of Workers* and become a ring of politicians.

"The signal of alarm was given a long time ago; but the convention at Apollo Hall, nominating, *in the name of the International*, Madame Woodhull as candidate for the presidency, must henceforth open the eyes of even the least clairvoyant. Internationals of America, take care!"

* "*The World*", *May 20, 1872.*

Sitting of Counter Council, 19 May 1872. Maddox (of Apollo Hall) in the Chair. *Withdrawal of 8 delegates (for 8 sections) (French and German).*

"*Herald*", *May 20, 1872**

brings the same session UNDER THE HEADING:

* "*The French* [*are*] *insulted and leave in disgust... Terrible slang used. But 1,500 Members in the United States. A Split among the Internationals of London. The Woodhull Crowd Victorious.*"

Resolution of General Council of 28 May 1872, by which—in reply to the questions put by the German Section of St. Louis and the

---

[a] This and the following extracts in the manuscript are in French.— *Ed.*

French Section of * New Orleans—* the old Council (*Provisional Federal Council for the United States*) *is alone recognised.**

Written after May 28, 1872

First published, in Russian, in *Generalny Sovet Pervogo Internatsionala. 1871-1872*, Moscow, 1965

Reproduced from the manuscript

Translated from the German and French

Published in English in full for the first time

Karl Marx

[EXTRACTS FROM THE MINUTES OF THE GENERAL COUNCIL FOR JUNE 1870-APRIL 1872][465]

COUNCIL SITTINGS

Sitting of Council June 28, 1870
Marx proposes Brussels for next General Council etc. Resolution to be sent to all sections.
Carried.
Hales announces reconsideration.
July 5. Continuation of debate. Debate adjourned.
July 12. Marx: "to write to the sections to ask them to consider the advisability of removing the Council from London. If they were favourable to a removal then Brussels should be proposed" (with mandates should the delegates come) (instruction to delegates). Only 3 vote for Hales amendment.
Mayence Congress Programme.
Sitting of Aug. 2.
Serraillier read letter from Belgium in which Amsterdam was proposed as the seat of the Congress. It would be near to all except Italy and Spain. Belgium wants the Council to remain at London, declines its transference to Brussels.
Debate on Congress.
Marx against the Brussels proposal for Amsterdam. All the sections ought to be written to and asked whether they would consent to a postponement. Instead of a Congress a Conference might perhaps be held as in 1865.
Jung against Congress. Swiss called to arms (60,000 men).
Hales (seconded by Eccarius) proposed that the sections should be appealed to to state whether they were in favour of postponement and if so to give the Council power to fix the date of convocation. (*Carried.*)
Marx: if the sections agreed, a conference might be held here, but he was for an appeal.
Aug. 9. Spaniards propose Barcelona as seat of the Congress.
Aug. 16. Jung communicated letter from the German Swiss

Committee agreeing to the postponement of Congress and leaving it to the Council to appoint time and place; to the same effect letter of the German Social Democratic Party. Both against removal of the Council from London.

Aug. 23. Serraillier read letter from the Belgian Council in which the postponement of the Congress agreed to. Ditto from Romance Geneva Committee, Council to remain at London.

Postponement of Congress resolved.

Sitting of Nov. 22 (documents found on the Bonaparte gvt).

"On the eve of the Plebiscite Ollivier had written to all the towns of France that the leaders of the International must be arrested else the voting could not be satisfactorily proceeded with."

Sitting of Nov. 29. Marx communicated that our Brunswick friends had been brought back from Loetzen in chains, to be tried for high treason. To frighten the middle class the police organs published long articles to tell the people these men were allies of the International Association—subvert everything, establish Universal Republic.

1871

March 14. Robin moves to convoke conference of delegates. (Rejected.)

July 25. Engels proposes convocation of conference, seconded by Robin.

In this month Archbishop *of Malines established* a Catholic Workingmen's International Association with a view to counteract the I.W.A.

[1872]

Feb. 20. Art. Utin.[a]

12 March. Resolutions on United States.[b]

16 April. Cochrane. Fawcett.[c]

Drawn up after August 27, 1872   Reproduced from the manuscript

First published, in Russian, in *Gaagsky kongress Pervogo Internatsionala, 2-7 sentyabrya 1872 g. Protokoly i dokumenty*, Moscow, 1970

---

[a] K. Marx and F. Engels, *Declaration of the General Council of the International Working Men's Association* (see this volume, pp. 77-78).— *Ed.*

[b] K. Marx, *Resolutions on the Split in the United States' Federation Passed by the General Council of the I.W.A. in Its Sittings of 5th and 12th March, 1872* (see this volume, pp. 124-26).— *Ed.*

[c] K. Marx, *Declaration of the General Council of the International Working Men's Association Concerning Cochrane's Speech in the House of Commons* (see this volume, pp. 140-45).— *Ed.*

Mandate issued to Marx by New York Section No. 1 for him to take part
in the Hague Congress

Vollmacht.

Die Breslauer Mitglieder der Internationalen Arbeiter-Association beauftragen Herrn Friedrich Engels in London mit ihrer Vertretung auf dem Congreß der Internationalen Arbeiter-Association am 2ten Septbr. dieses Jahres im Haag.

Breslau den 19ten August 1872.

Heinrich Oehme
Paul Bock
Hermann Kriemichen

Mandate issued to Engels by the Breslau Section for him to take part
in the Hague Congress

This is to certify that Mr. Fredr. Engels of London is duly elected to represent section six of the I. W. A of New York North America in the General Congress which is to be held at Hague from the 2 of Peptember 1872.

New York August 8th 1872.

76

pr. T. Bertrand
Chairman pro temp.

John Stock Secretary

To certify the genuineness of the above credentials I affix hereunto the seal of the Federal Council for North America and my signature

New York, August 9th, 1872.

F. Bolte, Gnl. Sy.
of the F. C. I. W. A. N. a.

Mandate issued to Engels by New York Section No. 6 for him to take part in the Hague Congress

NOTES
AND
INDEXES

NOTES

1 The original text of the *Rules of the International Working Men's Association* was written by Marx in English in October 1864 and approved by the Central Council (see present edition, Vol. 20, pp. 14-16). In 1867, an English text of the *Rules* and *Administrative Regulations* was printed in London, with the changes introduced at the Geneva and Lausanne congresses (ibid., pp. 441-46). The next congresses—in Brussels (1868) and Basle (1869)—adopted a number of resolutions which were additions to the Rules. However, the texts of the Rules then in circulation did not contain these additions and amendments and this led to inaccurate translations in a number of countries. The London Conference adopted the resolution, moved by Marx, on a new and authentic edition of the Rules and Administrative Regulations in English, German and French, and decided that in future all translations into other languages should be approved by the General Council. On Engels' proposition, a special meeting of the General Council of October 7, 1871 appointed a commission to prepare the new edition of the General Rules and resolutions of the conference. It included Karl Marx, Hermann Jung and Auguste Serraillier. On October 24, the General Council approved the work done on the new edition of the Rules.

The text of the Rules and Administrative Regulations was revised in accordance with the resolutions of all congresses and the London (1871) Conference of the International, the clauses which had become invalid being excluded. An "Appendix", which substantiated in detail all amendments and additions, was written anew. At the General Council meeting of October 31 Engels reported that the Rules and Administrative Regulations were almost ready for the press but that it was impossible to print them in three languages simultaneously as was decided at the conference. In view of that he proposed to publish them in each language separately. Marx and Engels directly supervised the translation of the Rules and Regulations into German and French.

The *London Conference* of the International was held from September 17 to 23, 1871. The Franco-Prussian war of 1870-71 and reaction in Europe, which intensified after the fall of the Paris Commune, frustrated the convocation of the regular congress in 1871. But the need to define the tasks of the working-class movement, to draw general conclusions from the experience of the Commune and the struggle against the sectarian elements, especially the Bakuninists, demanded collective decisions. Under those conditions, the General Council, headed by Marx and Engels, considered it expedient, having received the agreement of the majority of federations to hold a closed conference of the International's delegates.

The most important decision of the London Conference was formulated in Resolution IX, "Political Action of the Working Class", which declared the need to found, in each country, an independent proletarian party whose aim would be the conquest of political power by the working class. Other Conference decisions covered a wide range of tactical and organisational issues: the combination of various forms of proletarian struggle, legal and illegal, peaceful and non-peaceful; the alliance of the working class and the peasantry; the organisation of trade unions under the leadership of the International; the struggle against sectarianism and conspiracies, etc.   p. 3

2 The Geneva Congress resolution, cited below, on the statistical inquiry into the situation of the working classes reproduced almost word for word the relevant passages in the "Instructions for the Delegates of the Provisional General Council. The Different Questions" written by Marx on the eve of the Congress (see present edition, Vol. 20, p. 186).   p. 13

3 Jules Gottraux, a Swiss-born subject of Great Britain and a member of the International, was detained by the French police on the French-Swiss frontier on September 30, 1866, when he was returning to London from Switzerland. The police confiscated letters, printed matter, and other material entrusted to him by the International's leaders in Geneva for delivery to the General Council. The seized documents included the preliminary report on the work of the Geneva Congress which had been drawn up by Council member Joseph Card and published in French in Geneva as a pamphlet. (Later, this gave rise to rumours that the French authorities had confiscated the Congress minutes, which in fact had by that time been brought to London by Hermann Jung.) The General Council decided to lodge a complaint about this wanton act and to use the fact publicly to expose the regime of the Second Empire. At the beginning of December, the Council addressed the British Foreign Secretary, requesting him to make a corresponding démarche to the French government, which forced the French authorities to return, on December 21, the materials taken from Gottraux.   p. 15

4 The French edition of the Provisional Rules, issued by the Administration of the Paris Section (Henri Louis Tolain, Ernest Edouard Fribourg, Charles Mathieu Limousin) at the end of 1864-beginning of 1865, interpreted some principles of the Rules in a Proudhonist spirit and distorted them in translation.   p. 15

5 When Marx edited the General Rules of 1871 he deleted the following sentence: "They hold it the duty of a man to claim the rights of a man and a citizen, not only for himself, but for every man, who does his duty", previously included on the insistence of the other members of the Sub-Committee (see Marx's letter to Engels of November 4, 1864, present edition, Vol. 42, pp. 16-18).   p. 17

6 Marx has in mind the resolution of the Basle Congress of 1869 which approved the decision of the General Council of September 24, 1867 to abolish the post of President of the General Council.   p. 17

7 The question of Gustave Durand was considered at a special meeting of the General Council on October 7, 1871, at which Durand's correspondence with the French police officers was produced. Durand was instructed to participate in the London Conference of the International with espionage as an ulterior

motive and also to become a member of the General Council. The resolution on Durand's expulsion was drawn up and submitted to the meeting by Engels. He also translated it into French and Italian. p. 21

8 The *Federal Chamber of Working Men's Societies*—an association of trade unions and other workers' societies in Paris—was formed on the International's initiative in 1869. The Chamber organised aid for workers on strike and maintained close ties with the International. p. 21

9 This letter was published in English for the first time in *The General Council of the First International. 1870-1871. Minutes*, Progress Publishers, Moscow, 1967. p. 22

10 On October 7, 1871, the General Council, in accordance with the London Conference decision, instructed Marx to draw up a declaration to the effect that the International Working Men's Association had nothing to do with the so-called Nechayev conspiracy. The text of the declaration was approved at the General Council meeting on October 16, 1871. The declaration is written on the form of the General Council together with Marx's letter to John Hales of October 14, 1871.

In 1869 Nechayev established contacts with Bakunin and developed activities for the purpose of founding in Russia a secret society, Narodnaya Rasprava (People's Judgment). The study circles organised by Nechayev advocated anarchist ideas of "absolute destruction". Sharp criticism of the Tsarist regime and the call to wage resolute struggle against it attracted revolutionary-minded students and middle-class intellectuals (*raznochintsy*) to the Nechayev organisation. Nechayev received from Bakunin the credentials of the European Revolutionary Union and used them to pass himself off as a representative of the International, thereby misleading the members of the organisation.

When Nechayev's organisation was broken up and its members tried in St. Petersburg in the summer of 1871, his adventurist methods were made public—blackmail, intimidation, deception and the like. The bourgeois press made use of the trial to denigrate the International, which was, in fact, not associated with Nechayev in any way.

The General Council's declaration was translated into French and Italian by Engels. It was published in German in *Der Volksstaat*, No. 88, November 1, 1871 (signed by Marx as Corresponding Secretary for Germany and Russia); in French, in *Qui vive!* No. 14, October 18, and in *L'Égalité*, No. 21, November 5; in Italian, in *Gazzettino Rosa*, No. 306, November 3, *L'Eguaglianza*, No. 18, November 12 and in *La Plebe*, No. 122, October 19, 1871; in Russian, in *Недѣля*, No. 16, October 19 (31), *С.-Петербургскія вѣдомости*, No. 292, October 23 (November 4), *Биржевые вѣдомости*, No. 290, October 23 (November 4), *Донъ*, No. 83, November 4(16), 1871; in English, in *The Daily News* (between October 16 and 30, 1871) (the Institute of Marxism-Leninism does not have the issue at its disposal; the fact of publication is known from the Russian newspaper *Недѣля*, No. 16, October 19 (31), 1871). p. 23

11 The *Resolution on the Rules of the French Section of 1871* was written by Marx and adopted unanimously at the General Council meeting of October 17, 1871.

The French Section of 1871 was formed in London in September 1871 by French refugees, mostly petty-bourgeois intellectuals. It also included proletarians, among them former Communards Albert Félix Theisz, Augustin Avrial and Zéphyrin Camélinat. The spy Durand insinuated himself into the Section but was soon exposed by the General Council. The leaders of the

Section established close contacts with Bakunin's followers in Switzerland and joined them in attacking the organisational principles of the International. The Rules of the French Section of 1871 were submitted to the General Council at its special meeting on October 16 and referred to the Council's commission for examination. At the General Council meeting of October 17 Marx made a report on the Rules and submitted this Resolution, which is extant as a manuscript in the hand of Auguste Serraillier, Secretary for France.

The Resolution was published in English for the first time in *The General Council of the First International. 1870-1871. Minutes,* Progress Publishers, Moscow, 1967.   p. 24

[12] The resolution adopted on the recommendation of the London Conference on September 22, 1871 provided for the establishment of a Federal Committee (Council) for England (see present edition, Vol. 22, p. 428). Until then Marx was of the opinion that the General Council, better than any other body, could function as the leading organ of the International Working Men's Association in Britain, since it promoted the education of the British workers in an internationalist spirit and helped them to overcome the influence of bourgeois ideology. However, the General Council's vastly extended activities in 1871 made Marx consider it advisable to set up a special Federal Council for England.   p. 26

[13] The minutes of the General Council meeting of October 17, 1871 have only a brief entry on Engels' speech: "Citizen *Engels* reported the progress of the Association in Italy and Spain." Engels handed his own record of the speech, as in other cases, to Secretary of the General Council John Hales for publication in *The Eastern Post.* The manuscript is not extant.   p. 28

[14] A secret conference of the delegates from the local Spanish federations of the International Working Men's Association took place in Valencia on September 10-18, 1871. It adopted the Rules of the Spanish branch of the International and model rules for local federations and sections. The conference decisions bore the stamp of anarchist and anarcho-syndicalist ideas (it adopted the Bakuninist thesis of abstention from the political struggle, formation of the International's organisations according to the trade principle and others). However, the Spanish Federal Council elected at the conference included several General Council supporters (Francisco Mora, Pablo Iglesias, José Mesa).
                                                                                              p. 29

[15] Engels wrote this statement in connection with a letter from Alexander Baillie Cochrane, a British Conservative M. P., published in *The Times,* No. 27208, October 31, 1871. Cochrane reproduced allegations by the bourgeois French and British papers and libelled the International by ascribing to it the documents of Bakunin's Alliance of Socialist Democracy. Engels read out the statement at the General Council meeting of October 31, and it was approved. Since the *Times* editors refused to publish it, the statement appeared in *The Eastern Post.*   p. 31

[16] See Note 6.   p. 31

[17] A reference to the excerpt from the General Council's confidential circular letter to the Federal Council of Romance Switzerland published by Oscar Testut in the police collection of the International's documents early in 1871. Written by Marx, the circular letter (see present edition, Vol. 21, pp. 84-91) was sent to all sections. The excerpt published by Testut had been taken from the copy seized by the French police; this copy was signed by Eugène Dupont

as Corresponding Secretary for France (see O. Testut, *L'Internationale*, 3rd edition, Paris-Versailles, 1871, pp. 237-38).   p. 32

[18] The *Customs Union* (Zollverein) of German states (it initially included 18 states) was founded in 1834 to establish a common customs frontier, and was headed by Prussia. By the 1840s, the Union embraced all the German states except Austria, the Hanseatic towns (Bremen, Lübeck, Hamburg) and some small states. Formed under the pressure for an all-German market, the Customs Union subsequently promoted Germany's political unification, completed in 1871.
                                    p. 35

[19] A reference to the consequences of the Anglo-Chinese war of 1840-42, known as the First Opium War. The British imposed the Nanking Treaty on China in 1842, the first of a series of treaties concluded by the Western powers with China, which reduced it to the level of a semi-colony. The Nanking Treaty made China open five of its ports to British commerce—Canton, Shanghai, Amoy, Ningpo and Foochow.   p. 35

[20] The French Section rejected the General Council's Resolution on the Rules of the French Section of 1871 (see Note 11). It attacked the General Council and demanded that all the principles of the General Rules concerning the Council's rights and functions should be completely revised. The Section's reply signed by Augustin Avrial was discussed by the General Council on November 7, 1871. Auguste Serraillier, Corresponding Secretary for France, made a report on this matter and also submitted a resolution written by Marx which was adopted unanimously. The stand taken by the General Council prompted such working-class leaders as Albert Félix Theisz, Avrial, Zéphyrin Camélinat and other former Communards to dissociate themselves from the Section. By the beginning of 1872 the French Section split up into several hostile groups. A new section of French émigrés supporting the General Council was set up in London.

This resolution is extant in two manuscripts, one in Marx's hand, the other in Pierre Louis Delahaye's and signed by Serraillier (this being presumably the final version of the resolution). The second manuscript has a note pencilled on it by Engels: "Conseil Général 7 nov. 71. Section française de Londres."

It was published in English for the first time in *The General Council of the First International. 1871-1872. Minutes*, Progress Publishers, Moscow, 1968.
                                    p. 37

[21] A reference to the Sixth half-yearly congress of the Belgian Federation of the International Working Men's Association which took place in Brussels on December 25 and 26, 1870. Alfred Herman was coopted into the General Council on Engels' proposal at the meeting of July 18, 1871. He was recommended for the post of Corresponding Secretary for Belgium by the Belgian Federal Council.   p. 41

[22] The minutes of the General Council meeting of November 7, 1871 have the following record of Engels' report: "Citizen *Engels* reported that he had a great deal of information from the sections in Italy, which he would hand over to the Secretary for the weekly report in the *Eastern Post*. Garibaldi's letter, in which he had finally broken with Mazzini, had exercised great influence in Italy and as (soon as) it (had) been received, it would be included in the report." Engels' manuscript is not extant.   p. 43

[23] The regular (twelfth) congress of the Italian workers' societies (mainly mutual aid societies), most of which were under Mazzini's influence, was held in Rome

from November 1 to 6, 1871. A split followed when the delegates from the International's sections in Naples and Girgenti (Cafiero, G. de Montel and A. Tucci) opposed the Mazzinists' principles. For details about the congress see this volume, pp. 46-48.   p. 43

24 A reference to the main stages in the revolutionary activity of Garibaldi and his comrades-in-arms: the independence struggle of the republics of Rio Grande and Uruguay (South America) in the 1830s-40s; the 1848-49 revolution in Italy, in particular, the heroic defence of the Roman Republic in 1849; the military operations against the Austrians in Northern Italy in 1859 and the "expedition of the Thousand" to Sicily in 1860, which led to the unification of Italy. In 1870-71 Garibaldi headed the Italian and international volunteers who fought in the Franco-Prussian war on the side of the French Republic.   p. 43

25 The minutes of the General Council meeting of November 14, 1871 have the following entry on Engels' report: "Citizen *Engels* gave a full report of the Working Men's Congress which was held in Rome. The whole affair was a sham organised by Mazzini to revive his waning influence, and had been a complete failure." Engels' manuscript is not extant.   p. 46

26 The Declaration was intended for the defence of Wilhelm Bracke and other members of the Committee (administrative board) of the German Social-Democratic Workers' Party (Eisenach) at the trial which took place in Brunswick on November 23-25, 1871. The Committee members were arrested in September 1870 as a result of the internationalist position taken by the Party during the Franco-Prussian war; they were accused of "infringement upon public order". The main accusation was their involvement with the International Working Men's Association. But the Social-Democratic Workers' Party at its inaugural congress in Eisenach in 1869 took into account the German legislation on the workers' unions and, while supporting the International's programme, did not join it officially; the legislation, however, did not prohibit German citizens' individual membership of foreign societies. The accused were sentenced to a few months' imprisonment.   p. 50

27 In accordance with the organisational structure of the Eisenach Party, the seat of the Committee was named at its annual meeting, it being in turn one of the main German cities; the Council was elected from the members of the local organisation. Brunswick was the first seat of the Committee. At the time the Declaration was written the newly elected Council had been based in Hamburg (since August 1871).   p. 50

28 The Statement was published in English for the first time in *The General Council of the First International. 1871-1872. Minutes*, Progress Publishers, Moscow, 1968.   p. 52

29 The *Universal Republican League*—an international organisation founded in London in April 1871. Its leaders included bourgeois radical Charles Bradlaugh, trade-unionist George Odger, petty-bourgeois journalists Victor Le Lubez, Pierre Vésinier and others. The League put forward a mixed programme in which democratic demands (the nationalisation of the land, universal suffrage) were placed side by side with a call for the establishment of a world federative republic. The League's activists claimed leadership in the international working-class movement and, together with other anti-Marxist elements, waged a struggle against the General Council of the International.   p. 52

30 Engels is referring to the Bakuninists who, within the International, set up branches of their secret Alliance of Socialist Democracy in a number of Spanish cities in 1870-71 and tried to seize the leadership in the Spanish Federal Council.

The letters, sent by Engels to the Spanish Federal Council, after the London Conference, in particular that of November 8, 1871, are not extant.   p. 53

31 Engels wrote this letter in reply to the publication by *Il Proletario Italiano*, on November 23, 1871, of the Bakuninists' charges against the General Council of the International and the London Conference decisions, allegedly made by the Turin workers.

The letter appeared in *Il Proletario Italiano* (see M. Nettlau, *Bakunin e l'Internazionale in Italia dal 1864 al 1872*, Geneva, 1928, p. 269).

The letter was published in English for the first time in *The General Council of the First International. 1871-1872. Minutes*, Progress Publishers, Moscow, 1968.

p. 54

32 A reference to the congress of the Bakuninist Jura Federation in Sonvillier on November 12, 1871 which adopted the "Circulaire à toutes les fédérations de l'Association Internationale des Travailleurs".

The Sonvillier circular countered the decisions of the London Conference of the International with the anarchist dogmas on political indifferentism and complete autonomy of sections; it also calumniated the General Council of the International. The Bakuninists suggested that all federations should demand an immediate congress to revise the General Rules of the International and to condemn the General Council's actions.   p. 55

33 This document was drawn up by Engels in reply to a letter from Enrico Bignami, a leader of the International's section in Lodi, dated November 14, 1871. The latter informed the Council that sections of the International had been formed in Ferrara and other Italian towns and asked it to send the documents authorising certain citizens of Romagna, Giuseppe Boriani among them, to form new sections.

This document was published in English for the first time in *The General Council of the First International. 1871-1872. Minutes*, Progress Publishers, Moscow, 1968.   p. 56

34 This report, made by Engels at the General Council meeting of December 5, 1871 and submitted in written form for insertion in the newspaper report on the meeting, was not recorded in the Minutes. Engels' manuscript is not extant.

p. 57

35 On September 10, 1869, the Basle Congress of the International (September 6-11) adopted the resolution, confirming the one already adopted by the Brussels Congress (1868), in favour of the collective ownership of the land.

p. 57

36 This item was published in *La Plebe* in the section "The Latest News" and began with the words: "A member of the International writes us from London". The item, apparently, is part of Engels' letter to the editor of the paper, Enrico Bignami, which is not extant.   p. 59

37 This Declaration of the General Council, written by Engels on December 5, 1871 was sent to *La Roma del Popolo* with the covering letter of December 6 and, according to Engels' note in the rough manuscript, between December 5 and 7 also to a number of other Italian newspapers.

The Declaration was published in English for the first time in *The General Council of the First International. 1871-1872. Minutes*, Progress Publishers, Moscow, 1968.   p. 60

38 The Brussels Congress of the International (September 5-13, 1868) refused to accept the invitation of the League of Peace and Freedom to participate officially in its forthcoming congress in Berne. The resolution of the Brussels Congress recommended members of the International to attend it only in an individual capacity.

The *League of Peace and Freedom* was a pacifist organisation set up in 1867 with the active participation of Victor Hugo, Giuseppe Garibaldi and other democrats. Voicing the anti-militarist sentiments of the masses, the League's leaders did not reveal the social sources of wars. In 1867-68 Bakunin took an active part in the work of the League; under his influence it tried to use the working-class movement and the International Working Men's Association for its own purposes. At the League's second congress which took place in Berne between September 21 and 25, 1868, Bakunin moved a resolution on the necessity for the economic and social "equalisation of classes". Having failed to win support at the congress, Bakunin and his followers withdrew from the League and that same year set up the Alliance of Socialist Democracy.
                                                                              p. 61

39 This letter was occasioned by the slanderous attacks the publisher of *The National Reformer*, radical Charles Bradlaugh made against Marx in his public lecture in London on December 11, 1871, and also in his letter to *The Eastern Post* (published on December 16). At the General Council meeting of December 19, Marx drew attention to the close connection of Bradlaugh's attacks with the campaign of persecution the bourgeois politicians and the press waged against the International, which especially intensified after the Paris Commune and the publication of the General Council's address *The Civil War in France*; he pointed out Bradlaugh's affinity with the venal journalists in France.   p. 62

40 Engels wrote this article for *Der Volksstaat*, in reply to the circular to all sections of the International (see Note 32) adopted at the Sonvillier Congress and directed against the decisions of the London Conference. In his letters to Wilhelm Liebknecht of January 3 and 18, 1872, Engels wrote that he intended to have that article distributed (in translation and as copies of *Der Volksstaat* carrying it) in the countries which had become centres of Bakuninist propaganda, namely, Belgium, Italy and Spain.

This article was published in English for the first time in Marx, Engels, Lenin, *Anarchism and Anarcho-Syndicalism*, Progress Publishers, Moscow, 1972.
                                                                              p. 64

41 *Versailles* was the seat of the Thiers Government which in the spring of 1871 fought and defeated the Paris Commune, killing many thousands of Communards.

Brunswick criminal court—a district court where the members of the Committee (administrative board) of the Social-Democratic Workers' Party, arrested by the Prussian authorities, were tried in November 1871 (see Note 26).   p. 66

42 *Black Cabinet* (Cabinet noir), or *Black Bureau*—a secret institution, established at the postal departments in France, Prussia, Austria and several other states to inspect private correspondence. It existed since the time of the absolute monarchies in Europe.   p. 67

[43] Engels wrote this letter after a campaign of slander against the International in the newspaper *Il Libero Pensiero*, edited by Luigi Stefanoni.

To undermine the influence of the International Working Men's Association, Stefanoni presented himself in November 1871 as the initiator of the "Universal Society of Rationalists", allegedly destined to put into practice the principles of the International but without "its negative features". He put forward a utopian idea of redeeming land from landowners and setting up agricultural colonies as a universal means to solve the social question. His programme was rejected by the Italian workers and his scheme for founding the Society of Rationalists was never implemented.

Engels nicknamed the rationalists "prebendaries" (from the Latin word "praebenda"—possessions of the Catholic Church accumulated through gifts and legacies), alluding to their plan of solving the social problem by creating a land fund out of donations.

This letter was published in English for the first time in *The General Council of the First International. 1871-1872. Minutes*, Progress Publishers, Moscow, 1968.

p. 74

[44] A reference to the *Communist League*, the first international communist organisation of the proletariat, formed under the leadership of Marx and Engels in London early in June 1847, as a result of the reorganisation of the League of the Just (a secret association of workers and artisans that appeared in the 1830s and had communities in Germany, France, Switzerland and England). The programme and organisational principles of the Communist League were drawn up with the direct participation of Marx and Engels. The League's members took an active part in the bourgeois-democratic revolution in Germany in 1848-49. In the summer of 1850, disagreements arose in the League between the supporters of Marx and Engels and the Willich-Schapper sectarian group which tried to impose on the League the adventurist tactic of embarking on revolution immediately, irrespective of the actual situation. The discord resulted in a split within the League. Owing to police persecution and arrests of League members in May 1851, the activities of the Communist League as an organisation in Germany practically ceased. On November 17, 1852, on a motion by Marx, the London District announced the dissolution of the League.

p. 75

[45] The *Cologne Communist trial* (October 4-November 12, 1852) was organised and stage-managed by the Prussian government. The defendants were members of the Communist League, arrested in the spring of 1851 on charges of "treasonable plotting". The forged documents and false evidence presented by the police authorities were not only designed to secure the conviction of the defendants but also to compromise the proletarian organisation as a whole. Seven of the defendants were sentenced to imprisonment in a fortress for terms ranging from three to six years. The dishonest tactics of the Prussian police state to combat the international working-class movement were exposed by Engels in his article "The Late Trial in Cologne" and, in greater detail, by Marx in his pamphlet *Revelations Concerning the Communist Trial in Cologne* (see present edition, Vol. 11).

p. 75

[46] The rough draft of this document was written by Engels on the letter from Arturo Guardiola of January 23, 1872, in which he reported that the Barcelona commercial employees had formed a section of the International and asked for addresses of similar sections in other countries. Engels communicated this news at the General Council meeting of January 30.

p. 76

[47] This Declaration was approved at the General Council meeting of February 20, 1872. A copy of the Declaration in Hermann Jung's hand is extant.　　p. 77

[48] At the General Council meeting of March 5, Marx set forth the main points of the circular and stated that the great value of the document consisted in the "historical development of the principles and policy of the Association".

Fictitious Splits in the International exposed to the international proletariat the genuine aims of the anarchists and their ties with the circles alien to the working class cause; it described Bakunin's Alliance as a sect hostile to the workers' movement.

Fictitious Splits in the International was published late in May 1872 as a pamphlet in French under the signature of all the General Council members and sent to all the federations of the International. It was published in English for the first time in *The General Council of the First International. 1871-1872. Minutes*, Progress Publishers, Moscow, 1968.　　p. 79

[49] In reply to the slanders heaped on the International by the bourgeois press after the publication of the General Council's address *The Civil War in France*, Marx and Engels sent to *The Times*, *The Standard*, *The Daily News* and other English newspapers a number of statements and letters on behalf of the General Council in defence of the Paris Commune, explaining the stand taken by the International (see present edition, Vol. 22, pp. 364-68, 370-71).

　　p. 80

[50] In June 1871, on Marx's initiative, the General Council began to raise funds and distributed them among the Communards who had fled from France to England to escape persecution by the Versailles government; it also helped to find jobs for many of them. In July, the General Council formed a special Relief Committee which included Marx, Engels, Jung and others. In September 1871 the Communards themselves formed a Committee to provide direct aid for the refugees, but the General Council and its individual members (Marx, Engels, Dupont, Jung and Stepney among them) continued to collect money and find jobs for them.　　p. 80

[51] Since the late 1850s, the nine-hour working day had become a major demand of the English workers. In May 1871, a big strike of the building and engineering workers headed by the Nine Hours' League, started in Newcastle. Burnett, the Chairman of the League, requested the General Council of the International to help resist the importation of strike breakers. The General Council sent its two members, Georg Eccarius and James Cohn, to the Continent to explain the importance of the struggle in Newcastle. Thus the importation was checked. In October the strike in Newcastle ended with victory for the workers; a 54-hour working week was introduced.　　p. 80

[52] After the defeat of the Paris Commune, a number of its leaders who had emigrated to England were coopted into the General Council of the International: Antoine Arnaud, André Bastelica, Frédéric Cournet, Pierre Louis Delahaye, Leo Frankel, Margueritte, Constant Martin, Benjamin Le Moussu, Gabriel Ranvier, Vitale Regis, Charles Rochat, Joséf Rozwadowski, Albert Félix Theisz, Edouard Vaillant, Walery Wróblewski.　　p. 80

[53] On Engels' motion, the General Council resolved to convene a closed conference of the International in London. Since that time Marx and Engels had done a great deal of organisational and theoretical work to prepare it: they outlined its programme and drafted resolutions, which had been previously discussed at the General Council meetings.　　p. 80

54 The General Council's decision to hold the next congress in Mainz instead of Paris was taken on May 17, 1870. On July 12, acting on Marx's proposal, the General Council approved the draft programme of the Mainz Congress (see present edition, Vol. 21, pp. 143-44). p. 83

55 At the General Council meeting of June 28, 1870 Marx proposed that all sections of the Association should discuss the question of moving the seat of the General Council so as to avoid creating privileged conditions for workers of one particular country. The proposition had been discussed at several meetings of the Council and then adopted; on July 14, 1870 Marx wrote "Confidential Communication to All Sections" (see present edition, Vol. 21, p. 142). The sections, however, opposed the transfer of the Council's seat, considering London the most suitable place for the leading body of the International Working Men's Association. p. 83

56 On September 25-29, 1865, a preliminary conference was held in London in lieu of a scheduled congress in Brussels. The General Council's decision to postpone the congress and convene the conference was taken at Marx's insistence, who held that local organisations of the International were yet not strong enough either ideologically or organisationally. p. 83

57 On May 26, 1871, Jules Favre, Foreign Minister of France, sent a circular dispatch to French diplomatic representatives abroad, which ordered them to press European governments for arrest and extradition of the Commune refugees as common criminals.

Minister of Justice Dufaure tabled a law, drafted by a specially appointed commission of the National Assembly, under which affiliation with the International was punishable by imprisonment. The law was passed on March 14, 1872. p. 83

58 On June 7, 1871, Bismarck sent a message to Schweinitz, German Ambassador to Vienna, recommending that he and the Austrian government co-ordinate action against the workers' organisations. On June 17, Bismarck sent Beust, the Chancellor of Austria-Hungary, a memorandum on the measures taken in Germany and France against the International. Emperor of Germany William I and Emperor of Austria Francis Joseph met in Gastein in August 1871 and in September in Salzburg for a special discussion of measures to be taken against the International.

The Italian government joined the general anti-International campaign: in August 1871, it banned the Naples section and began persecuting members of the International, Theodor Cuno in particular (see this volume, pp. 151-52).

The Spanish government, too, adopted repressive measures against the workers' organisations and the sections of the International in the spring and summer of 1871; this forced Francisco Mora, Tomás Morago and Anselmo Lorenzo, members of the Spanish Federal Council, to emigrate temporarily to Lisbon. p. 83

59 In Austria-Hungary Oberwinder, Andreas Scheu, Most and Papst, active members of the Austrian Social-Democratic Party, were arrested and brought to trial for high treason in July 1870; some workers' societies were likewise persecuted.

On September 9, 1870, Wilhelm Bracke, Leonhard Bornhorst, Samuel Spier and other members of the Brunswick Committee of the German Social-Democratic Workers' Party were arrested and brought to trial for the publication, on September 5, of a manifesto against the militarist plans of the Prussian government (see Note 26).

In the latter half of December 1870, Wilhelm Liebknecht and August Bebel were arrested for their opposition to the predatory war; they were charged with conspiring to commit treason and, in March 1872, sentenced to a two-year term of imprisonment in the fortress.   p. 84

60 On August 12, 1871, the Central Committee of the North American Federation of the International Working Men's Association decided against sending its delegates to the London Conference and to spend the money at its disposal on the assistance to the Commune refugees. A special commission was appointed to draw up the report for the Conference. A memorandum describing the conditions of the workers in the USA and difficulties in the work of the Committee itself was unanimously adopted by the Central Committee on August 20; it was then sent to the General Council. Marx briefly reported on it at the sitting of the Conference on September 22, 1871.   p. 84

61 The London Conference, on Marx's proposal, instructed the General Council to form a Federal Council (Committee) for England (see Note 12). The London Federal Council was founded on October 25, 1871. It consisted of representatives of the London sections and trade unions affiliated with the International. After a number of local sections joined the Federation in March 1872, it began to function as the British Federal Council. From the very beginning, a group of reformists, headed by John Hales, were among its leaders. The reformists sought to oppose the British Council to the General Council and did not recognise its internationalist stand; they also refused to recognise the decisions of the Hague Congress. Some members of the British Council (Samuel Vickery, William Harrison Riley, George Milner, Friedrich Lessner among them) came out against the reformists and actively supported Marx and Engels. In early December 1872, a split occurred in the Federal Council; the part of it that still supported the decisions of the Hague Congress constituted the British Federal Council. Marx and Engels actively assisted it in its organisational work. The reformists failed in their attempts to lead the British Federation of the International.   p. 84

62 This refers to Resolution IX of the London Conference of 1871—"Political Action of the Working Class"—which stressed the necessity to organise a workers' political party as an indispensable condition for the victory of the socialist revolution and the attainment of its ultimate aim: a classless society (see this volume, pp. 105-06).   p. 84

63 This refers to Resolution II of the London Conference of 1871—"Designations of National Councils, etc."—which barred various sectarian, conspiratorial and such like groups from the International (see present edition, Vol. 22, pp. 423-24).   p. 84

64 On the *League of Peace and Freedom* and the resolution moved by Bakunin at its congress in Berne in September 1868 see Note 38.   p. 85

65 Johann Philipp Becker, a member of the Provisional Committee of the Alliance, sent the Alliance's Programme and the Rules to the General Council on November 29, 1868. Both these documents were read out at its meeting on December 15. On that day Marx forwarded them to Engels asking for his comments. On December 18 Engels complied with this request and on December 22 Marx's draft reply with Engels' remarks taken into account, was read out by Hermann Jung at the General Council meeting and adopted, with

slight changes, as a circular letter. The circular letter was sent out as a confidential communication; it was first published by Marx and Engels in the *Fictitious Splits in the International*.   p. 85

66 This circular was written in reply to the second application of the Alliance's Central Bureau (of February 27, 1869) to the General Council with the statement that it was ready to dissolve the international Alliance, provided the General Council approved its programme and admitted its local sections into the International. The circular was written by Marx who obtained Engels' approval; it was accepted unanimously by the General Council on March 9, 1869 (see present edition, Vol. 21, pp. 45-46). The document was first published by Marx and Engels in the *Fictitious Splits in the International*.
                                                                                                 p. 87

67 On the *Nechayev trial* see Note 10.   p. 90

68 The *League of Public Welfare* (*Ligue* (universelle) *du bien public*)—an association of bourgeois pacifists of various social strata and political convictions. It was founded in 1863 by the French journalist Edmond Potonié and later merged with the League of Peace and Freedom (see Note 38).   p. 90

69 "*Factory workers*", i.e. those who worked for La Fabrique, the production of watches and jewellery in Geneva and its environs carried on in large and small manufactory-type workshops; also home-workers in these trades.   p. 91

70 This refers to the *Manifeste aux Sections de l'Internationale* written by the Bakuninists James Guillaume and Gaspard Blanc and published in Neuchâtel as a supplement to the newspaper *La Solidarité*, No. 22, September 5, 1870.
                                                                                                 p. 93

71 The capitulation of the French army at Sedan, on September 2, 1870 (see Note 293) and the fall of the French Empire that followed sparked off revolutionary workers' uprisings in a number of French cities. In Lyons, Marseilles and Toulouse, people formed their own government bodies, communes, which, despite the short terms of their existence, carried out important revolutionary measures. On September 15 Bakunin arrived at Lyons and tried to take over the leadership of the movement and implement his anarchistic programme. On September 28 the anarchists attempted a coup d'état, which failed.   p. 93

72 In a letter of August 10, 1871 to Hermann Jung, Corresponding Secretary for Switzerland, Nikolai Zhukovsky, Secretary of the Bakuninist section in Geneva named "The Alliance of Socialist Democracy. Central Section", sent the resolution of August 6 on the voluntary dissolution of the section.
                                                                                                 p. 93

73 In April 1870, Paul Robin, a follower of Bakunin, proposed to the Paris Federal Council that it should recognise the Federal Committee formed by the anarchists at a congress in La Chaux-de-Fonds as the Romance Federal Committee and announce in *La Marseillaise* that its supporters were only *bona fide* members of the International. The Paris Council refused to examine the matter as coming within the competence of the General Council.   p. 94

74 This refers to Resolution XVII of the London Conference of 1871—"Split in the French-Speaking Part of Switzerland" (Vol. 22, pp. 430-31).

It was published in abridged form in the separate edition of the resolutions of the Conference and in full in *L'Égalité*, No. 20, October 21, 1871 (see present edition, Vol. 22, pp. 419-22).   p. 94

[75] The *Section of Propaganda and Revolutionary Socialist Action* was founded in Geneva on September 6, 1871 in place of the Geneva section, Alliance of Socialist Democracy, dissolved in August. It was organised by its former members, Nikolai Zhukovsky, Charles Perron and others and some French refugees, Jules Guesde and Benoît Malon in particular. On September 8, October 4 and 20, 1871, the section applied to the General Council with the request to be admitted into the International; the General Council refused to comply because it had received a negative opinion on the matter from the Romance Federal Committee in Geneva.   p. 94

[76] On June 28, 1870, the General Council adopted the resolution moved by Marx to let the Romance Federal Council keep its name and suggested that the Chaux-de-Fonds Council should adopt another name. The London Conference confirmed the resolution of June 28, 1870, and recommended that the Jura sections should join the Romance Federation and, in case this was impossible, should be called the Jura Federation.   p. 96

[77] The conflict between the members of the old Lyons Section (Adrien Schettel among them), close to the French Republicans, and the group headed by the Bakuninist Albert Richard was discussed by the General Council on March 8, 1870. The Council adopted Marx's report on this question which declared all the accusations of the parties in the conflict to be without the least foundation and based on a mode of procedure aimed at exciting personal animosities and producing divisions in the ranks of the International Working Men's Association (see present edition, Vol. 21, pp. 108-09). The General Council decision, signed by the Corresponding Secretary for France, Eugène Dupont, was published in *L'Internationale*, No. 63, March 27, 1870.   p. 96

[78] The public meeting to celebrate the anniversary of the June 1848 insurrection of the Paris workers was held on June 29, 1868 in London. Félix Pyat, described in certain newspapers as a leader of the International, made a speech in which he called for terrorist acts against Napoleon III. At its meeting of July 7 the General Council resolved, on Marx's proposal, to disavow Pyat's behaviour (see present edition, Vol. 21, p. 7). When the resolution appeared in the press, a split took place in the London French Section, of which Pyat was a member. Eugène Dupont, Hermann Jung, Paul Lafargue and other proletarian members withdrew from it. A group of petty-bourgeois French refugees, headed by Pyat, lost ties with the International but retained its name and repeatedly supported anti-proletarian elements in opposition to Marx's line in the General Council.

The question of official dissociation from this group was raised in the General Council more than once. In the spring of 1870 when a third trial against members of the International, charged with a conspiracy to assassinate Napoleon III, was in preparation in France, this dissociation became all the more necessary since the incriminatory material included documents of the so-called French Section in London, in which the International was identified with a secret republican society, headed by Pyat. This prompted Marx to draw up a resolution to the effect that the International had nothing to do with that group, and it was adopted by the General Council on May 10, 1870.   p. 97

[79] The reference is to Resolution 2 in the section "Special Votes of the Conference" which declared that the German working men had done their internationalist duty during the Franco-German war of 1870-71 (see present edition, Vol. 22, p. 428).   p. 100

[80] At a meeting of the Geneva sections of December 2, 1871, Benoît Malon, Gustave Lefrançais and François Charles Ostyn proposed a resolution directed against the General Council and the London Conference decisions and based on the French translation of the International's Rules that had been distorted in a Proudhonist spirit. The meeting, however, rejected the proposal and adopted a resolution approving the decisions of the London Conference and expressing solidarity with the General Council. The draft of Malon's anarchist resolution was published in *La Révolution Sociale*, No. 7, December 7, 1871.

p. 103

[81] The *Icarians* were the followers of Etienne Cabet, champion of peaceful utopian communism and the author of *Voyage en Icarie*, which gave a fantastic picture of a future communist society.   p. 106

[82] In a circular letter of June 6, 1871 to the diplomatic representatives of France, Foreign Minister Jules Favre called upon all the governments to join forces in the struggle against the International. Marx and Engels wrote "Statement by the General Council on Jules Favre's Circular" (see present edition, Vol. 22, pp. 361-63).

Sacase made his report in the National Assembly on February 5, 1872, on behalf of the commission appointed to consider the Dufaure law (see Note 57).

p. 107

[83] The *Working Men's Federation* was founded in Turin in the autumn of 1871 and was influenced by the Mazzinists. In December 1871, the proletarian elements split away from the Federation and formed the *Emancipation of the Proletarian Society*, later admitted to the International as a section; up to February 1872, it was headed by a secret police agent, Carlo Terzaghi.   p. 111

[84] This refers to the *International Foundrymen's Union* which, as its leader William Sylvis wrote in a letter read out at the General Council meeting of July 9, 1867, had spent a lot of money in 1866-67 in support of the strikers.

The Union was founded in 1859 and took final shape in 1863 under the leadership of Sylvis, who became its president. The Union amalgamated the local foundrymen's associations on a national scale, had its organisations in British Columbia and Canada and led strikes. It did much to strengthen other US trade unions.   p. 112

[85] The quotations below are taken from the Programme of the Alliance of Socialist Democracy drawn up by Bakunin and published as a leaflet in Geneva in 1868 in French and German. The full text of the Programme is given by Marx and Engels in "The Alliance of Socialist Democracy and the International Working Men's Association" (see this volume, pp. 577-78).   p. 115

[86] On Luigi Stefanoni's attempts to undermine the International's influence on the Italian workers by establishing the "Universal Society of Rationalists" see Note 43. Marx's and Engels' articles in the Italian press (see this volume, pp. 74-75 and 160-63) helped to frustrate his attempts to subject the Italian working-class movement to bourgeois influence.   p. 119

[87] By the Bismarck socialists, Marx and Engels meant the leaders of the Lassallean General Association of German Workers (founded in May 1863) and they called their newspaper, the *Neuer Social-Demokrat*, the police mouthpiece because both pursued a policy of accommodation to the Bismarck regime and attacked the revolutionary proletarian wing in the German workers' movement and in the International.

The name *"white shirts"* (les blouses blanche) refers to the gangs of declassed elements recruited by the police of the Second Empire. Pretending to be workers, they staged provocatory demonstrations and disturbances, thus providing the authorities with pretexts for persecuting genuine workers' organisations.   p. 119

88 The Congress of the Belgian Federation of the International Working Men's Association, held in Brussels on December 24 and 25, 1871, when discussing the Sonvillier circular, did not support the Swiss anarchists' demand for the immediate convocation of a general congress of the International, though it did instruct the Belgian Federal Council to draft new General Rules for the Association. True to its anarchist spirit, this draft abolished the General Council.

At the Hague Congress of the International (September 1872) the Belgian delegates together with the anarchist minority voted against the decisions of the General Council on the changes in the Rules and Administrative Regulations, aimed at strengthening the Association organisationally and widening the powers of its leading body.   p. 119

89 The workers' insurrection in Lyons on April 30, 1871, in support of the Paris Commune, was suppressed by the army and police on May 1. It was preceded by the unsuccessful attempt by the workers of Lyons on March 22-25 to overthrow the local administration of the Versailles government and establish a local Commune. Both insurrections failed largely because the anarchists, who claimed leadership, fell victim to spontaneity, denied the role of the revolutionary leaders and adopted wrong tactics.   p. 120

90 In December 1870 in New York representatives of several sections formed a Central Committee as the leading body of the International in the United States. In July 1871, Sections No. 9 and No. 12, headed by the bourgeois feminists Victoria Woodhull and Tenessee Claflin, joined these sections and began campaigning, in the name of the International, for bourgeois reforms. On September 27, 1871, without the knowledge of the New York Central Committee, Section No. 12 demanded that the General Council recognise it as the leading section in the United States. At the same time it conducted a campaign in the newspapers against those sections which maintained the proletarian character of the organisation. In its resolution of November 5 the General Council rejected the claims of Section No. 12 and confirmed the powers of the New York Central Committee. Nevertheless Section No. 12 continued to attack the Central Committee which led to a split in December 1871 between the proletarian and petty-bourgeois sections. Two councils were formed in New York: the Provisional Federal Council (committee No. 1) which included Friedrich Sorge, Friedrich Bolte and others, and committee No. 2 headed by Woodhull and other bourgeois reformers from Section No. 12. The General Council resolutely supported the proletarian wing of the North American Federation, and Section No. 12 was suspended from the International pending the next congress. On May 28, 1872, the General Council announced the Provisional Federal Council the only leader of the International in the USA. The North American Federation Congress in July 1872 elected the standing Federal Council, its members being almost all those of the Provisional Council. For causes of the split in the North American Federation, see Engels' "The International in America" and Marx's draft manuscript "American Split" (this volume, pp. 177-83 and 636-43).

The resolutions have survived in two manuscripts: Marx's rough manuscript in English and the French translation of these resolutions in Charles Rochat's hand with Marx's corrections on a form with the stamp "International Working Men's Association".   p. 124

91 Under the direct influence of anarchists, Serbian and Bulgarian students in Zurich organised a small group "Slavenski Savez" within the Alliance of Socialist Democracy. After several attempts in the spring of 1872 to constitute itself as a section of the International and the General Council's refusal to recognise it, the group (whose programme was drawn up by Bakunin) affiliated to the Jura Federation in June-July 1872 and ceased to exist in the summer of 1873.   p. 126

92 On March 14, 1871, the French reactionary *Paris-Journal* stated in its article "Le Grand Chef de l'International" that it had at its disposal Marx's letter to Auguste Serraillier which testified to the contradictions between the French and German members of the International; on March 19, the forged letter was published in the newspaper. The libel of the French press was taken up by the London newspapers, *The Times* included. It was refuted at the General Council meeting of March 21, 1871, and also in a special letter to the editor of *The Times* drafted by Marx and Engels (see present edition, Vol. 22, p. 285) and Marx's statement to the editor of *Der Volksstaat* (ibid., pp. 288-90). Moreover, the *Paris-Journal* provocative fiction was exposed in the *Courrier de l'Europe* on March 18 by Serraillier.   p. 127

93 At its meeting of February 20, 1872, the General Council adopted Hermann Jung's proposal to celebrate the anniversaries of the Paris Commune by mass meetings in London. To prepare the first meeting, a special committee was appointed which included Jung. J. Patrick MacDonnell, George Milner, Alfred Taylor and Martin James Boon. Marx was to be one of the chief organisers and Engels, on Jung's request, was to draft resolutions. The meeting, however, did not take place because at the last moment the owner of the hall refused to let it. Nevertheless, the members of the International and the former Communards held a ceremonial meeting on March 18, 1872 to mark the first anniversary of the Paris Commune. The meeting, on the proposal of the Communards Albert Félix Theisz and Zéphyrin Camélinat and the General Council member Milner, adopted three resolutions which coincide word for word with the French manuscript in Jenny's (Marx's daughter) hand with Marx's corrections.

On the occasion of the second anniversary of the Paris Commune in March 1873, the British Federal Council of the International adopted a special declaration consisting of a collection of extracts from Marx's *The Civil War in France*.   p. 128

94 Engels communicated the contents of the letter from the Spanish Federal Council at the General Council meeting of March 26, 1872.   p. 129

95 On the *Dufaure law* see Note 57.   p. 129

96 The *Ferré Section*, named after the Communard Theophil Ferré who was shot by the Versaillists, was one of the first French sections of the International set up in Paris after the defeat of the Commune. The section took its final form in April 1872; its foundation was confirmed by the Sub-Committee of the General Council, on Marx's proposal, on July 27, 1872, after its Rules had been examined by the General Council standing committee for revising rules.
                                                                        p. 129

97 For the persecution of the members of the German workers' movement see notes 26 and 59.   p. 129

98 Marx was prompted to write this work by the discussion of the nationalisation
   of the land question in the Manchester Section of the International. In his
   letter to Engels of March 3, the organiser of the section Eugène Dupont wrote
   about the confusion among the members over the agrarian question. He also
   formulated five points of his future speech and asked Marx and Engels to
   comment on them so that he could take them into account before the meeting
   of the section. Marx substantiated his views in detail. Dupont made his report
   (which coincided almost word for word with Marx's rough manuscript) at a
   meeting of the section on May 8, 1872; it was published in *The International
   Herald* on June 15, 1872, under the heading "The Nationalisation of the Land.
   A Paper read at the Manchester Section of the International Working Men's
   Association"; neither the author nor the speaker were named.   p. 131

99 This letter was written by Engels on the instruction of the General Council and
   read out at the congress of the Spanish Federation of the International on
   April 7, 1872.
      The congress was held at Saragossa from April 4 to 11, 1872. It was
   attended by 45 delegates representing 31 local federations. The police, on
   government instructions, wrecked its public sittings.
      A sharp struggle developed at the congress between the followers of the
   General Council of the International, whose mouthpiece was the newspaper *La
   Emancipacion*, and the adherents of the Bakuninist Alliance. The latter
   managed to have some of their anarchist resolutions adopted and secured seats
   for the Alliance members in a newly elected Spanish Federal Council which,
   after having moved from Madrid to Valencia, became wholly Bakuninist.
   Further sharpening of the contradictions among the Spanish organisations of
   the International resulted in a break of the *Emancipacion* group with the
   Bakuninists.
      Apart from publications in *La Emancipacion*, No. 44, April 13, *La Liberté*,
   No. 17, April 28 and *Der Volksstaat*, No. 36, May 4, 1872 and also in the
   pamphlet *Estracto Internacional de las actas del Segundo Congreso Obrero de la
   Federacion Regional Española, celebrado en Zaragoza en los dias 4 al 11 de Abril de
   1872, segun las actas y las notas tomadas por la comision nombrada al effecto en el
   mismo*, Engels' rough manuscript in French has also survived.
      The letter was published in English for the first time in *The General Council
   of the First International. 1871-1872. Minutes*, Progress Publishers, Moscow, 1968.
                                                                               p. 137

100 On the *Saragossa Congress* see Note 99. The telegram was published in English
    for the first time in *The General Council of the First International. 1871-1872.
    Minutes*, Progress Publishers, Moscow, 1968.   p. 139

101 This declaration occasioned by Alexander Cochrane-Baillie's slanderous speech
    in the House of Commons, was read out by Marx at the General Council
    meeting on April 16, 1872. By the Council's decision, it was published in the
    name of the International Working Men's Association as a leaflet and also in
    the newspapers *The Eastern Post*, No. 186, April 20, *The International Herald*,
    No. 5, April 27 (the beginning was omitted), *La Emancipacion*, No. 49, May 18,
    O Pensamento Social, No. 14, May 1872. In the leaflet the text was preceded by
    the words: "At a full meeting of the General Council of the above Association,
    held at the Council-room, 33, Rathbone-place, on Tuesday evening, citizen
    Longuet in the chair, the following declaration was unanimously adopted, in
    reply to the strictures in the late debate in the House of Commons." p. 140

[102] The preamble to the Provisional Rules of the Association, containing the basic programmatic principles of the first international organisation of the working class, was incorporated unchanged in the General Rules approved by the Geneva Congress of 1866. The tasks of the proletariat's political struggle were formulated in Paragraph 3, reading, in part, as follows: "...The economical emancipation of the working classes is therefore the great end to which every political movement ought to be subordinate as a means" (see present edition, Vol. 20, p. 14). The Inaugural Address of the Working Men's International Association, drawn up simultaneously with the Provisional Rules, demonstrated the proposition that "to conquer political power has ... become the great duty of the working classes" (ibid., p. 12). The International called upon the working class "to master themselves the mysteries of international politics; to watch the diplomatic acts of their respective Governments; to counteract them, if necessary, by all means in their power" (ibid., p. 13).   p. 141

[103] On *Sacase's report* see Note 82.   p. 143

[104] The *act for the establishment of a federal Labour Statistics Office* was adopted by the House of Representatives of the US Congress but afterwards turned down by the Senate.   p. 145

[105] At the General Council meeting of March 19, 1872, Engels announced that he had received a letter from Ferrara of March 3 which stated that the Ferrara workers' society was going to join the International, provided it retained its own autonomy. Engels explained in his reply that the recognition of the General Rules and Administrative Regulations was an indispensable condition for the admission of a new section to the International. Engels' letter, as well as the International's documents forwarded by him to the Ferrara society, helped its members to overcome the anarchist influence. On May 7, acting on Engels' proposal, the General Council recognised the Ferrara society as a section of the International.   p. 146

[106] This article marked the beginning of Engels' regular contributions to the Italian newspaper *La Plebe* which continued until the end of 1872. Before this, in 1871, the newspaper published extracts from Engels' letters and some documents of the General Council of the International which he had sent to Italy. At the request of the editor Enrico Bignami, Engels wrote several articles. The first article was supplied with the note: "Under this heading we shall henceforth print letters which one respected citizen has pledged to write to us from London." Engels discontinued his contributions at the beginning of 1873 because government persecution made the regular publication of the newspaper impossible, and resumed them in 1877. In this volume the editorial subtitles of this and most of the other articles of the series correspond to their titles in Gianni Bosio's collection *Karl Marx. Friedrich Engels. Scritti italiani*, Milan-Rome, 1955. This article was published in English for the first time in Marx and Engels, *Articles on Britain*, Progress Publishers, Moscow, 1971.   p. 148

[107] In 1830-31, extremely hard conditions caused spontaneous rebellions of agricultural workers in the south and east of England. The new agricultural machines led to mass unemployment among the farm-hands who, in protest, burned hay ricks and damaged machines. The rebels were severely dealt with by the army.   p. 148

[108] In late March 1872, the agricultural workers of Warwickshire formed a union which headed a strike that soon spread to the neighbouring counties. The strike was supported by the trade unions of industrial workers. Their financial

aid and the need for extra workers promoted the struggle of the agricultural workers. A national union of agricultural workers headed by Joseph Arch was founded in May 1872 and by the end of 1873, it numbered about 100,000 members. The struggle for a shorter working day and higher wages went on till 1874 and was victorious in a number of counties.   p. 148

[109] At the General Council meeting of April 23, 1872, Engels communicated details concerning the police persecution of Theodor Cuno, the German socialist and a leader of the Milan Section of the International. Engels drew on the Italian newspapers and Cuno's letter of April 22. Engels regarded this persecution as a concrete expression of the conspiracy of the European reactionary governments against the International and thought it very important to expose it.   p. 151

[110] Engels wrote this draft after the General Council recognised the Ferrara workers' society as a section of the International (see Note 105). Engels put it down on the clean third page of the letter from the Ferrara society of April 27, in which its members, in reply to Engels' letter of April 16 (see this volume, pp. 146-47), agreed to interprete their autonomy in accordance with the Rules of the International. There is a note by Engels on the fourth page: "Ferrara 27 aprile 72. Sezione di Ferrara. Btw. 10 Mai" (Ferrara, April 27, 72. Section of Ferrara. Answered May 10). The full text of Engels' letter to the Ferrara society has not been found.

An excerpt from this document was published in English for the first time in *The Hague Congress of the First International. September 2-7, 1872. Reports and Letters*, Progress Publishers, Moscow, 1978.

                                     p. 153

[111] At its meeting of May 14, 1872, the General Council discussed the relations between the Irish sections emerging in England and Ireland and the British Federal Council. Engels exposed the chauvinism of John Hales and some other English members of the General Council and British Council who opposed an independent Irish organisation and its struggle for Ireland's independence. During the discussion the majority of the General Council supported Engels.

Engels' speech is extant in the form of his own record made for the newspaper and, in part, as the entry in the Minute Book of the General Council. It was not published because the General Council decided not to include the discussion of the Irish question in the report for the press. The General Council feared that the publication of certain speeches, that of Hales, in particular, would damage the International's reputation.

Engels' record of his report was published in English for the first time in *The General Council of the First International. 1871-1872. Minutes*, Progress Publishers, Moscow, 1968.   p. 154

[112] On March 8, 1842, a clash between the Chartists and the Irish was provoked in Manchester by the bourgeois nationalist leaders of the Irish National Association of Repealers who advocated abrogation of the Union of 1801 and were hostile to the working-class movement in England, Chartism in particular. The Repealers drove out a group of Chartists and Feargus O'Connor from the Hall of Science where O'Connor was to deliver a lecture.   p. 155

[113] This declaration was read out by Marx at the General Council meeting of May 21, 1872, and adopted by the Council. It was occasioned by the pamphlet *Conseil fédéraliste universel de l'Association Internationale des Travailleurs et des*

sociétés républicaines socialistes adhérentes, which was published in London in April 1872 in French, English and German and contained libels against the leaders of the International.

The *Universal Federalist Council* was set up early in 1872 and included the remaining members of the French Section of 1871 (see notes 11 and 20), members of various bourgeois and petty-bourgeois organisations, a few Lassalleans expelled from the German Workers' Educational Society in London and other people who strove to worm their way into the leadership of the International. They concentrated their attacks on the London Conference resolutions relating to the political action of the working class and to the struggle against sectarianism. The Hague Congress of the International decided to include the resolution on political action of the working class in the General Rules and so inflicted a decisive blow on the elements hostile to the International. The Universal Federalist Council summoned its congress in London in late September 1872 and tried to pass it off as a congress of the International Working Men's Association. Further activity of the Federalist Council developed into a struggle between various groups for the leadership of the "movement".

Apart from *The Eastern Post,* the declaration was published in nearly all the press organs of the International, including *The International Herald,* No. 9, June 1, *Der Volksstaat,* No. 44, June 1, *La Liberté,* No. 22, June 22, *La Emancipacion,* No. 52, June 8, *O Pensamento Social,* No. 16, June, *L'Égalité,* No. 13, June 23, 1872.

In *La Emancipacion* it ended with the following editorial comment: "This important document, exposing as it does the intrigues of the bourgeois parties, reveals their desire to split the ranks of the International and paralyse its activities. In all countries, in Britain and Germany, in Belgium and Switzerland, in America and Italy, the bourgeoisie strives to distort the principles of workers' solidarity so as to wreak havoc in our Association. Let it serve us as a lesson."   p. 157

114 See Note 29.   p. 157

115 The *Land and Labour League* was founded, with the participation of General Council members, in London in October 1869. Along with general democratic demands, its programme included those for the nationalisation of land, a shorter working day, and Chartist demands for universal suffrage and home colonisation. By the autumn of 1870, however, the influence of the reformists had increased in the League and by 1872 it had lost contact with the International.   p. 157

116 In late 1871, a group of Lassalleans who slandered the General Council were expelled from the *German Workers' Educational Society* in London.

This Society was founded in February 1840 by Karl Schapper, Joseph Moll and other leaders of the League of the Just. After the Communist League came into existence in 1847, members of the League's local communes played the leading role in the Society. In 1847 and 1849-50 Marx and Engels took an active part in its work, but they, as well as a number of their supporters, abandoned the Society on September 17, 1850, since most of its members sided with the sectarian Willich-Schapper group. Marx and Engels resumed their work in the Society in the late 1850s. When the International was founded, the Society became the German Section of the International Association in London and, since the end of 1871, a section of the British Federation. The Educational Society existed till 1918, when it was closed down by the British government.
                                                                          p. 157

[117] Drawing on the protests against Pierre Vésinier's slanders against the French members of the International, the Brussels Congress of 1868 instructed the Brussels Section to demand proofs of his accusations from Vésinier and, should they be insufficient, expel him from the International.

On October 26, 1868, the Brussels Section resolved to expel Vésinier from the International.   p. 157

[118] Marx wrote this article in reply to Luigi Stefanoni's libellous item "Marx-Vogt-Herzen" printed in the *Libero Pensiero* on April 18, 1872, and directed against the International and Marx. Engels exposed Stefanoni in the press earlier (see this volume, pp. 74-75). Stefanoni's continuous attacks and his direct contacts with the Bakuninist Alliance and the Lassalleans compelled Marx to follow suit. Exposures made by Marx, Engels and the Italian members of the International frustrated Stefanoni's attempts to subjugate the Italian workers' movement to bourgeois influence.   p. 160

[119] Planning to organise the Universal Society of Rationalists (see Note 43), Luigi Stefanoni tried to secure support of prominent members of the republican and workers' movement. With this aim in view he applied to Wilhelm Liebknecht. Liebknecht, unaware of Stefanoni's plans and being in the dark about his contacts with the Bakuninist Alliance and the Lassalleans, replied with a letter of greetings which was published in *Libero Pensiero* on January 18, 1872, of which fact he informed Engels. In his reply of February 15, Engels explained the state of affairs to Liebknecht; the latter wrote a sharp letter to Stefanoni on February 29 to say that he refused to have anything to do with Stefanoni and, in the name of the German Social-Democracy, to declare full solidarity with the General Council of the International Working Men's Association. Engels translated this letter into Italian and had it published, through Carlo Cafiero, in the *Gazzettino Rosa* of April 20, 1872.   p. 160

[120] A reference to those accused in the *Cologne Communist trial* of 1852 (see Note 45).   p. 161

[121] After the fall of the Second Empire, the collection of documents *Papiers et correspondance de la Famille impériale*, was published in Paris in 1871. It had a note (Vol. II, p. 161) which confirmed the payment of 40,000 francs to Karl Vogt in 1859.   p. 161

[122] On the articles by Marx and Engels on the war of France and Piedmont against Austria, see present edition, Vol. 16. Mazzini's manifesto *La Guerra* (mentioned below) was translated by Marx and published, somewhat abridged, in *The New-York Daily Tribune* (see K. Marx, "Mazzini's Manifesto", ibid., pp. 355-59).
                                                                      p. 162

[123] A collection of Herzen's posthumous articles contained excerpts from his memoirs *Byloye i Dumy* (My Past and Thoughts), in particular the chapter "The Germans in Emigration".   p. 162

[124] This letter was prompted by a libellous article published anonymously in the *Concordia*, No. 10, March 7, 1872. The author was the German bourgeois economist Luigi Brentano, who sought to discredit Marx as a scientist by accusing him of misquoting the sources. On March 30, Liebknecht sent Engels the relevant copy of the *Concordia* and insisted on a reply to it in *Der Volksstaat*. Marx's reply appeared in *Der Volksstaat* on June 1, and the *Concordia* responded with another article by Brentano, again published anonymously, to which Marx answered with an article in *Der Volksstaat*, No. 63, August 7, 1872

(see this volume, pp. 190-97). After Marx's death, the accusation was repeated by the English bourgeois economist Sedley Taylor. The allegation that Marx had misquoted the sources was completely refuted by his daughter Eleanor in two letters to the *To-Day* journal in February and March 1884 and by Engels in the Preface to the fourth German edition of *Capital* in June 1890 and in the pamphlet *Brentano contra Marx*, published in 1891.   p. 164

125 The phrase from Gladstone's speech of April 16, 1863, quoted by Marx, was printed in almost all the reports of parliamentary debates published by the London newspapers (*The Times, The Morning Star, The Daily Telegraph* and others of April 17, 1863); it was omitted in the semi-official *Hansard's Parliamentary Debates* (Vol. 170, London, 1863) where the texts were corrected by the speakers themselves.   p. 164

126 Marx refers to the pages of the first German edition of Volume One of *Capital* (1867) that correspond to pp. 667 and 668 of the 1887 English edition of *Capital* edited by Engels.   p. 166

127 In a polemic with August Bebel in the German Reichstag on November 8, 1871, the National-Liberal Lasker said that should the German Social-Democratic workers dare to follow the example of Paris Communards, the "respectable and propertied citizens would club them to death". In the stenographic report, however, he replaced the last few words with the milder "would keep them in hand". Bebel brought this substitution to light, and Lasker became a laughing-stock among the workers. He was nicknamed "little Lasker" because of his diminutive stature.   p. 167

128 On the Emancipation of the Proletarian Society see Note 83.

The draft was published in English for the first time in *The Hague Congress of the First International. September 2-7, 1872. Reports and Letters*, Progress Publishers, Moscow, 1972.   p. 168

129 This apparently refers to Engels' letters to Carlo Cafiero which the latter passed to one of the leaders of the Bakuninist Alliance, James Guillaume. The *Bulletin de la Fédération jurassienne*, No. 6, May 10, 1872, stated that it had at its disposal some letters written by Engels "to his Italian friends" in the autumn of 1871.   p. 168

130 At its meeting of June 11, 1872, the General Council, on Marx's proposal, resolved to convene the next congress in Holland on September 2, 1872; the main question on the agenda was to be that of strengthening the International organisationally (revision of the General Rules and Administrative Regulations). At its next meeting, on June 18, the General Council decided to hold the congress at The Hague and appointed a special Committee (Engels, Edouard Vaillant and J. Patrick MacDonnell) to prepare an official announcement on the coming congress. It was written by Engels and, apart from *The International Herald*, was published in *Der Volksstaat*, No. 53, July 3, *Die Tagwacht*, No. 27, July 6, *L'Internationale*, No. 182, July 7, *L'Égalité*, No. 14, July 7, *La Emancipacion*, No. 57, July 13, *Le Mirabeau*, No. 156, July 14, *La Liberté*, No. 28, July 14, *Bulletin de la Fédération jurassienne*, No. 13 (Supplement), July 15, *O Pensamento Social*, No. 18, July, *La Plebe*, No. 88, August 3, 1872.

Engels' rough manuscript in French and English is extant.   p. 170

131 The *Manifesto of the Communist Party* was written by Marx and Engels as the programme of the Communist League (see present edition, Vol. 6, pp. 477-519) and first published in German in February 1848 in London as a pamphlet. In

March-July 1848, the *Manifesto* was published in the *Deutsche Londoner Zeitung*, the democratic press organ of the German refugees. That same year it was reprinted in pamphlet form in London; certain misprints of the first edition were corrected and this text was used by Marx and Engels for subsequent authorised editions.

The 1872 German edition of the *Manifesto* with Marx's and Engels' preface and slight corrections in the text was brought out on the initiative of the editors of *Der Volksstaat*.

This preface was included into many editions in other languages.

This preface was published in English for the first time in K. Marx and F. Engels, *Manifesto of the Communist Party*, Glasgow, 1909.   p. 174

132 See Note 44.   p. 174

133 Besides German editions of the *Manifesto of the Communist Party* mentioned in Note 131, between 1848 and 1872 the work was also published in German, in full and in part, in Germany, Austria, Britain and the USA in the periodicals: *Die Hornisse, Neue Rheinische Zeitung. Politisch-ökonomische Revue, Republik der Arbeiter, Die Revolution, Arbeit-Blatt*; in the collections: *Wermuth-Stieber. Die Communisten-Verschwörungen des neunzehnten Jarhunderts. Leipziger Hochverrathprozeß* and in pamphlet form: *Das Manifest der Kommunistischen Partei*, London and Berlin, 1860 and Chicago, 1871.   p. 174

134 A reference to "Manifesto of the German Communist Party", *The Red Republican*, Nos. 21-24, November 9, 16, 23 and 30, 1850, London; "Manifesto of the German Communist Party", *The World*, November 21, 1871, New York (in fragments); "Manifesto of the German Communist Party", *Woodhull & Claflin's Weekly*, No. 7, December 30, 1871.

In England, besides the translation by Helen Macfarlane mentioned in the text, fragments from the introduction and chapters I and II were translated by William Stepney and published in *The Social Economist*, August 1 and September 1, 1869.   p. 174

135 The reference is to the heroic insurrection of the Paris workers in June 1848 (see present edition, Vol. 7, pp. 124-28, 130-64).

The French translation of the *Manifesto* of 1848 has not been found.

In New York, the French Section of the International published the translation of chapters I and II: "Manifest de Karl Marx", *Le Socialiste*, Nos. 16-17, 19-24 and 26, January 27, February 10, 17 and 24, March 2, 9, 16 and 30, 1872.   p. 174

136 The Russian translation of the *Manifesto of the Communist Party* was published in Geneva in 1869 in Chernetsky's printshop. Recently doubts have arisen whether the Russian translation was done by Bakunin; some scholars believe it might have been done by N. N. Lyubavin.

This translation contained certain mistakes, distorting the meaning. The shortcomings of the first publication were eliminated in the translation by Georgi Plekhanov, which appeared in Geneva in 1882.

The Polish and Danish translations of 1848 have not been found. p. 174

137 This is the record of Engels' proposals tabled at the meeting of the Sub-Committee of the General Council on July 5, 1872. Marx and Engels were instructed to give the General Council their opinion of the Alliance's secret activity. In line with this resolution, Engels drew up the draft address to all the members of the International Association, and this was discussed at a General Council meeting in August 1872 (see this volume, pp. 205-10).

The *Sub-Committee* (Standing Committee) or the *Executive Committee* was formed out of the Committee appointed simultaneously with the foundation of the International Association to draw up its programme and the Rules. It included the General Secretary of the Association, the Treasurer and the corresponding secretaries for different countries. The Sub-Committee had a wide range of duties: it carried on the routine management of the Association and drew up documents which were later considered by the General Council.

This document was published in English for the first time in *The General Council of the First International. 1871-1872. Minutes*, Progress Publishers, Moscow, 1968.   p. 176

138 The reference is to Bakunin's letter in response to the private circular *Fictitious Splits in the International* which was full of spiteful attacks on the General Council.   p. 176

139 Engels wrote this article for *Der Volksstaat*; he drew on Marx's extracts from the newspapers and letters of the members of the International concerning the split in the North American Federation (see this volume, pp. 636-43). One of his sources was an article in the Madrid newspaper *La Emancipacion*, No. 54, June 22, 1872: "La burguesia y la Internacional en los Estados-Unidos" (The bourgeoisie and the International in the United States) which exposed the attempts of bourgeois reformers to use that American organisation in their own interests.

Engels' article was published in English for the first time in Marx and Engels, *On the United States*, Progress Publishers, Moscow, 1979.   p. 177

140 The *Shakers*—members of a religious sect in the USA.   p. 179

141 A reference to the resolution of the General Council of May 28, 1872, which was not recorded in the Minute Book. It is reproduced in Marx's extracts on the split in the North American Federation (see this volume, pp. 642-43). p. 183

142 Engels drafted this rough letter (first published, in Russian, in 1935) on the margins of the letter from the *Committee for the Emancipation of the Working Classes* in Parma of July 7, 1872, addressed to the General Council; the document bears a note in Engels' hand: "Received 16 Juli. Beantwortet 18 Juli." (Received July 16. Answered July 18.) The fair copy of the letter was found in Parma and first published, in the language of the original, in *La corrispondenza di Marx e Engels con italiani, 1848-1895*, Milan, 1964.   p. 184

143 About 20,000 miners of the Ruhr Valley went on strike on June 18, 1872. They demanded a 25 per cent increase in wages and an eight-hour working day. After five weeks of struggle, the workers were defeated.   p. 185

144 This document was written by Marx who communicated its contents at the General Council Sub-Committee meeting of July 27, 1872.

The document was published in English for the first time in *The General Council of the First International. 1871-1872. Minutes*, Progress Publishers, Moscow, 1968.   p. 188

145 Marx wrote this letter because the *Concordia*, No. 27, July 4, published anonymously a second article by Luigi Brentano, entitled "Wie Karl Marx sich vertheidigt" (How Karl Marx defends himself). (See Note 124.) Adolf Hepner, an editor of *Der Volksstaat*, sent this new article to Marx c/o Engels and asked for a prompt reply stressing the importance of the struggle against the pseudo-socialist bourgeois trend (Katheder-Socialism) to which the author of the article belonged.   p. 190

[146] Here and below Marx quotes and refers to the first German edition of Volume One of *Capital*, Hamburg, 1867. In the 1887 English edition, published in London and edited by Engels, the relevant passages are to be found on p. 668.

p. 191

[147] This note in the first German edition of Volume One of *Capital* refers to Molière; the poetical quotation is from Boileau, *Satirae*, VIII. p. 191

[148] *Blue Books*—a series of British parliamentary and foreign policy documents published in blue covers since the seventeenth century. p. 193

[149] This refers to the words of the Prussian Minister of the Interior von Rochow. In an address of January 15, 1838, to the citizens of Elbin, dissatisfied with the expulsion of seven oppositional professors from the Hanover Diet, Rochow wrote: "Loyal subjects are expected to exhibit due obedience to their King and sovereign, but their limited thinking should keep them from interfering in the affairs of heads of state." p. 197

[150] The draft General Rules and Administrative Regulations, revised, on Marx's proposal, by the General Council in June-August 1872, were supposed to be confirmed by the Hague Congress of the International (September 2-7, 1872). Lack of time and the general situation at the Congress, compelled Marx, Engels and their associates to propose only a few major amendments and additions to the Rules.

The original document is a copy of the official 1871 French edition of the General Rules and Administrative Regulations with the amendments and additions approved by the General Council, inserted by Marx himself.

Only articles with Marx's amendments are published in this volume. Changes approved by the General Council are set in italics. p. 198

[151] The former General Rules had: "to afford a central medium of communication and co-operation between Working Men's Societies existing in different countries" (see this volume, p. 4). Marx proved the expediency of the alteration at the General Council meeting on July 16, 1872, and this was recorded in the Minute Book: "Upon Rule I Citizen *Marx* proposes to strike out the words relative 'to a central medium' upon the ground that the development of the Association has changed the conditions and he moves the insertion of the following words instead: 'To organise common action between the working classes of different countries.' He says the alteration was rendered necessary to prevent misinterpretations." p. 198

[152] Article 8 of the former Rules read: "Every section has the right to appoint its own secretary corresponding with the General Council." The new draft of the article was a version of Resolution IX "Political Action of the Working Class" adopted by the London Conference of 1871 (see present edition, Vol. 22, pp. 426-27). The draft was approved by the Hague Congress that included it in the Rules as Article 7a (see this volume, p. 243). According to the Minutes of the General Council meeting on July 23, 1872, Marx and Engels substantiated the inclusion of the article in the Rules as follows: "Citizen *Engels* seconds it—the same reasons that made us adopt it at the Conference still exist and we shall have to fight it out at the Congress.

"Citizen *Marx* says there is another view; we have two classes of enemies: the abstentionists, and they have attacked the resolution more than any other; the working class of England and America let the middle classes use them for political purposes; we must put an end to it by exposing it." p. 201

[153] Marx proposed this addition to Article 9 of the Rules at the General Council meeting of July 23, 1872, drawing on the experience of the North American sections which successfully employed this principle in the struggle against bourgeois reformists. p. 201

[154] Article 12 on the terms for the revision of the Rules and Article 13 on the additions to the Administrative Regulations remained unchanged (cf. this volume, p. 8). p. 201

[155] A separate sheet of paper has survived in the Minute Book of the General Council with the text of this article written in English by Engels:

"6. The General Council has also the right of suspending, till the meeting of next Congress, any branch, section, Federal Council, or Federation of the International.

"Nevertheless, with regard to branches belonging to a federation, it will exercise this right only after having consulted the respective Federal Council.

"In case of the dissolution of a Federal Council, the General Council shall, at the same time, call upon the branches composing such federation to elect a new Federal Council within thirty days.

"In the case of the suspension of a whole federation, the General Council is bound to inform thereof immediately all the remaining federations. If the majority of the federations should demand it, the General Council shall convoke an extraordinary Conference composed of the delegate for each federation, which Conference shall meet within a month and decide finally on the matter. It is well understood that the countries where the International may be prohibited, shall have the same rights as the regular federations." p. 203

[156] In the summer of 1872, after the circular *Fictitious Splits in the International* had been published, Marx and Engels received from Paul Lafargue, José Mesa, Nikolai Utin and others a large number of documents proving the existence of the secret Bakuninist Alliance of Socialist Democracy within the International Working Men's Association. The preparations for the Hague Congress made the exposure of the Alliance's subversive activities all the more important. At a meeting on July 5, 1872, the Sub-Committee decided to request the General Council to propose the expulsion of Bakunin and other members of the Alliance at the coming congress of the International (see this volume, p. 176 and Note 137). On August 6, Engels submitted to the Council a draft address to all members of the Association, written on behalf of the Sub-Committee. A heated discussion ensued and by a majority vote Engels' draft was adopted.

The document has survived in the form of Engels' two manuscripts in French, one of them with insertions in Charles Longuet's hand, and also in the form of Engels' manuscript in English which is reproduced in this volume.

The document was published in English for the first time in *The General Council of the First International. 1871-1872. Minutes*, Progress Publishers, Moscow, 1968. p. 205

[157] The *New Madrid Federation* was formed on July 8, 1872, by the editors of *La Emancipacion* expelled from the Madrid Federation by the anarchist majority for having exposed the secret Alliance's activities in Spain. Paul Lafargue was very active in organising the New Madrid Federation and in its work. When the Spanish Federal Council refused to admit the New Madrid Federation, the latter appealed to the General Council, on behalf of which the Executive Committee (the Sub-Committee) recognised it as a Federation of the International on August 15, 1872 (see this volume, p. 215). The New Madrid Federation campaigned determinedly against anarchist influences, propagated

the ideas of scientific socialism and fought for an independent workers' party
in Spain. p. 208

158 This document was adopted at the meeting of the Sub-Committee of the
General Council on August 8, 1872. As is seen from the rough manuscript in
French, the first paragraph was written by Marx (in the manuscript it is
supplied with the subtitle "Introduction") and the rest by Engels.

It was published, besides *La Emancipacion*, in *La Federacion*, No. 157,
August 18, *Bulletin de la Fédération jurassienne de l'Association Internationale des
Travailleurs*, Nos. 15-16, August 15-September 1 and, in excerpts, in *The
Times*, No. 27476, September 7, 1872 (in Eccarius' report).

The document was first published in English in full in *The General Council
of the First International. 1871-1872. Minutes*, Progress Publishers, Moscow, 1968.

The *Sub-Committee*—see Note 137. p. 211

159 Marx wrote this letter because *The Times*, No. 27456, August 15, 1872,
reprinted from the Paris newspapers a forged circular of the General Council
of the International on the coming Congress at The Hague. p. 214

160 The New Madrid Federation (see Note 157) published this letter together with
the information that it had been recognised by the General Council of the
International.

The letter was published in English for the first time in *The General Council
of the First International. 1871-1872. Minutes*, Progress Publishers, Moscow, 1968.
p. 215

161 The conference of the Italian anarchist groups (Bakunin helped to prepare it) took place in Rimini on August 4-6, 1872. It resolved to set up an
Italian national anarchist organisation, the self-styled Italian Federation of the
International, and to sever all relations with the General Council. No section in
other countries, not even Bakuninist organisations, supported the attempt of
the conference to counter the coming Hague Congress of the International
with an "anti-authoritarian" congress in Neuchâtel. p. 216

162 Engels sent this address of the General Council to the Italian sections of the
International in Milan, Turin, Ferrara and Rome, which were officially
recognised by the General Council and were in constant contact with it.

The editors of *Il Popolino*, the Turin Section's weekly, published in
April-October 1872, prefaced it with the following note: "In printing this letter,
we inform the reader that we could not do so earlier since the editorial board
of the *Emancipazione del proletario*, to whom it was addressed, had been
imprisoned because of a strike; the interrupted contacts with them were only
resumed recently."

Engels' rough copy of the letter in Italian bears the inscription: "Rome,
Ferrara, Milan, Turin."

The address was published in English for the first time in *The General
Council of the First International. 1871-1872. Minutes*, Progress Publishers,
Moscow, 1968. p. 217

163 The Resolution was published in English for the first time in *The General
Council of the First International. 1871-1872. Minutes*, Progress Publishers,
Moscow, 1968. p. 218

164 The task of the Hague Congress was to adopt the resolutions of the 1871
London Conference on the political activity of the working class and against the
sectarian sections. Marx and Engels devoted much effort to preparing the

Congress. With their active participation the General Council discussed and adopted the proposals to the Congress on the changes in the Rules and Regulations of the International, first of all, on the inclusion in the Rules of the resolution on the political activity of the working class and on the extension of the General Council's powers.

The Hague Congress was the most representative. Sixty-five delegates from 15 national organisations were present. The Congress summed up the many years' struggle waged by Marx, Engels and their associates against all kinds of petty-bourgeois sectarianism in the workers' movement, Bakuninism above all. The anarchist leaders were expelled from the International. The Hague Congress decisions laid the foundation for future independent political parties of the working class in various countries.

At its meeting of July 19, 1872, the Sub-Committee instructed Marx to write the General Council's report and to deliver it at the Hague Congress. The report was confirmed by the General Council at the end of August. Before reading it in German at the open session of the Congress on September 5, Marx warned those present that he would only outline the work of the International since the report was intended for the press. The report was then read by the Congress secretaries in French, English and Dutch and adopted by all delegates except those from Spain.   p. 219

165 On April 23, 1870, the French government published a decree on holding a plebiscite, the purpose of which was to bolster up the shaky position of the government of Napoleon III. The questions were so worded that it was impossible to express disapproval of the Second Empire's policy without also opposing all democratic reforms. The plebiscite took place on May 8, 1870 and demonstrated a considerable growth of opposition to the Bonapartist regime.
                                                                                p. 219

166 This refers to the third trial of the members of the Paris organisation of the International, held from June 22 to July 8, 1870. Thirty-eight people, active in the workers' movement, were put on trial, including Eugène Varlin (he managed to flee), Leo Frankel, Jules Johannard, Augustin Avrial, Louis Chalain. The accused were sentenced to various terms of imprisonment—from two months to a year—and were fined.   p. 220

167 An ironical allusion to the outward semblance of historical events preceding the establishment and the fall of the two empires in France, i. e. of Napoleon I and of Napoleon III. In both cases the empires were established after coup d'états (on November 9, 1799 and on December 2, 1851) and fell after military defeats and the capture of the emperors (Napoleon I was defeated at Waterloo on July 18, 1815 and Napoleon III together with the French Army capitulated at Sedan on September 2, 1870, during the Franco-Prussian war).   p. 221

168 On September 5, 1870, the Brunswick Committee of the German Social-Democratic Workers' Party issued a manifesto "An alle deutschen Arbeiter". It was published as a leaflet and also in *Der Volksstaat*, No. 73, September 11, 1870. All the members of the Committee were arrested on September 9 (see notes 26 and 59).   p. 221

169 *Wilhelmshöhe* (near Kassel)—a castle of the Prussian Kings where Napoleon III, former Emperor of France, was held prisoner by the Prussians from September 5, 1870 to March 19, 1871.   p. 222

170 On November 26, 1870, when the German Reichstag discussed the question of new loans for the war with France, August Bebel and Wilhelm Liebknecht

refused to vote for them and demanded that a peace treaty without annexations should be concluded with the French Republic as soon as possible. Bebel was arrested on December 17 and Liebknecht somewhat later (see Note 59).

Despite this, Bebel was again elected deputy to the Reichstag during the general elections in March 1871.   p. 222

171 The Franco-Prussian war ended with the preliminary peace treaty of Versailles (February 26, 1871), and the final peace was signed in Frankfurt on May 10, 1871. Under its terms, France lost Alsace and Eastern Lorraine; part of France remained occupied by German troops until the war indemnity of 5,000 million francs was paid out.   p. 222

172 On Jules Favre's circular of June 6, 1871 see Note 82; for his circular dispatch of May 26, 1871 on the extradition of the Commune refugees see Note 57.
                                                                                p. 223

173 The *General Working Men's Union*, the first socialist organisation in Hungary set up in Pesth in February 1868, conducted the socialist propaganda in major industrial towns and directed workers' strikes. Its leaders (Károly Farkas, Antal Ihrlinger) were also members of the Hungarian Section of the International Association and had contacts with Austrian and German Social-Democrats and directly with Marx. On June 11, 1871, the Union organised a demonstration of solidarity with the Paris Commune. The government dissolved the Union, and its leaders and representatives of the Austrian working class who had come from Vienna were arrested on charge of treason. They were acquitted, however, for lack of evidence and under pressure of public opinion.
                                                                                p. 223

174 On the *Dufaure law* see Note 57.   p. 223

175 On the persecution of the leaders of the Austrian Social-Democratic Party in the summer of 1870 see Note 59.   p. 224

176 The *Fenians* were Irish revolutionaries who named themselves after the "Feni" — the name of the ancient inhabitants of Ireland. Their first organisations appeared in the 1850s in the USA among the Irish immigrants and later in Ireland itself. The secret Irish Revolutionary Brotherhood, as the organisation was known in the 1860s, aimed at establishing an independent Irish republic by means of an armed uprising. The Fenians, who objectively expressed the interests of the Irish peasantry, came chiefly from the urban petty bourgeoisie and intelligentsia and believed in conspiracy tactics. The British government attempted to suppress the Fenian movement by severe police reprisals. The Fenians in British prisons were brutally treated, the cruelties becoming even worse after the abortive uprising of Fenians in February-March 1867. The General Council of the International more than once came out in defence of the Fenians and condemned the punitive measures taken against them by the British government (see present edition, Vol. 20, p. 339 and Vol. 21, pp. 3-4, 407-10).   p. 224

177 Louis Pio, Paul Johansen Geleff and Harold Brix, the leaders of the Danish Federation of the International, were arrested as early as May 1872, and sentenced in March 1873 to various terms of imprisonment (from four to six years) for an attempt "to organise a coup d'état and establish a socialist state". In August the authorities banned the sections of the International in Denmark.
                                                                                p. 224

178 For the meeting of William I and Francis Joseph in Salzburg see Note 58.
p. 225

179 In his circular of August 14, 1871, Giovanni Lanza, Italian Minister of the Interior, ordered the dissolution of the International's sections. On August 20, the Naples Section was disbanded.

In January 1872, Práxedes Mateo Sagasta, Spanish Minister of the Interior, issued a similar circular. Lanza's and Sagasta's circulars were a reply by the Italian and Spanish governments to Jules Favre's call for a joint struggle against the International. p. 225

180 Between January 26 and 28, 1872, the house of Nikolai Utin was searched and his private papers and the documents of the International Association were inspected. On February 20, the General Council expressed its resolute protest against this act of arbitrariness in a special declaration written by Marx and Engels (see this volume, pp. 77-78). p. 225

181 The Emperors of Germany (William I), Austria-Hungary (Francis Joseph) and Russia (Alexander II) met in Berlin in September 1872 to resurrect the reactionary alliance of these countries. An important point in the discussion was a joint struggle against the revolutionary movement. p. 227

182 At the very first sittings of the Hague Congress when the mandates were discussed, a question was raised on the Bakuninist Alliance of Socialist Democracy as a secret sectarian organisation the existence of which within the International contradicted the Rules. Marx and other delegates proposed to appoint a special committee to inquire into the secret activities of the Alliance. The committee included Theodor Cuno, Roch Splingard, Walter, Lucain (Frédéric Potel) and Paul Vichard. Engels' report and the documents mentioned in it were submitted to the committee on September 5, 1872. It also heard reports on the Alliance by other delegates but could not bring its work up to the end in view of the abundance of documents and testimonies; however, drawing on the material examined, it came to the conclusion that the Alliance was incompatible with the International and proposed on September 7, to expel Bakunin, James Guillaume and other Alliance members from the International Association.

On the whole, the Congress adopted the motion and also resolved to make public the documents on the Alliance which were in the possession of the committee (see this volume, p. 250).

Engels' report has survived as a rough manuscript in French. It was published in English for the first time in The General Council of the First International, 1871-1872. Minutes, Progress Publishers, Moscow, 1968. p. 228

183 A reference to the circular, written by Victor Pagés in the name of the New Madrid Federation (see Note 157), to members of the Spanish Federation of the International. The circular was published in La Emancipacion, No. 61, August 10, 1872. A clipping from this issue is extant with Engels' note in red pencil: "No. 4." p. 229

184 The circular of June 2, 1872, was drawn up by José Mesa, Victor Pagés, Francisco Mora, Pablo Iglesias and other editors of La Emancipacion who were at that time also members of the Alliance. It was published in issue No. 59, July 27, 1872. p. 230

185 On the conference of the Spanish Federation in Valencia see Note 14. p. 235

24—1006

[186] In March 1872, editors of *La Emancipacion* Francisco Mora, José Mesa, Pablo Iglesias, Victor Pagés, Inocente Calleja and Hipolito Pauly, then members of the Spanish Federal Council, elected by the Valencia Conference, were expelled from the local Madrid Federation by its anarchist majority. The cause was the editors' open letter of February 25, 1872, to the representatives of the Republican Federalist Party who gathered in Madrid. The letter showed that its authors had abandoned the anarchist principle of abstention from politics, and this was considered by the Bakuninists as "a violation of the principles" of the International Association.   p. 235

[187] On the *Saragossa Congress* see Note 99.   p. 235

[188] The Spanish sections of the International held their first *congress at Barcelona* on June 19, 1870; it was attended by 90 delegates representing 150 workers' societies. The Congress founded the Spanish Federation of the International Working Men's Association and elected the Federal Council. It adopted an address to the General Council in which it declared its recognition of the General Rules of the International; it drafted the Rules of the Spanish Federation, as well as of local federations and sections (the final version of the Rules was adopted by the 1871 conference in Valencia). However, influenced by its anarchist participants, the Congress adopted a resolution recommending abstention from political struggle.   p. 235

[189] There has been preserved a copy of the pamphlet with extracts from the Saragossa Congress papers, which Engels submitted to the committee of the Hague Congress. The copy bears Engels' notes.   p. 236

[190] By sending delegates from small, and very often non-existent, sections the anarchists tried to secure an artificial majority and take over the leadership of the International (at the Basle Congress in 1869) and of the Romance Federation (at its congress in La Chaux-de-Fonds on April 4-6, 1870) (see this volume, pp. 89, 91).   p. 237

[191] Engels submitted this motion on September 6, 1872, so as to concentrate the delegates' attention on those changes in the General Rules and Administrative Regulations which were to strengthen discipline and centralisation of the International and to extend the powers of its leading body, the General Council. Marx also spoke at the same sitting in favour of the extension of the General Council's powers. During the discussion of the organisational question on September 5-6, the majority of the delegates supported Marx and Engels and rebuffed the Bakuninists' attempts to deprive the General Council of its function and to transform it into a mere statistical and correspondence bureau.

Engels' motion was published in English for the first time in *The Hague Congress of the First International. September 2-7, 1872. Minutes and Documents*, Progress Publishers, Moscow, 1976.   p. 239

[192] The European reaction prevented the General Council from having its seat anywhere but London. However, the growing activity of sectarian and reformist elements had led to a sharp struggle within the International, and a danger arose that the General Council might be seized either by the French Blanquist refugees, who sought to turn the International into the tool of their adventurist and voluntarist policy of immediate "arrangement of a revolution", or by the English reformists. Under these circumstances, it was expedient to temporarily transfer the seat of the General Council to the USA. Engels substantiated this motion in his speech on September 6, 1872. The Blanquist delegates, who voted on other points with Marx and Engels against the Bakuninists and

reformists, tried to turn down this motion and, having failed to do so, walked out.

A copy of this proposal, certified by Theodor Cuno, is extant in the Congress documents. A facsimile of Marx's manuscript in French was first published in H. Schlüter, *Die Internationale in Amerika*, Chicago, 1918. It was published in English for the first time in *The Hague Congress of the First International. September 2-7, 1872. Minutes and Documents*, Progress Publishers, Moscow, 1976.   p. 240

[193] The official text of the resolutions adopted by the Hague Congress was compiled in French and edited by Marx and Engels, members of the committee appointed to prepare the minutes and resolutions of the Congress for publication. It also included Eugène Dupont, Leo Frankel, Auguste Serraillier and Benjamin Le Moussu.

Most of the resolutions were based on the proposals by Marx and Engels which were adopted by the General Council during the preliminary discussion of the Congress agenda in the summer of 1872.

Engels' manuscript of the full French text of the resolutions prepared for the press is extant/ The present volume reproduces the resolutions from *The International Herald*. The differences in reading between the newspaper publication, the French pamphlet (which, in contrast to the English text, gives almost all the voting lists) and Engels' manuscript are given in footnotes.
                                                                                        p. 243

[194] On the invitation of the Dutch Federal Council most delegates to the Hague Congress went to Amsterdam when the Congress was over to meet the local section of the International. The meeting took place on September 8, 1872. Speeches were made by Marx, Friedrich Sorge, Paul Lafargue and other delegates. Marx delivered his speech in German and French; it was published in the Dutch, Belgian, French, German, Spanish and English press, in particular, in *The Times*, No. 27479, September 11, 1872, in Eccarius' record. The Belgian and French newspapers gave the most accurate records of Marx's speech, which tally. *Der Volksstaat* published it, with certain changes, according to the Belgian *Liberté*. Adolf Hepner wrote to Marx on September 26 that they could not print his speech verbatim, for in the conditions prevailing in Germany mention of the need for a violent revolution would immediately provide a pretext for a case against the newspaper. The Dutch *Algemeen Handelsblad* gave a résumé of Marx's speech. Its correspondent wrote: "After Citizen Sorge, there was a speech by Citizen Marx... The speaker said that formerly The Hague had been a centre of European diplomacy. Here, hardly had peace treaties been signed when plans of all sorts of war had been made. In sharp contrast to that was the congress of workers, whose purpose was to make war impossible. The International had been told that The Hague was the most reactionary city in Holland and that its ignorant population would 'tear to pieces' the 'scum of the Paris Commune'. But that was all the more reason for choosing precisely that 'blood-thirsty' city to show that the International did not fear any reactionary excesses. Moreover, it hoped to find here, too, people who sympathised with it, such as were to be found wherever there were working people.

"Citizen Marx went on to consider the results of the Congress, which had just finished work. He qualified them as important. A strong concentration of power in the hands of the General Council was an imperative necessity in the face of the conference in Berlin, which, in the speaker's opinion, presaged a general attack on the proletariat, persecution and repression of the working class. Until the International came forward as a closely united organisation, it would not be able to make the movement universal, to succeed in making it arise everywhere simultaneously, and its efforts would produce no significant results. The speaker cited the example of the Paris Commune. Why had it been defeated? Because it had remained isolated. If, simultaneously with the uprising in Paris, revolutions had flared up in Berlin, Vienna and other capitals, there would have been a greater chance of success.

"The speaker defended the use of force when other means produce no result. Barricades were not necessary in North America because there the proletarians would, if they wanted, achieve victory through elections. The same applied to England and some other countries where the working class enjoyed freedom of speech. But in the enormous majority of states revolution must replace legality because otherwise—by false magnanimity, a wrongly directed sense of justice—it would not be possible to achieve the necessary goal. Vigorous, energetic propaganda must prepare and support this revolution. For these reasons it was also extremely necessary to have an enormous centralisation of power in the hands of the General Council.

"Citizen Marx said that the Congress decided yesterday (Saturday) to transfer the General Council from London to New York. He approved this decision. America was a country of working men. Every year hundreds of thousands of people went there, driven out of Europe or forced to go by privation. What a new and beneficial field of activity for the efforts of the International. The speaker hoped that this step would produce good results.

"As for himself, he was giving up the title of member of the General Council, but—contrary to rumours—not the title of member of the International! Quite the contrary. Having freed himself of the burden of administrative activity, he would devote himself with new energy to the task to which he had given 25 years of his life and to which he would devote himself to his very last breath: the emancipation of labour. (*Stormy applause.*)"

Marx's speech, as reported by *La Liberté*, was published in English for the first time in K. Marx and F. Engels, *On Britain*, Second Edition, Foreign Languages Publishing House, Moscow, 1962.   p. 254

195 For the meeting of the three emperors see Note 181.   p. 255

196 The letter was published in English for the first time in Karl Marx, *On the First International.* Arranged and edited, with an introduction and new translations by Saul K. Padover, New York, 1973, pp. 310-11.   p. 257

197 After the Hague Congress Marx and Engels, as members of the commission appointed to edit the minutes and resolutions of the Congress, prepared these documents for publication. In October-December 1872 the resolutions of the Congress were published in French and English (see Note 193). The work on preparing the minutes for publication remained unfinished.   p. 259

198 A series of articles on the Hague Congress of the International for *Der Volksstaat* was to be written by one of its editors, Adolf Hepner, who was a delegate to the Congress. The first article was published on September 25, 1872. Soon Hepner was arrested and the editors asked two other delegates, Engels and Fritz Milke, a printer, to write reports on the Congress for them. Both complied with the request. Engels' report was published in the newspaper as the second article of the series with the following editorial note: "Article II is not written by the author of Article I. When, owing to the arrest of our correspondent, we were unable to receive some of his papers—which was also the reason for our reports appearing so late—we

asked two other participants in the Congress for reports. When the two reports arrived, *Hepner*'s papers relating to the Congress were also found and so we are in a position to present our readers with a choice of three different reports." *Der Volksstaat* published Milke's article and the beginning of Engels' article in the same issue on September 28 and Hepner's material, as the continuation of the series, i.e. as articles III and IV, on October 19, November 6, 13 and 27, 1872. Engels' article was published in the newspaper on September 28 and October 9; at the end of the first instalment the editors noted: "The end of Article II in the next issue", and the concluding part had the editorial heading: "The Hague Congress (End of Article II)".

The minor differences between the resolutions quoted by Engels and their official version are due to the fact that when Engels wrote the article there was no official text of the resolutions, adopted by the editorial committee on October 21.

The article was published in English for the first time in *The Hague Congress of the First International. September 2-7, 1872. Reports and Letters,* Progress Publishers, Moscow, 1978. p. 260

199 The data given by Engels here and in his article on the Hague Congress published in *La Plebe* (see this volume, p. 271.), differ somewhat from the list of delegates and from Friedrich Sorge's record which says that the Congress was attended by 65 delegates, among them 18 Frenchmen, 15 Germans, 7 Belgians, 5 Englishmen, 5 Spaniards, 4 Dutchmen, 4 Swiss, 2 Austrians, 1 Dane, 1 Hungarian, 1 Australian, 1 Irishman and 1 Pole. p. 260

200 The original has *Kriegs-, Haupt- und Staatsaktion.* The term has a double meaning. First, in the 17th and the first half of the 18th century, it denoted plays performed by German touring companies. The plays were rather formless historical tragedies, bombastic and at the same time coarse and farcical.

Second, the term can denote major political events. It was used in this sense by a trend in German historical science known as "objective historiography". p. 262

201 By the time the Hague Congress was convened in September 1872, the General Council comprised 50 members; 18 of them took part in the work of the Congress: six as the delegates from the General Council and 12 had mandates of different sections. Twelve voted for the motion by Marx and Engels to transfer the seat of the General Council to New York. p. 265

202 Here and below the original has *Sonderbund.* Engels ironically gives this name to the anarchists and their allies by analogy with the separate union of reactionary Catholic cantons in Switzerland in the 1840s. Marx and Engels often applied this name to the sectarian Willich-Schapper group which split from the Communist League in 1850 (see Note 44). p. 269

203 After *La Plebe* published Engels' articles "The Congress at The Hague" and "Letters from London.—II" (see this volume, pp. 283-84), Enrico Bignami, the editor of the newspaper, wrote to Engels on October 17, 1872: "As you see from the *Plebe*, I published your reports, which aroused great interest. Costa speaks of them in the *Favilla*, others in other newspapers."

This article was published in English for the first time in *The Hague Congress of the First International. September 2-7, 1872. Reports and Letters,* Progress Publishers, Moscow, 1978. p. 271

204 José Mesa, an editor of *La Emancipacion*, informed Engels in his letter of October 5, 1872, that he had received Engels' article on October 4 and found it "very good and very opportune". The editors tried to make it look like an article written in Spain and published it unsigned. It was published in English for the first time in *The Hague Congress of the First International. September 2-7, 1872. Reports and Letters*, Progress Publishers, Moscow, 1978.   p. 277

205 This article was published in English for the first time in *The Hague Congress of the First International. September 2-7, 1872. Reports and Letters*, Progress Publishers, Moscow, 1978.   p. 283

206 The Portuguese Federal Council sent a letter to the British Federal Council c/o Engels, with the request to take urgent measures to prevent the importation of strike-breakers from Britain. The threat of importation arose because all the foundry workers of Lisbon went on strike on September 19, 1872. The strikers were joined by the workers of other trades and they demanded shorter working hours. The Portuguese Federation of the International supported the strike in Lisbon. Its letter was read out at the meeting of the British Federal Council on September 26 and published in *The International Herald* on October 5, 1872.   p. 285

207 This letter was published in English for the first time in *The Hague Congress of the First International. September 2-7, 1872. Reports and Letters*, Progress Publishers, Moscow, 1978.   p. 286

208 When publishing Marx's letter, the editors of *Der Volksstaat* gave the following footnote here: "Unfortunately the words 'of the Alliance' have been omitted by negligence here. Because of this misprint one could really think that Marx tabled the motion to expel Schwitzguébel, which was not the case." Marx quoted from one of the articles on the Hague Congress written by Adolf Hepner (see Note 198).   p. 286

209 The article "On the Hague Congress. III" criticised Karl Biedermann's article in the *Deutsche Allgemeine Zeitung* saying that Paul Lafargue was the Barcelona delegate to the Hague Congress.   p. 287

210 Engels' letter of October 5, 1872, to Friedrich Sorge (on October 11 Sorge was co-opted into the General Council in New York and elected its General Secretary), shows that he wanted to send to America his report on the position of the International in Spain, Portugal and Italy. On November 2, however, Engels wrote that he enclosed only the report on Spain. That Engels intended to send reports on Italy and Portugal later is seen from the extant manuscript in which the material on Spain is marked "1". There is no information whether the reports were sent or not.   p. 288

211 For the *Congress at Barcelona* see Note 188.
    For the *Conference of Valencia* see Note 14.   p. 288

212 For the *London Conference of the International* see Note 1.   p. 289

213 For *Sagasta's circular* see Note 179.   p. 289

214 For the *Saragossa Congress* see Note 99.   p. 289

215 For the *circular of June 2, 1872* see Note 184.   p. 290

216 Engels wrote about the formation of the Lodi Section in October 1872, the Rules of which corresponded to the General Rules of the International, to the General Secretary Friedrich Sorge in his letter of November 2, 1872. On

December 22, the General Council accepted the section into the International on Engels' proposal. In early 1873, the section ceased its activity because of police persecution.   p. 293

217 This article was published in English for the first time in Marx and Engels, *Ireland and the Irish Question*, Progress Publishers, Moscow, 1971, and in Marx and Engels, *Articles on Britain*, Progress Publishers, Moscow, 1971.   p. 294

218 In his letter to Engels of December 6, 1872, Auguste Serraillier wrote that E. Larroque, a leader of the International's section in Bordeaux, had requested a provisional mandate in the name of the New York Council for the Midi. Engels drafted the mandate on the blank fourth page of Serraillier's letter. The fair copy of the mandate, probably sent by Engels to Serraillier for signature, is not extant.

Larroque's mandate was confirmed by the General Council at its meeting of December 22, 1872.   p. 297

219 Engels is referring to the congress of representatives of several Dutch sections of the International convened in Amsterdam on November 24, 1872, by the Dutch Federal Council in connection with the anarchists' opposition to the decisions of the Hague Congress. The congress resolved to support the General Council.   p. 299

220 The congress of Spanish anarchists in Cordova was held between December 25, 1872 and January 2, 1873. The congress turned down the decisions of the Hague Congress and the General Rules of the International Working Men's Association and supported the resolutions of the international congress of anarchists in Saint-Imier, Switzerland (September 1872).

On the *Saragossa Congress* see Note 99.   p. 299

221 A congress of representatives of secret organisations of the Bakuninist Alliance from various countries was held in Saint-Imier on September 15-16, 1872, on the initiative of the Jura Federation. The congress decided to reject the resolutions of the Hague Congress and the authority of the General Council. It adopted a special resolution against the political struggle of the working class and the necessity of an independent political party of the proletariat. Its address called upon sections to oppose the General Council and to convene their own "anti-authoritarian" congress in six months' time. The decisions of the Saint-Imier Congress signified an actual split in the International. p. 299

222 The Gracia Federation meeting took place on November 4-6, 1872. On hearing the report on the Hague Congress delivered by an Alliance leader Charles Alerini it rejected the anarchists' proposal to support the Saint-Imier Congress decisions and approved the Hague Congress resolutions by a majority vote.

The Valencia Federation meeting was held on November 9, 1872. It rejected the Alliance members' proposal to include the demand to support the decisions of the Saint-Imier Congress in the imperative mandate of the delegate to the Cordova Congress.   p. 300

223 After the Hague Congress English reformists and Swiss anarchists attacked all the Congress decisions, in particular, the resolutions on the political action of the working class and on the extension of the General Council's powers. When the *Bulletin de la Fédération jurassienne*, No. 23 of December 1, 1872, published John Hales' letter of November 6 and the reply to it by Alliance member Schwitzguébel, Marx and Engels decided to rebuff Hales and his supporters in the press. When publishing their letter, the editors of *La Emancipacion* prefaced it with the note:

"Below we give the letter which Citizens Marx and Engels, our comrades and friends, forwarded to *The International Herald*, a newspaper published in London, in protest against Mr. John Hales' false assertions, the assertions which the Alliance organs here, always ready to support lies, reproduce with great pleasure."   p. 301

224 See Note 137.   p. 302

225 That John Hales abused his powers as General Secretary of the General Council was more than once discussed at the Council meetings. Since the spring of 1872, Hales had been opposing the Council majority that supported Marx. At the Nottingham congress of the British Federation held on July 21-22, 1872, he urged the adoption of the resolution on the "autonomy" of the British Federal Council. Taking this fact into consideration and the support he gave to bourgeois reformists expelled from the International in the USA, the General Council unanimously decided, on July 23, 1872, to suspend Hales as Council Secretary until the final investigation of his case. The correspondence with the British sections and trade unions which had been neglected by Hales was temporarily entrusted to George Milner as the Corresponding Secretary.
                                                                            p. 302

226 See Note 206.   p. 303

227 The *Manchester Foreign Section* of the International Association was formed in August 1872 mostly from the refugee workers. It waged a vigorous struggle against the reformist wing of the British Federal Council that rejected the decisions of the Hague Congress, and supported efforts made by Marx and Engels to strengthen the British Federation and rid it of the disorganising elements. Engels wrote the present address at the Section's request in response to the circular of December 10, 1872, issued by the reformists who had split from the British Federal Council. The circular called upon the British sections of the International to defy the Hague Congress resolutions and to convene the Federation's extraordinary congress in London in January 1873. Approved by the Manchester Foreign Section, Engels' address was published as a leaflet and forwarded to all members of the International in Britain.

   The address was also published in *La Emancipacion*, No. 82, January 11, 1873, and in *Arbeiter-Zeitung*, Nos. 5 and 6, March 8 and 15, 1873.   p. 304

228 A reference to the British Federal Council meeting of December 5, 1872, which was to abolish the post of Council General Secretary, held by Hales, and to appoint a Corresponding Secretary, Treasurer, a secretary responsible for the minutes and other officials. The intention of the British Federal Council to prevent abuse of power on the part of its reformist leaders was a direct pretext for the split in the Council that followed.   p. 304

229 On the congress of the Dutch Federation see Note 219.   p. 308

230 The congress, convoked in London on January 26, 1873 (instead of January 5 as originally planned) by the reformists who had seceded from the British Federation, showed that they had failed to take with them the majority of the English sections of the International Working Men's Association. The congress, attended by 12 men only, refused to recognise the Hague Congress resolutions and thus actually placed itself outside the International. A Federal Council formed by the secessionists discontinued its meetings in the spring of 1873, and the sections which supported it either disintegrated or returned to the British Federation.   p. 308

231 This address, like the address of the Manchester Foreign Section written by Engels (see Note 227), was a reply to the reformists' splitting activities in the British Federation. The address, read out by Council member John Mitchell at the meeting of the British Federal Council on December 23, 1872, was unanimously approved by that body, published as a leaflet and sent to the sections. p. 309

232 The regular congress of the Belgian Federation of the International took place in Brussels on December 25 and 26, 1872. Influenced by the anarchists, the congress rejected the resolutions of the Hague Congress and supported those of the anarchist congress at Saint-Imier.

On the congress of Spanish anarchists in Cordova held from December 25, 1872 to January 2, 1873 see Note 220. p. 310

233 On the General Council's preparation of a draft of the revised General Rules and Administrative Regulations for submission to the Hague Congress and the proposal (made by Edouard Vaillant) to include into the Rules the resolution of the 1871 London Conference on the political action of the working class see notes 150 and 152.

On the suspension of Hales from the post of General Secretary see Note 225. p. 311

234 The first congress of the British sections of the International Working Men's Association was held in Nottingham on July 21 and 22, 1872. The congress approved the resolutions of the London Conference of the International and the activities of the General Council. The congress adopted a resolution "On Political Action" which considered it necessary for the working class to wage political struggle for its social emancipation and with this in view to create an independent workers' party. The reformist delegates tried to impose on the congress their narrow interpretation of political action of the working class in the spirit of liberal labour policy, and to distract the general attention from formulating the socialist aims of the working-class movement. They succeeded in having a number of their representatives elected to the British Federal Council. p. 311

235 This resolution was proposed by Leo Frankel and supported by Engels; it was discussed as an amendment to Article 2, Section II of the Administrative Regulations and adopted at a meeting of the General Council on June 25, 1872. p. 312

236 On the congress of the Dutch Federation see Note 219. p. 312

237 The second congress of the British Federation of the International Working Men's Association was held in Manchester on June 1 and 2, 1873. Marx and Engels took an active part in the preparation for the congress and in the working out of its political platform. The congress was attended by 26 delegates from 23 sections, who—in contrast to the reformist secessionists of the British Federation—recognised the resolutions of the 1872 Hague Congress. It adopted resolutions which stressed the necessity to create an independent political party of the proletariat, demanded socialisation of the land and all the means of production, and corroborated adherence to the principles of proletarian internationalism. Engels highly appreciated the results of the Manchester congress in his article "From the International" (see this volume, p. 449). p. 313

238 In his work *The Housing Question* Engels substantiated the basic tenets of
scientific socialism and criticised the utopian views of petty-bourgeois socialists
and bourgeois social reformers. The work consisted of three parts, each of
which appeared in the course of Engels' acute polemics with advocates of
petty-bourgeois and bourgeois projects for solving the housing question.

Part I was an immediate answer to anonymous articles under the general
heading "Die Wohnugsfrage", reprinted by *Der Volksstaat* (Nos. 10, 11, 12, 13,
15 and 19 of February 3, 7, 10, 14, 21 and March 6, 1872) from the Austrian
Volkswille. It became known later that the author was doctor of medicine,
Proudhonist Arthur Mülberger. On May 7, 1872, Engels wrote to Liebknecht:
"As soon as I have time, I shall write you an article on the housing shortage
and against the absurd Proudhonist stories that have appeared in a series of
articles on the subject in the *Volksstaat*." By May 22, 1872, Part I was finished
and published in *Der Volksstaat*, Nos. 51-53, June 26 and 29 and July 3, 1872.
A fragment of the manuscript of Part I is extant.

In October 1872 Engels wrote Part II in which he criticised the philanthropic views of social problems presented in the spirit of bourgeois socialism
by E. Sax in *Die Wohnungszustände der arbeitenden Classen und ihre Reform*.
Part II was published in *Der Volksstaat*, Nos. 103 and 104, December 25 and
28, 1872, and Nos. 2 and 3, January 4 and 8, 1873.

Part III appeared as a new reply to Mülberger to whom the editors of *Der
Volksstaat* granted space for objections to Engels. Engels had been working over
this part in January 1873 and it was published in *Der Volksstaat*, Nos. 12, 13, 15
and 16, February 8, 12, 19 and 22, 1873.

Following the publication in *Der Volksstaat*, all the three parts of Engels'
work were successively brought out by the *Volksstaat* Publishers in Leipzig in
three separate prints; two of them— *Zur Wohnungsfrage* and *Zur Wohnungsfrage.
Zweites Heft: Wie die Bourgeoisie die Wohnungsfrage löst*—appeared in 1872, and
the last— *Zur Wohnungsfrage. Drittes Heft: Nachtrag über Proudhon und die
Wohnungsfrage*—in 1873. Part II was also printed by the *Volkswille*, Nos. 3-9,
January 1873.

In 1887, a second edition of Engels' work came out in Hottingen and Zurich
under the title *Zur Wohnungsfrage*. Engels made a number of changes and
additions in the text and wrote a Preface for it (see present edition, Vol. 26).

The work was published in English for the first time as a pamphlet:
F. Engels, *The Housing Question*, Lawrence, London, 1935.   p. 317

239 See Note 135.   p. 324

240 According to the biblical legend (Exodus 16:3), during the Israelites' flight
from Egypt the most faint-hearted among them were driven by the hardships
of the journey and by hunger to recall the flesh pots of Egypt, longing for the
days of captivity when at least they had enough to eat.   p. 324

241 The attempt to organise an exchange bank on the basis of the utopian
principle of non-monetary exchange, was made by Proudhon during the
1848-49 revolution. Proudhon believed that such a bank would eliminate,
through a credit reform, social injustice and help achieve his ideal—a society of
equal commodity-producers freely exchanging services and the products of
their labour. However, the Banque du peuple, founded by him on January 31,
1849 in Paris, went bankrupt even before it began to function regularly and
was closed down early in April of the same year.   p. 328

242 *Labour Exchange Bazaars*, or *Equitable Labour Exchange Bazaars or Offices*, were
organised by cooperative workers' societies in various cities of England. The

first such bazaar was arranged by Robert Owen in London in September 1832 and existed till mid-1834. Products of labour were exchanged there for labour paper money, its unit of value being a working hour. Such enterprises were a utopian attempt to organise a non-monetary exchange under the conditions of capitalist commodity economy, and they soon went bankrupt.   p. 329

243 Proudhon proposed such a solution of the housing question in his *Idée générale de la révolution au XIXe siècle* (the first edition appeared in Paris in 1851; in the Paris edition of 1868, see pp. 199-204). As early as 1851 Engels, at Marx's request, made a detailed critical analysis of the book. Having shown the infeasibility of Proudhon's general reformist idea and his anarchist views, Engels also noted the utopian character of his project for turning a house tenant into an owner, which Proudhon proposed as a measure to implement the so-called "social liquidation"—a peaceful transformation of society in the spirit of petty-bourgeois ideals (see present edition, Vol. 11, pp. 560-61). Engels had in his library a copy of the 1868 edition of Proudhon's book. The notes in the margins of that volume were probably made by Engels when he worked on *The Housing Question*.   p. 329

244 The reference is to the decree signed by Louis Bonaparte on January 22, 1852. By this decree, the state issued a loan of 10,000,000 francs (one-third of the necessary capital) for building dwellings for the workers. In Mulhouse (Alsace) the manufacturer Jean Dollfus founded the Société des cités ouvrières for this purpose. The workers became the owners of the houses built by this society after they paid an increased monthly rent for about 15 years.

Below, in Part II, Engels elaborated on the true aims of this enterprise and its results (see p. 354).   p. 330

245 In his book Emil Sax refers to numerous works by the authors mentioned, among them to the following: Ed. Ducpétiaux, "De l'amélioration des habitations de la classe ouvrière en Angleterre" in *Congrès général d'hygiène de Bruxelles. Session de 1852. Compte-rendu des séances*. Brussels, 1852; idem, *Projet d'Association financière pour l'amélioration des habitations et l'assainissement des quartiers habités par la classe ouvrière à Bruxelles*, Brussels, 1846; idem, *Texte des résolutions votées.—Appendice. Plans*, Brussels, 1852; James Hole, *The Homes of Working Classes with Suggestions for Their Improvement*, London, 1866; V. A. Huber, *Genossenschaftliche Briefe aus Belgien, Frankreich u. England*, Vols. 1, 2, Hamburg [1855]; idem, *Sociale Fragen*. IV. Die latente Association, Nordhausen, 1866; idem, "Ueber die geeignetsten Maßregeln zur Abhülfe der Wohnungsnoth" in *Die Wohnungsfrage mit besonderer Rücksicht auf die arbeitenden Klassen*, Berlin, 1865; idem, "Ueber innere Colonisation" in *Janus*, Vol. 1, Nos. 7, 8, Berlin, 1846; idem, "Die Wohnungsfrage" in *Concordia*, Nos. 2, 3, Leipzig, 1861; idem, "Die Wohnungsfrage in Frankreich und England" in *Zeitschrift des Central-Vereins in Preußen für das Wohl der arbeitenden Klassen*, Vol. 2, No. 1, Leipzig, 1859; idem, *Die Wohnungsnoth der kleinen Leute in großen Städten*, Leipzig, 1857; H. Roberts, *The Dwellings of the Labouring Classes, Their Arrangement and Construction*, London [1850]; idem, "The dwellings of the labouring classes, their improvement through the operation of government measures, by those of public bodies and benevolent associations, as well as by individual efforts" in *Transactions of the National Association for the Promotion of Social Science. 1858*, London, 1859; idem, *The Essentials of a Healthy Dwelling, and the Extension of Its Benefits to the Labouring Population*, London, 1862; idem, *Home Reform: or, What the Working Classes May Do to Improve Their Dwellings*, London

[1852]; idem, "The measures adopted in England for promoting improvement in the dwellings of the labouring classes" in *Congrès international de Bienfaisance de Londres. Session de 1862*, Vol. 2, London, Brussels, Ghent, Leipzig, Paris, 1863; idem, "On the progress and present aspect of the movement for improving the dwellings of the labouring classes" in *Transactions of the National Association for the Promotion of Social Science. 1860*, London, 1861; idem, *The Physical Condition of the Labouring Classes, Resulting from the State of Their Dwellings, and the Beneficial Effects of Sanitary Improvements Recently Adopted in England*. Rev. Ed., London, 1866.　　　　　　　　　　　　　　　　　p. 338

246 In 1859, a French manufacturer, Jean Baptiste André Godin, founded a socialist colony in Guise (Aisne Department in the north of France) on a model of Fourier's phalanstery, with production and everyday life organised on a cooperative basis. By the 1880s the colony, named Familistère, turned into a capitalist joint-stock enterprise.　　　　　　　　　　　　　　　　　p. 348

247 *Harmony Hall* was a communist colony established in Hampshire (South England) at the end of 1839 by English utopian socialists headed by Robert Owen. It existed until 1845. Engels characterised it in one of his earlier articles, "Description of Recently Founded Communist Colonies Still in Existence" (see present edition, Vol. 4, pp. 223-27).　　　　　　　　　　　　　　　p. 348

248 In June 1869, the Reichstag of the North German Confederation, established after Prussia's victory in the Austro-Prussian war of 1866, adopted the new Trades Rules which came into force on October 1, 1869. These Rules eliminated all the limitations of free enterprise previously in existence in Prussia and other German states. The bourgeoisie had long been pressing for this concession on the part of Bismarck's government. At the same time the Reichstag had to abolish the articles of the former Trades Rules which prohibited the creation of workers' coalitions (trades unions).　　　　p. 352

249 Engels is referring to an idea spread by Schulze-Delitzsch, a German economist, that the creation of workers' cooperative societies would peacefully solve the social question within the framework of a capitalist society. Schulze-Delitzsch and his supporters used this idea and tried to put it into practice as a means of distracting the workers from the proletarian revolutionary movement. p. 357

250 A reference to the 5,000-million francs indemnity which France had to pay to Germany under the terms of the Frankfurt Peace Treaty of May 10, 1871 (see Note 171).　　　　　　　　　　　　　　　　　　　　　　　　　p. 365

251 Engels is referring to the statements made by Adolf Wagner in a number of his books and speeches (see, for example, his *Rede über die sociale Frage*, Berlin, 1872, pp. 55-58) to the effect that the revival of economic activity in Germany after the 5,000-million francs indemnity had been received would considerably improve the condition of the working people.

On the talks between Bismarck and Beust, Chancellor of Austria-Hungary, and also between the Emperors William I and Francis Joseph in Gastein and Salzburg in August-September 1871 see Note 58. Calling them Stieber's conferences after a senior police official of that name, Engels emphasised their anti-worker and police character.　　　　　　　　　　　　　　　p. 365

252 Among Engels' manuscripts the excerpts have survived which he made early in 1873 from Proudhon's *La guerre et la paix* (published in 1869) when he was preoccupied with Part III of *The Housing Question*. Engels supplied these excerpts with his own comments in which he stressed Proudhon's idealistic views, his misunderstanding of the laws of social development, and his

pretentious unsubstantiated judgments. "Everywhere there is nothing but pretentiousness and sheer assertion instead of proof and development of thought," Engels stated. As regards Proudhon's explanation of the origin of social inequality, he noted, "It is not deduced from the laws of economic and historical development, but, as everything else, wars included, from psychological reasons..." Engels also pointed out that Proudhon's theory of population was close to Malthus' false doctrine which stated that population tends to increase faster than the means of subsistence for natural reasons, and, therefore, alleged that the distress of the working people cannot be explained by social conditions.   p. 380

253 The District Regulations for the provinces of Prussia, Brandenburg, Pomerania, Posen, Silesia and Saxony, adopted in December 1872, were part of an administrative reform in Prussia. It abolished patrimonial power of the Junkers and introduced certain elements of local self-government (community elders were to be elected and district councils under government officials were introduced). The reform aimed at greater centralisation of the Junker bourgeois state in the interests of the Junkers in general and preserved, in fact, all the privileges of individual representatives of this class. They were given an opportunity to be elected or nominated to most of the offices in local government or have their protégés there. Nevertheless the reform met with strong resistance of conservative nobility and landed aristocracy, especially in the Prussian Upper House. For details see Engels' article "The 'Crisis' in Prussia" (this volume, pp. 400-05).   p. 381

254 As the editorial board of La Plebe intended to start a yearbook Almanacco Repubblicano in 1873, the newspaper editor Enrico Bignami requested Engels on July 31, 1872 and Marx on October 10, 1872 to write articles for this collection. Engels wrote an article "On Authority" (see Note 295), and Marx wrote the present article, "Political Indifferentism". Marx's original, which was probably written in French, is not extant. Translated by Bignami, the article was published in the Almanacco Repubblicano per l'anno 1874 only in December 1873. The publication could not be started earlier because of the police persecution. In Engels' lifetime Marx's article was reprinted by the Milanese La Battaglia (Vol. 1, No. 15, July 14) in the summer of 1894.

The article was published in English for the first time in The Plebs, Vol. XIV, No. 11, London, 1922.   p. 392

255 In May 1864, the Corps législatif repealed the so-called Le Chapelier Law of 1791 on the prohibition of workers' associations and adopted, on May 24, another one after the project of a moderate republican Emile Ollivier. It granted workers the right of combination but prohibited assemblies.   p. 395

256 The strike of stone-masons and miners in Rive-de-Gier (a town south of Lyons) broke out in the spring of 1844. The strike, caused by hard labour conditions and low wages, was suppressed by the troops.   p. 395

257 The reference is to the act of the British Parliament which in 1824 cancelled the prohibition of workers' coalitions and provided the basis for the legalisation of trades unions.   p. 396

258 Engels is alluding to the growing desire of the French reactionaries to restore the monarchy after the fall of the Paris Commune. Monarchist elements prevailed in the National Assembly (nicknamed the Rural Assembly) which was elected in February 1871 and had its seat in Versailles. However, the attempts at restoration were hampered by the quarrels continuing between various

monarchist factions and, above all, by the fear felt by the greater part of the bourgeoisie of a new revolutionary action by the republican-minded masses. Therefore many bourgeois politicians, Thiers, President of the Republic, among them, preferred to leave the republican form of government intact, preserving at the same time the monarchist institutions ("a republic without republicans").   p. 400

259 See Note 253.   p. 400

260 Engels is referring to the restoration of patrimonial jurisdiction (that is, the landlord's right to exercise police and legal functions with respect to peasants dependent on him), which was abolished in 1848-49 but actually sanctioned by the law of April 14, 1856, for the six provinces of the Kingdom of Prussia lying east of the Elbe (Prussia, Brandenburg, Pomerania, Posen, Silesia and Saxony).

On February 9, 1849, the Prussian government issued two decrees prescribing changes in the Trades Rules, which introduced Trades Councils (Gewerberäte) and Trades Courts (Gewerbegerichte), thus virtually restoring medieval trade legislation. These decrees nullified attempts to eliminate the medieval barriers to industrial and commercial activities which were made in the period of liberal reforms in Prussia after its defeat in the war against Napoleonic France. In particular, they actually annulled the decree of October 24, 1808 on the elimination of guild restrictions and monopolies, and also the order of December 26, 1808 which declared, in general terms, the freedom of industry and commerce.   p. 401

261 Engels is referring to the June insurrection of the Paris proletariat, see Note 135.   p. 401

262 In 1856, the head of the Prussian police department Hinckeldey was killed in a duel by Baron Rochow, a representative of an ultra-conservative grouping interested in the business of a gambling-house closed down by the police. A number of bourgeois newspapers, the Berlin *National Zeitung* (No. 119/120, March 11, 1856) in particular, responded to this event with laudatory articles about Hinckeldey, describing him as a champion of liberty and progress.
                                                                              p. 401

263 The reference is to the "liberal" course announced by Prince William of Prussia (King of Prussia since 1861) when he became regent in October 1858. He made the Manteuffel ministry resign and called the moderate liberals to power. The bourgeois press dubbed this the policy of the "New Era". It was, in fact, solely intended to strengthen the position of the Prussian monarchy and the Junkers. This soon became clear to the representatives of the liberal opposition whose hopes had been deceived and who refused to approve the government project of a military reform.   p. 401

264 A reference to the war waged by France and the Kingdom of Sardinia (Piedmont), on the one side, and Austria, on the other, from April 29 to July 8, 1859. Austria suffered a defeat and was compelled to cede Lombardy to Piedmont, while Piedmont, in its turn, ceded Savoy and Nice to Bonapartist France. During the war, the Prussian government, pursuing the "policy of having a free hand", declared neutrality.   p. 402

265 Engels is referring to the so-called constitutional conflict in Prussia which started in February 1860 when the liberal majority of the Provincial Diet refused to approve the projected army reorganisation moved by von Roon, Minister of War. The government, however, soon succeeded in obtaining allocations for the maintenance of the army in fighting trim, and this helped it to begin the planned reorganisation. In March 1862, the liberal majority

refused to approve the military expenditure and demanded that the ministry should be answerable to the Provincial Diet. The government dissolved the Diet and fixed a new election. In late September the Bismarck ministry was formed which, in October of the same year, dissolved the Diet again and began to effect a military reform without the Diet's sanction. The conflict was settled only in 1866, when after Prussia's victory over Austria the Prussian bourgeoisie gave in to Bismarck. For details see Engels' "The Prussian Military Question and the German Workers' Party" (present edition, Vol. 20).   p. 402

266 This refers to the war of Prussia and Austria against Denmark in 1864 over Schleswig and Holstein, duchies subject to Denmark but inhabited mainly by Germans. Austria joined the war in the fear that if its rival, Prussia, fought on its own, it would enjoy all the fruits of victory. Denmark was defeated. Schleswig and Holstein were declared joint possessions of Austria and Prussia, which aggravated the conflict between the two countries. After its defeat in the war against Prussia in 1866, Austria had to renounce its right to the duchies in Prussia's favour.   p. 402

267 On July 3, 1866, a decisive battle of the Austro-Prussian war took place near the village of Sadowa at Königgrätz (Hradec Králové), Bohemia. The Austrian troops suffered a major defeat.   p. 402

268 Engels, apparently, refers to the idea of the recurrence of historical events which Hegel expressed in his work *Vorlesungen über die Philosophie der Geschichte*, the first edition of which was published in Berlin in 1837 (see Part 3, Section 2, entitled "Rom vom zweiten punischen Krieg bis zum Kaiserthum"). Hegel also repeatedly expressed the idea that in the process of dialectical development there is bound to be a transition from the stage of formation and efflorescence to that of disintegration and ruin (see, in particular, G.W.F. Hegel, *Grundlinien der Philosophie des Rechts* (Part 3, Section 3, § 347).

Hegel's idea was developed by Marx in *The Eighteenth Brumaire of Louis Bonaparte* (see present edition, Vol. 11, p. 103), *Contribution to the Critique of Hegel's Philosophy of Law. Introduction* (Vol. 3, p. 179), *The Deeds of the Hohenzollern Dynasty* (Vol. 9, p. 421), and by Engels in his letter to Marx of December 3, 1851 (Vol. 38, p. 505).   p. 403

269 As a result of Prussia's victory in the Austro-Prussian war of 1866, Prussia annexed the Kingdom of Hanover, the Electorate of Hesse-Kassel, the Grand Duchy of Nassau, the free city of Frankfort on the Main, and the duchies of Holstein and Schleswig.   p. 403

270 The Stahl-Gerlach party, or party of the *Kreuz-Zeitung* (as the *Neue Preußische Zeitung* was called), was formed during the revolution of 1848-49 and consisted of representatives of the counter-revolutionary court clique and feudal Junkers. Striving to restore limited absolutism, the party defended privileges of the aristocracy and nobility. It opposed Bismarck's policy of Germany's unification from above seeing it as a threat to feudal privileges.   p. 403

271 The *North German Confederation* was a federative state formed in 1867 under Prussia's supremacy after its victory in the Austro-Prussian war. It replaced the German Confederation which was established in 1815. The North German Confederation incorporated 19 German states and three free cities. The King of Prussia was declared president of the Confederation and commander-in-chief of the confederate armed forces; he was also in charge of foreign policy. The creation of the North German Confederation was an important stage in

implementing the so-called Little Germany plan for the unification of Germany (without Austria) which was carried out by Bismarck. In 1870 the Confederation was joined by Bavaria, Baden, Württemberg and Hesse-Darmstadt. In January 1871 upon the formation of the German Empire the Confederation ceased to exist.   p. 403

272 As a rule, the British Parliament created new peers when the government sought to form a majority in the House of Lords which would support its measures. The ruling circles in several other countries also used this device to influence the upper chambers (the Prussian Upper House, in particular).
                                                                               p. 404

273 The Prussian bourgeoisie was pressing its demands with increased force in 1845-46, its hopes for liberal reform having failed to materialise at Frederick William IV's ascension to the throne in 1840. In 1845, almost all the provincial diets demanded a constitution. In his memorandum of 1846 David Hansemann, a wealthy bourgeois of the Rhine Province, suggested that an all-Prussian parliament should be summoned, the Customs Union strengthened and enlarged, patrimonial jurisdiction and a number of other privileges of the nobility abolished, freedom of the press and the jury system introduced, etc.
                                                                               p. 405

274 This reply was published together with the official communication of the British Federal Council which read as follows: "A circular having appeared, signed by a former Corresponding Secretary of the British Federal Council, and others, convening a so-called Congress for the 26th inst., we hereby declare that the time of assemblage and purpose of the said proposed Congress are illegal, and that members of the Association taking part in the said so-called Congress, as well as Sections authorising members to take part in it will render themselves liable to expulsion from our Association."

On the secessionist congress of the reformist elements of the British Federation see Note 230.   p. 406

275 The First Congress of the North American Federation of the International Working Men's Association which took place in New York between July 6 and 8, 1872, elected the Federal Council consisting of: C. Carl, F. Bertrand, F. Bolte, E. David, E. Levièle, S. Cavanagh, Saint-Clair, Laurell and Cetti. When the seat of the General Council was transferred to New York by decision of the Hague Congress, all these persons, except Cetti, became Council members; David, however, soon left it and Saint-Clair and Levièle actually did not take part in its activities. The co-optation into the Council of Friedrich Sorge, Marx's and Engels, associate, and his election as General Secretary on October 11, 1872, were conducive to unity among the efficient and stable proletarian elements in the Council.   p. 408

276 See Note 221.   p. 408

277 In December 1872, after the split in the British Federation of the International Working Men's Association, *The International Herald* became an official newspaper of the new British Federal Council. Wishing to support the paper, Engels considered it necessary to keep it as well informed as possible about the development of the international working-class movement, and especially about the activities of the International on the Continent. The paper published his communications on the subject in the reports on the meetings of the British Federal Council written by Samuel Vickery. Some of Engels' communications

were published, apparently, in abridged form. In a letter to Engels of February 15, 1873, which is extant, William Riley, the newspaper's editor, apologised for the incomplete publication of the material received.   p. 409

278 See Note 220.   p. 410

279 On the meeting of the Gracia Federation see Note 222.

Mariano Rodriguez, delegate of the Federation of Granada to the Congress at Cordova, had an imperative mandate which required full approval of the Hague Congress resolutions. Engels obtained this information from José Mesa's letter of December 29, 1872.   p. 410

280 Apparently, Engels is referring to one of the letters he received from Nobre Franca, Secretary of the Lisbon Section.   p. 410

281 Obviously, Engels means the participation of members of the International's federations of Gracia and Cadiz in the armed insurrection of republican federalists in Andalusia in November 1872 and of members of the New Madrid Federation in the armed insurrection in Madrid in late November-early December 1872.   p. 411

282 In his letter to Engels of January 18, 1873, José Mesa asked Engels to inform the workers in England and Belgium, through the International's periodicals, about the railwaymen's strike in Spain in order to prevent the importation of strike-breakers.

The strike by the engine-drivers and stokers on the railway lines Almansa-Valencia and Tarragona-Almansa began on December 23, 1872, and successfully ended in early April 1873. The strikers demanded shorter working hours and higher wages.

A committee appointed by the British Federal Council to prevent the importation of strike-breakers, reported at the Council meeting of January 30, 1873, that it had sent notices on the strike to a number of English newspapers, in particular, to *The Standard, Reynolds's Newspaper* and *Railway Servant's Gazette.* One of these notices was published in *Reynolds's Newspaper,* No. 1173 on February 2, 1873.   p. 411

283 On July 6, 1872, August Bebel was sentenced by the Leipzig circuit court to the nine months imprisonment (in addition to two years in the fortress to which he and Liebknecht had been sentenced earlier) and was deprived of his powers as deputy to the Reichstag on the charge of *lèse majesté.* Bebel's speeches at the meetings on February 19 and 26, 1872, served as grounds for the sentence. Bebel won a victory at the additional elections to the Reichstag in the district of Glauchau-Meerane, where he had been elected before. Engels most likely drew this information from *Der Volksstaat,* Nos. 9 and 10, January 29 and February 1, 1873.   p. 411

284 By decision of the Committee of the Jura Federation, the *Bulletin de la Fédération jurassienne,* No. 20/21, November 10, 1872, published Jules Montels' letter with a protest against the expulsion from the International, by the Beziers section, of an anarchist Abel Bousquet, Secretary of Police.   p. 412

285 The *Notes for the General Council,* and Engels' letters to the General Council of the International Working Men's Association of April 15 and June 14, 1873 (see this volume, pp. 437-38 and 447), show that Engels as well as Marx rendered immediate support to the leading body of the International in New

York, supplied it with the necessary information and assisted in taking the correct decisions. The *Notes* have survived as a manuscript by Engels. This text does not fully coincide with the one first published in part in *Briefe und Auszüge aus Briefen von Joh. Phil. Becker, Jos. Dietzgen, Friedrich Engels, Karl Marx u. A. an F. A. Sorge und Andere*, Stuttgart, 1906. p. 414

286 The first part of the report on the secessionist London Congress of the British Federation—"Congress of the International Working Men's Association"—was published in *The Eastern Post*, No. 227, February 1, 1873. The second and concluding part of the report appeared in the second edition of No. 228 of February 9, 1873, on the next day after the *Notes* were written. p. 414

287 The Second Congress of the Italian anarchists who had formed their federation at the Rimini Conference (see Note 161) was set for March 15 in Mirandola; later, however, it was transferred to Bologna. It took place on March 15-17, 1873. p. 414

288 By its decision of January 5, 1873, the International General Council in New York suspended the anarchist Jura Federation from the Association until the next Congress.

The critical remarks made by Marx and Engels in their letters to Sorge and Engels' statement here concerning the unsatisfactory character of this decision, made the General Council in New York revise it. On January 26, 1873, the Council adopted a resolution which stated that all the societies and individuals refusing to recognise the Hague Congress decisions and comply with the demands of the International's Rules and Administrative Regulations, thereby put themselves outside its ranks. Another resolution of the Council of May 30, 1873 confirmed and elaborated on this decision.

On Sonderbund see Note 202. p. 415

289 After the Hague Congress Theodor Cuno emigrated to America. He signed an appeal of Section 29 of the International Working Men's Association to the New Madrid Federation of January 10, 1873 with the assumed name of Capestro. The Brussels *Internationale*, No. 212, February 2, 1873 reported on this fact, stating that Cuno and Capestro were one and the same person.

p. 415

290 Membership stamps were issued by decision of the London Conference of 1871 and were affixed to the membership card to indicate payment of the annual subscription. By decision of the General Council of December 22, 1872 these stamps continued to be issued in London. The French émigré Le Moussu, an engraver, undertook to manufacture a cliché and print them. p. 416

291 This article was published as a leader in *Der Volksstaat*, No. 18, March 1, 1873. The term "Caesarism" which is not to be found in any other work by Engels shows the interference—though slight—of an editor. In the Spanish translation the last paragraph was omitted. José Mesa, editor of *La Emancipacion*, wrote in this connection to Engels on March 11, 1873: "You must have seen that I allowed myself to omit the last paragraph in your article from the *Volksstaat* which I thought somewhat discouraging. I apologise a thousand times to you."

While working on the article, Engels apparently discussed with Marx the problems that arose in it. Consequently, a number of the conclusions and points it contains—on the essence of Bonapartism, on the republic as a form of the bourgeois state, on the attitude of the working class to it—may have been the result of their cooperation. p. 417

292 In September 1868, the fifth bourgeois revolution began in Spain and continued till 1874. This struck a blow at the absolutist reactionary forces which supported the survivals of feudalism in the country. Queen Isabella II fled and the liberals came to power, advocating a constitutional monarchy. In 1870, Amadeo, representative of the Savoy dynasty, was elected to the throne. His position, however, proved very unstable in the situation of a deepening domestic crisis, growth of pro-republican moods among the masses and, at the same time, constant attacks from the right, i.e. of the reactionary monarchist elements. On February 9, 1873, Amadeo abdicated, and on February 11 a republic was proclaimed in Spain. This opened up a new stage in the development of the revolution and led to the further exacerbation of the class struggle and to deeper contradictions in the republican camp itself.   p. 418

293 The surrender of the French army under MacMahon and the capture of Emperor Napoleon III by the Prussians during the Franco-Prussian war of 1870-71, took place on September 2, 1870 at Sedan.

The Sedan disaster hastened the collapse of the Second Empire and led to a republic in France being proclaimed on September 4, 1870.   p. 418

294 The *Carlists*—a clerical-absolutist group which supported the claims of Don Carlos, King Ferdinand VII's brother, to the Spanish throne in the first half of the 19th century. Leaning for support on the reactionary military circles and Catholic clergy, as well as the backward peasantry from the mountainous regions of Spain, the Carlists unleashed a civil war in 1833 which lasted till 1840 (the 1st Carlist war). When Don Carlos died in 1855, the Carlists supported the candidature of his grandson, Don Carlos, Jr. In 1872, during the political crisis, the Carlists became more active and this led to another civil war (2nd Carlist war) which did not end until 1876.   p. 420

295 Engels wrote this article after repeated requests by Enrico Bignami to Marx and Engels to send him articles for the collection *Almanacco Repubblicano* (see Note 254). Bignami addressed Engels for the first time on July 31, 1872. On November 3, 1872, Bignami informed Engels that he had received his article written, apparently, in October. However, Bignami was arrested and the manuscript was lost. Bignami wrote to Engels about this loss on March 2, 1873, and asked him to send, if possible, either a copy of that article or something else for the collection planned. In March 1873 Engels sent Bignami the second version of the article "On Authority" which was published in December of that year in the *Almanacco Repubblicano per l'anno 1874.*

The article was published in English for the first time in *The New Review*, No. 4, New York, 1914.   p. 422

296 Engels' notes on the labour movement in Europe and America are thematically linked with his "News on the Activities of the International on the Continent" which was published in the same newspaper, *The International Herald*, in January-February 1873 (see this volume, pp. 409-13). As distinct from the "News on the Activities of the International on the Continent", published in the reports on the meetings of the British Federal Council of the International, the "News on the International Labour Movement" was published separately under the headings "Continental Trade News" and "Foreign Trade News". The labour press of different countries, notably the Leipzig *Volksstaat* and the Madrid *Emancipacion*, as well as the information Engels drew from the extensive correspondence with his friends and associates, served as a source for the "News on the International Labour Movement".   p. 426

297 The first strike won through the assistance of the International was the strike of Geneva builders; it took place in March-April 1869. The campaign of support organized by the International forced the employers to meet the workers' demands: introduce a common pay by the hour and raise wages from 15 to 25 centimes per hour.   p. 427

298 The congress of Swiss Working Men took place in Olten between June 1 and 3, 1873. Apart from the Swiss sections of the International Working Men's Association, it was attended by representatives of trades unions, cooperatives, educational and other workers' societies. The congress founded the Swiss Workers' Union, which existed until 1880 and amalgamated various workers' organisations on the principles of the International.   p. 428

299 The reference is to the Hungarian General Working Men's Union (see Note 173).
   On March 23, 1873, the meeting at Budapest proclaimed the foundation of the Hungarian Workers' Party whose aim was to unite representatives of all trends in the Hungarian workers' movement. The Workers' Party was dissolved by a governmental decree of May 10, 1873.   p. 432

300 See Note 290.   p. 437

301 See Note 1.   p. 437

302 On the preparing the Hague Congress minutes for publication see Note 197.   p. 438

303 The last issue of *La Emancipacion* came out on April 12, 1873.   p. 438

304 This refers to the Second Congress of the British Federation of the International fixed for June 1 and 2, 1873 in Manchester (see Note 237).
                                                                           p. 438

305 This article is part of Engels' letter to Adolf Hepner, editor of *Der Volksstaat*, written in late April 1873 in connection with the libellous article about the International Working Men's Association in the *Neuer Social-Demokrat*, No. 49, April 27, 1873. The letter was not meant for the press, but the newspaper editors published a part of it without mentioning the author in *Der Volksstaat*, No. 37, May 7, 1873. On May 2, Engels wrote "The International and the *Neuer*", specially for the *Volksstaat*, which appeared in No. 38 on May 10, 1873 (see this volume, pp. 442-45).   p. 439

306 See Note 57.   p. 439

307 In many French cities at the end of 1872 and the beginning of 1873, the police, who had obtained information from their informers and spies (in particular, from Van-Heddeghem), made numerous arrests of members of the International's sections. Trials were organised in a number of cities. The first took place in Paris in February-early March 1873. The four accused were sentenced to imprisonment from one to three years. A major trial of members of the International was held in Toulouse from March 10 to 26. The organisers of the trial widely used the testimony of Dentraygues, a member of the Toulouse section, who had divulged, during the preliminary investigation and at the trial itself, information about the composition and activities of nearly all the sections of the International in the Midi. Twenty-two out of the 38 accused were sentenced to various terms of imprisonment. Police and court reprisals inflicted a heavy blow on the French organisations of the International Working Men's Association.   p. 440

308 See Note 307.   p. 442

309 The *reptile press fund*—a special money fund at Bismarck's disposal for bribing the press. It got this name after Bismarck's speech in the Prussian Provincial Diet in January 1869 when he applied the word "reptiles" to mercenary agents. After this, the left press began to use the expression to denote the government-bribed semi-official press.   p. 442

310 *The International Herald* included this communication in its report on the regular meeting of the British Federal Council, which took place on May 8, 1873.   p. 446

311 This is an allusion to the attempts made by John Hales, former General Secretary of the General Council of the International, after the transfer of the General Council from London to New York, to turn the breakaway reformist wing of the British Federal Council into a sort of centre for all the federations opposing the decisions of the Hague Congress. Hales' claims to leadership in the international working-class movement did not find support on the Continent.   p. 446

312 A reference to the General Council decision of January 26, 1873, published in *La Plebe*, No. 14, June 1, 1873.

The address of the General Council of the International Working Men's Association to Spanish workers of February 23, 1873 was occasioned by the proclamation of a republic in Spain. It was published in *La Plebe*, No. 13, May 26, 1873.

After a temporary suspension from March 23, 1873, caused by police persecution, *La Plebe* resumed publication after May 15, 1873.   p. 447

313 Engels is referring to the draft General Rules and Administrative Regulations of the International, revised by the General Council in the summer of 1872 for the Hague Congress (see Note 150).   p. 447

314 One fragment of this article was published in English for the first time in Marx and Engels, *Ireland and the Irish Question*, Progress Publishers, Moscow, 1971, and another in Marx, Engels, Lenin, *Anarchism and Anarcho-Syndicalism*, Progress Publishers, Moscow, 1972.   p. 448

315 On the split in the British Federation of the International and the London Congress of its breakaway reformist wing in January 1873 see notes 228 and 230.   p. 448

316 See Note 237.   p. 449

317 See Note 176.   p. 449

318 On the application of the words "Sonderbund", "Sonderbündler", etc., to the anarchist secessionists in Engels' works of the period see Note 202.   p. 449

319 A reference to the draft of the new Rules of the International Working Men's Association, worked out by the Belgian Federal Council in the anarchist spirit before the Hague Congress of the International (see Note 88).   p. 451

320 Renan's book *L'Antéchrist* (Paris, 1873) was the fourth volume of his comprehensive *Histoire des origines du christianisme*, Vols I-VIII, Paris, 1863-1883. A review of this book was included in an anonymous report marked "Paris, June 26" and published in *Kölnische Zeitung*, No. 181, Supplement 3, July 2, 1873. Engels' note on the review was freely translated into Serbo-Croat by an anonymous author in the Belgrade Church journal Православље (Orthodoxy),

No. 9, September 1873. The author referred to the *Kölnische Zeitung* and mentioned Engels.

Engels mentions Prof. Ferdinand Benary's lectures, which he attended at Berlin University as an external student when he did military service as a volunteer in Berlin from September 1841 to October 1842.

Engels examined in detail the problem of the dating and composition of the last book in the New Testament, the Revelation of St. John the Divine or the Apocalypse (from Greek *apokálypsis*, revelation), in his articles "The Book of Revelation" and "On the History of Early Christianity", written in 1883 and 1894. p. 452

321 Engels attached great importance to Giuseppe Garibaldi's criticism of anarchist doctrines and did his best to make known the ideas Garibaldi had expressed on that score in his letter to Prospero Crescio. Engels quoted from his letter in the German translation in his article "From the International", published in *Der Volksstaat* in early July 1873. He inserted it as a footnote in the pamphlet *The Alliance of Socialist Democracy and the International Working Men's Association* written in French (see this volume, pp. 451, 504). To familiarise the members of the British Federation of the International with the letter, Engels translated it into English for the meeting of the British Federal Council on July 8, 1873. It was included in the report on the meeting, published in *The Eastern Post* on July 13, 1873. Engels supplied the translation with a short comment which he may have written after the meeting of the Council, when the report on it was being prepared for the press. p. 453

322 Marx and Engels wrote this work, with the assistance of Paul Lafargue, between April and July 1873, drawing on a large number of documents presented to the commission of inquiry into the activities of the secret Alliance, appointed by the Hague Congress. Among them was the material sent by Lafargue, José Mesa and others from Spain, J. Ph. Becker from Switzerland, N. F. Danielson and N. N. Lyubavin from Russia, and a large report written by N. I. Utin on the instructions of the London Conference of 1871. Some of the documents reached Marx and Engels only after the Hague Congress.

A number of preparatory materials are extant, including a list of documents used in the process of work. This list, drawn up by Engels, shows that the authors had at their disposal French translations of a few Russian editions sent in by Utin. That is why a number of Bakunin's documents are quoted according to their French translation.

The Alliance of Socialist Democracy and the International Working Men's Association was published as a pamphlet in French in late August-early September 1873; in the summer of 1874 it came out in Brunswick in German (in S. Kokosky's translation) under the title "Ein Complot gegen die Internationale Arbeiter-Association" (A Conspiracy Against the International Working Men's Association). Engels took a direct part in the editing of the German translation. In October 1873-January 1874, the Introduction and the first four chapters of this work were published in the New York *Arbeiter-Zeitung*. The work was published in English for the first time in *The Hague Congress of the First International, September 2-7, 1872. Minutes and Documents*, Progress Publishers, Moscow, 1976. p. 454

323 A reference to the commission which was to prepare the minutes and resolutions of the Hague Congress of the International for publication. It was elected at the Congress sitting on September 7, 1872, and consisted of Karl

Marx, Frederick Engels, Eugène Dupont, Leo Frankel, Benjamin Le Moussu and Auguste Serraillier (see Note 197).   p. 457

324 A reference to the second congress of the bourgeois pacifist League of Peace and Freedom held in Berne in September 1868. The congress rejected a resolution moved by Bakunin on September 23 and supported by an insignificant minority, after which Bakunin and his followers withdrew from the League (see Note 38).   p. 458

325 A reference to the confidential circular of the Bureau of the Permanent Committee of the League of Peace and Freedom, written by Bakunin in August 1868 and signed by Gustav Vogt, President of the Bureau. Marx and Engels had a copy of the circular sent to Mikhail Elpidin. This copy with notes by Bakunin and Utin is inscribed "No. 1" in Engels' hand.   p. 460

326 The decision of the Brussels Congress (September 6-13, 1867) to reject the offer from the League of Peace and Freedom to merge with the International Working Men's Association derived from the position of the General Council towards the League worked out by Marx as early as August 1867 (see present edition, Vol. 20, p. 204).   p. 461

327 Gustav Vogt's letter to Bakunin and a fragment from Bakunin's reply (below) are quoted according to the report on the Alliance written by Nikolai Utin for the Hague Congress on the instructions of the London Conference (see Note 322). Utin's report was published in English for the first time in *The Hague Congress of the First International, September 2-7, 1872. Minutes and Documents*, Progress Publishers, Moscow, 1976.   p. 461

328 On the Lyons events of September 1870 and Bakunin's role in them see Note 71.   p. 467

329 The Basle Congress of the International (September 6-11, 1869) became the scene of the first clash between the adherents of Marx's scientific socialism and the followers of Bakunin's anarchism over the abolition of the right of inheritance. With the discussion on this point Bakunin sought to distract the workers from solving urgent problems of the programme and tactics. Preparing for the Congress, Marx drew up a report of the General Council on the right of inheritance (see present edition, Vol. 21). It was read at the Congress by Johann Eccarius. The report branded as erroneous the attempts, originally made by the followers of Saint-Simon, to regard the right of inheritance not as a juridical consequence but as a cause of the existing economic organisation of society. The Congress took no decision on this point, since not a single proposal gained the necessary absolute majority of votes. However, Bakunin's well-prepared attempt to impose his ideas on the International failed.   p. 472

330 This refers to the struggle between the Lassalleans and the Eisenachers in Germany which intensified after the Basle Congress of the International. The Bakuninist press organs used this to accuse the General Council of allegedly holding aloof from settling the conflict. In October 1869, in a series of anonymous articles in *Der Social-Demokrat*, Johann Baptist Schweitzer, a Lassallean leader, heaped libels upon the leaders of the Social-Democratic Workers' Party (Eisenachers), in particular, upon Wilhelm Liebknecht. He alleged that they had rejected the socialist programme and the resolutions of the Basle Congress on the social property in land, for the benefit of the petty-bourgeois People's Party which opposed these decisions. Leonhard

Bonhorst, member of the Brunswick Central Committee of the Social-Democratic Workers' Party, used the columns of *Der Volksstaat* to refute Schweitzer (Nos. 8 and 9, October 27 and 30, 1869). The position of the General Council of the International in the conflict between the Eisenachers and the Lassalleans, Liebknecht and Schweitzer, was explained by Marx in the circular letter "The General Council to the Federal Council of Romance Switzerland" (see present edition, Vol. 21, pp. 90-91).   p. 473

[331] The declaration of Duplaix, Weyhermann, Perret and Utin, Geneva delegates, to the congress of the Romance Federation in La Chaux-de-Fonds, is quoted according to the report on the Alliance written by Utin for the Hague Congress on the instructions of the London Conference.   p. 474

[332] See Note 69.   p. 474

[333] On the Section of Propaganda and Revolutionary Socialist Action see Note 75.
    The resolution of the Basle Congress of 1869 on the order of admittance of new sections to the International Working Men's Association empowered the General Council to admit or refuse to admit new sections. Where federal councils existed, their opinion had to be taken into account when this question arose.   p. 477

[334] In early April 1871, trying to prevent the execution of captured Communards by the Versailles counter-revolutionaries, the Paris Commune proclaimed persons guilty of dealings with Versailles to be hostages. On May 23 and 24, 1871, in reply to the atrocities committed by the Versailles troops after they had entered Paris, several hostages were shot by the Communards.   p. 477

[335] On Jules Favre's circular and Sacase's report see Note 82.
    In October 1871, the Chamber of Deputies of the Spanish Cortes debated the intention of the bourgeois government legislatively to dissolve the Spanish organisations of the International. Right-wing deputies taking part in the discussion used the Alliance documents and police-forged material to calumniate the International. Although the Republican representatives (Castelar, Garrido and others) resisted and proved that the proposed measures contradicted the Constitution, the government was given support. In January 1872, Sagasta, Minister of the Interior, published a circular which ordered a dissolution of the International in Spain (see Note 179).   p. 480

[336] On the *Toulouse trial* of members of the International see Note 307. The reference is to the report on a court session of March 17, published in *La Réforme*, No. 669, March 18, 1873.   p. 483

[337] A reference to the letter from the Alliance member Charles Alerini to André Bastelica of November 14, 1871, sent by the Barcelona Section to all the sections of the International in Spain (see below, pp. 488-89). The Pope here means Bakunin. A copy of the letter was presented by Engels to the Hague Congress among other documents on the Alliance.   p. 483

[338] The draft General Rules of the International drawn up in the anarchist spirit by representatives of the Belgian Federal Council (see Note 88), were discussed at the regular congress of the Belgian Federation on May 19 and 20, 1872, and at its extraordinary congress on July 14 of the same year in Brussels. At both congresses part of the delegates opposed the abolition of the General Council proposed in the draft. The extraordinary congress decided by a majority vote to retain the General Council, but with very limited powers. The draft Rules, adopted with this amendment, reflected on the whole the growing influence of

anarchism within the Belgian Federation. In accordance with the draft, the Belgian delegates to the Hague Congress supported the Bakuninists and sided with them against the revolutionary proletarian wing of the International.

p. 483

339 The meeting of the International's sections held in Geneva on December 2, 1871, adopted a resolution censuring the decisions of the anarchist congress at Sonvillier. On December 20, 1871, the Federal Committee of Romance Switzerland adopted a special address, "Réponse du Comité fédéral romand à la circulaire des 16 signataires, membres du Congrès de Sonvilliers", which was published in *L'Égalité*, No. 24 of December 24, 1871. The editors of *L'Égalité* also published their own protest.

p. 483

340 See Note 43.

p. 484

341 See Note 87.

p. 484

342 This is a quotation from the letter written on August 2, 1872 by Jósef Tokarzewicz, member of the Polish Section of the International in Zurich, to Walery Wróblewski, the General Council's Corresponding Secretary for Poland. The translation of the letter into French made by Engels is extant.

The *Programme of the Socialist-Revolutionary Polish Society in Zurich* was written by Bakunin and published on July 27, 1872 in the supplement to the *Bulletin de la Fédération jurassienne*, No. 13. The Polish Social-Democratic Association, which appeared under the influence of the anarchist elements, first adopted this programme but later rejected it on the initiative of Tokarzewicz.

The newspaper *Wolność* (Freedom) was not published.

p. 485

343 See Note 188.

p. 486

344 See Note 14.

p. 487

345 This statement addressed to the delegates of the international Congress at The Hague and containing facts which revealed the existence of the secret Alliance in Spain, José Mesa sent to Engels who handed it over to the commission of inquiry into the Alliance activities. The statement was published in English for the first time in *The Hague Congress of the First International, September 2-7, 1872. Minutes and Documents*, Progress Publishers, Moscow, 1976.

p. 488

346 A reference to the handwritten confidential circular of the Valencia section ("Seccion internácional de Valencia. Circular") to the Spanish sections of the International, which proposed a fight for total decentralisation and an "anarchist commune" in the event of a revolution.

p. 488

347 The circular of the Seville section of the Alliance of Socialist Democracy, written by Nicola Marselau, was sent to the Madrid Section of the International on October 25, 1871. It formulated decisions adopted by the section in view of the government repressions.

p. 489

348 A reference to the open letter of *La Emancipacion*'s editors "A los representantes del Partido Republicano Federal reunidos en Madrid". The letter was dated February 25, 1872, and published in *La Emancipacion*, No. 38 of March 3, 1872. The anarchist members of the Council of the Madrid Federation of the International demanded that the editors should withdraw the letter, but Mesa, who was *La Emancipacion*'s editor and also acting Secretary of the Spanish Federal Council, flatly refused to comply with this demand. On March 9, 1872, after consultation with other members of the Council, he sent the Republicans a similar letter in the name of the Federal Council.

p. 490

349 On March 7, 1872, the anarchist Council of the Madrid Federation addressed a letter to the meeting of representatives of the Republican Federalist Party, in which it dissociated itself from the letter of *La Emancipacion*'s editors (see Note 348) and stated that it contradicted the principles of the International. The Madrid Council's letter was published in the radical Republican newspaper *La Igualdad*, No. 1059, March 9, 1872, and in *La Emancipacion*, No. 40, March 16, 1872.   p. 490

350 See Note 99.   p. 491

351 See Note 184.   p. 491

352 The government of Napoleon III held a plebiscite on May 8, 1870 (see Note 165).   p. 496

353 See Note 221.   p. 496

354 The *Unión de las tres clases de vapor* (Union of the Three Categories of Factory Workers) was one of the first trades unions in Catalonia and amalgamated weavers, spinners and day-labourers employed at textile mills. The Union was a collective member of the International.   p. 497

355 This letter was addressed to Engels and described the state of affairs in the Naples Section of the International (see *La Corrispondenza di Marx e Engels con italiani. 1848-1895*, Milan, 1964). It is also quoted in the text below.
                                                                  p. 497

356 Quoted from Stefano Caporusso's letter to George Odger, dated January 21, 1872.   p. 498

357 The Milan section of the International was formed by Theodor Cuno who acted on Engels' advice. In December 1871, under Cuno's influence, some members of the local Mazzinian Society of Moral and Mutual Assistance and Education of the Workers withdrew from this organisation and formed an Emancipation of the Proletarian Society which declared itself a section of the International on January 7, 1872. On January 30, 1872, Engels reported to the General Council on the formation of the Milan Section stating that its Rules conformed to the International's principles; thereupon the section was admitted to the Association. Under Engels' guidance, Cuno persistently opposed the anarchist members of the section, and as a result, prior to and at the Hague Congress, the section did not support the anarchists in their struggle against the General Council.   p. 499

358 See Note 83.   p. 499

359 Here and above the quotations are from Carlo Terzaghi's letter to Engels of October 10, 1871. Terzaghi's messages to the General Council of December 4, 1871 and March 10, 1872 were also written in the form of letters to Engels.
                                                                  p. 499

360 On Engels' proposal, Vitale Regis, member of the General Council and former Communard, was sent to Italy in February 1872 to establish contacts between the Italian sections and the Council and counteract the Bakuninist influence. In the latter half of February, Regis spent ten days in Milan and Turin where he studied the situation in the local sections and popularised the decisions of the International Working Men's Association. Drawing on Engels' instructions, Regis

explained to the members of the Milan and Turin sections the radical difference between the anarchist views and the principles and tasks of the International. Regis' report on his trip to Italy was written in the form of the letter to Engels of March 1, 1872. p. 500

361 On the *Conference of Rimini* see Note 161. Its resolution against the decisions of the London Conference and the General Council is given below (see pp. 502-03). p. 501

362 Jules Guesde's letter to the members of the Montpellier section of the International was addressed to Gironis, one of the section's leaders. On November 20, 1872, Gironis sent this letter to the General Council. p. 506

363 The original has "Ruraux"—a contemptuous nickname for members of the Versailles National Assembly of 1871, which consisted mainly of monarchist conservatives: provincial landlords, officials, rentiers and tradesmen elected in rural electoral districts. p. 507

364 A reference to a letter addressed by André Calas and other leaders of the Montpellier section on August 18, 1872 to the General Council of the International c/o Louis Monnesau. Engels refers to it in his article "The International and the *Neuer*" (see this volume, p. 443). p. 507

365 A reference to the slaughter of Communards in the last week of May 1871 by the Versailles troops after their invasion of Paris. p. 507

366 This letter was written by J. Martin to Auguste Serraillier. p. 508

367 On September 15, 1872, a short extraordinary congress of the Jura Federation was held in Saint-Imier, where a secessionist congress of the anarchists (see Note 221) opened on the same day. All delegates of the extraordinary congress also took part in the secessionist congress. For that reason, the New York General Council resolved on January 5, 1873 to suspend the Jura Federation from the International Working Men's Association until the next congress. Marx and Engels regarded this resolution as rather inconsistent in the struggle against anarchist disorganisers, since the Jura Federation actually placed itself outside the International by its refusal to comply with the resolutions of the Hague Congress (see F. Engels, "Notes for the General Council", this volume, p. 415). Acting on advice from London, the New York General Council adopted new, more radical resolutions of January 26 and May 30, 1873, against the dissidents. p. 509

368 See Note 237. p. 513

369 See Note 298. p. 514

370 Nikolai Chernyshevsky was arrested on July 7, 1862. Until 1864 he was kept in the Peter and Paul Fortress in St. Petersburg and then sentenced to deportation for life to Siberia with seven years' hard labour. p. 516

371 *Frères ignorantins*—the name of a religious order founded in Reims in 1680; its members undertook to dedicate their lives to teaching the children of the poor; in the schools organised by this order the pupils received mainly religious instruction and acquired but meagre knowledge of other subjects. p. 519

372 An excerpt from this letter was quoted in Nikolai Utin's report to the Hague Congress of the International. Utin did not name the author but noted that his devotion to the people's cause must have been known to Bakunin, to whom the letter was communicated. p. 527

373 *The Revolutionary Catechism*—a document which was written in Geneva in the summer of 1869, enciphered and printed in several copies. A copy was discovered in 1869, during the search of the apartment of P. G. Uspensky, a member of the Nechayev organisation. The text was deciphered by the police and reproduced in *Pravitelstvenny Vestnik* (The Government Bulletin), No. 162, July 9 (21), 1871. Marx and Engels had this issue at their disposal.

   The French translation of this document is extant; it was made by Utin and enclosed with his report to the Hague Congress of the International under the title "'The Catechism' written by Bakunin in Russian". It was this translation that was used here and in more detail below, in section 2 of this chapter. Some researchers attribute the authorship of the document to Bakunin, others to Nechayev (in the latter case, probably written with Bakunin's help or drawing on his works and ideas). Utin was convinced that it had been written by Bakunin.
p. 527

374 Originally Nikolai Ogarev dedicated his poem *The Student* to his and Herzen's friend S. I. Astrakov, who died in 1866. When Bakunin received the manuscript, he wrote back to Ogarev that it would be "more useful for the cause" if the poem were dedicated to Nechayev. With this dedication, the poem was published as a leaflet (Geneva, 1869), and Nechayev used it as a sort of credentials from Ogarev.
p. 529

375 The proclamation *Благородное российское дворянство!* (Appeal to Russian Nobility) was published anonymously in Geneva in 1870. Its authors were Sergei Nechayev and Nikolai Ogarev. The French translation of the excerpts from this proclamation is extant; it was made by Utin and enclosed with his report to the Hague Congress of the International. This translation was used by Marx and Engels. Utin thought that Bakunin had participated in writing the proclamation. It was probably based on the appeal *Русское дворянство* (The Russian Nobility), drawn up by Bakunin in 1869.
p. 535

376 Bakunin's letter (given here in a free rendering) to Charles Louis Chassin, editor of *La Démocratie*, was written in April 1868 for the sample off-prints published from March 1868. The proposed newspaper contributors were to expound their views in them. Bakunin's letter was published in late April 1868 in several off-prints and then reprinted in a number of other newspapers, in particular, in the Berlin *Die Zukunft*, No. 230, June 19, 1868 (under the title "Zum Programm der Demokratie"). Engels had this German reprint at his disposal.
p. 540

377 The reference is to the money which was handed over to Alexander Herzen in 1858 by the Russian landlord Pavel Bakhmetyev for revolutionary propaganda (the so-called Bakhmetyev Fund). In May 1869, under pressure from Bakunin and Ogarev, Herzen agreed to divide the fund into two parts, one of which Ogarev gave to Nechayev. In March 1870, after Herzen's death, Nechayev received the second half from Ogarev, too.
p. 540

378 See Note 136.
p. 543

379 James Guillaume spoke at the sitting of the Hague Congress on September 6, 1872, when the inclusion of Resolution IX of the London Conference "On the Political Action of the Working Class" into the General Rules of the International was discussed. In opposition to it, Guillaume advocated the Bakuninist principles of abstention from politics and of the abolition of state and declared that an erroneous, from his point of view, authoritarian idea of

replacing bourgeois power with workers' power, had been moved as early as in the *Communist Manifesto*. (Guillaume's speech was summarised in the Belgian *La Liberté*, No. 31, September 15, 1872, in the report "Le Congrès de la Haye".)   p. 544

380 The *Escobars*—followers of the Spanish Jesuit Escobar y Mendoza (1589-1669) who preached that pious intentions justify actions condemned by ethics and laws (the end justifies the means).   p. 545

381 On December 14 (26), 1825, members of secret societies of Russian revolutionary nobles opposed to the autocracy and the feudal-serf system headed the insurrection of the St. Petersburg garrison units. They are known in history as the *Decembrists*. The Decembrists sought to prevent the oath of allegiance being taken to the new Emperor, Nicholas I, and to secure the introduction of civic liberties and the convocation of a Constituent Assembly to decide the question of a Constitution. The insurrection was suppressed by Tsarist troops. The same fate befell an uprising in the Ukraine in late December 1825. The Decembrists were subjected to severe reprisals. Five of their leaders were hanged and 121 men sentenced to hard labour and exile in Siberia.   p. 551

382 A reference to members of the secret revolutionary society organised in Moscow in September 1863 by Nikolai Ishutin. Originally, it was a circle affiliated with the underground revolutionary-democratic organisation Zemlya i Volya (Land and Freedom) (1862-64), but when the latter ceased to exist it acted on its own. The society had contacts with underground circles in St. Petersburg and a number of provincial towns, and kept in touch with Polish revolutionaries. The society's aim was to work for a peasants' revolution which, in the opinion of its members, would lead to the establishment of socialism. The idea of seizing power by a revolutionary organisation with the purpose of handing the government of the state over to the people, was very popular among them. Individual terror was proposed as one of the means of struggle. Dmitry Karakozov was a member of the society; after his abortive attempt on the life of Alexander II in April 1866, the organisation was partly discovered by the police and some of its leaders were subjected to repression.   p. 551

383 A reference to the Jesuit theocratic state which was formed in 1610 in South America, mainly on the territory of what is now Paraguay, and existed until 1768. The domination of the Jesuit Order assumed a form of cruel colonial exploitation of the local Indians who were driven by Jesuit missionaries by force or deceit to special settlements.   p. 554

384 *Hegira*—the flight of Muhammad, founder of Islam, and his followers from Mecca to Medina to escape persecution which took place in September 622. This year is regarded as the beginning of the Muslim era.   p. 556

385 This refers to a group of young people, mainly intellectuals, who rallied round Mikhail Butashevich-Petrashevsky in St. Petersburg in 1844. From 1845 their meetings became regular ("Petrashevsky's Fridays"). They held democratic views and condemned the autocracy and serfdom. The most radical among them regarded a popular revolution as the main means for changing the existing order. The young people vigorously championed utopian socialism, and discussed social and political problems as well as—particularly under the influence of the 1848 revolution in Europe—plans for setting up an active revolutionary organisation. However, the members of the Petrashevsky circle failed to put their plans into effect: in April 1849 they were arrested and

subjected to repression. The court martial sentenced 21 of them to be shot, but at the last moment the death sentence was commuted to exile and hard labour. Fyodor Dostoyevsky, Mikhail Saltykov-Shchedrin and some other prominent figures in the Russian culture were members of the Petrashevsky circle.

p. 556

386 M. S. Neklyudov, an official serving under the Governor-General of Eastern Siberia in Irkutsk, N. N. Muravyov-Amursky, was systematically baited by the latter's entourage, particularly by F. A. Beklemishev. On April 16, 1859, a duel between Neklyudov and Beklemishev took place with the connivance of the administration; Neklyudov was killed. This caused a protest on the part of broad democratic circles in Irkutsk. Butashevich-Petrashevsky made a denunciatory speech at Neklyudov's graveside. Neklyudov's funeral turned into a huge demonstration. The *Kolokol* reported the details of the duel in the supplement "Подъ судъ!" (Put Them on Trial!). Muravyov's hangers-on protested against these accusations and sent, through Bakunin, their refutations to Herzen, editor of the *Kolokol*. Bakunin's letter, mentioned here, was published by Herzen unsigned and with editorial notes on July 1 and 15, 1860.

p. 557

387 The Manifesto on the abolition of serfdom was signed by Alexander II on February 19 (March 3), 1861, and made public on March 6 (18) of the same year. It marked the beginning of the peasant reform introduced by the ruling classes in the conditions of the profound crisis of the serf system and the growing threat of a popular revolution. The peasants were granted personal freedom but deprived of a considerable part of the land toiled by them. They were to buy back the plots they still kept. The terms of redemption made the peasants debtors to the state, which paid a lump redemption sum to the landowners and then exacted heavy payments from the peasants for several decades, making the village commune collectively responsible for the timely payment.

Progressive, revolutionary-democratic circles in Russia severely criticised the anti-popular reform. Before long even those Russian democrats (e.g. Alexander Herzen) who initially cherished liberal illusions about the emancipatory intentions of the Tsarist government towards the peasants were disappointed in the Manifesto.

p. 558

388 The manifesto *Молодая Россiя* (Young Russia) was written by Pyotr Zaichnevsky, a member of a revolutionary student circle which lithographed and distributed illegal literature. It was published in mid-May 1862 on behalf of the so-called Central Revolutionary Committee. The manifesto expressed the views of the most radical Russian revolutionaries and was widely circulated in Moscow, St. Petersburg and the provinces.

The following words from Herzen's *My Past and Thoughts*, Part Six, "England (1852-1854)", Chapter IX, "Robert Owen", served as the epigraph: "Do you understand now on whom the future of individuals and nations depends?... On *you and me*, for example. How can we be idle after that?"

p. 561

389 A reference to the disagreements between Herzen, on the one hand, and Chernyshevsky and Dobrolyubov, on the other, caused by Herzen's liberal attitudes in appraising the emancipation of the serfs, then in preparation by the Tsarist government. For some time Herzen hoped that the educated and sober-minded section of the nobility would succeed in persuading the Tsar to

resolve the peasant question radically and peacefully. He regarded the revolutionary tactics of the radicals in the democratic movement as extremist and dangerous, and therefore likely to play into the hands of the reactionary serf-owners. It was in this spirit that he argued against Chernyshevsky and Dobrolyubov (the article "Very Dangerous!!!", *Kolokol*, June 1, 1859, and others). The revolutionary democrats, for their part, vigorously attacked Herzen's vacillations in *Sovremennik* and in letters to *Kolokol*. In the 1860s Herzen broke with liberalism and joined the revolutionary democrats in their active struggle for the consolidation of the Russian revolutionary forces.

p. 562

390 Among the documents submitted by Marx and Engels to the special commission of the Hague Congress elected to investigate the activities of the secret Alliance, was a letter written by Nechayev in February 1870 on Bakunin's instructions and addressed, on behalf of the non-existent Russian revolutionary organisation, to Lyubavin who was preparing the publication of the first volume of *Capital* in Russia. Lyubavin was threatened with violence unless he released Bakunin from his obligations concerning the translation of Volume I of *Capital* into Russian. Lyubavin sent the letter to Marx c/o Danielson in August 1872.

p. 580

391 The series of articles *The Bakuninists at Work* was written in the wake of the events in Spain during the summer of 1873, which were the culmination of the Spanish bourgeois revolution of 1868-74 (see Note 292). Engels focussed his attention on the involvement of the Spanish Bakuninists in the abortive cantonal revolts (July-September) organised in the south and south-east of the country by the Intransigents, an extremist republican grouping that advocated the partition of Spain into independent cantons. The Intransigents and their Bakuninist allies were dissatisfied with the radical social measures undertaken by the Left republican government of Pi y Margall (sale of state and Church lands, establishment of mixed commissions to regulate labour conditions, a free regime in the colonies, etc.) and with the Constitution drawn up by the Cortes, which proclaimed a federative republic. They weakened the republican camp by forcing Pi y Margall to resign on July 18, 1873, and thus paved the way for the establishment of a military dictatorship in Spain early in 1874 and then for the restoration of the Bourbon monarchy.

Engels drew his information from the periodical press and various documents of the Spanish sections of the International, above all from a report submitted by the New Madrid Federation to the Geneva Congress of the International held on September 8-13, 1873.

Following the publication in *Der Volksstaat*, Engels' series of articles came out as a pamphlet entitled *Die Bakunisten an der Arbeit. Denkschrift über den letzten Aufstand in Spanien* (Leipzig, November 1873); in April-May 1874 it was published in the New York *Arbeiter-Zeitung* (Nos. 11-13 and 15-16). In 1894 *The Bakuninists at Work* was included in the collection of Engels' articles *Internationales aus dem "Volksstaat" (1871-75)* published by *Vorwärts* Publishers in Berlin. For that publication Engels provided the Preliminary Remark (see present edition, Vol. 27) and made several corrections.

The work was published in English for the first time in K. Marx, F. Engels, *Revolution in Spain*, Lawrence & Wishart, International Publishers, London-New York, 1939.

p. 581

392 The text published in *Der Volksstaat* in 1873 and the reprint of the same year had no author's note, but a reference in brackets: "see the article 'Cagliostro

Bakunin' in *Der Volksstaat*, No. 87 et seqq." This anonymously published article
contained a brief summary in German of Marx's and Engels' *The Alliance of
Socialist Democracy and the International Working Men's Association* with excerpts
from different chapters. It was written by Adolf Hepner and published in *Der
Volksstaat*, Nos. 87-90 of September 19, 21, 24 and 26, 1873. Engels referred to
it because a full German translation of the work about the Alliance was then
just being prepared.   p. 581

393 On July 1, 1873, the General Council in New York officially announced the
convocation of the regular congress of the International in Geneva on
September 8. It was to discuss revision of the Rules, organisation of an
international trades union association, the political activity of the organised
workers, labour statistics, and other questions. Initially Marx and Engels
intended to be present at the congress and take part in its work but after an
analysis of the situation within the International, concluded that the congress
could not be really representative. Almost all the organisations of the
International, being unable to send delegates, transferred their mandates to
members of the Romance Federation of Switzerland. This was also the case with
the New Madrid Federation (see Note 157) whose leaders sent a copy of their
report to the Geneva Congress to Engels in London. What prompted Marx and
Engels to change their attitude towards the congress was mainly their growing
awareness that the IWMA as a form of international association could no longer
meet the needs of the expanding proletarian movement.

At the sixth congress of the International Association in Geneva (September 8-13, 1873) 28 delegates out of 31 belonged to the Swiss organisations of
the International or its émigré sections in Switzerland. Only 3 delegates
represented other countries.

The congress heard the report of the General Council and reports from the
localities. While discussing the Rules the majority of the delegates led by
J. Ph. Becker confirmed the decisions of the Hague Congress of 1872 on
expanding the functions of the General Council. The congress underlined the
need for the working class to carry on a political struggle, and adopted a
resolution on further measures to establish an international association of trades
unions. New York remained the seat of the General Council. The Geneva
Congress of 1873 was the last congress of the International.   p. 581

394 A reference to the liberal-constitutional monarchists who supported the protégé
of the European powers on the Spanish throne, King Amadeo of Savoy.
                                                                           p. 583

395 The *Alfonsists*—a reactionary political grouping in Spain who backed Alfonso
(son of Isabella II), the Bourbon pretender to the Spanish throne. He was
proclaimed King (Alfonso XII) in 1874. The Alfonsists relied on the big
landowners, the clergy and the upper crust of the bourgeoisie.   p. 583

396 See Note 294.   p. 583

397 A reference to the congress, held in Geneva from September 1 to 6, 1873, of
representatives of the anarchist and reformist organisations which had
challenged the resolutions of the Hague Congress and thereby placed
themselves outside the International, as stated in the decisions of the General
Council of January 26 and May 30, 1873. The congress was convened by the
Bakuninist Geneva Section of Propaganda and Revolutionary Socialist Action
(see Note 75). The congress proclaimed the negation of all authority the basic
principle of the international anarchist association, abolished the General

Council, denied congresses the right to adopt resolutions on questions of principle, and dropped Article 7a, on the political action of the working class, from the General Rules.   p. 584

398 See Note 87.   p. 587

399 By decision of the congress of Spanish anarchists in Cordova (see Note 220) of December 30, 1872, the Spanish Federal Council was replaced by a Federal Commission with limited powers (for details see K. Marx and F. Engels, *The Alliance of Socialist Democracy and the International Working Men's Association*, this volume, p. 510).   p. 587

400 See Note 221.   p. 588

401 A reference to the great insurrection of the German peasants in 1524-25 known as the German Peasant War, and to the uprisings in Saxony, the Rhine Province of Prussia, the Palatinate and Baden in May 1849 in defence of the Imperial Constitution drawn up by the Frankfurt National Assembly but rejected by the German princes. The struggle for the Imperial Constitution (in the Palatinate and Baden it continued until July 1849) was the final stage of the bourgeois-democratic revolution of 1848-49 in Germany.

See Engels' *The Peasant War in Germany* and *The Campaign for the German Imperial Constitution*, present edition, Vol. 10, pp. 397-482, 147-239.   p. 592

402 On the initiative of the New Madrid Federation the adherents of the General Council of the International in Spain formed, in January 1873, a new Spanish Federal Council in Valencia to counterbalance the actions of the anarchist federations, which had substituted the Federal Commission for the Federal Council (see this volume, pp. 511-12).   p. 593

403 These manuscripts show that Engels intended to write a treatise on German history. He gave his attention to the subject on repeated occasions, particularly in 1873-74. He wrote to Wilhelm Liebknecht on January 27, 1874: "I wanted to write something on Germany for the *Volksstaat*, but to do so immersed myself into economic and statistical research so deeply that the result will probably be a booklet, if not a whole book." Engels' plan, however, remained unfulfilled. Apart from the preparatory materials, two draft manuscripts are extant. The first one is divided into two sections. The "Introduction. 1500-1789", outlines the opening part of the planned work, in which Engels intended to trace German history up to the French Revolution. The second section of this manuscript, "1789-1815", is a plan for the study of German history of that period. The second manuscript, entitled "Varia on Germany. 1789-1873", deals mainly with the 19th century up to contemporary developments. Unlike the first one, this manuscript consists of separate notes unconnected chronologically and touching upon individual aspects of the historical development of Germany both in the period indicated by the title, and in earlier times.

Excerpts from *Varia on Germany* were published in English in *V.O.K.S.- Bulletin*, Nos. 11 and 12, Moscow-Riga, 1945, and in F. Engels, *The Peasant War in Germany*, Foreign Languages Publishing House, Moscow, 1956.

p. 599

404 *The Hansa. The Hanseatic League*—a commercial and political alliance of medieval German towns along the southern coasts of the North and Baltic seas, and the rivers running into them; its aim was to establish a trade monopoly in Northern Europe. The Hanseatic League reached its prime in the latter half of the 14th century, and began to decay at the end of the 15th century.

The *Rhenish League of Cities* and the *Swabian League of Cities* of Western and Southern Germany were formed in the 1370s for the protection of the trade routes and for the defence of the cities against feudal lords. The two leagues merged in 1381. At the end of the 14th century these unstable associations dissolved.   p. 599

405 *The Wars of the Roses* (1455-85)—wars between the royal houses of York and Lancaster fighting for the throne, the white rose being the badge of York, and the red rose that of Lancaster. The Yorkists were supported by some of the big feudal landowners from the south-eastern, more economically developed part of the country and also by the knights and townspeople, while the Lancastrians were backed by the feudal aristocracy of the backward North and of Wales. The wars almost completely wiped out the ancient feudal nobility and brought Henry VII to power to form a new dynasty, that of the Tudors, who set up an absolute monarchy in England.   p. 599

406 Applying the term "Kulturkampf" to the struggle between the German emperors and the popes in the Middle Ages, Engels hints at the Bismarck government's conflict with the Pope and the Catholic circles in 1872-79, which was known by that name. On the pretext of secularising national culture the Bismarck government introduced anti-Catholic reforms directed against the opposition Centre party which expressed the separatist, anti-Prussian views of the landowners, the bourgeoisie and part of the peasantry in the Catholic regions of Germany (above all South-West Germany). One of the aims of the Kulturkampf was to intensify national oppression in the Polish lands under Prussian rule. In order to consolidate the forces of reaction against the growing workers' movement, Bismarck repealed most of the reforms in the late 1870s and early 1880s.   p. 600

407 A reference to Franche-Comté and French Lorraine which were initially part of the German Empire but then passed to France.   p. 600

408 A reference to the support lent by the Council of Ulm to the Swabian rulers in their punitive expeditions against the rebellious peasants during the 1524-25 Peasant War in Germany.   p. 600

409 *Little Germany*—a plan for the unification of Germany from above under Prussia's aegis and excluding Austria; supported by the majority of the German bourgeoisie.   p. 601

410 *The Thirty Years War* (1618-48)—a European war, in which the Pope, the Spanish and Austrian Habsburgs, and the Catholic German princes rallied around the banner of Catholicism and fought the Protestant countries: Bohemia, Denmark, Sweden, the Republic of the Netherlands, and a number of Protestant German states. The rulers of Catholic France—rivals of the Habsburgs—supported the Protestant camp. Germany was the main battle scene and object of plunder and territorial claims. The Treaty of Westphalia (1648) sealed the political dismemberment of Germany.   p. 601

411 The reference is to the participation of Irish emigrants in the Thirty Years War as mercenaries of the Imperial army and to the use of German mercenaries by the English for police service in Ireland and the suppression of the Irish national liberation movement.   p. 601

412 Engels has in mind the claims of German chauvinists to Alsace and Lorraine on the pretext that by "historical" right these provinces belonged to the German

with the English government, had become an impediment to the national liberation struggle. p. 613

The reference is to the National Charter Association, the first mass working-class party, which was founded in 1840 and had about 50 thousand members in its heyday. The Left wing of the party strove to combine the struggle for its political programme—the People's Charter—with social demands. With the decline of the Chartist movement after 1848 the National Charter Association lost its mass character. However, it continued to play an important part in the attempts of the revolutionary elements (Ernest Jones and others), made in the first half of the 1850s, to reorganise Chartism on socialist lines. p. 613

35 The *Labour Representation League* was founded in November 1869. It included trades union leaders who sought to secure the election of worker candidates to the House of Commons largely through compromise with the Liberal Party. The League ceased to exist in about 1880. p. 614

436 See Note 176. p. 616

437 From the 1820s, the Repeal movement became widespread in Ireland. Its aim was to revoke the Anglo-Irish Union of 1801, which had eliminated all traces of Irish autonomy. In the early 1840s, the Repealers' Association was formed; the Liberals who headed it (Daniel O'Connell and others) regarded the agitation for the repeal of the Union only as a means to obtain individual concessions from the British government for the benefit of the propertied upper crust of Irish society. Following the defeat of the Irish national uprising of 1848 and the advance of reaction in England and Ireland, the Repealers' Association was dissolved. p. 616

438 This series of articles was written by Engels in connection with the Reichstag debates on a bill calling for an increase in the strength of the peacetime army. Known as the Septennate Law, it endorsed for the coming seven years the military budget and a 401.5-thousand-strong peacetime standing army. The law imposed the Prussian military system on the whole of Germany and reflected the growth of German militarism and aggressive aspirations of the German ruling circles concealed behind the fuss about "war danger" on the part of France. p. 617

439 *The Men of Progress*—members of the Party of Progress formed in June 1861. It demanded the unification of Germany under the aegis of Prussia, the convocation of an all-German parliament, and the formation of a liberal ministry responsible to the Chamber of Deputies. After the unification of Germany in 1871 the men of Progress, unlike the National Liberals, went into opposition, if only in words. Their fear of the working-class movement made them reconcile themselves to the rule of the Prussian Junkers in semi-absolutist Germany. Their vacillations in policy reflected the political instability of the sections they relied on—the commercial bourgeoisie, the small factory-owners and, in part, the artisans.

The *National Liberals*—a party of the German big bourgeoisie formed in the autumn of 1866 as a result of a split in the Party of Progress. The main goal of the National Liberals was to unite the German states under Prussia's supremacy. Their policy reflected the German liberal bourgeoisie's capitulation to Bismarck and increasingly took on traits of allegiance after the unification of Germany. They practically renounced their earlier liberal demands, including

Empire in the Middle Ages. Marx and Engels repeatedly stressed that the historical destinies of Alsace, which had passed to France during the Thirty Years War, and of Lorraine, finally annexed by the French in 1766, had been indissolubly linked with France since the time of the French Revolution. They sharply criticised the Bismarck government for the annexation of these provinces in 1871. p. 601

413 A reference to the American War of Independence (1776-83) and the wars France waged against the counter-revolutionary coalitions of European states for a number of years since the French Revolution. p. 602

414 Engels refers to several German princes (dukes Leopold of Dassau, Ernst Friedrich of Coburg and others) who patronised the 18th-century German agronomist Johann Christian Schubart and applied his agricultural methods on their estates. p. 602

415 A confederation of the states of Western and Southern Germany founded in 1806 under the protection of Napoleon I. These states officially broke with the Holy Roman Empire of the German Nation, which soon ceased to exist. The confederation fell apart after Napoleon I lost the military campaign of 1813. p. 602

416 This refers to the estates of the German imperial princes (mainly ecclesiastical) in Alsace and Lorraine. After the two provinces were annexed by France, the princes became vassals of both the French king and the German emperor. The secularisation of Church property by the French Revolution, extended to Alsace and Lorraine, served as a pretext for a declaration of war on the French Republic by the coalition of European powers (Austria, Prussia, etc.) in 1792. p. 603

417 On September 20, 1792, at Valmy (North-Eastern France), the French revolutionary forces halted the Austro-Prussian interventionists commanded by the Duke of Brunswick. The interventionists were compelled to retreat and on October 5 were thrown back over the French border. p. 603

418 In the battle of *Jemappes* (Belgium) on November 6, 1792, the French revolutionary army won a major victory over the Austrians.

At *Fleurus* (Belgium) on June 26, 1794, the French revolutionary army routed the Austrian army. p. 603

419 The *Peace of Amiens* was concluded by Napoleonic France and Britain on March 27, 1802. It marked the end of the war between France and the second European coalition (formed in late 1798-early 1799). The Peace of Amiens was but a short respite in the Anglo-French struggle for world domination. In May 1803 the war between Britain and France recommenced.

Napoleon I took advantage of his victory over Austria (a member of the coalition) and the Lunéville peace treaty of February 9, 1801, which gave France the left bank of the Rhine, to establish his hegemony in Germany. Under his pressure a special Imperial deputation at the Imperial Diet of the Holy Roman Empire of the German Nation in Regensburg adopted, in February 1803, a decree which secularised the Church estates, reduced the number of free cities and annexed the small secular principalities to the large ones (the so-called mediatisation). In all, 112 small states were abolished in Germany, their territory being turned over to Bavaria, Baden, Württemberg and Nassau (they later constituted the Confederation of the Rhine), which were to form, under Napoleon I's plan, a counterbalance to Austria and Prussia. The implementation of the Imperial deputation's resolutions undermined the foundations of the Holy Roman Empire of the German Nation, which was finally abolished in August 1806 after Austria had suffered a series of defeats in the war of the third European coalition against Napoleonic France.

p. 603

420 The *Continental System*, or the *Continental Blockade*, proclaimed by Napoleon I after the crushing defeat of the Prussian army by the French in 1806, prohibited trade between the countries of the European Continent and Great Britain.

p. 603

421 A reference to the so-called great mobilisation of the Prussian army in November 1850 during the Austro-Prussian conflict when the two powers attempted to intervene in an uprising in the Electorate of Hesse. This conflict was part of the struggle between Prussia and Austria for supremacy in Germany. Engels described the mobilisation, which revealed grave shortcomings in the Prussian army, in his work *The Role of Force in History* (see present edition, Vol. 26).

On the *Italian war of 1859* see Note 264.

p. 604

422 A reference to the financial transactions of Mayer Amschel Rothschild, owner of the Frankfurt banking-house. During the Napoleonic wars he added to his fortune by putting into circulation the assets of his debtor William, the Elector of Hesse.

p. 604

423 In 1852-56, Georg Weerth made several trips to the West Indies and Latin America as representative of a trading firm. Engels possibly alludes to what Weerth told his friends.

p. 607

424 The *Prussian Rules concerning servants* (Gesinde-Ordnung für sammtliche Provinzen der Preußischen Monarchie) were issued on November 8, 1810; they defined the legal status of landowners' servants who had been freed by an edict of 1807. The Rules preserved many features of feudal dependence in the relations between servants and masters.

p. 607

425 This refers to the wars fought by the French Catholics and the Calvinists (Huguenots), with short intervals, between 1562 and 1598. The religious struggle reflected the deep social and political contradictions in France—the growing discontent of the masses, the clashes between different groupings within the ruling class, the feudal aristocracy's opposition to the centralising policy of absolutism (assertion by the Huguenot nobility in the southern and western provinces of their medieval liberties, and later the struggle of the Catholic nobles against the King). The religious wars ended with the Edict of Nantes, signed by King Henry IV in 1598. It left Catholicism as the dominant religion, but Huguenots were allowed to hold services in their castles and in some towns and villages, and were granted certain civil rights. Clashes between Catholics and Huguenots continued, however, in later years. In 1685 the Edict of Nantes was repealed.

p. 608

426 The *Old Catholics*—followers of a Christian trend which broke away from official Catholicism after the Vatican Council of 1869-70. They refused to recognise the supreme authority of the Pope as well as papal infallibility and certain other dogmas of the Catholic Church. Old Catholicism originated in Germany, and then spread to Austria, Switzerland, the Netherlands, the USA and other countries.

p. 608

427 Under the Verdun treaty of 843, the Carolingian Empire was divided into three kingdoms. The lands west of the Rhine, Flanders included, formed part of the West Frankish Kingdom.

p. 608

428 German girls who came to England in the 1820s-40s to sel markets.

429 This article was published in English for the first time i F. Engels, *On Britain*, Foreign Languages Publishing House,

430 On January 26, 1874, Gladstone, the leader of the Liberal Parliament and called for new elections with a view to obtain a majority in the House of Commons. As a result 350 Conservative and 58 Irish MPs were elected to the House of Commons. On Conservative government was formed with Disraeli at the head.

A Bill on the second electoral reform in England was passed 1867. It extended the suffrage to house and flat tenants in th considerably lowered the property qualification for rural voters. A number of voters increased from one to two million. The extensio rights benefited the petty bourgeoisie and the top layer of the w

The Act on secret ballot was passed by Parliament on July 18

431 The *Irish Church Bill* was moved by Gladstone and passed by Pa July 26, 1869. Like other Liberal measures, it was intended to weake national movement by combining repression with certain conc some sections of Irish society. Under this Bill, the Church of Engla parated from the state in Ireland and made equalised in status Catholic and Presbyterian churches. It remained, however, th landowner, exploiting the labour of the Irish peasants.

The *Land Bill* was submitted by Gladstone under the pretext of Irish tenants and was passed on August 1, 1870. Its numerous reserva qualifications virtually left intact the powers of the big English lan Ireland who retained the right to raise the rent and evict tenants. stipulated that in the latter case the landlords were to pay the tenant improvement, and laid down a court procedure for determining the si compensation. The Bill considerably hastened the concentration of property in Ireland and the ruin of small Irish tenants.

432 A reference to the army reform act passed in 1871, which among other banned the purchase of officers' commissions. This caused an obstruction House of Lords, but Gladstone secured the ban by the royal decree of J 1871.

433 The *Home Rulers*—members of the Home Rule party, founded in the au of 1872. They expressed the interests of the progressive Irish bourgeoisi demanded self-government for Ireland, i.e. the autonomous Irish parlia and national administrative bodies within the framework of the U Kingdom. From 1874 onwards they constituted a large opposition faction i House of Commons of the English Parliament and gradually becam considerable political force. The Home Rulers intended to carry out t programme by peaceful parliamentary means but soon the more radical am them adopted the tactics of obstruction and made common cause with revolutionary-democratic wing of the national movement in organising m actions for agrarian reforms in Ireland. By the turn of the century the Ho Rule party, now dominated by the Right Liberal advocates of a comprom

those of the 1866 programme on the necessity "above all to defend the budgetary rights" of the representative bodies. p. 617

440 The Prussian army was reorganised in 1859-61.
On the constitutional conflict in Prussia see Note 265. p. 617

441 Engels quotes from Manteuffel's speech in the Second Chamber of the Prussian Diet on December 3, 1850, concerning the Olmütz agreement with Austria under which Prussia had to temporarily renounce its claims to domination in Germany (see *Stenographische Berichte über die Verhandlungen der durch die Allerhöchste Verordnung vom 2. November 1850 einberufenen Kammern. Zweite Kammer*, Vol. I, Berlin, 1851, p. 44). p. 617

442 On the *Danish War* see Note 266.
On the *Battle of Sadowa* see Note 267.
In September 1867, the Prussian Chamber of Deputies passed by a majority vote a bill on indemnity introduced by the Minister of Finance. It relieved the Bismarck government of responsibility for the funds it had spent on military purposes without legal sanction during the constitutional conflict. p. 617

443 The North German Imperial Diet, in session from February 24 to April 17, 1867, approved the formation of the North German Confederation (see Note 271) and adopted its Constitution. p. 618

444 This refers to the Imperial Diet, which first met on March 21, 1871 and endorsed the Constitution of the German Empire on April 14. p. 618

445 See Note 293. p. 619

446 The *Venetian Quadrilateral* was a strongly fortified position in North Italy formed by the fortresses of Verona, Legnago, Mantua and Peschiera. It played an important role as an operational base in the wars of the 19th century.
p. 620

447 A reference to the meeting of the emperors William I and Francis Joseph in Salzburg in September 1871 and to that of the emperors William I, Francis Joseph and Alexander II in Berlin in September 1872 (see notes 58 and 181).
p. 620

448 Blücher's expression "Landwehr-Patteljohns" (militia battalions) cited by Engels is to be found in I. Scherr's *Blücher. Seine Zeit und sein Leben*. Vol. 3, Leipzig, 1863, pp. 178-79.
The *Landwehr*, first raised in Prussia in 1813 as a people's militia to fight against Napoleon I's troops, embraced men of older age groups liable for call-up who had completed their service with the regular army and the reserve. In peacetime Landwehr units were only called up sporadically for training courses. In wartime the Landwehr of the first levy (men aged from 26 to 32) was used to replenish the army in the field; the Landwehr of the second levy (men from 32 to 39) was employed for garrison duty. Under the law of the North German Confederation of November 9, 1867 on universal conscription, the Landwehr of the second levy was dissolved, the Landwehr now being confined to a contingent of men aged from 27 to 32. p. 622

449 The *Landsturm*—a militia first set up in Prussia in 1813-14. It was formed of men aged 17 and older who served neither in the regular army nor in the navy

and was only raised when there was a threat of foreign intervention. Under the law of 1814 the age of men liable for Landsturm service was limited to 50 years, under that of 1867—to 42 years.   p. 622

450 A reference to the abortive attempt by the Prussian government to call up the Landwehr reservists in the western provinces of Prussia for the suppression of the uprising in defence of the Imperial Constitution, which engulfed Western and Southern Germany in May 1849. The Landwehr reservists in Rhenish Prussia and Westphalia refused to obey orders on the grounds that under the laws of September 3, 1814 and November 21, 1815 the Landwehr could only be called up in the event of foreign aggression. Moreover, in a number of cases they sided, arms in hand, with the insurgent people.   p. 622

451 This refers to the army recruitment law of July 27, 1872 which introduced universal conscription in France (with a five-year term of service); however, its application allowed for a great number of exemptions.   p. 623

452 While preparing the third edition of his *Peasant War in Germany*, written in 1850 (see present edition, Vol. 10), Engels amplified the preface to the second edition, written in February 1870. The new version of the preface was published in the third edition of *Der deutsche Bauernkrieg*, Leipzig, 1875 (the book actually came out late in October 1874). This volume contains the second part of the preface, dated by Engels July 1, 1874. The first part, in accordance with the time when it was written, is to be found in Volume 21 of the present edition, pp. 93-100.   p. 626

453 Engels means the proclamation of the German Empire on January 18, 1871, at Versailles, which made King William I of Prussia the German Emperor.

  Here Engels parodies the name of the Holy Roman Empire of the German Nation (962-1806) thus stressing that the unification of Germany was effected under Prussian supremacy and was followed by the Prussification of the German provinces.

  On the *battle of Sadowa* see Note 267.
  On the *battle of Sedan* see Note 293.   p. 626

454 On Engels' use of the term "Haupt- und Staatsaktion" see Note 200.
                                                                                   p. 626

455 See Note 269.   p. 626

456 See Note 271.   p. 627

457 The South-West German states of Baden, Hesse, Bavaria and Württemberg joined the North German Confederation in the course of the Franco-Prussian war even before the official proclamation of the German Empire in January 1871. Their accession was formalised by special treaties, signed in November 1870. The federal state thus formed was officially called the German Union (Deutscher Bund), and from December 9, 1870, the German Empire (Deutsches Reich).   p. 627

458 See Note 253.   p. 627

459 A reference to the 1873 crisis, which put an end to the period of rapid industrial expansion in Germany, marked by an unprecedented development of business speculation, profiteering and stock-jobbing.   p. 629

460 In the battle of *Spichern* in Lorraine (also called the battle of *Forbach*) on

August 6, 1870, the Prussian troops defeated the French units. It was one of the first major engagements of the Franco-Prussian war of 1870-71.

In the battle of *Mars-la-Tour* (also known as the battle of *Vionville*) on August 16, 1870, the German troops succeeded in stopping and cutting off the retreat of the French Rhenish army from Metz. p. 629

[461] Nine Social-Democrats were elected to the Imperial Diet on January 10, 1874, polling more than 350,000, or 6 per cent of the vote. Among the elected were August Bebel and Wilhelm Liebknecht, who were then serving prison terms. p. 630

[462] These notes were presumably written by Marx in connection with the measures taken by the General Council of the International to organise aid for the refugees of the Paris Commune (see Note 50). p. 635

[463] These notes and excerpts in English, German and French were written by Marx when he was studying the reports and letters of the leaders of the US sections of the International, as well as American newspaper reports on the split in the North American Federation. Marx intended to use this material for the further unmasking of the bourgeois reformists and other sectarians in the US sections of the International, who had responded to the General Council resolutions of March 5 and 15, 1872 on the split in the US Federation (see this volume, pp. 124-26) with fierce attacks on the leaders of the International. Marx's notes were also widely used by Engels for his work "The International in America" (see this volume, pp. 177-83).

In the languages of the original the notes were first published in *The General Council of the First International. 1871-1872. Minutes,* Progress Publishers, Moscow, 1968. p. 636

[464] See Note 140. p. 637

[465] These extracts were drawn up by Marx at the end of August 1872 shortly before the Hague Congress of the International. Earlier, when preparing for the London Conference of 1871, he and Engels made extracts from the Minutes of the General Council for the period from September 1869 to early September 1871 (see present edition, Vol. 22, pp. 554-64). Marginal lines and marks on both manuscripts show that Marx and Engels used these extracts in their work on the relevant documents of the International.

These extracts were published in English for the first time in *The Hague Congress of the First International, September 2-7, 1872. Minutes and Documents,* Progress Publishers, Moscow, 1976. p. 644

NAME INDEX

A

Abeele, Henri van den (b. 1847)—
Belgian anarchist, merchant; delegate
to the Hague Congress of the International (1872); expelled from the
International in 1873; agent of the
French and Belgian police.—244,
245, 247, 249, 250

Ackroyd (Akroyd), Edward—English
manufacturer, Liberal M.P.—351,
352

Albarracin, Severino (d. 1878)—Spanish
anarchist, teacher; member of the
Spanish Federal Council (1872-73); a
leader of an uprising in Alcoy
(1873).—208, 589

Albors, A. (d. 1873)—Spanish Republican; the alcalde of Alcoy in 1873.—
587, 588

Alerini, Charles (b. 1842)—French
anarchist; Corsican by birth, teacher;
member of the section of the International in Marseilles; took part in
the Marseilles Commune (April
1871); emigrated to Italy, then to
Spain; editor of *La Solidarité Révolutionnaire* (Barcelona); delegate to
the Hague Congress of the International (1872).—245, 247-50, 291, 488,
495, 510, 586

Alexander II (1818-1881)—Emperor of
Russia (1855-81).—506, 525, 535,
557, 558, 561, 563, 564, 625

Alexandrovskaya (née *Chirikova*), *Varva-
ra Vladimirovna* (born c. 1833)—
member of the Nechayev organisation; in 1871 was sentenced to deportation to Siberia.—539

Alexei (Alexis) Mikhailovich (1629-
1676)—Tsar of Russia (1645-76).—
518

Allen, George R.—American Radical.—
182, 640

Amadeo (Amadeus) I (1845-1890)—son
of King Victor Emmanuel II of
Italy; King of Spain (1870-73).—418,
496, 583

Amberny—Swiss lawyer.—77

Antonelli, Giacomo (1806-1876)—Italian
cardinal; counsellor of the Pope
Pius IX.—497

Applegarth, Robert (1833-1925)—a
leader of the British trade unions,
cabinet-maker; General Secretary of
the Amalgamated Society of Carpenters and Joiners (1862-71), member
of the London Trades Council;
member of the General Council of
the International (1865, 1868-72);
delegate to the Basle Congress of the
International (1869); subsequently
abandoned the working-class movement.—19, 145, 159

Argaing, Ferdinand—French worker, member of the International; from the end of 1872 an authorised representative of the General Council in Toulouse.—444

Arnaud, Antoine (1831-1885)—French revolutionary, Blanquist; member of the Central Committee of the National Guard and the Paris Commune; emigrated to England; member of the General Council of the International (1871-72), delegate to the Hague Congress of the International (1872); withdrew from the International in view of the decision by the Congress to transfer the General Council to New York.—19, 122, 145, 159, 243-47, 250, 253, 441

Ashton, Thomas—manufacturer in Lancashire, Liberal.—351, 354

Ashworth, Edmund (1801-1881)—English manufacturer, Liberal.—351, 354

Attila (Etzel) (d. 453)—King of the Huns (433-53).—610

Avrial, Augustin Germain (1840-1904)—prominent figure in the French working-class movement; mechanical engineer; Left Proudhonist; member of the Federal Council of the Paris sections of the International; member of the Paris Commune; emigrated to England.—101

Ayrton, Acton Smee (1816-1886)—English politician, Liberal M.P. (1857-74); Chief Commissioner of Works and Public Buildings (1869-73).—612

B

Bacave, Henri—police agent, insinuated himself into the Narbonne Section of the International; supported anarchists; was exposed in 1873.—507

Bach, Johann Sebastian (1685-1750)—German composer.—602

Bakunin, Mikhail Alexandrovich (Bakounine, Michael) (1814-1876)—Russian revolutionary, took part in the 1848-49 revolution in Germany; an ideologist of Narodism and anarchism; opposed Marxism in the International; was expelled from the International at the Hague Congress (1872) for his divisive activities.—32, 61, 64, 66-68, 85, 89-92, 96, 105, 112, 115, 118, 120, 121, 141, 142, 168, 176, 205-07, 228, 230, 231, 238, 249, 257, 267, 268, 274, 275, 283, 290, 413, 439, 440, 442, 445, 446, 451, 457, 459-62, 464, 466-70, 472, 475-76, 478, 480, 482, 485-86, 488, 496, 497, 499, 503, 505, 506, 509, 516-25, 526-32, 535-37, 539-41, 543, 544, 549, 551-55, 556-60, 562-68, 571, 579-81, 584, 592, 595, 630

Banks, Theodore H.—member of the International in the USA, housepainter; bourgeois Radical.—182, 640, 641

Barni, Jules Romain (1818-1878)—French idealist philosopher, Republican; an organiser of the League of Peace and Freedom; deputy to the National Assembly from 1872.—460

Barry, Maltman (1842-1909)—English journalist, socialist; member of the International; member of the General Council (1872) and British Federal Council (1872-74); delegate to the Hague Congress of the International (1872); supported Marx and Engels in the struggle against Bakuninists and English reformists.—145, 159, 240, 244, 245, 250

Bassi, Ugo (1801-1849)—Italian revolutionary, democrat; took part in the 1848-49 revolution; shot by the Austrians.—44

Bastelica, André Augustin (1845-1884)—a leading figure in the French and Spanish working-class movement, Corsican by birth, printer; Bakuninist; member of the General Council of the International (1871), delegate to the London Conference of 1871.—92, 93, 97, 102, 474, 476, 488, 504-05

Bayard, Pierre Terrail, seigneur de (c. 1475-1524)—French warrior, glorified by his contemporaries as *Le chevalier sans peur et sans reproche* (the Knight Without Fear and Without Reproach).—466

Bayle, Pierre (1647-1706)—French sceptic philosopher, critic of religious dogmatism.—608

Bebel, August (1840-1913)—a leading figure in the international and German working-class movement; turner; President of the Union of German Workers' Associations from 1867; member of the International, deputy to the Reichstag from 1867; one of the founders and leaders of German Social-Democracy; opposed the Lassalleans; took an internationalist stand during the Franco-Prussian war of 1870-71; came out in support of the Paris Commune; friend and associate of Marx and Engels.—46, 48, 129, 167, 222, 224, 411-12

Becker, Bernhard (1826-1891)—German journalist, follower of Lassalle, President of the General Association of German Workers (1864-65); subsequently supported the Eisenachers; delegate to the Hague Congress of the International (1872).—243, 244, 250

Becker, Hermann Heinrich (1820-1885)—German lawyer and journalist, member of the Communist League from 1850; one of the accused at the Cologne Communist Trial (1852); member of the Party of Progress in the 1860s; later National-Liberal.—75

Becker, Johann Philipp (1809-1886)—prominent figure in the international and German working-class movement, took part in the 1848-49 revolution in Germany; organised sections of the International in Switzerland and Germany; delegate to the London Conference (1865) and all the congresses of the International; editor of *Der Vorbote* (1866-71);

friend and associate of Marx and Engels.—160, 243-50

Beesly, Edward Spencer (1831-1915)—British historian and politician, Radical, positivist philosopher; professor at London University, in 1870-71 supported the International and the Paris Commune.—165, 193

Beethoven, Ludwig van (1770-1827)—German composer.—603

Beghelli, Giuseppe (1847-1877)—Italian journalist, democrat; took part in Garibaldi's campaigns; in 1871 member of the Working Men's Federation in Turin.—500

Beklemishev, Fyodor Andreyevich—clerk in the office of Governor-General of Eastern Siberia Muravyov-Amursky.—556

Benardaki, Dmitry Yegorovich (1799-1870)—Russian landowner and manufacturer.—557

Benary, Franz Simon Ferdinand (1805-1880)—German Orientalist, philologist, and Bible scholar, professor in Berlin.—452

Benedek, Ludwig August von (1804-1881)—Austrian general, Commander-in-Chief of the Austrian army during the Austro-Prussian war of 1866.—624

Bennett, George—member of the British Federal Council of the International (1872-73).—414

Bergenroth, Gustav Adolph (1813-1869)—German historian and journalist; petty-bourgeois democrat, took part in the 1848-49 revolution; left Germany in 1850.—609

Bert, Cesare—Italian mechanic, an organiser of the Turin Section of the International; in 1871-72 supported the General Council; later joined the anarchists; delegate to the anarchist Congress in Geneva (1873).—500

Bertrand, Francis J.—cigar-maker; German by birth; member of the North American Federal Council of the

International (1872) and the editorial board of the *Arbeiter-Zeitung*; member of the General Council elected by the Hague Congress (1872).—240, 253, 266

Bervi, Vassily Vassilyevich (pseudonym *Flerovsky, N.*) (1829-1918)—Russian economist and sociologist; democrat; Narodnik utopian socialist; author of the book *The Condition of the Working Class in Russia.*—521

Beust, Friedrich Ferdinand, Count von (1809-1886)—Saxon and Austrian statesman, opposed the unification of Germany under the supremacy of Prussia; in 1849-66 held several ministerial posts in the Government of Saxony; Foreign Minister (1866-71) and Chancellor of Austria-Hungary (1867-71), Ambassador to London (1871-78) and to Paris (1878-82).—64, 83, 223, 225

Biedermann, Friedrich Karl (1812-1901)—German historian and journalist, Liberal; a National-Liberal in the 1860s; editor of the *Deutsche Allgemeine Zeitung* (1863-79).—287

Bignami, Enrico (1846-1921)—prominent figure in the Italian democratic and working-class movement, journalist; took part in Garibaldi's campaigns; organiser of the Lodi Section of the International; editor of *La Plebe* (1868-82); from 1871 regularly corresponded with Engels; opposed anarchism.—22, 271, 409, 415, 437, 447

Bismarck-Schönhausen, Otto, Prince von (1815-1898)—statesman of Prussia and Germany, diplomat; Prime Minister of Prussia (1862-72, 1873-90), Chancellor of the North German Confederation (1867-71) and of the German Empire (1871-90); carried through the unification of Germany by counter-revolutionary means.—62, 64, 75, 83, 95, 116, 119, 161, 222, 225, 262, 352, 360, 364, 402-05, 411, 446, 477, 484, 617, 618, 620, 622, 624

Blanc, Gaspard Antoine (b. 1845)—French Bakuninist; took part in the Lyons uprising in 1870; after the suppression of the Paris Commune, sided with the Bonapartists.—92, 93, 96, 119-21, 300, 467, 474, 476, 505, 567

Blanc, Jean Joseph Charles Louis (1811-1882)—French petty-bourgeois socialist, historian; member of the Provisional Government and President of the Luxembourg Commission in 1848; pursued a policy of conciliation with the bourgeoisie; a leader of petty-bourgeois refugees in London in the 1850s-60s; deputy to the National Assembly of 1871; opposed the Paris Commune.—524, 562

Blanqui, Louis Auguste (1805-1881)—French revolutionary, utopian communist; organised secret societies and plots; sentenced to imprisonment several times.—265

Blind, Karl (1826-1907)—German journalist, petty-bourgeois democrat; a leader of the German petty-bourgeois refugees in London in the 1850s; National-Liberal from the 1860s.—162, 418

Blood, James—American Radical.—641

Blücher, Gebhard Leberecht von (1742-1819)—Prussian field marshal; took part in wars against the French Republic and Napoleonic France.—622

Böhme, Jakob (1575-1624)—German artisan, pantheist philosopher; expressed ideas on the dialectical development of the world.—602

Bolte, Friedrich—prominent figure in the American working-class movement; cigar-maker; Secretary of the North American Federal Council of the International (1872), member of the *Arbeiter-Zeitung* editorial board; member of the General Council (1872-74) elected at the Hague Congress.—240, 253, 266

Bonança—Portuguese anarchist.—487

Bonaparte—see *Napoleon III*

Boon, Martin James—British mechanic; follower of the social-reformist views of James Bronterre O'Brien, a Chartist; member of the General Council of the International (1869-72); member of the British Federal Council (1872).—19, 122, 145, 159

Boriani, Giuseppe—participant in the Italian working-class movement of the 1870s; member of the International.—56

Börne, Ludwig (1786-1837)—German critic and writer.—604

Borrel(l), Enrique—Spanish anarchist, tailor; a founder of the first sections of the International in Spain; member of the Spanish Federal Council (1870-71).—486, 487

Bousquet, Abel—French anarchist, expelled from the Béziers Section of the International as a police agent.—249, 300, 399, 412, 508

Bové, Clementé—Spanish anarchist, weaver; Chairman of the factory workers' trade union of Catalonia.—497

Bracke, Wilhelm (1842-1880)—German Social-Democrat; publisher of socialist literature in Brunswick; a founder and leader of the Social-Democratic Workers' Party; deputy to the Reichstag (1877-79).—50

Bradlaugh, Charles (1833-1891)—English Radical, editor of the *National Reformer*; sharply attacked Marx and the International Working Men's Association.—62, 71-73

Bradnick, Frederick—member of the General Council of the International (1870-72), delegate to the London Conference (1871); following the Hague Congress (1872) joined the reformist wing of the British Federal Council.—19, 122, 145, 159, 306, 311, 312

Bray, John Francis (1809-1897)—English utopian socialist, follower of Robert Owen.—394

Brentano, Lujo (1844-1931)—German vulgar economist; a representative of Katheder-Socialism.—164, 190

Bright, John (1811-1889)—British manufacturer; one of the Free Trade leaders and founders of the Anti-Corn Law League; leader of the Left wing of the Liberal Party from the early 1860s; held several ministerial posts in Liberal cabinets.—144

Brismée, Désiré Jean François (1822-1888)—prominent figure in the Belgian democratic and working-class movement; printer; Proudhonist; a founder of the Belgian Section of the International (1865); member of the Belgian Federal Council from 1869; joined Bakuninists at the Hague Congress (1872), subsequently dissociated himself from the anarchists.—243, 245-50

Brix, Harald Frederik Valdemar (1841-1881)—Danish journalist; a founder of the sections of the International in Copenhagen; editor of the *Socialisten*; an organiser of the Danish Social-Democratic Party (1876).—224

Brousse, Paul Louis Marie (1854-1912)—French petty-bourgeois socialist: physician; participant in the Paris Commune; sided with the anarchists; in 1879 became a member of the French Workers' Party; a leader of the opportunist trend of the Possibilists.—399, 443, 507, 586

Bruce, Henry Austin, 1st Baron Aberdare (1815-1895)—British statesman, Liberal, Home Secretary (1868-73).—149, 612

Brunetti, Angelo (nicknamed *Ciceruacchio*) (1800-1849)—Italian revolutionary; took part in the 1848-49 revolution; shot by the Austrians.—44

Brutus, Lucius Junius (6th cent. B.C.)—according to legend, founder of the Roman Republic, Roman Consul (509 B.C.); condemned his own sons to death for conspiring against the Republic.—395

Bürgers, Heinrich (1820-1878)—German radical journalist; member of the Communist League; an editor of the *Neue Rheinische Zeitung*; from 1850 member of the Communist League Central Authority; one of the accused at the Cologne Communist Trial (1852); member of the Party of Progress in the 1860s-70s.—75

Burt, Thomas (1837-1922)—English trade-unionist, miner; Secretary of the Northumberland Miners' Association; M.P. (1874-1918); supported the Liberal Party.—613, 615

Butt, Isaac (1813-1879)—Irish lawyer and politician, Liberal M.P. (1852-65, 1874-78); counsel for the defence at the trial of the Fenians (1860s); leader of the Irish Home Rule League in 1872-75.—616

Buttery, G. H.—member of the General Council of the International (1871-72).—19, 122, 145, 159

Buttner, Hugo—Swiss whitesmith; participant in the League of Peace and Freedom; member of the Bakuninist Alliance.—461

C

Cabet, Étienne (1788-1856)—French writer, utopian communist; author of *Voyage en Icarie*.—524

Cafiero, Carlo (1846-1892)—participant in the Italian working-class movement, member of the International; in 1871 corresponded with Engels, pursued the General Council's line in Italy; one of the founders of the Italian anarchist organisations from 1872; abandoned anarchism at the end of the 1870s.—48, 262, 275, 280, 283, 497, 498, 503, 509

Cagliostro, Alessandro, Count (*Giuseppe Balsamo*) (1743-1795)—Italian adventurist and hoaxer.—89

Cagnon (*Cognon*), *Émile*—French anarchist, engraver; lived in Switzerland; member of the Romance Federal Committee; in 1870 expelled from the International for embezzlement.—474

Calas, André (born c. 1825)—French upholsterer; Secretary of the section of the International in Montpellier; supported the policy of the General Council; in 1873 was sentenced to one-year imprisonment.—443, 507, 508

Calleja, Inocente—prominent figure in the Spanish working-class movement, jeweller; member of the Spanish Federal Council of the International (1871-72), the *Emancipacion* editorial board (1871-73) and the New Madrid Federation (1872-73); opposed the anarchists.—493

Camélinat, Zéphyrin Rémy (1840-1932)—prominent figure in the French working-class and socialist movement, bronze-worker; a leader of the Paris sections of the International; participant in the Paris Commune.—40, 101

Campos—see *Martinez de Campos, Arsenio*

Caporusso, Stefano (*Étienne*)—Italian anarchist, tailor; one of the founders of the Neapolitan Section of the International and its chairman; delegate to the Basle Congress (1869); in 1870 was expelled from the section for embezzlement.—497, 498

Carl, Conrad (d. 1890)—German refugee in the USA from 1854; tailor; member of the North American Federal Council of the International; elected to the General Council at the Hague Congress (1872); in 1873 editor of the *Arbeiter-Zeitung*; after 1875 abandoned the working-class movement.—240, 253

Castelar y Ripoll, Emilio (1832-1899)—Spanish politician, historian and writer; leader of the Right-wing Republicans; in September 1873-January 1874 head of the government which paved the way for the restoration of monarchy in Spain.—496

Catherine II (1729-1796)—Empress of Russia (1762-96).—567

Cervera, Rafael (1828-1908)—Spanish politician; Federal Republican; deputy to the Constituent Cortes (1873).—589

Cetti—member of the North American Federal Council of the International.—240

Chalain, Louis Denis (1845-1888)—prominent figure in the French working-class movement, metal-turner; member of the Paris Commune; emigrated to England, where for some time he was a member of the French Section of 1871, which opposed the General Council; later joined the anarchists.—101

Charles Augustus (*Karl August*) (1757-1828)—duke of Saxe-Weimar (from 1758); grand duke of Saxe-Weimar-Eisenach (from 1815).—602

Chassin, Charles Louis (1831-1901)—French journalist and historian, Republican; participant in the League of Peace and Freedom; founder and editor of the *Démocratie* (1868-70).—540

Chautard, B.—French police agent who found his way into workers' organisations; member of the French Section of 1871 in London; was exposed and expelled from the section.—40, 98

Chernyshevsky, Nikolai Gavrilovich (1828-1889)—Russian revolutionary democrat and utopian socialist; materialist philosopher; writer and literary critic, one of the predecessors of Russian Social-Democracy.—516, 524, 526, 558, 559, 561-62

Cherval, Julien (real name *Joseph Crämer*)—police spy for Prussia and France; gained entry into the Communist League and led one of the Paris communities belonging to the sectarian Willich-Schapper group; ac-

cused of complicity in the so-called Franco-German plot in Paris in February 1852; escaped from prison with the connivance of the police.—160

Chevalley, Henri—Swiss anarchist, tailor.—92, 474, 475

Cicero (*Marcus Tullius Cicero*) (106-43 B.C.)—Roman orator, statesman and philosopher.—619

Ciceruacchio—see *Brunetti, Angelo*

Cincinnatus (*Lucius Quinctius Cincinnatus*) (c. 519-438 B.C.)—Roman patrician, Consul (460 B.C.), dictator (458 and 439 B.C.); according to legend, was an ordinary man and worked his own small farm.—621

Claflin, Tennessee Celeste (1845-1923)—American bourgeois feminist; sought to use the International's organisation in the USA for her own ends; together with her sister, Victoria Woodhull, published *Woodhull & Claflin's Weekly.*—178

Claris, Aristide (1843-1916)—French journalist, anarchist; took part in the Paris Commune; emigrated to Switzerland, where he joined the anarchist Section of Propaganda and Revolutionary Socialist Action; editor of the *Révolution Sociale* (1871-72).—485

Cochrane-Baillie, Alexander Dundas Ross Wishart (1816-1890)—British politician and man of letters; Conservative M.P.—31, 33, 140-43, 145, 149-50, 645

Coenen, Philip(pe) (1842-1892)—a leading figure in the Belgian working-class movement, shoe-maker; Secretary of the editorial board of the Antwerp newspaper *De Werker*; delegate to the Brussels Congress (1868), London Conference (1871) and Hague Congress (1872) of the International; at the latter he joined the anarchist minority; subsequently one of the organisers of the Belgian

Socialist Party (1879).—243, 245-47, 249, 250

Cordova y Lopez, Francisco—Spanish journalist, Republican; from 1868 member of the Bakuninist Alliance in Madrid.—486

Costa, Andrea (1851-1910)—prominent figure in the Italian working-class and socialist movement; in the 1870s a leader of the anarchist organisations in Italy; in 1879 criticised anarchism; subsequently worked for the establishment of a political workers' party.—503, 509

Cournet, Frédéric Étienne (1839-1885)— French revolutionary, Blanquist; member of the Paris Commune; emigrated to England; member of the General Council of the International (1871-72); delegate to the Hague Congress (1872); withdrew from the International in view of the decision by the Congress to transfer the General Council to New York.— 19, 122, 145, 159, 213, 243-47, 250, 253, 441

Cremer, William Randal (1838-1908)— active participant in the British trade union and pacifist movement; a founder of the Amalgamated Society of Carpenters and Joiners (1860); member of the London Trades Council, participant in the inaugural meeting of the International held at St. Martin's Hall (September 28, 1864); member of the General Council of the International and its General Secretary (1864-66); in 1870-71 opposed the campaign in defence of the French Republic; subsequently Liberal M.P.—31, 615

Crescio, Prospero—Italian journalist; supporter of Garibaldi; joined the Bakuninists; editor of the newspaper Avvenire Sociale in Piacenza.—451, 453, 504

Cuno, Edward Heinrich—engineer and architect; father of Theodor Friedrich Cuno.—151

Cuno, Theodor Friedrich (pseudonym Capestro, Frederico) (1846-1934)— prominent figure in the German and the international working-class movement, engineer; actively opposed the anarchists in Italy; organiser of the Milan Section of the International; delegate to the Hague Congress (1872); after the Congress, emigrated to the USA and took part in the International's activities there.— 151-52, 244, 245, 246-47, 249-50, 415, 457, 499

Cyrille, Marie Antoine Victor—French anarchist, shop assistant; took part in the Paris Commune; refugee in Italy, Switzerland, Belgium; delegate to the Hague Congress of the International (1872); subsequently became a police agent.—245, 250, 253, 279

D

Dante, Alighieri (1265-1321)—Italian poet.—72, 143, 600

Darboy, Georges (1813-1871)—French theologian, archbishop of Paris from 1863; shot by the Commune as a hostage in May 1871.—143, 149

Dave, Victor (1847-1922)—member of the Belgian Federal Council of the International, journalist; delegate to the Hague Congress (1872); sided with the anarchist minority.—244-50

David, Edouard—prominent figure in the French and American working-class movement; was elected to the General Council at the Hague Congress of the International (1872), but refused.—253, 266

Davis, Ira—American Radical.—641

Delahaye, Victor Alfred (1838-1897)— French mechanic, Proudhonist; member of the International from 1865, participant in the Paris Commune; emigrated to England; member of the General Council of the International (1871-72); delegate to the London Conference (1871).— 19, 122, 145

Dentraygues, Émile Jean Philippe (pseudonym *Swarm*) (b. 1836)— French railway worker; member of the section of the International in Toulouse; delegate to the Hague Congress (1872); betrayed his friends at the Toulouse Trial (1873).—243, 245, 247, 249, 250, 438-40, 442-44, 507

De Paepe, César Almé Désiré (1841-1890)—Belgian socialist, compositor, subsequently physician; one of the founders of the Belgian sections of the International, delegate to the London conferences (1865 and 1871), the Lausanne (1867), Brussels (1868) and Basle (1869) congresses of the International; following the Hague Congress (1872) supported the Bakuninists for some time; a founder of the Belgian Workers' Party.—135

Dereure, Louis Simon (1838-1900)— prominent figure in the French and the international working-class movement, shoe-maker; Blanquist, member of the Paris Commune, emigrated to the USA; delegate to the Basle (1869) and Hague (1872) congresses of the International; member of the General Council (1872-74); from 1882, member of the French Workers' Party.—243-50, 253, 266

De Wolfers, Alfred Charles Daniel Edouard (b. 1841)—took part in the Paris Commune, refugee in London; member of the General Council of the International (1871-72).—145, 159

Dickens, Charles John Huffam (1812-1870)—English novelist.—196

Diderot, Denis (1713-1784)—French philosopher of the Enlightenment, atheist, leader of the Encyclopaedists.—608

Dietzgen, Joseph (1828-1888)—German Social-Democrat, leather-worker; self-taught philosopher who independ-

ently arrived at dialectical materialism; delegate to the Hague Congress of the International (1872).—246

Dilke, Charles Wentworth (1843-1911)— British politician and writer; a leader of the Radical wing of the Liberal Party, M.P.—52, 265

Dolgov, Nikolai Stepanovich (born c. 1844)—Russian revolutionary Narodnik; took part in student disturbances in 1869; member of the Nechayev organisation; in the 1870s was close to the Land and Freedom society.—531, 533

Dollfus, Jean (1800-1887)—Alsace manufacturer, bourgeois philanthropist; Mayor of Mulhouse.—329, 383

Douglass, Frederick (c. 1817-1895)— outstanding leader of the Abolitionist movement; participant in John Brown's raid in 1855 and in the American Civil War; active advocate of women's rights.—641

Ducpétiaux, Édouard (1804-1868)— Belgian journalist and statistician; bourgeois philanthropist; inspector of prisons and charity institutions.—338

Dufaure, Jules Armand Stanislas (1798-1881)—French lawyer and politician, Orleanist; in the 1840s held several ministerial posts; one of the organisers of the suppression of the Paris Commune; Minister of Justice (1871-73, 1875-76 and 1877-79); Prime Minister (1876, 1877-79).—83, 107, 122, 129, 223-24, 439

Dumont—see *Faillet, Eugène Louis*

Dupont, Eugène (c. 1837-1881)— prominent figure in the international working-class movement; musical instrument maker; took part in the June 1848 uprising in Paris; from 1862 on lived in London; member of the General Council of the International (November 1864 to 1872), Corresponding Secretary for France (1865-71); participant in the majority of congresses and conferences of the International; associate of Marx; became a member of the British Federal Council of the International in 1872; moved to the USA in 1874.— 19, 32, 122, 132, 145, 159, 240, 243-46, 249-50, 253, 265, 273, 283, 314, 556

Dupont, Jean Martial Aminthe (b. 1841)—French revolutionary; sided with the Blanquists; bank clerk; member of the Paris Commune.— 142

Durand, Gustave—member of the section of the International in Lyons; police agent; after the suppression of the Paris Commune, went to London, where he passed himself off as a refugee; Secretary of the French Section of 1871; in October 1871 was expelled from the International.— 21, 38, 67, 97, 103

Duval, Théodore—prominent figure in the Swiss working-class movement, joiner; a founder of the Alliance of Socialist Democracy; at the beginning of 1870 left the Bakuninists; member of the Romance Federal Committee of the International; opposed the Bakuninists; delegate to the Hague (1872) and Geneva (1873) congresses.—243-50, 253

E

Eastwick, Edward Backhouse (1814-1883)—British diplomat and Orientalist, Conservative M.P. (1868-74).— 143

Eberhardt—Belgian tailor; delegate to the Hague Congress (1872) of the International; sided with the anarchist minority.—244-47, 250, 253

Eberstein, Mangold von—West-German knight; engaged in hostilities with Nuremberg and other towns from 1516.— 600

Eccarius, Johann Georg (1818-1889)—prominent figure in the international and German working-class movement, tailor; refugee in London; member of the Communist League, member of the General Council of the International (1864-72), Council's General Secretary (1867-May 16, 1871); Corresponding Secretary for America (1870-72); from 1865 to 1872 delegate to all the International's conferences and congresses; associate of Marx up to 1872; after the Hague Congress, joined the reformist wing of the British Federal Council.— 16, 20, 122, 145, 159, 243, 245, 247, 449, 615

Elliott, John T.—American democrat; member of the International.— 640

Elpidin, Mikhail Konstantinovich (1835-1908)—took part in the student movement in Russia in the 1860s; then emigrated to Switzerland; member of the Bakuninist Alliance.— 36, 460

Engels, Frederick (1820-1895)—19, 22, 30, 36, 53, 55, 56, 59-61, 74-76, 122, 129-30, 137-39, 145-47, 150, 154, 159, 168, 175, 176, 184, 211, 213, 215, 217, 239, 240, 243-50, 253, 265, 273, 276, 283-85, 292, 293, 296, 297, 298, 300, 302, 303, 315, 319, 321, 325, 326, 327, 330, 338, 342, 344, 348, 349, 353, 359, 360, 362, 364-66, 369-71, 373-80, 382, 383, 385-90, 391, 415, 416, 418, 422-25, 437, 438, 447, 556, 581, 591, 627, 632, 636, 637, 645

Estévanez y Murphy, Nicolás (1838-1914)—Spanish politician and writer; Republican; took part in the 1868-74 revolution; Governor of Madrid (1873).— 490

F

Faillet, Eugène Louis (pseudonym Dumont) (1840-1912)—prominent figure in the French working-class movement; took part in the Paris Commune; delegate to the Hague Congress of the International (1872) from the sections in Paris and Rouen; subsequently member of the

French Workers' Party.—243-45, 247-50

Fanelli, Giuseppe (1827-1877)—Italian democrat; participant in the 1848-49 revolution and Garibaldi's campaign of 1860; Mazzinist; close friend of Bakunin from the mid-1860s; organiser of the first sections of the International and anarchist groups in Spain (1868); delegate to the Basle Congress of the International (1869); deputy to the Italian parliament from 1865.—288, 467, 486, 490, 497, 509

Farga Pellicer, Rafael (1840-1903)—Spanish anarchist, printer and journalist; an organiser and leader of anarchist groups and first sections of the International in Spain, one of the leaders of the secret Alliance, editor of the Federacion (1869-72); delegate to the Basle (1869) and Hague (1872) congresses of the International.—245, 247, 249, 250, 291, 486, 489, 495, 496, 510, 586

Farkas, Károly (Carl) (1843-1907)—prominent figure in the Hungarian working-class and socialist movement; exponent of Marxism, metal-worker; an organiser and leader of the section of the International in Hungary; delegate to the Hague Congress of the International (1872).—243-50, 432

Faucher, Julius (Jules) (1820-1878)—German journalist, Young Hegelian; advocate of Free Trade; refugee in England from 1850 till 1861; author of works on the housing question; member of the Party of Progress.—339

Favre, Claude Gabriel Jules (1809-1880)—French lawyer and politician; a leader of the republican bourgeois opposition from the late 1850s; Foreign Minister (1870-71), an organiser of the suppression of the Paris Commune and of the struggle against the First International.—32, 45, 83, 107, 161, 223, 224, 421, 480

Favre, Henri—watch-maker; chairman of the section of the International in Moutier-Grandval (Switzerland); opposed the principles of the Bakuninist Jura Federation and complied with the decisions of the Hague Congress (1872).—512

Fawcett, Henry (1833-1884)—English vulgar economist; follower of John Stuart Mill; M.P. from 1865; Liberal.—143-45, 645

Ferdinand I (1503-1564)—Austrian Archduke; Holy Roman Emperor (1556-64).—326

Ferdinand II (1810-1859)—King of Naples (1830-59), nicknamed King Bomba for the bombardment of Messina in 1848.—294

Ferré, Théophile Charles (1846-1871)—French revolutionary, Blanquist; member of the Paris Commune; member and later leader of the Committee of Public Safety and Deputy-Procurator of the Commune; shot by the Versaillese.—95, 477

Flerovsky, N.—see Bervi, Vassily Vassilyevich

Florinsky, Ivan Ivanovich (born c. 1845)—student of the Agricultural Academy in Moscow; member of the Nechayev organisation; in 1871 sentenced to six months' imprisonment.—533

Fluse, Pierre Joseph (1841-1909)—Belgian Proudhonist, weaver; delegate to the London Conference (1871) and the Brussels (1868) and Hague (1872) congresses of the International, supported the Bakuninists.—244-46, 249, 250

Fornaccieri—participant in the American working-class movement, Italian by birth; member of the General Council of the International, elected at the Hague Congress (1872).—253, 266

Foster, Robert—Secretary of the British Federal Council of the International

(1871-72), member of its reformist wing.—406

Fourier, François Marie Charles (1772-1837)—French utopian socialist.—347, 348, 394, 524, 630

Franca—see Nobre Franca, José Correia

Frankel, Léo (1844-1896)—a leading figure in the Hungarian and the international working-class movement, jeweller; member of the Paris Commune; member of the General Council of the International (1871-72); delegate to the London Conference (1871) and the Hague Congress (1872); associate of Marx and Engels.—19, 122, 145, 159, 213, 243-47, 249-50, 253, 284, 556

Frederick II (the Great) (1712-1786)—King of Prussia (1740-86).—401, 602

Frederick William II (1744-1797)—King of Prussia (1786-97).—604

Frederick William III (1770-1840)—King of Prussia (1797-1840).—604

Frederick William IV (1795-1861)—King of Prussia (1840-61).—401

Friedländer, Hugo—German Social-Democrat; delegate to the Hague Congress of the International (1872) from the section in Zurich.—243, 244, 246, 250

Fries, Jakob Friedrich (1773-1843)—German idealist philosopher.—610

Fusté, Luis—Spanish cooper; member of the section of the International in Sans.—495

G

Gambetta, Léon (1838-1882)—French statesman, bourgeois Republican, member of the Government of National Defence (1870-71); Prime Minister and Minister of Foreign Affairs (1881-82).—482

Gambuzzi, Carlo (1837-1902)—Italian lawyer; Mazzinist at the beginning of the 1860s; then anarchist; a leader of the secret Bakuninist Alliance and anarchist organisations in Italy.—461, 497

Gameter, Charles—Swiss anarchist; member of the Bakuninist Jura Federation.—450, 514

Garcia Fraile, Dionisio—Spanish anarchist, member of the group of the Bakuninist Alliance in Saint-Sebastien, police agent; expelled from the International in 1872 for embezzlement of section funds.—497

Garibaldi, Giuseppe (1807-1882)—Italian revolutionary, democrat; participant in the revolution of 1848-49; in the 1850s and 1860s headed the struggle for national liberation and the unification of the country; defended the Paris Commune; welcomed the establishment of sections of the International in Italy.—29, 43-45, 47, 48, 451, 453, 504, 579

Garrido y Tortosa, Fernando (1821-1883)—Spanish Federal Republican, utopian socialist, deputy to the Cortes (1869-73).—486

Gavrishev, Georgi Yakovlevich (born c. 1846)—student of the Agricultural Academy in Moscow; member of the Nechayev organisation; in 1871 sentenced to four months' imprisonment.—532

Geleff, Paul Johansen (1842-1921)—an organiser of sections of the International in Denmark (1871); a founder of the Danish Social-Democratic Party (1876); subsequently abandoned the working-class movement.—224

Gerhard, Hendrick (1829-1886)—one of the founders and leaders of the Dutch sections of the International; delegate to the Hague Congress of the International (1872); sided with the Bakuninists.—245, 247, 250, 253

Gerlach, Ernst Ludwig von (1795-1877)—Prussian reactionary politician, one of the founders of the Conservative Party and its organ *Neue Preussische Zeitung* (1848).— 403

Gibbons, Sills John—Lord Mayor of London in 1871.— 51

Girardin, Émile de (1806-1881)— French journalist and politician, lacked principles in politics.— 62

Gladstone, Robert (1811-1872)—English businessman; bourgeois philanthropist; cousin of William Ewart Gladstone.— 144

Gladstone, William Ewart (1809-1898)— British statesman, Tory; later Peelite; a leader of the Liberal Party in the latter half of the nineteenth century; Chancellor of the Exchequer (1852-55 and 1859-66) and Prime Minister (1868-74, 1880-85, 1886, 1892-94).— 164-66, 190-97, 225, 265, 284, 294-95, 611, 612, 615

Gluck, Christoph Willibald von (1714-1787)—German composer.— 603

Goethe, Johann Wolfgang von (1749-1832)—German writer and thinker.— 386, 582, 603, 620

Gondres, Eugène (b. 1825)—police agent, insinuated himself into the Narbonne Section of the International; was exposed in 1873.— 507

Gorchakoff (*Gorchakov*), *Alexander Mikhailovich, Prince* (1798-1883)— Russian statesman and diplomat; Foreign Minister (1856-82); State Chancellor (1867-82).— 64

Grant, James (1802-1879)—English journalist; editor of *The Morning Advertiser* (1850-71).— 351

Greg, Robert Hyde (1795-1875)— English manufacturer, Liberal.— 352, 354

Grimm, Jacob Ludwig Carl (1785-1863)—German philologist; a founder of comparative linguistics.— 604

Gromeka, Stepan Stepanovich (1823-1877)—Russian journalist, moderate Liberal; during the Polish uprising in

1863-64, was Chairman of the Commission on peasant questions in Poland, later Governor.— 562

Grosse, Eduard—German refugee in the USA, Lassallean; member of the International.— 183, 641

Grout, John—member of the British Federal Council of the International (1872), member of its reformist wing.— 406

Guesde, Jules (*Basile, Mathieu*) (1845-1922)—prominent figure in the French and the international working-class and socialist movement; sided with the anarchists in the first half of the 1870s; later a founder of the French Workers' Party (1879) and exponent of Marxism in France.— 442-44, 506, 507

Guillaume, James (1844-1916)—Swiss teacher, anarchist, participant in the Geneva (1866), Lausanne (1867), Basle (1869) and Hague (1872) congresses of the International; one of the organisers of the Alliance of Socialist Democracy; editor of the newspapers *Le Progrès*, *La Solidarité* and *Bulletin de la Fédération jurassienne*; at the Hague Congress (1872) was expelled from the International for his divisive activities.— 67, 91, 92, 102, 113, 118, 244-46, 249, 250, 257, 267, 268, 275, 280, 286, 287, 446, 450, 457, 473-76, 478, 485, 500, 504, 505, 509, 514, 540, 544, 580

Gülich, Gustav von (1791-1847)— German economist and historian; author of works on the history of economics.— 604

H

Hales, John (b. 1839)—British trade unionist, weaver; member of the General Council of the International (1866-72) and its Secretary (1871-72); delegate to the London Conference (1871) and the Hague Congress (1872) of the International; headed the reformist wing of the British Federal Council in 1872.—20, 32, 123, 145, 154, 159, 301-03, 306, 309, 311, 312, 406, 408, 414, 415, 446, 615, 644

Hales, William—member of the General Council of the International (1867, 1869-72).—19, 122, 145, 159

Halliday, Thomas (1835-1919)—a leader of British trade unionists, Chairman of the Amalgamated Association of Miners (1869-75); supported the policy of the Liberal Party.—615

Händel, Georg Friedrich (George Frederick) (1685-1759)—German composer, citizen of Great Britain from 1726.—603

Hansard, Thomas Curson (1776-1833)— English publisher; printed reports on the Parliamentary sittings; after his death they continued to be published under his name.—166-67, 195-97

Hansemann, David Justus Ludwig (1790-1864)—big German capitalist; a leader of the Rhenish liberal bourgeoisie; Minister of Finance of Prussia in March-September 1848.—342

Harcourt, W. E.—miner; delegate to the Hague Congress of the International (1872) from Australia.—247, 250

Hardenberg, Karl August von, Prince (1750-1822)—Prussian statesman and diplomat; Foreign Minister (1804-06, 1807), Chancellor of State (1810-22); champion of moderate reforms; supported the policy of the Holy Alliance after 1815.—401

Harris, George—active in the British working-class movement, follower of James Bronterre O'Brien, a Chartist; member of the General Council of the International (1869-72), Finance Secretary of the Council (1870-71).—19

Hartmann, Karl Robert Eduard von (1842-1906)—German idealist philosopher.—610

Hasenclever, Wilhelm (1837-1889)— German Social-Democrat, Lassallean; President of the General Association of German Workers in 1871-75.—451

Hasselmann, Wilhelm (b. 1844)—one of the leaders of the Lassallean General Association of German Workers; in 1871-75 editor of the *Neuer Social-Demokrat*; member of the Socialist Workers' Party of Germany from 1875; expelled from the party as anarchist in 1880.—451

Haussmann, Georges Eugène, Baron (1809-1891)—French politician, Bonapartist; prefect of the Seine Department (1853-70); directed work on the reconstruction of Paris.—319, 365

Heddeghem—see *Van-Heddeghem, L.*

Hegel, Georg Wilhelm Friedrich (1770-1831)—classical German philosopher.—370, 403, 600, 610, 630

Heim, Ludwig—see *Oberwinder, Heinrich*

Heine, Heinrich (1797-1856)—German revolutionary poet.—607

Henry III (1551-1589)—King of France (1574-89).—608

Henry IV (1553-1610)—King of France (1589-1610).—608

Hepner, Adolf (1846-1923)—German Social-Democrat; an editor of *Der Volksstaat*; delegate to the Hague Congress of the International (1872).—243-45, 247, 249, 250, 286, 439

Herbart, Johann Friedrich (1776-1841)— German idealist philosopher and teacher.—610

Herder, Johann Gottfried von (1744-1803)—German writer and literary theorist of the Enlightenment, a founder of the *Sturm-und-Drang* movement.—603

Herman, Alfred (1843-1890)—active in the Belgian working-class movement, sculptor; an organiser of sections of the International in Belgium; member of the General Council and Corresponding Secretary for Belgium (1871-72); at the Hague Congress (1872) joined the anarchist minority.—19, 41, 103, 122, 145, 159, 244-45, 247, 249, 250

Herzen, Alexander Alexandrovich (1839-1906)—Russian physiologist; son of Alexander Ivanovich Herzen.—162

Herzen, Alexander Ivanovich (1812-1870)—Russian revolutionary democrat, materialist philosopher and writer; emigrated in 1847.—162, 529, 540, 541, 557, 558, 561-62

Hills, Edmund—Secretary of the British Federal Council of the International (1872), opposed its reformist wing.—285, 313

Hinckeldey, Karl Ludwig Friedrich von (1805-1856)—Prussian official, Chief Commissioner of Berlin police from 1848; President of the Police Department in the Ministry of the Interior from 1853.—401

Hoffmann, Gotthelf (pseudonym *Füsilier Kutschke*) (1844-1924)—German poet, author of the nationalist soldier's songs.—339

Hole, James (1820-1895)—English publicist, author of a book on housing conditions of the working class.—338

Hollinger, Fidelio—German refugee, owner of a printing-house in London.—162

Höpfner, Friedrich Eduard Alexander von (1797-1858)—Prussian general, military writer.—604

Hout, Isaak Salomon van der (b. 1843)—Dutch worker; delegate to the Hague Congress of the International (1872) from the sections in Amsterdam.—243, 245, 247, 250, 253, 278

Howell, George (1833-1910)—a leader of the British trade unions, mason; participant in the Chartist movement, Secretary of the London Trades Council (1861-62), participant in the inaugural meeting of the International held on September 28, 1864 at St. Martin's Hall; member of the General Council of the International (October 1864 to 1869); opposed revolutionary tactics.—615

Huber, Victor Aimé (1800-1869)—German publicist and historian of literature, conservative.—338, 348, 349

Hubert, Joseph—Belgian miner, member of the International; at the extraordinary Congress of the Belgian Federation in July 1872 came out for preserving General Council's functions.—483

Hugo, Victor Marie (1802-1885)—French writer, Republican; after the Bonapartist coup d'état of December 2, 1851 emigrated from France.—562

Huleck, Maria—member of the General Council of the International (1868); emigrated to the USA, joined the group of bourgeois reformers.—641

Hume, Robert William—American Radical; one of the leaders of the National Labour Union; member of the International and correspondent of the General Council; subsequently joined the group of bourgeois reformers.—182, 640

Hurliman—member of the General Council of the International (1871-72); delegate from the Swiss Society in London.—19, 122, 145, 159

Hurry, F.—member of the British Federal Council of the International (1872-73), opposed its reformist wing.—313

I

Iglesias, Pablo (1850-1925)—prominent figure in the Spanish working-class and socialist movement, printer;

member of the Spanish Federal Council of the International (1871-72), the *Emancipacion* editorial board (1871-73), and the New Madrid Federation (1872-73); opposed anarchists; a founder of the Spanish Socialist Workers' Party (1879).—493

Ishutin, Nikolai Andreyevich (1840-1879)—Russian revolutionary; founder and leader of the secret revolutionary society in Moscow (1863-66); was arrested in 1866 and sentenced to death, commuted to penal servitude for life.—551

Itzenplitz, Heinrich August Friedrich, Count (1799-1883)—Prussian statesman, Minister of Trade (December 1862-May 1873).—404

Ivanov, Ivan Ivanovich (d. 1869)—student of the Agricultural Academy in Moscow; participant in the student movement in the 1860s and the Nechayev organisation; was murdered by Nechayev.—528, 530, 531, 535-38, 541, 553

J

Jacoby, Pavel Ivanovich—Russian refugee, physician, friend of Bakunin; propagated anarchism in Italy in the early 1870s.—500

Jalvo, Juan—Spanish anarchist; founded the groups of the Bakuninist Alliance in Spain; Chairman of Madrid Section of the International.—486

Johannard, Jules Paul (1843-1892)—active in the French working-class movement, lithographer, member of the General Council of the International (1868-69, 1871-72) and Corresponding Secretary for Italy (1868-69); member of the Paris Commune, Blanquist; emigrated to London; delegate to the Hague Congress (1872).—19, 122, 145, 159, 243-45, 247, 249, 250, 253

Jung, Hermann (1830-1901)—prominent figure in the international and Swiss working-class movement, watch-maker; member of the General Council of the International and Corresponding Secretary for Switzerland (November 1864 to 1872); Treasurer of the General Council (1871-72); Vice-President of the London Conference (1865); Chairman of the Geneva (1866), Brussels (1868) and Basle (1869) congresses and of the London Conference (1871) of the International; member of the British Federal Council (1872); supported Marx before the Hague Congress (September 1872), later joined the reformist wing.—20, 122-23, 129, 145, 158, 159, 189, 213, 302, 303, 306, 311, 312, 406, 449, 644

K

Kameke, Arnold Karl Georg von (1817-1893)—Prussian general, fought in the Franco-Prussian war of 1870-71; War Minister (1873-74).—404

Kamensky, Gavriil Pavlovich (1824-1898)—agent of the tsarist government abroad; in 1872, was, in his absence, sentenced to imprisonment by the Swiss court for the forgery of bank notes.—77

Kant, Immanuel (1724-1804)—founder of the German classical philosophy.—603, 610

Karakozov, Dmitry Vladimirovich (1840-1866)—Russian revolutionary; in April 1866 made an attempt upon Alexander II's life; was hanged.—525, 534

Katkov, Mikhail Nikiforovich (1818-1887)—Russian journalist; in the 1830s and 40s was close to democratic circles; later moderate Liberal; sided with reaction from 1863; editor of the *Moscow Gazette* (*Московскія вѣдомости*) (1850-55, 1863-87).—557

Kavanagh, Samuel—participant in the American working-class movement, Irishman by birth; member of the General Council elected at the Hague Congress of the International (1872).—240, 253, 266

Keen, Charles—participant in the British working-class movement; Chartist in the past; member of the General Council of the International (1872).—145, 159

Kepler, Johannes (1571-1630)—German astronomer.—602

Klein, Johann Jacob (1817-c. 1896)—doctor in Cologne, member of the Communist League, defendant at the Cologne Communist Trial (1852); acquitted by the jury.—75

Klimin, Innokenty Fyodorovich (b. 1847)—student of the Agricultural Academy in Moscow, member of the Nechayev organisation; in 1871 sentenced to one-year imprisonment.—532, 534

Kolachevskaya, Alla Nikolayevna (born c. 1845)—sister of Andrei Kolachevsky; prosecuted in the Nechayev organisation's case; was released in 1870 under police surveillance.—534

Kolachevskaya, Lyudmila Nikolayevna (born c. 1850)—sister of Andrei Kolachevsky; prosecuted in the Nechayev organisation's case; was released in 1870 under police surveillance.—534

Kolachevsky, Andrei Nikolayevich (c. 1848-1888)—participant in the student movement in Russia in the 1860s; prosecuted in the Nechayev organisation's case; acquitted by the jury.—534

Kossuth, Lajos (1802-1894)—leader of the Hungarian national liberation movement; head of the Hungarian revolutionary government in 1848-49; after the defeat of the revolution emigrated from Hungary.—52

Krug, Wilhelm Traugott (1770-1842)—German idealist philosopher, follower of Kant.—610

Krupp, Alfred (1812-1887)—German manufacturer.—187, 353

Kugelmann, Ludwig (1828-1902)—German physician, participant in the 1848-49 revolution; member of the International; delegate to the Lausanne (1867) and Hague (1872) congresses of the International; friend of Marx.—243, 244, 247, 249, 250

Kupper, F.—Secretary of Manchester Foreign Section of the International (1872); opposed reformists.—308

Kuznetsov, Alexei Kirillovich (1845-1928)—Russian revolutionary, student of the Agricultural Academy in Moscow, member of the Nechayev organisation; in 1871 was sentenced to ten years of penal servitude.—532, 537-40

Kuznetsov, Semyon Kirillovich (born c. 1847)—student of the Agricultural Academy in Moscow in 1869; member of the Nechayev organisation; arrested in December 1869; discharged in 1871; brother of Alexei Kuznetsov.—532

L

Lafargue, Paul (1842-1911)—prominent figure in the international and French working-class movement, member of the General Council of the International; Corresponding Secretary for Spain (1866-69), helped to organise the International's sections in France (1869-70), Spain and Portugal (1871-72); delegate to the Hague Congress (1872); a founder of the French Workers' Party; disciple and associate of Marx and Engels.—236, 243-45, 247-50, 261, 266, 271, 286, 287, 290, 437, 493, 496

La Fontaine, Jean de (1621-1695)—French fabulist.—526

Landeck, Bernard (b. 1832)—French jeweller, refugee in London; member of the French Section of 1871 and the Universal Federalist Council, both of which opposed the General Council of the International.—101, 157

Langethal, Christian Eduard (1806-1878)—German botanist and historian of agriculture.—609

Lanza, Giovanni (1810-1882)—Italian statesman, Liberal; Minister of Finance (1858-59), Minister of the Interior (1864-65), Prime Minister and Minister of the Interior (1869-73).—225

Larroque, Charles (Édouard) (b. 1829)—participant in the French working-class movement and in the Paris Commune, a leader of the International's section in Bordeaux; in 1873 fled to Spain where he conducted the work of Bordeaux sections as a representative of the General Council.—297, 415, 444

Lasker, Eduard (1829-1884)—German politician, a founder and a leader of the National-Liberal Party; deputy to the Reichstag from 1867.—167, 619

Lassalle, Ferdinand (1825-1864)—German journalist, lawyer, in 1848-49 took part in the democratic movement; founder of the General Association of German Workers (1863), adherent of the unification of Germany under Prussia's supremacy, one of the originators of the opportunist trend in the German working-class movement.—144, 379, 380

Laugrand, P.—French refugee in the USA.—641

Laurel(l), Carl Malcom Ferdinand—took part in the American working-class movement, Swede by birth, member of the General Council elected at the Hague Congress of the International (1872).—240, 253, 266

Law, Harriet (1832-1897)—a leading figure in the democratic and atheist movement in England, member of the General Council (1867-72) and the International's Manchester Section (1872).—19, 122, 145, 159

Ledru-Rollin, Alexandre Auguste (1807-1874)—French journalist and politician, democrat; member of the Provisional Government (1848), deputy to the Constituent and Legislative Assemblies where he headed the petty-bourgeois Montagne Party; emigrated to England after the demonstration of June 13, 1849.—562

Lefrançais, Gustave Adolphe (1826-1901)—took part in the 1848 revolution in France; member of the International from the late 1860s; Left Proudhonist, member of the Paris Commune, emigrated to Switzerland where he sided with the anarchists.—103, 105, 119, 127

Leibniz, Gottfried Wilhelm, Baron von (1646-1716)—German idealist philosopher and mathematician.—600, 602

Le Moussu, Benjamin Constant (b. 1846)—participant in the French working-class movement, engraver; member of the Paris Commune, emigrated to London; member of the General Council of the International and Corresponding Secretary for the French-speaking sections in America (1871-72); delegate to the Hague Congress (1872); supported Marx and Engels in their struggle against the Bakuninists.—20, 122, 145, 159, 213, 240, 243-45, 247, 249-50, 253, 416, 437, 447, 556

Léo, André (real name Léodile Champseix) (1832-1900)—French writer, took part in the Paris Commune, emigrated to Switzerland, supported the anarchists.—95, 477, 488

Lessing, Gotthold Ephraim (1729-1781)—German writer, critic and philosopher of the Enlightenment.—603

Lessner, Friedrich (1825-1910)— prominent figure in the German and the international working-class movement, tailor; member of the Communist League, participant in the revolution of 1848-49, a refugee in London from 1856; member of the General Council of the International (November 1864 to 1872); took part in the London conferences of 1865 and 1871, and the Lausanne (1867), Brussels (1868), Basle (1869) and the Hague (1872) congresses of the International; member of the British Federal Council; friend and associate of Marx and Engels.—19, 75, 122, 145, 159, 240, 244, 247, 250, 294, 313

Levièle, E.—member of the American working-class movement, French by birth, member of the General Council elected at the Hague Congress of the International (1872).—240, 253, 266

Liebig, Justus, Baron von (1803-1873)— German chemist, a founder of agricultural chemistry.—384, 609

Liebknecht, Wilhelm (1826-1900)— prominent figure in the German and the international working-class movement, took part in the 1848-49 revolution; member of the Communist League and of the International, delegate to the Basle Congress (1869); from 1867 deputy to the Reichstag; a founder and leader of the German Social-Democracy, editor of the *Volksstaat* (1869-76); during the Franco-Prussian War took an internationalist stand, supported the Paris Commune; friend and associate of Marx and Engels.—75, 129, 160, 164, 222, 224, 473, 496

Likhutin, Ivan Nikitich (born c. 1848)— took part in the student movement in 1869, founded a circle connected with Nechayev in Petersburg, sentenced to sixteen months' imprisonment (1871).—534

Lochner, Georg (born c. 1824)—active member of the German and the international working-class movement, joiner; member of the Communist League and of the General Council of the International (November 1864 to 1867 and 1871-72); delegate to the London conferences of 1865 and 1871; friend and associate of Marx and Engels.—19, 122, 145, 159

Longuet, Charles (1839-1903)— prominent figure in the French working-class movement, journalist, Proudhonist; member of the General Council of the International (1866-67, 1871-72), delegate to the Lausanne (1867), Brussels (1868) and Hague (1872) congresses and the London Conference (1871); member of the Paris Commune, emigrated to England; later joined the opportunist group of Possibilists.—19, 20, 123, 145, 159, 240, 243-45, 249, 250

Lorenzo, Anselmo (1841-1914)—active member of the Spanish working-class movement, printer; a founder of the International's sections in Spain, member of the Spanish Federal Council (1870-72), delegate to the London Conference (1871).—53, 207, 234, 236, 289, 290, 302, 303, 486, 491, 493-94

Lostau, Baldomero (born c. 1845)— Spanish mechanic, federal Republican, member of the International; elected to the Cortes in 1871.—495

Louis XIV (1638-1715)—King of France (1643-1715).—94

Louis XV (1710-1774)—King of France (1715-74).—34

Louis Bonaparte—see *Napoleon III*

Louis Napoleon—see *Napoleon III*

Louis Philippe I (1773-1850)—Duke of Orleans, King of the French (1830-48).—417

Loyola, St. Ignatius of (*Inigo López de Recalde*) (1491-1556)—Spanish nobleman, in 1540 founded and headed the Society of Jesus.—470, 525

Lucain—see *Potel, Frédéric*

Lucraft, Benjamin (1809-1897)—a leader of the British trade unions, furniture-maker; participant in the inaugural meeting of the International held on September 28, 1864 at St. Martin's Hall; member of the General Council of the International (1864-71), delegate to the Brussels (1868) and Basle (1869) congresses; in 1871 refused to sign the General Council's address *The Civil War in France* and left the Council.—80

Ludwig, Gustav—German Social-Democrat, delegate to the Hague Congress of the International (1872) from the Mainz Section.—245, 250, 253

M

Macdonald, Alexander (1821-1881)—British trade unionist, miner, President of the National Union of Mineworkers; member of Parliament from 1874, supported Liberal Party's policy.—613, 615

M(a)cDonnell, Joseph Patrick (1845-1906)—active member of the Irish working-class movement; member of the General Council of the International, Corresponding Secretary for Ireland (1871-72); delegate to the London Conference (1871) and the Hague Congress (1872), member of the British Federal Council (1872); in December of 1872 emigrated to the USA, took part in the American working-class movement.—19, 122, 145, 159, 213, 240, 244-46, 249, 250, 265, 284, 294, 416

Macfarlane, Helen—a Chartist on the staff of *The Democratic Review* (1849-50) and *The Red Republican* (1850); translated the *Manifesto of the Communist Party* into English.—174

Machiavelli, Niccolò (1469-1527)—Italian politician, philosopher, historian and writer.—488

Mac-Mahon, Marie Edmé Patrice Maurice, duc de Magenta (1808-1893)—French military figure and politician, marshal, Bonapartist; during the Franco-Prussian War commanded the First Corps, then the Châlon Army, was captured at Sedan; Commander-in-Chief of the Versaillese Army, an organiser of the suppression of the Paris Commune; President of the Republic (1873-79).—623

Maddox (Maddock or *Maddoss), G. W.*—American Radical.—182, 640-42

Mahomet—see *Mohammed*

Malon, Benoît (1841-1893)—French socialist, member of the International and of the Paris Commune; emigrated to Italy, then to Switzerland where he sided with the anarchists; later a leader of the opportunist trend of the Possibilists.—94, 101, 103, 104, 117, 119, 249, 267, 275, 485, 506, 507

Malou, Jules Edouard, François Xavier (1810-1886)—Belgian statesman, belonged to the Catholic Party, Minister of Finance (1844-47, 1870-78), Chairman of the Council of Ministers (1871-78).—83, 224

Malthus, Thomas Robert (1766-1834)—British vulgar economist, founder of the misanthropic theory of population.—380

Manteuffel, Otto Theodor, Baron von (1805-1882)—Prussian statesman; Minister of the Interior (1848-50), Prime Minister and Minister of Foreign Affairs (1850-58).—401, 402, 617

Marchand, Louis Joseph Gabriel (1842-1901)—French Bakuninist; from 1871 refugee in Switzerland, contributed to *La Révolution Sociale*; expelled from the International.—249, 399

Marguerittes, Édouard Louis Marie (b. 1835)—French revolutionary, Blanquist, took part in the Paris Commune, emigrated to London; member of the General Council of the International (1871-72).—122, 145, 159

Marselau, Nicolás Alonso—Spanish anarchist, a leader of the Spanish organisation of the Bakuninist Alliance, editor of the Razon in Seville (1871-72); delegate to the Hague Congress of the International (1872).—244-45, 247, 249, 250, 253, 291, 495, 510

Marshall, Alfred (1842-1924)—British economist.—351, 352

Martin, Constant (1839-1906)—French revolutionary, Blanquist, took part in the Paris Commune, emigrated to London; member of the General Council of the International (1871-72), delegate to the London Conference (1871).—19, 122, 145, 159

Martin, Felipe—Spanish anarchist.—490

Martinez de Campos, Arsenio (1831-1900)—Spanish general; in 1873 suppressed a cantonal uprising in Catalonia and Valencia, headed the monarchical coup d'état which brought to power Alfonso XII (December 24, 1874); War Minister (1881-83).—593, 594

Martinez, Franco (Francisco)—Spanish anarchist, dyer, member of the Spanish Federal Council of the International (1872-73).—208, 493

Marx, Karl (1818-1883)—19, 50-52, 63, 71-73, 75, 103, 122, 127, 131, 132, 145, 159-67, 175, 187, 188, 190-94, 197, 199, 213, 214, 240, 243, 244, 247, 249-50, 253, 254-59, 265, 273, 284, 286, 287, 303, 317, 318, 322, 333, 336, 370, 379, 390, 395, 397-99, 440, 445, 448, 461, 488, 501, 556, 644-45

Marx-Aveling, Eleanor (1855-1898)—participant in the British and international working-class movement, Karl Marx's younger daughter, married to Edward Aveling.—330

Mavritsky, Vasily Abramovich (c. 1847-1910)—student of the Kiev theologi-

cal seminary, prosecuted in the Nechayev organisation's case, the investigation was stopped for lack of evidence.—527

Mayo, Henry—took part in the British working-class movement, member of the General Council of the International (1871-72) and the British Federal Council (1872); in the latter he joined the reformist wing.—19, 122, 145, 159, 306, 311, 312, 406

Mazzini, Giuseppe (1805-1872)—Italian revolutionary, democrat, a leader of the national liberation movement in Italy; when the International was founded in 1864, tried to bring it under his influence; in 1871 opposed the Paris Commune and the General Council.—28, 29, 43-48, 60, 61, 141, 162, 480, 497, 504, 562, 579

Mechnikov, Lev Ilyich (1838-1888)—Russian geographer, sociologist and journalist; took part in Garibaldi's campaign (1860); contributed to Kolokol and Sovremennik; in the second half of the 1860s was close to Bakunin.—506

Méndez, Juan—Spanish anarchist.—495

Menke, Heinrich Theodor (1819-1892)—German geographer and ethnographer.—601, 602

Mesa y Leompart, José (1840-1904)—participant in the Spanish working-class and socialist movement, printer; an organiser of the International's sections in Spain, member of the Spanish Federal Council (1871-72), of the Emancipacion editorial board (1871-73), the New Madrid Federation (1872-73), fought anarchism; a founder of the Spanish Socialist Workers' Party (1879); translated works by Marx and Engels into Spanish.—290, 292, 438, 487, 488, 493

Milke, Fritz—German Social-Democrat, printer, delegate to the Hague Congress of the International (1872) from the Berlin Section.—245, 247, 250, 253

Mill, John Stuart (1806-1873)—British economist and positivist philosopher, follower of the classical school of political economy.—144

Millot, Théodore—French refugee in the USA, bookbinder, member of the International; took bourgeois radicalist stand.—182, 640

Milner, George—took part in the British working-class movement, Irish by birth, tailor; follower of the Chartist O'Brien's views; member of the General Council of the International (1868-72) and the British Federal Council (1872-73), came out against its reformist wing.—19, 122, 145, 159, 302, 313

Mitchell, John—member of the British Federal Council of the International (1872-73), came out against its reformist wing.—313

Mohammed (or *Muhammed, Mahomet*) (c. 570-632)—semi-legendary founder of Islam.—107, 558

Molière, Jean Baptiste (real name *Poquelin*) (1622-1673)—French dramatist.—191, 192

Moltke, Helmuth Karl Bernhard von, Count (1800-1891)—Prussian field marshal, military writer, Chief of the Prussian (1857-71) and the Imperial (1871-88) General Staff.—222, 592, 619-24

Montel, Guglielmo—member of the International in Italy.—48

Montoro, Peregrin (pseudonym *Damon*)—Spanish anarchist, weaver, member of the Spanish Federal Council of the International (1872-73).—208, 488, 493, 496

Mora, Angel—participant in the Spanish working-class movement, carpenter; member of the Spanish Federal Council of the International (1870-72), of the *Emancipacion* editorial board (1871-73) and the New Madrid Federation (1872-73); fought against anarchist influence.—486, 493

Mora, Francisco (1842-1924)—took part in the Spanish working-class and socialist movement, shoe-maker; an organiser of the International's sections in Spain and Portugal; member of the Spanish Federal Council of the International (1870-72), of the *Emancipacion* editorial board (1871-73), and the New Madrid Federation (1872-73); fought against anarchist influence; an organiser of the Spanish Socialist Workers' Party (1879).—235, 236, 290, 413, 486, 487, 491-93, 503, 578

Morago, González, Tomás (d. 1885)—Spanish anarchist, engraver; a founder and leader of the Bakuninist Alliance in Spain, member of the Spanish Federal Council of the International (1870-71); delegate to the Hague Congress (1872).—236, 245, 247, 249, 250, 287, 289-91, 486-90, 495, 497, 510

Morley, Samuel (1809-1886)—British manufacturer and politician, Liberal M.P. (1865, 1868-85).—265, 412, 446, 615

Mottershead, Thomas G. (c. 1826-1884)—British weaver, participant in the Chartist movement, member of the General Council of the International (1869-72); Corresponding Secretary for Denmark (1871-72), delegate to the London Conference (1871) and the Hague Congress (1872); a representative of the reformist wing of the British Federal Council, opposed Marx.—19, 122, 145, 159, 243, 247, 305, 306, 309, 311, 312, 615

Mozart, Wolfgang Amadeus (1756-1791)—Austrian composer.—603

Mülberger, Arthur (1847-1907)—German petty-bourgeois journalist, Proudhonist, physician.—368-79, 381-83, 385-91

Mundella, Anthony John (1825-1897)—British manufacturer and statesman, M.P. (from 1868), held several ministerial posts.—167

Muravyov, Mikhail Nikolayevich, Count (1796-1866)—Russian statesman, during the Polish uprising (1863) was Governor-General in Poland, for the brutal suppression of the uprising was called "hangman".—536, 556

Muravyov-Amursky, Nikolai Nikolayevich, Count (1809-1881)—Russian statesman, Governor-General of Eastern Siberia (1847-61).—556, 557

Murray, Charles Joseph—member of the British working-class movement, shoe-maker; took part in the Chartist movement, follower of O'Brien's views; member of the General Council of the International (1870-72) and the British Federal Council (1872-73); supporter of Marx and Engels.—19, 122, 145, 159, 294, 313

N

Napoleon I Bonaparte (1769-1821)—Emperor of the French (1804-14 and 1815).—340, 419, 420, 602, 603, 604, 624

Napoleon III (Charles Louis Napoleon Bonaparte) (1808-1873)—Emperor of the French (1852-70).—60, 92, 96, 107, 120, 157-58, 161, 219, 220, 300, 330, 350, 354, 361, 364, 401, 402, 417, 420, 438, 440, 461, 466, 467, 567, 624

Navarre, E.—Secretary of the French Section of 1871 (London) which the General Council did not admit to the International.—100

Nechayev (Netschajeff), Sergei Gennadyevich (1847-1882)—Russian revolutionary, conspirator, representative of the extremely adventurist trend in anarchism; in 1869-71 was connected with Bakunin; in 1872 was extradited by the Swiss authorities to the Russian government, sentenced to twenty years' imprisonment, died in the Peter and Paul Fortress in St. Petersburg.—23, 30, 77, 89, 459, 463, 478, 485, 515-17, 519, 522-24, 527-41, 544, 549, 552, 553, 557

Negreskul, Mikhail Fyodorovich (c. 1843-1871)—took part in the student movement in the 1860s, in 1869 arrested in connection with the Nechayev organisation's case, discharged because of illness (1870).—535

Neklyudov, Mikhail Sergeyevich (d. 1859)—Russian lawyer, employee in the office of the Eastern Siberian Administration in Irkutsk, killed by Beklemishev at a duel.—556

Nero (Nero Claudius Caesar Augustus Germanicus) (37-68)—Roman Emperor (54-68).—452

Nicholas I (1796-1855)—Emperor of Russia (1825-55).—560, 567

Nikolayev, Nikolai Nikolayevich (born c. 1850)—member of the Nechayev organisation, in 1871 sentenced to seven years and four months' imprisonment and to settlement in Siberia.—538, 539

Nobre Franca, José Correia—took part in the Portuguese working-class movement, an organiser of the International's sections in Lisbon.—413

Notker, Labeo (c. 952-1022)—German monk, taught at the monastic school of St. Gallen, Switzerland; translated into German and annotated a number of works by ancient and medieval authors.—604

O

Oberwinder, Heinrich (1846-1914)—participant in the Austrian working-class movement, journalist; Lassallean in the early 1860s, later joined the Eisenachers; delegate to the Basle (1869) and the Hague (1872) congresses of the International; in the late 1870s abandoned working-class movement, subsequently exposed as a police agent.—249, 250, 253, 415

O'Connell, Daniel (1775-1847)—Irish lawyer and politician, leader of the Liberal wing of the national liberation movement; organiser and leader of the Repeal Association.—616

O'Connor, Feargus Edward (1794-1855)—a leader of the Left wing of the Chartist movement, founder and editor of *The Northern Star*; reformist after 1848.—155

Odger, George (1820-1877)—a leader of the British trade unions, shoe-maker; member of the London Trades Council; participant in the inaugural meeting of the International held on September 28, 1864 at St. Martin's Hall; member of the General Council of the International (1864-71), its President (1864-67), took part in the London Conference (1865) and the Geneva Congress (1866); in 1871 refused to sign the General Council's address *The Civil War in France* and left the Council.—31, 80, 87, 615

Ogarev, Nikolai Platonovich (1813-1877)—Russian revolutionary democrat, poet and journalist, friend and associate of Alexander Herzen.—529

Ol(l)ivier, Émile (1825-1913)—French politician, moderate Republican, Bonapartist from the end of the 1860s; head of the government (January-August 1870).—220, 395, 645

Otto(n)s—first emperors of the Holy Roman Empire; its founder Otto I (962-73), German King of the Saxon dynasty, and his followers Otto II (973-83) and Otto III (983-1002).—600

Outine—see *Utin (Outine), Nikolai Isaakovich*

Owen, Robert (1771-1858)—British utopian socialist.—347, 348, 394, 561, 630

P

Pagés, Victor (born c. 1850)—participant in the Spanish working-class movement, shoe-maker; member of the Spanish Federal Council (1871-72), of the *Emancipacion* editorial board (1871-73), the New Madrid Federation (1872-73); fought against anarchist influence in Spain.—290, 493

Palladino, Carmelo (1842-1896)—Italian anarchist, barrister, a leader of the Bakuninist Alliance, a founder of anarchist organisations in Italy, member of the International's Neapolitan Section.—498

Pape, Fletcher—member of the International's British Federal Council (from 1871), belonged to the reformist wing.—406

Pauly, Hipolito—participant in the Spanish working-class movement, printer; member of the International's Spanish Federal Council (1871-72), of the *Emancipacion* editorial board (1871-73), the New Madrid Federation (1872-73); fought against anarchist influence in Spain.—290, 493

Pavía y Rodriguez de Alburquerque, Manuel (1827-1895)—Spanish general and politician, in 1873 suppressed the cantonal uprising in Andalusia, carried out the coup d'état (January 2-3, 1874) which brought the monarchist Serrano to power; Senator from 1880.—590, 593

Pavlov, Platon Vasilyevich (1823-1895)—Russian historian, professor; in 1862 deported from Petersburg for the connection with revolutionary circles.—561

Pène, Henri de (1830-1888)—French journalist, monarchist; founder and chief editor of the *Paris-Journal* (1868-88).—127

Péniche, count—Portuguese aristocrat, head of a masonic lodge, organiser of a secret society in 1872.—487

Péreire, Isaac (1806-1880)—French banker, Bonapartist, founded the joint-stock bank Crédit Mobilier together with his brother Émile (1852).—364

Perron—chocolate manufacturer.—94

Perron, Charles Eugène (1837-1919)— Swiss anarchist, member of the Central Bureau of the Bakuninist Alliance of Socialist Democracy, editor of *L'Égalité* (1869), an editor of *La Solidarité* and a leader of the Jura Federation; later abandoned the working-class movement.—229

Pestel, Pavel Ivanovich (1793-1826)—a leader of the Decembrist movement, founder and leader of the Southern Society.—567

Peter I (the Great) (1672-1725)—Tsar of Russia (1682-1721), Emperor of Russia (1721-25).—518, 563

Petrashevsky (*Butashevich-Petrashevsky*), *Mikhail Vasilyevich* (1821-1866)— Russian revolutionary, utopian socialist, organiser of the progressive Russian intellectuals' circle in Petersburg (1844); in 1849 was arrested and sentenced to death, then commuted to penal servitude for life.—556, 557

Petroni, Giuseppe (1812-1888)—Italian journalist and politician, Mazzinist; took part in the 1848-49 revolution; sentenced to life imprisonment in 1853, released in 1870; editor of the *Roma del Popolo.*—43, 44, 47

Petzold, Ernst—German lawyer, legal officer, Liberal, candidate for election to the Reichstag in Glauchau-Meerane (1873).—411

Pfänder (Pfander), Karl (c. 1819-1876)—prominent figure in the German and international working-class movement, painter; refugee in London from 1845; member of the Communist League's Central Authority, of the International's General Council (1864-67 and 1870-72); friend and associate of Marx and Engels.— 19, 122, 145, 159

Piétri, Joseph Marie (1820-1902)— French politician, Bonapartist, Prefect of police in Paris (1866-70).— 101, 463

Pihl, Sophus Theodor (1840-1881)— delegate to the Hague Congress of the International (1872) from the Copenhagen Section.—243, 245, 247, 249-50

Pindy, Jean Louis (1840-1917)—French engraver, member of the International (from 1867), of the Paris Commune; emigrated to Switzerland where he sided with the anarchists; member of the Bakuninist Jura Federation's Committee.—450, 514

Pino, Miguel—Spanish anarchist, mechanic, founder of the Bakuninist Alliance group in Malaga.—490

Pio, Louis (1841-1894)—participant in the Danish working-class and socialist movement; an organiser of the International's Danish sections (1871); editor of *Socialisten*; a founder of the Danish Social-Democratic Party (1876); in 1877 emigrated to America.—57, 224

Pius IX (Giovanni Maria Mastai-Ferretti) (1792-1878)—Pope (1846-78).—45, 64, 225

Pi y Margall, Francisco (1824-1901)— Spanish politician, historian, lawyer, philosopher and writer; leader of the Left federalist Republicans, was influenced by utopian socialist ideas; took part in the revolutions (1854-56 and 1868-74), Minister of the Interior (February 13-June 11, 1873), temporary President of the Republic (June 11-July 18, 1873).—585, 589, 590, 592

Pompadour, Jeanne-Antoinette Poisson, marquise de (1721-1764)—Louis XV's mistress.—34

Potel, Frédéric (pseudonym *Lucain*) (died in December 1872)—French refugee in Belgium, engineer; took part in the Paris Commune; member of the International, delegate to the Hague Congress (1872).—244-45, 247, 249, 250, 437, 457

Potter, George (1832-1893)—a leader of the British trade unions, carpenter;

member of the London Trades Council and a leader of the Amalgamated Union of Building Workers; editor of *The Bee-Hive Newspaper*; pursued a policy of compromise with the liberal bourgeoisie.—615

Proudhon, Pierre Joseph (1809-1865)— French journalist, economist and sociologist, a founder of anarchism.— 317, 319, 320-23, 324, 325, 327-29, 331, 332, 334-35, 336-37, 341, 343, 369-71, 372, 373-74, 376-80, 381, 384, 385, 387, 388, 391, 394-95, 397

Pryzhov, Ivan Gavrilovich (1829-1885)— Russian historian, ethnographer and journalist, member of the Nechayev organisation; in 1871, sentenced to twelve years of penal servitude and life settlement in Siberia.—531, 537-39

Pugachev, Yemelyan Ivanovich (c. 1742-1775)—leader of the anti-serfdom uprising of peasants and Cossacks in Russia (1773-75); executed in Moscow.—567

Pyat, Félix (1810-1889)—French journalist, dramatist and politician; democrat, took part in the 1848 revolution; in 1849 emigrated to Switzerland, then to Belgium and England; conducted a slander campaign against Marx and the International, using for this purpose the French Section in London; member of the Paris Commune.—96

R

Ranvier, Gabriel (1828-1879)—French revolutionary, Blanquist, member of the Paris Commune, emigrated to England; member of the General Council of the International (1871-72), delegate to the Hague Congress (1872); left the International after the decision to transfer the General Council to New York.—19, 122, 145, 159, 243, 245-47, 250, 253, 439, 441, 444

Razin, Stepan Timofeyevich (c. 1630-1671)—leader of an anti-serfdom uprising of peasants and Cossacks in Russia (1670-71); executed in Moscow.—518, 524, 549

Razoua, Angèle Eugène (1830-1878)— French journalist, Republican, sided with neo-Jacobins; took part in the Paris Commune, emigrated to Geneva, contributed to several newspapers.—83

Regis, Vitale (pseudonyms *Carlo Boggio, Étienne Péchard*)—Italian revolutionary, member of the International's Italian section in London; participant in the Paris Commune, member of the General Council (1871-72); took part in the 1873 revolutionary events in Spain.—19, 122, 145, 159, 499, 500

Renan, Joseph Ernest (1823-1892)— French historian, idealist philosopher, author of works on the origins of Christianity.—452

Reschauer, Heinrich (b. 1838)— Austrian writer and journalist, Liberal.—383

Reuter, Fritz (1810-1874)—German humorous writer and poet, wrote in Low German dialect.—380

Ricardo, David (1772-1823)—British economist.—396

Richard, Albert Marie (1846-1925)— French journalist, a leader of the International's section in Lyons; member of the Bakuninist Alliance, took part in the Lyons uprising in September 1870; after the suppression of the Paris Commune became a Bonapartist.—91, 93, 96, 119-21, 300, 440, 444, 461, 467, 472, 474, 476, 505, 567

Rigaut, Raoul (1846-1871)—Ftench revolutionary, Blanquist; member of the Paris Commune, member of the Public Safety Committee, Procurator of the Commune, shot by the Versaillese troops.—95, 477

Riley, William Harrison (1835-1907)—British journalist, Republican, socialist, editor and publisher of the *International Herald*; member of the International's British Federal Council (1872-73), opposed the reformist wing.—313, 314

Ripman, Fyodor Fyodorovich (b. 1842)—student of the Agricultural Academy in Moscow, member of the Nechayev organisation; in 1871 sentenced to one-year imprisonment.—531, 533

Ripoll—took part in suppression of cantonal uprisings in Spain in the summer of 1873.—593

Roach, Thomas John—member of the British working-class movement; member of the General Council of the International (1871-72), delegate to the Hague Congress (1872); Corresponding Secretary of the British Federal Council (1872), belonged to its reformist wing.—19, 122, 145, 159, 245-47, 250, 306, 310-12

Robert, Fritz (1845-1899)—Swiss teacher, Bakuninist, member of the editorial board of *La Solidarité*.—92, 113, 475

Roberts, Henry (d. 1876)—British architect, philanthropist.—338

Robin, Paul Charles Louis Jean (1837-1912)—French teacher, Bakuninist, a leader of the Alliance of Socialist Democracy; member of the International's General Council (1870-71); delegate to the Basle Congress (1869) and the London Conference (1871).—93, 102, 476, 645

Rochat, Charles Michel (b. 1844)—took part in the French working-class movement; member of the Paris Federal Council of the International, participant in the Paris Commune; member of the General Council of the International and Corresponding Secretary for Holland (1871-72), delegate to the London Conference of 1871.—19, 122, 145, 159

Rodriguez, Mariano—member of the International's Granada Federation (1872-73), joined Bakuninists in 1873.—410

Romanovs—dynasty of the Russian tsars and emperors (1613-1917).—567

Roon, Albrecht Theodor Emil, Count von (1803-1879)—Prussian statesman and military figure, from 1873 field marshal-general, War Minister (1859-73) and Naval Minister (1861-71), Minister-President of Prussia (January-November 1873).—404

Rossell, Vicente—Spanish anarchist, weaver, member of the Spanish Federal Council (1872-73).—208

Rothschild, Mayer Amschel (or Meyer Anselm) (1743-1812)—head of the banking firm in Frankfurt am Main.—604

Roy, Henry—English physician and economist.—165

Rozwadowski, Józef (1846-c. 1878)—Polish revolutionary, participant in the 1863-64 uprising in Poland; took part in the Paris Commune, emigrated to England; member of the General Council of the International (1872).—122, 145, 159

Rubau Donadeu, José—Spanish anarchist, lithographer, a founder and leader of the Bakuninist Alliance in Spain.—486

Rühl, J.—German worker, member of the General Council of the International (1870-72).—19, 122, 145, 159

S

Sacase, Jean François (1808-1884)—French legal officer, monarchist, deputy to the National Assembly from 1871.—107, 122, 143, 480

Sadler, Michael Thomas—participant in the British working-class movement, member of the General Council of the International (1871-72).—19, 122, 145, 159

Sáenz, Valentin—took part in the Spanish working-class movement, commercial employee; member of the Spanish Federal Council of the International (1871-72), of the *Emancipacion* editorial board (1871-73), and the New Madrid Federation (1872-73); fought against anarchist influence in Spain.—493

Sagasta, Práxedes Mateo (1827-1903)— Spanish statesman, leader of the Liberal Party, Minister of the Interior (1871-72), Foreign Minister (1874), Prime Minister (1881-83, 1885-90, 1892-95, 1897-99, 1901-02).—225, 289, 491, 497, 596

Saint-Clair, E. P.—participant in the American working-class movement, Irish by birth, member of the General Council elected at the Hague Congress of the International (1872).—240, 253, 266

Saint-Germain, Claude-Louis, comte de (1707-1778)—French general, War Minister (1775-77).—622

Saint-Martin, D., de—French barrister, Bakuninist.—507

Saint-Simon, Claude Henri de Rouvroy, comte de (1760-1825)—French utopian socialist.—89, 394, 472, 630

Salt, Sir Titus (1803-1876)—English manufacturer.—351

Sauva, Arsène—French socialist, tailor; follower of Cabet, an organiser of the Icarian colonies in the USA; took part in the Paris Commune, emigrated to the USA; delegate to the Hague Congress of the International (1872), where he supported the anarchist minority; participant in the socialist movement in America in the 1870s.—244-45, 247, 249, 250, 260, 280

Sax, Emil (1845-1927)—Austrian economist.—338-55, 359-61

Scheu, Heinrich (1845-1926)—Austrian Social-Democrat, member of the International; delegate to the Hague

Congress (1872), emigrated to England in 1873.—245, 247

Schiller, Johann Christoph Friedrich von (1759-1805)—German writer.—167, 522, 603

Schlözer, August Ludwig von (1735-1809)—German historian and statistician.—603

Schneider, Josef—German worker, Lassallean, member of the German Workers' Educational Society in London, at the end of 1871 expelled from it for divisive activities; libelled Marx and his supporters in the German press.—75

Schneider, Joseph Eugène (1805-1875)— French manufacturer, owner of the metallurgical plants in Creusot.—353

Schopenhauer, Arthur (1788-1860)— German idealist philosopher, exponent of voluntarism, irrationalism and pessimism.—610

Schubart, Johann Christian (1734-1787)—German agronomist.—602

Schulze-Delitzsch, Franz Hermann (1808-1883)—German economist and liberal politician, supporter of unification of Germany under Prussia's supremacy, a founder of the National Association and leader of the Party of Progress; tried to divert workers from revolutionary struggle by organising co-operative societies.—357, 384

Schumacher, Georg (1844-1917)— German Social-Democrat, tanner, later businessman; delegate to the Hague Congress of the International (1872) from the Solingen Section; expelled from the Social-Democratic Party in 1898.—245, 247, 250, 253

Schweitzer, Johann Baptist von (1833-1875)—German barrister, a leader of the Lassalleans; editor of the *Social-Demokrat* in 1864-67; President of the General Association of German Workers (1867-71), supported the policy of unification of Germany under Prussia's supremacy, fought against the Social-Democratic Workers' Party; expelled from the General Association for his contacts with the Prussian authorities (1872).—180, 183, 445, 473, 641

Schwitzguébel, Adhémar (1844-1895)— Swiss anarchist, engraver, member of the International; a leader of the Bakuninist Alliance of Socialist Democracy and the Jura Federation; delegate to the Hague Congress (1872).—67, 68, 113, 188, 243-47, 267-68, 275, 280, 286, 287, 474, 478, 580

Schwitzguébel, Léon—Swiss anarchist, member of the Bakuninist Jura Federation.—36, 450, 514

Selchow, Werner von—Prussian statesman, Minister of Agriculture (December 1862-January 1873).—404

Sentiñon, Gaspar (d. 1903)—Spanish anarchist, physician, a founder and leader of the Bakuninist Alliance in Spain; delegate to the Basle Congress of the International (1869).—486, 496

Serno-Solovyovich, Alexander Alexandrovich (1838-1869)—Russian revolutionary democrat, follower of Chernyshevsky, took part in the revolutionary movement in Russia in the early 1860s, then emigrated to Geneva; member of the International, participant in the Swiss working-class movement.—163

Serraillier, Auguste Daniel (b. 1840)— participant in the French and international working-class movement, shoe-maker; member of the General Council of the International (1869-72), Corresponding Secretary for Belgium (1870) and France (1871-72); member of the Paris Commune; delegate to the London Conference (1871) and the Hague Congress of the International (1872), member of the British Federal Council (1873-74); supporter of Marx and Engels.— 19, 27, 42, 122, 127, 145, 159, 213,

240, 243, 247, 249-50, 253, 265, 273, 283, 297, 415, 439, 444, 507-08, 556, 644, 645

Sexton, George—British socialist, physician; member of the General Council of the International (May-August 1872), delegate to the Hague Congress (1872); fought against the reformist wing in the British Federal Council (1872-73).—159, 240, 245, 247, 250

Shakespeare, William (1564-1616)— English poet and dramatist.—470, 588

Shaw, Robert (d. 1869)—participant in the British working-class movement, house-painter; took part in the inaugural meeting of the International held at St. Martin's Hall on September 28, 1864; member of the General Council of the International (1864-69), Council's Treasurer (1867-68); Corresponding Secretary for America (1867-69); took part in the London Conference (1865) and the Brussels Congress (1868).—87

Shimanovsky—Russian army officer, was close to the Nechayev organisation.— 531

Dr. Simpson—member of the German Reichstag.—49

Smith, Adam (1723-1790)—Scottish economist.—191

Sorge, Friedrich Adolf (1828-1906)— prominent figure in the international and American working-class and socialist movement, took part in the 1848 revolution in Germany, emigrated to the USA in 1852; organised the International's American sections, delegate to the Hague Congress (1872), member of the General Council in New York and its General Secretary (1872-74); friend and associate of Marx and Engels.—243-47, 249, 250, 253, 292, 398

Soriano, Trinidad (d. after 1913)— Spanish anarchist.—467, 495, 496

Soria Santa Cruz, Federico de (1815-1891)—Spanish general, suppressed the cantonal uprising in Andalusia in 1873; Military Governor of Cadiz (1874-75).—590

Speyer, Karl (b. 1845)—German carpenter; in the 1860s Secretary of the German Workers' Educational Society in London, in 1870 emigrated to the USA; member of the General Council of the International in New York from October 1872.—253, 266

Spichiger, Auguste (d. 1919)—Swiss anarchist, Chairman of the Bakuninist sections' Congress in Sonvillier (1871).—479

Splingard, Roch Jules Jean Baptiste (1843-1889)—Belgian anarchist, barrister, delegate to the Hague Congress of the International (1872).—245, 247, 249, 250, 457, 458

Spotti, Vincenzo—member of the International in Parma (1872).—184

Spruner von Merz, Karl (1803-1892)—German historian and cartographer.—601

Stahl, Friedrich Julius (1802-1861)—German lawyer, philosopher and reactionary politician, a founder of the Prussian Conservative Party.—403

Stanley, Edward Henry, Earl of Derby (1826-1893)—British statesman, Tory; Conservative in the 1860s-70s, later Liberal; Secretary of State for Colonies (1858, 1882-85) and Secretary for India (1858-59); Foreign Secretary (1866-68, 1874-78).—15

Statuti, Michelangelo—Italian clergyman, after renouncing orders took part in the activities of the Neapolitan Section of the International.—498

Stefanoni, Luigi (1842-1905)—Italian writer and journalist, democrat, rationalist, took part in Garibaldi's campaigns, founder and editor of *Il*

Libero Pensiero, supported Bakuninists.—74, 119, 160-62, 484

Stein, Heinrich Friedrich Karl, Baron von (1757-1831)—Prussian statesman, in 1804-08 held several high-ranking posts, an initiator of moderate reforms.—401

Stepney, Cowell William Frederick (1820-1872)—participant in the British working-class movement, member of the General Council of the International (1866-72) and its Treasurer (1868-70); delegate to the Brussels (1868) and Basle (1869) congresses and the London Conference (1871), member of the British Federal Council (1872).—19, 122, 145, 159

Stieber, Wilhelm (1818-1882)—Prussian police officer, Chief of the Prussian political police (1850-60), an organiser of the Cologne Communist Trial (1852); during the Franco-Prussian war Chief of military police and of the German intelligence on French territory.—67, 161, 225, 463

Strousberg, Bethel Henry (or *Barthel Heinrich*) (real name *Strausberg, Baruch Hirsch*) (1823-1884)—railway entrepreneur; till 1855 lived in London, then in Berlin; went bankrupt in 1875.—364

Strutt, Edward, Baron Belper (1801-1880)—British liberal politician, member of the House of Commons.—351, 352

Svyatsky, Vladimir Ivanovich (born c. 1847)—student of the Agricultural Academy in Moscow, prosecuted as a member of Nechayev's Petersburg circle, acquitted in 1871.—532

Swarm—see *Dentraygues, Émile ·Jean Philippe*

T

Taylor, Alfred—British worker, member of the General Council of the International (1871-72) and the

British Federal Council (1872).—19, 122, 145, 159

Terzaghi, Carlo (b. 1845)—Italian barrister and journalist, Secretary of the Emancipation of the Proletarian society in Turin; became police agent in 1872.—112, 168, 275-76, 483, 499-501

Testut, Oscar—French lawyer, close to police circles; author of a book on the organisation and history of the International, published in 1871-72 with a police-informative purpose.—32

Theisz, Albert Frédéric Félix (1839-1881)—participant in the French working-class movement, engraver, Proudhonist; member of the Paris Commune, emigrated to England; member of the General Council of the International (1871-72) and its Treasurer.—97, 101

Thiers, Louis Adolphe (1797-1877)—French historian and statesman, Orleanist, Prime Minister (1836, 1840); head of the executive power (Chairman of the Council of Ministers) (1871); President of the Republic (1871-73), chief organiser of the suppression of the Paris Commune.—44, 59, 64, 98, 119, 122, 128, 223, 225, 262, 300, 412, 418, 420, 446, 507, 623

Tokarzewicz, Józef (pseudonym J. T. Hodi) (1840-1919)—Polish revolutionary, journalist and writer; in 1863 emigrated to France and later to Switzerland; member of the Polish Section of the International in Zurich; fought against Bakuninist influence on the Polish refugees.—484

Tolain, Henri Louis (1828-1897)—participant in the French working-class movement, engraver, Right Proudhonist, a leader of the Paris Section of the International, delegate to its several congresses; after February 8, 1871 deputy to the National Assembly, during the Paris Commune took sides of the Versaillese; in

1871 was expelled from the International; later a senator.—67, 142

Tomás Oliver (Tomas), Francisco (c. 1850-1903)—Spanish anarchist, bricklayer, member of the Spanish Federal Council of the International (1872-73).—208, 589

Tomilova (née Drittenpreis), Yelizaveta Khristianovna (born c. 1839)—prosecuted in the Nechayev organisation's case, acquitted in 1871; in the 1880s took part in the People's Will circle in Saratov.—527

Townshend, William—British worker, member of the General Council of the International (1869-72), participant in the socialist movement in the 1880s.—19, 122, 145, 159

Trochu, Louis Jules (1815-1896)—French general and politician, Orleanist, head of the Government of National Defence and Commander-in-Chief of the Paris armed forces (September 1870-January 1871), sabotaged city's defence.—45

Tucci, Alberto—member of the Neapolitan Section of the International.—48

U

Us, Vasily Rodionovich (d. 1671)—Don Cossack, associate of Stepan Razin, a leader of the peasants' uprising in Russia (1670-71).—524

Uspensky, Pyotr Gavrilovich (c. 1847-1881)—a member of the Nechayev organisation, in 1871 sentenced to fifteen years of penal servitude and to settlement in Siberia.—528, 530, 532, 536-38

Utin (Outine), Nikolai Isaakovich (1845-1883)—Russian revolutionary, took part in the student movement, member of the Land and Freedom society; refugee from 1863, an organiser of the Russian Section of the International in Geneva, delegate to the London Conference (1871); supported Marx and the General Council in their struggle against Bakunin and his adherents; in the mid-1870s abandoned the revolutionary movement.—77, 100, 225, 485, 517, 526, 540, 562, 645

V

Vaillant, Marie Edouard (1840-1915)— French revolutionary, Blanquist, member of the Paris Commune, member of the General Council of the International (1871-72), delegate to the London Conference (1871), Lausanne (1867) and the Hague (1872) congresses; withdrew from the International in connection with the decision to transfer the General Council to New York; a founder of the Socialist Party of France.— 19, 122, 145, 159, 243-47, 250, 253, 441

Van-Heddeghem, L. (pseudonym *Walter*) (born c. 1847)—police agent who penetrated the Paris sections of the International, delegate to the Hague Congress (1872); exposed in 1873.— 244, 247, 249-50, 438-41, 444, 457

Varlin, Louis Eugène (1839-1871)— prominent figure in the French working-class movement, bookbinder, Left Proudhonist, a leader of the International in France, delegate to the London Conference (1865), Geneva (1866) and Basle (1869) congresses; member of the Paris Commune, shot by the Versaillese at the end of May 1871.— 101

Velarde, José Maria—Spanish general, captain-general of Catalonia in April-September 1873.— 589

Vermersch, Eugène Marie Joseph (1845-1878)— French petty-bourgeois socialist, participant in the republican movement; during the Paris Commune published the newspaper *Père Duchêne*; emigrated to England where he published the newspaper *Qui Vive!* attacking the International and the General Council.— 143

Vésinier, Pierre (1824-1902)—French

journalist, an organiser of the French Section of the International in London, expelled from the Central Council for slander (1866) and in 1868 from the International; member of the Paris Commune, emigrated to England, Secretary of the French Section of 1871 and member of the Universal Federalist Council, opposed Marx and the General Council of the International.— 101, 157

Vichard, Paul Eugène (1835-1883)— participant in the French working-class movement, took part in the Paris Commune, delegate to the Hague Congress of the International (1872).—244, 245, 247, 249, 250, 457

Vickery, Samuel—Secretary of the British Federal Council (1872-73), fought against its reformist wing; Chairman of the British Federation Congress in Manchester (1873).—304, 309, 314, 414

Victor Emmanuel (Vittorio Emanuele) II (1820-1878)—King of Piedmont (Sardinia) (1849-61), King of Italy (1861-78).—45, 64, 83

Viñas, Garcia José (1848-1931)—Spanish medical student, anarchist, an organiser of the Bakuninist Alliance in Spain (1868), took part in the revolutionary events of 1873.—486, 496, 586

Virgil (Publius Vergilius Maro) (70-19 B.C.)—Roman poet.—166

Vogel von Falckenstein, Eduard (1797-1885)—German general, during the Franco-Prussian war Governor-General of the coastal regions of Germany.—221-22

Vögele, August—compositor at the Hollinger printing shop in London (1859).—162

Vogelweide, Walther, von der (1170-1230)—German medieval poet.—610

Vogt, Gustav (1829-1901)—Swiss lawyer, writer and radical politician, pacifist, an organiser of the League of Peace and Freedom; Karl Vogt's brother.—85, 461

Vogt, Karl (1817-1895)—German naturalist, vulgar materialist, petty-bourgeois democrat; in 1849 left Germany; in the 1850s-60s Napoleon III's secret agent, a participant of slanderous campaign against proletarian revolutionaries.—160-62, 440

Voltaire (real name *François Marie Arouet*) (1694-1778)—French philosopher, writer and historian of the Enlightenment.—405, 608

W

Wagner, Adolf (1835-1917)—German vulgar economist, Katheder-Socialist.—365, 620

Wakefield, Edward Gibbon (1796-1862)—British statesman and economist, proposed a theory of colonisation.—166, 193

Waldersee, Friedrich Gustav, Count von (1795-1864)—Prussian general and military writer, War Minister (1854-58).—604

Walter—see *Van-Heddeghem, L.*

Ward, Osborne—participant in the American working-class movement, mechanic, member of the International's section in Brooklyn, was influenced by bourgeois reformists; at the Hague Congress of the International (1872) was elected member of the General Council, but refused.—253, 266

Weerth, Georg (1822-1856)—German proletarian poet and journalist, member of the Communist League; an editor of the *Neue Rheinische Zeitung* (1848-49); friend of Marx and Engels; in the 1850s visited Latin American states as a travelling agent of the British trade firm.—607

Weiler, G. Adam (1841-1894)—German refugee in the USA and from 1862

in England, cabinet-maker, member of the International (from 1865), member of the British Federal Council (1872-73) and its last Secretary; supported Marx and Engels in their struggle against reformists, later member of the Social-Democratic Federation.—313

Wenker, Henri—Swiss anarchist, joiner, member of the Bakuninist Jura Federation.—450, 514

West, William—American Radical, Secretary of Section No. 12 in New York, expelled from the International by the General Council and the Hague Congress (1872).—178, 179, 182, 261, 272, 514, 636-39, 640

Weston, John—participant in the British working-class movement, carpenter, then businessman, Owenite; took part in the inaugural meeting of the International held on September 28, 1864 at St. Martin's Hall, member of the General Council of the International (1864-72), member of the British Federal Council (1872).—19, 122, 145, 157, 159

Wheeler, George William—took part in the British working-class movement, participant in the inaugural meeting of the International held on September 28, 1864 at St. Martin's Hall, member of the General Council of the International (1864-67), Treasurer of the Council (1864-65, 1865-67).—31

Wiehe, Johann Friedrich—compositor at the Hollinger printing shop in London (1859).—162

Wieland, Christoph Martin (1733-1813)—German writer of the Enlightenment.—603

William I, the Conqueror (c. 1027-1087)—Duke of Normandy, King of England (from 1066).—222

William I (1743-1821)—Landgrave of Hesse-Cassel (under the name of

William IX) (1785-1803), Elector of Hesse-Cassel (1803-07, November 1813 to 1821).—604

William I (1797-1888)—King of Prussia (1861-88), Emperor of Germany (1871-88).—128, 417

William IV (1765-1837)—King of Great Britain and Ireland (1830-37).—50

Wilmart, Raimond (pseudonym *Wilmot*)—French revolutionary, took part in the Paris Commune, delegate to the Hague Congress of the International (1872) from Bordeaux sections; in 1873 emigrated to Buenos Aires where he propagated the International's principles.—243-47, 249, 250, 253

Wilmot—see *Wilmart, Raimond*

Wolf—owner of a shoe factory in Mainz.—434

Woodhull, Victoria Claflin (1838-1927)—American feminist, in 1871-72 tried to become a leader of the International's North American Federation; headed Section No. 12 in New York, expelled from the International by the General Council and the Hague Congress (1872).—178-80, 182, 183, 636, 638-42

Wróblewski, Walery (1836-1908)—prominent figure in the Polish and international working-class movement, revolutionary democrat, a leader of the Polish uprising (1863-64); general of the Paris Commune, member of the General Council of the International and Corresponding Secretary for Poland (1871-72), delegate to the Hague Congress (1872), fought against Bakuninists.—19, 122, 145, 159, 213, 240, 244, 247, 249, 250, 265, 273, 284

Wyss, O.—French secretary of the Manchester foreign section of the International, supported Marx and Engels in their struggle against reformists; later emigrated to the USA.—308

Y

Yarrow (*Jarrow*), *F. J.*—prominent figure in the British trade-unionist movement, cabinet-maker; member of the General Council of the International (1866-68 and 1872).—122, 145, 159

Yenisherlov, Georgi Petrovich (born c. 1849)—student at the Petersburg Technological Institute, took part in the student disturbances in 1868-69, prosecuted in the Nechayev organisation's case, released for lack of evidence.—534

Z

Zabel, Friedrich (1802-1875)—German liberal journalist, editor of the Berlin *National-Zeitung* (1848-75).—160

Zaichnevsky, Pyotr Grigoryevich (1842-1896)—Russian revolutionary, organised the student movement in the early 1860s in Moscow and a circle to disseminate illegal literature; author of the *Young Russia* proclamation; sentenced to penal servitude and exile to Siberia where he continued revolutionary propagandist activities.—561

Zévy, Maurice—member of the General Council of the International (1866-72), Corresponding Secretary for Hungary (1870-71).—19, 122, 145, 159

Zhukovsky (*Joukowsky, Joukowski*), *Nikolai Ivanovich* (1833-1895)—Russian anarchist, participant in Petersburg revolutionary circles in the early 1860s; refugee in Switzerland from 1862; a leader of the Bakuninist Alliance.—94, 249, 272, 461

Zürcher, P.—member of the Manchester foreign section of the International (1872), opposed the reformist wing in the British Federal Council.—308

INDEX OF LITERARY AND MYTHOLOGICAL NAMES

Achates—character in Virgil's *Aeneid,* Aeneas' loyal fellow-traveller, whose name is symbolical of true friendship.—476

Anthony—Christian saint, according to legend, hermit in the Nubian desert.—493

Aymon's sons—heroes in the French early medieval legends; Alard, Richard, Guichard and Renaud de Montauban, sons of Count Dordona Aymon, took part in the vassals' struggle against Charles the Great (8th-9th cent.).—509

Christ, Jesus (Bib.).—497

Daniel—Old Testament prophet.—562

Dogberry—a character in Shakespeare's comedy *Much Ado About Nothing,* a pretentious ignoramus.—143

Don Quixote—the title character in Cervantes' novel.—223, 599

Etzel—a character in the German medieval poem *Nibelungenlied,* Huns' King; Attila, the Huns' leader (433-53) was his prototype.—610

Falstaff, Sir John—a character in Shakespeare's *King Henry IV* and *Merry Wives of Windsor,* a sly, fat braggart and jester.—470, 588

Gargantua—the title character in Rabelais' *Gargantua et Pantagruel.*—493

John—one of the Twelve Apostles, according to Christian tradition, author of the *Revelation of John* (Apocalypse), one of the Canonic gospels, and three Epistles actually written by different persons.—452

John Bull—the title character in John Arbuthnot's book *The History of John Bull* (18th cent.). His name is often used to personify England and Englishmen.—611

Karl Moor—the main character in Schiller's drama *Die Räuber.*—522, 548

Kri(e)mhild—a character in the German medieval poem *Nibelungenlied;* sister of Gunter, King of Burgundy; fiancée, then wife of Siegfrid; after his death, wife of Etzel, King of the Huns.—610

Leviathan (Bib.)—a sea monster.—104

Mary Magdalene (Bib.)—according to the evangelical legend, a sinner who repented.—439

Mephistopheles—a character in Goethe's tragedy *Faust.*—386

Monte-Christo de, count—the title character in Alexander Dumas' novel.—548

Peter (Bib.)—one of Christ's Twelve Apostles; according to the evangelical legend, he renounced his Teacher three times.—497

Robert Macaire—typical villain, a character created by the French actor Frédéric Lemaître and immortalised in Honoré Daumier's caricatures.—548

Rodolphe, Prince of Gerol(d)stein—the main character in Eugène Sue's *Les Mystères de Paris.*—548

Rüdiger of Bechelaren—a character in the German medieval poem *Nibelungenlied,* margrave.—610

Siegfri(e)d—hero of the old German epics and a medieval poem *Nibelungenlied.*—610

Uncle Bräsig—a character in the German humorous writer Fritz Reuter's novel *Ut mine Stromtig.*—380

INDEX OF QUOTED
AND MENTIONED LITERATURE

WORKS BY KARL MARX AND FREDERICK ENGELS

Marx, Karl

Address of the British Federal Council to the Sections, Branches, Affiliated Societies and Members. London, December 23, 1872, leaflet (this volume).—406

Capital. Vol. I (present edition, Vol. 35)
— *Das Kapital. Kritik der politischen Oekonomie.* Von Karl Marx. Erster Band. Buch I: Der Produktionsprocess des Kapitals. Hamburg, 1867.—166, 167, 191, 192, 318, 322, 333, 390

The Civil War in France. Address of the General Council of the International Working Men's Association. [London,] 1871 (present edition, Vol. 22).—31, 62, 79, 142
— *Der Bürgerkrieg in Frankreich.* Adresse des Generalraths der Internationalen Arbeiter-Assoziation an alle Mitglieder in Europa und den Vereinigten Staaten, Leipzig, 1871.—175, 370

Concerning the Persecution of the Members of the French Sections (present edition, Vol. 21)
— Declaration of the General Council of the International Working Men's Association. [London, 1870] leaflet; Association Internationale. Conseil Général de Londres. Aux membres de l'Association Internationale des Travailleurs. *La Marseillaise,* No. 138, 7 mai 1870.—106, 219

Confidential Communication to All Sections (present edition, Vol. 21).—37

[Declaration of the General Council of the International Working Men's Association Concerning Cochrane's Speech in the House of Commons,] [1872,] leaflet (this volume). In: *The Eastern Post,* No. 186, April 20, 1872; *The International Herald,* No. 5, April 27, 1872.—645

[Draft Resolution of the General Council on the "French Federal Section in London"] (present edition, Vol. 21)
— Association Internationale des Travailleurs (Conseil Général). Londres, 10 mai 1870. In: *La Marseillaise,* No. 145, 14 mai 1870.—97; [Resolution.] In: *Le Réveil.*—97

[*First Address of the General Council of the International Working Men's Association on the Franco-Prussian War.*] *To the Members of the International Working Men's Association in Europe and the United States.* [London,] July 23, 1870, leaflet (present edition, Vol. 22).—220, 221

The General Council of the International Working Men's Association to the Central Bureau of the International Alliance of Socialist Democracy (present edition, Vol. 21).—87-89, 91, 205, 471

The General Council Resolution on the Federal Committee of Romance Switzerland (present edition, Vol. 21)
—Le Conseil Général au Comité fédéral romand. In: *Le Mirabeau*, No. 53, 24 juillet 1870; *La Solidarité*, No. 16, 23 juillet 1870.—92, 475

The General Council to the Federal Council of Romance Switzerland (present edition, Vol. 21).—90, 473

Herr Vogt (present edition, Vol. 17)
—Herr Vogt. London, 1860.—160, 161

Inaugural Address of the Working Men's International Association, Established September 28, 1864, at a Public Meeting Held at St. Martin's Hall, Long Acre, London (present edition, Vol. 20)
—Address. In: *Address and Provisional Rules of the Working Men's International Association, Established September 28, 1864, at a Public Meeting held at St. Martin's Hall, Long Acre, London*, [London,] 1864.—16, 54-56, 106, 164, 165, 167, 190, 192-94, 407

The International Working Men's Association and the International Alliance of Socialist Democracy (present edition, Vol. 21).—32, 85-87, 91, 205, 471

[Manteuffel's Speech.—Religious Movement in Prussia.—Mazzini's Address.—London Corporation.—Russell's Reform.—Labor Parliament] (present edition, Vol. 12). In: *New-York Daily Tribune*, No. 3948, December 12, 1853.—161

Mazzini and Napoleon (present edition, Vol. 15)
—In: *New-York Daily Tribune*, No. 5321, May 11, 1858.—162

The Poverty of Philosophy. Answer to the "Philosophy of Poverty" by M. Proudhon (present edition, Vol. 6)
—Misère de la philosophie. Réponse à la philosophie de la misère de M. Proudhon. Par Karl Marx. Paris, Bruxelles, 1847.—317, 336, 395

Provisional Rules of the Association (present edition, Vol. 20). In: *Address and Provisional Rules of the International Working Men's Association, Established September 28, 1864, at a Public Meeting held at St. Martin's Hall, Long Acre, London*, [London,] 1864.—13, 105, 106, 114, 141, 454

[Reply to Brentano's Article] (this volume)
—An die Redaktion des *Volksstaat*. In: *Der Volksstaat*, Nr. 44, 1. Juni 1872.—191, 193-94

[*Resolution of the General Council on Félix Pyat's Provocative Behaviour*] (present edition, Vol. 21)
—Communication du Conseil Général de Londres de l'Association Internationale, Londres, 7 juillet. In: *La Liberté*, No. 55, 12 juillet 1868.—97

Resolution of the General Council [*on the Rules of the French Section of 1871*] *adopted at the meeting of October 17, 1871* (this volume)
— Résolution Séance du Conseil Général du 17 Octobre 1871. Aux Citoyens membres de la Section française de 1871.—38-42, 98

Resolutions of the General Council [*on the French Section of 1871*] *adopted at the meeting of November 7, 1871* (this volume)
—Association Internationale des Travailleurs. Résolutions du Conseil Général. Séance du 7 novembre 1871.—98-99

Resolutions of the London Conference relating to the Split in Romance Switzerland (present edition, Vol. 22)
— *Résolutions de la Conférence des délégués de l'Association Internationale des Travailleurs—relatives au différend suisse.* In: *L'Égalité,* No. 20, 21 octobre 1871.—94, 104, 107

Resolutions on the Split in the United States' Federation Passed by the General Council of the I.W.A. in Its Sittings of 5th and 12th March, 1872 (this volume). In: *Woodhull & Claflin's Weekly,* No. 25/103, May 4, 1872.—183, 638, 645; *Der Volksstaat,* Nr. 37, 8. Mai 1872.—183

Revelations Concerning the Communist Trial in Cologne (present edition, Vol. 11)
— Enthüllungen über den Kommunisten-Prozeß zu Köln. Basel, 1853.—161, 440

Second Address of the General Council of the International Working Men's Association on the Franco-Prussian War. To the members of the International Working Men's Association in Europe and the United States. [London, 1870] (present edition, Vol. 22).—92

To the Editor of "The Eastern Post" (this volume). In: *The Eastern Post,* No. 173, January 20, 1872.—72

Engels, Frederick

[*The Address "The Civil War in France" and the English Press*] (present edition, Vol. 22)
—London, 30. Juni 1871. In: *Der Volksstaat,* Nr. 54, 5. Juli 1871.—36

The Condition of the Working-Class in England (present edition, Vol. 4)
— Die Lage der arbeitenden Klasse in England. Nach eigner Anschauung und authentischen Quellen. Leipzig, 1845.—323, 349, 352, 366, 389, 584
— Die Lage der arbeitenden Klasse in England. Zweite Auflage. Stuttgart, 1892.—584

Declaration Sent by the General Council to the Editors of Italian Newspapers Concerning Mazzini's Articles About the International (this volume).—480

The Housing Question (this volume)
—Wie Proudhon die Wohnungsfrage löst. In: *Der Volksstaat,* Nr. 51-53, 26., 29. Juni, 3. Juli 1872.—368-69, 372, 373
—Zur Wohnungsfrage. Separatabdruck aus dem *Volksstaat,* Leipzig, 1872.—375, 390
—Zur Wohnungsfrage. Heft 2: Wie die Bourgeoisie die Wohnungsfrage löst. Sonderabdruck aus dem *Volksstaat,* Leipzig, 1872 [1873].—627

The General Council to the New Madrid Federation (this volume).
— Consejo general. A la nueva federacion madrilena. In: *La Emancipacion,* Núm. 63, 24 de Agosto de 1872.—261, 271

The International in America (this volume)
— Die Internationale in Amerika. In: *Der Volksstaat,* Nr. 57, 17. Juli 1872.—261

Letters from London [III. Meeting in Hyde Park] (this volume)
— Lettere da Londra. In: *La Plebe,* Num. 117, 17 Novembre 1872.—298

The Manchester Foreign Section to All Sections and Members of the British Federation. Leaflet, December 23, 1872 (this volume).—406

The Peasant War in Germany (present edition, Vol. 10)
— Der deutsche Bauernkrieg. In: *Neue Rheinische Zeitung. Politisch-ökonomische Revue.* London-Hamburg-New York, 1850. Heft 5-6, Mai-Oktober 1850.—599
— Der deutsche Bauernkrieg. 2. Auflage. Leipzig, 1870.— 599, 626

[*The Position of the Danish Internationalists in the Agrarian Question*] (this volume). In: *The Eastern Post,* No. 167, December 9, 1871.—389

Preface to the Second Edition of "The Peasant War in Germany" (present edition, Vol. 21)
— Der deutsche Bauernkrieg. 2. Auflage. Leipzig, 1870.—626, 629

Report on the Alliance of Socialist Democracy Presented in the Name of the General Council to the Congress at the Hague. Manuscript (this volume).— 268-69

Resolution of the General Council Expelling Gustave Durand from the International Working Men's Association (this volume)
— Resolution. In: *The Eastern Post,* No. 159; *Der Volksstaat,* Nr. 83, 14. Oktober 1871.—22, 97

To Citizen Delegates of the National Spanish Congress Assembled at Saragossa (this volume)
— A los ciudadanos delegados del Congreso regional español constituido en Zaragoza. In: *La Emancipacion,* Núm. 44, 13 de Abril de 1872.—129-30

To the British Federal Council, International Working Men's Association [Concerning Portuguese Strikes] (this volume).—303

To the General Council of the International Working Men's Association. London, April 15, 1873. Manuscript (this volume).—447

[*To the Saragossa Congress*] (this volume). In: *La Emancipacion,* Núm. 44, 13 de Abril de 1872.—129

To the Spanish Federal Council, July 24, 1872 (this volume)
— Al Consejo federal español. In: *La Emancipacion,* Núm. 62, 17 de Agosto de 1872.—176, 237, 494

Marx, Karl and Engels, Frederick

The Alliance of Socialist Democracy and the International Working Men's Association. Report and Documents Published by Decision of the Hague Congress of the International (this volume)

—L'Alliance de la démocratie socialiste et l'Association Internationale des Travailleurs. Rapport et documents publiés par ordre du Congrès International de la Haye. Londres-Hambourg, 1873.—268, 269, 302, 437, 438, 581
— Ein Complot gegen die Internationale Arbeiter-Association. Im Auftrage des Haager Congresses verfaßter Bericht über das Treiben Bakunin's und der Allianz der socialistischen Demokratie. Deutsche Ausgabe von "L'Alliance de la démocratie socialiste et l'association internationale des travailleurs". Uebersetzt von S. Kokosky. Braunschweig, 1874.—454, 581, 583, 585

Declaration of the General Council of the International Working Men's Association (this volume). In: *The Eastern Post,* No. 178, February 24, 1872; *The International Herald,* No. 1, March 2, 1872.—645

Fictitious Splits in the International. Private Circular from the General Council of the International Working Men's Association (this volume)
—Les prétendues scissions dans l'Internationale. Circulaire privée du Conseil Général de l'Association Internationale des Travailleurs. Genève, 1872.—168, 206, 211, 228, 233, 234, 236, 302, 467, 471, 481-84, 502, 503

General Rules and Administrative Regulations of the International Working Men's Association. London, 1871 (this volume).—3-20, 84, 437, 438
—Allgemeine Statuten und Verwaltungs-Verordnungen der Internationalen Arbeiterassoziation. Amtliche deutsche Ausgabe, revidirt durch den Generalrath. Leipzig, 1872.—11, 14, 19, 20, 84, 437
—Statuts généraux et reglements administratifs de l'Association Internationale des Travailleurs. Édition officiele, revisée par le Conseil général. Londres, 1871.—7, 9, 11, 13, 14, 15, 16, 17, 19, 84, 146-47, 437

Manifesto of the Communist Party (present edition, Vol. 6)
— Manifest der Kommunistischen Partei. Veröffentlicht im Februar 1848. London, 1848.—174-75, 340, 370
—Manifesto of the German Communist Party (published in February 1848). In: *The Red Republican,* Nos. 21-24, November 9, 16, 23, 30; London, 1850.—174
—Манифестъ Коммунистической партіи (Женева, 1869).—174, 543
—Manifesto of the German Communist Party. In: *The World,* November 21, 1871.—174
—Manifesto of the German Communist Party. In: *Woodhull & Claflin's Weekly,* No. 7, December 30, 1871.—174
—Manifeste de Karl Marx. In: *Le Socialiste,* Nos. 16-17, 19-24, 26; 20, 27 janv.; 10, 17, 24 fevr.; 2, 9, 16, 30 mars 1872.—174
—Das Kommunistische Manifest. Neue Ausgabe mit einem Vorwort der Verfassers. Leipzig, 1872.—340, 373

Resolutions of the Conference of Delegates of the International Working Men's Association Assembled at London from 17th to 23rd September 1871. (Circular issued by the General Council of the Association). London, 1871 (present edition, Vol. 22).—16, 32, 38, 53, 55, 56, 59, 65, 84, 103-05, 130, 181, 234, 254, 264, 273-74, 290, 305-06, 311, 407, 478, 490, 502, 512, 579

Resolutions of the General Congress Held at The Hague from the 2nd to the 7th of September 1872 (this volume). In: *The International Herald,* No. 37, December 14, 1872.—272-73, 304-07, 310-12, 407, 415, 510, 511-12, 582

[Statement by the General Council on Jules Favre's Circular.] To the Editor of *The Times* (present edition, Vol. 22). In: *The Times*, No. 27088, June 13, 1871; To the Editor of the *Eastern Post*. In: *The Eastern Post*, No. 142, June 17, 1871; An den Redakteur der *Times*. In: *Der Volksstaat*, Nr. 50, 21. Juni 1871.—32

WORKS BY DIFFERENT AUTHORS

Bakounine, M. *Ai-je besoin...* In: *La Voix de l'Avenir*, No. 21, 24 mai 1868; *Zum Programm der Demokratie.* "Ein Schreiben Bakunins an la Démocratie, ein von Chassin neubegründetes *Pariser Blatt.*" In: *Die Zukunft*, Nr. 230, 19. Juni 1868.—540

— *Aux Compagnons rédacteurs...* In: *Bulletin de la Fédération jurassienne de l'Association internationale des travailleurs*, No. 10/11, 15 juin 1872.—176, 485
— *Discours de Bakounine et de Mroczkowski au deuxième Congrès de la Paix, à Berne.* In: *Kolokol*, No. 14/15, December 1, 1868.—461
— *L'Empire knouto-germanique et la révolution sociale.* Genève, 1871.—525
— *Le Fédéralisme, le Socialisme et l'Antithéologisme.* Proposition motivée au Comité Central de la Ligue de Paix et de la Liberté. Bern, 1867-1868 [unfinished work published in separate instalments].—460
— *Herzen.* In: *La Marseillaise*, No. 72, 2 mars 1870.—540
— *Lettres à un Français sur la crise actuelle.* Septembre 1870. [Neuchâtel, 1870].—525, 592
— [Letter to F. Mora of April 5, 1872.] Manuscript.—413, 491, 578-80
— *Programme de la Société Socialiste-Révolutionnaire polonaise de Zurich.* In: *Bulletin de la Fédération jurassienne de l'Association internationale des travailleurs*, No. 13, 27 juillet 1872. Supplement.—484-85
— *Quelques paroles—A mes jeunes frères en Russie.* Bruxelles [1870].—525
— *République française. Fédération Révolutionnaire des Communes. Lyon, 26 septembre 1870.* Lyon, 1870.—525
— *Risposta d'un Internazionale a Giuseppe Mazzini.* Milano, 1871.—141

[Bakunin] Бакунинъ, М. *Къ офицерамъ русской армiи.* [Женева, 1870].—506, 544, 549-54
— *Народное Дѣло. Романовъ, Пугачевъ или Пестель?* Лондонъ, 1862.—506, 560, 562-67
— *Нѣсколько словъ къ молодымъ братьямъ въ Россiи.* Женева, 1869.—517-19, 528, 535, 544, 549, 550
— *Письмо въ редакцiю по поводу дуэли Беклемишева съ Неклюдовымъ.* In: *Колоколъ.* Приложенiе «Подъ судъ!» л. л. 6, 7; 1 и 15 iюля 1860.—557
— *Постановка революцiоннаго вопроса* [Женева, 1869].—519-21, 549
— *Русскимъ, польскимъ и всѣмъ славянскимъ друзьямъ.* In: *Колоколъ*, л. л. 122, 123, supplement, 15 февраля 1862.—85, 559-60

Bastelica, A. *Mon cher Guillaume.* In: *La Solidarité*, No. 5, 7 mai 1870.—91, 474
— [Letter to P. Lafargue of December 13, 1870.] Manuscript.—505

Bebel, A. [Speech at the Reichstag sitting]
— on October 30, 1871. In: *Der Volksstaat*, Nr. 91, 11. November 1871.—46, 48-49
— on November 8, 1871. In: *Der Volksstaat*, Nr. 92, 15. November 1871.—46, 48

Beesly, E. S. *The International Working Men's Association.* In: *The Fortnightly Review*, Vol. XLVII, November 1, 1870.—165, 192-93

Benary, F. *Erklärung der Zahl 666 <χχσ'>* in der Apocalypse <13, 18> und ihrer Variante 616 <χισ'>. In: *Zeitschrift für spekulative Theologie* ... hrsg. von Bruno Bauer. Berlin, Bd. 1, H. 2, 1836.—452

Bible
  The Old Testament
    Exodus.—324
  The New Testament
    The Revelation of St. John the Divine.—452

Bradlaugh, C. *Rough Notes and Readings*. In: *The National Reformer*, No. 1, January 7, 1872.—71
— *To the Editor of "The Eastern Post"*. In: *The Eastern Post*, No. 168 (second edition), December 17, 1871, reprinted in No. 169, December 23, 1871.—72
— *To the Editor of "The Eastern Post"*. In: *The Eastern Post*, No. 173, January 20, 1872.—72

Bray, J. Fr. *Labour's Wrongs and Labour's Remedy; or, the age of might and the age of right*. Leeds, 1839.—394

[Brentano, L.] *Wie Karl Marx citirt*. In: *Concordia*, Nr. 10, 7. März 1872.—164, 165, 167, 190-94
— *Wie Karl Marx sich vertheidigt*. In: *Concordia*, Nr. 27, 4. Juli 1872.—190-94, 197

Cervantes Saavedra, M. de. *Don Quixote*.—223, 599

Chadwick, Ed. *Report on Dwellings Characterised by Cheapness Combined with the Conditions Necessary for Health and Comfort*. In: *The Illustrated London News*. Vol. 51, No. 1434/1435, July 6, 1867.—339

[Chernyshevsky] Чернышевскій, Н. Г. *Народная безтолковость*. In: *Современникъ*, № 9/10, сентябрь/октябрь 1861.—559
— *Національная безтактность*. In: *Современникъ*, № 7, июль 1861.—559
— *Политика. Похвала миру.—Сраженія при Маджентѣ и Сольферино. Причины слабости австрійской арміи.— Причина, по которой былъ заключенъ миръ*. In: *Современникъ*, июль 1859.—562

Cicero, Marcus Tullius. *Oratio pro Q. Ligario*.—619

Claris, A. *La bonne foi* ... Genève, 13 juin 1872. In: *Bulletin de la Fédération jurassienne de l'Association internationale des travailleurs*. No. 10/11, 15 juin 1872.—485

Cochrane, A. B. [Speech in the House of Commons, April 12, 1872.] In: *The Times*, No. 27350, April 13, 1872.—140-43, 149, 150
— *To the Editor of "The Times"*. In: *The Times*, No. 27208, October 31, 1871, p. 6.—31, 32-33, 140

Dante Alighieri. *La Divina Commedia*.—72, 143, 423
— *De Monarchia*.—600

Dickens, Ch. *Little Dorrit*.—196

Dictionnaire anglais-français et français-anglais. Abrégé de Boyer. Paris, 1854.—407

Dufaure, J. [Speech in the National Assembly on April 26, 1871.] In: *Le Mot d'Ordre*, No. 65, 26 avril 1871.—223

Dumas, A. *Le Comte de Monte-Cristo*.—548

[Eccarius, J. G.] *The International Working Men's Association.* In: *The Times,* No. 27205, October 27, 1871.—31

Faucher, J. *Die Bewegung für Wohnungsreform.* In: *Vierteljahrschrift für Volkswirthschaft und Kulturgeschichte.* Jg. 3, Bd. 4, 1865; Jg. 4, Bd. 3, 1866.—339
— [Speech at the 9th Congress of German Economists.] In: *Bericht über die Verhandlungen des neunten Kongresses deutscher Volkswirthe zu Hamburg am 26., 27., 28. und 29. August 1867.* In: *Vierteljahrschrift für Volkswirtschaft und Kulturgeschichte.* Berlin, Jg. 5, Bd. 3, 1867.—339

Fawcett, H. [Speech in the House of Commons on April 12, 1872.] In: *The Times,* No. 27350, April 13, 1872.—143, 144

La Fontaine, J. de. *La grenouille qui se veut faire aussi grosse que le boeuf.* In: *Fables choisies.* Pt. 1, Paris, 1779.—526

[Flerovsky] Флеровскій, Н. [В. В. Берви] *Положеніе рабочаго класса въ Россіи.* Наблюденія и изслѣдованія. С.-Петербургъ, 1869.—521

Garibaldi, G. *Altra lettera di Garibaldi.* In: *L'Eguglianza,* Num. 13, 8 Ottobre 1871.—29
— *Caro Crescio.* In: *La Favilla,* Num. 134, 5 Giugno 1873.—451, 453, 504
— *Lettere.* In: *La Favilla,* Num. 255, 31 Ottobre 1871.—43-45, 47
— *Garibaldi a Petroni.* In: *Avvenire de Sardegna,* Ottobre 1871.—47
— *Garibaldi e l'Internazionale.* In: *L'Eguglianza,* Num. 9, 10; 10 e 17 Settembre 1871; in: *La Favilla,* Num. 215, 12 Settembre 1871.—29
— *Garibaldi on the International.* In: *The Echo,* No. 873, September 27, 1871.—29

Gladstone, W. [Speech in the House of Commons, April 16, 1863.] In: *The Times,* No. 24535, April 17, 1863.—164-66, 192-96; in: *Hansard's Parliamentary Debates.* Third Series. Vol. CLXX. London, 1863.—164-66, 195-96; in: *The Morning Advertiser,* No. 22418, April 17, 1863.—196, 197; in: *The Morning Star,* April 17, 1863.—196
— *Two Letters to the Earl of Aberdeen on the State Persecutions of the Neapolitan Government.* London, 1851.—294

Goethe, J. W. *Dichtung und Wahrheit. Aus meinem Leben.*—620
— *Faust.*—386
— *Zueignung.*—582

Guesde, J. *Les arrestations continuent...* Rome, 5 avril. In: *La Liberté,* No. 15, 13 avril 1873.—442
— *Le Congrès de Mirandola...* Rome, 22 mars. In: *La Liberté,* No. 13, 30 mars 1873.—444
— *Rien ou presque rien...* Rome, 14 octobre. In: *La Liberté,* No. 42, 20 octobre 1872.—443, 507

Gülich, G. von. *Geschichtliche Darstellung des Handels, der Gewerbe und des Ackerbaus der bedeutendsten handeltreibenden Staaten unsrer Zeit.* Zweiter Band. Jena, 1830.—604

Hansemann, D. [Speech at the 34th sitting of the First United Diet, June 8, 1847.] In: *Preußens Erster Reichstag.* Th. 7. Berlin, 1847.—342

Hegel, G. W. F. *Wissenschaft der Logik.* Hrsg. von Leopold von Henning. In 2 Th. Th. 1. Abth. 2. Berlin, 1834. (*Werke,* Bd. 4).—370

[Hepner, Ad.] *Vom Haager Kongress der Internationale. III.* In: *Der Volksstaat*, Nr. 84, 19. Oktober 1872.—286, 287

[Herzen] Герцен, А. И. *10 апрѣля 1861 и убійства въ Варшавѣ.* In: *Колоколъ* (The Bell), № 96, 15 апреля 1861.—562
— *Журналисты и террористы.* In: *Колоколъ* (The Bell), № 141, 15 августа 1862.—562
— *Лишніе люди и желчевики.* In: *Колоколъ* (The Bell), № 83, 15 октября 1860.—562
— *На Канунѣ.* In: *Колоколъ* (The Bell), № 93, 1 марта 1861.—559
— *Робертъ Оуенъ* included in *Былое и Думы* [My Past and Thoughts].—561
— *Сборникъ посмертныхъ статей Александра Ивановича Герцена* (съ портретомъ автора). Изданіе дѣтей покойнаго. Женева, 1870.—162
— *Very dangerous!!!* In: *Колоколъ* (The Bell), № 44, 1 июня 1859.—562
— *Vivat Polonia.* In: *Колоколъ* (The Bell), № 94, 15 марта 1861.—559

Höpfner, E. von. *Der Krieg von 1806 und 1807. Ein Beitrag zur Geschichte der Preußischen Armee nach den Quellen des Kriegsarchivs bearb.* In 4 Bden. Bd. 1. Berlin, 1850.—604

Катехизис революционера (by M. Bakunin or S. Nechayev), 1869.—527, 543-49, 552

[Katkov] [Катков, М. Н.] *Самое тяжелое впечатлѣніе....* In: *Московскія Вѣдомости*, № 4, 6 января 1870.—557

Die Krähwinkler Landwehr (folk-song).—627

Kutschkelied (soldiers' song).—339

Lafargue, P. *A los Internacionales de la region Española.* Madrid, 1872.—487
— (anon.) *Articulos de primera necesidad.* II. *La Habitacion.* In: *La Emancipacion*, Núm. 40, de 16 Marzo de 1872.—329-30
— *La burguesia y la Internacional en los Estados-Unidos.* In: *La Emancipacion*, Núm. 54, de 22 Junio de 1872.—177, 183

Langethal, Chr. Ed. *Geschichte der teutschen Landwirthschaft.* Th. 2. Buch 4. Jena, 1856.—609

Lassalle, F. *Das System der erworbenen Rechte. Eine Versöhnung des positiven Rechts und der Rechtsphilosophie.* In 2 Th. Th. 1. Leipzig, 1861.—379, 380

Lefrançais, G. *Étude sur le mouvement communaliste à Paris, en 1871.* Neuchâtel, 1871.—127

[Léo, A.] *Comment les socialistes honnêtes, intelligents et dévoués, sont expulsés de l'Internationale de Genève.* In: *La Révolution Sociale*, No. 2, 2 novembre 1871.—488
— *L'esprit de l'Association internationale.* In: *La Révolution Sociale*, No. 3, 9 novembre 1871.—488

Léo, A. *La guerre sociale.* Discours prononcé au Congrès de la Paix à Lausanne (1871). Neuchâtel, 1871.—95, 477

Liebig, Justus von. *Die Chemie in ihrer Anwendung auf Agricultur und Physiologie.* In zwei Theilen. 7. Aufl. Th. 1. Braunschweig, 1862.—384

Loyola, I. de. *Constitutio Societatis Jesu.*—470

Malon, B. *Je n'accorde pas ... Neuchâtel, 12 juin 1872.* In: *Bulletin de la Fédération jurassienne de l'Association internationale des travailleurs.* No. 10/11, 15 juin 1872.—485
— *La troisième défaite du prolétariat français...* Neuchâtel, 1871.—94

Manteuffel, O. Th. von. [Speech at the sitting of the Prussian Second Chamber, December 3, 1850.] In: *Stenographische Berichte über die Verhandlungen der durch die Allerhöchste Verordnung vom 2. November 1850 einberufenen Kammern.* Zweite Kammer. Bd. 1. Berlin, 1851.—617

Marseillaise (words and music by Claude Joseph Rouget de Lisle).—284, 295

Mazzini, G. *Agli operai italiani.* In: *La Roma del Popolo,* Num. 20, 13 Luglio 1871.—28
— *Documenti sull'Internazionale.* In: *La Roma del Popolo,* Num. 38, 39, 41; 16, 23 Novembre, 7 Dicembre 1871.—60, 61
— *Il Comune di Francia.* In: *La Roma del Popolo,* Num. 9, 26 Aprile 1871.—44, 46
— *La Guerra.* In: *Pensiero e Azione,* Num. 17, 12-16 Maggio, 1859.—162
— *L'Internazionale. Cenno storico.* In: *La Roma del Popolo,* Num. 30, 31; 21 e 28 Settembre 1871.—43
— *L'Internazionale Svizzera.* In: *La Roma del Popolo,* Num. 29, 14 Settembre 1871.—43
— *Il moto delle classi artigiane e il congresso.* In: *La Roma del Popolo,* Num. 28, 7 Settembre 1871.—43

Mill, J. St. *Principles of Political Economy with Some of Their Applications to Social Philosophy.* Vols. 1, 2. London, 1848.—144

Moltke, [H. von.] [Speech in the German Imperial Diet, February 16, 1874.] In: *Stenographische Berichte über die Verhandlungen des Deutschen Reichstages.* 2. Legislatur-Periode. 1. Session 1874. Bd. 1. Berlin, 1874.—619

Montels, [Jules.] *Comme je n'ai...* In: *Bulletin de la Fédération jurassienne de l'Association internationale des travailleurs.* No. 10/11, 15 juin 1872.—485
— *Compagnons rédacteurs...* In: *Bulletin de la Fédération jurassienne de l'Association internationale des travailleurs.* No. 20/21, 10 novembre 1872.—508

[Mülberger, A.] *Die Wohnungsfrage.* In: *Der Volksstaat,* Nr. 10-13, 15, 19; 3., 7., 10., 14., 21. Februar, 6. März 1872.—317, 319-23, 327, 330, 331, 334, 335, 373, 388

Mülberger, A. *Die Wohnungsfrage. Eine sociale Skizze.* Separat-Abdruck aus dem *Volksstaat.* Leipzig, 1872.—371, 373, 375, 378-79, 383, 385-88, 390, 391
— *Zur Wohnungsfrage.* (Antwort an Friedrich Engels.) In: *Der Volksstaat,* Nr. 86, 26. Oktober 1872.—368, 373, 374, 376-79, 381-85

Начала Революціи. [Женева, 1869.] [Presumably written by Bakunin or Nechayev,] leaflet.—519, 521, 549

[Nechayev] Нечаевъ, С. Г. Письмо къ Огареву и Бакунину. In: *Община,* № 1, 1 сентября 1870.—541
— *Студентамъ университета, академіи и тех[нологическаго] института въ Петербургѣ.* Второй оттискъ. [Женева, 1869].—517, 535

[Нечаев, С. Г., Огарев, Н. П.] *Благородное россійское дворянство!* [Женева, 1870].—535

Das Nibelungenlied.—610

[Ogarev] Огаревъ, Н. П. *Студентъ. Молодому другу Нечаеву* [Женева, 1869].—
529, 535

Petrus. *Ai lettori!* In: *La Plebe*, Num. 119, 4 Dicembre 1872.—409

Pio, L. [Om vore Landboforhold.] In: *Socialisten*, Nr. 17, 4 november 1871.—57

Pius IX [Allocution to the deputation of Swiss Catholics].—225

Proudhon, P.-J. *De la capacité politique des classes ouvrières*. Nouvelle édition. Paris,
1868.—395-97
— *De la justice dans la révolution et dans l'église*. Nouveaux principes de philosophie
pratique adressés à Son Éminence Monseigneur Mathieu, Cardinal-Archevêque
de Besançon. T. 1-3. T. 1. Paris, 1858.—378, 379
— *La guerre et la paix*. Recherches sur le principe et la constitution du droit des
gens. Nouvelle édition. T. I, II. T. II. Paris, 1869.—379, 380
— *Idée générale de la révolution au XIXe siècle*. Choix d'études sur la pratique
révolutionnaire et industrielle. Nouvelle édition. Paris, 1868.— *Œuvres com-
plètes*. T. 10.—329, 343, 369-70, 377, 387, 388
— *Système des contradictions économiques, ou Philosophie de la misère*. T. 1-2. Paris,
1846.—335, 336, 378, 395

Renan, Ernest. *L'Antéchrist*. Paris, 1873.—452

Reschauer, H. *Die Wohnungsnoth und ihr schädlicher Einfluß auf die Kleingewerbetreibenden und Lohnarbeiter*. Wien, 1871.—383

Reuter, F. *Ut mine Stromtid*.—380

Ricardo, D. *On the Principles of Political Economy, and Taxation*. London, 1817.—396

Richard, A., Blanc, G., Bastelica, A. *Au Pilori!* In: *L'Égalité*, No. 3/4, 15 février
1872.—120-21

[Richard, A., Blanc, G.] *La Commission fédérale...* In: *La Solidarité*, No. 3, 23 avril
1870, No. 5, 7 mai 1870.—91, 474
— *L'Empire et la France nouvelle. Appel du peuple et de la jeunesse à la conscience
française*. Bruxelles, 1872.—119-20, 505

[Roy, H.] *The Theory of the Exchanges. The Bank Charter Act of 1844*. The abuse of
the metallic principle to depreciation. Parliament mirrored in debate, supplemen-
tal to `"The Stock Exchange and the Repeal of Sir J. Barnard's Act". London,
1864.—165, 190-92

Sax, Em. *Die Wohnungszustände der arbeitenden Classen und ihre Reform*. Wien,
1869.—338-56, 359-62

Scherr, J. *Blücher. Seine Zeit und sein Leben*. In 3 Bden. Bd. 3. *Blücher, 1813-1819*.
Leipzig, 1863.—622

Schiller, Fr. *Die Räuber*.—522
— *Die Worte des Glaubens*.—167

Schlözer, A. L. [von.] *Briefwechsel meist historischen und politischen Inhalts*. Bd. 1-10.
Göttingen, 1776-1782.—603
— *Stats-Anzeigen*. Bd. 1-18. Göttingen, 1782-1793.—603

Schwitzguébel, A. *An die Redaktion des Volksstaat in Leipzig.* In: *Der Volksstaat,* Nr. 81, 7. Oktober 1871.—35

[Serno-Solovyovich] Серно-Соловьевичъ, А. *Наши домашнія дѣла. Отвѣтъ г. Герцену на статью «Порядокъ торжествуетъ»* (Ш. *Колоколъ,* № 233). Vevey, 1867.—163

Shakespeare, W. *King Henry IV.* Part 1.—470
— *Much Ado about Nothing.*—143

Smith, A. *An Inquiry into the Nature and Causes of the Wealth of Nations.* Vol. 2. London, 1776.—191

Spruner, [K. von] und Menke, [H.Th.] *Hand-Atlas für die Geschichte des Mittelalters und der neueren Zeit.* 3. Aufl. ..., neu bearb. v. Th. Menke. Gotha, [1871-]1880.— 601

Stefanoni, L. *L'Internationale e il Consiglio Supremo di Londra.* In: *Il Libero Pensiero,* Num. 4, Gennaio 1872.—74, 75
— *Marx-Vogt-Herzen.* In: *Il Libero Pensiero,* 18 Aprile 1872.—161, 162-63
— [article] In: *Il Libero Pensiero,* 28 Marzo 1872.—160

Sue, E. *Les mystères de Paris.*—548

[Terzaghi, C.] ["Correspondence from Turin"signed: Ateo.] In: *La Favilla,* Num. 184, 3 Settembre 1872.—275-76

Testut, O. *L'Internationale. Son origine. Son but. Son caractère. Ses principes. Ses tendances. Son organisation. Ses moyens d'action. Ses ressources. Son rôle dans les grèves. Ses statuts. Ses congrès. Son développement. Tableau de la situation actuelle de l'Internationale en France, en Europe et en Amérique.* 3. éd. revue et augm. Paris, Versailles, 1871.—32

Teulière, Er. *Citoyens rédacteurs...* Lausanne, 10 juin 1872. In: *Bulletin de la Fédération jurassienne de l'Association internationale des travailleurs.* No. 10/11, 15 juin 1872.—485

Transactions of the National Association for the Promotion of Social Science. Ed. by George W. Hastings. London, 1859-1865.—338

Ueber die Verbesserung der Wohnungen der arbeitenden Klassen in England von Ducpetiaux zu Brüssel, nach den durch Herrn Roberts mitgetheilten Nachrichten. In: *Zeitschrift des Central-Vereins in Preussen für das Wohl der arbeitenden Klassen.* Leipzig, 1858. [Bd. 1.] H. 2.—338

Universal Federalist Council of the International Working Men's Association and of the Republican Socialist Societies Adhering. London, 1872.
— Conseil fédéraliste universel de l'Association Internationale des Travailleurs et des Sociétés républicaines socialistes adhérentes. Londres, 1872. [Also published in German.] [Signed: R. D. Butler, Hayes, P. Vésinier].—157, 159

[Vaillant, Ed.] *Internationale et révolution.* À propos du congrès de La Haye par des réfugiés de la Commune, Ex-membres du Conseil Général de l'Internationale. Londres, 1872.—370, 441

Virgil. *Aeneid.*—166

Vogt, C. *Mein Prozess gegen die Allgemeine Zeitung.* Stenographischer Bericht, Dokumente und Erläuterungen. Genf, im December 1859.—160, 440
— *Studien zur gegenwärtigen Lage Europas.* Genf und Bern, 1859.—161

Wagner, A. *Elsass und Lothringen und ihre Wiedergewinnung für Deutschland.* Leipzig, 1870.—620

— *Rede über die Sociale Frage.* Gehalten auf der freien kirchlichen Versammlung evangelischer Männer in der K. Garnisonkirche zu Berlin am 12. October 1871. Separatabdruck aus den "Verhandlungen der kirchlichen October-Versammlung in Berlin". Berlin, 1872.—365

[Wakefield, E. G.] *England and America.* A comparison of the social and political state of both nations. Vols. I-II. London, 1833.—166, 193

Walesrode, L. *Eine Arbeiter-Heimstätte in Schwaben.* In: *Über Land und Meer, Allgemeine illustrirte Zeitung.* 1868. Jg. 10, Bd. 2, Nr. 35, 36, 44 u. 45.—339

Walther von der Vogelweide. *Die Gedichte* ... 4 Ausg. Berlin, 1864.—610

[Woodhull, V. C. et al.] *The Party of the People to Secure and Maintain Human Rights, to Be Inaugurated in the U.S., in May, 1872.* [Signed] Victoria C. Woodhull, Horace H. Day... Theodore H. Banks... R. W. Hume... In: *Woodhull & Claflin's Weekly,* Nos. 21-25 (99-103), April 6, 13, 20, 27, May 4, 1872.—182, 640-41

[Zaichnevsky] [Зайчневский, П. Г.] *Молодая Россия* [Рязан, 1862].—561, 565

DOCUMENTS OF THE INTERNATIONAL WORKING MEN'S ASSOCIATION

Address to the Workingmen of America [proposed by Section 1, at the meeting of the Central Committee of the United States, October 15, 1871].—637

[*Announcement by Turin workers.*] "Dalle officine 18 novembre Amici cari del Proletario...". [Signed:] "Parigi Antonio—Ferrero—Durando Agostino..." In: *Il Proletario Italiano,* Num. 39, 23 Novembre 1871.—54

A los representates del Partido Republicano Federal reunidos en Madrid. [Signed:] El Consejo de redaccion. Madrid. 25 de Febrero de 1872. In: *La Emancipacion,* Núm. 38, 3 de Marzo de 1872.—490

Aux travailleurs de toutes les nations. In: *Le Réveil,* No. 409, 12 juillet 1870.—220

Bert, C. *Associazione Internazionale dei Lavoratori Società l'Emancipazione del Proletario Regione Piemontese.* Torino, 5 Aprile 1872. Manuscript.—500

[*Circular of Committee No. 1,* December 4, 1871.] In: *New-Yorker Democrat,* December 9, 1871.—180, 638

Comitato per l'Emancipazione delle Classi Lavoratrici. Statuto. Parma [1872].—184

Compte-rendu du Congrès de Genève. In: *Le Courrier international,* Nos. 8-17; 9, 16, 23, 30 mars et 6, 13, 20, 27 avril 1867.—16

Compte-rendu du IVe Congrès international, tenu à Bâle, en septembre 1869. Bruxelles, 1869.—16, 18, 24, 40, 93, 95, 96, 104, 112-13, 125, 233, 267, 486

Congrès ouvrier de l'Association Internationale des Travailleurs, tenu à Genève du 3 au 8 septembre 1866. Genève, 1866.—15, 16, 17, 101, 110-12

Congrès Ouvrier Belge. Des 19 et 20 mai. In: *L'Internationale,* No. 176, 26 mai 1872.—483

— *Projet de Statuts Generaux.*—451, 483

Congrès Ouvrier Belge du 14 juillet. In: *L'Internationale*, No. 184, 21 juillet 1872.—483

Il Consiglio Generale.... [Signed:] (February 23, 1873.) F. A. Sorge, Segretario Generale. In: *La Plebe*, Num. 13, 26 Maggio 1873.—447

Il Consiglio Generale alle federazioni, alle società affigliate, alle sezioni ad a tutti i membri dell'Associazione Internazionale dei lavoratori. [Signed:] Il Consiglio Generale [October 20, 1872.] F. J. Bertrand, F. Bolte, F. A. Sorge. In: *La Plebe*, Num. 118, 27 Novembre 1872.—409

Consejo Federal Español al Consejo General. Valencia 1 de agosto de 1872. Ai Consejo General residente en Lóndres. [Signed:] Francisco Tomàs. Valencia, 3 de Agosto de 1872. In: *La Federacion*, Núm. 157, 18 de Agosto de 1872.—237, 494

Consejo Federal de la Region Española. Valencia 2 de febrero de 1873. [Signed:] José Arcos, Pedro Marqués [et al.]. In: *La Emancipacion*, Núm. 85, 8 de Febrero de 1873.—511

[Cuno, Th.] *La Section 29 à la rédaction du "Socialiste". Paterson, 10 janvier 1873.* [Signed:] Frederico Capestro. In: *Le Socialiste*, New York, No. 17, 2 février 1873.—415

Déclaration de la minorité. [Signed:] Alerini, Farga Pelicer, Morago [et al.]. In: *La Liberté*, No. 37, 15 septembre 1872.—269, 508

De Paepe, C. *Rapport de la section Bruxelloise sur la question de la propriété foncière.* [11 septembre 1868.] In: *Troisième Congrès de l'Association Internationale des Travailleurs. Compte-rendu officiel.* Supplément au journal *Le Peuple Belge.* 15 septembre. Bruxelles, 1868.—135

Estatutos de la Federacion Regional Española de la Asociacion Internacional de los Trabajadores. De las federaciones locales. In: *Asociacion Internacional de los Trabajadores. Organizacion social de las secciones obreras de la Federacion Regional Española adoptada por el Congreso Obrero de Barcelona en Junio de 1870, y reformada por la Conferencia Regional de Valencia celebrada en Setiembre de 1871.* Barcelona, 1871.—492, 511

Estracto de las actas del segundo Congreso Obrero de la Federacion regional Española, celebrado en Zaragoza en los dias 4 al 11 de abril de 1872, segun las actas y las notas tomadas por la comision nombrada al efecto en a el mismo. Valencia, 1872.—236

Federación Regional Española, Circular. [Signed:] Vicente Rosell, Vicente Torres et al. In: *La Federacion*, Núm. 155, 4 de Agosto de 1872.—494

— *Federación Regional Española, Circular reservada. Valencia, 7 de Julio de 1872.*—208, 212, 236-37, 494, 496

Der Generalrath der Internationalen Arbeiter-Assoziation an alle Föderationen, Sektionen. Comites und Mitglieder der Internationalen Arbeiter-Assoziation in Deutschland. New-York, den 1. Dez. 1872. [Signed:] F. A. Sorge. In: *Der Volksstaat*, Nr. 103, 25. Dezember 1872.—398

Hales, J. *International Working Men's Association.* In: *The Eastern Post*, No. 168, December 16, 1871.—62

Hill, E. *International Working Men's Association. Federal Council.* In: *The International Herald*, No. 27, October 5, 1872.—285

Holtmann, F. *An die Böttcher-Gesellen Deutschlands!* In: *Der Volksstaat*, Nr. 24, 22. März 1873.—428

Liste nominale des délégués composant le 5-me Congrès universel, tenu à la Haye, (Hollande), du 2 au 7 septembre 1872. Amsterdam, 1872.—283, 406

Mandat impératif donné aux délégués jurassiens pour le Congrès de la Haye. In: *Bulletin de la Fédération jurassienne de l'Association internationale des travailleurs*, Nos. 15 et 16, 15 août-1 septembre 1872.—268, 279-80

Mandato Imperativo que la Federacion regional española da á los compañeros Nicolás Alonso Marselau, Tomás González Morago, Rafar Farga Pellicer y Carlos Alerini... delegados de la Misma al Congreso internacional. Valencia 22 de Agosto de 1872. In: *Asociacion Internacional de los Trabajadores. Federacion Regional Española.* Circular. Valencia, 22 de Agosto de 1872.—277, 278, 281, 282, 495, 510

Manifeste antiplébiscitaire des sections parisiennes fédérées de l'Internationale et de la chambre fédérale des sociétés ouvrières. A tous les travailleurs français. In: *La Marseillaise*, No. 125, 24 avril 1870, leaflet.—219

Manifest des Ausschusses der sozial-demokratischen Arbeiterpartei. "An alle deutschen Arbeiter!..." [Signed:] Braunschweig-Wolfenbüttel, 5. September 1870. Der Ausschuss. Braunschweig, 1870.—221, 222

Memoria. A todos los Internacionales Españoles. In: *Asociacion Internacional de los Trabajadores. Federacion Regional Española. Consejo Federal, Circular a todas las federaciones locales.* Valencia, 1872.—510

Mesa, J. *Declaracion. A los delegados del Congreso internacional del Haya.* Madrid, 1 de Septiembre de 1872. Manuscript.—488

Mitchell, J., Vickery, S. *International Working Men's Association. British Federal Council.* In: *The International Herald*, No. 45, February 8, 1873.—414

Nobre França, J. C. [Carta de los delegados de las secciónes obreras de Lisboa a la Nueva federacion madrilenã.] In: *La Emancipacion*, Núm. 84, 1 de Febrero de 1873.—413

La Nueva Federacion Madrileña
— *A todas las federaciones, secciones é individuos de la Asociacion Internacional en España.* [Signed:] Victor Pagés. Madrid. 1° de Noviembre de 1872. In: *La Emancipacion*, Núm. 73, 9 de Noviembre de 1872.—299, 410, 511
— *A todas las federaciones y secciones de la Asociacion Internacional en España.* [Signed:] Victor Pagés. In: *La Emancipacion*, Núm. 76, 30 de Noviembre de 1872.—409
— *A los delegados al sexto congreso general. Madrid, 24 de Agosto de 1873.* [Signed:] José Mesa, Paulino Iglesias. Manuscript.—581-83, 595-96
— *Circular. 2 de Junio de 1872.* In: *La Emancipacion*, Núm. 59, 27 de Julio de 1872.—229-230, 491-92
— *Circular. Madrid. 22 de Julio de 1872.* In: *La Emancipacion*, Núm. 59, 27 de Julio de 1872.—492
— *Companeros...*, Madrid, 21 de Julio de 1872. [Signed:] Victor Pagés. In: *La Emancipacion*, Núm. 59, 27 de Julio de 1872.—495

Nueva Federacion Madrileña. [Signed:] Victor Pagés. In: *La Emancipacion*, Núm. 61, 10 de Agosto de 1872.—229

Nueva Federacion Madrileña. In: *La Emancipacion*, Núm. 78, 14 de Diciembre de 1872.—511

Outine, N. *Au Vme Congrès de l'Association Internationale des Travailleurs à La Haye.* Confidentiel. [Berne, 1872.] Manuscript.—485-86, 562

Procès-verbaux du Congrès de l'Association Internationale des Travailleurs réuni à Lausanne du 2 au 8 septembre 1867. Chaux-de-Fonds, 1867.—16-18, 55, 105, 111, 311

Procès-verbaux du Congrès Romand tenu à La Chaux-de-Fonds au Cercle des ouvriers du 4 au 7 avril 1870. In: *L'Égalité*, Nos. 17, 18; 23 et 30 avril 1870.—473, 540

Protokoll des ersten allgemeinen schweizerischen Arbeiter-Kongresses zu Olten am 1., 2. und 3. Juni 1873. Zürich, 1873.—450

Rapport de la commission d'enquête sur la Société l'Alliance secrète. [Th. F. Cuno, Lucain, R. Splingard, P. Vichard.] Manuscript. In: *La Liberté*, Nos. 37 and 42, 15 septembre and 20 octobre 1872.—457

Regis, V. [Report to the General Council. March 1, 1872.] Manuscript.—500

Réponse du Comité fédéral romand à la Circulaire des 16 signataires, membres du Congrès de Sonvilliers. In: *L'Égalité*, No. 24, 24 décembre 1871.—104, 489

Report of the British Federal Congress, held at Manchester, June 1 and 2, 1873. In: *General and British Federative Rules of the International Working Men's Association, together with a Report of the Second Annual Congress of the British Federation, held at Manchester, June 1st and 2nd, 1873.* Published by the British Federal Council. [London, 1873].—449

Report of the Fourth Annual Congress of the International Working Men's Association, Held at Basle, in Switzerland. From the 6th to the 11th September 1869. Published by the General Council. London [1869].—16, 66

Resolution of the General Council of the International Working Men's Association in reply to an application of Section 12 of New York. [November 5, 1871. Signed: J. G. Eccarius.] In: *Woodhull & Claflin's Weekly*, No. 81, December 2, 1871 (this volume).—638

Resolution of the General Council of 28 May 1872. In: *New York Union*, No. 17, 1872.—642-43

Résolutions administratives votées par le Congrès de Bâle. In: *Association Internationale des Travailleurs. Compte-rendu du IVe Congrès international, tenu à Bâle, en septembre 1869.* Bruxelles, 1869.—307, 312

Resolutions adopted at the First Congress. In: *The International Herald*, No. 33, November 16, 1872.—311

Resolutions of the Congress of Geneva, 1866, and the Congress of Brussels, 1868. London [1869].—16, 19, 86-87, 110

Resolutions of the Manchester Congress. In: *General and British Federative Rules of the International Working Men's Association, together with a report of the Second Annual Congress of the British Federation, held at Manchester, June 1st and 2nd, 1873.* Published by the British Federal Council [London, 1873].—441, 449, 513

Rules of the British Federation of the International Working Men's Association. In: *General and British Federative Rules of the International Working Men's Association, together with a report of the Second Annual Congress of the British Federation, held at Manchester, June 1st and 2nd, 1873*. Published by the British Federal Council. [London, 1873].—313

Rules of the International Working Men's Association. Founded September 28th, 1864. London, [1867] (present edition, Vol. 20).—13, 15-19

La Section 2. Resolution. In: *La Socialiste*, 18 mai 1872.—641

Serraillier, A. *A la rédaction de "L'Emancipation" de Toulouse.* London, 13 décembre 1871. In: *L'Emancipation*, No. 1243, 19 décembre 1871.—508

— *Au citoyen Vermersch, rédacteur du Qui Vive!* In: *Qui Vive!* No. 39, 16 novembre 1871.—100

— [Letter to A. Calas of December 18, 1872.] Manuscript.—443, 507

— *Monsieur le Rédacteur.* In: *Courrier d'Europe*, 18 mars 1871.—127

— [Speech at the Hague Congress on September 6, 1872.] In: Le Moussu, *Procès-Verbaux.* Manuscript.—506

Statuto e Regolamento della Società Internazionale degli Operai seguiti dal Regolamento interno della Sezione Girgentina. Girgenti, 1871.—28

Statuts et reglements. 1866. London [1866].—28

Statuts pour la Fédération des Sections Romandes adoptés par le Congrès Romand, tenu à Genève au Cercle international des Quatre-Saisons, les 2, 3 et 4 janvier 1869. Genève [1869].—475

To all Members of the International Workingmen's Association. Resolution of the General Council. [Signed:] New York, Jan. 26th, 1873. F. A. Sorge, General Secretary (this volume). In: *The International Herald*, No. 52, March 29, 1873.—447, 512

— *A tutti i membri dell'Associazione.* In: *La Plebe*, Num. 14, 1 Giugno 1873.—447

To all members of the International Working Men's Association. Resolution of the General Council. [Signed:] New York, May 30, 1873, F. A. Sorge, General Secretary (this volume).

— *Der Generalrath der Internationalen Arbeiterassociation an alle Mitglieder derselben.* New York, 30. Mai 1873. In: *Der Volksstaat*, Nr. 51, 25. Juni 1873; *Arbeiter-Zeitung*, Nr. 18, 7. Juni 1873.—512

To the federations, affiliated societies, sections and all members of the International Working Men's Association. [Signed:] The General Council: F. J. Bertrand, F. Bolte [etc.], F. A. Sorge. In: *The International Herald*, No. 34, November 23, 1872.—409

— *Il Consiglio Generale.* In: *La Plebe*, Num. 118, 27 Novembre 1872.—409

Troisième procès de l'Association Internationale des Travailleurs à Paris. Paris, juillet 1870.—101, 158

Troisième Congrès de l'Association Internationale des Travailleurs. Compte-rendu officiel. In: Supplément au journal *Le Peuple Belge*. Bruxelles, septembre 1868.—16, 19, 87, 112, 135, 141

Wylding, Jno. *South Lambeth Section.* In: *The International Herald*, No. 30, October 26, 1872.—309

* * *

* *Address of the British Federal Council to the Branches, Sections, Affiliated Societies, and Members of the Federation. British Federation of the International Working Men's Association.* [Signed:] H. Jung, H. Mayo, F. Pape, R. Foster, J. Grout, J. Hales (London [1873]).—406-07

Alianza de la Democracia Socialista [Rules.] In: *La Federacion*, Núm. 155, 4 de Agosto de 1872.—230

Appeal of Section No. 12. [Signed:] New York, Aug. 30, 1871. William West. In: *Woodhull & Claflin's Weekly*, No. 19 (71), September 23, 1871.—125, 178-79, 636-37

Associazione Internazionale dei Lavoratori. Fascio Operaio. Federazione Italiana— Regione di Bologna. Primo Congresso Regionale. Sunto del Processo Verbale. In: *Il Fascio Operaio*. Num. 13, 24 Marzo 1872.—502

Circulaire à toutes les Fédérations de l'Association Internationale des Travailleurs. (Sonvillier, le 12 novembre 1871.) Leaflet and in: *La Révolution Sociale*, No. 5, 23 novembre 1871 (extracts) and No. 8, 14 décembre 1871 (in full).—65, 67, 68, 102-03, 105, 108-09, 113, 234, 236, 267, 290, 442, 473, 479, 480, 482, 483, 489, 499, 506

Circular à todas las federaciones y secciones de la Asociacion Internacional de los Trabajadores. [Signed:] Abhémar Schwitzguébel. In: *La Federacion*, Núm. 168, 2 de Noviembre de 1872.—510

Le Comité fédéral jurassien a adressé la réponse suivante au Conseil fédéral anglais. [Signed:] Le Secrétaire-correspondant, Adhémar Schwitzguébel. In: *Bulletin de la Fédération jurassienne de l'Association internationale des travailleurs*, No. 23, 1 décembre 1872.—301

Le Congrès Jurassien, des 27 et 28 avril 1873. In: *Bulletin de la Fédération jurassienne de l'Association internationale des travailleurs*, No. 9, 1 mai 1873; *L'Internationale*, No. 228, 18 mai 1873; *La Liberté*, No. 23, 8 juin 1873.—450, 514

Congress of the International Working Men's Association [report on the London Congress held by the secessionists of the British Federation]. In: *The Eastern Post*, No. 227, February 1, 1873.—414, 441, 448-49, 512

Congrès Ouvrier Belge des 25 et 26 décembre 1872. In: *L'Internationale*, No. 207, 29 décembre 1872.—441, 511-12

Congrès régional des sections du Jura, tenu à Sonvilliers le 12 novembre. In: *La Révolution Sociale*, No. 5, 23 novembre 1871.—478-79

Conseil fédéral belge. Séance du 26 janvier 1873. In: *L'Internationale*, No. 212, 2 février 1873.—415

Déclaration de la Section française fédéraliste de 1871, siégeant à Londres. Londres, 1871. [Signed:] Le Secrétaire E. Navarre.—100

---

* Below is a list of documents drawn up by groups and organisations opposing the General Council of the I.W.A., not admitted into the Association or expelled from it.— Ed.

Les deux Congrès de Saint-Imier. In: *Bulletin de la Fédération jurassienne de l'Association internationale des travailleurs,* No. 17-18, 15 septembre-1 octobre 1872.—408, 509, 589

Federacion Regional Española. Circular. Valencia, 22 de Agosto de 1872. [Signed:] Vicente Rossell, Vicente Torres ... Leaflet.—495

Federacion Regional Española. Consejo Federal. Circular á todas las federaciones locales [November 14, 1872]. [Signed:] Vicente Rossell, Vicente Torres. In: *La Federacion,* Núm. 171, 23 de Noviembre de 1872.—511

Federazione Italiana, 1ª Conferenza. Risoluzione. Rimini, 6 Agosto 1872. [Signed:] Carlo Cafiero, Andrea Costa. Leaflet.—216, 237, 275-76, 414, 502-03

Federazione Italiana. Commissione di corrispondenza. Circolare a tutte la sezioni e federazioni locali. Bologna, 10 Gennaio 1873. [Signed:] Andrea Costa. In: *La Plebe,* Num. 3, 19 Gennaio 1873.—414

Guillaume, J. *Au Comité fédéral jurassien.* Neuchâtel, 10 juin 1872. In: *Bulletin de la Fédération jurassienne de l'Association internationale des travailleurs.* Nos. 10/11, 15 juin 1872.—476, 485
— *Le Congrès de la Chaux-de-Fonds.* In: *Le Progrès,* No. 14, 2 avril 1870.—540
— *Le Congrès de la Haye.* In: *Bulletin de la Fédération jurassienne de l'Association internationale des travailleurs,* No. 17-18, 15 septembre-1 octobre 1872.—278, 287
— *Le Conseil général...* In: *La Solidarité,* No. 16, 23 juillet 1870.—476
[Guillaume, J., Blanc, G.] *Manifeste aux Sections de l'Internationale.* In: *La Solidarité,* No. 22, 5 septembre 1870, supp.—92-93, 476

Hales, J. *Au Comité fédéral de la Fédération jurassienne. Londres, le 6 novembre 1872.* In: *Bulletin de la Fédération jurassienne de l'Association internationale des travailleurs,* No. 23, 1ᵉʳ décembre 1872.—301-03

Lista de los delegados al Congreso de Córdoba. In: *La Federacion,* Núm. 179, de 18 Enero de 1873.—510

Officious interference with the local government of the several sections properly rebuked—section 12 vindicated. [Signed:] W. West. In: *Woodhull & Claflin's Weekly,* No. 27(79), November 18, 1871.—637

Organisation de l'Alliance des Frères Internationaux [Genève, novembre 1868] [by M. Bakunin].—457-59, 461-70, 480-81, 505-06, 518-20, 525, 532, 544, 548-49, 568-77

Palladino, C. *Relazione Sulla Sezione Napoletana dell'Associazione Internazionale dei Lavoratori. Napoli,* 13 novembre 1871. Manuscript.—498-99

Programme de la Section de l'Alliance de la Démocratie Socialiste. Genève, 1869 [by M. Bakunin].—88, 89, 525

[*Programme et règlement de l'Alliance internationale de la Démocratie Socialiste.* Genève, novembre 1868] [by M. Bakunin].—32, 85-89, 107, 205, 577-78

Protest of Section 12. In: *Woodhull & Claflin's Weekly,* No. 2 (80), November 25, 1871.—179-80, 637

Rapport du Comité Fédéral Jurassien présenté au congrès annuel de la Fédération Jurassienne, tenu à Neuchâtel, les 27 et 28 avril 1873. Sonvillier, le 25 avril 1873. [Signed:] Adhémar Schwitzguébel et al. In: *Bulletin de la Fédération jurassienne de l'Association internationale des travailleurs.* No. 9, 1 mai 1873.—513

Rapport du Comité Fédéral romand. Siégeant à St.-Imier-Sonvillier, présenté au Congrès régional de la fédération romande de l'Internationale, tenu à Sonvillier, le 12 novembre 1871. [Signed:] Adhémar Schwitzguébel. In: *La Révolution Sociale*, No. 5, 23 novembre 1871.—68-69, 478

Section française à Londres de 1871, Statuts. In: *Qui Vive!*, No. 6, 8 et 9 octobre 1871 and as a leaflet.—24-27, 38-42, 98-99

Seccion internácional de Valencia Circular. [Signed:] El Secretario Damon. Enero 30/72. Manuscript.—488

Section 12 sustained. The decision of the General Council. In: *Woodhull & Claflin's Weekly*, No. 3(81), December 2, 1871.—638

Seccion Sevillana de la Alianza Democrática Socialista. 25 octubre 1871. Circular. [Signed:] El Secretario Evaristo.—489

Terzaghi, C. to the General Council, October 10, 1871. Manuscript.—111-12, 499

To the Branches, Sections and Members of the British Federation of the International Working Men's Association. [Signed:] Hales, J., Bennett, G. [London,] December 10th, 1872.—304-10, 313, 414

To the Workingmen of America. [Address of the Central Committee of the United States. New York, October 15, 1871.] In: *Woodhull & Claflin's Weekly*, No. 25(77), November 4, 1871.—636

To the United States Central Committee of the I.W.A. In: *Woodhull & Claflin's Weekly*, No. 27(79), November 18, 1871.—179, 638

Travailleurs, compagnons! Nous... [Signed:] Les commissions ouvrières de Barcelone et des environs. In: *La Solidarité Révolutionnaire*, No. 6, 16 juillet 1873.—585-86

The United States Federal Council versus the delegate of the twelfth section. To the Members of Section Twelve of I.W.A. In: *Woodhull & Claflin's Weekly*, No. 16(94), March 2, 1872.—179, 639

DOCUMENTS

An Act for the Regulation of the Royal Parks and Gardens (27th June 1872).—612

An Act Further to Amend the Laws Relating to the Representation of the People in England and Wales (15th August, 1867).—611, 613

An Act to Amend the Law Relating to Procedure at Parliamentary and Municipal Elections (18th July 1872).—611, 613

An Act to Amend the Law Relating to the Occupation and Ownership of Land in Ireland (1st August 1870).—612

An Act to Amend the Public Health Act, 1848, and to Make Further Provision for the Local Government of Towns and Populous Districts (2nd August 1858).—360

An Act to Consolidate and Amend the Acts Relating to the Regulation of Coal Mines and Certain Other Mines (10th August 1872).—615

An Act to Consolidate and Amend the Nuisances Removal and Diseases Prevention Acts, 1848 and 1849 (14 August 1855).—360

An Act to Enable the Public Works Loan Commissioners to Make Advances Towards the Erection of Dwellings for the Labouring Classes (18th May 1866).—361

An Act to Provide Better Dwellings for Artisans and Labourers (31st July 1868).—360

An Act to Put an End to the Establishment of the Church of Ireland (26th July 1869).—612

An Act to Repeal an Act of the Present Session of Parliament intituled An Act for the more effectuell abolition of Oaths and Affirmations taken and made in various departments of the State, and to substitute Declarations in lieu thereof, and for the more entire suppression of voluntary and extra judicial Oaths and Affidavits and to make other provisions for the abolition of unnecessary Oaths [the fifth and sixth years of the reign of his Majesty King William the Fourth].—50-51

[*Arrêté sur l'abolition des amendes ou retenues sur les salaires. Paris, 27 avril 1871.*] In: *Journal officiel de la République française*, No. 119, 29 avril 1871.—370

[*Arrêté sur la suppression du travail de nuit dans les boulangeries, Paris, 20 avril 1871.*] In: *L'Avant-Garde*, No. 451, 22 avril 1871.—370

Atto di fratellanza. In: *Il Giornale delle Associazione Operaie.* Luglio, 1864.—47

Bericht über die Welt-Ausstellung zu Paris im Jahre 1867. Herausgegeben durch das k.k. österreichische Central-Comité. Wien, 1869.—338

Божіею Милостію Мы, Александръ Вторый... [Manifesto on the Emancipation of the Serfs.] In: *Санктпетербургскія Вѣдомости*, № 52, 6 марта 1861.—558

Children's Employment Commission (1862). First Report of the Commissioners. With appendix. Presented to both Houses of Parliament by Command of Her Majesty. London, 1863.—193

[Decree of April 16, 1871 on handing over the workshops and manufactories to cooperative workmen societies.] In: *The Daily News*, No. 7790, April 18, 1871; *Journal officiel de la République française*, No. 107, 17 avril 1871.—370

L'Enquête du dixième groupe. Catalogue analytique des documents, mémoires et rapports. Exposés hors classe dans le dixième groupe et relatifs aux institutions publiques et privées créées par l'état, les départements, les communes et les particuliers pour améliorer la condition physique et morale de la population. Paris, 1867.—339

Entwurf eines Gesetzes betreffend die Ertheilung der Idemnität in Bezug auf die Führung des Staatshaushalts vom Jahre 1862 ab und die Ermächtigung zu den Staats-Ausgaben für des Jahr 1866. In: *Stenographische Berichte des preußischen Abgeordnetenhauses. 1866-1867.* Bd. 1. Anl. Berlin, 1866.—617

Entwurf eines Reichs-Militär Gesetzes. In: *Stenographische Berichte über die Verhandlungen des Deutschen Reichstages. 2. Legislatur-Periode. 1. Session 1874.* Bd. 3. Berlin, 1874.—617

Falckenstein, V. von. [Ukase on the interdiction of all meetings of the Democratic Socialist Party.] In: *Der Volksstaat*, Nr. 80, 5. Oktober 1870.—222

— [Ukase cancelling the interdiction of the meetings of the Democratic Socialist Party.] In: *Der Volksstaat*, Nr. 83, 15. Oktober 1870.—222

Favre, J. [Circular to the diplomatic representatives of the French Republic.] Versailles, le 6 juin 1871. In: *Journal officiel de la République française*, No. 159, 8 juin 1871.—32, 107, 223, 224, 480

Geschäfts-Instruktion für die Regierungen in sämmtlichen Provinzen. In: *Sammlung der für die Königlichen Preußischen Staaten erschienenen Gesetze und Verordnungen von 1806 bis zum 27sten Oktober 1810.* Berlin, 1822, Nr. 64.—401

Gesetz, betreffend den außerordentlichen Geldbedarf der Militair- und Marine-Verwaltung und die Dotirung des Staatsschatzes. In: *Gesetz-Sammlung für die Königlichen Preußischen Staaten.* Berlin, 1866, Nr. 6431.—617

Gesetz, betreffend die Friedenspräsenzstärke des deutschen Heeres und die Ausgaben für die Verwaltung desselben für die Jahre 1872, 1873 und 1874. In: *Reichs-Gesetzblatt.* Berlin, 1871. Enthält die Gesetze, Verordnungen etc. vom 1. Januar bis 29. Dezember 1871, nebst einem Vertrag und einem Allerhöchsten Erlasse aus dem Jahre 1870, Nr. 751.—618

Gesetz, betreffend die ländlichen Ortsobrigkeiten in den sechs östlichen Provinzen der Preußischen Monarchie. In: *Gesetz-Sammlung für die Königlichen Preußischen Staaten.* Berlin, 1856, Nr. 4413.—401

Gesinde-Ordnung für sämmtliche Provinzen der Preußischen Monarchie. Vom 8. November 1810. In: *Gesetz-Sammlung für die Königlichen Preußischen Staaten.* Berlin, 1810, Nr. 13.—607

Hansard's parliamentary debates. Third series, commencing with the accession of William IV. 26° Victorae, 1863. Vol. CLXX. Comprising the period from the twenty-seventh day of March 1863, to the twenty-eighth day of May 1863. Second Volume of the Session. London, 1863.—164-67, 195-97

Kreisordnung für die Provinzen Preußen, Brandenburg, Pommern, Posen, Schlesien und Sachsen. Vom 13. Dezember 1872. In: *Gesetz-Sammlung für die Königlichen Preußischen Staaten.* Berlin, 1872, Nr. 8080.—400, 403-04, 627

Loi qui établit des peines contre les affiliés de l'association internationale des travailleurs.— 223, 224, 439

— Dufaure, J. [Circulaire aux procureurs généraux. Versailles, 23 avril 1871.] In: *Le Mot d'Ordre*, No. 62, 26 avril 1871.—223

Общее положеніе о крестьянахъ, вышедшихъ изъ крѣпостной зависимости. In: *Санктпетербургскія Вѣдомости*, № 53, 7 марта 1861.—558

Papiers et correspondance de la Famille impériale. Édition collationnée sur le texte de l'imprimerie nationale. T. 1-2. Paris, [1870-]1871.—220

The People's Charter; being the Outline of an Act to provide for the Just Representation of the People of Great Britain in the Commons' House of Parliament. Embracing the principles of Universal Suffrage. No Property Qualification, Annual Parliaments, Equal Representation, Payment of Members, and Vote by Ballot. Prepared by a committee of twelve persons, six members of Parliament and six members of the London Working Men's Association, and addressed to the People of the United Kingdom. London, 1838.—613

Public Health. Sixth report of the medical officer of the Privy Council. With appendix. 1863. Presented pursuant to Act of Parliament. London, 1864.—193

Report addressed to Her Majesty's Principal Secretary of State for the Home Department, relative to the Grievances complained of by the Journeymen Bakers. London, 1862.—193

Report of the Commissioners appointed to inquire into the operation of the Acts (16 & 17 Vict. c 99 and 20 & 21 Vict. c. 3) Relating to Transportation and penal Servitude. Vol. I. Report and appendix. Vol. II. Minutes of evidence. Presented to both Houses of Parliament by Command of Her Majesty, London, 1863.—193

Report to Her Majesty's Principal Secretary of State for the Home Department, from the Poor Law Commissioners, on an inquiry into the sanitary condition of the labouring population of Great Britain. With app. Presented to both Houses of Parliament by command of Her Majesty, July, 1842. London, 1842.—338

Royal Warrant, dated 20th July 1871, to cancel and determine all regulations authorizing the purchase or sale or exchange for money of commissions in the army, from the 1st November 1871. [London], 1871.—612

Sacase, J. Fr. *Rapport fait au nom de la commission chargée d'examiner le projet de loi ayant pour objet d'établir des peines contre les affiliés à l'Association internationale des travailleurs* [5 février 1872]. In: *Annales de l'Assemblée nationale. Compte-rendu in extenso des séances.* Annexes. T. VII. Du 15 janvier au 22 février 1872. Paris, 1872.—107, 143, 480

[Sagasta.] *La circular del ministro de la gobernacion.* In: *La Emancipacion*, Núm. 32, 21 de Enero de 1872.—225

[Trial of members of the Nechayev organisation. Sessions of the St. Petersburg law-court.] In: *С.-Петербургскія Вѣдомости*, №№ 179-181, 185-188, 190, 194, 198-200, 202, 225-226, 229-230 и 238, июль-август (сентябрь)—515-16, 527-34, 538-39
— Общія правила организаціи. In: *С.-Петербургскія Вѣдомости*, № 187, 10(22) июля 1871.—530
— *Отношеніе революціонера.* In: *С.-Петербургскія Вѣдомости*, № 187, 10(22) июля 1871.—544-49

Tribunal de police correctionnelle de Toulouse. L'affaire de l'Internationale. 38 prévenus. Audience du 17 mars 1873. In: *La Réforme*, No. 663, 18 mars 1873.—483

Verordnung, betreffend die Errichtung von Gewerberäthen und verschiedene Abänderungen der allgemeinen Gewerbeordnung. In: *Gesetz-Sammlung für die Königlichen Preußischen Staaten.* Berlin, 1849, Nr. 3102.—401

Verordnung über die Errichtung von Gewerbegerichten. In: *Gesetz-Sammlung für die Königlichen Preußischen Staaten.* Berlin, 1849, Nr. 3103.—401

Verordnung wegen Aufhebung des Zunftzwangs und Verkauf-Monopols der Bäcker-, Schlächter- und Hölzergewerke in den Städten der Provinzen Ost-, Westpreußen und Litthauen. In: *Sammlung der für die Königlichen Preußischen Staaten erschienenen Gesetze und Verordnungen von 1806 bis zum 27sten Oktober 1810.* Berlin, 1822, Nr. 53.—401

Die Verfassung des Norddeutschen Bundes, in vergleichender Zusammen-Stellung mit der Entwurf. Berlin, 1867.—618

Verfassung des Deutschen Reichs. In: *Reichs-Gesetzblatt. Berlin 1871. Enthält die Gesetze, Verordnungen etc. vom. 1. Januar bis 29. Dezember 1871, nebst einem Vertrage und einem Allerhöchsten Erlasse aus dem Jahre 1870, Nr. 628.*—49, 618

Verfassungs-Urkunde für den Preußischen Staat. In: *Gesetz-Sammlung für die Königlichen Preußischen Staaten.* Berlin, 1850, Nr. 3212.—617

ANONYMOUS ARTICLES AND REPORTS
PUBLISHED IN PERIODIC EDITIONS

Arbeiter-Zeitung, Nr. 2, 15. Februar 1873: *An die Mühevollen und Geplagten!*—429
— Nr. 3, 22. Februar 1873: *Fabrikantenspiegel.*—429

Bulletin de la Fédération jurassienne de l'Association internationale des travailleurs, No. 3, 15 mars 1872: *Les socialistes n'ayant plus d'organes....*—482-83
— No. 4, 20 mars 1872: *Le 18 mars.*—484
— No. 10/11, 15 juin 1872; *Réponse à M. Lafargue.*—544
— No. 20/21, 10 novembre 1872: *Nous recevons la lettre suivante....*—412
— No. 8, 15 avril 1873: *Les proconsuls marxistes en France.*—440

The Daily News, No. 8179, July 15, 1872: *The position of the British coal trade.*—185-87
— No. 8230, September 12, 1872: *The New Constitution of the International* (From our special correspondent).—259
— No. 8258, October 15, 1872: *The miners' right to vote.*—350
— No. 8268, October 26, 1872: *Fall of Six Houses at Manchester.*—360

The Economist, No. 1507, July 13, 1872: *The Great Rise in the Price of Coal.*—187

La Emancipacion, Núm. 24, 27 de Noviembre de 1871: *La politica de la Internacional.*—59
— Núm. 51, 1 de Junio de 1872: *Informacion revolucionaria.*—492

La Federacion, Núm. 120, 3 de Deciembre de 1871: *La politica de la Internacional* (a reprint from *La Emancipacion,* Núm. 24, 27 de Noviembre de 1871).—59
— Núm. 149, 28 de Julio de 1872: *Nuestro querido colega....*—497
— Núm. 163, 18 de Septiembre de 1872: *El meeting de Bruselas.*—508
— Núm. 164, 5 de Octubre de 1872: *El Congreso de la Haya.*—544
— Núm. 177, 4 de Enero de 1873: *Tercer Congreso Regional de la Federacion Española.*—412
— Núm. 178, 11 de Enero de 1873: *Movimiento obrero universal. España.*—412
— Núm. 179, 18 de Enero de 1873: *El Congreso de Córdoba.*—510
— Núm. 206, 26 de Julio de 1873: *Á los Trabajadores.*—587, 589

Le Figaro, 11 septembre 1872: *On continue à ne pas voir...* [Signed:].:—257

Frankfurter Zeitung und Handelsblatt, Nr. 326, 24. November 1871: *London, 18. Nov.*—52

Gazzettino Rosa, Num. 360, 28 Dicembre 1871: *Movimento operajo.* [Signed:] Nicodemo.—499

La Igualdad, Núm. 1069, 19 de Marzo de 1872: *Segun dice el combate....*—491
— Núm. 1074, 24 de Marzo de 1872: *No quieron acabas.*—491

L'Internationale, No. 223, 20 avril 1873: *Nous extrayons les lignes suivantes...*—442

Изданія Общества «Народной Расправы», № 1. Москва, лѣто 1869 [Женева, 1869].—519, 522-24, 530, 535, 539-42, 544, 549
— *Взглядъ на прежнее и нынѣшнее пониманіе дѣла.*—524
— *Всенародное возстаніе...*—522-23
— № 2, С.-Петербургъ, 1870 [Женева]: I. *В послѣднихъ числахъ...*—539, 541
— II. *Кто не за насъ, тотъ противъ насъ.*—506, 522, 541-43
— III. *Главныя основы будущаго общественнаго строя.*—542
— № 2. *Прибавленіе. Извѣщеніе и предостереженіе отъ Комитета.*—530

Journal de Genève, No. 3, 5 janvier 1870: *On s'occupe. ...*—539
— No. 254, 27 octobre 1871: *La Liberté dans l'Association Internationale des Travailleurs. Confédération Suisse. Genève, le 27 Octobre 1871.*—32

Kölnische Zeitung, Nr. 181, 2. Juli 1873, Drittes Blatt: [Review of E. Renan's *L'Antéchrist.*]—452
— Nr. 48, 17. Februar 1874: *Die französische Heer- und Flottenstärke für 1874.*—623

Il Libero Pensiero, Num. 1, 4 Gennaio 1872: *L'Internazionale e il Consiglio Supreme di Londra.*—74, 75
— Num. 18, 2 Novembre 1871: *Società Universale dei Razionalisti.*—484

The Manchester Weekly Times, No. 763, July 20, 1872: *The Floods in the Medlock. Charles-Street Pit.*—366-68

Neuer Social-Demokrat, Nr. 45, 18. April 1873: *Internationale Arbeiterassoziation.*—440
— Nr. 49, 27. April 1873: *Internationale Arbeiterassoziation.*—439-42, 444, 445
— Nr. 68, 18. Juni 1873: *Internationale Arbeiterassoziation.*—451

O Pensamento Social, Núm. 25, 6 Outubro 1872: *O Congresso da Internacional na Haya.*—410
— Núm. 51, 5 Abril 1873.— *Da commissão de correspondencia.*—438

Paris-Journal, No. 76, 19 mars 1871: *Lettre du Grand Chef de l'Internationale.*—127

La Plebe, Num. 119. 4 Dicembre 1872: *Sequestro LIX.*—409
— Num. 120, 8 Dicembre 1872: *Uno post unum.*—409
— Num. 121, 11 Dicembre 1872: *Jeri é stato.*—409

Le Progrès, No. 25, 4 décembre 1869: *On sait que la presque totalité...*—473
— No. 6, 5 février 1870: *Événements de Russie.*—540

La République française, No. 125, 11 mars 1872: *Questions ouvrières.*—482

La Révolution Sociale, No. 4, 16 novembre 1871: *Le Congres de Sonvillier.*—116

Reynolds's Newspaper, No. 1173, February 2, 1873: *Labour and wages.*—411

The Saturday Review of politics, literature, science, and art, No. 785, November 12, 1870: *Mr. Beesly and the International Association.*—192

Le Socialiste (New York), 18 mai 1872: *Internationaux, prenez garde à vous!*—641-42

Le Socialiste (Paris), No. 45, 3 juillet 1886: *Le Familistère de Guise.*—348
— No. 48, 24 juillet 1886: *Le programme de Godin.*—348

La Solidarité, No. 5, 7 mai 1870: *Deux organes socialistes...*—91, 474
— No. 14, 9 juillet 1870: *Communications du Comité fédéral romand.*—92, 474
La Solidarité Révolutionnaire, No. 6, 16 juillet 1873: *Le mouvement révolution-naire....*—588, 590

Die Tagwacht, Nr. 11, 16. März 1872: *Diese Anmerkungen....*—459

The Times, No. 27200, October 21, 1871: *A society which calls itself...*—84
— No. 27456, August 15, 1872: *The International.*—214
— No. 27576, January 2, 1873: *Karl Marx and the International..*—398, 399

Woodhull & Claflin's Weekly, No. 23(75), October 21, 1871: *The Internationals.*—179, 637
— No. 2 (80), November 25, 1871: *Meetings of the Sections.*—637
— No. 5 (83), December 16, 1871: *Addendum—Reorganization.*—181, 639
— No. 16 (94), March 2, 1872: *The coming combination convention.*—179, 182, 639
— No. 21 (99), April 6, 1872: *The May convention.*—640
— No. 25 (103), May 4, 1872: *Remarks.*—181, 639
— No. 28 (106), May 25, 1872: *The Convention.*—641
— *Official report of the equal rights convention, held in New York city, on the ninth, tenth and eleventh of May, 1872.*—641

The World, May 13, 1872.—641
— May 20, 1872: *Secession from the International.*—642

INDEX OF PERIODICALS

Almanacco Repubblicano per l'anno 1874—a yearly published in Lodi by the editorial board of *La Plebe* in late 1873.—397, 425

Almanach du Peuple pour 1872—an anarchist annual published in Geneva in late 1871.—116

Arbeiter-Wochen-Chronik—a socialist weekly published under this title in 1873-90 in Budapest in German and in Hungarian (Hungarian title *Munkás-Heti-Krónika*).—432

Arbeiter-Zeitung—a workers' weekly, organ of the German Section No. 1 and of the Federal Council of the International in the USA published in New York from February 1873 to March 1875 (from October 1874 under the title *Neue Arbeiter-Zeitung*). The paper published reports on the sittings of the General Council and documents of the International, and also some of the works by Marx and Engels. In summer 1874 began to deviate from the principles of the International.—429, 437

La Asociacion—a Spanish republican paper published in Léon in the early 1870s.—29

L'Avvenirre Sociale—an Italian weekly organ of the Bakuninists, published irregularly in Piacenza from April to October 1873.—450, 453, 504

Belletristisches Journal und New-Yorker Criminal-Zeitung—a weekly founded by German petty-bourgeois emigrants in New York in 1851 and published under the title *New-Yorker Criminal-Zeitung*. From March 18, 1853 to March 10, 1854 it appeared as *Belletristisches Journal und New-Yorker Criminal-Zeitung*. In 1853 published slanderous articles against Marx and other proletarian revolutionaries.—72

Bulletin de la Fédération jurassienne de l'Association internationale des travailleurs—organ of the Swiss anarchists, published under the editorship of James Guillaume in 1872-78, at first, twice a month, and from July 1873, weekly.—176, 189, 278, 279, 287, 300, 301, 408, 412, 415, 440, 450, 476, 482-85, 508, 509, 513, 544, 580, 589

La Campana—an Italian anarchist weekly published in Naples in 1872.—580

La Capitale—an Italian democratic daily paper published in Rome in 1872.—48

Ciceruacchio. Il Tribuno—an Italian Left-wing republican daily, close to the International, published in Rome from July 15, 1871 to December 31, 1872.—48

El Combate—a Spanish republican daily, organ of the Federalists, published in Madrid.—486

El Comunero—a Spanish republican paper published in Madrid in the early 1870s.—29

Concordia. Zeitschrift für die Arbeiterfrage—organ of the German industrialists and Katheder-Socialists, founded in 1871; published in Berlin until 1876.—164, 190-94, 197

El Condenado—a Spanish weekly, organ of the anarchists, published in Madrid in 1872-74 by Morago.—490-91

La Constitution—a French republican daily published in Paris in 1871.—100

Le Corsaire—a French republican daily published in Paris from 1871.—257, 258

Courrier de l'Europe—a French paper, organ of the Orleanists, published in London in 1840-89.—100, 127

Criminal-Zeitung—see *Belletristisches Journal und New-Yorker Criminal-Zeitung*

The Daily News—a liberal newspaper, organ of the British industrial bourgeoisie, published under this title in London from 1846 to 1930.—185-87, 259, 350, 360

La Démocratie—a French democratic weekly published in Paris from November 1868 to 1870.—540

Deutsche Allgemeine Zeitung—a daily published under this title in Leipzig from 1843 to 1879, until the summer of 1848 it was conservative but later adopted liberal views.—287

Les Droits de l'Homme—a French Left-wing republican daily published by J. Guesde in 1870-71 in Montpélier.—507

The Eastern Post—an English workers' weekly published in London from 1868 to 1873, organ of the General Council of the International from February 1871 to June 1872.—21, 29, 31, 33, 45, 49, 58, 62, 71-73, 78, 152, 159, 414, 453

The Echo—an English liberal paper published in London from 1868 to 1907.—29

The Economist—an economic and political weekly published in London since 1843, organ of the big industrial bourgeoisie.—187

L'Égalité—a Swiss weekly, organ of the Romance Federation of the International, published in Geneva from December 1868 to December 1872. In November 1869-January 1870 Bakunin, Pérron, Robin and others, who were on the editorial board of the paper, tried to use it for the attacks on the General Council. However, in January 1870 the Romance Federal Council expelled the Bakuninists from the editorial board, and after that the paper once again began to support the line of the General Council.—77, 90-91, 93-94, 104, 120, 225, 408, 472-74, 476, 489, 540

L'Eguaglianza—an Italian weekly published in Agrigento (Sicily) from July 1871 to 1872, organ of the local section of the International.—30, 579

La Emancipacion—a Spanish workers' weekly, organ of the Madrid sections of the International, published in Madrid from 1871 to 1873; waged struggle against Bakuninism in Spain. In 1872-73 the paper printed the *Manifesto of the Communist Party* by Marx and Engels, parts of *Poverty of Philosophy* and of *Capital* by Marx, and a series of articles by Engels; in 1872 Paul Lafargue was on the editorial board of the paper.—59, 126, 138, 139, 177, 183, 213, 215, 229, 230, 236, 237, 256, 258, 290, 292, 299, 303, 329, 408, 409, 413-15, 438, 490-92, 495, 511

L'Emancipation—a French republican paper published in Toulouse from 1867.— 100, 508

Il Fascio Operaio—an Italian anarchist weekly published in Bologne from December 1871 to September 1872.—502-03, 580

La Favilla—an Italian paper, at first, democratic, published in Mantua in 1866-94, in 1871-72, daily; in the first half of the 1870s was under the influence of anarchists.—43, 275-76, 451, 453, 504

La Federacion—a Spanish workers' weekly, organ of the Barcelona Federation of the International, published in Barcelona from 1869 to 1873; was under the Bakuninists' influence.—59, 230, 236, 237, 281, 412, 415, 497, 510-11, 544, 587, 589, 596

Le Figaro—a French conservative paper published in Paris from 1854, from 1866, daily; was connected with the Government of the Second Empire.—75, 95, 257, 477, 504

The Fortnightly Review—an English historical, philosophical, and literary magazine founded in 1865 by a group of radicals, subsequently it became liberal in character, under this title it was published in London till 1934.—165, 192

Frankfurter Zeitung und Handelsblatt—a democratic daily published in Frankfurt am Main from 1856 (under this title from 1866) to 1943.—52

Die Gartenlaube. Illustriertes Familienblatt—a literary weekly published in Leipzig in 1853-1903 and in Berlin in 1903-43.—339

La Gaulois—a conservative-monarchist daily, organ of the big bourgeoisie and aristocracy, published in Paris from 1867 to 1929.—75, 95, 477

Gazzettino Rosa—an Italian daily, organ of the Left Mazzinists, published in Milan from 1868 to 1873; in 1871-72 came out in defence of the Paris Commune, printed documents of the International; in 1872 was under the influence of anarchists.—30, 61, 74, 75, 152, 160, 163, 258, 499, 580

Herald—see *The New-York Herald*

La Igualdad—a Spanish radical daily published in Madrid in 1868-70; a number of utopian socialists and republicans contributed to the paper, from the early 1870s it also expressed anarchist ideas.—491

The Illustrated London News—a weekly magazine published since 1842.—339

L'Internationale—a Belgian weekly, organ of the Belgian sections of the International, published in Brussels from 1869 to 1873; in 1873 took an anarchist stand.—219, 227, 415, 442, 483, 514

The International Herald—an English republican weekly published in London from March 1872 to October 1873, from May 1872 to May 1873 (with intervals) was organ of the British Federal Council of the International; published documents and correspondences by Marx and Engels.—78, 128, 136, 173, 219, 221, 224, 227, 285, 301, 303, 305-07, 309, 314, 408-14, 426, 427, 429, 431, 433, 434, 438, 446

Изданія Общества «Народной Расправы» (Publications of the "People's Judgment" Society)—anarchist publication, which appeared in two issues in 1869 under the editorship of Bakunin and Nechayev; both issues were printed in Geneva.— 506, 519, 522, 523, 530, 540-44

Janus, Jahrbücher deutscher Gesinnung, Bildung und That—a German conservative yearly published in Berlin from 1845 to 1848.—348

Journal de Genève national, politique et littéraire—a Swiss conservative daily, founded in 1826.—32, 75, 105, 539

La Justicia—a Spanish republican paper published in Malaga in 1871-73.—29

Kladderadatsch—an illustrated satirical weekly published from 1848 to 1944 in Berlin; in the 19th century held liberal positions.—339

Kölnische Zeitung—a German daily, under this title it was published in Cologne from 1802 to 1945; organ of the Rhenish bourgeoisie and National-Liberal party; in the 1870s was Bismarck's mouthpiece.—452, 607, 623

Колоколъ (The Bell)—a revolutionary-democratic newspaper, was published by Alexander Herzen and Nikolai Ogarev from 1857 to 1867 in Russian and in 1868-69 in French under the title *Kolokol* (La Cloche) with Russian supplements; until 1865 was published in London, later in Geneva.—85, 163, 461, 529, 557, 559, 562-63

Колоколъ. Органъ русскаго освобожденія, основанный А. И. Герценомъ—was the title under which Sergei Nechayev and Vladimir Serebrennikov published six issues of the paper in spring 1870 in Geneva.—544, 549

Il Ladro—an Italian paper published in Florence from August 20, 1872.—217

Il Libero Pensiero—an Italian weekly magazine, organ of the republican rationalists, published in Florence in 1866-76, attacked the International and its General Council.—74, 75, 160, 163

La Liberté—a Belgian democratic paper published in Brussels from 1865 to 1873, in 1872-73, weekly; from 1867, organ of the International in Belgium.—127, 128, 219, 256, 442-44, 457, 507, 508

The Manchester Weekly Times—an English liberal paper published in Manchester since December 1857.—366

La Marseillaise—a French daily, organ of the Left-wing republicans, published in Paris with the participation of Blanquists from December 1869 to September 1870, printed materialis on the activity of the International and on the working-class movement.—97, 219, 540

Il Martello—an Italian paper published in Milan in February-March 1872, organ of the Milan Section of the International.—580

The Morning Advertiser—a daily published in London from 1794 to 1934; in the 1850s and 1860s reflected the interests of the radical bourgeoisie.—196

The Morning Star—an English daily, organ of the Free Traders, published in London from 1856 to 1869.—196

Московскія вѣдомости (Moscow Gazette)—a Russian paper published from 1756 to 1917; from 1859, daily; from the 1850s assumed a reactionary character.— 72, 75, 557

Munkás-Heti-Krónika—see *Arbeiter-Wochen-Chronik*

Народное дѣло (*La Cause du Peuple*)—a magazine (from April 1870, newspaper) published in Geneva in 1868-70 by a group of Russian revolutionary émigrés, the first issue was prepared by Bakunin; in October 1868, the editors, among whom was Nikolai Utin, broke off relations with Bakunin and opposed his views; in April 1870 it became the organ of the Russian Section of the International Working Men's Association which pursued the policy of Marx and the General Council.—523, 526, 551

The National Reformer—an English weekly magazine of bourgeois radicals published in London from 1860 to 1893.—71

National Zeitung (*National-Zeitung*)—a German liberal daily published under this title in Berlin in 1848-1915.—160

Neue Rheinische Zeitung. Organ der Demokratie—a daily published in Cologne under the editorship of Marx from June 1, 1848 to May 19, 1849 (with an interval between September 27 and October 12, 1848), organ of the revolutionary-proletarian wing of the democrats during the 1848-49 revolution in Germany; Engels was among its editors.—161

Neuer Social-Demokrat—a German daily published in Berlin from 1871 to 1876 three times a week, organ of the Lassallean General Association of German Workers; from sectarian stance waged a struggle against the leaders of the International and of the German Social-Democratic Labour Party, supported Bakuninists and representatives of other anti-proletarian trends.—75, 119, 439, 440, 442, 444, 445, 451, 484

New-York Daily Tribune—an American daily published from 1841 to 1924, organ of the US Left-wing Whigs until the mid-1850s and later of the Republican Party; it voiced progressive views and opposed slavery. Marx and Engels contributed to it from August 1851 to March 1862.—161-62

New-Yorker Demokrat—a weekly of German democratic émigrés in the USA published under different titles from 1845 to 1876.—180, 638

The New-York Herald—a US daily of the Republican Party published from 1835 to 1924, favoured compromise with the slave-owners of the South during the Civil War.—181, 642

Norddeutsche Allgemeine Zeitung—a conservative daily published in Berlin from 1861 to 1918, in the 1860s-80s, semi-official organ of the government of Bismarck.—225

Obshchina (Commune)—the paper, the first issue of which came out under this title in September 1870 in London and was edited by Sergei Nechayev and Vladimir Serebrennikov; the second issue, published in 1871, was destroyed by the publishers themselves.—541

Paris-Journal—a conservative daily connected with the police, was published by Henri de Pène from 1868 to 1874 in Paris, libelled the International and the Paris Commune.—95, 127, 477

O Pensamento Social—a Portuguese socialist weekly newspaper published from February 1872 to April 1873 in Lisbon; organ of the International sections.— 408, 410, 421, 438

Pensiero e Azione—organ of the Italian democrats, published under the editorship of Mazzini, appeared twice a month in 1858-59 in London and in 1860 in Lugano and Genoa.— 162

Le Père Duchêne—a French daily published in Paris by Eugène Vermersch from March 6 to May 21, 1871; was close in its trend to the Blanquist press.— 143

Le Petit Journal—a French bourgeois daily published in Paris from 1863 to 1944.— 75

La Plebe—an Italian paper published under the editorship of Enrico Bignami in Lodi from 1868 to 1875 and in Milan from 1875 to 1883; before the early 1870s, was of democratic trend, later of socialist; in 1872-73, organ of the International sections; supported the General Council in its struggle against anarchists, published the documents of the International and articles by Engels.— 22, 59, 61, 150, 217, 276, 284, 293, 296, 300, 408, 409, 414, 438, 447

Il Popolino—a weekly, official organ of the Turin Section of the International, published in Turin from April 15 to October 6, 1872.— 217, 258

Le Progrès—a Swiss paper, organ of the Bakuninists; opposed the General Council of the International, published in Le Locle from December 1868 to April 1870 under the editorship of James Guillaume.— 90, 104, 472, 473, 540

Le Progrès de Lyon—a French bourgeois daily published in Lyon from 1860.— 104

Il Proletario—see *Il Proletario Italiano*

Il Proletario Italiano—an Italian paper published in Turin under the editorship of a secret police agent Terzaghi in 1871, organ of the Turin Section of the International, supported Bakuninists; from 1872 to 1874 was published under the title *Il Proletario*.—28, 29, 54, 111, 499

Qui Vive!—a daily published in London in 1871, organ of the French Section of 1871.— 23, 100

Le Radical—a French republican daily published in Paris in 1871-72.— 100

La Razon—a Spanish weekly, organ of the anarchists, was published in Seville in 1871-72.— 211, 236, 494

The Red Republican—a Chartist weekly published in London by George Harney from June to November 1850; the English translation of the *Manifesto of the Communist Party* by Marx and Engels appeared in it.— 174

La Réforme. Journal du Midi—a French paper published in Toulouse from 1870.— 483

Reichs-Gesetzblatt—a German government paper, organ of the Ministry of Home Affairs, was founded in Berlin in 1867, published under this title from 1871.— 618

La République Française—a French daily of the radical trend, founded by Léon Gambetta in Paris in November 1871 as organ of the parliamentary faction of the Republican League, was published up to (and including) 1924.— 482

La Réveil—a French weekly, a daily from May 1869, organ of the Left republicans, was published under the editorship of Charles Delescluse in Paris from July 1868 to January 1871; printed documents of the International and materials on the working-class movement.— 97, 220

La Révolution Sociale—an anarchist weekly published in Geneva from October 1871 to January 1872; from November 1871, official organ of the Bakuninist Jura Federation.— 55, 68, 69, 95, 116, 119, 121, 477, 478, 484, 488

La Roma del Popolo—a weekly on questions of religion, philosophy, politics, and literature, organ of the petty-bourgeois democracy, published in Rome from 1871 to 1872; published articles by Mazzini against the International.— 28, 43, 44, 46, 60, 61, 480

Il Romagnolo—an Italian democratic weekly published in Parma with intervals from September 1868 to October 1871.— 29

С.-Петербургскія вѣдомости (St. Petersburg Gazette)—a Russian daily, official government organ, published from 1728 to 1917; under this title appeared from 1728 to 1914.— 516, 527-35, 539

The Saturday Review of Politics, Literature, Science and Art—an English conservative weekly magazine published in London from 1855 to 1938.— 192

Der Social-Demokrat—organ of the Lassallean General Association of German Workers, under this title was published in Berlin from December 15, 1864 to 1871; Johann Baptist Schweitzer was its editor in 1864-67; under the title *Neuer Social-Demokrat* was published from 1871 to 1876.— 473

Le Socialiste—a daily published in New York from October 1871 to May 1873; organ of the French sections of the International in the USA; after the Hague Congress (1872) broke off with the International.— 174, 641-42

Le Socialiste—a French weekly, founded by J. Guesde in Paris in 1885; up to 1902, organ of the Workers' Party, later organ of the French Socialists; Engels was its contributor in the 1880s and 90s.— 348

Socialisten—a Danish workers' paper published in Copenhagen from July 1871 to May 1874, first as a weekly and from April 1872, as a daily; organ of the Danish sections of the International.— 57, 408

Le Soir—a French bourgeois daily published in Paris from 1869 to 1932.— 257

La Solidarité—a Swiss daily, organ of the Bakuninists, was edited by James Guillaume from April to September 1870 in Neuchâtel and from March to May 1871 in Geneva.— 91, 92, 95, 104, 120, 474, 476-77

La Solidarité Révolutionnaire—a weekly published in Barcelona in French from June to September 1873, organ of the Committee for Revolutionary Socialist Propaganda for Southern France, founded by Alerini and Brousse for popularising anarchist ideas in France and among the refugees of the Paris Commune.— 586-88, 590

Современникъ (Contemporary)—a Russian literary and political magazine published in St. Petersburg from 1836 to 1866 (from 1843, a monthly); was founded by Pushkin; from 1847, its editors were Nekrasov and Panayev;

Belinsky, Dobrolyubov, Chernyshevsky contributed to it; organ of the Russian revolutionary democracy in the 1860s.—559

The Spectator—an English weekly published in London from 1828; at the beginning was liberal in character, later, conservative.—187

The Standard—an English conservative daily founded in London in 1827.—75

Die Tages-Presse—an Austrian daily published in Vienna from 1869 to 1878.—72, 75

Die Tagwacht—a Swiss social-democratic paper published in Zurich from 1869 to 1880; in 1869-73 organ of the German sections of the International in Switzerland, later, of the Swiss Workers' Union and of the Social-Democratic Party of Switzerland.—408, 459

The Times—an English conservative daily founded in London in 1785.—31, 32, 84, 104, 127, 140, 143, 166, 193-96, 214, 395, 398, 399

El Trabajo—a Spanish republican paper published in El Ferrol in the early 1870s.—29

Le Travail—a French daily of the Paris sections of the International published in Paris from October 3 to December 12, 1869; Louis Eugène Varlin was among its major contributors.—90, 473

Il Tribuno—see *Ciceruacchio. Il Tribuno*

Über Land und Meer—a German illustrated weekly magazine published in Stuttgart from 1858 to 1923.—339

Vierteljahrschrift für Volkswirthschaft und Kulturgeschichte—a German liberal magazine published in Berlin from 1863 to 1893.—339

Der Volksstaat—central organ of the German Social-Democratic Workers' Party, published in Leipzig from October 2, 1869 to September 29, 1876 twice a week (from July 1873, three times a week) under the general editorship of Wilhelm Liebknecht, August Bebel played an important role in its publishing, Marx and Engels were among its contributors.—21, 23, 35, 48, 70, 126, 164, 167, 181, 183, 185, 187, 190, 191, 193, 194, 197, 216, 219, 223, 226-27, 255, 256, 260-62, 264, 266, 270, 286, 287, 317, 319, 321-23, 327, 331, 334, 335, 368, 371, 374-78, 383, 388, 390, 391, 398, 405, 408, 421, 437, 441, 445, 448, 451, 473, 584, 588, 591, 598, 616, 617, 619, 625, 629

Die Volksstimme—an Austrian workers' paper published in Vienna twice a month from April to December 1869, supported the General Council of the International.—142

Volkswille—an Austrian workers' paper published in Vienna from January 1870 to June 1874 (once a week up to October 1872, later, twice a week); printed documents of the International.—408

De Werkman—a Dutch workers' weekly published in Amsterdam from 1868 to 1874, organ of the Amsterdam Section of the International from 1869.—408

Wiesbadener Zeitung—a German paper published from 1872 to 1881.—75

Woodhull & Claflin's Weekly—a paper published by bourgeois feminists Victoria Woodhull and Tenessee Claflin in New York from 1870 to 1876; organ of the

US Section No. 12 excluded from the International by the General Council and the Hague Congress (1872).— 125, 126, 178, 180-82, 636-41

The World—an American daily of the Democrats published in New York from 1860 to 1931.— 641-42

Zeitschrift des Central-Vereins in Preussen für das Wohl der arbeitenden Klassen—a German philanthropic magazine published by Guido Weiß in Leipzig.— 338

Zeitschrift für spekulative Theologie—a German theoretical magazine of the Hegelian trend published under the editorship of Bruno Bauer in Berlin from 1836 to 1838.— 452

Die Zukunft—a German democratic paper, organ of the petty-bourgeois People's Party, published in Königsberg (Kaliningrad) in 1867 and in Berlin from 1868.— 127

SUBJECT INDEX

A

Agricultural labourers—48, 57, 148-49, 422
Agriculture—58, 131-36, 148, 384, 389, 422, 424
Alsace—155, 221, 601, 603, 607, 620
America—607, 609
Anarchism, anarchists—121, 264-65, 267, 268, 288, 332, 392-94, 425, 446, 466-69, 470, 476, 497, 525-26, 559-60, 581-82, 588-91, 597
See also Bakuninism, Bakuninists; International alliance of anarchists; Sectarianism
Anti-communism—160-61, 224-25, 445
Army—66, 363, 402-04, 419-20, 592-93, 601, 603, 612, 617-18, 620-24, 626
Australia—324
Austria—80, 161, 223, 601-03, 604, 610, 619
Austria-Hungary (from 1867)—35, 223-25, 365
Austro-Italo-French war, 1859—162, 402, 604, 607
Austro-Prussian war, 1866—402, 617, 624
Authority—67, 95-96, 110, 206, 233-36, 255, 274, 279-82, 310, 422-25, 472-76, 500-01, 508-10, 525, 543-44, 554

B

Bakuninism, Bakuninists—61, 66, 67, 85, 86, 88-90, 92-93, 107-08, 114-15, 121, 205, 231-32, 264-65, 268, 275, 281, 369, 393, 394, 457, 458, 460-62, 465-70, 471-75, 480, 490, 492-93, 497, 503-04, 506-07, 518-20, 523-24, 526, 544-49, 553-60, 572-80
— theoretical views—61, 89, 107-08, 114-15, 121, 205, 230, 288, 369, 458, 461, 466-71, 472, 473, 478, 480, 490, 517-26, 535-36, 542-56, 559-60, 562-67, 572-74, 579-80, 596-97, 630
— views on the state—93, 288, 392-93, 425, 466-70, 476, 497, 505, 509, 519-21, 544, 545, 547-48, 554, 559-60, 572-76, 578-79, 581-83, 585, 589, 597
— abstention from political action by the proletariat—209, 233, 254, 274, 288, 392-94, 397, 462, 474, 478, 483, 497, 509, 540, 555, 568, 578, 582, 584-85, 596-97
— federalist ideas, negation of authority—66, 67, 92, 94-95, 97-98, 105, 114-16, 206, 208-10, 216, 233-36, 267-68, 274, 279-82, 288, 310, 394, 414, 422-25, 450, 460, 465-69, 473, 475-76, 480-84, 489, 493, 496-97, 500-03, 505-07, 510-11, 513-14, 524, 525, 528, 543-55, 566, 573-76, 578-81, 590-92, 595-97
— on revolution—233, 466-70, 472, 476, 481, 518-27, 540, 544-51, 553, 555, 563-64, 568, 572-77, 582, 584, 586-87, 590-92, 595, 597, 598

— orientation on lumpenproletariat—555, 595
— ideas of a future society—66-68,
115, 394, 468-70, 482, 490, 521,
524, 542-43, 547-48, 552, 554,
572, 575-76
— attitude to the working class and
its movement—114, 168, 231,
233, 279, 392-94, 460-61, 467,
469-70, 481, 488, 541-44, 555,
572, 575-79, 581, 582
— and general strike—584-86, 591
— and the nationalities question—
85, 95, 517-18, 559-60, 566, 578
— attitude to scientific communism—502, 519-21, 544
— attitude to various socialist and
communist trends—121, 492,
524, 551, 565-66, 574, 577, 630
— disorganising activity in the working-class movement—32, 66-68,
79, 84-122, 168, 188, 205-12, 215,
216, 217, 228-38, 247-50, 254,
260-65, 267-69, 272, 274-75, 279-
82, 286-92, 294, 299-300, 302,
312, 408, 439-46, 456-598
— and the Paris Commune—95,
477, 496, 509
— revolutionary phrase-mongering,
adventurism and voluntarism—
92, 107-08, 207, 264, 267-69, 281,
465-68, 475-77, 480, 498, 505, 526,
581-98
— and Nechayevism—23, 89, 463,
515-19, 524, 526-41, 549, 552-55,
557
— blocs with reformists—118-19,
484, 513-14
See also Anarchism, anarchists; International alliance of anarchists; International Alliance of Socialist Democracy;
International Working Men's Association
(First International)
Basle Congress of the International Working Men's Association, 1869—18, 19,
24, 40, 57, 66-67, 93-96, 102, 112, 125,
188, 233-34, 267, 307, 312, 477, 642
Bavaria—428
Belgium—83, 620
Blanquism, Blanquists—265, 284, 370,
439-41
Bonapartism—319, 354, 363-65, 417,
627-28

Border tariffs—420
Bourgeois political economy—321-22,
331-33, 394-97
See also Vulgar bourgeois political
economy
Bourgeoisie—3, 106, 243, 264, 274, 325,
337, 339-40, 362, 376, 395, 400-01,
417, 419, 628
Bourgeoisie, Danish—57
Bourgeoisie, English—149, 186, 284,
349, 351, 612, 614-15, 616
Bourgeoisie, French—177, 363, 401,
405
Bourgeoisie, German—49, 223, 338, 357,
362-63, 426-31, 436, 628, 629
Bourgeoisie, Italian—28
Bourgeoisie, Prussian—363-64, 400-05,
617-19, 626-28
Bourgeoisie, Spanish—29, 418-20
Brussels Congress of the International
Working Men's Association, 1868—16,
19, 61, 85, 87, 101, 112, 135, 141,
460, 479
Bureaucracy—255, 363, 364, 403

C

Capital—34-35, 331-32, 342, 343, 345,
385-87, 390
Capitalism—331
See also Capitalist mode of production;
Society, bourgeois
Capitalist—49, 204, 318-20, 337, 343,
346, 348, 362, 396, 422-23, 426-27,
616
Capitalist mode of production—132, 136,
318, 323, 327, 338, 350, 360, 368,
383-87, 389-91
Catalonia—419-20
Catholicism—608
Centralisation of the state—599-600
Chartism, Chartist movement—106-07,
155, 306, 372, 481, 584, 613-14
Chauvinism—116, 155-56, 402, 519,
629, 631
Chemistry—107, 322, 381-82, 384, 394,
519
Child labour—392, 394, 497
China—35
Christianity—67, 255, 397, 484, 608
Civil rights—3-4, 44, 48, 435
Class(es)—3, 66, 88, 106-07, 121, 128,

131, 135, 138, 140, 154, 158-59, 166, 193-95, 201, 226, 243, 246, 273, 317, 318, 323-28, 339-40, 361-64, 370, 372, 375, 377, 384, 394, 417-21, 467, 470, 471, 585, 604, 613
Class struggle—3, 55, 106, 233, 243, 274, 419, 481, 631
See also Economic struggle of workers; Political struggle; Revolution, proletarian, socialist; Tactics of the proletarian class struggle; War, civil; Working-class movement
Clergy, the—28, 46, 48, 58, 645
Coalitions, workers'—352, 394-96
Cologne Communist trial—75, 161
Commodity, commodity production—320, 322, 374
Commune—388, 558
Communism—3, 4, 35, 54, 55, 66-68, 88, 106, 121, 126, 128, 131-36, 175, 201, 221, 226-27, 243, 246, 255-56, 264, 274, 317, 318, 323-27, 330, 336, 341, 347-49, 368, 370, 372, 377, 383-91, 393-94, 407, 422-26, 467, 471, 542-44, 581-82
— transitional period from capitalism to communism (socialism)— 330, 348, 370, 386, 389, 393
See also Dictatorship of the proletariat; Revolution, proletarian, socialist
Communism (theories and trends)— 543-44, 639
Communism, Icarian—106, 481
Communism, scientific—317, 368, 370, 377, 389, 391
See also Marxism
Communist League—75, 161, 174-75
Communists, communist movement—8, 175
Competition—396
Compromise (in politics)—392, 619
Concept(ion)—190, 380-81
Confederation of the Rhine, the—602, 603
Connection (between different facts)— 55, 106, 322, 332, 384, 390, 600
Conquest—131, 283, 599-600
Consciousness—364, 394
Conservative Party (Britain)—611
Conspiracy—265, 267, 420, 439, 441, 458
Constitutions, bourgeois—49, 402, 417
Consumption—320, 324-26, 374, 543

Contradiction, antagonism—12, 25-27, 47, 87-88, 96, 98, 125, 135, 146-47, 151-52, 184, 212, 220, 257, 273-74, 321, 326, 339, 383, 395, 471, 481, 494
Control over production—422-25
Corruption—360, 363-64, 417
Counter-revolution—128, 223-25, 420, 588
Court, legal system—64, 609
Crafts, craftsmen—323, 329, 340, 419, 422
Criticism—88, 106, 197, 368, 371, 391, 394, 481, 526, 548, 604, 608
Culture—325, 400
Customs Union (1834-37)—35

D

Danish war, 1864—402, 617, 619
Democracy, democratic movement, bourgeois—43, 48, 96-97, 294, 418
See also Constitutions, bourgeois; Suffrage
Denmark—601
Despotism—120, 219, 403
See also Bonapartism
Development—58, 88, 106, 131-32, 175, 324, 377, 380-81, 396, 419, 424, 452, 481, 582, 608, 627-29
Dictatorship, bourgeois—222-23, 393
Dictatorship of the proletariat—55, 106, 121, 128, 136, 175, 201, 226, 243, 255, 256, 264, 274, 330, 370-72, 386, 393, 407, 425
See also Communism; Paris Commune of 1871; Party, proletarian; Revolution, proletarian, socialist
Diplomacy—255
Discipline—67, 422-25, 451, 501, 519-20, 554, 572-73, 579, 589
Discussions in working-class movement— 88, 107-08, 272, 470, 482
Diseases (as social phenomenon)—337, 343, 361
Distribution—318, 326-27, 389
Division of labour—325, 381, 393
Dogmatism, doctrinairism—91, 119, 281, 371, 393-94, 458, 484, 602

E

Economic crises—35, 340-41
Economic relations—320-21, 373, 377-81, 422
Economic struggle of workers—3, 54-55, 106, 201, 243, 264, 274, 393-95, 397, 426-36, 555, 631
Economics and the state—54-55, 106, 243, 264
Education, training—14, 144, 392, 419, 607-08, 610, 621
Emigration
— of Paris communards—80, 83, 94, 101, 102, 223, 225, 265, 283, 442, 591, 635
— French—260, 265, 637-38, 642-43
— German—116, 178, 429, 607, 609-10, 637, 642-43, 645
— Irish—638
— Italian—44, 435
— Russian—517, 519, 522
Ends and means—3, 4, 54-55, 88, 105, 106, 121-22, 126, 136, 201, 243, 255, 256, 264, 274, 467
Engels, Frederick—74-75, 155, 174, 368
England (Great Britain)—34, 35, 195, 294, 298, 299, 359-61, 401, 407, 611-13, 615-16
— Wars of Red and White Roses—599
— industry—34, 35, 185-86, 360, 396, 602, 613
— towns—337, 352, 355, 360, 362
— legislation—50, 51, 294-95, 360-62, 611-12
— suffrage, Reform Bills of 1832 and 1867—361, 611-15
— bourgeois-republican movement—157, 484
— possibility of a peaceful proletarian revolution—255
— colonial policy in Ireland—154-56, 295, 612
— and France—154
Enlightenment, Enlighteners, the—603, 608
Equality—3, 88, 418-19
Estates—600, 604
Exchange—320-22, 324-25, 380
Exploitation—57, 201, 264, 317-18, 323, 327, 331, 333, 336, 345, 348, 429
Expropriation—58, 330, 348, 390

F

Factory, factory system—324, 426, 430
Factory legislation—144
Family and marriage—135, 347, 352, 360-61
Federalism—590-92, 595
Female labour—394, 497
Fenians—294-96, 449, 616
Feudalism—403, 404, 599-600, 602-08, 627-28
See also Guilds; Serfdom; State, feudal
Foreign policy—116, 220-21, 283-85
See also Diplomacy; International relations
Foreign trade—600-02
Fourierism, Fourierists—106-07, 347-48, 394, 481, 630
France—400, 599-601, 607-09, 620
— July monarchy—417
— Second Empire—96, 106, 219-21, 402, 417
— Revolution of September 4, 1870, the Lyons uprising—93, 476, 504-05
— Third Republic—122, 222, 224, 400, 417-19, 482-83, 622-23
— industry, transport, agriculture—132-35, 353, 388-89
— foreign policy—154, 402, 601, 603-09
Franco-Prussian war of 1870-71—43, 44, 83, 92-93, 100, 116, 158, 219-23, 262, 305, 365, 402, 604, 619, 624, 629
Freedom—49, 222, 294-96, 344, 417, 581-82, 603, 639
Freemasonry—472, 487
French Revolution of 1789-94—277, 377, 381, 400, 417, 603
Funds, social—325-26

G

General Association of German Workers—75, 107, 119, 442, 444-45, 451, 481, 484, 587
Geneva Congress of the International Working Men's Association, 1866—13, 15-19, 86, 100-01, 110, 310
Geneva Congress of the International

Working Men's Association, 1873—253, 263, 266-67, 269, 308, 312, 581, 584

German Conservative Party—403

German Empire (from 1871)—49, 363, 618, 621-22, 626
— economy—426-34, 629
— political system—49, 362-65, 618
— home policy—400, 403-05, 627-28
— and annexation of Alsace and Lorraine—619-20
— and prospects of a European war—604, 620-21, 625
— prospects of the revolution—622
— participation in Poland's oppression—627
— and France—625
— and Russia—225, 625

German Peasant War—592, 599-600

German philosophy—600, 602-03, 610, 630

German Social-Democracy—48-49, 66, 92, 101, 116, 221-24, 372, 389, 415, 619, 629-31, 645

Germans, ancient—405

Germany—401, 599-604, 617, 626-28, 630
— fragmentation of the country and tasks of its unification—599-601
— economy—35, 344, 351-53, 363, 388-89, 403, 599-603, 607-10, 628, 629
— classes, estates, social development—361, 363, 364, 600-02, 609, 622, 627-28
— taxes—602, 628
— political system—363, 599-602
— cultural development, science, education—452, 601-03, 607-10, 630
— press, censorship—160, 161, 221, 286
— religion and the church—600-01, 608
— oppression of other peoples—599-600
— and foreign policy—161, 599-601, 607, 608

Greece—381, 566

Ground rent—321, 327, 386-87

Guilds—382, 401

H

The Hague Congress of the International Working Men's Association, 1872—119, 170-71, 176, 188, 208-10, 212, 215, 219-27, 240-56, 260-62, 265, 267-75, 277-84, 287, 291, 300, 302, 304-05, 310-11, 432, 443, 483, 487, 494-96, 507-11, 556
— struggle against Bakuninism—176, 188, 228-38, 249-50, 257, 264, 265, 267-69, 274-75, 286-87, 290-91, 302, 445, 454, 457-59, 483-85, 487, 511, 543-44, 580
— struggle against reformists—265, 266, 448
— and Blanquists—265, 266, 284, 439-41
— its decisions—243-58, 263-67, 269-70, 272-76, 283-84, 291, 305-07, 311-12, 407, 450
— approvement of its decisions by local organisations—291, 299-300, 304, 308, 312-13, 407-08, 409-10, 426, 440-41, 513-14
— actions of Bakuninists and reformists against decisions of the Congress—188, 189, 291-92, 307-12, 406-08, 414, 415, 440, 448-50, 508-12

Historical approach—321, 381, 608

Historical materialism—379
See also *Class(es)*; *Class struggle*; *Consciousness*; *Economics and the state*; *Production*; *Productive forces*; *Relations of production*

History—131, 175, 323-24, 329, 379, 418, 419, 608, 626

Holy Roman Empire of the German nation (962-1806)—600, 603

Housing question, the—204, 317-24, 326-68, 371-79, 382-83, 385-91

Huguenots, Huguenot wars—608

Humanitarian goal of the socialist transformation of society—136

Hungary—566

I

Ideal, idealisation—329, 349, 391, 417, 590

Ideas—88, 107, 115, 224, 256, 322, 380, 458, 470, 492, 516, 526, 603

Ideology, bourgeois—331, 376

Impoverishment of the working class—191
See also *Industrial reserve army of labour; Pauperism; Workers' labour and living conditions under capitalism*

Industrial reserve army of labour—98, 340-41

Industrial revolution—323

Industry—135-36, 175, 319, 323-26, 329, 353, 360, 362, 369, 373, 384, 389, 419, 422-24

Inquisition—223

Instruments of production—339-40, 386

Interests
— as economic relations—379
— and production—132
— and state—295, 363, 425, 626, 628
— and law—132, 363-64
— and social development—377
— common—137, 299
— private—132
— individual—341
— of society—363, 425
— of estates—600
— class—295, 363
— of landowners—626
— of bourgeoisie, capital—295, 336-37, 343, 346, 363-64, 395, 628
— of petty bourgeoisie—336-37, 372-73
— *of proletariat*—372-73, 411, 454
— *in communist society*—425

International alliance of anarchists—217, 299, 309-10, 408, 410-12, 415, 440-41, 450-51, 496, 503, 508-15, 555-56, 585, 588-89

International Alliance of Socialist Democracy—32, 79, 85-97, 102-08, 111-17, 119-22, 176, 205-13, 228-38, 247, 249-50, 261, 267-69, 278-80, 286-90, 302, 437-41, 442, 444-45, 448, 451, 454-580, 583, 586-88
— secret—206-12, 215, 229-38, 249-50, 257, 261, 267-68, 274-75, 281, 283, 287-92, 299-300, 302, 412-13, 442, 445, 448, 457-70, 472-74, 480, 481, 486-88, 494-95, 499, 505-06, 509, 519-21, 525, 527, 530, 532, 536, 548, 554-55, 567-77, 581, 585, 596

International relations—608

International solidarity of workers—3-8, 46, 80, 94, 107, 110, 112, 116, 198, 201, 220-21, 226, 255-56, 262, 264, 266, 283, 303, 305, 310, 411, 430-32, 435-36, 482, 554, 635
See also *International Working Men's Association (First International); Internationalism, proletarian; Paris Commune of 1871*

International Working Men's Association (First International)—88, 106-07, 226, 255, 275, 283, 454, 457, 482, 554-56
— foundation of and first programme documents—3-20, 22, 54, 87-88, 96, 105-07, 141, 146, 162, 207, 232, 243, 254, 257, 274-75, 280, 311, 407, 454
— struggle for class character of Association—74-86, 108-09, 110-11, 114-15, 118-19, 126, 137-38
— struggle for international solidarity—3-4, 7, 64, 66-67, 88, 109, 198, 201, 226, 256, 262, 266, 267, 283-84, 454, 469-70, 482, 554
— economic and political struggle of the working class—3-4, 54-55, 57, 65-66, 87-88, 105-07, 126, 141, 178, 198, 201, 226, 243, 254-55, 257-58, 273-75, 407, 449, 477
— socialist principles in its programme—131-36, 449
— demand for the creation of the proletarian party in individual countries—57, 106, 201, 243, 264, 274, 306
— and Paris Commune—29, 46, 64, 68-69, 93-94, 102, 116, 128, 141-43, 158, 223, 225, 283, 288, 370, 477, 496
— struggle against Lassalleans—119, 439-45
— struggle against Mazzinists—60-61, 480, 499
— struggle against Proudhonism—12, 370-71, 481
— struggle against reformism—80, 260-65, 306, 446, 448, 449
— struggle against Bakuninists—53, 61, 64-70, 79, 84-96, 102-22, 176, 188-89, 205-12, 215, 228-38, 247-48, 267-69, 277-82, 286-87, 301-02, 415, 437, 438, 467, 470, 509-13, 544-49, 557-71

— and Blanquists—265, 284, 370, 439-40
— and League of Peace and Freedom—61, 85, 87, 460-62
— organisational principles—3-4, 7-11, 14, 22, 24-27, 38-41, 65-67, 83, 84, 86-88, 98-100, 102-05, 109-13, 124-25, 137, 146-47, 158, 170, 173, 198, 201-03, 216, 244-47, 260, 261, 264, 265, 272-74, 276-78, 280-81, 283, 291-92, 305-07, 310, 312, 313, 482
— General Rules and Administrative Regulations—3-20, 24-27, 40, 83, 84, 86-88, 90, 98-103, 105-11, 114, 124-26, 146-47, 154, 158, 170, 173, 184, 198-204, 211, 212, 214, 216, 217, 232, 243-45, 260-61, 263, 264, 268, 269, 272, 273, 276, 280, 281, 299, 305, 310-13, 437-38, 440, 447, 454, 482, 493, 496, 512
— General Council—4, 7, 9-11, 24-26, 31, 37, 38, 40-41, 61, 65-68, 83, 86, 88-93, 95-97, 99-100, 104, 105, 108-14, 158, 170, 176, 180-81, 198, 201, 202-04, 206, 216, 218, 234, 240, 244-45, 248, 255-56, 260-63, 265, 267-69, 271-75, 284, 296, 302-03, 306-07, 311, 312, 448, 471-73, 475-77, 480, 495, 554-55, 556, 638, 639, 642-44, 645
— Sub-Committee—176, 211-13
— General Council in New York—240, 249-50, 256, 257, 265, 267, 269, 273, 283, 291, 292, 299, 306-07, 311-12, 398, 399, 408, 409, 414-16, 447, 448, 450, 509, 511-12
— local organisations—7, 8, 12-16, 19, 25-26, 94, 103-04, 111-13, 124-26, 137, 154, 181, 201-04, 209, 261, 263, 269, 272-73, 305, 307, 310, 312
— membership, money resources—7, 8, 11, 22, 25, 39, 52, 98, 108, 125-26, 181, 202-03, 206, 211, 232, 244-45
— its press—104, 141, 408, 438, 499, 523-24
— role played by Marx and Engels—19, 22, 43-53, 55, 57-58, 60-61, 74-75, 122, 129-30, 137-39, 145-47, 159, 176, 184, 187, 211-13, 215, 217, 259, 265, 284, 285, 288-93,

302-03, 398, 409-16, 437-38, 440, 448, 644-45
— and bourgeois press—31-32, 48, 62, 74-75, 80, 84, 127, 158-59, 312, 477, 482
— and ruling classes, police persecution—21, 28, 32, 62-64, 74, 77-78, 80-84, 103, 111, 114, 128, 129, 137-38, 140, 142-44, 149-52, 170, 177, 203, 219-21, 223, 225-26, 255, 283, 288, 312, 409, 412, 415, 437, 439, 442-44, 480, 487, 489, 491, 497, 507-08, 554, 645
See also Basle Congress, 1869; Brussels Congress, 1868; Geneva Congress, 1866; Geneva Congress, 1873; The Hague Congress, 1872; International Working Men's Association (in different countries); Lausanne Congress, 1867; London Conference, 1865; London Conference, 1871; Mainz (Mayence) Congress
International Working Men's Association and revolutionary movement in Poland—155, 260, 262, 263, 271, 275, 307, 312, 407
International Working Men's Association and Russia—77, 89, 122, 145, 159, 213, 458-59, 463, 485, 515-54
International Working Men's Association in Argentina—226
International Working Men's Association in Australia—84, 260, 262, 271, 275
International Working Men's Association in Austria—83, 111, 137, 151-52, 223, 224, 260, 263, 307, 312, 407-08, 415, 514
International Working Men's Association in Belgium—26, 41, 85, 99, 103, 119, 260, 266, 273, 275, 441, 483, 512, 513, 644-45
International Working Men's Association in Denmark—57-59, 224, 226, 260, 262, 271, 275, 312, 389, 407, 408
International Working Men's Association in England—25-26, 84, 95-100, 116, 118, 130, 154-57, 265-66, 285, 301-14, 406, 410-12, 414, 438, 441, 448-49, 512, 513
International Working Men's Association in France—19, 26, 59, 64, 79-80, 83, 91-93, 95-98, 99, 102, 111-12, 129-30,

137, 221, 223, 260, 262, 264-66, 275,
283, 307, 312, 370, 399, 407, 412,
439-45, 472, 481, 504-07, 513
International Working Men's Association in
Germany—50, 59, 92, 100-01, 112,
116, 129-30, 221-22, 275, 307, 407,
411, 415
International Working Men's Association in
Holland—59, 130, 226, 260, 262, 269,
271, 275, 299, 308, 312, 408, 513
International Working Men's Association in
Hungary—19, 137, 223, 224, 260, 262,
263, 275, 307, 312, 407, 408, 432, 514,
International Working Men's Association in
India—84
International Working Men's Association in
Ireland—130, 154-56, 225-26, 260,
262, 263, 275, 294
International Working Men's Association in
Italy—43, 45, 83, 111, 146-47, 184,
260, 275, 276, 283, 293, 312, 408,
409, 414, 437, 438, 440, 447, 497-99,
504, 512
International Working Men's Association in
New Zealand—226
International Working Men's Association in
Portugal—226, 260, 262, 263, 266,
275, 285, 287, 303, 307, 312, 407, 408,
410, 412, 415, 438, 487
International Working Men's Association in
Spain—26, 54, 99, 129-30, 137-38,
207-08, 215, 234-37, 247-48, 260-62,
267-69, 271-72, 281, 288-92, 299-300,
308, 312, 408-13, 415, 417-18, 426-28,
438, 441, 459, 486-87, 490-96, 510-13,
581-98
International Working Men's Association in
Sweden—266
International Working Men's Association in
Switzerland—55, 68-70, 77, 80, 89-94,
100-05, 108, 118, 122, 130, 188, 189,
225, 247, 260-62, 275, 307, 312, 407,
415, 427, 449-50, 472-76, 478, 479,
483, 485, 489, 514, 540, 584-85,
645
International Working Men's Association in
the USA—84, 112, 124-26, 130, 177-
83, 226, 240, 246, 260-62, 265, 266,
269, 272, 275, 280, 307, 312, 407, 408,
429, 513, 636-43, 645
Internationalism, proletarian—3-4, 46,
116, 154-56, 198, 201, 256, 283-84,
295-96, 631, 632

See also International solidarity of
workers
Ireland—154, 155, 295, 449, 612, 613,
616
See also Fenians; Working-class movement, Irish
Italy—43-48, 162, 294, 402, 451, 566,
599-600, 609

J

Jesuits—459, 470, 545, 553, 554
Jews—604
Joint-stock societies—333, 351, 364
Journalism, journalists—104, 499
See also Press, the
Junkers, Prussian—363, 364, 381, 382,
400-01, 403-04, 626-28
Jurisprudence—375-76

K

Kingdom of Sardinia (Piedmont)—43

L

Labour—135-36, 221, 226, 255, 324-26
Labour aristocracy—284, 357, 613-15
Labour power—318, 320, 327, 339, 345
Land and Labour League (England)—157
Landed property—57, 131-35, 318, 321,
344, 386-89, 419, 423
Language—601-02, 607
Lassalleanism, Lassalleans—75, 107, 119,
144, 380, 444-45, 481-82, 484
See also General Association of German
Workers
Lausanne Congress of the International
Working Men's Association, 1867—55,
105, 311
Law(s)
— of nature—322
— of society—341, 347
— economic—35, 320-22, 332, 374-
75, 377, 378
Lawyers—49, 131, 380-81
League of Peace and Freedom—61, 85, 87,
95, 460-62, 464, 477, 482, 496
Lease, farmer—149, 376
Legislation—131, 132, 332, 380-81, 628
See also Factory legislation

Liberal Party (England)—294, 306, 361, 612-15
Liberalism—45, 49, 284, 401, 460
Literature—72, 167, 338, 522, 602-07, 610
Logic—326, 383
Lombardy—44
London—353-54, 358-59, 375, 384
London Conference of the International Working Men's Association, 1865—83
London Conference of the International Working Men's Association, 1871—14-16, 18, 19, 23, 25-26, 32, 37, 38, 55, 59, 80-84, 93, 100-08, 118, 121, 126, 130, 181, 206-07, 232-34, 243, 254, 257, 264, 267, 273, 289-90, 306-06, 311, 407, 477-82, 485, 490
Lorraine—221, 603, 607, 620
Lumpenproletariat—454, 555, 595

M

Machinery—131-32, 324-25, 340-41, 422-24
Mainz (Mayence) Congress—80-83, 158, 170, 644-45
Malthusianism—380
Man, humanity—128, 136, 324-25, 378, 380, 381, 384, 423, 543, 603
Manchester—366
Marx, Karl (biographical data)—62, 71-73, 161-62, 259, 283-84
— as a scientist—265
— Engels on Marx's role—391
Marxism—174-75, 317, 370, 389, 391, 630-31
Mazzinism, Mazzinists—43-48, 497, 499-500
Means of communication—384, 420
See also Railways
Means of labour—126, 368
Means of production—136, 326, 368, 386, 423, 449
See also Instruments of production; Means of labour
Means of subsistence—340, 346, 429, 639
Middle Ages, the—418, 608-09
Militarism—48-49, 401, 419-20
Mind—145, 197, 226, 325, 592, 631
Mode of production—136, 327, 347-48, 368, 373, 384-85, 389

Monarchy—363-64, 417-19, 599-600, 608, 627
Monasteries—608
Monopolies—3, 48
Morals—4, 25, 98, 223, 232, 255, 291, 341, 347, 495, 524-25, 544-53, 555, 626-27
Mortgages—344
See also Usury
Music—602-03

N

Napoleonic wars—420, 602-04, 621-24
Nation, nationality—116, 154-55, 198, 203, 305-06, 599, 607-08
National Liberals, Germany—618-19, 621
National movement—154-55
National question—154-56, 227, 600
See also Fenians; Ireland; National movement; Polish question
National Reform League—313
Nationalisation of land—57-58, 131-136, 386-87, 389, 449
Nationalism—154-56, 607-08
See also Chauvinism
Natural science—337, 608
Nature—384, 423
Navigation—599
Necessity and chance—132, 324, 338, 340-41, 363, 402
Needs—66, 107, 132, 170, 264, 355, 358, 370, 380, 393, 482, 613
Netherlands, the—608-10
Neutrality—418, 620
New York—240, 260, 261, 265, 266, 429, 434-35, 638-38, 641
Nobility, landowners—149, 177, 363, 393, 400, 419, 600, 602 612, 628
North German Confederation (1867-71)—221, 403, 618, 627

O

Owenism, Owenites—106-07, 347-48, 394, 481, 630-31

P

Pan-Slavism—85, 558-60
Papacy—45, 600

Papal States (Roman State)—225, 600
Parcel, parcelling—132, 135
Paris Commune of 1871—44, 46, 48, 80-83, 94, 128, 142-43, 175, 219, 225, 256, 370, 425, 451, 468, 477, 504, 591, 593, 631, 635
Parliament—48, 411, 583
Parliament, British—145, 197, 360, 612-16
Party of Progress, Germany—617
Party, political—48, 372, 425
Party, proletarian—4, 7, 12, 24, 52, 57-58, 66-67, 88, 105-08, 119, 125-26, 136, 174-75, 201, 222-23, 243, 255, 264-65, 274-75, 281-83, 305-08, 372, 424-25, 449, 459, 470, 490, 614, 629-31
See also *Communists, communist movement; Communist League*
Pauperism—380
Peace as the most important demand of the working-class movement—220-21
Peasantry—48, 57-59, 132-35, 148-49, 344, 362, 373, 376, 384, 389, 400, 401, 403, 419, 520-21, 602
People, popular masses—401, 420
Petty bourgeoisie—318-19, 336, 372-73
Philanthropy—110, 338, 343, 349, 350, 352, 354, 357, 383, 394
Philistinism—525, 597
Philosophy—131, 379-80, 600-03, 608, 630
See also *German philosophy; Marxism*
Phoenicia—608
Plebeians, plebs—405
Police, the—255, 393, 400, 401, 435, 516, 518, 628
Policy, politics—201, 255, 264, 371-72, 379, 418-19, 425, 601, 629
Polish question—560
Political struggle—3, 54-55, 89, 105-08, 120, 198, 201, 209, 234, 243, 254-55, 264, 273-74, 290, 343, 370, 372, 392-97, 419, 477-78, 482, 555, 582-85, 631
Population—131-32, 380, 384-85
Portugal—599
Positivism—96
Press, the—101, 158-59, 222, 226, 312, 429, 432, 442, 484, 645
Prevision, prediction—384-91
Private property—132, 323, 382, 386
Product of labour, of production process—324-26

Production—35, 132, 135-36, 322, 326, 332, 380, 384
Productive forces—325-26, 377
Productivity of labour—324
Profit—331, 429
Progress—135, 377, 418-19, 602
Propaganda—80, 106, 112, 137-38, 265, 289, 470, 555, 631
Property—135, 328, 339, 368, 389
See also *Private property; Public property*
Prostitution—609
Protestantism—601, 608
Proudhonism, Proudhonists—317, 319-37, 341, 343, 346, 368-91, 394, 351, 630
Prussia—352, 363-64, 401-03, 601-03, 604, 607, 617-18, 621-22, 626-28
— after the foundation of the German Empire—400, 403-05, 627-29
— industry, commerce and agriculture—363-64, 401, 403-04, 627-29
— political system—363-64, 401-03, 419, 627
— Constitution, constitutional question, the—401-04, 617-18
— legislation, law—364, 609
— foreign policy—161, 221, 402, 418, 602-04, 607, 624, 626
Public opinion—46, 149, 608
Public property—135, 388
Publicity—459

R

Race—121, 637
Radicalism, radicals—48, 266, 284, 482, 614, 639
Railways—422, 424
Rate of profit—332
Rate of surplus value—332
Red flag—449
Reform, reformers (bourgeois)—144, 345, 361, 403, 405, 628
Reformation in Germany—600-01
Reformism—154-56, 265-66, 284, 448, 613-15
Relations of production—340, 385
See also *Economic relations*
Religion—379, 608
See also *Catholicism; Christianity; Protestantism*
Rentier—332, 333
Republic—46, 400, 417-21, 469, 582, 585

Republican movement (bourgeois)—44, 46-48, 118-19, 158-59, 418-19, 459-60, 484, 505, 583, 585, 597

Research—167, 321-22, 332, 350, 373-75, 381, 389-91, 596

Revolution—425, 470, 596-98

Revolution, bourgeois, bourgeois-democratic—401, 582-84, 596-97, 628

Revolution, proletarian, socialist—3, 35, 46-47, 55, 67, 106, 128, 135-36, 175, 198, 201, 243, 255-56, 264, 274, 330, 347-48, 368, 372, 377, 384, 386, 389, 419, 420, 423, 425, 469-70, 587, 631, 636

See also *Communism* (theories and trends); *Dictatorship of the proletariat*; *Paris Commune of 1871*

Revolution, social—106, 128, 243, 274, 318, 324, 330, 348, 377, 423-25

Revolution of 1848 in France—175, 401

Revolution of 1848-49 in Germany—161, 400-01, 592, 604, 607, 628

Revolution of 1848-49 in Italian states—44-45

Right—89, 326, 373-74, 380-81
— of inheritance—472
— of property—131, 135, 373

Russia
— before the 19th cent.—405, 518, 520, 567
— the rising of the Decembrists (1825)—566
— followers of Mikhail Butashevich-Petrashevsky—556-57
— reform of 1861, Russia after 1861—225, 558, 561-65
— development of revolutionary radical thought under the influence of Nikolai Chernyshevsky—516, 524-26, 558-59, 561-62
— revolutionary actions of the student youth in the 1860s-70s—89-90, 515-20, 523-24, 526, 561, 565-66
— tsarist persecution of the revolutionaries, political trials—515-18, 524, 561-63
— liberal constitutional movement—556-59, 561-62
— and Poland—155
— foreign policy—77-78, 602, 604, 624-25

S

Saint-Simonism, Saint-Simonians—89, 106-07, 394, 472, 481, 630-31

Scandinavia—607

Schleswig-Holstein—155, 607

Science—85, 115, 132, 144-45, 167, 191, 259, 284, 325, 337, 339, 381, 388-89, 394-95, 452, 482, 519, 526, 529, 549, 557, 602-03, 630-31
See also *Communism, scientific*; *Natural science*

Sectarianism—12, 61, 84, 89, 105-07, 126, 232, 234, 274-75, 369-70, 391, 394, 458, 481-82

Sects, religious—608

Serfdom—602, 604

Silesia—429

Social formation—332

Social labour—136, 324, 422-25

Social question—330, 339, 346-47, 368, 516

Social relations—331, 390-91, 394, 424

Social system—34, 318, 338-41, 361, 542

Socialism (theories and trends)—121, 175, 319, 340-50, 353, 372-73, 467, 639-40

Socialism in Germany—317, 389

Socialism, scientific—see *Communism, scientific*

Socialism, socialists in England—394

Socialism, socialists in France—584

Socialism, socialists in Russia—516, 523-24

Socialism, utopian—106-07, 347, 348, 394, 481, 630-31

Societies, secret—47-48, 161, 174, 232, 267, 439, 441, 454, 516

Society—131-32, 135-36, 325, 329, 340, 362-65, 379-80, 424-25
See also *Social formation*; *Social relations*; *Social system*

Society, bourgeois—128, 135, 177, 220-21, 243, 274, 322, 327, 330-33, 339-41, 363-64, 377, 383, 384, 389, 391-94, 397, 417, 422-25, 481, 627-28

Spain—417-21, 581-82, 586, 587, 591-93, 596
— fifth revolution in Spain (1864-74)—408, 418, 420-21, 449, 490, 581-86

State, the—107, 121, 128, 135, 136, 175, 255, 362-65, 370, 380-81, 392-

93, 422-25, 467-68, 482, 599-602, 627
See also *Dictatorship of the proletariat*; *Monarchy*; *Republic*; *State, bourgeois*; *State, feudal*; *State power*
State, bourgeois—107, 121, 128, 201, 264, 362-63, 417-19, 467, 586, 627
See also *Bonapartism*; *Constitutions, bourgeois*; *Dictatorship, bourgeois*; *Parliament*
State debt—336, 388
State, feudal—599
State power—201, 264, 417, 421, 586, 607
Statistics—13-14, 19, 145
Strikes—106, 112, 148-49, 281, 394, 418, 481, 585-86
Students—499, 516
Suffrage—361, 417, 640
Surplus value—318, 320, 327, 331-32
See also *Rate of surplus value*
Switzerland—83, 85, 144

T

Tactics of the proletarian class struggle—391-92, 583-84, 631-32
Taxes, taxation—135, 336, 388, 404-05, 420, 468, 602
Terror, counter-revolutionary—128, 223, 225-26, 563
Theory and practice—3, 66, 88-89, 96, 106-09, 115, 143-44, 174-75, 283, 292, 322, 329, 337, 369-70, 375, 378, 381-82, 388-91, 393, 480, 482, 526, 544, 555, 630-31
Thinking—470, 526
Thirty Years War (1618-1648)—601-02
Town and country—28, 43, 46, 57, 317, 324, 328, 330, 337, 341, 344, 347-50, 352, 368, 375, 383-86, 388, 418-19, 603, 609
Trade—318, 609
See also *Foreign trade*; *World market*
Trade unions, trade-union movement—106-07, 246, 266, 365, 393, 394, 481, 631
See also *Coalitions, workers'*; *Trade unions in England*
Trade unions in England—80, 106-07, 112, 148-49, 306, 481, 613-16, 631

Traditions—394, 419, 604-05, 614
Truth, the—4, 207, 212, 232, 322, 394, 495, 642
Turkey—625

U

United States of America, the—144, 177-78, 255, 392
Uprising, armed—420, 421, 586, 587-88, 592-95
Usury—135, 332, 334, 344, 388
Utopism—330, 384-86, 389, 630-31

V

Violence—222-23, 255, 371, 386, 417, 420, 425
Vulgar bourgeois political economy—88, 341-44

W

Wage labour—35, 201
Wages—149, 340, 345, 399, 426-36
War(s)—116, 220-21, 227, 283, 420, 561, 601-02, 604, 620, 625, 627,
See also *Army*; *Conquest*; *Militarism*; *War, civil*
War, civil—219, 418, 420, 469
See also *Class struggle*; *Paris Commune of 1871*; *Revolution, proletarian, socialist*
Wars of the First French Republic—602-03
War of North American colonies for independence, 1775-83—603
Westphalia—610
Women's question—12-13, 178, 461, 636-43
See also *Family and marriage*; *Female labour*
Worker—49, 57-58, 260-62, 318-20, 327-28, 336-37, 339-40, 395-97, 636, 639, 642
Workers' associations and combinations—352, 394-96
See also *Trade unions, trade-union movement*; *Workers' societies*

Workers' labour and living conditions under capitalism—14, 148-49, 204, 343, 377, 424

Workers' societies—4, 7, 12, 47, 88, 107, 125, 148-49, 161, 174, 198, 201, 203, 246, 266, 439, 482, 491

Working class—3-7, 46-48, 57, 88, 106-07, 111, 128, 135, 148-49, 154-56, 201, 220-21, 226-27, 255-56, 264, 319, 323-24, 336, 339-41, 371-73, 377, 391, 393-94, 396-97, 581-82, 629-31

Working class in Austria—430, 432, 434, 435

Working class in Belgium—433

Working class in Denmark—57-58

Working class in England—148-49, 155, 255, 265-66, 284, 294-96, 306, 357, 359, 613-16, 630

Working class in France—46, 220, 262, 319, 350-51, 353-55, 359, 365

Working class in Germany—49, 266, 337, 351-52, 364, 365, 403, 426-34, 436

Working class in Italy—43-46, 48

Working class in Prussia—363-65, 626-27

Working class in Spain—419-21, 426-28, 449, 586-89, 593-94

Working class in Switzerland—91, 427, 428, 430-31, 433, 436, 474-75

Working class in the USA—116, 255, 429, 434-35

Working-class movement—3-7, 54-55, 57-58, 105, 109-110, 116-17, 121, 126, 135, 138-39, 154-56, 175, 198-200, 210, 226-27, 243, 255-56, 262, 264, 273-74, 283-84, 295-96, 369-70, 391, 393-94, 427-36, 467, 469-70, 555, 584, 613-14, 629-32

— ideological struggle in it—88-89, 106-08, 482, 631

See also *Class struggle*; *International*

Working Men's Association (First International); *Party, proletarian*; *Trade unions, trade-union movement*; *Working-class movement* (in different countries)

Working-class movement in Canada—431

Working-class movement in England—80, 148-49, 328-29, 392, 449, 613-14, 630-31

Working-class movement in Germany—92, 100-01, 116, 221-22, 262, 426-32, 433-34, 436, 444, 629-32

Working-class movement in Roumania—433

Working-class movement in the USA—434-35

Working-class movement, Irish—155-56, 295-96

Working-class and socialist movement in Austria—430, 432, 434, 435

Working-class and socialist movement in Belgium—370, 430, 433, 584, 630

Working-class and socialist movement in Hungary—223, 224, 262, 433, 435-36

Working-class and socialist movement in Italy—28-29, 43, 45-48, 216, 369-70, 498-99, 630

Working-class and socialist movement in Spain—369-70, 410-11, 420-21, 486, 582, 585-89, 591-94, 597, 630

Working-class and socialist movement in Switzerland—428, 430-31, 433, 436, 450, 514

Working day—144, 185, 392, 394, 426-36, 449, 497

World market—602, 607, 609, 613

Y

"Young Russia" manifesto—561, 565

Youth—497, 504, 516, 520